ROAD ATLAS
OF THE
BRITISH ISLES

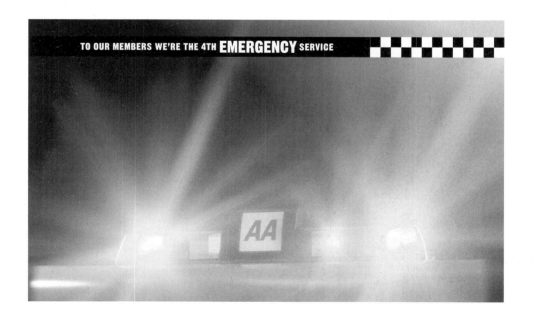

TO OUR MEMBERS WE'RE THE 4TH **EMERGENCY** SERVICE

BCA

LONDON   NEW YORK   SYDNEY   TORONTO

7th edition September 1996
6th edition September 1995
5th edition September 1994
4th edition September 1993
Reprinted October 1993
3rd edition September 1992
Reprinted October 1992
2nd edition September 1991
Reprinted October 1991
1st edition September 1990

Published by AA Publishing (a trading name of Automobile Association Developments Limited, whose registered office is Norfolk House, Priestley Road, Basingstoke, Hampshire RG24 9NY. Registered number 1878835).

Mapping produced by the Cartographic Department of The Automobile Association. This atlas has been compiled and produced from the Automaps database utilising electronic and computer technology.

This edition published 1996 by BCA by arrangement with AA Publishing.

CN 5377

Printed by: Printers Trento, S.R.L., Italy.
Bound by L.E.G.O. SpA, Vicenza, Italy.

The contents of this atlas are believed to be correct at the time of printing. Nevertheless, the publishers cannot be held responsible for any errors or omissions, or for changes in the details given. They would welcome information to help keep this atlas up to date; please write to the Cartographic Editor, Publishing Division, The Automobile Association, Norfolk House, Priestley Road, Basingstoke, Hampshire RG24 9NY.

As a result of the Local Government Review, changes to some counties and county boundaries will take place when new Unitary Authorities are introduced in England, Wales and Scotland during 1996, 1997 and 1998. New and revised County, County Borough and Council Area boundaries have been added to the atlas where appropriate, and included in the index to place names. New Unitary Authorities for towns and cities in England which are within an existing county (eg Portsmouth) are not shown on this mapping.

Information on National Parks provided by the Countryside Commission for England and the Countryside Council for Wales.
Information on National Scenic Areas in Scotland provided by the Scottish Natural Heritage.
Information on Forest Parks provided by the Forestry Commission.
The RSPB sites shown are a selection chosen by the Royal Society for the Protection of Birds.
National Trust properties shown are those open to the public as indicated in the handbooks of the National Trust and the National Trust for Scotland.

contents

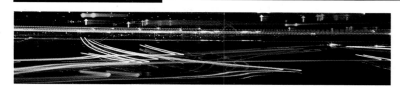

THE TOURIST'S BRITISH ISLES

· SYMBOLS ·

Rochester Castle, in Kent, is a fine example of Norman military architecture.

WHETHER you are looking to spend an afternoon with the family or want to plan a holiday, knowing exactly where to go and what you can see when you get there can often be a problem. The following pages have been designed to give you an idea of what is on offer wherever you happen to be visiting.

Your needs could be as simple as locating a suitable place to enjoy a picnic, where to launch your boat for a day's sailing or where you can find further information about the area.

Whatever your requirement, some 50 symbols, highlighting over 8,000 features of interest, give you a chance to choose what interests you.

Pages 6 to 48 give a taste of what can be seen and where to find it.

Each place located on the atlas by the use of red symbols, has been chosen because it is open and has reasonable access for the public. Although some places may not be open to the public, they have been included simply because they are an interesting feature or landmark, waterfall, windmill etc.

The AA is constantly checking and updating these entries in its atlases and other publications to ensure accurate, up-to-date information is given. All the attractions featured in *Days Out in Britain*, published annually by the AA, are highlighted in this atlas by the red symbols. The atlas, however, includes even more places and the information on locations such as country parks, nature reserves, nature trails, RSPB sites and Forest Parks, is supplied by the numerous authorities and national bodies such as the Countryside Commission, the Forestry Commission and many others.

There is a wide range of interests to choose from.

For cultural tastes, museums, art galleries, historic houses, castles, abbeys and cathedrals are featured. A stately home like Stourhead, in Wiltshire, may be more famous for its garden than its house and will therefore be depicted by the red garden symbol. Others, like Chatsworth in Derbyshire, which are better known for the architectural splendour of the house, even though they are also renowned for their garden features, will be indicated by the red house symbol. Larger, specific garden features, classified as arboreta, are depicted accordingly. Major sporting venues such as athletics stadiums, county cricket grounds and horse racing courses are located by appropriate symbols. It is not possible to indicate league football grounds because of their large numbers and the limitations of the map scale. However, some are shown on the town plans at the back of the atlas where appropriate.

For those who like to participate rather than spectate, outdoor and leisure-type facilities, such as ski slopes, golf courses and coastal launching sites for boats are located.

If you have a particular interest in Ancient Britain, you can choose from the various hill-forts, Roman antiquities and prehistoric monuments which are found throughout the country. Even battle

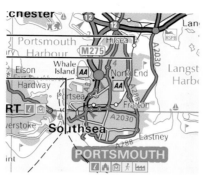

The places behind Portsmouth's tourist symbols. Left Tourist Information at The Hard. Below left Industrial Interest with restored steam pumping engines at Eastney. Below right The Cathedral. Right HMS Warrior, just one of the city's many Museums.

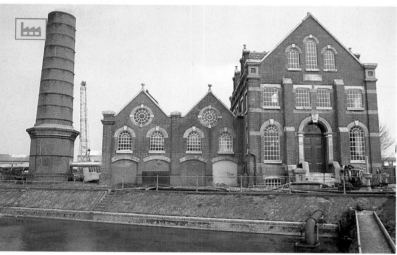

sites, where the course of history has often been changed, are shown. Some of these have interpretative centres which help you to relive and understand the events that occurred there.

Animal lovers can visit the major wildlife collections (both mammals and birds), zoos, and aquariums, or see nature in the wild at one of the numerous nature reserves, Forest Parks and RSPB sites. Another option is to follow one of the nature trails through the countryside. The more adventurous can attempt part or all of one of the national trails which traverse some of Britain's most spectacular scenic areas.

Industrial interest covers a wide spectrum from heritage centres and museums to mills, mines and slate caverns. Old railways, many of which served these industries in the past, now delight the public with a taste of the golden days of steam.

Family days out are catered for by the theme parks. The AA has selected eight of these for inclusion on the basis that they provide multi-purpose entertainment and leisure facilities

and have numerous fairground attractions that are unnervingly described as 'white knuckle' rides. Along with the country parks, they make ideal places to spend the whole day rather than just a quick visit.

Picnic sites are selected and inspected by the AA on a regular basis and are easily accessible, being sited on or by A and B roads. Viewpoints are shown if they offer vistas of at least 180 degrees, and many have panoramic 360 degree views.

Other places of interest which are worth visiting but do not fall easily into the categories symbolised are indicated by a small red star alongside their name. There is a great variety of these – waterfalls, water mills, visitor centres and market crosses, among others.

New additions for the 1990s include the National Parks of England and Wales and the National Scenic Areas of Scotland, along with 930 miles of Heritage Coasts along the shores of England and Wales.

When the red symbols are boxed, this indicates the attractions are in

urban areas. Some of these places may seem bare compared to the surrounding countryside. However, it may be that one symbol for a museum covers several museums in the town, but it is not practical to include them all because of space limitations.

Ireland is included in this special tourist section, and places of interest are located in the atlas, but the scale of mapping does not allow a large selection. Nevertheless, all the most important of Ireland's many tourist attractions are clearly marked.

Wherever possible, the red pictorial symbols used in the atlas are based on the Department of Transport's brown tourist signposts, so that the maps correspond with the road signs. In addition to all this information in the special tourist spreads, a month by month calendar on pages 46 and 47 tells you which customs and events occur throughout the year. This can assist you in deciding when to go. Page 48 describes the services offered by Britain's Tourist Information Centres to help you get the most out of your visits

Abbey, cathedral
or priory

Ruined abbey,
cathedral or
priory

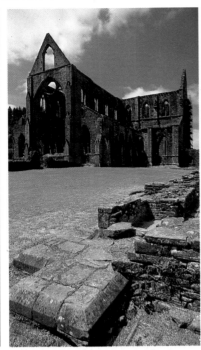

Top *Tintern Abbey: majestic roofless ruin beside the River Wye in Gwent.* Above *St David's Cathedral, Dyfed, where the bones of St David lie.*

| **Abbeys**
| **Cathedrals**
| **Priories**
Augustinian, Benedictine, Cistercian and Dominican – the monastic orders which preserved ideals and scholarship after the fall of Rome have left a rich heritage in stone across Britain. Each imposing ruin or active place of worship tells its own story. All evoke a sense of wonder at the faith and industry of the medieval builders and monks. Which of any of them is the loveliest, however, will for ever be a matter of personal preference.

Burnt down in 1174, four years after Becket's murder, the choir of **Canterbury Cathedral** was rebuilt in a manner worthy of the martyr and appears today much as it was in the early 16th century. The 'Altar of the Sword's Point' and a modern cruciform sculpture, dedicated in 1986, mark the site of Becket's martyrdom. The long vistas back to the nave, at a lower level than the choir aisles, show the evolution of Gothic style over three centuries.

The west front of **York**, the largest Gothic church north of the Alps, presents an almost 13th-century 'French' outline, with its glorious façades. The Minster contains the largest single collection of medieval stained glass in England – the West Window painted in 1339 by Master Robert and the East Window, the work of John Thornton of Coventry, between 1405 and 1408. The Pilgrim Window dates from about 1312 and the Bellfounders' Window was given by Richard Tunnoc, buried in the Minster in 1330.

A fire, started by lightning on 9 July 1984, destroyed much of the south transept. Craftsmen, incorporating 20th-century improvements for future safety, restored the medieval beauty of the transept, reopened by the Queen in October 1988.

Embodiment of the spirit of the nation, **Westminster**, the Norman abbey of Edward the Confessor, took on its Gothic appearance after its rebuilding by Henry III. Fortunately, when the 600-year-old Benedictine community was disbanded, the buildings were spared. The Lady Chapel houses the Confessor's shrine, ringed by the tombs of five kings and three queens. In the centre is the Coronation Chair and below the oaken seat the Stone of Scone.

In the Sanctuary beyond the choir every monarch since the Conqueror has been crowned, with the exception of Edward V and Edward VIII. Early Parliaments met in the Chapter House, and the Henry VII Chapel has a superb fan-vaulted roof – the most glorious, some would say, in the country. Near the West Door lies the 'Unknown Warrior', brought back from France after World War I to sleep among the nation's great.

On its rocky promontory dominating the city and a loop in the River Wear, the Norman architecture of **Durham Cathedral** gives an impression, inside as well as out, of overwhelming power. Huge, deeply grooved columns alternating with massive piers support gallery, clerestory and beautiful vault. The Early English Chapel of the Nine Altars is a 13th-century addition, its tall lancet windows paralleled only in the now ruined Fountains Abbey. In the Treasury are evocative relics of the 7th-century St Cuthbert, including his tiny portable altar, his delicate gold pectoral cross and the remains of his original carved oak coffin.

One of the most delicate of England's cathedrals must be **Salisbury**, built in the 40 years following 1220 of local silver-grey limestone with pointed arches and soaring windows. The spire, at 404 feet (123m), is the tallest in the country. It is such inspired work that it blends perfectly with the rest, though crossing piers of clustered black marble had to be reinforced in the 15th century to support the added 6,500 tons of the spire.

Wells is the first cathedral church in the Early English style. Its west front is still, despite Puritan vandalism, one of England's richest displays of 13th-century sculpture. Inside, the most striking feature is the inverted arches, built from 1338 to 1348 to combat subsidence of the tower.

The Norman crypt and transepts of **Winchester Cathedral** survive, the rest being 13th and 14th century. At 556 feet (169m) it is the longest Gothic church in Europe. Saved from demolition in 1652 by a petition of the citizens, it was again saved at the beginning of this century by a diver, William Walker. Working alone, from 1906 to 1912, in pitch dark waters of the marshy foundations, he replaced the rotting 13th-century beech tree raft (on which the cathedral had originally been built) with cement.

Near York are three jewels – Beverley, Selby and Ripon. **Beverley Minster** houses the Percy Tomb, the most splendid of British Decorated funerary monuments. It shares, with St Mary's Church nearby, wonderful misericords and the largest collection of carvings of medieval musical instruments anywhere in the world.

Benedictine **Selby Abbey**, founded in 1069, predates Durham. The west front ranges in style from strength and simplicity to later elegance. The easternmost arches of the nave have distorted spectacularly, due to a high water table. High up above the south side of the choir is a 14th-century window with the arms of the Washington family – the 'Stars and Stripes' motif of the American flag.

Ripon Cathedral is built over the tiny 11 by 8 ft (3.4 x 2.4m) Saxon crypt of St Wilfrid's Church, one of the few Saxon structures left in England. The cathedral has a beautiful Early English west front. One woodcarver, working from 1939 to 1945, replaced all the 'idolatrous images' on the choir screen, destroyed by Puritans in 1643.

There are modern cathedrals, too. The new **Coventry Cathedral** appears to grow out of the old St Michael's and the overwhelming impression is of height, light and colour. South-facing angled windows enable sunlight to flood the nave with colour. Dominating the whole cathedral is the huge tapestry designed by Graham Sutherland, *Christ in Glory*.

Liverpool's **Anglican Cathedral** is, in the words of Sir John Betjeman, 'vastness, strength and height no words can describe'. Sir Giles Gilbert Scott designed Britain's largest cathedral in medieval style but on a scale which no medieval builder would have attempted. His memorial is set in the floor of the central space under the tower. He, a Catholic, is buried just outside the West Door.

The **Metropolitan Cathedral of Christ the King** in Liverpool, often irreverently called 'Paddy's Wigwam', stands above the huge crypt of the cathedral which Sir Edwin Lutyens started before the war. Inside the 194ft (59m) circular nave, completed by Sir Frederick Gibberd, every member of the 2,300 congregation has an uninterrupted view of the white marble high altar.

A cathedral conveys 'city status' on a town, however small. Pass through the gatehouse at **St David's,** Dyfed, and the lichen-encrusted purple stone of Wales's greatest church is dramatically revealed. It was restored in Decorated Gothic style after an earthquake in 1248 and the whole building slopes upwards some 14 feet (4m) from west to east – an unnerving first glimpse for the visitor entering at the western end

of the nave. The relics of St David rest in an oak and iron reliquary, hidden at the Reformation and discovered during restoration work in 1866.

St Asaph Cathedral, in Clwyd, is on the site of a monastic community founded in AD570. It houses the tomb of Bishop William Morgan, translator of the Bible into Welsh, and the 16th-century Bible itself, which was used at the Investiture of the Prince of Wales in 1969.

Henry VIII's Dissolution left a legacy of ruined religious centres across the country, many of which still survive today in all their shattered glory.

Perhaps one of the most magnificent monastic ruins is **Rievaulx Abbey**, two miles north-west of Helmsley. It was founded in 1131 and is the first Cistercian house in the north of England. The name, pronounced 'Reevo', comes from Rye Vallis or valley of the River Rye, above which it stands, surrounded by wooded hills. Its chief glory is its choir built *c.* 1225. The scale of the buildings gives an idea of the activities and work of the 600 and more monks and lay brothers who lived here in the 13th century.

The Cistercian community of **Fountains Abbey**, near Ripon, became the centre of an enormous enterprise, with fish-farms, forestry,

Right The ancient kings of Northumbria lie buried near Tynemouth Priory. Below Cistercian Fountains Abbey, now part of the Studley Royal estate.

iron-workings and, above all, sheep, which funded its building. It was one of the first foundations to be sold by Henry VIII in 1540. In 1768 the Aislabie family bought it as a picturesque addition to their Studley Royal estate.

The condition of the Benedictine **Whitby Abbey** cannot wholly be blamed on King Henry. The gaunt ruins of the clifftop site, chosen by St Hilda in AD657, became the setting for Bram Stoker's *Dracula* and suffered further indignity when they were bombarded by German warships during World War I.

The 7th-century buildings at **Much Wenlock** were destroyed by the Danes and later refounded by Leofric, husband of Lady Godiva. Today's ruins are the remains of the church built in the 1220s by Prior Humbert, whose lodging is one of the finest examples of English domestic architecture from around the 1500s.

Abbey, cathedral or priory

Ruined abbey, cathedral or priory

Castle

Castles

Maiden Castle to Balmoral, Mousa Broch to Dover – Britain is rich in castles dating from Bronze to Victorian ages. The very name 'castle', conjuring up visions of power, of menace and later of opulence, has often been affected by builders of lesser dwellings.

Castles begin with the hillforts of the Bronze Age and stone brochs of pre-Christian Scotland, primarily refuges for men and cattle in time of local warfare. The ruins of Norman timber-built motte and bailey castles – a stone keep on a mound, surrounded by a defensive wall – later converted by the Plantagenets to stone fortresses, still dominate many towns, river crossings and strategic points across the country.

These were not solely refuges, but administrative headquarters, stores and living quarters. Even in times of peace they would have been bustling centres of activity; in time of war, life must have been pretty chaotic, with garrisons, stores, cattle and weaponry increased and as many of the local population as

Below Orford Castle, in Suffolk, has a remarkable 18-sided polygonal keep. *Inset* The Welsh border castle of Goodrich, in the Wye Valley.

could be squeezed in taking refuge in the bailey. Castles were not designed for passive defence but for vigorous action. They were not safe refuges in which to avoid conflict, but ingeniously contrived to make the enemy fight at a disadvantage – they were meant to be costly to capture – both in time and in lives. Henry II (1154-1189), after the mayhem of Stephen's reign 'took every castle of England into his hands', destroyed about 500 unlicensed castles and founded a line of castle-building kings – Richard, John, Henry III, Edward I and III.

Visiting some of these castles, it needs only a little imagination to bring to life the history of their times. The castles of Edward I (1272-1307) around the coast of North Wales are symbols of the organising ability and engineering skills as well as reminders of the vast expense of castle building in the Middle Ages.

Norman and Plantagenet castles vary to suit the site on which they are built but the first criterion was always that of aggressive defence. Where possible a ditch or moat – dry or flooded – was dug to prevent besiegers tunnelling under the walls. Towers without sharp

corners were less likely to be undermined, and so became the fashion.

From about 1268, the date of **Caerphilly Castle** in Mid Glamorgan, the defenders of the outer curtain wall and its towers would be supported by covering fire from higher inner walls. A formidable array of outworks defends gateways and sluices, further protected by drawbridge and portcullis. Barbicans and towers ensured that attackers were subjected to murderous flanking crossfire before they got anywhere near anything so flammable as a wooden gate.

Caerphilly, at 30 acres the largest castle in Wales, surpassed only by **Dover** and **Windsor**, is sufficiently well preserved to give a vivid idea of the way these defensive ideas worked together. It has wide water defences, in imitation of those which Henry III had built at **Kenilworth** and which Simon de Montfort held so successfully against him. Edward I, on his return from the Crusades, liked what he saw at Caerphilly and began to turn the **Tower of London** into a concentric castle. He also introduced at **Caernarfon** and **Conwy** an idea from his campaigns in Gascony –

the 'bastide' – an extension of the bailey to enclose a small town in which traders, labourers and craftsmen could live under the protection of the castle.

Edward I's castle building in North Wales is well documented and throws fascinating light on the feudal power and organisation at the King's command. Ditch diggers were recruited from the Fens and marched across by mounted serjeants – to discourage deserters – to dig the canal around **Rhuddlan Castle.**

At **Conwy**, Edward's young Spanish queen, Eleanor, homesick for the courts and fountains of her native Castile, had a small garden and fishpond built in the castle's east barbican. In the hot summer of 1283 a labourer hauled water from the well, to 'water the Queen's new grass'. Here at Conwy it is believed that Eleanor introduced one of our favourite summer flowers – the sweet pea.

At **Caernarfon Castle** where his son, later Edward II, was born on 25 April 1284, Edward sought to bring Arthurian and Welsh legends to life and make the seat of his government in Wales a new imperial Constantinople. Octagonal towers are set in a single curtain wall, banded with red sandstone in imitation of those of the 5th-century Turkish capital. Defended passages within the thickness of the masonry and ingenious triple arrow slits allowed three bowmen a wide angle of fire through only one external opening.

The more settled times of the Tudor dynasty after the Wars of the Roses reduced the military significance of the castle. Gunpowder played no little part in this. Castles continued to be built, but design changed. Henry VIII began a series of symmetrically planned coastal 'artillery forts' from the Thames to Dorset in 1538. **Deal, Walmer** and **Sandgate** are three, but these were garrisoned rather than lived in – the garrisons complaining that 'they stank of gunpowder and dogs'. Comfort and elegance dictated the style of Elizabethan and Jacobean buildings, though many were still castellated and defensible.

The Civil War saw many castles used again as strongpoints. They stood up so well, even to improved 17th-century firepower, that the victorious Parliamentarians decreed that those which had been so vigorously defended should be 'slighted' – demolished so as to make them useless for military purposes. Some of these 'ruins Cromwell knocked about a bit', if not too badly damaged, became the

Above *Caernarfon Castle, Gwynedd, built by Edward I to subdue the Welsh.* Right *St Andrews' 13th-century castle overlooks the North Sea.*

local prison and the Norman word for the keep – *donjon* – became the English dungeon.

In Scotland, Northumberland, Cumbria and the troubled lands of the Borders, there are over 1,100 'castles' of one sort or another, excluding the baronial houses of the last 200 years. Most are tower houses or 'peles', built in stone, for timber was always short in the region, and usually several storeys high. **Craigievar**, west of Aberdeen, is the masterpiece of this uniquely Scottish style. Seven storeys high with, even today, few windows in its pink granite walls, it must have been a formidable sight for any would-be attacker.

Many peles have been absorbed into later houses. **Traquair House** west of Galashiels, now more 'château' than castle, claims to be the oldest continuously inhabited house in Scotland. Buried within the north-east corner is a pele tower dating back to the reign of Alexander I (1107-24).

Stirling Castle, which looked down on Edward II's ignominious defeat at Bannockburn in 1314, was still an earthen and timber construction. The 'Gateway to the Highlands' was transformed under the Stuarts, first into a stone fortress, then into a splendid Renaissance royal palace.

Castles lived on in the romantic imaginations of later centuries. Sir Charles Cavendish, son of Bess of Hardwick, built his mansion at **Bolsover**, Derbyshire, in the 1620s with the turrets, crenellations and medieval fancies so popular with the Elizabethans. As tastes began to rebel against Classical symmetry and long for 'the good old days', mock medieval 'castles' were built

and some genuine 14th-century castles, such as **Croft**, in Shropshire, were 'gothicised'.

William Burges built two for the Marquess of Bute, at **Cardiff** and **Castell Coch**, reconstructing the motte and bailey castle the Normans had built at Cardiff within a Roman fort into an extravaganza rivalling the creations of Ludwig of Bavaria – with a medieval tower suite complete with smoking room, Gothic chapel and banqueting hall. At Castell Coch, to the north of Cardiff, Burges transformed the ruins of a keep destroyed in the 15th century into a mock 13th-century retreat. Its conical roofs recall the illustrations in the Duc de Berry's 'Book of Hours' but the thick walls have arrow slits and 'murder holes' and a portcullis and drawbridge which function.

The last such conceit built in Britain was designed by Edwin Lutyens, who in 1901 had made a comfortable home for the publisher of *Country Life* magazine within the ramparts of **Lindisfarne**, off the Northumbrian coast. For 20 years, from 1910, **Castle Drogo**, Lutyen's composite Norman and Tudor 'castle' arose overlooking the River Teigne in Devon, home to the founder of the Home & Colonial Stores and is – to date, at any rate – Britain's 'last castle'.

Historic house

National Trust properties

Historic Houses

The Greek historian, Thucydides said 'Men, not walls, make a city'. The same holds true for a house and the human stories of the builders, owners or residents add interest to it, however humble, however grand. Membership of the National Trust and English Heritage – an outlay quickly recouped if you are going to visit even half a dozen properties in a season – will give you a wonderful selection from which to choose, rich in architecture and in treasures, but above all in personalities.

The name 'Mote' at **Ightham Mote** in Kent recalls the 'moot', the council which met here, in the Great Hall, dating from 1340. Three centuries of continuous ownership by the Selby family have left their mark, from Jacobean fireplaces through 17th-century wallpaper to Victorian bedrooms. All told there are 600 years of England's history to be discerned at Ightham.

Ightham Mote, Kent, is one of the best examples of a medieval manor house.

Built in 1340 by a Lord Mayor of London, the Great Hall at **Penshurst Place** in Kent is the finest to have survived. Birthplace of the Elizabethan courtier, soldier and poet, Sir Philip Sidney, the house remains in the same family today. Later ranges of building have left it light and airy. The Long Gallery marries house to garden and medieval to Renaissance, a fitting memorial to the man who personified all that was best in the Elizabethan age.

The Elizabethan house Bess of Hardwick built with Sir William Cavendish at **Chatsworth** in Derbyshire has been absorbed into the present house. Chatsworth is the home of the Cavendish family, the Dukes of Devonshire, the first of whom, in the early 1700s, transformed the house into a baroque palace, a second Versailles. Treasures are everywhere – in the Painted Hall, the State Rooms, Sculpture Gallery – works by famous artists, painters and sculptors abound. The Library has over 17,000 volumes, among them those of Henry Cavendish, the 18th-century discoverer of hydrogen. Capability Brown laid out much of the garden, but retained Grillet's 1696 Cascade, the sound of the water varying as it falls over steps of different height. Joseph Paxton, too, worked here, and his Great Conservatory was the forerunner of the Crystal Palace.

Montacute in Somerset is one of the least altered of late Elizabethan houses. Begun in the year of the Armada, it expresses the rise to power of an astute lawyer, Edward Phelips. He led the prosecution of Guy Fawkes and became Speaker of the House of Commons. The house, with its mullioned front and statues standing in their lofty niches, is the masterpiece of a local genius, William Arnold. No one, though, who has seen the charming Elizabethan pavilions can ever doubt the delicacy and humour of this Elizabethan mason who has so completely captured his master's wish to display his continuing good fortune.

After a spell in the Tower and a stiff fine, Sir John Thynne retired to his Wiltshire estate at **Longleat**, following his support of the disgraced Lord Protector to Edward VI. He began Longleat in about 1546, and today it is still home to the Thynne family, now the Marquesses of Bath. The Great Hall, with its 16th-century fireplace and hunting scenes, is the least altered part of the house. Sir John broke from the tradition of the Elizabethan 'E-shaped' house and built around two inner courts. The top floor of the house was the library and home of Thomas Ken, Bishop of Bath and Wells, who was given refuge

here when he fell foul of both James II and William and Mary. Lord Bath, an innovator like his ancestor, opened his house to the public in 1949 and in 1966 introduced the 600-acre safari park, a 'drive-through' reserve of giraffes, rhinoceroses, elephants, tigers – and the well-known 'lions of Longleat'.

Bess of Hardwick married four times, each time increasing her fortune. She married Sir William Cavendish when she was 27 and their second son inherited Chatsworth. She left her fourth husband, the Earl of Shrewsbury, for his alleged infatuation with his prisoner, Mary, Queen of Scots. Then, aged 70, she began to build **Hardwick Hall**. The accounts of the building reflect the imperiousness of the owner who, living a hundred yards away in her old hall, strode across to inspect and criticise every day. Her descendants preferred Chatsworth and Hardwick remained, frozen in time, one of the purest examples of 16th-century design and decor in the country, a memorial to the indomitable woman whose portrait stares down from the tapestried wall of the Long Gallery.

Robert Cecil, first Earl of Salisbury, builder of **Hatfield House**, Hertfordshire, was adviser to both Elizabeth I and James I. James suggested that Robert Cecil exchange the house his father, Lord Burghley, had built at Theobalds, for the palace at Hatfield – a 'suggestion' he could scarcely refuse. Between 1607 and 1611, Cecil built himself a vast new house nearby.

Great Halls and Long Galleries were by then going out of fashion, but Hatfield would have lost much had Cecil not been traditionalist enough to include them. His own quarters and the guest wing, however, have smaller rooms. Here conversation and gracious living could flourish. The style of the great house was changing. It was a later Cecil, Marquess of Salisbury, three times Prime Minister to Queen Victoria and amateur scientist, who installed electricity in 1881 and it is reported that 'the naked wires on the Gallery ceiling tended to burst into flame, being extinguished by members of the family who threw cushions a them before returning to their conversation'.

By the time **Petworth** was built, 70 years or so after Hatfield, Long Galleries and Great Halls had gone completely from the English building scene. The house passed by marriage from the Percys to the 'Proud Duke' of Somerset, who began building – using his wife's fortune – in 1688. The name and skill of Grinling Gibbons will always be associated with Petworth. His mastery of limewood carving is complete. The house also

Historic house

National Trust
properties
Scotland

boasts excellent tracery work by Jonathan Ritson, and the Marble Hall has wonderful carving by John Selden, the Duke's estate carpenter.

Just to the south of Wrexham lies **Erddig**. It was completed by a local mason in 1689 and owned by the Yorke family since 1733, who collected much and threw little away! Subsidence from coal mining almost destroyed the house and restoration began in 1973. The interest of the house is not in its architecture or its treasures, but in the relationship that a local family maintained with their servants. Portraits of master and servant hang in drawing room and servants' hall, many with little poems and descriptions. There are frequent group photographs of the whole staff, enabling us to follow some servants right through their careers. Erddig is one of the few houses to show the public the maids' bedrooms as well as the public rooms. Here, 200 years of the running of a self contained estate come vividly to life.

Soldier turned dramatist on his return to England in 1692, John Vanbrugh came to the notice of Charles Howard, 3rd Earl of Carlisle, perhaps through his popular and bawdy plays. Howard chose this enthusiastic amateur to build him a home fitted to the position of an Earl, and so Castle Howard came about. Vanbrugh was widely helped by one of Sir Christopher Wren's assistants, Nicholas Hawksmoor, who turned Vanbrugh's ideas into working drawings. Castle Howard impresses

but does not overawe, as does their later work at Blenheim. At the heart of the house is the Great Hall, rising 70 feet (21m) through two storeys into the painted dome. It is the most light-hearted but impressive concept of English architecture. Treasures and portraits abound, including one of a stricken Henry VIII, painted by Holbein just after the execution of Catherine Howard, and a portrait of her uncle, Thomas Howard, who escaped the block because the king died on the day of his execution.

The story of **Blenheim Palace** is full of powerful men and women. It was built for John Churchill, Duke of Marlborough. Queen Anne instigated the idea of the palace as a reward for Churchill's victory over the French and Bavarians at the battle of Blenheim. She later quarrelled with Sarah, Duchess of Marlborough, as did Vanbrugh, the architect. Sarah wanted a comfortable country house and Vanbrugh wanted something even greater than Castle Howard. Sir Winston Churchill, born here, became Prime Minister at a time when a man of Marlborough's character was again needed.

William Adam began to build **Mellerstain** in the Scottish borders for George Baillie in 1725 and his son, Robert, finished it in 1770. It is the interiors, by Robert, that are the main attraction, for William was never able to finish the exterior as planned and it lacks a noble central block. The colours Adam used in his decorations make the rooms particularly attractive.

Above *Vanbrugh's spectacular Castle Howard, in North Yorkshire.*
Right *The beautiful Georgian mansion of Mellerstain, in the Borders.*

The National Trust

Many of the historic houses mentioned on these two pages are in the care of the National Trust of England, Wales and Northern Ireland and the National Trust for Scotland. Apart from maintaining many of Britain's finest buildings the Trust also owns gardens such as the renowned Hidcote Manor Garden near Chipping Campden, ruins such as **Fountains Abbey** in North Yorkshire, tracts of especially scenic shoreline, such as 110 miles of spectacular Cornish coast, follies, windmills, locks and even pubs, of which *The Fleece Inn* at Bretforton, on the edge of the Cotswolds, is a particularly attractive example. The letters 'NT' designate where the Trust owns property or land.

*Concorde 01 is on show at the Imperial
War Museum, Duxford, Cambridgeshire.*

Museums
Art Galleries

Among the prized possessions of
the British Museum in its early days
were a landscape painted on a
spider's web, a two-headed chicken,
Chinese shoes, figures of King
William III and Queen Mary carved
out of walnut shells and various
unpleasant-looking things preserved
in spirits and hidden in the
basement in case they might
frighten pregnant women. A far cry
from the British Museum of today
with its Elgin Marbles, Assyrian
winged bulls and the Sutton Hoo
treasure included in its fabulous
array of objects from every corner of
the globe.

The ancestors of today's museums
and art galleries were the collections
of classical sculptures and
antiquities formed during the
Renaissance period by rulers,
wealthy churchmen and merchant
princes like the Medicis of Florence.
They were inspired by the
devouring interest which had
sprung up in ancient Greece and
Rome. With interest also rapidly
developing in science, others
assembled natural history collections
and 'cabinets of curiosities', which
contained animal bones, weapons,
coins, shells, oddly shaped plants or
stones – anything that took the
collector's fancy.

In England the two John
Tradescants, father and son, who
were keen naturalists, plant-hunters
and gardeners to Charles I in the
17th century, formed a substantial
collection, or 'museum' as it was
called: one of its star pieces was a
stuffed dodo. The collection passed
to Elias Ashmole, the antiquary,
herald and pioneer Freemason, who
added to it and passed it on in turn
to Oxford University. Twelve wagon
loads of objects were conveyed to
Oxford, to form the nucleus of the
Ashmolean Museum, opened to the
public in 1683 and the oldest
museum in Britain.

The Ashmolean today glories in
its Egyptian mummy cases and
medieval jewellery, its Old Master
paintings and British art, but it still
honours Ashmole's memory and
items from the original Tradescant
collection can be seen, with other
curiosities such as Guy Fawkes's
lantern.

The **British Museum** opened its
doors in London to 'studious and
curious persons' in 1759, the word
'museum' now meaning the
building in which a collection was
kept rather than the collection itself.
It was established by Parliament and
funded by a state lottery to house
the collections of Robert Harley, Earl
of Oxford, and the books and
manuscripts assembled by Sir
Robert Cotton – which included the
Lindisfarne Gospels and two copies
of Magna Carta. Also included was
the astonishing collection of no less
than 79,575 objects put together by
Sir Hans Sloane. A successful
London doctor, Sloane's fanatical
zeal as a collector extended to
classical antiquities, coins, jewels,
fossils, plants, butterflies, zoological
specimens and oddities of every
kind. Those who came to feast their
eyes on these items consisted, as
the Trustees reported in 1784,
'chiefly of Mechanics and persons of
the lower Classes'.

Zeal to improve and educate
'persons of the lower classes' gained
strength in the 19th century,
especially in the heavily populated
towns created by the industrial
revolution, and prompted the
establishment of numerous
museums and art galleries. The
splendid **City Art Gallery** in
Manchester, for example was
opened in 1834 and is today noted
for its superb Victorian and Pre-
Raphaelite paintings. The
**Birmingham Museum and Art
Gallery** was founded in 1867 and
the building it now occupies was
opened in 1885. Approximately a
hundred museums opened in Britain
in the 1870s and '80s.

The Victorian boom in museums
and art galleries was also stimulated
by an ambition to promote scientific
and technological advance and to
improve standards of design. This
was why the **Victoria & Albert
Museum** in London was founded by
the Prince Consort in 1852,
originally as a 'museum of
manufactures', in the wake of the
Great Exhibition of the previous
year.

National and civic pride were also
a factor. The **National Gallery** in

London is now the country's premier collection of Western painting down to 1900 (developments since then are the preserve of the **Tate Gallery**). It was founded in 1824 to emulate the national art galleries already established in Vienna, Paris, Berlin and other European capitals. The government bought 38 paintings to start it off from the collection of a banker, Sir John Julius Angerstein: they included the Rubens *Rape of the Sabine Women*, two Rembrandts and Raphael's *Portrait of Julius II*.

Major museums and galleries generally have two functions and there is often a tension between them. The obvious function is to instruct and entertain the public. The other, carried on out of the public eye, is the advancement of scholarship. An example of this dual role is the **National Museum of Wales** in Cardiff, opened in 1927 (in a building which has leaked ever since). It was founded to inform both the Welsh and the rest of the world about Wales, which it does. However, its own staff and visiting academics also work behind the scenes on collections far too voluminous for public display – 230,000 pressed plant specimens, more than 300,000 fossils, serried multitudes of dead beetles.

The museum is also a good example of the fact that the functions of an institution of this kind today go far beyond the display of objects in showcases. Activities include lectures, the loan of items to schools, and guided family walks with experts from the staff discoursing learnedly along the way.

Museums like this take a wide range of subjects for their province. Others concentrate on specialised areas. There is a museum of Scottish tartans at **Comrie**, for example, of stained glass at **Ely**, of horse racing at **Newmarket**. Military museums concentrate on regiments: the **Durham Light Infantry** in Durham, the **Staffordshire Regiment** in Lichfield, the **Royal Green Jackets** at Winchester. Some museums concentrate on World War II, such as the **German Occupation Museum** in Guernsey. Portsmouth has an unrivalled battery of naval attractions, with the excellent **Royal Naval Museum**, Nelson's flagship **HMS** *Victory*, the Tudor warship *Mary Rose* and the **Submarine Museum** in Gosport among others.

There are museums which concentrate on a single famous person: **John Bunyan** in Bedford, **Jane Austen** at Chawton, **Captain Cook** in Middlesbrough, **Barbara Hepworth** at St Ives. There are also galleries which preserve a collection formed by a single person or family – the enchanting **Lady Lever Art Gallery** at Port Sunlight, for instance, or the gorgeous **Bowes Museum** at Barnard Castle. Some of the most rewarding preserve a collection accumulated by a business firm: **Colman's Mustard** in Norwich, the **Harvey's Wine Museum** in Bristol, the **Pilkington Glass Museum** in St Helen's, the **Bass Museum of Brewing** at Burton upon Trent, treasures of **Minton** at Stoke-on-Trent, **Wedgwood** at Barlaston, **Royal Crown Derby** in Derby.

There are agricultural museums, costume museums, museums which collect whole buildings, like the **Weald and Downland Museum** in Sussex. So does the sparkling **Welsh Folk Museum** in St Fagans, founded in 1947 and an example of the growing post-war interest in the lives of ordinary people in the past.

The **North of England Open Air Museum** at Beamish in County Durham, which is showered with awards like confetti, re-creates the way of life of working-class people in the North around the turn of the century.

Since the 1950s there has been a second museum boom, on a far greater scale than the first. There were perhaps 700 museums all told in Britain when World War II ended. There are now more than 2,000. A substantial number of these, about a third, are independent institutions, not set up by the government or the local authorities, but by private operators. To survive, they depend on their ability to attract and please paying customers and among them are some of the best museums in the country. The **National Motor Museum** at Beaulieu in Hampshire has more than 250 historic vehicles on show and visitors are carried in moving 'pods' past displays which show how motoring developed in Britain from the late 19th century on and how it may develop in the future. In Shropshire there is the marvellous **Ironbridge Gorge** complex of museums, bringing one of the key sites of the industrial revolution to life. In the old canal docks at Gloucester is the immensely enjoyable and nostalgic **Robert Opie Collection** of packets, wrappers, tins and advertising material, a museum of all our domestic yesterdays.

The best independents have contributed to the general enlivening of museums over the last 20 years. The old, musty institution of yore, full of mournful stuffed birds, prehistoric flint implements and dauntingly uninformative captions, is now a collector's item, if you can find one.

Some of the newest museums and galleries have been encouraged or funded by local authorities bent on developing tourist attractions to bring visitors and money into an area. In Bradford, for example, the **National Museum of Photography, Film and Television** opened in 1983, with the biggest cinema screen in Britain. It has galleries with 'interactive displays', where you can see yourself reading the news on TV!

There are teapots to admire in **Norwich**, trams to ride at **Crich** in Derbyshire, pork pies in **Melton Mowbray** and buns in **Abingdon**, voices in Lincolnshire dialect to listen to on the telephone in **Lincoln**, while the **Town Docks Museum** in Hull echoes to the voices of whales moaning in the deep. Certainly no one could sensibly complain of a lack of variety and interest in Britain's museums and galleries today.

Museum or art gallery

Below *The ship's wheel of HMS Warrior on show at Portsmouth.* Bottom *One of the locomotives at the National Railway Museum, in York.*

Industrial interest

Tourist railway or steam centre

Industrial Interest Tourist Railways and Steam Centres

Agriculture, industry and transport are the three principal activities through which successive generations have altered the appearance and character of Britain's landscape. Far back in the Stone Age there were axe factories in the Lake District and men wielding deer antlers as picks were digging shafts 40ft (12m) deep to mine for flint in Norfolk and Sussex. Since then the face of the land has been scarred wherever opportunity offered, by quarrying for building stone and mining for coal, iron ore, copper, lead and tin.

The great majority of Britain's sites of industrial interest today are legacies from the industrial revolution. They date roughly from the 1750s on, when water power and subsequently steam power were harnessed to the mass production of goods in mills and factories. The products were efficiently transported to customers along

Below Handsome 18th-century Quarry Bank Mill, at Styal in Cheshire. Bottom The splendid iron bridge in Ironbridge in Shropshire.

improved roads, later by canals and in the 19th century by railways.

Interest in preserving what was left of the old industrial heritage gathered strength after World War II. The term 'industrial archaeology' was coined in about 1950 and since then some exceptionally impressive sites have been rescued from dereliction or threatened destruction.

Perhaps the single most important one is the **Ironbridge Gorge** in Shropshire, where the River Severn cuts its way through steep, wooded hills. Here in the mining village of Coalbrookdale, the Darby dynasty of ironmasters succeeded in 1709 in smelting iron with coke – a fundamental advance in technology which led to the mass production of iron. It was in Coalbrookdale that the great Iron Bridge across the Severn was cast, the first important iron bridge in the world. The bridge is still there and the complex of museums and sites in the area today includes blast furnaces and engines, and a charmingly restored 1890s industrial community at Blists Hill, with a working foundry, a candle mill, other installations and railway exhibits.

The Darby family and other ironmasters pressed on to exploit the use of steam. One of the pioneers was John Wilkinson, known as 'Iron-Mad Wilkinson' because of his passionate advocacy of iron for every conceivable use. He wore an iron hat, was buried in an iron coffin when he died in 1808, and an iron obelist was raised to his memory. It was Wilkinson who patented the method of boring cylinders which made James Watt's steam engine a practical proposition. His ironworks at **Bersham**, near Wrexham in North Wales, is today the centrepiece of an industrial heritage centre. This itself is on an eight-mile trail which traces the industrial history of this area from Roman times to the present day.

Another pioneer was Richard Arkwright, the Lancashire barber turned textile magnate, who built a water-powered cotton mill in the 1770s at **Cromford** in Derbyshire, with model housing for his factory hands. The site is being restored by the Arkwright Society. In Cheshire the National Trust owns **Quarry Bank Mill** at Styal, where another factory town was created round the cotton mill by the Greg family from the 1780s on. The machinery is running again, cotton goods woven in the mill are on sale and visitors can see the huge 85ft (26m) water-wheel, the village and the house where the pauper children lived.

The vast, dinosaur-like wheels and engines of the early industrial age always attract and awe visitors. Lead mining was long an important industry on the northern moors and an enormous wheel is the most striking feature of the **Killhope Lead Mine** in Weardale, County Durham. In Cornwall giant engines were needed to pump water out of the shafts of tin mines driven 2,000ft (610m) deep and sometimes far out under the sea. The ruined engine houses and chimney stacks of abandoned tin mines are a dramatic and melancholy feature of the Cornish landscape. The National Trust preserves two of the engines at **East Pool Mine**, near Camborne. North of St Austell, in the strange white moonscape of china clay heaps, the 19th-century **Wheal Martyn** pit is a museum of the industry.

The titanic 1876 steam engine which pumped Brighton's water up from 160ft (49m) below ground has been restored, with many other engines, at the **British Engineerium** in Hove. Machinery clatters and rattles energetically away at the **Stott Park Bobbin Mill** in Cumbria, now in the care of English Heritage. This bobbin factory built in the 1830s is virtually unchanged. Wheels turn and fan-belts flap alarmingly at **Camden Works** in Bath, in the former brass foundry of J B Bowler. Here the most elementary safety precautions were ignored. The firm also made dubious aerated soft drinks. Nothing was ever thrown away at Bowler's and the whole ramshackle place is a delight.

Scotland is not as rich in industrial sites as it might be, but drinks of quite a different kind can be sampled in a clutch of whisky distilleries in the Dufftown area. There is a 70-mile, eight-distillery Whisky Trail for enthusiasts, who are urged to let someone else do the driving.

Coal mining and ironworking were carried on for centuries on a small scale in the Forest of Dean. One of the eerier experiences in Britain is to make your way down into the echoing tunnels and caverns of the **Clearwell Caves Iron Mine**, which had its heyday between 1850 and 1900.

In Wales, among the mountains of Snowdonia, there are dramatic sites where the hillsides are torn and broken by quarrying for slate, the principal industry of the area for 200 years until quite recently. At the **Llechwedd Slate Caverns** near Blaenau Ffestiniog, visitors are taken deep underground into the tunnels and caverns, and there are demonstrations of the skilled art of slate-splitting. Close by is the **Gloddfa Ganol Slate Mine**, once the biggest in the world. At Llanberis there is a museum of the industry in the workshops of the now-closed **Dinorwic Quarry**.

The country's most dramatic and convincing coal mining museum is in South Wales. This is **Big Pit**, near Blaenafon in Gwent, in a colliery which closed in 1980. You go down almost 300ft (90m) in the cage, wearing your miner's helmet with lamp – which you need – and an ex-miner guides the party through the tunnels.

The application of steam power to transport created the great age of railways in Britain in the 19th and 20th centuries. The landscape was changed for every by the Herculean works involved; the construction of embankments, cuttings and tunnels, the throwing of noble bridges and soaring viaducts across rivers and valleys. The sight of a powerful steam locomotive hammering along the rails at full tilt under a plume of smoke, the screaming of its whistle echoing across country, became part of the right order of things. When steam gave way to diesel and electric power, and much-loved branch lines were closed down in the 1950s and '60s, preservation societies were formed to keep steam lines running or restore them to operation.

Many of the preserved lines go through particularly attractive stretches of country. The **Severn Valley Railway** runs more trains than any other, for 16 miles close to the River Severn between Bridgnorth, Bewdley and Kidderminster. Among its steam warhorses are some fine old Great Western locomotives.

The **Bluebell Railway** in Sussex has five miles of track between Sheffield Park and Horsted Keynes, through woods shining with bluebells in the spring. The **North Yorkshire Moors Railway** steams the 18 miles from Pickering to Grosmont through superlative scenery in the North York Moors National Park and runs a Pullman service regularly. There are gaslit stations on the **Keighley and Worth Valley Railway**, whose headquarters are at Haworth in the Brontë Country. The **Lakeside & Haverthwaite Railway** puffs amicably through the Cumbrian woods to connect with the steamers on Lake Windermere.

In 19th-century England and Scotland the standard gauge of 4ft 8$\frac{1}{2}$in held sway, but elsewhere, especially in mountainous areas, a narrow gauge might be better suited

to the terrain – the **Isle of Man Railway's** 15-mile line from Douglas to Port Erin, has a 3ft gauge. Wales has a special reputation for its 'great little trains', on which the traveller can enjoy the steam, the shining paintwork and polished brass, and extremely spectacular scenery.

The **Vale of Rheidol Railway**, for instance, which opened in 1902, clanks its way along the mountainsides and round sharp bends from Aberystwyth to the famous beauty spot of the Devil's Bridge. The **Ffestiniog Railway**, originally built to haul slate, clambers up into Snowdonia from the harbour of Porthmadog past lakes and waterfalls and into the mountains. Some of its genial, round-faced engines have been making the trip for a hundred years. The **Talyllyn Railway**, which has been running since 1865, travels seven miles inland from Tywyn on Cardigan Bay, with splendid mountain prospects. This was the first railway in Britain to be saved by volunteers from destruction. It set an example many were glad to follow.

A vintage steam engine on the Brecon Mountain Railway near Merthyr Tydfil.

Industrial interest

Tourist railway or steam centre

Garden

Arboretum

Gardens
Arboreta

'An Englishman's home is his castle' and round his castle he creates a garden. Despite – or perhaps because of – the vagaries of our climate, the closeness of the Gulf Stream and the collections brought back from all over the world particularly in the 18th and 19th centuries, Britain has a wonderful heritage of gardens and arboreta.

The **Royal Horticultural Society**, inaugurated in 1804, has gardens at **Wisley**, near Woking, **Rosemoor**, in Devon, as well as close affiliations with the College of Horticulture, at **Pershore** and Liverpool University Botanic Garden, at **Ness**, on the Wirral. The RHS has, since 1889, published *'The Garden'*, describing what can be seen, when and where. At all these places, keen gardeners can readily obtain advice and information.

The **Royal Botanic Garden** at Kew was established in 1759, in the reign of George II. Joining the traditional Victorian Palm and Temperate Houses, is Kew's latest feature, the Princess of Wales Conservatory, a

The gardens at Bodnant, Gwynedd, are among the most beautiful in Britain.

complex of 10 independently controlled climatic environments, growing a range of plants from desert to tropical forest species.

Since 1965 the National Trust property at **Wakehurst Place**, near Ardingly, has been 'Kew in the country' and it is here that a national seed bank is maintained.

As we become increasingly aware of the fragile nature of our planet's eco-system, plant collections and gene banks are more and more a vital part of horticulture. The National Council for the Conservation of Plants and Gardens has, since 1982, co-ordinated collections such as the magnolias at **Savill Garden**, near Windsor, violas at **Leicester University**, clematis at **Tenbury**, peonies at **Hidcote** and rhododendrons at **Leonardslee**, **Nymans** and at **Exbury**. **Abbotsbury,** in Devon, looks after eucalyptus and in scores of smaller gardens, amateurs as well as professionals nurture border plants, primroses, celandines, buddleias and asters. For bigger specimens, arboreta play their part. Seventeen miles of pathways lead through the 500 acres of the Forestry Commission's **Westonbirt Arboretum** in Gloucestershire, where plantings have been

continuous for 150 years. Oak, chestnut, pine and beech shelter more exotic specimens, such as acers and willows, azaleas and rhododendrons.

The **Granada Arboretum**, in Manchester, and the National Trust's **Winkworth Arboretum**, in Surrey, maintain sorbus and malus. Winter-flowering plants such as daphnes, honeysuckle, camellias and viburnum can be seen at the **Hillier Arboretum**, near Romsey, and plants which flourish on chalky soils are the specialty of **Hidcote Manor Garden**, north of Chipping Campden.

Many of the gardens lovingly tended in the past have now been restored. At **New Place**, in Surrey, the Edwardian garden of Gertrude Jekyll was recovered from beneath couch grass and poppies. At East Grinstead, the mullioned windows of 16th-century **Gravetye Manor** now reflect the glory of a Victorian garden created by William Robinson. At **Erddig**, near Wrexham, another 18th-century design has been re-created in the grounds of the National Trust house and **Culpeper Flower Garden** now flourishes at **Leeds Castle**, in Kent, 17th-century home of the Culpeper family. The 18th-century garden at

Painshill Park in Surrey was laid out in the 1740s by Charles Hamilton. Sadly decayed, the combination of classical architecture, lake and landscaping is being restored and it may once again rival the garden of Hamilton's friend, Henry Hoare at Stourhead.

Gardens stretch the length and breadth of the British isles. **Inverewe,** in Wester Ross, despite its northern latitude, enjoys frost-free conditions, due to the warm North Atlantic Drift, and **Tresco Abbey Gardens** in the Scilly Isles, created and maintained since 1834 by successive generations of the same family, relishes mild, moist weather. In the 1790s garden of 13th-century **Drum Castle**, near Aberdeen, a collection illustrating the development of roses from the 17th-century has recently been created by the National Trust for Scotland.

The **University Botanic Gardens** at St Andrews, training ground for future professionals, also provide a well laid out and informative garden for the visitor. Its high point is the peat, water and rock complex simulating the natural progression from mountain crag to scree to meadow and bog. The **Royal Botanic Garden**, in Edinburgh, second oldest in the country after Oxford, also has a superb rock garden and, like the new conservatory at Kew, grows the astonishing *Victoria Amazonica* water lily, its huge leaves capable of supporting a small child, but which grow from seed annually.

Across on the west coast are the gardens of **Brodick Castle**, on the Isle of Arran. Sir John Ramsden, then owner of **Muncaster Castle**, in Cumbria, after a visit to Brodick sent his hostess some rhododendrons for her garden – in all 80 tons! In 1953 an expedition to Burma brought back hundreds more plants and yet more varieties, most of which flourish in the mild climate.

At **Belsay**, north of Newcastle, English Heritage has restored the gardens, partly in the quarry used by Charles Monck, a keen member of the Horticultural Society. At **Thorp Perrow**, near Ripon, there is a cherry avenue which is a riot of blossom in May. Several 'autumn bays' provide colour from September to November and there is a rowan avenue, with spring blossom and autumn berries.

John Aislabie, Chancellor of the Exchequer at the time of the South Sea Bubble, retired to his estate at **Studley Royal**, in Yorkshire, albeit under something of a cloud. The garden he designed is a work of true inspiration, anticipating

Stourhead by 40 years. It now incorporates the ready-made 'folly', so essential to Romantic landscaping, acquired when his son purchased the nearby Fountains Abbey.

Harlow Carr Botanical Garden, near Harrogate, has been since 1948 the headquarters of the Northern Horticultural Society, working closely with the RHS and offering a similar range of walks, workshops and demonstrations as Wisley. **Newby Hall**, near Ripon, has something to delight the eye all year round, but is best known for its display of roses in early summer and its herbaceous border plants.

At **Eaton Hall**, Eccleston, near Chester, there is an unheated glasshouse 360 feet (110m) long, with camellias which are usually at their best in April. **Bodnant**, near Llandudno, always associated with the Aberconway family, has rhododendrons, azaleas, magnolias and camellias. Here, too, there is a wonderful laburnum walk where, on a sunny day in May, you can walk through a tunnel of glorious yellow blossom. Near Welshpool is **Powis Castle**, once the home of Clive of India. Its terraces are one of the few remaining medieval-style gardens in the country.

Doddington Hall, south-west of Lincoln, was built by the Elizabethan architect, Smythson, who designed Longleat and Hardwick Hall. The garden, even as late as 1919, had cattle grazing on the lawns, but now the walled west garden is full of the old-fashioned roses for which Doddington is famous, as well as a profusion of irises.

Near Colchester, **Beth Chatto's Garden** covering 12 acres, has developed into a centre where gardeners can pick up hints on what grows best in hard-baked sandy soil, sour silt or waterlogged clay. At **Sissinghurst**, in Kent, the garden of this Tudor house is a monument to Vita Sackville-West who, in the 1930s, created walks where each of the gardens opening off had its own colour scheme.

In **Sheffield Park**, near East Grinstead, famous for its autumn colours, you can wander away from the lakeside rhododendrons and discover the wonderful collection of conifers. One group of maritime pines is reputed to have been planted by Sir Joseph Banks, a founder of the RHS. David Douglas, after whom the Douglas fir is named, brought Monterey pines here from California and there is a dwarf Siberian pine planted in the 1920s, which has just about reached five feet (one and a half metres) and can thus be highly recommended for the small garden!

The National Trust property at **Kingston Lacy** in Dorset, has a delightful fernery planted with snowdrops for an early effect and the Cedar Walk has carefully recorded plantings by the Duke of Wellington, King Edward VII, the Kaiser and King George V, who planted an oak here to commemorate his Coronation. At **Stourhead**, north of Shaftesbury, lake, bridge, temples and grottoes combine to achieve one of the finest 'landscaped' gardens in the world, the creation of Henry Hoare in the 1740s, a generation before Capability Brown began diverting rivers and moving mountains around many of the great houses of his day.

Penjerrick, in Cornwall, was begun in the 1830s and many exotic plants here were grown from seed brought into nearby Falmouth by clipper captains, but rhododendrons remain one of its glories.

Wherever you go, at no matter what season of the year, there are gardens to be enjoyed all over Britain. Provided you do not pick a Bank Holiday weekend, in most cases you will find someone ready to pass on the secret of their success to you.

Garden

Arboretum

Hillier Arboretum in Hampshire.

Country park

The forested slopes at Afan Argoed resemble those in Switzerland.

Country Parks

In the 1960s and '70s, increasing affluence, more leisure time, more cars and faster roads combined to bring the open countryside within the reach of far more people. The number of townspeople and suburbanites driving out for a day in the country was growing rapidly and there was a need to accommodate the demand without spoiling the countryside which everyone was eager to enjoy.

In 1966 a government white paper on 'Leisure in the Countryside' suggested the establishment of country parks and the idea was taken up in the Countryside Acts which followed. The two Countryside Commissions, one for England and Wales, the other for Scotland, were given the responsibility for stimulating the creation of country parks, providing advice and grants of taxpayers' money to projects they approved.

Most of the country parks have been set up by local authorities. One of their fundamental functions is to make available country places where visitors know they have a right to be. Opinion polls and studies have shown time and time again that people are held back from enjoying the countryside by an uneasy feeling that they may be trespassing or at least not wanted. A country park is a place where you are welcome. It is also a place where there will be toilets and somewhere to park the car.

There are now more than 200 country parks in Britain, varying considerably in size and character. The larger ones have visitor centres where you will find information about the landscape, the wildlife and often the area's history; wardens or rangers who keep an eye on things and provide help and information when needed; way-marked paths; amusements for children, and refreshments.

Country parks are usually open every day during daylight hours, and in the great majority of them admission is free, though boating, bowls or other special facilities may have to be paid for. Activities vary from one park to another – from riding, fishing, hang-gliding and grass-skiing to orienteering, golfing, boating and sailing.

Some of the earliest country parks were areas which were already heavily visited and where better facilities were needed. An example is **Box Hill**, near Dorking in Surrey, named after the rare wild box trees on the chalk hill. For centuries past people have loved to walk there and admire the views of the Weald. Much of the area is owned by the National Trust and there is a car park, information room and shop.

Another case in point is **Butser Hill**, a much-visited beauty spot on the A3 south of Petersfield where

Hampshire County Council created the **Queen Elizabeth Country Park,** opened by the Queen in 1976. The park covers 1,400 acres of downs, Forestry Commission beechwoods and stands of yew at the western edge of the South Downs Way footpath. There are splendid views from the top of Butser Hill, a nature reserve and waymarked trails, with downland plants and flowers to see, woodpeckers, butterflies and deer. The Ancient Farm Research Project here farms the way Iron Age man did 2,000 years ago and the park has an information centre with an audio-visual programme, a café and a picnic area.

Another heavily visited area is the **Brimham Rocks Country Park** on the moors near Pateley Bridge in North Yorkshire. The rocks, weathered into strange shapes over the centuries, drew sightseers in such numbers that the area was in danger of being badly damaged. It is owned by the National Trust and the threat to the rocks has been brought under control.

Since country parks were intended primarily for town dwellers, they tend to be more numerous close to heavily populated urban areas. They are not thick on the ground in Norfolk and Suffolk, for example, but there is quite a concentration of them in Essex, nearer London. One of these is the attractive **Hatfield Forest Country Park**, near Bishop's Stortford, an area of ancient hunting forest which was only just rescued from the developer's grasp in the 1920s and which is famous for its hornbeams and its nightingales.

Similarly, there are fewer country parks in North and Central Wales than in the former mining and industrial areas of South Wales. One of the biggest and best is **Margam Country Park**, near Port Talbot. Its 850 acres include what were once the stately grounds of the Mansel family's fine house. There are landscaped gardens, a deer park, a handsome orangery which is used for concerts, a theatre, a large maze and boating on the lake, which is also occupied by swans, coots and moorhens. A herd of Glamorgan cattle and an Iron Age hillfort with commanding views over the Bristol Channel add to its enormous appeal. There is an adventure playground, a heronry in the nature reserve and there are skylarks and buzzards. Just outside the park is the ruined church of 12th-century Margam Abbey.

Many other parks have solved the problem of what to do with fine country estates the owners can no longer keep up. **Mount Edgcumbe Country Park**, which looks out over Plymouth Sound, preserves the formal gardens with their statues and fountains laid out for the Edgcumbe family in the 18th century. Stretching for miles along the coast, it boasts follies, woods, a deer park and a fabulous collection of camellias.

Many country parks, by contrast, have contributed to the reclamation of derelict industrial wasteland. East of Sheffield, on the border of Yorkshire and Derbyshire, the **Rother Valley Country Park** has arisen phoenix-like from an area of opencast coal mining, with 350,000 freshly planted trees and no less than three lakes for fishing and watersports. There are footpaths and visitors can hire cycles to ride along the network of bicycle tracks.

The **Strathclyde Country Park** in the south-eastern outskirts of Glasgow was formally opened in 1978. Millions of pounds were spent to take a derelict, stagnant wasteland of exhausted colliery workings and desolate spoil heaps and turn it back into pleasant countryside. The River Clyde was diverted to create a 200-acre loch, trees and shrubs and long stretches of grass were planted, paths were laid out by the loch and picnic areas and car parks provided.

Now the trees have matured. The loch, almost two miles long, is a watersports centre for sailing, canoeing and waterskiing. There is a golf course and sports pitches, an interpretation centre and a nature reserve which attracts wintering whooper swans and other waterfowl. Also inside the park are the remains of a Roman fort and a peculiar 19th-century mausoleum, which was constructed for the Dukes of Hamilton but turned out to have such a noisy echo in the chapel inside that it was impossible to use it.

Country park landscapes vary from the heath and scrub of **Cannock Chase** in Staffordshire to the giant trees in **Sherwood Forest**, the ducal landscape by Capability Brown not far away in **Clumber Park** in Nottinghamshire and on to the deer and rugged rocks of **Bradgate Park** in Leicestershire, with the ruins of the house in which the tragic Lady Jane Grey grew up. On top of **Ham Hill** in Somerset, the grassed-over stone quarries make a wonderful arena for hide-and-seek. On **Berry Head**, south of Torbay in South Devon, towering cliffs command bracing views of the English Channel and the nests of kittiwakes and guillemots. The need to protect the wild orchids and other rare plants here was one reason why the local council bought the land in 1968. Further on along the Channel coast, at the **Lepe Country Park** in Hampshire, you can look across the Solent to the Isle of Wight and idly watch the ships and the black-headed gulls go by.

One question which remains is: are the visitors at country parks enjoying real countryside or a mock-up? Nowadays the Countryside Commission believes that the parks should be treated less as ends in themselves and more as gateways to the true countryside beyond.

Brimham Rocks, in North Yorkshire, where the rocks form weird shapes.

Theme park

The 'Thunder River' rapid-water ride, for all the family, at Thorpe Park.

Theme Parks

The British theme park has its spiritual ancestor across the Atlantic. Disneyland, which opened in Anaheim in the southern suburbs of Los Angeles in 1955, combined four basic characteristics. First there was a central theme – the world of Disney cartoons and films. Second, there were illusions, using the latest technology, and visitors experienced a simulated river trip in the African jungle, or thought they were going deep underwater in a submarine, when in fact they were only a few inches beneath the surface. Next, there were 'white knuckle' rides – an exciting roller-coaster, a terrifying helter-skelter and other thrilling fairground rides, again using the latest technology. And last, Disneyland catered for the motor car, the family with children and modern mass tourism, with a parking lot of gargantuan proportions and an ample supply of toilets and places to eat.

The lessons of Disneyland were absorbed and put to use at **Alton Towers**, the 500-acre 'leisure park' in Staffordshire which is now attracting two and a half million visitors a year. Alton Towers employs a staff of 1,400 people during the summer and has six different restaurants, of varying types and price levels, with innumerable kiosks scattered about the grounds selling ice-creams and soft drinks. There is no single central theme, but six 'themed areas', which include Fantasy World, Aqualand and Kiddies Kingdom. Among the 'white knuckle' rides are the gravity-defying Corkscrew Roller-coaster, which lives up to its name, as well as the New Black Hole, the Alton Beast, and the water-based Log Flume

and Grand Canyon Rapids Ride.

There are gentler rides for those of nervous disposition or with small children, with a beautiful carousel, and a mass of indoor attractions and Disney-style parades with bands, floats and performers in life-size animal costumes.

In addition to all this is a wonderful Victorian Gothic ruin and some of the most spectacular gardens in the country, inherited from the Earls of Shrewsbury, whose country seat Alton Towers used to be. The 15th and 16th Earls constructed an enormous pseudo-medieval fantasy palace here, replete with towers and spires, turrets and battlements. A W Pugin himself, the high priest of Victorian Gothic, was called in to preside over the interior decor. Outside, meanwhile, a fortune was spent to lay out a magnificent park and gardens. Lakes and pools were dug out, fed by water brought from a spring two miles off. Terraces, miles of walks, giant stairways and grand glasshouses were built at colossal expense by an army of workmen.

The future Queen Victoria visited Alton in 1832, at the age of 13, and was entertained to luncheon on gold plates. The Chinese-style Pagoda Fountain was built, and shoots a jet of water 70ft (21m) high. A Swiss cottage was erected on the hillside to provide a fine prospect over the grounds while a blind Welsh harper was stationed there to play soothing music. Today it is a restaurant.

In later years it proved impossible to keep the house up and the mansion fell into the condition of picturesque ruin in which visitors see it now. The gardens were properly maintained, however, and are a delight to walk in today.

More 'white knuckle' rides can be found by the adventurous at the **Chessington World of Adventures**, in Surrey. 'This Ride Is Not For The

Faint-Hearted' one sign warns. There is a blood chilling roller-coaster called the Vampire, which zooms along at tree-top height and dives underground. It is set in a 'Transylvania' village which also has a bubble works fantasy ride for children through a simulated fizzy pop factory, and a restaurant wittily named the Black Forest Chateau.

The theme areas at Chessington feature encounters with horrible science fiction monsters, and Calamity Canyon, where there's a Wild West trading post, a shooting gallery and a roller-coaster called the Runaway Mine Train. In the Mystic East area visitors see the Palace of the Nine Dragons, the Giant Buddha and the Cambodian temple of Angkor Wat, and go on a 'dragon river' water ride through a bamboo jungle, where the boat is attacked by a crocodile. In addition, Chessington has a zoo, a circus, a miniature railway, plenty of eating places and live entertainment with bands, dancers, clowns, street performers and 'madcap' characters in costume.

Halfway between Derby and Nottingham may seem an odd place to meet cowboys and shoot-outs, but the Wild West is one of the main themes at the **American Adventure**, near Ilkeston in Derbyshire. Pistol-packing posses career through town, bullets fly and saloon girls squeal as badmen get their come-uppances. There is live entertainment in Lazy Lil's Saloon and jazz on a Mississippi riverboat.

The numerous rides include a double-drop log flume in Thunder Canyon and a charge through the raging torrents of the Great Niagara Rapids. Or you can take a triple-looping roller-coaster called the Missile and blast off to the stars from Space Port USA. There are special attractions to keep small children happy in Pioneer Playland, including a cartoon cinema.

At the **Pleasurewood Hills American Theme Park**, near Lowestoft in Suffolk, southern fried chicken is on the menu, and attractions range from the evil Rattlesnake roller-coaster and the New Tempest, which hangs you upside down 100ft (30m) in the air, to a waterborne voyage to Aladdin's Cave, a land of dinosaurs, fairground big wheels, a spooky haunted castle and shows by performing sea lions and parrots.

In Yorkshire, near Ripon, the **Lightwater Valley Theme Park**, in the 1970s a peaceful pig farm, prides itself on the sheer appalling terror of its 'white knuckle' rides. It opened the longest roller-coaster ride in the world in 1990, at a cost of over £5 million, running close to

1¹/₂ miles (2.4km) with a drop of 158ft (48m) and a top speed of about 60mph. This joined a nightmare ride called The Rat, which runs entirely underground in pitch darkness, 'through smelly sewers alive with the shrieks and shrills of rats' – rated tops for sheer horror by the *Daily Mirror*.

There are calmer pleasures at Lightwater Valley, too – a nine-hole golf course, three boating lakes, an old-fashioned fairground, a miniature railway and a shopping centre. There is skateboarding, a go-kart track, an adventure playground for smaller children and a theatre with live entertainment.

At Charnock Richard in Lancashire, there awaits 'an enchanted day out for the whole family' in 'the magical kingdom' of **Camelot.** The theme here is the world of King Arthur and his heroic knights of the Round Table. Knights in full armour thunder into combat on their chargers in the jousting arena. Jesters and grotesque animal figures wander about. A chilling roller-coaster hurtles into the Tower of Terror, where something unspeakable called the Beast lurks in its dark lair. Guinevere's swan ride negotiates Merlin's magic mountain, the Grail trail crosses a swinging rope bridge and Sir Bedevere's Bridge leads to the enchantments of the Wild Wood.

You can eat at the Round Table Burger Bar, naturally, but altogether Camelot has 28 outlets selling food and drink. It reckons to cook 2¹/₂ miles of sausages every season, as well as 250,000 pounds of dragon burgers and 315,000 pounds of chips.

The 'family leisure park' at **Thorpe Park**, near Chertsey in Surrey, is close to both the M3 and the M25. It opened in 1979 on the site of old gravel workings, which gave it plenty of lakes and pools. Water skiing, windsurfing and other watersports rank high among its pleasures, water barges carry visitors from one area of the park to another and there are river-boat restaurants.

The original theme was Britain's maritime history, but now, with the need to attract repeat visitors, the emphasis has changed. 'White knuckle' rides are not particularly important here and the park concentrates more on entertainments and amusements which families with children aged about four to 14 can all enjoy together. There is live entertainment at two theatres, lots of street entertainment, musicians, clowns and giant sub-Disney animal grotesques, and a large amusement centre with

video games and one-armed bandits. The log flume ride in the Canadian Rockies theme area has a drop of 50ft and there is a fast Space Station Zero ride, but more typical is the complete working farm, which operates as it did in the 1930s. A simulated medieval town square has a double-decker carousel and other attractions include a nature trail, miniature railway, roller skating rink, crazy golf and a cartoon cinema.

All theme parks are geared to a

safe, enjoyable family day out, and you pay once, on entry, and get the rides and other attractions thrown in. Alton Towers is the kingpin in terms of visitor figures, but the numbers rung up at the other parks – over a million and a quarter at Thorpe Park and a similar figure at Chessington – suggest that this type of transatlantic family attraction is in Britain to stay.

The 'Runaway Mine Train' at Chessington World of Adventures.

Theme Park

Zoo

Wildlife collection – mammals

Wildlife collection – birds

Aquarium

Zoos
Wildlife Collections
Aquariums

The oldest picture of an elephant in England is in Exeter Cathedral, a 13th-century wood carving under one of the choir seats. It is quite likely to be a portrait of a real African elephant, the one which was presented to Henry III by the King of France in 1253. Its arrival in England created a sensation and people flocked to see the great beast as it tramped from the port of Sandwich to London.

Zoos
The century before, Henry I had established a menagerie at Woodstock in Oxfordshire. It was later moved to the Tower of London and survived there until well into the 19th century. The public was let in to see the animals, which in 1609 consisted of 11 lions, two leopards, a jackal, two mountain cats, three eagles and two owls.

Kings and noblemen continued to keep private menageries, but the 19th century saw the creation of public zoological gardens – zoos for short – as part of the same educational and improving impulse responsible for the establishment of so many museums. The first in the field was the **Regent's Park Zoo** in London, laid out by Decimus Burton and opened in 1828 by the recently founded Zoological Society of London. The animals from the Tower were moved here.

Municipal zoos now opened, combining serious study of animals with public instruction and entertainment. In Dublin, for example, the Royal Zoological Society of Ireland opened a zoo in **Phoenix Park** in 1830. It gained a substantial reputation for breeding lions, as **Glasgow Zoo** breeds porcupines and Edinburgh Zoo is famous for its penguins.

Wildlife Collections
After World War II, a tide of disapproval set in against the old-fashioned 19th-century zoo, which seemed little better than a prison with its cramped cages and unnatural conditions, and against the whole attitude to animals which this type of zoo was felt to represent. The consequence was the modernisation of many zoos and the coming of the safari park and a new style of wildlife collection.
The development of the open-range zoo, where animals roam in large enclosures instead of being penned in cages, had begun in 1931, when the Zoological Society of London opened a country branch at **Whipsnade Park** in Bedfordshire, near Dunstable. Whipsnade covers

The famous lions of Longleat.

more than 500 acres, most of the animals live in herds in sizeable paddocks and well over 90 per cent of them were born in the zoo. In the last 30 years many other zoos have moved closer to the open-range system.

Britain's first safari park opened in 1966 at **Longleat** in Wiltshire, the palatial Elizabethan seat of the Marquess of Bath. The prime movers in the enterprise were the Marquess himself and Jimmy Chipperfield, of the well-known circus family, an experienced supplier of wild animals to zoos. The idea was for visitors to drive through the spacious enclosures where the animals roamed: in other words, for a change, the animals would be free and the public confined. The project proved extremely popular.

Lions were the first and have always been the foremost attraction at Longleat, but many other animals can be seen there today – including the country's only white Bengal tiger, as well as white rhinos, camels, giraffes and gorillas. The monkeys enjoy riding on visitors' cars and there are boat trips to see hippos and sea lions. In some areas visitors can leave their cars and stroll about or even have a picnic among the animals. Like other safari parks, Longleat depends on and provides for the motor car and there is plenty of parking with no problem about finding a restaurant or a toilet.

The Duke of Bedford was not far behind in opening a safari park of his own at his stately Bedfordshire mansion of **Woburn**. Jimmy Chipperfield was again involved. But Woburn already had a distinguished history of keeping and breeding wild animals. Père David's deer are named after a French missionary, who saw the only remaining herd of them in the imperial park outside Peking where they were kept in the 19th century. A few animals were grudgingly shipped out to European zoos and

Flamingoes at Slimbridge Wildfowl Trust

when the Chinese herd was wiped out, the 16 Père David's deer in Europe were the only ones left. The 11th Duke of Bedford rounded all 16 up in 1894 and settled them in his park at Woburn, where they prospered and multiplied. All the Père David's deer in the world are descended from them, and in 1985 some were sent back to China, to the same park outside Peking.

Woburn also played a part in saving the European bison from extinction. The Père David's deer are still there, and so are the bison, and the **Woburn Wild Animal Kingdom** today is Britain's largest drive-through collection of wild creatures. A ride in aerial cars gives a bird's eye view of the park and there are performing sea lions, and even performing macaws.

A wildlife collection of an entirely different flavour can be enjoyed at **Chillingham**, in Northumberland, where visitors can cautiously inspect the 50-strong herd of wild white cattle. With their wicked, curving horns, they are the nearest thing to prehistoric cattle still in existence. They have been kept in the park at Chillingham for centuries and have never been crossbred.

John Aspinall has set up two Kent

Zoo

Wildlife collection – mammals

Wildlife collection – birds

Aquarium

zoo parks: **Howletts**, near Canterbury, famous for breeding gorillas and African elephants, and its sister at **Port Lympne**, near Hythe. Here magnificent Siberian tigers, black rhino and the country's only breeding colony of majestic Barbary lions loll about in aristocratic splendour.

Breeding animals, and especially breeding species which in the wild are threatened with extinction, has become an important function of zoos, safari parks and wildlife collections, and a key justification of their existence. **Chester Zoo**, for example, which ranks second only to London in its tally of visitors and has a wide range of animals in attractive grounds, has successfully bred orang-utans, Madagascan tree boas and rare fruit bats, among other species. **Bristol Zoo**, where the creatures on view range from tigers to tarantulas and penguins to piranhas, counts gorillas and orang-utans, Persian leopards, colobus monkeys and long-tailed macaques among its breeding successes. **Twycross Zoo**, near Atherstone in Warwickshire, a small zoo with a remarkable collection of apes and monkeys, has a notable breeding record and **Marwell**, near Winchester, breeds rare Sumatran tigers and the endangered oryx.

In 1947 there were only 50 breeding pairs of the Hawaiian geese (called nene) left in the world, all of them in Hawaii. The species was saved by successful breeding at the Wildfowl & Wetlands Trust reserve at **Slimbridge** in Gloucestershire, founded by the late Sir Peter Scott. Some of the birds from here were later sent back to Hawaii in the hope of re-establishing them in their native land.

The splendid Slimbridge reserve is on the bank of the River Severn. Other Wildfowl Trust reserves include those at **Arundel** in Sussex, **Washington** in Tyne and Wear, and **Caerlaverock**, near Dumfries in Scotland. At **Stagsden** in Bedfordshire is one of the first specialist bird collections in Britain. The Bird Gardens concentrate on cranes, but there are 150 species or more on view in all. **Birdworld**, near Farnham in Surrey, has a collection ranging from tiny hummingbirds to outsize ostriches, and is successfully breeding Humboldt penguins.

Aquariums
The first public aquarium in Britain opened in London in 1853. It was not until a hundred years later that the first massive sea aquariums, or oceanariums, opened in the United States, with huge tanks containing

The 'Penguin Parade' – the star attraction at Edinburgh Zoo.

hundreds of fish of different species swimming together. The example has been followed in Britain, for example at the **Sea Life Centre** in Weymouth, which opened in 1983 with the biggest display tank in Europe. Visitors can see dolphins and porpoises, British sharks, octopus and squid and evil-looking conger eels, and fish in drifting droves. There is a special flatfish tank and a tank with a simulated sunken wreck and the marine life that would gather around it. There are also 'touch pools' and plenty of fun for children.

Of the same genre, but on a much more modest scale, is **Anglesey Sea Zoo**, near Brynsiencyn, close to the shore of the Menai Strait, with its tanks of fish, lobsters and crabs from the local waters and 'touch tanks' for the children.

There is plenty of enjoyment and discovery at other sea life centres in seaside towns, like Brighton, Blackpool and Southsea and at Barcaldine in Scotland where young seals can be viewed prior to their release back into the wild. While wildlife is increasingly threatened in the wild, it flourishes in British zoos, safari parks and aquariums.

Nature reserve

RSPB site

Nature Reserves
Nature Trails
RSPB Sites

Brownsea Island is a much-treasured Dorset beauty spot, a 500-acre island in Poole Harbour, accessible only by boat. It has an honoured place in the history of the Boy Scouts, as it was here in 1907 that General Baden-Powell held his first scout camp. A succession of wealthy and sometimes eccentric owners preserved the island from contamination by development until, with the death of the last of them in 1961, it passed to the National Trust. It was then a wildly overgrown paradise for red squirrels, the late owner's peacocks, Sika deer, herons and seabirds. The National Trust has protected it ever since and thousands of visitors go there every year to enjoy the beaches, walk the heathland and woodland glades and admire stunning views of the Dorset coast.

A substantial area of the island is sealed off against casual visitors dropping in, though parties are guided round at regular intervals. This is a nature reserve, managed by the Dorset Trust for Nature Conservation, with a heronry, two lakes and a marsh fringed with reeds, where wildfowl congregate in

A view from a hide overlooking Welney Wildfowl Refuge, in Norfolk.

safety – terns and oystercatchers, godwits and sandpipers, dunlins and redshanks.

Nature Reserves
Unlike a National Park or a country park, a nature reserve is not protected for the sake of human visitors, but for the sake of the wild creatures, birds, insects and rare plants, and the habitats and conditions they need to survive and flourish. Many nature reserves are open to the general public; at others a permit may be needed or access may be limited, but some are closed altogether.

As long ago as 1912 the need to set aside areas in which threatened species could survive was recognised with the founding of the Society for the Promotion of Nature Reserves by the pioneering naturalist Charles Rothschild. When he died the movement lost impetus. After World War II, however, the pressure of expanding population and expanding leisure time bore so heavily on the country's wildlife that something plainly needed to be done. In 1949 the government set up the Nature Conservancy Council (NCC) as its wildlife protection arm, and one of the new body's responsibilities was 'to establish, manage and maintain nature reserves'.

At the same time vigorous county and local wildlife protection trusts were forming and establishing nature reserves of their own. Charles Rothschild's society re-emerged into the limelight as the national organisation and mouthpiece of these groups, as the Royal Society for Nature Conservation.

Today Britain has more than 2,000 nature reserves, occupying more than half a million acres of land between them. Some are managed by the NCC, but a far larger number are run by the county or local trusts for nature conservation, naturalists' trusts or wildlife trusts. Others are owned and managed by the Forestry Commission, others again by local authorities and conservation bodies.

From a visitor's point of view, nature reserves supply a way of seeing and coming close to the full range of Britain's wildlife and plant life without any danger of trespassing or going where one is not wanted. They can be found on the coast and inland, on high ground and on low, in a great variety of countryside.

At **Caerlaverock**, for instance, on the Solway Firth coast of Scotland, the NCC established a reserve in 1957 on the low-lying saltmarshes among muddy flats and creeks. Multitudes of birds feed and roost there: golden plovers in legions,

greylag geese, pintail and all manner of ducks and waders. Thousands of barnacle geese fly in from the Arctic every winter, and there are birds of prey, as well as saltmarsh plants in abundance. This is also one of the breeding grounds of the rare and noisy natterjack toad. Visitor access is limited, partly because the flats and creeks are dangerous when the tide sweeps in suddenly. There is also a Wildfowl Trust refuge close by and the romantic pink ruin of Caerlaverock Castle to visit.

By contrast, not so many miles away inland, east of Newton Stewart, the NCC runs the **Cairnsmore of Fleet** nature reserve, largely a trackless waste of peat and heather moorland, bog and mountainside. It is important as the home of the red deer, wild goats and ravens. Access is again restricted.

Similarly, there is a cluster of contrasting nature reserves in the Gower Peninsula of South Wales, which is famed for packing a remarkable variety of scenery into a small area, and for the accompanying wealth of wildlife. At **Cwmllwyd Wood**, west of Swansea, for instance, West Glamorgan County Council has a reserve of oak woods, grassland and marsh, with hides from which to watch snipe and woodcock. At **Oxwich** on the south coast there is an NCC reserve of quite different character in an area of sand dunes, wooded headlands and marshes, explored by nature trails. Keep an eye out for adders on the slopes.

RSPB Sites

Some of the most rewarding nature reserves in the country belong to the Royal Society for the Protection of Birds (RSPB). Founded in 1889, the RSPB is devoted to the conservation of wild birds. It has built up a portfolio of well over a hundred reserves in which the habitats of breeding and wintering birds and birds of passage are preserved.

Some of the RSPB reserves are as far flung as the **Orkneys** and **Shetlands**, but most of them are more accessible. There is one at **Dungeness** on the Kent coast, where the nuclear power station broods over a desolate landscape of shingle beach, ponds and abandoned gravel workings, and tangled gorse and brambles. But there is plenty of life here – marsh frogs, plants like viper's bugloss, and waterfowl in huge numbers, with many migrating birds making a landfall at this point.

Up in Lancashire, at **Leighton Moss** near Silverdale, the RSPB preserves an area of swamp,

The 300ft (91m) high cliffs of Marwick Head's RSPB reserve, Orkney.

shallow meres and scrubland. Here bitterns boom and breed among the reeds and marsh harriers pass by in spring, while below are otters, deer, bats and beautiful wild orchids.

The Forest of Dean is one of the few remaining ancient royal forests left in England. Although commercial forestry plantations have replaced much of the original oak woods, there are still a few areas where magnificent oaks over 150 years old can be found. One of these is at the RSPB **Nagshead Reserve** which covers some of the best remaining oak woodland and has a rich bird community. Summer visitors include wood warblers, redstarts and pied flycatchers as well as the whole range of woodland species including all three species of woodpecker, sparrowhawks, treecreepers and nuthatches.

At **Nene Washes** in Cambridgeshire the RSPB reserve, saved from drainage and ploughing, is an example of a landscape now nearly lost. Once, hay meadows like these – rich in flowers in spring and full of birds in winter – were common; now there are only scattered remnants left. It is ironic that the washes are entirely man-made, created in the 18th century as part of flood control and drainage schemes. Breeding birds here include redshanks, snipe, sedge warblers, yellow wagtails and shovelers. Winter brings Bewick's swans, wigeon, teal and pintails in large numbers.

On the north-west tip of Holy Island, is the RSPB reserve of **South Stack Cliffs**. This reserve consists of two separate areas: the dramatic sea cliffs and heathland of Holyhead Mountain make up the northern part, while the maritime heathland of Penrhosfeilw Common is the

southern section. The most numerous seabirds are guillemots but there are razorbills, puffins and kittiwakes. The reserve is one of the foremost migration watchpoints in North Wales, both for landbirds and seabirds. On most summer days, especially with a westerly wind, Manx shearwaters and gannets may be seen flying past, while in spring and autumn large movements of passerines can be recorded in suitable weather conditions. Hundreds of wheatears and swallows may pass through daily, with smaller numbers of willow and grasshopper warblers, whinchats and ring ouzels. In early winter thousands of starlings, chaffinches and other species pass westward to the warmer climate of Ireland.

One of the RSPB's most celebrated reserves is **Bempton Cliffs** near Goole. These spectacular 445ft chalk cliffs hold the largest breeding colony of seabirds in England. Puffins and guillemots nest here but the most famous of Bempton's seabirds is the gannet, whose colony is the only mainland one in Britain. Seawatching can be exceptionally good, especially in the autumn, when the terns and skuas are moving south. The narrow band between the cliffs and the cliff-top fields is an excellent place for wild flowers.

Though the primary purpose of a reserve is protection, the RSPB welcomes visitors – the general public as well as its own members – in order to encourage public sympathy and support for conservation. Trails and hides are provided to help visitors see as much as possible, while interfering as little as possible with the birds.

National trail

National Trails

Enthusiasm for long distance walking has grown apace in Britain since World War II, as part of a general quickening of appetite for exploring and enjoying the countryside at first hand, away from main roads and crowded tourist spots. The first national long distance walking route, the Pennine Way, was declared open in 1965. Since then many more paths have been established. Ten of them are now classified by the Countryside Commission as 'national trails'. These are continuous routes over substantial distances, which can take a week or more to traverse though, of course, many people enjoy walking for only a few hours or a day or two on part of one of the routes.

The ten national trails in England and Wales are: the Cleveland Way; the North Downs Way; the Offa's Dyke Path; the Peddars Way and Norfolk Coast Path; the Pembrokeshire Coast Path; the Pennine Way; the Ridgeway Path; the South Downs Way; the South

Below Offa's Dyke Path *traces the 8th-century English – Welsh boundary.* *Bottom* The 50 miles of the Peddar's Way, in Norfolk, follow a Roman road.

West Coast path; and the Wolds Way. Placed end to end, these 10 routes together cover approximately 1,750 miles. Three of them are in the South of England, one is in East Anglia, two are in Wales and the Marches, and three in the North. There are also three more long distance walking routes in Scotland.

The founding father of this whole network was the late Tom Stephenson of the Ramblers' Association, who in 1935 put forward the idea of a continuous public footpath running the whole length of the Pennine Chain to the Cheviots and the Scots Border. It took 30 years during which much opposition had to be overcome, but he lived to see his brainchild brought safely to birth as the Pennine Way.

The **Pennine Way** runs 250 miles up the backbone of England from the High Peak in Derbyshire to the Scottish border. It starts in the Peak District National Park and crosses two other National Parks – the Yorkshire Dales and Northumberland – as well as an Area of Outstanding Natural Beauty in the North Pennines.

You can walk it either way, naturally, but travelling from south to north keeps the weather at the walker's back and the route is usually described in this direction. It starts at Edale in the delectable valley of the River Noe, close to Castleton and its deep, eerie limestone caverns. The Way goes up across the Kinder Scout plateau (there are alternative routes here and elsewhere along the trail) to the aptly named wasteland of Bleaklow. It then passes by Blackstone Edge, with its exceptionally well preserved stretch of Roman road, and across the Calder Valley close to Hebden Bridge, where the rows of millhands' houses cling to the steep hillsides, to the beauty spot of Hardcastle Crags. North from here are the wild moors of the Brontë Country, near Haworth, and the bleak scenery and atmosphere of *Wuthering Heights* at the ruined farmhouse at Withins.

The Way crosses the Craven district to reach the tremendous limestone scenery of the Yorkshire Dales National Park: 'a strange landscape,' as the great fell-walker Wainwright has written, 'almost lunar, in places awesome, in places beautiful, and everywhere fascinating.' From Malham, the beetling gorge of Gordale Scar is a mile or so off the path, which scrambles up the sheer curving cliff of Malham Cove, close to 250ft (76m) high, to the cracked and fissured limestone 'pavement' on top. Malham Tarn is the lake where Charles Kingsley was inspired to

create *The Water Babies*. Further on is the isolated hump of Pen-y-ghent, 2,273ft (693m).

On to Ribblesdale and to Wensleydale, at Hawes, and close to Hardraw Force, where the water tumbles over a 100ft (30m) rock. Further on is Middleton in Teesdale and the Way follows the swirling, rock-strewn Tees to three spectacular waterfalls in succession: Low Force, High Force and Cauldron Snout, where the river boils and rages down the rock ledges for 200ft (61m). At the stupendous horseshoe of High Cup Nick an immense abyss opens, whose sides are sheer for almost 1,000ft (305m).

Northwards again, up the valley of the South Tyne to Hadrian's Wall, getting on for 1,900 years old now, but still swooping athletically over the crags. The Way follows it for nine miles, passing Housesteads, where there are the remains of a substantial Roman fort, with legionary latrines and a museum. Then the route lies on north over heathery moors to Bellingham, across Redesdale and through the forest to the high Cheviots, the lonely open spaces of the Northumberland National Park, and the Border at last, coming to a final grateful halt at Kirk Yetholm.

The **Wolds Way** in the old East Riding of Yorkshire is about as unlike the Pennine Way as two walking routes in the same country could conceivably be. In length, by comparison, the Wolds Way is a mere pygmy of 79 miles all told. It is easy going where the Pennine Way is hard. And instead of daring the wild and lonely places, and scenes of spectacular grandeur, the Wolds Way walker is in placid, pretty country and never far from a small town or a village, a bed, a meal, a drink.

Open since 1982, the Wolds Way begins at Hessle on the north bank of the Humber and runs under the northern end of the mighty Humber Suspension Bridge. Then the route heads north to the Yorkshire Wolds, rounded chalk hills with attractive valleys. The path lies through farming country and woods, over gentle slopes, along farm tracks and roads. A point of special interest is the deserted village of Wharram Percy, north of Thixendale. It was abandoned in Tudor times and only the ruined church is still standing.

From the northern scarp of the Wolds there are fine views across the Vale of Pickering to the North York Moors, and later to the North Sea as the footpath comes to the Victorian seaside resort of Filey. It passes close to Filey Brigg, a mile-long finger of rock protruding into the sea, going on along the cliffs to

National trail

join the Cleveland Way.

The **Cleveland Way** was the second long distance footpath to be opened, in 1969. It steers its course northwards along the Yorkshire coast by Scarborough and Whitby to Saltburn. There it turns inland and changes course to the south-west, to spend the rest of its energies in the Cleveland Hills and the North York Moors National Park before coming to an end at Helmsley, not far from the haunting ruins of Rievaulx Abbey.

The **Pembrokeshire Coast Path**, 180 miles round Wales's south-western corner, and the **South West Coast Path** both take the walker through heroic coastal scenery of massive sea-beaten cliffs, coves and sandy beaches, lighthouses, vast seaward panoramas and superlative sunsets. The South West Coast Path follows the entire coastline from Minehead on the Bristol Channel in Somerset, along the North Devon shore, all round Cornwall by Land's End and the Lizard, back along the South Devon coast and the Dorset shoreline to finish on the edge of Poole Harbour.

The longest of the Scottish long distance paths is the **Southern Upland Way**, 212 miles clear across the country between Cockburnspath, east of Dunbar on the North Sea shore, and Portpatrick, looking out over the Irish Sea from the Rhinns of Galloway. This is a demanding route over a great variety of Border landscape, and positively dripping in history – passing through the Lammermuirs and the Scott Country, by the austere Jacobite mansion of Traquair, past St Mary's Loch and across the wild country of the Galloway Forest Park.

The 95 miles of the **West Highland Way**, opened in 1980, also make a romantic pilgrimage. The route is by Loch Lomond, across bleak Rannoch Moor and past the grim mountain gates of Glen Coe to Kinlochleven and Fort William, in the shadow of Ben Nevis.

The English and Welsh paths, too, have historic roots. **Offa's Dyke Path**, which is quite heavily trampled in some sections but satisfactorily lonely in others, runs the whole length of the Welsh Marches for 168 miles. From Chepstow on the River Severn it goes up the entrancing Wye Valley and long the edge of the Brecon Beacons National Park, then makes its way through the solitary, eerie Shropshire Hills and over the Clwydian Range to reach the coast of North Wales at Prestatyn. For about one-third of a distance it follows the line of the formidable bank and ditch constructed by Offa, 8th-century King of Mercia, to mark and defend his frontier with the Welsh.

The **North Downs Way**, similarly, 140 miles from Farnham to Dover and Folkestone, in part runs along the traditional medieval pilgrims' route to Canterbury, to the shrine of St Thomas à Becket. The **South Downs Way** runs 106 miles on pre-historic tracks from towering Beachy Head across Sussex and Hampshire to Winchester, commanding on the way wonderful views over the English Channel and across the Sussex Weald. The **Peddars Way**, again, follows an ancient track from the Suffolk border across Norfolk to the coast, and the **Ridgeway Path** across Wiltshire is an immensely ancient route, passing close to the important prehistoric monuments of Avebury, Wayland's Smithy and the White Horse of Uffington. On these timeworn, well-trodden ways, today's walkers tread in the footsteps of travellers of long ago.

A view from Benbrack Hill, along the Southern Upland Way in Galloway.

Cave

Prehistoric monument

Hillfort

Roman antiquity

Stonehenge is one of the most famous prehistoric monuments in Europe.

Caves
Prehistoric Monuments
Hillforts
Roman Antiquities
As the last great Ice Age held Britain in its grip, early man and the animals he hunted with increasingly sophisticated stone weapons followed shifts of climate. Small family groups took refuge from the sleet-lashed tundra in many natural limestone caverns.

Caves
Creswell Crags, in Derbyshire, one of the most important Palaeolithic sites in Britain, has a visitor centre which illustrates the life they must have led, both in the main cave and in nearby **Pin Hole** and **Robin Hood's Cave**. At **Cheddar Gorge**, Gough's Cave and Cox's Cave have displays in a nearby museum. Other caves worth visiting are the remains of mine workings for lead and later for semi-precious fluorspar near Castleton, Derbyshire – the **Treak Cliff** and **Speedwell Caverns**, near Buxton, as well as the **Blue John Cavern** itself.

Prehistoric Monuments
Long after the retreating glaciers and rising sea levels had submerged the mud flats to the east of Britain, agriculturalists arrived from Europe.

By about 5000BC, they had given the British upland landscape a basic appearance which was to remain largely unchanged until the introduction of intensive farming methods in the 20th century. But in that landscape began to appear burial mounds and much larger monuments.

Most famous must be **Stonehenge**, but from **Callanish**, on the Isle of Lewis, through **Arbor Low** and the **Nine Ladies**, near Matlock, to the **Rollright Stones**, north of Oxford, similar circles have filled later generations with awe. Possibly built, like **Castlerigg** in Cumbria and the **Ring of Brodgar** on Orkney, in connection with solar or lunar observation and associated rituals, the 'alignments' so often attributed to these circles, and to groups such as the **Devil's Arrows**, near Boroughbridge, should be treated with caution. Stonehenge pre-dates the Druid cult by 3,000 years and yet, in the Romantic age and the 19th century was thought to have been a Druid temple. In today's 'computer climate' it has become, for some, an astronomical calculator.

Orientation to the rising and setting sun does appear to have influenced the builders of most of the megalithic burial mounds in Britain. One of these, at **Newgrange**, north of Dublin, a splendid example of Neolithic

carving in its own right, is so aligned that the midwinter sunrise casts a beam directly into the tomb chamber. Newgrange predates Stonehenge by a thousand years and the positions of earth and sun, of sunrise – midwinter or midsummer – have changed, but the east–west alignments remain an intriguing facet of the study of all these monuments.

The village of **Avebury**, in Wiltshire, is set within another huge stone circle and earthwork rampart. A museum here displays finds and explains the way in which rampart and circle were constructed. **Stonehenge** has seen many phases in its construction, from its origins in 3000BC to its present form, which dates from around 1800BC. The sheer manpower involved is amazing. Four million cubic feet of chalk were dug out at Avebury, using antler picks. This and the hauling on raft and sledge of the Stonehenge bluestones from the Preseli Mountains in Wales and the transport of the 80 huge sarsens from the Marlborough Downs, tells us something of the beliefs and about the organisational ability of the builders of both monuments. Illiterate agriculturalists they may have been – certainly they were ignorant of the use of iron – and yet their kings and priests were able to organise and plan huge civil engineering projects.

Associated with Stonehenge is the huge circular timber building – **Woodhenge**. It is not difficult to imagine a conical thatched roof supported by timber uprights, their positions now marked by concrete posts. When was it built? Around 2750BC – that at least is known. Why was it built? Who used it? There is no scatter of the usual debris associated with hut circles and their domestic middens, so Woodhenge and the nearby **Durrington Walls** site would seem to have a public and ceremonial function. Perhaps the forest of tree trunk pillars recalled forest groves which had long had religious significance. At Woodhenge a three-year-old child, its skull split, was buried, perhaps as a dedication, at the centre of the complex. When the timbers at last decayed, a memorial stone was placed at the centre of the circle.

Silbury Hill, near Avebury, has so far yielded up few of its secrets. Why this 130ft (40m) mound, covering over five acres at its base, was raised is still a mystery. Trenches have been dug, seeking a burial somewhere within, but all these excavations have found is that it was very carefully built. Inside the turf mound is a stepped cone of compacted chalk rubble, each layer being finished with smooth chalk blocks. The steps were later filled with earth except for the topmost one, still visible as a terrace. The fact that the whole of the Stonehenge circle would fit comfortably within this topmost terrace gives an idea of the scale of the mound.

Carbon-14 dating has placed its construction at around 2600BC – and the trenches have told us that it was started in July or August, for right at the core have been found winged ants – but maybe there is a more important burial still to be discovered. Nearby is **West Kennet Long Barrow** and its sarsen façade – burial chamber perhaps, of the chieftains who commanded the building of Avebury.

Hillforts

The 'Beaker Folk', so called from the distinctive pottery vessels found in their graves, arrived in Britain around 2700BC. They brought with them the Aryan roots of our language and their knowledge of metal working was gradually learnt by the established communities into which they merged. By 1800BC the British climate was deteriorating and tribes vied for workable land. Local chiefs gained power and protected their arable land and pasture from the safety of upland hillforts, which gradually became tribal 'capitals'

rather than merely bolt holes in case of war.

Thousands of these hillforts dot the landscape, and many were inhabited well into the Roman age. **Ingleborough**, just north of the National Park Centre at Clapham, North Yorkshire, is the highest in Britain. Life must have been very hard on this high windswept plateau. Earlier settlers in the area possibly make themselves a warmer home in the cave systems nearby, at **Ingleborough Show Cave** and **Gaping Gill**. One of the largest and most important hill-forts in Britain is **Maiden Castle**. Built initially around 300BC, it finally fell to Vespasian's troops in AD43. Boards around the two-mile perimeter provide much information and the museum in nearby Dorchester displays finds from the site.

Often associated with these hill-forts are the figures carved into the chalk hillsides – horses and giant figures – but only a handful can be said with certainty to be 'pre-historic'. **Uffington White Horse**, between Swindon and Wantage, certainly is. Overlooking the Ridgeway Path, an ancient trade route across the north Berkshire Downs, its disintegrated simplicity resembles the horses – tribal totems, perhaps – which feature on Celtic coinage. The **Cerne Abbas Giant,** north of Dorchester, is probably not more than 1,500 years old, but its club-wielding phallic figure possibly represents Hercules, part of a god-cult which flourished around AD100. The iron Age enclosure above him was used for May Day and fertility ceremonies long after the foundation of the nearby Benedictine priory in the 10th century. **Wilmington Long Man**, near Alfriston, inland from Beachy Head, could well be Romano-British, too.

From 700BC onwards, Celtic settlers brought their language, their chariots and a love of finery, gold and ornaments. Iron swords gave them an ascendancy in battle over the native Britons, who were pushed westwards. Celtic immigrant groups shared a common dialect but their lack of any concept of 'nationhood' left their society an easy prey to the civilising might of Rome.

Roman Antiquities

The lure of corn, gold, iron, slaves and hunting dogs was enough to make the Romans decide that an invasion of Britannia in the summer of AD43 was worthwhile. By AD70 50 or more towns were linked by a network of roads. *Lex Romana* tamed the unruly land and Latin became yet another rootstock from

which English would eventually spring. Evidence of Roman military occupation is everywhere – from **Hadrian's Wall** and the lighthouse in **Dover Castle**, to the legionary fortress at **Caerleon** in Gwent.

Many of the civilising influences of Rome can still be seen today – an aqueduct which supplied fresh water 12 miles along the Frome Valley to Dorchester, sewers in Lincoln, Colchester and York, and bath houses. The finest of these, at **Bath**, is rivalled by the complex of baths and exercise halls at Viroconium, near **Wroxeter**. Theatres such as those of Verulamium and Caerleon, and the busy shopping centres which developed around the forum or the town gates, attracted people to the towns. Mosaic floors like those at **Aldborough**, in Yorkshire, reflect a very comfortable style of life. This wealth is mirrored, too, by the remains of many Roman villas such as those at Lullingstone, near **Eynsford** in Kent, **Fishbourne** in Sussex and **Chedworth** in Gloucestershire.

Below *Westbury White Horse, on Bratton Down, Wiltshire.* Bottom *Housesteads Fort along Hadrian's Wall, in Northumbria.*

Cave

Prehistoric monument

Hillfort

Roman antiquity

Battle site with year

THE BATTLE OF FLODDEN FIELD
9th September 1513

Above *The site of the Battle of Flodden. Inset A display board at Flodden chronicles the battle which was fought here.* Top right *According to tradition, men watched London's Great Fire from Outwood Mill, Surrey.* Bottom *Porthcurno's Minack open-air theatre.*

Windmill

Other place of interest

Battlefields
Windmills
Other Places of Interest

Normans and Plantagenets, wars in Scotland and Wales, the Wars of the Roses, the Civil War and the Jacobite risings, have all left the map of Britain dotted with 'crossed swords' symbols. In the 250 years that separate us from Culloden, in 1746, the last battle on British soil, farming, roads and railways, canals and houses have changed the fields on which the history of the nation was written.

Battlefields

We do not commemorate our battles as lavishly as the Visitor Centres at places such as Waterloo or Gettysburg, but there are still fields where there is something to be seen today. Facilities are available, mainly in the tourist season, for organised groups to be taken round and it is worth telephoning to see whether you can join one.

The Battle of **Hastings**, on 14 October 1066, certainly changed things in England. Stories of the battle are well enough known – Harold's forced march of 250 miles from battle against the Norwegian king at Stamford Bridge, near York, to meet the Norman invaders; the Norman minstrel Taillefer charging

the shield-wall; the hail of arrows harassing the axemen; the final stand of the house-carles around the royal standard of Wessex. All are vividly recalled in an audio-visual presentation in the Tourist Office on the green just opposite the gateway of the Abbey which William founded, its altar traditionally on the spot where Harold fell. Now an English Heritage property, the pathways around and overlooking main sectors of the battlefield are well signposted, with information boards at regular intervals.

In the **Bannockburn** Heritage Centre the full story of the battle of 24 June 1314, is graphically told in an audio-visual entitled *The Forging of a Nation.* On the field itself is preserved the Borestone, where Robert the Bruce raised his banner before this decisive culmination of the Wars of Independence.

From the top of the Durham Cathedral tower the battlefield of **Neville's Cross** can be seen as it was by the monks who gave 'moral support' by singing hymns there in 1346. A leaflet explaining the battle is available from the Tourist Office and a half mile walk from the city brings the visitor to the battlefield itself.

An exhibition is mounted on **Bosworth** battlefield, near Sutton

Cheney, with an audio-visual presentation including scenes from Laurence Olivier's *Richard III.* There is a battlefield trail, with another information centre halfway round at Shenton Station. Here, Richard of Gloucester, uncle of the Princes in the Tower, met his end, having found no one to answer his cry 'My kingdom for a horse!'

At a call from France for help from the 'auld alliance', James IV of Scotland marched into England. On Pipers' Hill, at **Flodden Edge**, is a monument 'To the Brave of both Nations', with the battlefield spread out below. A booklet and map from nearby Coldstream enable you to follow the course of the battle. King Henry VIII had left the old Earl of Surrey, a veteran of Bosworth, to defend the north. Surrey had borrowed the banner of St Cuthbert, obviously a powerful morale raiser, from Durham Cathedral. But it was artillery fire that stung the Scots into premature offensive action, allowing English archers to reach the crest of Pipers' Hill and pour a murderous arrow storm into the massed pikemen below. Flodden was the last major battle won largely by the longbow.

The Castle Inn, in **Edgehill,** was built on the spot where King Charles raised his Standard. There

is a memorial on the field below and a map and guidebook will enable you to follow the course of the fighting. Neither side seemed willing to strike the first blow until a Parliamentary gunner spotted the King on the hill, fired – and missed. Prince Rupert charged – found an ally in the inaptly named Sir Faithful Fortescue, one of the Parliamentary cavalry commanders – and they all dashed the two miles or so to Kineton, where they rested their horses and indulged in a little light looting. Roundhead foot soldiers were about to finish off the exhausted Royalists when they were attacked owing to the opportune return of Prince Rupert and the cavalry. Captain John Smith, of the King's Lifeguard, met a party of Roundheads escorting a Royalist prisoner and the Royal Standard which they had just captured. The prisoner recognised Smith and called to him. Smith charged, killed one Roundhead, wounded another and the other four fled. He was knighted on the spot by the King for recovering the Standard, which had not been in Parliamentary hands above fifteen minutes.

In the village of **Naseby** is a museum with dioramas and a ten minute commentary of different stages of the battle of 14 July 1645.

Should the museum be closed, then try the village shop or the church for the descriptive leaflet and map, which will make the whole encounter more easy to follow.

A drive up the Naseby-Sibbertoft road takes you to a monument marking the position from which Cromwell led his cavalry to win the day and from where there is a good view over the whole battlefield.

Information about the battle of **Worcester**, 3 September 1651, is available from both the Tourist Office and the Civil War Centre at the Commandery. Worcester was the scene of the first and last battles of the war. During the summer, frequent 're-enactments' are staged by several groups, particularly in September.

Sedgemoor, the last battle fought on English soil, on 6 July 1685, followed the landing by the Duke of Monmouth, illegitimate son of Charles II, to claim the throne of James II. A stone monument marks the site of the battle, and information can be obtained from the Admiral Blake Museum in Bridgwater.

The Battle of **Culloden**, on the moors outside Inverness, ended the Jacobite Rising in 1746. Bonnie Prince Charlie, with the help of Flora Macdonald, escaped 'over the sea to Skye' and the Stuart cause was swept away. The whole story is graphically told in the visitor centre on the battlefield, which has been restored to its 18th-century appearance, but now dotted with emotive memorial cairns and the Graves of the Clans, on which no heather ever grows.

Since Culloden, we may be thankful that no armies have fought on British soil – only *above* it, in 1940. Aerial bombardment brought the realities of war much closer to the public than did any of the very localised combats of the previous 700 years.

Windmills

Few things add as much atmosphere to the countryside as a windmill. They have drained marshlands and ground corn since medieval times. One tradition suggests that they were introduced by crusaders returning home from the wars. Whether or not this is true, we know for a fact that they were first built here some eight centuries ago. None of the original structures remain, but some have survived a few hundreds years. Still in working order is **Berney Arms Mill**, in Norfolk, from the top of which there is a splendid view and the working wind pump at **Wicken Fen**, a remnant of the wetlands drained by Dutch engineers, which

became England's first nature reserve, in 1899. **Bourn Mill**, near Cambridge, is a 17th-century 'post mill', the oldest surviving mill in the country. Unlike the conical tower windmills with a rotating cap, here the sails and machinery all turn together, revolving round a central post. A tide mill has stood on the river bank at **Woodbridge** in Suffolk since the 12th century and the present one was working until 1956, when the shaft of the waterwheel broke. Careful restoration has successfully restored it to working condition.

Other Places of Interest

There is a wide range of other places of interest which are well worth visiting. From waterfalls, wells, bridges and towers to dovecotes, follies, monuments and parks, Britain has something to offer every visitor.

Not far from Land's End, on the cliffs near Porthcurno, is the **Minack Theatre**, carved out of the living rock in the 1930s, with the sea as a backdrop for the stage. North of Tavistock is **Lydford Gorge**, a deep wooded gorge with the lovely White Lady Waterfall at the end of a mile or so walk.

Further along the coast, north-west of Weymouth, the extraordinary Chesil Beach, a 12-mile long pebble bank, shelters the **Abbotsbury Swannery**, where swans were bred for the table by the monks as long ago as the 14th century. Today it is a breeding haven for hundreds of wild mute swans. At St Fagans, to the west of Cardiff, is the **Welsh Folk Museum,** a collection of rural buildings from the 17th century onwards from all over Wales, carefully re-erected in the grounds of St Fagans Castle, an elegant Elizabethan mansion.

Waterfalls abound, but one not to be missed is **Hardraw Force**, north of Hawes, North Yorkshire, a spectacular 90ft (27m) drop into a glen which has been used for brass band contests – a great local tradition – on account of its splendid acoustics. Further north, near Moffat on the A708, is one of Scotland's highest falls, the **Grey Mare's Tail**, where Loch Skeen plunges 200ft (61m) to meet Moffat Water.

Shire horses, Clydesdales and Suffolk Punches have ploughed England's fields – and delivered England's beer – for centuries. In the **National Shire Horse Centre**, at Plymouth, there is stabling dating back to 1772 and three parades a day are staged in summer. Courage Breweries have a **Shire Horse Centre** near Maidenhead, as do Whitbread at their **Hop Farm**, on the B2015, east of Tonbridge.

Viewpoint

Picnic site

Agricultural showground

Viewpoints
Picnic Sites
Agricultural Showgrounds
The **Clee Hills** of Shropshire, in the Welsh Marches, are in a remote and exceptionally attractive area of the country – an official Area of Outstanding Natural Beauty, in fact. They are 'young' hills, geologically, jagged and more impressive than their official height statistics would suggest, and in the past were heavily quarried for coal, building stone, iron and copper. A wealth of folklore still attaches to them, with sinister tales of witches and evil forces. They are also the site of a spectacular viewpoint.

Viewpoints
The viewpoint is on the A4117, six miles east of Ludlow. In the immediate foreground to the north is the bulk of Titterstone Clee, 1,750ft (533m) with its aerials and radar dishes, and one of the biggest Iron Age hillforts in Britain on its summit. Beyond the hill is the long,

Below The picnic site at David Marshall Lodge, Aberfoyle.
Bottom View of South Stack lighthouse from the viewpoint on Anglesey.

wooded ridge of Wenlock Edge and to the west beyond Ludlow rise the mountains of Wales.

Viewpoints, as marked in AA Road Atlases, are all easily accessible by car and have a plaque to identify landmarks and places of interest in the area. Each viewpoint has a prospect of at least 180 degrees and some command wider vistas still. The **Cockleroy** viewpoint, two miles south of Linlithgow in the Lothian region of Scotland, has marvellous views over the full 360 degrees. To the east the eye ranges over Edinburgh to the Firth of Forth, to the south-east lie the Pentland Hills, in the west is Glasgow and in the north the outlying bastions of the Highlands.

The viewpoint is in the Beecraigs Country Park, among the Bathgate Hills, with trails through the woodland, a reservoir with hides for watching the numerous waterfowl and a deer farm with a viewing platform. At Linlithgow are the romantic ruins of the palace of the Stuart kings, where Mary, Queen of Scots was born, and the church where she was christened. Not far away is Torphichen Preceptory, once the Scottish base of the crusading order of the Knights of St John of Jerusalem. A little to the south there are superlative views again, from Cairnpapple Hill, where prehistoric men buried their dead over a period of 2,500 years and more.

On the other side of Glasgow, the **Lyle Hill** viewpoint is just outside the former shipbuilding town of Greenock, the birthplace of James Watt, and during World War II the principal Free French naval base. The viewpoint is near the war memorial to those sailors, an anchor surmounted by a Cross of Lorraine. Down below is the Firth of Clyde and its swarming ferries. To the north and north-west lie Holy Loch and the woods and mountains of the Argyll Forest Park on the Cowal Peninsula, with the serrated crests of The Cobbler in the distance. West and south-west are the Isle of Bute, separated from the mainland by the narrow Kyles of Bute, the Isle of Arran rising to Goat Fell and, beyond Arran, the Kintyre Peninsula.

Far away at the other end of the country, in Cornwall, the majestic harbour of Carrick Roads was an important United States Navy base during the war. The viewpoint is on **Pendennis Point**, outside Falmouth, commanding a sweeping prospect of the harbour and out to the English Channel and the Lizard Peninsula. Close at hand is the round keep of Pendennis Castle,

one of the artillery strongpoints built along the coast in Henry VIII's time against attack by the French. Across the water is its other half, St Mawes Castle. These twin fortresses have done their job, and no enemy force has ever attempted to penetrate Carrick Roads.

Another viewpoint with naval connections lies eastward along the coast, on **Portsdown Hill** in Hampshire, a mile north of Cosham. Immediately to the south sprawls Portsmouth, with its historic harbour and the Royal Navy dockyard where Nelson's HMS *Victory* rests in honourable retirement. Birds wheel above the Farlington Marshes at the northern end of Langstone Harbour and the eagle eye pierces 10 miles across the Solent to the Isle of Wight. For visitors who would like something to eat as well as watch, there is a picnic site here.

So there is at the viewpoint at **David Marshall Lodge**, the Forestry Commission visitor centre in the scenic Trossachs area, in the Central region of Scotland, a mile north of Aberfoyle on A821. There are spectacular views here of Ben Lomond, the Highland mountains and the valleys of the Forth.

The haunting beauty of the Trossachs – 'So wondrous wild, the whole might seem the scenery of a fairy dream' – with its lochs, peaks and 'wildering forest' – was praised by Sir Walter Scott in 1810 in his immensely popular poem *The Lady of the Lake*. To add to its romantic attractions, much of the area was Rob Roy country.

Strictly speaking, the Trossachs ('the cross places' in Gaelic) means the narrow belt of land between Loch Katrine and Loch Achray, but the name is more often used broadly for the whole area between Loch Lomond and Callander. Much of it is now in the Forestry Commission's enormous Queen Elizabeth Forest Park. After Scott, tourists began to flock to the area in such numbers that the local landowner, the Duke of Montrose, built the road north from Aberfoyle which is now the A821, or Duke's Road. There are parking places and a picnic site along it, and more along the Forestry Commission's one-way Achray Forest Drive, which leaves the Duke's Road to make its way seven miles through the woods, by Loch Drunkie and Loch Achray. There are more scenic viewpoints here and a waymarked forest walk.

Picnic Sites
One of the Countryside Commission's achievements has been to stimulate local authorities to

provide places where motorists could pull off the road to enjoy a picnic. Opinion surveys and studies repeatedly made it clear that many people were deterred from enjoying the countryside by an uneasy fear of trespassing or going where they were not wanted; an official picnic spot is somewhere where you know you are entitled to be. Although most sites have been organised by county councils, many have been provided by the Forestry Commission, others by the National Trust and by private landowners.

Many sites provide a view of attractive scenery or are close to an outstanding attraction. There is one near the ruins of **Mount Grace Priory**, for instance, the medieval Carthusian monastery near Osmotherley in North Yorkshire (where each of the tiny hermit-like cells had running water, incidentally) and there is one close to the **Hardraw Force** waterfall, off the Pennine Way. In Wales there are several with views of **Llyn Clywedog**, near Llanidloes in Powys, a three-mile long reservoir. An old iron mine can also be visited here, and not far away is another picnic site beside the infant River Severn, as it starts its long journey to the sea from the high moors of Plynlimon. There are more looking over **Lake Vyrnwy** in Powys, a beautiful 1880s reservoir with wooded shores and a striking Victorian Gothic tower. In England too, reservoirs make pleasing picnic spots, as at **Rutland Water** in Leicestershire, or **Grafham Water** in Cambridgeshire.

Agricultural Showgrounds

The 'traditional' English landscape of green fields, hedgerows and narrow lanes was created by the agricultural revolution of the 18th century, which introduced improved farming methods. County agricultural societies were formed to spread knowledge of the new ways and raise standards. They organised annual county shows at which farmers and breeders showed off their achievements and competed against each other. For 200 years and more these agricultural shows have been part of the accustomed round of country life, with their marquees and bands, their displays of the latest farm machinery and equipment, and their classes for heavy horses, cattle and sheep. One of the oldest is the **Royal Bath and West Show**, which can trace its history back to 1777 and draws 100,000 people every year to its permanent showground near Shepton Mallet in Somerset. Before the War, the county shows normally moved around from one

Viewpoint

Picnic site

Agricultural showground

country estate or farmer's fields to another, year by year. After 1945 the cost of staging a show escalated alarmingly. Some shows folded up, some amalgamated and others established permanent showgrounds. The leader in the field was the Yorkshire Agricultural Society, which planted its **Great Yorkshire Show** on a permanent site at Harrogate. The **Royal Highland Show** chose a location at Ingliston, a few miles west of Edinburgh, for its shows.

Other leading shows which have equipped themselves with fixed locations include the **Three Counties** at Great Malvern (the three counties being Herefordshire, Worcestershire and Gloucestershire), the **South of England** at Ardingly in Sussex, the **Royal Cornwall** at Wadebridge, the

A plaque marking the viewpoint on Sugar Loaf Mountain in Wales.

East of England near Peterborough and the **Royal Welsh** at Builth Wells. The Royal Agricultural Society of England, founded in 1838, held its first show at Oxford the following year. The 'Royal' moved about the country every year until 1963, when it settled at Stoneleigh in Warwickshire, in a permanent home where the **National Agriculture Centre** evolved in the 1970s. The agricultural shows have had heavy weather to come through in recent years, but they have survived, and altogether are estimated to attract about three million visitors a year to share country triumphs and pleasures.

Horse racing

Show jumping and equestrian circuit

**Horse Racing
Show Jumping and
Equestrian Circuits
Athletics Stadiums
Motor Racing Circuits**
Becher's Brook . . . Valentine's . . .
the Canal Turn . . . the Chair. The
familiar litany of names conjures up
Aintree on Grand National Day –
the jostle at the start, the crash and
crackle of horse meeting thorn-and-
fir fence, horses and jockeys falling,
the clamour of the crowd. The early
history of the great race is obscure,
but it is usually traced back to the
Grand Liverpool Steeplechase of
1839. That race was won by a horse
appropriately named Lottery and
that was the year the gallant
Captain Becher, a well-known
gentleman rider of the day, fell into
the brook that bears his name. His
horse, named Conrad, fell in as
well.

Horse Racing
A steeplechase as the name
implies, did not originally take place
on a course at all. A by-product of
hunting, it was a wild pell-mell
gallop across country over hedges
and ditches, towards a distant
steeple or other agreed marker. Not

*World famous Derby Day, at Epsom
Race Course in Surrey.*

until the 19th century did organised
racing over artificial jumps on a set
course begin. Racing started at
Aintree in 1829, on the course
owned by the Earls of Sefton for
another 120 years. The course, in a
dreary northern suburb of
Liverpool, has the most formidable
fences in the sport and in 1928 a
horse named Tipperary Tim won
the Grand National simply by being
the only finisher of 42 starters. Far
and away the most famous horse
associated with Aintree and the
National, however, is Red Rum, the
only three-time winner (in 1973,
1974 and 1977).

The most prestigious steeplechase
course in England is at **Cheltenham**,
in a delightful country situation
outside the town, at Prestbury Park,
under the looming Cotswold
bulwark of Cleeve Hill. It is a
testing track on heavy clay. The
major event of the year is the
Cheltenham Gold Cup in March,
first held in 1924. The great horse
Golden Miller won it five years in
succession from 1932 to 1936 (and in
1934 won the Grand National as
well). The Champion Hurdle at
Cheltenham is the premier hurdle
event in the country.

The capital of the flat racing
industry is across the other side of
the country at **Newmarket**. The

town developed as a racing and
breeding centre for 'the sport of
kings' under royal patronage.
Charles II rode his own horses in
races there: hence the name Rowley
Mile for one of Newmarket's two
courses, from the king's nickname,
Old Rowley. In the mid-18th
century the aristocratic Jockey Club
was founded at Newmarket. It owns
the two courses and Newmarket
Heath, the open country around the
town on which strings of
staggeringly valuable racehorses can
be seen exercising. It occupies a
suitably august red brick building in
the centre of the town, and nearby
is the highly enjoyable National
Horseracing Museum, which
opened in 1983.

Two of the five 'classic' races are
held at Newmarket: the Two
Thousand Guineas, and the One
Thousand Guineas for fillies only,
inaugurated in 1809 and 1814
respectively. Both are run on the
Rowley Mile course, which has a
long flat straight, followed by a dip
and rise to the finish. Long races
cannot easily be seen from the
grandstands because the course was
laid out long before the days of
packed modern race crowds.

The most famous race in the
world is run early in June every year
at **Epsom.** It is named after the

12th Earl of Derby, though it might easily have been called the Bunbury. Lord Derby and Sir Charles Bunbury tossed a coin in 1780 to decide the name of a new race for three-year-old colts and fillies. As if in compensation, Bunbury's horse Diomed won the first Derby, and Lord Derby had to wait until 1787 to win with Sir Peter Teazle.

The other classic race at Epsom, the Oaks, restricted to fillies, was first run in 1779 and was named after a house which Lord Derby had taken nearby.

W P Frith's well-known painting *Derby Day* gives a vivid impression of the occasion in Victorian times, when it was virtually a public holiday. Huge numbers of people swarmed to enjoy a day out and all the fun of the fair on Epsom Downs. The Derby course is more or less level for the first three-quarters of a mile and then drops to a sharp turn at Tattenham Corner before the run-in.

The last of the classics, in September, is the oldest; the St Leger, which goes all the way back to 1776 and is named after a prominent Yorkshire sportsman of the time. It is run at **Doncaster,** on the Town Moor, the common land outside the town which, as at Epsom, was the natural place for the races.

One of the oldest courses in the country, and one of the oddest, is the Roodee at **Chester,** where there was apparently organised racing in Henry VIII's time. The course has the River Dee on one side with the old city wall on the other and is circular, with almost no straight. At **York,** there was racing on the Knavesmire, common land outside the city, early in the 18th century. Here in August is contested the Gimcrack Stakes, named in honour of a famous grey. The sport's most attractive setting is claimed by **Goodwood,** near Chichester in Sussex, where the course was laid out by the 3rd Duke of Richmond with the first meeting staged in 1801.

The smartest social occasion of the racing year is the **Royal Ascot** meeting in June, attended by the Queen, with a royal procession up the straight in carriages and much media fuss about fashionable hats. Races were first held at Ascot, in Berkshire, in 1711. The King George VI and Queen Elizabeth Diamond Stakes, run in July with the richest prize money in the sport, was inaugurated in 1951 to mark the Festival of Britain.

Showjumping and Equestrian Circuits
The first show jumping contest on record was held in London in 1869. From 1912 the sport was regularly included in the Olympic Games, but it is only since 1945 that it has attracted strong public and media interest. The popular Horse of the Year show, at **Wembley Arena** in London, dates from 1949. The same year saw the first horse trials at **Badminton,** in Avon, on a testing course laid out in the grounds of his palatial mansion by the Duke of Beaufort. Himself a redoubtable huntsman, the duke was determined to do something about the indifferent showing of the British equestrian team in the 1948 Olympics. The three day event at Badminton in the spring now draws spectators in thousands. In 1984 Lucinda Green won Badminton for a record sixth time, on six different horses. Another stately home course is the one at **Burghley House,** near Stamford, in the grounds of the palace of the Cecils, right-hand men to Elizabeth I and James I. The Marquess of Exeter, a former Olympic athlete, offered a home for a three day event here, first held in 1961. The Burghley Horse Trials in September are now firmly established as a prestigious occasion in the show jumping calendar.

The sport's equivalent of Aintree and Epsom combined is the course at **Hickstead** in Sussex, opened in 1960 at his home by a leading rider, Douglas Bunn, to provide a permanent arena with formidable obstacles. The first British Show Jumping Derby was held there in 1961.

Athletics Stadiums
Athletics is less well equipped with tracks and grounds than other major sports. The principal arena for international athletics is at the **Crystal Palace** in South London, where a 12,000-seater stadium was opened in 1964. Ten years later, an all-weather track was installed in the town stadium at **Gateshead,** and home-town athlete Brendan Foster set a new 3,000m world record to celebrate. The cross-country course at Gateshead is also well known.

Motor Racing Circuits
The magic name from the early history of motor racing in England is **Brooklands,** the track near Weybridge in Surrey which, sadly, closed in 1939. Every great figure of the early days raced there and John Cobb set a lap record of 143mph in a Napier-Railton in 1935. Another leading venue was **Donington Park,** near Derby, where Grand Prix events were held in the 1930s. During the war the site was taken over by the Army. Years later the circuit was reopened for racing, in the 1970s. The Motor Museum there has a notable collection of Grand Prix racing cars.

Since 1945 the two major British circuits have been Silverstone and Brands Hatch. **Silverstone**, in Northamptonshire near Towcester, opened in 1948 on a former airfield, hence the name Hangar Straight for part of the course. The British Grand Prix is staged there, but for many years it alternated with Brands Hatch, near Farningham in Kent. It opened for Formula Three racing in 1949 and in 1960 opened the Grand Prix course.

Athletics stadium

Motor racing circuit

A rider in the TT races, held every June on the Isle of Man.

Golf course

County cricket
ground

National rugby
ground

A scene at Lord's, the home of Middlesex County Cricket Club.

Golf Courses
County Cricket Grounds
National Rugby Grounds
Ski Slopes
Coastal Launching Sites

Of all the world's great golf courses, the most august is the venerable and venerated Old Course at **St Andrews** in Scotland, where the Victorian clubhouse of the Royal and Ancient Golf Club is the temple and citadel of the game. A links, or seaside course – as all the country's top courses are – the Old Course is four miles in length and so many golfers are keen to play it that it normally opens at six o'clock in the morning. The notorious par 4 17th, or Roadhole, is said to have driven more great golfers to rage and bitter despair than any other golf hole in the world.

Golf Courses
Golf was played at St Andrews on the springy turf beside the North Sea as long ago as the 15th century, it seems, and when 22 noblemen and gentlemen founded the Society of St Andrews Golfers in 1754, they described the game as an 'ancient and healthful exercise'. The club was dubbed 'royal' in 1834 by King William IV and became the governing body of the game.

Another illustrious club is the Honourable Company of Edinburgh Golfers, which was founded in 1744 (as the Gentlemen Golfers of Leigh), ten years before the Royal and Ancient. It drew up the first set of rules, which the R and A adopted. The club now has its headquarters at **Muirfield**, a famous championship course on the outskirts of the village of Gullane, east of Edinburgh. It is close to the shore of the Firth of Forth, whose invigorating breezes are claimed to account for the great age which the Edinburgh Golfers commonly attain. The course is known for its meticulously constructed bunkers. Jack Nicklaus won his first British Open at Muirfield in 1966 and Nick Faldo won there in 1987.

There is a clutch of notable courses across on the Ayrshire shore, on hillocky ground on the sandy turf and coarse grass beside the sea. The **Prestwick** club organised the first British Open championship in 1860 and it was played there many times, but after 1925 the course was no longer big enough for the crowds which the event was beginning to attract. Few of them are these days.

Royal Troon, just to the north, has holes with names – they start with Seal and to on to Postage Stamp and Rabbit. In the 1973 Open two holes-in-one were scored at Postage Stamp. One was by the veteran American Gene Sarazen and the other by the amateur David Russell, who happened to be respectively the oldest and the youngest players in the field.

There is another group of redoubtable courses in England along the Lancashire coast. **Royal Lytham and St Anne's**, near Blackpool, was in open countryside when the club was founded in 1886, but is now an oasis in a desert of housing estates. Here, the first Ladies Open was played in 1893 and Tony Jacklin had his Open triumph in 1969. Near Southport is another crack course, **Royal Birkdale,** and further south on the tip of the Wirral Peninsula, is **Hoylake,** where the first British Amateur championship was contested in 1885. The demanding course is no longer considered adequate to cope with Open crowds. The Open is still played over the **Royal St George's** course at Sandwich on the Kent coast, one of the toughest in Britain, and the scene of a famous fictitious match in Ian Fleming's *Goldfinger.*

Other courses are celebrated not for the championships fought out over them, but for their associations with heroic figures of the past. The legendary James Braid, five times Open champion, was professional at **Walton Heath** in Surrey for 45 years until he died in 1950 at the age of 80. On his birthday he invariably went out and played the course in as many strokes as his age or less.

His contemporary, the incomparable John Henry Taylor, learned his golf at the **Royal North Devon's** links at Westward Ho!, on the bumpy sandy ground of the Burrows, frequented by horses, cows and sheep as well as golfers.

Speaking of animals on a course, in 1934 the professional at the **St Margaret's at Cliffe** club in Kent killed a cow with his tee shot to the 18th. And in 1975 at **Scunthorpe**, Humberside, a drive at the 14th hole, named the Mallard, hit and killed a mallard duck in flight.

Cricket Grounds
Cricket, like golf, emerged from the mists of obscurity into the light of history in the 18th century. The most famous ground in the country, and the world, is **Lord's** in the St John's Wood district of London. It takes its name from its original proprietor, a Yorkshireman named Thomas Lord, who came to London in 1787, was instrumental in the founding of the MCC (Marylebone Cricket Club) and opened the St John's Wood ground in 1812. Lord's is also the home of the Middlesex County Cricket Club. The original pavilion, a one-room hut, and the tavern provided by Thomas Lord have been replaced over the years by a Victorian pavilion and modern stands. The grand entrance gates to the ground were specially designed in 1923 as a memorial to W G Grace, the greatest cricketer of his age, and Lord's now has a good museum of cricket.

The other famous London ground is the **Oval**, in Kennington, south of the river. Originally a market garden, and long famed for a fine view of the local gasometers, the ground has been the headquarters of the Surrey county club since its formation in a nearby pub in 1845. Like Lord's, the Oval is a regular Test match arena. The highest innings ever recorded in Test cricket was notched up there in 1938, when England scored 903 for 7 declared, with Len Hutton making 364.

One of cricket's most attractive settings is the county ground at **Worcester,** where the cathedral rises nobly in the background across the Severn. The drawback is that when the river floods, as in 1990, the pitch is covered with tons of thick black mud. Another attractive county cricket arena is the St Lawrence ground at **Canterbury** in Kent. The Canterbury Week cricket festival has been held since 1847.

The ground at **Old Trafford** in the southern suburbs of Manchester has seen many a Test match and many a tussle between the red rose of Lancashire and the white rose of Yorkshire. The principal Yorkshire ground is at **Headingley,** a couple of miles from the centre of Leeds. Two other grounds regularly used for Test cricket are **Trent Bridge** in Nottingham, where cricket has been played since 1838, and **Edgbaston,** the Warwickshire county ground in Birmingham.

Rugby Grounds
Rugby's equivalent of Lord's is the 'cabbage patch' at **Twickenham,** a market garden bought by the Rugby Union in 1907. The choice was fiercely criticised for being too far from Piccadilly Circus, but the motor car changed all that and the ground has been developed into a spanking modern arena. For Welsh rugby men, however, the holy of holies of their national game is **Cardiff Arms Park**, beside the River Taff close to the heart of the city, where the stands echo on great occasions to the impassioned sound of Welsh singing. The Cardiff Football Club began to practise on a piece of meadow here beside the river in 1876. Today it is a thoroughly up-to-date arena with

Above *The clubhouse at St Andrew's.*
Right *Skiing in the Cairngorms, one of Scotland's busiest resorts.*

two stadiums. The two other home international grounds are Murrayfield in Edinburgh and Lansdowne Road in Dublin.

Ski Slopes
Increasing affluence since 1945 has brought skiing within the reach of far more people than before, and although all the major ski slopes are abroad, a skiing industry has developed in Scotland. The Highland village of **Aviemore**, a quiet haven for anglers and mountaineers, was transformed into a thriving winter sports resort in the 1960s. There are ski schools and dry-ski slopes, and Aviemore is the base for the nearby Cairngorms ski area, with its chairlifts and ski tows.

There are cross-country ski trails of varying degrees of difficulty in this area, too. The other main Scottish ski areas are **Glenshee**, south of Braemar on the A93, Britain's highest main road, the **Lecht** area on the A939 near Tomintoul and the **Glencoe** area above the A82, where the road crosses Rannoch Moor.

Coastal Launching Sites
Sailing has also become more popular. Most of its enthusiasts are weekend sailors, who do not go far from shore, and there are boat launching sites at harbours and marinas all round the coast, from **St Ives** harbour in Cornwall to **Thurso Bay** on the north coast of Scotland. They vary from the broad, sheltered expanses of **Carrick Roads** or **Plymouth Sound** to the flat shingle shore at **Deal** in Kent, close to the historic anchorage of The Downs, or the exposed Suffolk coastline at **Walberswick** or **Southwold.**

Natural ski slope

Artificial ski slope

Coastal launching site

Heritage Coast

Above *Looking across Embleton Bay, a view for Dunstanburgh Castle.*
Left *Spectacular rock formation at Elegug stacks, Pembrokeshire.*

Heritage Coasts

For centuries the white cliffs of Dover have stood as symbols of English nationhood, independence and pride, confronting foes across the Channel with unyielding defiance. It was the sight of the white cliffs which told generations of weary English travellers that they were nearing home. Today, to keep the white cliffs unspoiled, they have to be protected as two four-mile stretches of Heritage Coast, either side of Dover.

Heritage Coasts

Before World War II, concern was growing about the substantial areas of coastline which had been ruined by commercial development and the threat that what was left would go the same way, disappearing under an ever-rising tide of cliff-top bungalows and caravan sites. The Coastal Preservation Committee mounted a campaign in the 1930s. During the War, the distinguished geographer J A Steers surveyed the coast for the government, and his work would later be the basis on which Heritage Coasts were chosen.

In 1965 the National Trust, thoroughly alarmed, launched Enterprise Neptune, a campaign to raise money to buy threatened coastline. This campaign continues and the Trust now owns and protects more than one mile in every six along the shoreline of England, Wales and Northern Ireland, including the **Giant's Causeway** on the scenic North Antrim seacoast of Northern Ireland and more than a quarter of the entire coast of **Cornwall.**

In 1970 the Countryside Commission recommended to the government that scenically outstanding stretches of undeveloped coast should be designated as Heritage Coasts and protected against undesirable development. This was duly set in train and by the end of the 1980s there were some 850 miles of Heritage Coast in total, amounting to a little over 30 per cent of the coastline of England and Wales. In Scotland more than 20 stretches of coastline of scenic, ecological or environmental importance have been designated by the Scottish Development Department as Preferred Conservation Zones.

The Heritage Coasts reflect much of the wide variety of scenery and wildlife of the shores of England and Wales. Atop the sheer chalk cliffs of **Dover**, **Beachy Head** and the **Seven Sisters** orchids grow, and they make good places to watch jackdaws and swallows as well as seabirds. Right across on the other side of the country, the granite **Isles of Scilly** lie 28 miles out to sea off Land's End. In legend the islands are all that is left above the surface of the lost land of Lyonesse, which sank beneath the waves when King Arthur's reign came to an end.

The local environmental trust manages 40 miles of Heritage Coast in the Scillies, where the long Atlantic rollers cream on sandy beaches and rocky coves. The mild climate fosters a wealth of wildlife – snails and worms, sea urchins and anemones in the sand or in rock pools, seaweed trailing and undulating in the waves. Here Manx shearwaters, stormy petrels and puffins breed and there are multitudes of terns and gulls. Marram and sand sedge grow in the dunes, with the dwarf pansy – found only here and in the Channel Islands.

The **Suffolk** Heritage Coast is altogether different. This is an understated shore of low cliffs under enormous skies, and shingle beaches where the sea's melancholy retreating roar rattles the pebbles. The sea has swallowed up stretches of this coast, but contrariwise has constructed the shingle bulk of Orford Ness and the long shingle spit that runs six miles down the North Weir Point. Martello towers stud the shoreline. The country's principal breeding colony of avocets has been established by the RSPB in the reserve at Havergate Island. Further north is the Sizewell nuclear power station and beyond is the RSPB reserve at Minsmere. Here among the marshes and shallow 'scrapes', or lagoons, are more avocets, as well as bitterns, marsh harriers, nightingales and nightjars, all told the largest number of breeding bird species on any British reserve.

Bird sanctuaries are again a feature of the **North Norfolk** Heritage Coast between Holme-next-the-Sea and Weybourne. This is a hauntingly desolate coast and another shifting shoreline, which has left places 'next the sea' – like Holme, Cley and Wells – marooned some distance inland. Along the shore an almost unbroken succession of nature reserves protects the saltmarshes, sand dunes and shingle spits, where mats of sea lavender edge the muddy inlets. Hundreds of species of moths gladden the hearts of entomologists here, and there are birds in millions. Rarities sometimes seen include hoopoes and ospreys. The nature reserve on Scolt Head Island is famous for its nesting terns and there are more at Blakeney Point.

Though it faces the same North Sea, the **North Yorkshire and Cleveland** Heritage Coast is a different matter altogether. Lying north of Scarborough and on either side of Whitby, this is the seaward edge of the North York Moors National Park, a line of high cliffs and bays, dramatic headlands and narrow, wooded ravines. Fishing villages huddle in deep clefts, and this is where the great explorer Captain Cook first learned his seamanship. Geologically it is an area of unusual interest and pieces of jet picked up along the shore are the foundation of the trade in Whitby jet ornaments. At Robin Hood's Bay the village houses crowd above each other on a 1-in-3 gradient.

Further up the same coast is the **North Northumberland** area, where there is a different landscape again, with miles of delectable sandy beaches, many of them owned by the National Trust. There are no titanic cliffs here, but low, rocky headlands thrust into the sea. On one of them sprawls ruined Dunstanburgh Castle, lazily menacing like a lion lying in the sun. Bamburgh Castle looks out seawards to the Farne Islands bird

sanctuaries and there are memories here of gallant Grace Darling, the lighthouse keeper's daughter who in 1838 rowed out in a storm to rescue shipwrecked sailors. The tides race in across the gleaming mudflats to cut Lindisfarne off from the mainland.

The only Heritage Coast in Cumbria and Lancashire is the short section round **St Bees Head.** The sheer red sandstone cliffs here command views of the Isle of Man on a clear day and the seabirds wheel and cry – fulmars, herring gulls, black-headed gulls and kittiwakes. Thrift, harebell and wild thyme grow by the cliff path.

The Great Orme is another dramatic headland with stark cliffs looming above Llandudno on the North Wales coast. Further south, miles more of formidable cliff scenery have been designated as Heritage Coasts: around the **Lleyn Peninsula**, along the **Pembrokeshire** shore and in **Devon, Cornwall** and **Dorset**.

Heritage Coasts have a great variety of owners, not all of whom are equally conscientious in their stewardship: from the National Trust, the RSPB and other conservation bodies to county councils, local authorities, farmers, private estates and individuals. The Countryside Commission itself gives advice and financial help, but does not own any of the land.

Where a piece of Heritage Coast is owned by an organisation like the National Trust or the RSPB, the public can feel entirely certain there will be proper protection. Matters are not as straightforward along the other Heritage Coasts. Here, each area has a Heritage Coast plan,

drawn up by the local authority on Countryside Commission guidelines. The aim is to involve all local interests in a common approach to the management of the area, to conserve it and to encourage locals and visitors to take tender care of it.

Pollution Free Beaches
Quite apart from the physical constitution of the coastline, there is concern about polluted beaches. In 1988 one-third of the bathing beaches in England, Wales and Northern Ireland failed to meet EEC standards of cleanliness: sewage levels in the water were too high. This was at least an improvement on 1986, when half the beaches had failed the test. The great majority of bathing beaches in Cornwall, Devon, Dorset, East Anglia, Wales and Northern Ireland were passed as clean. Along the Kent, Sussex and Hampshire shore, in southern Northumberland and especially in the North-West, the situation was not so good.

Large amounts of money are being spent on the problem. The Marine Conservation society publishes *The Good Beach Guide,* which gives lists and details of the country's cleanest beaches. These include most of those which have won a Blue Flag award from the Tidy Britain Group. The Blue Flag winners were mostly town beaches; those which are cleaned every day during the season and where water cleanliness is high. More beaches in Britain are clean than are not, but there is still work to be done.

Alum Bay, Isle of Wight, whose colourful sands are sold as souvenirs.

Heritage Coast

National Park

National Parks

Wordsworth, in his *Guide to the Lakes* wrote: 'the Lakes are a sort of national property, in which every man has a right and interest who has an eye to perceive and a heart to enjoy'. In the 19th century 'being outdoors' was seen as being good for body and soul.

Earlier this century, on many wild moors shooting took precedence over amenities for walkers. In the Peak District, an area much appreciated by those wishing to escape for a while from nearby large industrial communities, a mass trespass took place on Kinder Scout in 1932 and five men were arrested and imprisoned.

The Standing Committee on National Parks (SCNP) met for the first time on 26 May 1936, the start of an organised effort to protect and to make available to all the wild landscapes of Britain. The Council for National Parks now oversees the 11 National Parks in Britain, which have been set up since the National Parks and Access to the Countryside Act became law in 1949.

Reservoirs, power lines, roads, quarrying, forestry, TV transmitter

A spectacular view towards Derwent Dale, in the Peak District.

masts, power boats, caravan sites, even the tourists themselves by eroding footpaths are all potential threats to the preservation of the National Parks. But, provided informed and responsible public opinion and a spirit of co-operation prevail, all these amenities will be available to future generations.

It is fitting that, after the Kinder Scout protest, the **Peak District** should have been established as the first National Park. The Pennine Way was opened on the anniversary of the protest in 1965 and follows the backbone of England from Edale in Derbyshire, across Hadrian's Wall, to Kirk Yetholm, in the Cheviots. Seventeen million people live within a couple of hours' drive of the park and many come to enjoy walking the deep dales of the White Peak or the dramatic moors and peat bogs of the Dark Peak. Fishing, cycling and rock climbing on the gritstone edges have been joined as leisure activities by gliding and hang-gliding. An Iron Age fort on Man Tor overlooks Roman lead workings and the mine near Castleton, where deposits of decorative fluorspar – blue john – have been worked since Roman times. Heather covers one third of the Park and provides food for the red grouse.

Largest of the National Parks, the **Lake District** combines mountain and lake, woodland and farmland. Moving ice shaped these troughs and corries and glacial rubble dammed the valleys, but the underlying rock dictated whether the hills were softly rounded, like Skiddaw, or wildly rugged, like Scafell and Helvellyn. Broad-leaved woodland like the Borrowdale and Witherslack woods, of great interest to conservationists, cover about five per cent of the Park.

The Snowdon massif is the heartland of the **Snowdonia National Park** and Cader Idris is one of the most popular areas. Half a million people reach Snowdon Summit each year and only a quarter of them admit to using the railway! Many fewer visit the Aran Mountains in the south, or the rugged Rhynogydd. Harlech Castle lies on part of the park's 20 or so miles of sweeping sandy coastline, backed by beautiful mountain scenery. For the 'railway buff' there are six narrow-gauge railways to enjoy and to the 5,000 acres of ancient broad-leaved woodland have been added another 5,000, which with commercial forestry, now cover over 10 per cent of the Park.

Two plateaux make up **Dartmoor,** the largest and wildest stretch of open country in southern Britain, rising to over 2,000ft (610m). Covered with

blanket bog and heather moorland, they are divided by the River Dart. Granite tors protrude near the edges, where other rivers have eroded deep valleys. Over a third of the Park is farmland and the high northern moors have been a military training area since the 1870s. The Dartmoor pony – descendant of ponies turned out to graze in the Middle Ages – grazes much of the lower lying heather moorland. There are hundreds of ancient sites – chambered tombs, hillforts and stone circles – in the Park and medieval crosses and waymarks can still be useful to today's traveller.

The **Pembrokeshire Coast National Park**, the smallest of the Parks, hugs the coast and is only three miles wide along most of its length. Steep cliffs display spectacularly folded and twisted rock formations, while sheltered bays invite bathing, and scuba diving. Offshore, islands such as Skomer and Skokholm support huge colonies of seabirds, among them the world's largest concentration of Manx shearwaters and puffins. Inland from the Milford Haven oil terminal, with its facilities for 300,000-ton tankers, is the Daugleddau, a drowned river valley with dense woodlands and in the north, the windswept moorlands of the Preseli Hills, source of the 'bluestones' of Stonehenge.

Though Middlesbrough and York are not far away, the **North York Moors** is a relatively quiet Park. The moors rise sharply from Pickering in the south, Teesside in the north and the Vale of York in the west. The eastern boundary is the sea, with Staithes, home of Captain Cook, and Whitby (outside the Park boundaries), famous for its clifftop Abbey and its jet – a fossilised black amber – so popular with the Victorians. Rievaulx and Rosedale Abbeys are within the Park, as is Mount Grace Priory, the best preserved Carthusian priory in Britain. Evidence of man's occupation of the high moors ranges from the burial mounds of the neolithic farmers who first cleared the land to the giant golf ball-like radar domes of the Fylingdales early warning system.

Nearly half of the **Yorkshire Dales** is farmland, but there is little woodland. Over four centuries the monasteries' sheep walks developed into the start of a road system across the fells, the best known today being the green lane between Kilnsey and Malham. Miles of dry stone walling are a man-made feature of the landscape, as is the Settle–Carlisle railway with its spectacular Ribblehead Viaduct. Public transport facilities being poor, the Dalesrail scheme makes recreational use of this line for walkers, who form the second largest group of visitors, after the touring motorist. As well as a part of the Pennine Way, there are popular areas for walkers and day trippers around Malham Cove and Tarn, with its fascinating limestone pavement 'grikes' – sheltered habitats for lime- and shade-loving plants. Aysgarth Falls, in Wensleydale, attract over half a million visitors a year. There is a 'Bunk House Barns' project, offering basic shelter for walkers in field barns which used to over-winter the dairy cattle.

R D Blackmore's *Lorna Doone* has made **Exmoor** known to many, as has Williamson's *Tarka the Otter*. The heartland, rising to 1,500ft (460m), from Chapman Barrows to Dunkery Beacon is still the windswept haunt of falcon and hawk. The 'hog's back' cliffs along the coast are broken by deep valleys with waterfalls which make protected breeding sites for seabirds. Exmoor is known for its Bronze and Iron Age sites, and a recent aerial survey has added over 2,000 fresh areas to be investigated. The medieval Tarr Steps bridge in the Barle Valley is a popular tourist attraction. With the Quantocks, Exmoor is the last secure habitat in the south of

England for the red deer. The number of Exmoor ponies, adapted to rough grazing and wild winters, is declining, but a small herd has been established to maintain the breed.

Cheviot sheep graze the open moorland which makes up most of the **Northumberland National Park.** Remote from all settlements and mostly above 1,000ft (300m), it is often a harsh environment and must have seemed the end of the world to Roman legionaries from sunny Spain and Italy who manned Hadrian's Wall, part of which runs along the southern edge of the Park. Housesteads fort and Vindolanda have interesting visitor centres and museums. Otterburn and other battles over the 300 years up to the Union of Crowns in 1603 have given rise to many a Border ballad.

The **Brecon Beacons,** four high red sandstone mountain blocks, divide the ancient rocks of mid-Wales from the coalfields and industrialisation further south. From the Black Mountains, near Hay-on-Wye, through the Brecon Beacons and Fforest Fawr, the Park stretches to Black Mountain in the west. Along its southern edge a limestone belt provides a dramatic change in scenery with hundreds of sink-holes and cave systems. The most

spectacular are the Dan-yr-Ogof Caves, on the A4067, at the head of the Tawe valley. The ruins of Carreg Cennen Castle, a 13th-century stronghold on sheer limestone cliffs, lie just off the A40, near Llandeilo.

The **Broads Authority** was rejected together with the Sussex Downs from the twelve candidates in 1949, but was established as a National Park on 1 April 1989. We owe Britain's most famous stretch of inland waterways to the peat-digging activities of our ancestors in the 9th century, which caused flooding in the 14th, and its survival as a recreational area to the strenuous efforts of the Broads Authority, in the 1980s, to halt the environmental degradation. Algae flourished on increased nutrients from effluents and fertilisers, the water 'died', reed cover was lost and the banks became eroded. Much has been done, but care is still needed.

The **New Forest** is the latest area to be granted the status of a National Park, although, as it is administered by the Forestry Commission, the status is not 'real'.

National Park

Hound Tor, an example of Dartmoor's striking landscape.
Inset *The deep waters of Llyn Cau, from Cader Idris, Gwynedd.*

National Scenic Area (Scotland)

National Scenic Areas (Scotland)
Where England and Wales have National Parks, Scotland has National Scenic Areas. There are 40 of them, designated in 1978 by the Countryside Commission for Scotland, established to conserve Scotland's natural beauty and improve public access to and enjoyment of it. Though the Commission's stated policy is not 'to see land in Scotland managed as though it were a museum', the National Scenic Areas are protected from development which would harm their scenic qualities. Between them they cover close to one eighth of the total area of Scotland.

Inevitably, the great majority of these National Scenic Areas lie in the Highlands and Islands, along or north of the Highland Line, the geological fault which separates Highland from Lowland Scotland. It runs diagonally from south-west to north-east clear across the country from the Isle of Arran to Stonehaven on the east coast. North and west of this line Scotland's wilder, more solitary, most spectacular and least spoiled landscapes are to be found. The land to the south and east is far more given to farming and industry, and some of it is heavily populated.

A few of the areas lie south of the Highland Line, however. In the Borders, for instance, the **Eildon and Leaderfoot** area includes the uncannily beautiful Eildon Hills. The Leader Water runs south to join the River Tweed below the three volcanic Eildon peaks, the highest rising to 1,385ft (422m). These

Looking out to Scarista Bay, from Borve on the west coast of Harris.

shapely hills are steeped in legend and romance. King Arthur and his gallant knights of the Round Table are said to lie sleeping beneath them, under an enchantment, awaiting the time of their recall to life. It was here that Thomas the Rhymer, the 13th-century poet and prophet, encountered the Queen of Fairyland. Dressed all in green, and very fair, she took him away to her magic realm for seven years and gave him the power to see into the future. Here, below the hills, lies ruined Melrose Abbey, where the heart of Robert the Bruce was buried, and close by is Abbotsford, the house Sir Walter Scott built for himself in the countryside he loved.

Scott's immensely popular poems and novels whetted the appetite of prospective tourists for his native land. The process was helped along by Queen Victoria and Prince Albert, who made themselves a Highland retreat at Balmoral in the 1840s. They loved to go stalking deer in the mountains, picnicking at the remote shielings, or shepherds' huts, and fishing for trout in a lumbering rowing boat on Loch Muick.

The region today is the **Deeside and Lochnagar** National Scenic Area, which is the only one in the Grampian Region. The high granite ridge of Lochnagar, a favourite with climbers, rises to 3,786ft (1,154m) to the south of Braemar, in an area of mountain and forest where the River Dee flows past Balmoral Castle on its way to the North Sea at Aberdeen. Lord Byron wrote rhapsodically of 'the crags that are wild and majestic, the steep frowning slopes of dark Lochnagar'. Ever since Queen Victoria's time,

the Highland Gathering at Braemar has been regularly attended by the royal family and marks the annual apogee of the Highland Games season.

From Deeside westwards, the pass called the Lairg Ghru runs through another National Scenic Area, negotiating the heart of the **Cairngorm Mountains** on its way to Speyside. This is the largest tract of land above 3,000ft (915m) in Britain. Rearing up between Braemar and the valley of the Spey, the lofty granite summits of Ben Macdhui, Braeriach, Cairn Toul and Cairn Gorm itself all clear 4,000ft (1,220m) and are outstripped in height only by Ben Nevis.

The lures of hill walking, rock climbing and wintersports draw visitors here. The Forestry Commission manages an extensive Forest Park and near Loch an Eilein are Scots pines at least 250 years old. A hundred square miles of nature reserve lie to the south of Glen More and includes both Braeriach and Cairn Toul. Arctic and alpine plant rarities grow here, with all sorts of mosses and ferns. Reindeer were reintroduced a few years ago and red deer and wildcat roam the mountainsides. Golden eagles soar above the corries and in the woods capercaillies make popping noises like corks.

Scottish scenery is renowned not only for its breathtaking grandeur, its harmony of sky and mountain and water, but for the romantic and often violent history which seems to cling still to every peak and corrie, every pass and glen. The **Ben Nevis** and **Glen Coe** areas contain both the highest mountain in Britain at 4,408ft (1,344m) and one of the most notorious localities in all Scotland's bloody and tragic past. Ben Nevis, which is more of a hump than a peak, can be climbed fairly easily in good weather, though it will take a good many hours up and down, and there are colossal views from the top on a clear day. In Fort William, down below the mountain, the West Highland Museum illuminates the natural and the human history of the district.

To the south are the peaks which tower above Glen Coe, on an overcast day one of the bleakest and most melancholy places in the British Isles. The celebrated and treacherous massacre of the local Macdonalds by a party of Campbell soldiery occurred on a bitter February night in 1692. The site of the Macdonald settlement and much of the surrounding country is now owned by the National Trust for Scotland, which has a visitor centre in the glen. There is also a folk museum in Glencoe village. Further

south still, and part of the National Scenic Area, is the brooding wasteland of Rannoch Moor, with its peaty bogs and lochans, vividly described in an episode of Robert Louis Stevenson's *Kidnapped*.

Famed again in song and story are the **Cuillin Hills** of the Isle of Skye, which reach up in savage splendour above dramatic Loch Coruisk. These are black, jagged, precipitous, sinister mountains, the highest peak being Sgurr Alasdair at 3,309ft (1,009m). The Cuillins are an irresistible magnet to rock climbers, but they have an old reputation for treachery – compasses go oddly astray, mists descend suddenly, climbers are lost and cut off. Among marginally safer attractions on Skye are Talisker malt whisky and the MacLeods' ancestral castle at Dunvegan with its singularly daunting dungeon.

There is wonderful mountain and loch scenery again to the north, where six massive ranges rear their peaks to the sky in the National Scenic Area of **Wester Ross.** The sun glitters on Loch Maree and its islands, and the warmth of the North Atlantic Drift fosters a subtropical paradise in the luxuriant gardens at Inverewe, at the head of Loch Ewe. The gardens were created from the 1860s on by Osgood Mackenzie on what was initially barren peat wasteland.

The island of Foula is included in the Shetlands National Scenic Area, and so is Fair Isle, familiar from weather forecasts. In the Orkneys the island of **Hoy** is protected, with its dramatic isolated 450ft (137m) stack, the Old Man of Hoy. Man-made Orkney attractions include the Stone Age village of Skara Brae and the enormous Stone Age tomb of Maes Howe, as well as the cathedral of St Magnus in Kirkwall.

Though most of the National Scenic Areas protect mountain scenery, one of them is centred on the old town of **Dunkeld** in the Tayside Region, where the River Tay sweeps past the ruined cathedral among its lawns and sheltering trees. There are memorials in the church to a renowned Scottish regiment, the Black Watch, and to the Scottish Horse, a regiment raised by the Duke of Atholl to fight in the Boer War. An attractive walk through the woods by the River Braan leads to a waterfall and an 18th-century folly. Not far away in the opposite direction is the Loch of the Lowes nature reserve, run by the Scottish Wildlife Trust, where visitors who are lucky may see ospreys. *Macbeth's* Birnam Wood is not far away either.

Lying across the Highland Line are the 'bonnie banks' of **Loch Lomond,** 24 miles long and the largest stretch of inland water in Britain. This is another National Scenic Area. The narrow northern end of the loch protrudes into the Highlands between Ben Vorlich and Ben Lomond, both over 3,000ft (915m). The southern end, with its numerous islands, lies in more

Top *The rocks and tumbling waters of the River Dee, in Royal Deeside.* Above *Beinn Alligin's peak, with Upper Loch Torridon in the foreground.*

placid country. The burial place of the outlawed Clan MacGregor is on the island of Inchaillach, which is part of the nature reserve at the lower end of the loch.

To the south-west there is a return to mountain landscape in the National Scenic Area of **North Arran**, among the jagged heights of this island in the Firth of Clyde. The highest is Goat Fell at 2,866ft (874m), which can be climbed from the town of Brodick and offers wonderful views, stretching on a clear day to England, Ireland and the Isle of Man. It is to be hoped that the National Scenic Areas will continue to reward Scots and their visitors for many generations to come.

Forest Park

Forest Drive

Forest Parks
Forest Drives

Long ago, before man began to make his mark, most of the land surface of Britain was thickly covered with trees. Far back in the New Stone Age, 6,000 years ago or more, farmers began to fell and burn the woodlands to make clearings for crops and pasture stock. By the Middle Ages more than 80 per cent of the original woodland cover had been cleared. Little is left today of the tangled Wealden forest through which the defeated English were chased by William the Conqueror's Normans after Hastings, or of the oaks and glades of Sherwood Forest where Robin Hood and his outlaws hunted.

In this century huge new man-made forests have been created by the Forestry Commission, set up in 1919 to repair the ravages of World War I, when no timber was imported. The Commission's principal purpose has always been a commercial one, to grow saleable timber. It planted pine, larch and spruce – fast-growing softwood trees that thrive in poor soil and are ready for harvesting in 25 or 30 years – and it has been fiercely criticised for its regimented ranks of

This vast, wooded region of Argyll became Scotland's first Forest Park.

conifers marching monotonously over hill and dale. Increasingly, however, the Commission has recognised the importance of its role as a provider of recreation and its responsibility to the environment.

Forest Parks
In Scotland, where it is the largest landowner, the Commission began to create Forest Parks in scenically attractive areas. The first of them, set under way as far back as 1935, was the **Argyll Forest Park,** extending over 100 square miles of the Cowal Peninsula in the Strathclyde region. Lying between Loch Fyne and Loch Long, it is mountain country, long dominated by the Campbell clan, who feuded with the local Lamonts. The ruined Campbell hold of Carrick Castle glowers out over Loch Goil and the churchyard of Kilmun on Holy Loch was the traditional burying place of the Campbell chiefs.

Visitors can enjoy driving the forest roads, walking on miles of tracks, pony trekking, fishing, sailing and waterskiing. Deer, wildcats, otters, golden eagles and ravens live here. Near the head of Loch Long are fine peaks, including The Cobbler at 2,891ft (881m) and the pass called 'Rest and be Thankful' on the A83, named from the inscription on a stone seat that used to be there. Close to the

southern end of Loch Eck, Benmore House, weirdly and wonderfully Scots Baronial, was given to the Forestry Commission in 1928. The Younger Botanic Garden here is open to the public and is celebrated for its marvellous azaleas and rhododendrons. A brook runs through Puck's Glen, a narrow cleft among the rocks with rare mosses and ferns.

Further south and more than twice as big in area is the **Galloway Forest Park,** designated in 1943, a wild area of wooded mountains, moorland, lochs and streams lying to the north of Newton Stewart. There are ten peaks above 2,000ft (610m), the highest being Merrick, 2,766ft (843m) near the centre of the park. There is climbing, walking, fishing and swimming to enjoy, and a tremendous richness of wildlife – deer, wild goats, pine martens, wildcats, red squirrels, golden eagles and hen harriers.

There are miles of trails for walkers, but motor roads are few and far between in this part of the world. North of Newton Stewart, Loch Trool, bowered among wooded slopes, has a good forest trail. The main road in the park is the Queen's Drive, or more prosaically the A712, from New Galloway to Newton Stewart. Bruce's Stone marks the place where Robert the Bruce scored an early

victory over the English and the man-made Clatteringshaws Loch is part of a hydro-electric scheme. The Galloway Deer Museum is informative not only about the deer but the park and its wildlife in general. The Raiders' Road Forest Drive turns off to the south and follows an old cattle thieves' route through the woods for 10 miles beside the Black Water of Dee, with bathing places and picnic spots.

The **Glen More Forest Park** is in the National Scenic Area of the Cairngorms. The **Queen Elizabeth Forest Park,** designated in 1953, links two National Scenic Areas, Loch Lomond and the Trossachs. In the Tayside Region there is pony trekking, mountain biking and fishing in the **Tummel Forest Park,** with numerous walks of varying length and degrees of difficulty. Forestry Commission walks are graded as 'Easy', 'Strenuous' or 'Difficult'. There are camp sites, picnic sites and plenty of car parks, with deer, red squirrels and capercaillies to watch. The forest here has mostly been planted since World War II, but a specially enticing attraction is a guided walk through the magically named Black Wood of Rannoch. On the south shore of Loch Rannoch, this is one of the rare remaining fragments of the great Caledonian pine forest, which once stretched for hundreds of miles. The visitor centre for the Forest Park is above Loch Tummel at the Queen's View, where you can stand in the footsteps of Queen Victoria, who admired the prospect in 1866. She also admired the Pass of Killiecrankie, not far away, a wooded gorge and battlefield where the National Trust for Scotland has a visitor centre.

The Forest Park idea spread from Scotland south into England. The **Border Forest Park,** designated in 1955, straddles the high sparse moors on both sides of the Anglo-Scots border, where so many raiding and rustling parties rode about their nefarious business in past centuries. Ruins of pele towers and castles testify to a violent history of feuding and marauding. At the heart of the park lies Kielder Water, a spectacular man-made reservoir seven miles long in the valley of the North Tyne, holding 40 million gallons of water. Ferry boats ply across it in the summer, and it is reached by the 12-mile Kielder Forest Drive from the A68. The drive runs past viewpoints and picnic spots to the Forestry Commission's visitor centre at Kielder Castle. In the remoter areas, you may catch sight of red deer, wild goats, blue hares and red squirrels.

On a much smaller scale is the **Grizedale Forest Park,** occupying a slice of Lake District scenery between Coniston Water and Esthwaite Water, south-west of Hawkshead. There are walks and guided tours, orienteering courses, cycle trails, a disabled trail, and a theatre. A trail bears witness to past industries: bloomeries where iron ore was smelted, charcoal pits, potash pits for soap-making, kilns, a tannery and a blast furnace.

The **North Riding Forest Park** lies north-east of Pickering in the rolling landscape of the North York Moors. Centred on the Dalby Valley, in the Middle Ages it was part of the much larger royal hunting forest of Pickering. A nine-mile forest drive takes the motorist gently through the woodland today, with an ample supply of parking pull-offs and places for a picnic. Leaflets detail forest walks for those who want to stretch their legs. Part of the drive follows the Staindale Beck, which was dammed to create an attractive lake, and there is a walk from here to the strange rock formations called the Bridestones, in a nature reserve run by the National Trust and the Yorkshire Wildlife Trust.

Forest Drives

Where there is no Forest Park, there is still occasionally a forest drive: as in the **Hamsterley Forest,** the largest area of woodland in County Durham. It covers 5,000 acres west of Bishop Auckland, off the A68. The Forestry Commission bought the estate from the last Surtees owner, a descendant of the famous Victorian sporting novelist R S Surtees. The drive runs for four miles along the Bedburn Beck and the Spurlswood Beck, through

Right Helpful information at the Visitor Centre in the Borders Forest Park. Below Kielder Forest Drive, between Kielder Castle and Redesdale.

woodland which sports much pine and fir, spruce and larch. There are no less than 60 varieties of tree here all told, with oak and ash, beech and thorn among them. Red squirrels and roe deer, bats and lizards frequent these woods and there are large numbers of woodpeckers and fungi. There are waymarked walks, though more adventurous visitors can explore wherever they like.

In South Wales, meanwhile, it takes a tough cyclist to manage the splendid **Cwmcarn Forest Drive.** The seven-mile drive starts at an excellent new visitor centre south of Abercarn, near Newport. Higher up are picnic places and barbecue spots with commanding views across country and to the Bristol Channel. Walks lead off at intervals, including one which climbs to the summit. The trees are mostly spruce, larch and pine, but oaks, beeches and rowans temper the conifers.

The drive runs through part of the Forestry Commission's Ebbw Forest, a distant man-made descendant of the ancient forest of Machen, which was eaten away over the centuries by sheep and charcoal burners and finally fell victim to the devouring demand for timber in the South Wales coal mines. So here man has put back something of what he has destroyed.

Forest Park

Forest Drive

THE TOURIST'S BRITISH ISLES
·CALENDAR·

SPRING

MARCH

Whuppity Scoorie
Lanark, Strathclyde
(March 1)

Ideal Home Exhibition
Earls Court, London
(early March to early April)

Belfast Musical Festival
Belfast
(March – 3rd week)

Oxford v Cambridge Boat Race
Putney to Mortlake,
London
(late March or early April)

APRIL

Midgley Pace Egg Play
Calder Valley, West
Yorkshire
(Good Friday)

Nutters Dance
Bacup, Lancashire
(Easter Saturday)

Easter Parade
Battersea Park, London
(Easter Monday)

Harness Horse Parade
Regent's Park, London
(Easter Monday)

Hare Pie Scramble and Bottle Kicking
Hallaton, Leicestershire
(Easter Monday)

Hocktide Festival
Hungerford, Berkshire
(Easter Tuesday)

Northumbria Gathering
Morpeth, Northumbria
(week after Easter)

The Grand National
Aintree, Merseyside
(April – 2nd Saturday)

Shakespeare's Birthday Celebrations
Stratford-upon-Avon,
Warwickshire
(April 21)

Spring Flower Show
Harrogate, North Yorkshire
(late April)

Badminton Three Day Event
Badminton, Avon
(late April or early May)

MAY

May Morning Ceremony
Oxford
(May 1)

Royal May Day Celebrations
Knutsford, Cheshire
(May – 1st Saturday)

Flower Parade
Spalding, Lincolnshire
(early May)

Furry Dance
Helston, Cornwall
(May 8)

Garland Day
Abbotsbury, Dorset
(May 13)

Goat Fell Race
Isle of Arran, Strathclyde
(May – 2nd or 3rd
Saturday)

Bath International Festival of the Arts
Bath, Avon
(late May to early June)

Chelsea Flower Show
Royal Hospital, Chelsea,
London
(late May to early June)

TT Motorcycle Races
Isle of Man
(late May to early June)

Arbor Tree Day
Aston on Clun, Shropshire
(late May)

Garland Day
Castleton, Derbyshire
(May 29)

Dickens Festival
Rochester, Kent
(late May or early June)

Royal Bath and West Show
Shepton Mallet, Somerset
(late May or early June)

Woolsack Races
Tetbury, Gloucestershire
(Spring Bank Holiday)

SUMMER

JUNE

The Derby
Epsom, Surrey
(June – 1st Wednesday)

Scuttlebrook Wake
Chipping Campden,
Gloucestershire
(Saturday following Spring
Bank Holiday)

Appleby Horse Fair
Appleby, Cumbria
(June – 2nd Tuesday and
Wednesday)

Trooping the Colour
Horse Guards Parade,
London
(June – 2nd Saturday)

Royal Cornwall Show
Wadebridge, Cornwall
(June – 2nd week)

Aldeburgh Festival of Music and the Arts
Aldeburgh, Suffolk
(June – 2nd to 4th
weeks)

Selkirk Common Riding
Selkirk, Borders
(mid-June)

Three Counties Agricultural Show
Great Malvern, Hereford &
Worcester
(mid-June)

Stour Music Festival
Boughton Aluph, Kent
(June – 2nd half)

Royal Highland Show
Ingliston, Lothian
(June – 3rd week)

Royal Ascot Race Meeting
Ascot, Berkshire
(late June)

Wimbledon Lawn Tennis Championships
Wimbledon, London
(late June to early July)

JULY

Tynwald Day
Isle of Man
(July 5)

Henley Royal Regatta
Henley on Thames,
Oxfordshire
(July – 1st week)

Cheltenham International Festival of Music
Cheltenham,
Gloucestershire
(July – 1st and 3rd weeks)

British Rose Festival
Gardens of the Rose,
Chiswell Green,
Hertfordshire
(July – 1st or 2nd week)

Royal International Agricultural Show
Stoneleigh, Warwickshire
(early July)

Great Yorkshire Agricultural Show
Harrogate, North Yorkshire
(July – 2nd week)

International Musical Eisteddfod
Llangollen, Clwyd
(early July)

Sham Fight
Scarva, Co Down
(July 13)

Royal Welsh Show
Builth Wells, Powys
(July – 3rd week)

Black Cherry Fair
Chertsey, Surrey
(July – 3rd Saturday)

Royal Tournament
Earls Court, London
(mid-July)

Buxton International Arts Festival
Buxton, Derbyshire
(mid-July to early August)

Tweedmouth Salmon Feast
Tweedmouth,
Northumberland
(Sunday after July 18)

Tolpuddle Martyrs Procession
Tolpuddle, Dorset
(July – 3rd Sunday)

Durham Miners Gala
Durham
(July – Saturday of 2nd
week)

Croagh Patrick Pilgrimage
Near Westport, Co Mayo
(July-last Sunday)

AUGUST

Royal National Eisteddfod
Varying locations in Wales
(August – 1st week)

The Burry Man Festival
Queensferry, Lothian
(August – 2nd Friday)

Cowes Week
Cowes, Isle of Wight
(August – 2nd week)

Puck Fair
Killorglin, Co Kerry
(August 10–12)

Marymass Festival
Irvine, Strathclyde
(August – 2nd or 3rd
weeks)

**Edinburgh International
Festival**
Edinburgh
(August – last three weeks)

Priddy Sheep Fair
Priddy, Somerset
(mid-August)

Grasmere Sports
Grasmere, Cumbria
(Thursday nearest
August 20)

Burning of Bartle
West Witton, North
Yorkshire
(Saturday nearest
August 24)

Oul' Lammas Fair
Ballycastle, Co Antrim
(August – last Tuesday)

Plague Sunday Service
Eyam, Derbyshire
(August – last Sunday)

Navy Days
Plymouth and Portsmouth
(August Bank Holiday)

AUTUMN

SEPTEMBER

Ben Nevis Hill Race
Fort William, Highland
(September – 1st Saturday)

Braemar Gathering
Braemar, Grampian
(September – 1st Saturday)

Hop Hoodening
Canterbury, Kent
(early September)

St Giles's Fair
Oxford
(September – 1st full week)

Horn Dance
Abbots Bromley,
Staffordshire
(Monday after 1st Sunday
following September 4)

Burghley Horse Trials
Burghley House, Stamford
(early September)

Blackpool Illuminations
Blackpool, Lancashire
(early September to early
November)

International Air Show
Farnborough, Hampshire
(September – 1st week)

**Clarinbridge Oyster
Festival**
Clarinbridge, Co Galway
(early or mid-September)

**World Carriage Driving
Championships**
Windsor, Berkshire
(September – 3rd week)

Victorian Festival
Llandrindod Wells, Powys
(September – 3rd week)

**Great Autumn Flower
Show**
Harrogate, North Yorkshire
(mid-September)

Dr Johnson's Birthday
Lichfield, Staffordshire
(on or near September 18)

Egremont Crab Fair
Egremont, Cumbria
(Saturday nearest
September 18)

Barnstaple Old Fair
Barnstaple, Devon
(September – 3rd week)

**Painswick Church
Clipping**
Painswick, Gloucestershire
(September – 3rd week)

Dublin Theatre Festival
Dublin
(late September to early
October)

OCTOBER

Nottingham Goose Fair
Nottingham
(early October)

Tavistock Goose Fair
Tavistock, Devon
(October 10)

Pack Monday Fair
Sherborne, Dorset
(1st Monday after
October 10)

Border Shepherds Show
Alwinton, Northumberland
(October – 2nd week)

Horse of the Year Show
Wembley Arena, London
(mid-October)

Stratford Mop Fair
Stratford-upon-Avon,
Warwickshire
(mid-October)

Wexford Opera Festival
Wexford, Co Wexford
(late October to
mid-November)

NOVEMBER

**London to Brighton
Veteran Car Run**
Hyde Park Corner, London
(November – 1st Sunday)

Guy Fawkes Night
Lewes, East Sussex, and
elsewhere
(November 5)

Tar-Barrel Rolling
Ottery St Mary, Devon
(November 5)

Lord Mayor's Show
Guildhall to the Strand,
London
(November – 2nd Saturday)

Belfast Festival at Queen's
Belfast
(mid to late November)

**Contemporary Music
Festival**
Huddersfield, West
Yorkshire
(late November)

WINTER

DECEMBER

Royal Smithfield Show
London
(early December)

**Festival of Carols and
Lessons**
King's College Chapel,
Cambridge
(December 24)

Ba' Games
Kirkwall, Orkney Islands
(December 25 and
January 1)

Greatham Sword Dance
Greatham, Cleveland
(December 26)

**Allendale Tar-Barrel
Ceremony**
Allendale, Northumberland
(December 31)

Fireball Ceremony
Stonehaven, Grampian
(December 31)

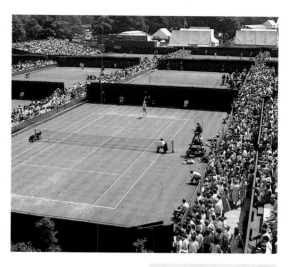

Flambeaux Procession
Comrie, Tayside
(December 31)

JANUARY

Haxey Hood Game
Haxey, Humberside
(January 5 or 6)

Straw Bear Festival
Whittlesey, Cambridgeshire
(Friday and Saturday
before Plough Monday)

Plough Stots Service
Goathland, North
Yorkshire
(Monday after January 6)

Burning the Clavie
Burghead, Grampian
(January 11)

Wassailing the Apple Tree
Carhampton, Somerset
(January 17)

Up Helly Aa
Lerwick, Shetland Islands
(January – last Tuesday)

FEBRUARY

Jorvik Viking Festival
York, North Yorkshire
(February – whole month)

Pancake Day Race
Olney, Buckinghamshire
(Shrove Tuesday)

Shrovetide Football
Ashbourne, Derbyshire
(Shrove Tuesday)

Shrovetide Skipping
Scarborough, North
Yorkshire
(Shrove Tuesday)

*Left Traditional maypole
dancing at Chipping Campden
in Gloucestershire.
Inset A familiar sight in The
Mall, the Household Cavalry.
Above Wimbledon draws the
crowds each summer.
Below May Day celebrations
in Oxford, which were started
in the mid-17th century.*

Tourist
Information
Centre

Tourist
Information
Centre
(Summer only)

▌Tourist Information Centres

▌With over 800 offices nationwide, Britain's Tourist Information Centres offer a free service, welcoming calls both in person and by phone.

Whatever your query – whether you are looking for something new to do on a Sunday, somewhere to take the family for the day or simply a good place to eat, your local Tourist Information Centre is only too willing to help.

The staff at each centre have details on just about everything within a 50-mile radius and this is backed up by a comprehensive range of brochures, pamphlets and guides both free and for sale.

They can help with excursions and outings, giving you details and route directions to a variety of places, from castles and craft centres to model villages and museums, tell you which bus to catch, the best place for a picnic, or a walk or a scenic drive. They can even advise on which restaurant is likely to provide a high-chair for the baby or which stately home involves a lot of walking about. They also have details of local events: concerts, carnivals, festivals and fêtes and

Inside the London Tourist Board Information Centre at Victoria.

what is on in town in the evenings.

Another invaluable service is to offer on-the-spot help with finding places to stay. Most centres have up-to-date lists of all kinds of holiday accommodation in the area such as hotels, holiday homes and campsites. They can make local reservations for you, if available, or reservations at any other town which has a centre offering this facility, for the same or the following day. A fee or deposit may be payable for these services.

Most of the centres keep regular office hours from 9 to 5, Monday to Friday, but many are also open at weekends or for longer periods, especially in the summer. Some, however, are open from Easter to September only, but you can always refer your enquiries to the nearest all-year-round centre.

Britain's Tourist Information Centres are at your service and are always happy to help, no matter what the query.

The following signs indicate where you will find a Tourist Information Centre in a town.

 – directional sign for road traffic

 – sign for pedestrians

 – this sign means a Tourist Information Centre is just a few yards away

ROAD ATLAS
—OF THE—
BRITISH ISLES

Tourism and leisure

Places of interest to note in the area you are

visiting.

Red pictorial symbols and red type highlight numerous places of interest, catering for every taste. Red symbols within yellow boxes show tourist attractions in a town. Use them to plan days out or places to visit on holiday. To avoid disappointment remember to check opening times before you visit.

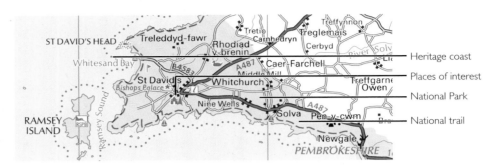

- Heritage coast
- Places of interest
- National Park
- National trail

Town plans

Up-to-date, fully indexed town plans show AA

recommended roads and other practical

information, such as one-way streets, car parks

and restricted roads,

making navigation much easier.

- One-way streets
- Major buildings and places of interest
- Town parking facilities

London

Easy-to-read, fully indexed street maps of inner

London provide a simple guide to finding your

way around the city.

- Underground railway stations
- Major places of tourist interest
- Garage parking
- One-way systems

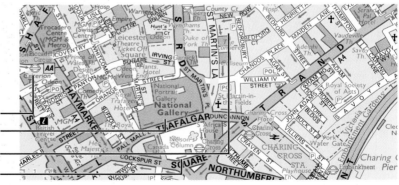

Ports and airports

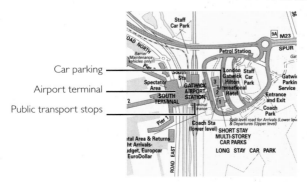

- Car parking
- Airport terminal
- Public transport stops

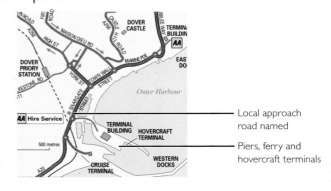

- Local approach road named
- Piers, ferry and hovercraft terminals

using this atlas

Road Maps

Clear, easy-to-read mapping helps you to plan more detailed journeys, and provides a wealth of information for the motorist.

All motorways, primary, A and B roads, and unclassified roads are shown. The atlas also identifies interchanges, roundabouts and those roads outside urban areas which are under construction.

Additional features include rivers, lakes and reservoirs, railway lines, interesting places to visit, picnic sites and Tourist Information Centres. To assist you in estimating journey length, distances are shown in miles between blue marker symbols.

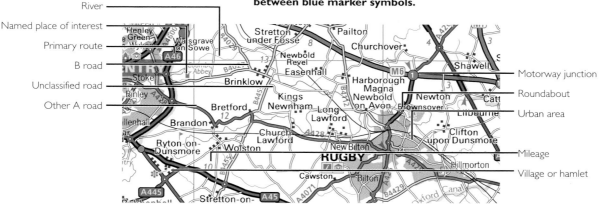

- River
- Named place of interest
- Primary route
- B road
- Unclassified road
- Other A road
- Motorway junction
- Roundabout
- Urban area
- Mileage
- Village or hamlet

Ferry and rail routes

Useful ferry and rail information.

To assist in planning journeys overseas mapping of coastal regions provides basic off-shore information including ferry routes. Throughout the atlas, railway lines with stations and level crossings are shown to assist with general navigation or rail travel requirements.

- Level crossing
- Railway station
- Railway line
- Continental ferry routes

Motorways – restricted junctions

Motorway junctions, displayed as diagrams, highlight individual restrictions.

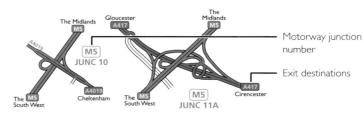

- Motorway junction number
- Exit destinations

Call AA Roadwatch

or listen to local radio

to avoid delays on

your journey.

Delays and hold-ups

Despite ever-increasing levels of traffic, motorways are still the quickest means of getting from A to B. Nevertheless, a hold-up on a motorway can easily delay your journey for several hours. There are a number of ways of gleaning information about the stretches of motoway to avoid: by phone, television (teletext), radio and newspaper.

AA Roadwatch

This service provides up-to-the-minute information on traffic conditions, roadworks and the weather for the whole country. See page XII for numbers to call.

Radio

Frequent radio bulletins are issued by both the BBC and independent local radio stations about road and weather conditions, and likely hold-ups. By tuning into the local radio stations you can prepare to make changes to your route and avoid delays. Local radio however, does not yet cover the entire country. A recent development is the Radio Data System Traffic Message Channel (RDS–TMC), which is becoming more widely available.

Carry out regular checks to make sure that you

and your car arrive safely.

Daily checks

Before you start every journey you should always ensure that:

- You check the dashboard warning lights before and after starting the engine
- There are no unusual noises once the engine is running
- All the lights are both clean and working
- The windscreen and all other windows are clean
- You have sufficient fuel for your journey

Weekly checks

Before you set out on a journey you should also ensure that:

- The engine oil level is correct, looking for obvious signs of leakage
- The coolant level is correct, checking the anti-freeze before the onset of winter
- The battery connections and terminals are clean and free from corrosion
- The brake (and clutch, if hydraulic) fluid is correct
- The tyres, including the spare, are properly inflated and not damaged
- The tyres are changed if the tread falls below 2mm
- The fan-belt is not worn or damaged, and that the tension is correct
- The windscreen wipers are clean and that the screen wash reservoir is full

Are you fit to drive?

Food, tiredness, drink

and medicine all affect

your driving.

Fit to drive

Many accidents are caused by one or more of the drivers involved being unfit to drive when the accident occurred. The most obvious reason for such accidents is alcohol; even the smallest quantity can affect driving. The only safe advice is: if you drive, don't drink – if you drink, don't drive. However, alcohol is just one of a number of factors that can make someone unfit to drive.

Tiredness

Some people become tired sooner than others, but the following are guidelines which you should aim to keep: for every three hours on the road, take 20 minutes rest; if possible, share the driving; limit yourself to a maximum of eight hours behind the wheel in any one day; and try to avoid driving at times when you would normally be asleep or resting. You should also avoid driving after hard exercise, a large meal and, of course, after consuming alcohol. Other factors which can contribute to tiredness are temperature inside the car and medication; a stuffy atmosphere – and some drugs – can induce drowsiness. If you are on medication, check with your doctor whether you should be driving at all. One final point: not driving during peak hours keeps delays to a minimum, reduces frustration and minimises journey time.

Driving abroad

Always ensure you know the specific legal requirements and road signs before you set out – and make sure your car conforms to such requirements. If you take an overnight ferry crossing you will probably be tired the next morning; do not set yourself too long a drive after arriving on the Continent. When you begin driving again after taking a break be especially careful to keep on the correct side of the road.

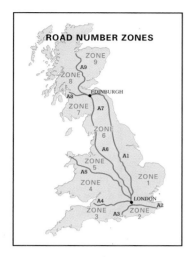

ROAD NUMBER ZONES

How to get there

Special route-planning maps on pages XII–XVII enable you to devise a basic route before referring to the main pages of the atlas for greater detail.

Road classification

London is the hub for the spokes of roads numbered A1 to A6, and Edinburgh the hub for A7, A8 and A9. Beginning with the A1, running north from London, the roads radiate clockwise from the capital: A2 runs roughly east, the A3 west, and so forth. The system has made the numbering of other roads very simple. Generally, the lower the subsequent number, the closer the road's starting point to London (or Edinburgh).

using the national grid

One of the unique

features of AA

mapping is the use of

the National Grid

System.

The National Grid

The National Grid covers Britain with an imaginary network of squares, using blue vertical lines called eastings and horizontal lines called northings. On the atlas pages these lines are numbered along the bottom and up the left-hand side.

The index

Each entry in the index is followed by a page number, two letters denoting an area on the map and a 4-figure grid reference. You will not need to use the two letters for simple navigation, but they come in useful if you want to use your map in relation to the rest of the country and other map series.

Quick reference

For quick reference, the four figures of the grid reference in the index are arranged so that the 1st and 3rd are in a bolder type than the 2nd and 4th. The 1st figure shows the number along the bottom of the grid, and the 3rd figure, the number up the left-hand side. These will indicate the square in which you will find the place name.

Pinpoint accuracy

However, to pinpoint a place more accurately you will also need to use the 2nd and 4th numbers. The second will tell you how many imaginary tenths along the bottom line to go from the first number, and the 4th will tell you how many tenths to go up from the third number. Where these two lines intersect, you will find your place name. For example: Skegness 77TF**5663**. Skegness is located on page 77 within grid square **56** in National Grid square TF. Its exact location is **56**63.

Skegness **77**TF**5663**

Skegness is located on page **77**

within grid square **56**

in National Grid square TF.

Its exact location is **56**63.

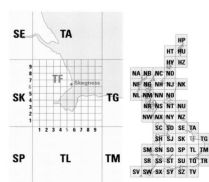

Classes of signs

A consistent and comprehensive set of road signs provides information and warning to the motorist.

These are based on an internationally agreed system, with variations specific to Britain. Signs which give orders and prohibitions are usually circular, and if the background is blue, their instructions are compulsory. Triangular signs carry warning messages and rectangular signs give information.

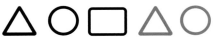
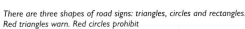

There are three shapes of road signs: triangles, circles and rectangles. Red triangles warn. Red circles prohibit

Blue circles give positive instruction. Blue rectangles give general information. Green rectangles are used for direction signs on primary routes.

Junctions and roundabouts

Warning signs lead up to a junction or roundabout, and provide information about the nature of the junction.

Warning signs will probably be followed by a give way or stop sign. The road markings at a stop sign consist of a solid white line identifying the farthest point to which you may drive. It is obligatory to stop and look to see that it is possible to enter the major road in safety. The give way sign has different road markings – a pair of white dashed lines – and drivers are required to delay joining the main road until it is safe to do so. If the main road is clear, there is no obligation to stop completely.

| Countdown markers approaching a major junction | Crossroads | T-junction | Staggered junction | Roundabout | Mini-roundabout (roundabout circulation) | No through road | No vehicles |

| Distance to 'STOP' line ahead | Distance to 'GIVE WAY' line ahead | Stop and give way | Give way to traffic on major road |

The road ahead

Advance warning of the road layout ahead helps a driver plan his/her approach.

The information given is generally precise about which side of the road is affected or which direction the road will take. The triangular signs give warnings, the circular signs must be obeyed.

| Bend to left | Double bend, first to left | Bend to right | Double bend, first to right | Road hump or series of road humps ahead | Worded warning sign | Dual carriageway ends | Steep hill downwards | Steep hill upwards |

| No goods vehicles over maximum gross weight shown (in tonnes) | Axle weight limit (in tonnes) | No vehicles over height shown | Sharp deviation of route | Traffic merges from left | Road narrows on left | Traffic merges from right | Road narrows on right | Road narrows on both sides |

road signs

Hazards ahead

The signs warning of hazards ahead should never be ignored, and provide valuable information about what is round the next corner or just ahead.

Pedestrian crossing

Hospital ahead with accident and emergency facilities

Slippery road

Road works

Uneven road

Wild animals

Wildhorses or ponies

Cattle

Other danger

Traffic signals

Failure of traffic light signals

Children

Children going to or from school

School crossing patrol ahead

School crossing patrol

Hump bridge

Opening or swing bridge ahead

Falling or fallen rocks

Quayside or river bank

Overhead electric cable

Traffic behaviour

Information about the way traffic should be organised is given in a series of specific signs.

These signs govern the speed and general approach at any situation. They are signs which must be obeyed.

No stopping (Clearway)

National speed limit applies

No U-turns

Give priority to vehicles from opposite direction

No overtaking

Motor vehicles prohibited except for access

No entry for vehicular traffic

Two-way traffic straight ahead

No right turn

No left turn

Turn left ahead

Turn left

Vehicles may pass either side to reach same destination

Ahead only

Keep left

Level crossings

There are several different types of level crossing. Many have barriers which may cross half or all of the road.

Level crossings may be worked automatically by the approach of the train or they may be operated by an attendant. When flashing lights and bell signals are in operation you should not pass. If you are already crossing when the amber lights flash and the bells start, keep crossing.

Level crossing without barrier

Level crossing without barrier or gate ahead

Level crossing with barrier or gate ahead

Alternately flashing red lights mean YOU MUST STOP

M1 London–Leeds

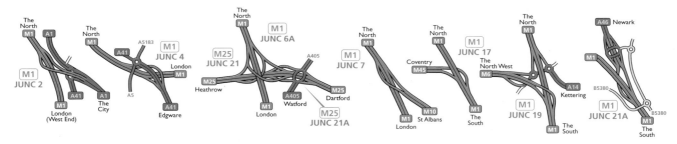

M1 London–Leeds   M2 Rochester–Faversham   M3 Sunbury–Southampton

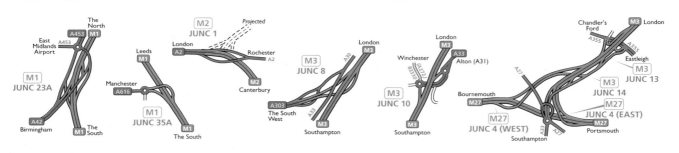

M4 London–South Wales   M5 Birmingham–Exeter

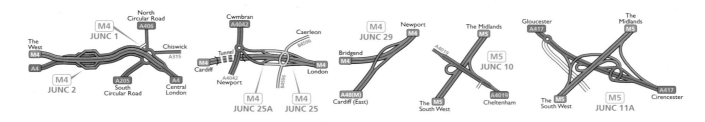

M5 Birmingham–Exeter   M6 Rugby–Carlisle

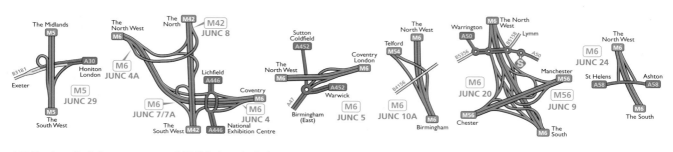

M6 Rugby–Carlisle   M8 Edinburgh–Bishopton

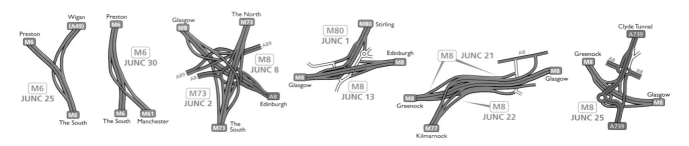

motorways –restricted junctions

Diagrams of selected motorway junctions which have entry and exit restrictions

M8 Edinburgh–Bishopton ## M9 Edinburgh–Dunblane ## M11 London–Cambridge

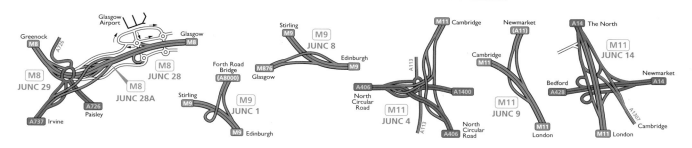

M20 Swanley–Folkestone   ## M25 London Orbital   ## M27 Cadnam–Portsmouth ## M40 London–Birmingham

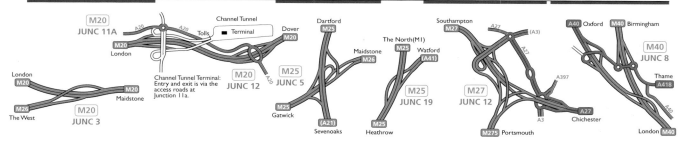

M42 Bromsgrove–Measham   ## M56 North Cheshire Motorway   ## M62 Liverpool–Humberside

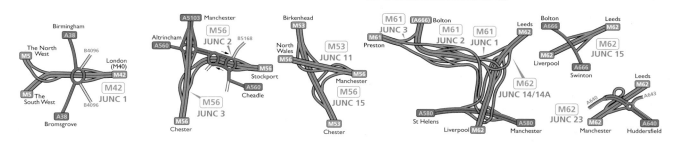

M63 Greater Manchester   ## M73 East of Glasgow   ## M74 Glasgow–Gretna

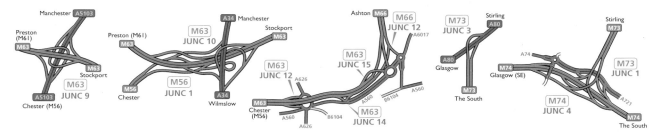

M74, A74(M) Glasgow–Gretna   ## M80 Glasgow–Stirling   ## M90 Forth Road Bridge–Perth   ## A1(M) Scotch Corner–Tyneside

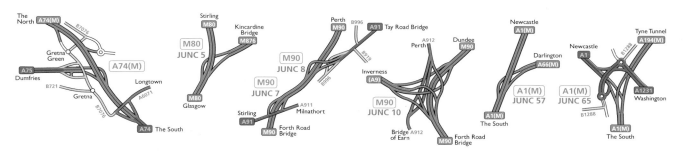

route planner

Planning your route

The route-planning maps on the following pages show principal routes throughout the country and pinpoint the major towns and cities. Detailed routes can be worked out from the maps in the main atlas section of this book. You may find it useful to make a note of road numbers and route directions. You are advised to avoid driving through towns and built-up areas whenever possible, even if such routes appear to be more direct on the map. Delays caused by traffic lights, one-way systems and other road-users will almost certainly be encountered in such areas.

The length of the journey is a fundamental consideration when planning a route. The mileage chart on the inside back cover gives the distances between main towns and can be used to make a rough calculation of the total journey length. The time needed for the journey can then be estimated.

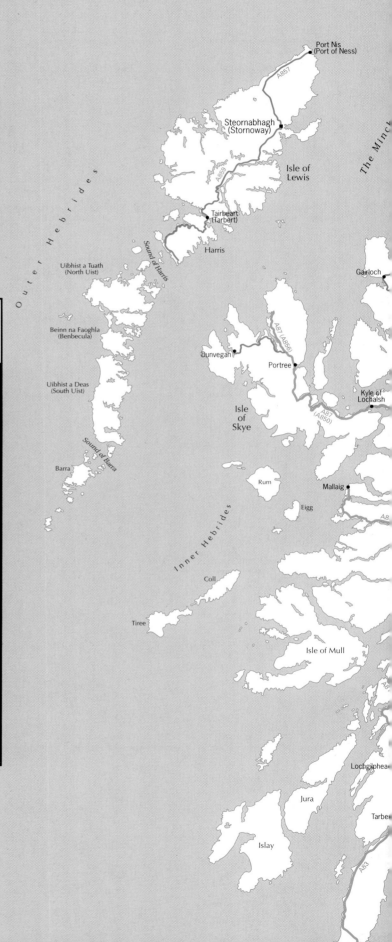

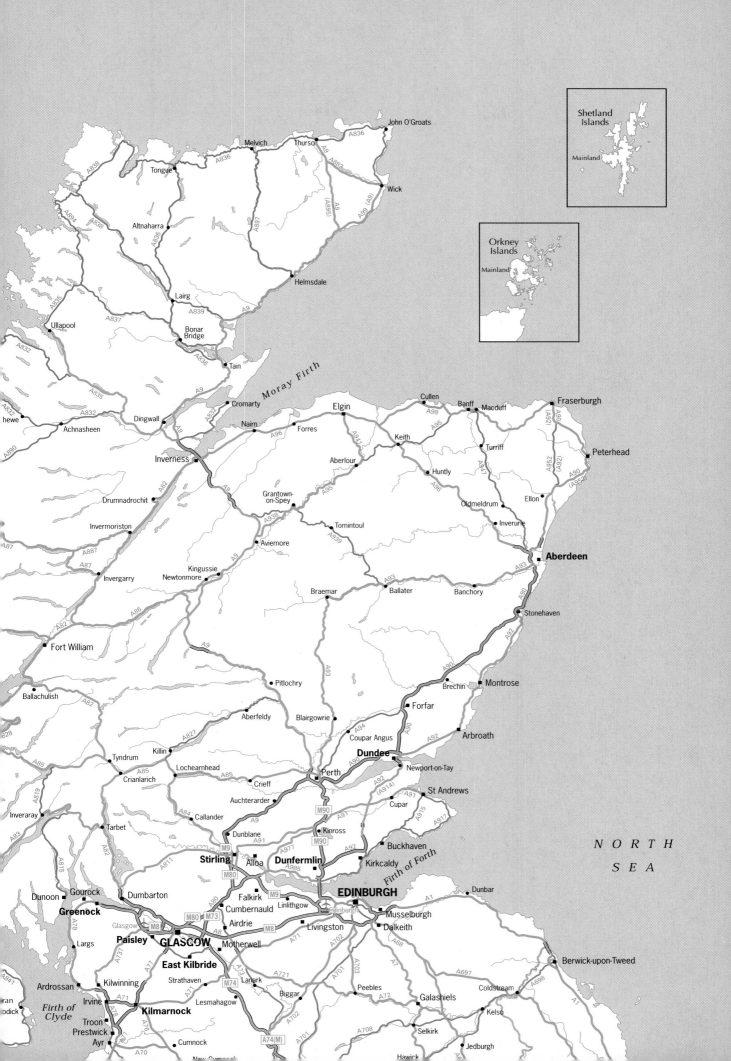

eed

Whitley Bay
Tynemouth
South Shields
NEWCASTLE UPON TYNE
Jarrow
anley
SUNDERLAND

A1(M)
Spennymoor
Hartlepool
A19
Stockton-on-Tees
Middlesbrough
Darlington
A66
A589
cotch Corner
A172
Whitby
A171
Northallerton
A19
A684
A169
A171
Thirsk
A168
A170
Scalby
Scarborough
ipon
A61
Pickering
A170
Filey
A64
A1(M)
A59
Malton
A165
gate
A59
A614 (A166)
Bridlington
York
A166
A614
(A163)
Driffield
Wetherby
A64
A19
A1079
A166
A165
LEEDS
A163
Market Weighton
A1035
A614
Beverley
Selby
A63
A1034
A63
A62
Hessle
HULL
M62
A1
A645
Goole
Barton-upon-Humber
ury
M62
Pontefract
M18
A160
Wakefield
Thorne
Scunthorpe
Immingham
ld
M1
M180
M180
Grimsby
Barnsley
A635
Doncaster
Brigg
A18
Cleethorpes
Rotherham
A159
A46
A1(M)
Bawtry
Gainsborough
A16
FFIELD
A631
A631
A15
A1031
onfield
M1
A57
Worksop
A156
Market Rasen
Louth
Mablethorpe
Staveley
A1
A619
A614
A57
A46
A16
A52
Chesterfield
A619
A60
Lincoln
A158
A15
Horncastle
A158
Mansfield
A617
Skegness
ck
Alfreton
A617
A52
bourne
A6097
Newark-on-Trent
A17
Sleaford
A17
Boston
The Wash
Sheringham
Cromer
52
Ilkeston
NOTTINGHAM
A52
A17
A149
A148
RBY
A52
Grantham
A16
Hunstanton
North Walsham
Long Eaton
A52
A148
A453
A607
Spalding
King's Lynn
A148
Fakenham
A140
A6
urton upon Trent
A606
A151
A17
A1065
East Dereham
A1067
A149
hby-de-Zouch
M1
Loughborough
Bourne
A1101
A47
Norwich
Caister-on-Sea
A50
Melton Mowbray
A16
A47
Swaffham
A47
A146
amworth
A6
Oakham
Stamford
Wisbech
A10
A1122
Great Yarmouth
A42
LEICESTER
A606
A47
Downham Market
A134
A11
Hinckley
Wigston
A605
Peterborough
A1101
Attleborough
Lowestoft
eaton
M1
Market Harborough
A141
March
A1165
A143
Bungay
Beccles
GHAM
M69
Corby
A6116
A605
A1
Chatteris
A1066
Diss
M6
A4304
(A427)
Kettering
Ely
A1101
Thetford
Southwold
COVENTRY
A45
A14
A14
A10
A142
A143
A12
Rugby
A508
A14
Huntingdon
A14
M45
Leamington Spa
A45
Bury St Edmunds

Motorway

Primary route
dual carriageway

Primary route
single carriageway

Other A roads

10   20   30 miles

0   10   20   30   40 kilometres

XV

map pages

Orkney
Islands
155

Shetland
Islands
155

Outer
Hebrides

Steornabhagh
(Stornoway)

154

148 149 150 151
Thurso
Wick

144 145 146 147
Ullapool
Gairloch
Dingwall
Tain

136 137 138 139 140 141 142 143
Portree
Mallaig
Elgin
Inverness
Banff
Peterhead

128 129 130 131 132 133 134 135
Aviemore
Aberdeen

120 121 122 123 124 125 126 127
Fort
William
Oban
Pitlochry
Perth
Montrose
Dundee

112 113 114 115 116 117 118 119
Stirling
Glasgow
Largs
Edinburgh
Berwick-
upon-Tweed

104 105 106 107 108 109 110 111
Peebles
Ayr
Moffat
Alnwick
Campbeltown

98 99 100 101 102 103
Stranraer
Dumfries
Newcastle upon Tyne

92 93 94 95 96 97
Carlisle
Workington
Penrith
Middlesbrough

156 157
Londonderry
Larne
Belfast
Sligo
Cavan
Newry

86 87 88 89 90 91
Kendal
Lancaster
Settle
Thirsk
Scarborough

80 81 82 83 84 85
Blackpool
Burnley
Leeds
Hull
Grimsby
York

153
Douglas
Isle of
Man

Westport
Galway
Athlone
DUBLIN

68 69 70 71 79 74 75 76 77
Colwyn
Bay
Caernarfon
Chester
Liverpool
Manchester
Sheffield
Newark
Lincoln
Boston
Stoke
Nottingham

156 157 158 159
Limerick
Tralee
Killarney
Waterford
Cork
Rosslare

56 57 58 59 60 61 62 63 64 65 66 67
Dolgellau
Shrewsbury
Stafford
Leicester
King's Lynn
Peterborough
Norwich
Great
Yarmouth
Aberystwyth
Newtown
Birmingham
Coventry

42 43 44 45 46 47 48 49 50 51 52 53 54 55
Cardigan
Ludlow
Worcester
Stratford-upon-
Avon
Northampton
Bedford
Cambridge
Bury St
Edmunds
Felixstowe
Fishguard
Brecon
Hereford

30 31 32 33 34 35 36 37 38 39 40 41
Pembroke
Carmarthen
Abergavenny
Gloucester
Oxford
Luton
Chelmsford
Swansea
Cardiff
Bristol
Swindon
Reading
Watford
LONDON
26 27

18 19 20 21 22 23 24 25 28 29
Barnstaple
Taunton
Bath
Salisbury
Andover
Guildford
Sevenoaks
Maidstone
Dover
Folkestone
Bude

14 15 16 17
Yeovil
Southampton
Brighton
Chichester
Hastings
Newhaven

8 9 10 11 12 13
Lyme
Regis
Weymouth
Bournemouth

4 5 6 7
Bodmin
Truro
Torquay
Plymouth
Exeter

2 3

Isles of
Scilly
2

The Channel
Islands
152

map symbols

motoring information

M4	Motorway with number
11	Motorway junction with and without number
3	Motorway junction with limited access
S Fleet	Motorway service area
	Motorway and junction under construction
A3	Primary route single/dual carriageway
S Oxford	Primary route service area
BATH	Primary route destination
A1123	Other A road single/dual carriageway
B2070	B road single/dual carriageway
	Unclassified road single/dual carriageway
	Roundabout
	Interchange
	Narrow primary, other A or B road with passing places (Scotland)
	Road under construction
⊧═══⊨	Road tunnel
→	Steep gradient (arrows point downhill)
Toll	Road toll
▽ 5 ▽	Distance in miles between symbols

— **V** —	Vehicle ferry – Great Britain
BERGEN **V**	Vehicle ferry – continental
— **H** —	Hovercraft ferry
✈	Airport
H	Heliport
F	International freight terminal
	Railway line/in tunnel
—○—✕—	Railway station and level crossing
┼┼┼┼┼┼┼	Tourist railway
AA	AA shop
☎	AA telephone
	Urban area/village
628 ▲	Spot height in metres
	River, canal, lake
	Sandy beach
	County/County Borough /Council Area boundary
	National boundary
85	Page overlap and number

tourist information

i	Tourist Information Centre
i	Tourist Information Centre (seasonal)
♠	Abbey, cathedral or priory
♠	Ruined abbey, cathedral or priory
♜	Castle
🏛	Historic house
🅼	Museum or art gallery
⛏	Industrial interest
❀	Garden
♣	Arboretum
♔	Country park
♖	Agricultural showground
♒	Theme park
🐘	Zoo
🐗	Wildlife collection – mammals
🐦	Wildlife collection – birds
🐬	Aquarium
🦆	Nature reserve
RSPB	RSPB site
··········	Forest drive
– – – – –	National trail
☀	Viewpoint
⛄	Picnic site
⁘	Hill-fort

♠	Roman antiquity
⛰	Prehistoric monument
✕ 1066	Battle site with year
🚂	Steam centre (railway)
⌒	Cave
✠	Windmill
⚑	Golf course
⚑	County cricket ground
⬮	Rugby Union national ground
🏃	International athletics ground
🐎	Horse racing
🐎	Show jumping/ equestrian circuit
🏁	Motor racing circuit
⛵	Coastal launching site
🎿	Ski slope – natural
🎿	Ski slope – artificial
NT	National Trust property
NTS	National Trust for Scotland property
★	Other places of interest
▢	Boxed symbols indicate attractions within urban areas
	National Park (England & Wales)
	National Scenic Area (Scotland)
	Forest Park
⌣	Heritage Coast

I

The Isles of Scilly

WHITE ISLAND

King Charles
'Cromwell's'
BRYHER 42
BRYHER

Old Grimsby
ST.MARTIN'S
St Martin's Head
38 49
Old Blockhouse
Higher Town
Lizard Point
New Grimsby
Pool
GREAT GANILLY

Isles of Scilly Heritage Coast

Crow Sound
Crow Bar

Tresco Abbey
TRESCO
GREAT ARTHUR

North West Channel

SAMSON

Bant's Carn Burial
Innisidgen Tomb
ST.MARY'S
A3110

Harry's Walls
Longstone Heritage Centre
Hugh Town
Deep Point
Garrison Walls
Porth Hellick Downs Tombs
Isles of Scilly (St Mary's)

SV

Old Town
Peninnis Head

ANNET
St Mary's Sound

Broad Sound

Middle Town
GUGH
ST AGNES

Smith Sound

Horse Point

Western Rocks

| 0 | 1 | 2 | 3 | 4 | 5 miles |
| 0 | 1 | 2 | 3 | 4 | 5 | 6 | 7 kilometres |

9

St Agnes H
ST AGNES HEAD
St A
Wheal Coates
Goonvr

Porthtowan
Menagis
Mawla
Camb
B3300
Bridge
Nort
Coun
Illogan

Godrevy – Portreath Heritage Coast
Portreath

Godrevy Island
Navax Point
Poynter's Lane End
Tehidy Woods
Park Bottom
Roseroggan
Coombe
Cornish
Pool
Carn Brea
Carn Brea
Tuckingmill
A30
Roseworth
Camborne
Penponds
Four

Godrevy Point

Gwealavellan
Reskadinnick
Treswithian
Kehelland

Gwithian
Upton Towans

The Island or St Ives Head

Carn Naun Point

Zennor Head
Treveal
Hellesveor
St Ives
Towans Railway
Phillack
Connor Downs
Troon
Bolenowe
Penhalve

Trendrine
Carbis Bay
The Towans
Hayle
Angarrack
Barripper
Carnhell Green
Croft Michael
Burras

Gurnards Head
B3306
Lelant
Copperhouse
High Lanes
Gwinear
Rosewarne
Praze-an-Beeble
Blackrock
Farms Common

Zennor
Halsetown
Merlins Magic Land
Penhale
Por

Treen
Towednack
Brunnian
Nancledra
Fraddam
B3303
Wall
Trenerth
Crowan
Lezerea

Porthmeor
Cripplesease
Georgia
Canonstown
St Erth
St Erth Praze
River Hayle
B3280
Horsedown
Drym
Releath

Pendeen Watch
14
Men-An-Tol
Mulfra
Chysauster
Whitecross
Cockwells
A30
Kerthen Wood
Leedstown
Townshend
Godolphin Cross
Nancegollan
Trenear
Crelly
Poldark
Mine

Lower Boscaswell
Morvah
New Mill
Castle Gate
Boswarthan
Badger's Cross
Crowlas
Trannack
Relubbus
Trescowe
Prospidnick
Wendron

Geevor Tin Mines
Bojewyan
Boskednan
Lanyon Quoit
Ludgvan
Gulval
Treneague St Hilary
Millpool
Balwest
Carleen
Crownton
Manhay

Trewellard
Pendeen
Great Bosullow
Trengwainton Garden NT
Bone Tolver
Penzance H
Longrock
Goldsithney
Trew
Sithney
Lower Town
Coverack Bridges

Botallack
Carnyorth
7
Newbridge
Madron
Trevarrack
Marazion
Newtown
A394
Germoe
Ashton
Sithney Green
Trewennack

Cape Cornwall
Tregeseal
B3318
Heamoor
Tremethick Cross
Chyandour
St Michael's Mount NT
Rosudgeon
Kenneggy
Crowntown

St Just
Ballowall Barrow
A3071
Bosavern
Sellan
Sancreed
Perranuthnoe
Prussia Cove
Rinsey Croft
Breage
Antron
Helston
B3304

with Heritage Coast
Kelynack
Grumbla
Tredavoe
Penzance
Cudden Point
Praa Sands
Rinsey
Trewavas
Mellangoose
Flambards

Nanquidno
Brane
Carn Euny
Drift
Newlyn
Perranuthnoe
Rinsey Head
Trewavas Head
Methleigh
A3083

Whitesand Bay
Land's End
10
Catchall
Kerris
Paul
MOUNT'S BAY
Higher Pentire
Porthleven
Mawgan Cross
Tregoose

Escalls
Crows-an-Wra
Sheffield
Mousehole
Carminowe
Gunwalloe
Berepper

Sennen Cove
Sennen
Trevorgans
Toldavas
Trevithal
Chyvarloe
White Cross
Gw
Cro
Wha

LAND'S END
Lands End
Trengothal
St Buryan
Trewoofe
Raginnis
SW
Chyanvounder
Cury

Trevescan
Trebehor
Bottoms
The Merry Maidens
Castallack
Lamorna
Bochym
Angrouse
Poldhu Point
Trewoon

Polgigga
Trethewey
Treen
Boskennal
Lamorna Cove
Mullion
Trenance
Mullion Cove

Raftra
Roskesta
Porthcurno
Cribba Head
Mullion Island
Mullion Cove

Porthgwarra
St Levan
Minack Open Air Theatre
Merthen Point
Predannack Head
Predannack Wollas

Gwennap Head
Mount Hermon

Vellan Head

The Lizard Heritage Coast
South West Coast Path
Lizard Head

LIZARD POINT
Lizard

4 **5** **6** **7**

6 **5** **4** **3** **2**

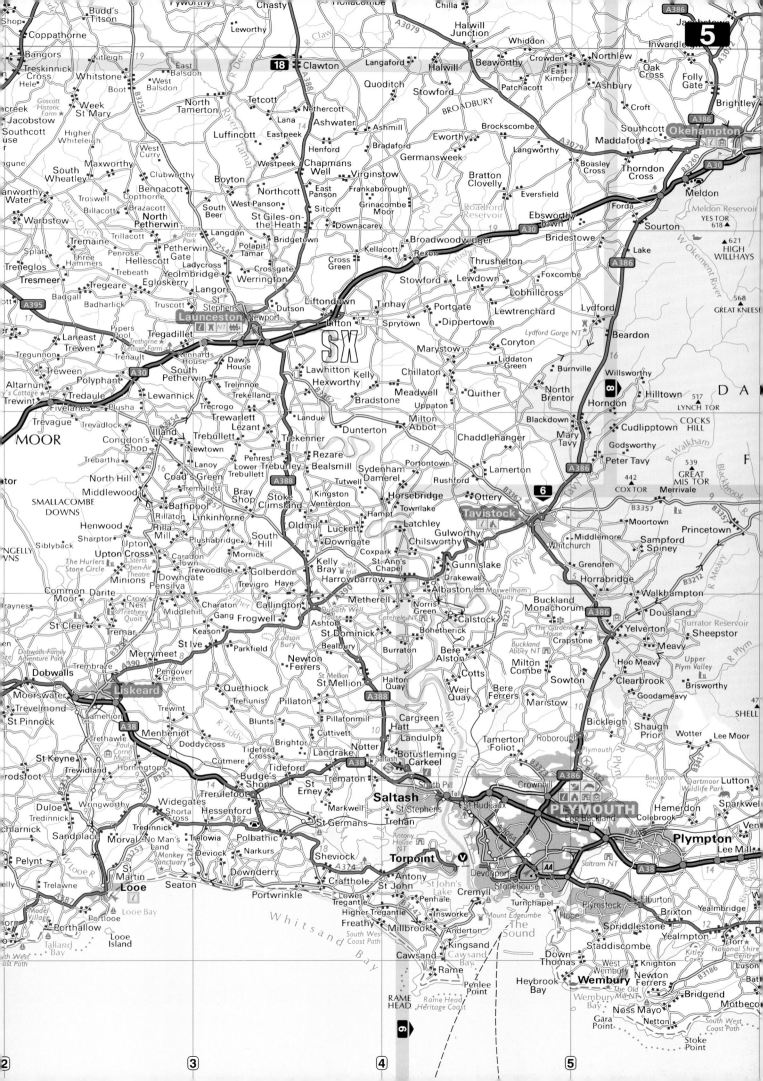

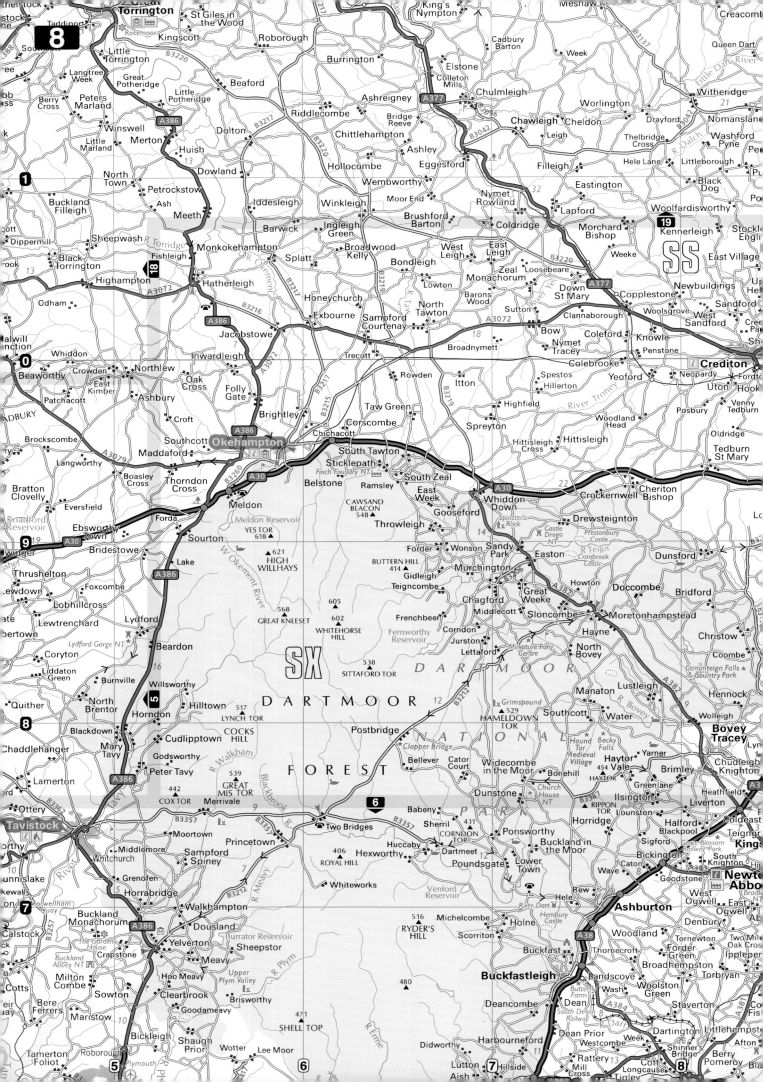

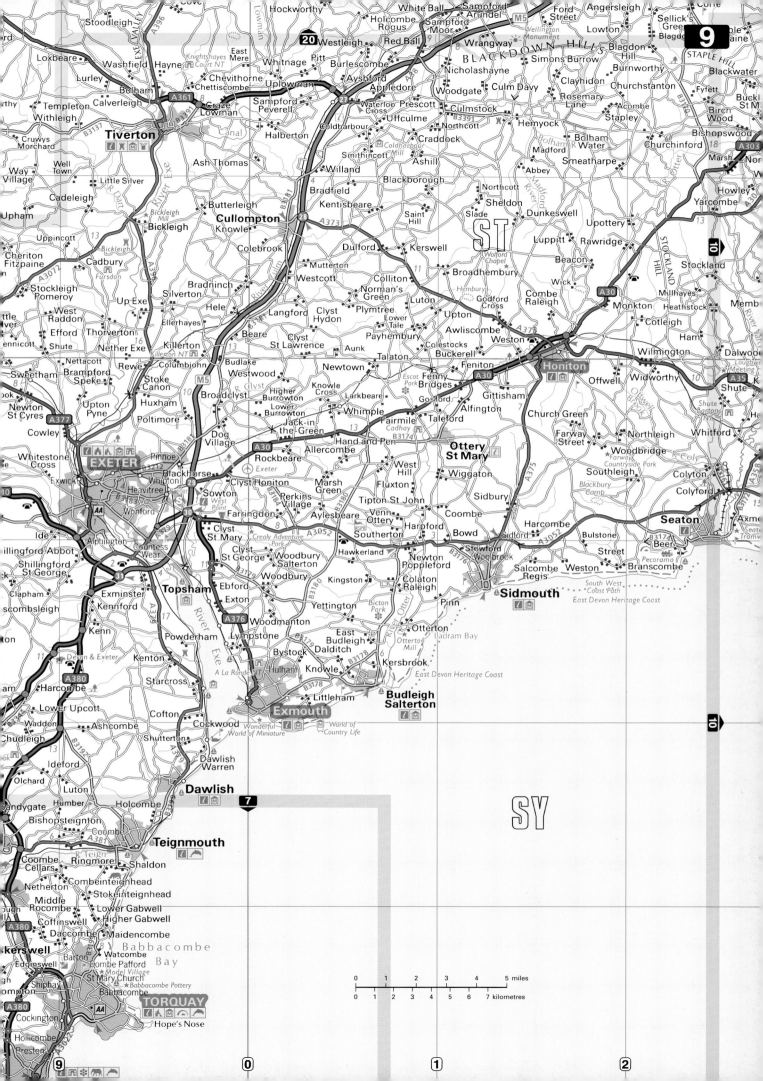

5

4

3

2

1

0

North West
Point
Lundy
Heritage Coast
LUNDY
▲142
Marisco
⚔
Surf Point

0   1   2   3   4   5 miles
0 1 2 3 4 5 6   7 kilometres

B A R N S T A P L E

O R

B I D E F O R D   B A Y

Bull Point
Rockham
Bay
Lee
Bay
Morte Point
Mortehoe
*North Devon
Heritage Coast*
Woolacombe
Morte Bay
Pickwell
Baggy Point
Putsborough
Croyde Bay
Bu
George
Darracott
Knov
Croyde Bay
Croyde
Lobb
Saunton
Braunto
Wraf

Westward Ho!
Appledore
Northam
Eastleig
Pi
East-the-W

HARTLAND
POINT
Shipload
Bay
*South West
Coast Path*
Titchberry
Brownsham
Damehole
Point
Hartland
Velly
Clovelly
*Hartland
Heritage Coast*
Abbotsham
*The Big
Sheep*
Fairy
Cross
Ford
Bideford
A386
Hartland
Quay
Stoke
Sierra
Dyke
Buck's
Mills
Horns
Cross
A39
Woodtown
Yeo
Vale
Landcro
*Spekes Mill
Mouth*
Milford
Philham
A39
4
B3248
*Milky
Way*
Buck's
Cross
Goldworthy
Cranford
Parkham
Littleham
11
Elmscott
Woolfardisworthy
Parkham
Ash
Cabbacott
Buckland
Brewer
Saltrens
Monkleig
Hardisworthy
Melbury
Frithelstock
South
Hole
Frithelstock
Stone
Taddipor
Welcombe
Mead
Darracott
Woolley
Meddon
Ashmansworthy
Thornehillhead
18
A388
Southcott
Gooseham
Eastcott
16
East
Youlstone
Dinworthy
West
Putford
East Putford
Langtree
Lan
Morwenstow
Higher Sharpnose
Point
Shop
West
Youlstone
Bradworthy
Colscott
Haytown
Bulkworthy
Stibb
Cross
Berry
Cross
Tamar Lakes
Kimworthy
Alfardisworthy
Sutcombe
Abbots
Bickington
Newton
St Petrock
Lower Sharpnose
Point
Kilkhampton
Darracott
Sutcombemill
Venngreen
Steeple
Point
Thurdon
Soldon
Cross
Soldon
River
Waldon
Milton Damerel
Sandy
Mouth
Stibb
B3254
Holsworthy
Beacon
Thornbury
Shebbear
Buckla
Filleig
Northcott
Mouth
Poughill
Hersham
Bush
Venn
Dunsdon
Little
Lashbrook
A388
Brendon
Bradford
Priestacott
Hole
Dippermill
Bude
Maer
Flexbury
Stratton
Grimscott
Lana
Kingford
Chilsworthy
Cookbury
Wick
Cookbury
Lashbrook
13
Black
Torrin
Bude
Bay
Bude
World of Nature
Lynstone
Launcells
Launcells
Cross
10
Pancrasweek
Holsworthy
Anvil
Corner
Holemoor
Upton
A3072
Red Cross
Buttsbear
Cross
Derril
Derriton
Whimble
A3072
Brandis
Corner
Odham
Helebridge
Marhamchurch
Bridgerule
Pyworthy
Chasty
Hollacombe
Chilla
Widemouth
Bay
Budd's
Titson
Lewthorn
Halwill
Junction
Whiddo
Box's Shop
Coppathorne
Millook
R Claw
A3079
Dizzard Point
Poundstock
Bangors
Kitleigh
19
East
Balsdon
R Deer
Clawton
Langaford
Halwill
Beaworthy
Dizzard
Penlean
Tregole
Treskinnick
Cross
Hele
Whitstone
West
Balsdon
Boot
A388
Quoditch
Stowford
Patchacot
St Gennys
ackington Haven
Cambeak
Coxford
Trencreek
*Goscott
Historic
Farm*
Week
St Mary
th
Tamerton
Tetcott
Nethercott
BROADBURY

Lynmouth Bay • Foreland Point • Countisbury Cove • Hurtstone Point

Woody Bay • Lynton • Brass Rubbing Centre • Countisbury • Exmoor Heritage Coast • Porlock Bay • Bossington

Combe • Hele Bay • Water Mouth • Combe Martin • Watermouth • Martinhoe • Trentishoe • Hunter's Inn • Woody Bay • Toll • Lynbridge • Lynmouth • Wilsham • Brendon • Culbone • Porlock Weir • Toll • West Porlock • Porlock • Ly

Two Pots • Hele • Haggington Hill • Hele Mill • Chambercombe Manor • Combe Martin • Heale • Kemacott • Dean • West Lyn • Barbrook • Watersmeet House NT • Rockford • Tippacott • Oare • Malmsmead • Horner • Luccomb

Mullacott Cross • Sterridge • Berrynarbor • Ruggaton • Bodstone Barton Farm Park • Patchole • Kentisbury • Killington • Parracombe • Churchtown • West Ilkerton • East Ilkerton • Cheriton • Furzehill • Woolhanger • Lucott • Lucott

West Down • Berry Down Cross • East Down • Kentisbury Ford • Arlington Beccott • Stowford • Barton Town • Swincombe • Challacombe • HOAROAK HILL 474 • DRY HILL 444 • Edgcott • DUNKERY HILL 519

EXMOOR FOREST • EXMOOR • NATIONAL PARK

Halsinger • Bittadon • Churchill • Arlington • Arlington Court NT • Exmoor Zoological Park • Knightacott • B3358 • River Exe • Simonsbath • Newland • Exford • Luckwell Bridge

Higher Muddiford • Milltown • Muddiford • Upcott • Loxhore Cott • Loxhore • Loxhore Lower • Leworthy • SPAN HEAD 493 • Kinsford Water • 410 • Blackland • Withypool • Winsford • Gre Nurc

Marwood • Guineaford • Kingsheanton • Prixford • Shirwell • Shirwell Cross • Bratton Fleming • Benton • Fullaford • Lydcott • Whitefield • WORTH HILL • WINSFORD HILL • Knaplock • Liscombe

Ashford • Bradiford • Pilton • Burridge • Northleigh • Goodleigh • Stoke Rivers • 12 • R Bray • Brayford • High Bray • Bentwichen • North Radworthy • Tarr Steps • Tarr

Derby • Barnstaple • Willesleigh • Gunn • Bradninch • Whitsford • Accott • Charles • Stoodleigh • North Heasley • South Radworthy • Heasley Mill • Twitchen • Hawkridge

Newport • Bickington • Swimbridge Newland • West Buckland • Elwell • East Buckland • Yarnacott • Bremridge • North Molton • Upcott • Molland • Slade • West Anstey • Northmoor • Dulverto

Lake • Landkey • Bishop's Tawton • Landkey Town • Swimbridge • A361 • Castle Hill • South Molton • Aller • Bish Mill • Newtown • Ash Mill • Crooked Oak • Knowstone • Oldways End • Yeo Mill • East Anstey • Nightcott • Battlet

Horsacott • Tawstock • St John's Chapel • Hannaford • Kerscott • Filleigh • Quince Honey Farm • B3227 • Radley • Bishop's Nympton • Roachill • Sowerhill • Ex

Harracott • Herner • Traveller's Rest • East Stowford • George Nympton • Newtown • Alswear • Mariansleigh • Yard • Rose Ash • Knowstone • Oldways End • Oakfordbr • Oakford • Westcott

Newton Tracey • Hiscott • Ensis • Week • Cobbaton • Chittlehampton • Umberleigh • Warkleigh • Clapworthy • Satterleigh • Romansleigh • Meshaw • Creacombe • Rackenford • Loxbeare

Huntshaw Cross • Langridge Ford • Atherington • A377 • Chittlehamholt • River • Mole • King's Nympton • Cadbury Barton • Queen Dart • Witheridge • Edgeworthy • Templet • Withleigh

High Bullen • Dodscott • St Giles in the Wood • Roborough • High Bickington • River Taw • Week • Worlington • Drayford • Nomansland • Great Torrington • Kingscott • Burrington • Elstone • Colleton Mills • Chulmleigh • Chawleigh • Cheldon • Thelbridge Cross • Washford Pyne • Pennymoor • Cruwys Morchard

Beaford • Little Potheridge • Riddlecombe • Ashreigney • A377 • Bridge Reeve • Leigh • Hele Lane • Littleborough • Puddington • Way Village • Well Town

Merton • Dolton • Chittlehampton • Ashley • Eggesford • Filleigh • Eastington • Black Dog • Poughill • Upham

Huish • Dowland • Hollocombe • Wembworthy • Nymet Rowland • Lapford • Woolfardisworthy • Cadele

Petrockstow • Ash • Meeth • Iddesleigh • Winkleigh • Moor End • Brushford Barton • Coldridge • Morchard Bishop • Kennerleigh • Stockleigh English • Uppincott

Monkokehampton • Barwick • Ingleigh Green • West Leigh • East Leigh • Weeke • East Village • Cheriton Fitzpaine • Chilton

Fishleigh • Splatt • Broadwood Kelly • Bondleigh • Zeal Monachorum • Loosebeare • A3220 • Newbuildings • Upton Hellions • Stockleigh Pomeroy

Hatherleigh • Honeychurch • Lowton • Barons Wood • Sutton • Down St Mary • Copplestone • Sandford • Lower Creedy • Little Silver • Raddor

Jacobstowe • Exbourne • North Tawton • Clannaborough • Woolsgrove • West Sandford • Efford • Pennicott • Shute

Inwardleigh • Sampford Courtenay • Bow • Nymet Tracey • Coleford • Knowle • Penstone • Creedy Park • Crediton • Fordton • Neopardy • Uton • Hookway • Smallbrook • Newton St Cyres • Sweetham

Oak Cross • Folly Gate • Brightley • Trecott • Rowden • Golebrooke • Yeoford • Spestos • Hillerton • Venny Tedburn • Wyke

SX • A386 • Northlew • Ashbury • Croft • Taw Green • Corscombe • Spreyton • Itton • Highfield • Woodland Head • River Troney • Neadbury

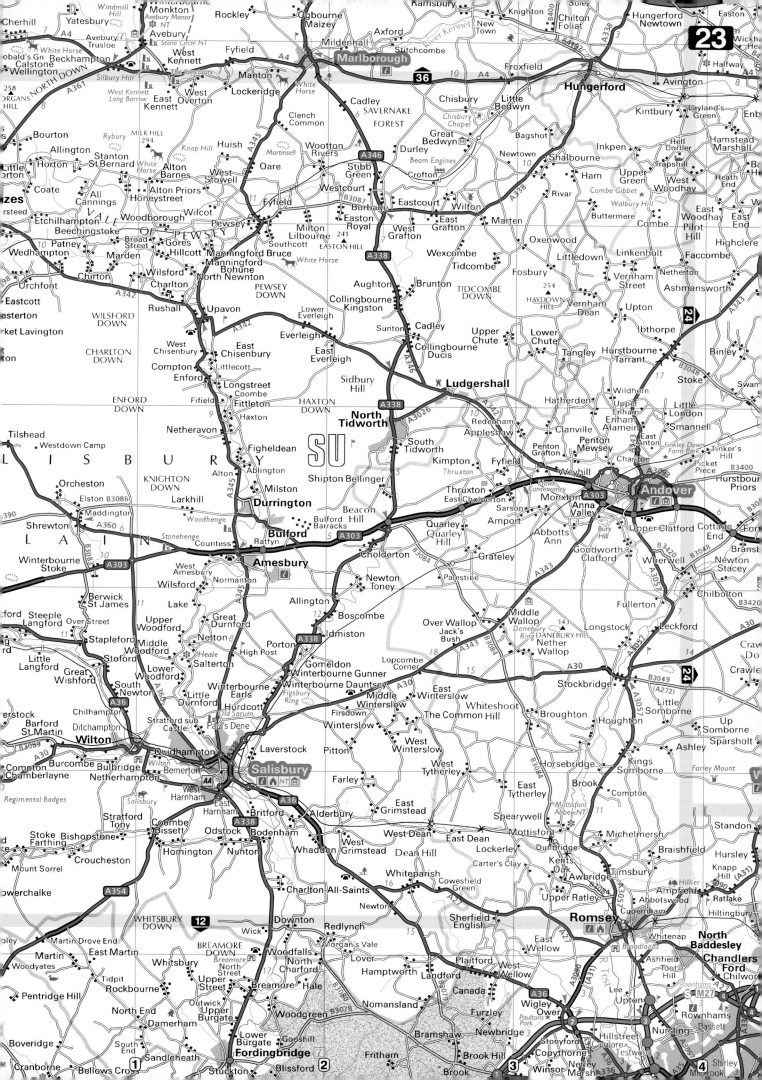

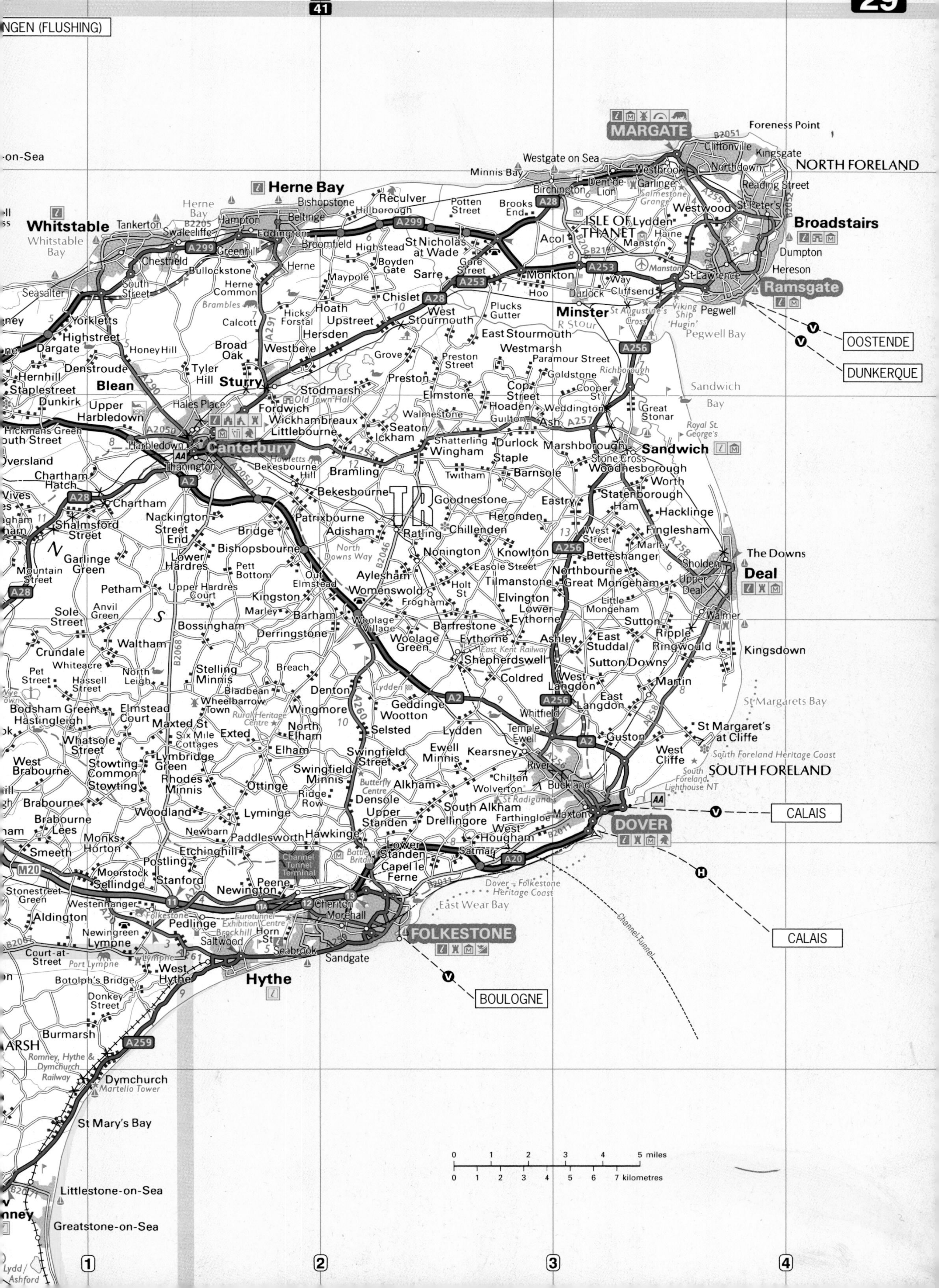

NGEN (FLUSHING)

-on-Sea

Whitstable
Whitstable Bay
Seasalter
ney
ne
Yorkletts
Highstreet
Dargate
Denstroude
Hernhill
Staplestreet
Dunkirk
Hickmans Green
outh Street
Oversland
Chartham Hatch
ves
Vives
ngham
ham
Shalmsford Street
Chartham
N
Garlinge Green
Mountain Street
Nackington Street End
Lower Hardres
Petham
Anvil Green
Sole Street
Waltham
Crundale
Whiteacre
Pet Street
Hassell Street
North Leigh
Bodsham Green
Hastingleigh
ok
Elmsted Court
Maxted St
Stelling Minnis
Six Mile Cottages
Bladbean
Wheelbarrow Town
West Brabourne
Whatsole Street
Stowting Common
Stowting
Lymbridge Green
Rhodes Minnis
Breach
Denton
Brabourne
Brabourne Lees
ham
Monks Horton
Smeeth
Woodland
Ottinge
Lyminge
Newbarn
Paddlesworth
Hawkinge
Aldington
Sellindge
Moorstock
Stanford
Newington
Peene
Stonestreet Green
WestenHanger
Lympne
Newingreen
Court-at-Street
Port Lympne
Botolph's Bridge
Donkey Street
West Hythe
Hythe
Burmarsh
ARSH
Romney, Hythe & Dymchurch Railway
Dymchurch
Martello Tower
St Mary's Bay
Littlestone-on-Sea
nney
Greatstone-on-Sea

Herne Bay
Herne Bay
Tankerton
Swalecliffe
Chestfield
Bullockstone
South Street
Hampton
Eddington
Greenhill
Herne
Herne Common
Broomfield
Beltinge
Bishopstone
Hillborough
Reculver
Highstead
Maypole
Hoath
Upstreet
Hicks Forstal
Hersden
Honey Hill
Broad Oak
Tyler Hill
Sturry
Westbere
Calcott
Blean
Upper Harbledown
Harbledown
Thanington
Hales Place
Fordwich
Stodmarsh
Old Town Hall
Wickhambreaux
Littlebourne
Canterbury
AA
Bekesbourne
Bekesbourne Hill
Bramling
Twitham
Patrixbourne
Adisham
Bishopsbourne
Bridge
Pett Bottom
Out Elmstead
Kingston
Marley
Barham
Derringstone
Bossingham
Woolage Village
Woolage Green
Womenswold
Frogham
Nonington
Ratling
Goodnestone
Chillenden
Knowlton
Easole Street
Aylesham
Holt St
Elvington
Eythorne
Lower Eythorne
Barfrestone
Shepherdswell
Coldred
Whitfield
Denton
Wingmore
Geddinge
Wootton
Selsted
Lydden
Ewell Minnis
Kearsney
Temple Ewell
Chilton
Wolverton
St Radigund's
Exted
Elham
North Elham
Rural Heritage Centre
Swingfield Street
Swingfield Minnis
Ridge Row
Densole
Upper Standen
Alkham
South Alkham
Drellingore
Farthingloe
West Hougham
Lower Standen
Capel le Ferne
Satmar
Battle of Britain
Channel Tunnel Terminal
Peene
Cheriton
Morehall
Eurotunnel
Exhibition Centre
Brockhill
Horn St
Saltwood
Pedlinge
Seabrook
Sandgate
FOLKESTONE
East Wear Bay
Dover - Folkestone Heritage Coast

St Nicholas at Wade
Potten Street
Brooks End
Boyden Gate
Gore Street
Sarre
Chislet
West Stourmouth
East Stourmouth
Grove
Preston
Preston Street
Elmstone
Hoaden
Guilton
Ash
Shatterling
Walmestone
Seaton
Ickham
Wingham
Staple
Durlock
Marshborough
Barnsole
Eastry
Heronden
West Street
Finglesham
Betteshanger
Northbourne
Great Mongeham
Tilmanstone
Ashley
East Studdal
Sutton
Sutton Downs
West Langdon
East Langdon
Guston
Buckland
Maxton

MARGATE
Westgate on Sea
Minnis Bay
Birchington
Dent-de-Lion
Westbrook
Garlinge
Salmestone Grange
Cliftonville
Kingsgate
Northdown
Reading Street
St Peter's
Broadstairs
Dumpton
Hereson
Ramsgate
ISLE OF THANET
Lydden
Haine
Acol
Manston
Monkton
Way
Cliffsend
St Lawrence
Hoo
Durlock
Minster
St Augustine's Cross
Viking Ship 'Hugin'
Pegwell
Pegwell Bay
Westmarsh
Paramour Street
Goldstone
Cooper St
Cop Street
Weddington
Great Stonar
Richborough
Sandwich Bay
Royal St George's
Sandwich
Woodnesborough
Worth
Statenborough
Ham
Hackinge
Sholden
Deal
The Downs
Upper Deal
Walmer
Ripple
Ringwould
Kingsdown
Martin
St Margarets Bay
St Margaret's at Cliffe
West Cliffe
South Foreland Heritage Coast
South Foreland Lighthouse NT
SOUTH FORELAND
Rivers
DOVER
AA

NORTH FORELAND
Foreness Point

East Kent Railway

TR

North Downs Way

North Downs Way

R Stour

M20
11
11A
12
13
A299
A299
A2050
A2
A28
A28
A2050
A28
A280
A291
A257
A255
A28
A2050
A2
A2
A20
A20
A260
A256
A256
A256
A258
A259
B2205
B2046
B2068
B2051

OOSTENDE
DUNKERQUE
CALAIS
CALAIS
BOULOGNE
Channel Tunnel
V
V
V
V
H

| 0 | 1 | 2 | 3 | 4 | 5 miles |
| 0 | 1 | 2 | 3 | 4 | 5 | 6 | 7 kilometres |

1
2
3
4

Lydd / Ashford

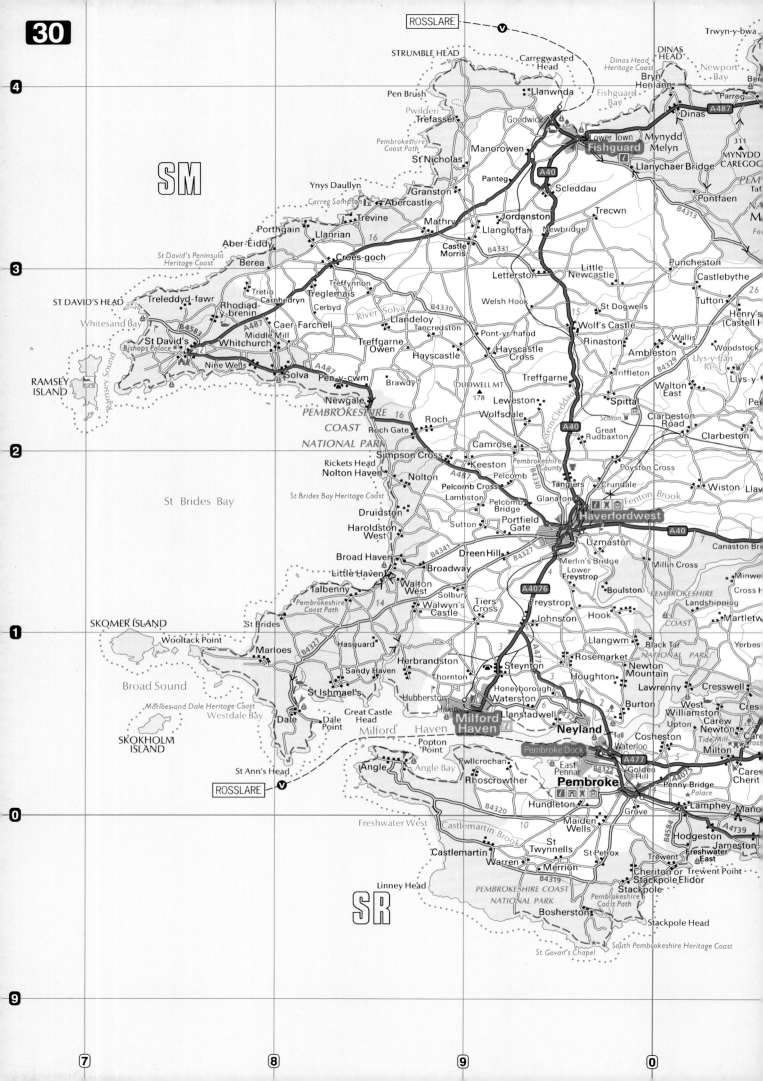

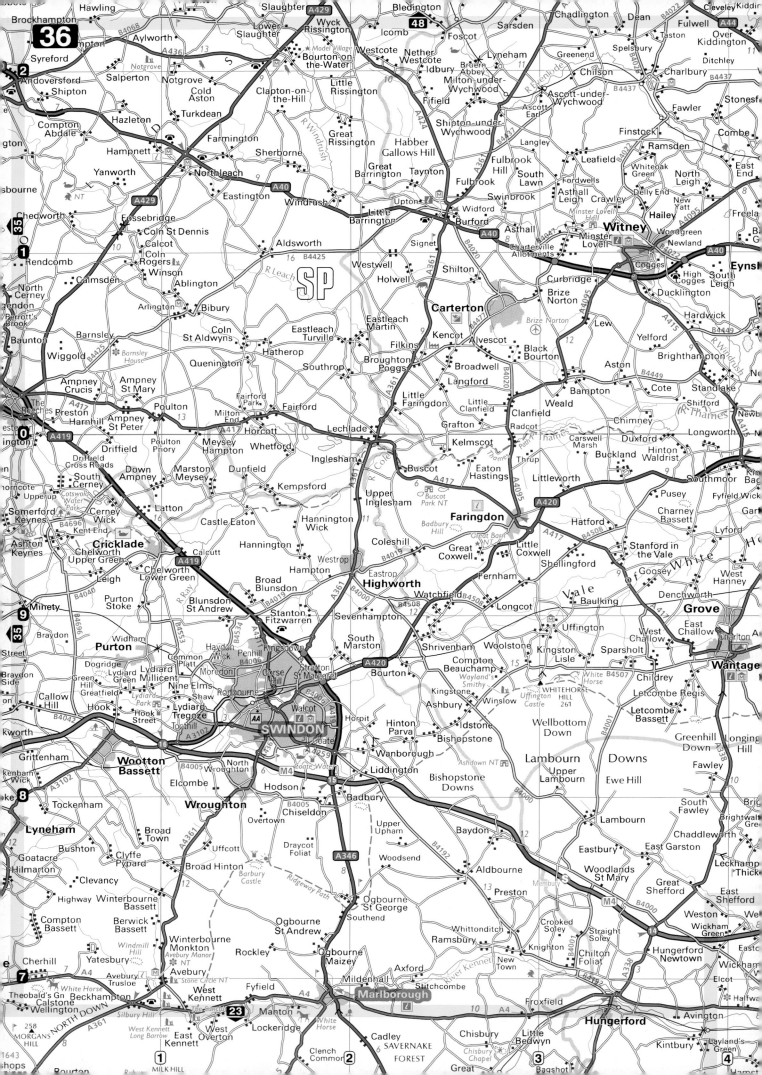

Boxted
Langham
Dedham
Brantham
Stutton
Erwarton
Shotley Gate
Felixstowe *i*

Horkesley Green
Boxted Cross
Castles House
Langham Moor
Flatford Mill & Lock
Cattawade
Holbrook Bay
55
AA
Parkeston Quay
Bath Side
The Redoubt

Boxted Heath
Boxted
Dedham Hatch
Langham Hatch
A12
Lawford
Manningtree
Mistley Towers
New Mistley
River Stour
Wrabness
AA
Parkeston
Harwich Harbour
Landguard Fort

Langham Wick
Ardleigh Heath
Mistley
Mistley Heath
Bradfield
Ramsey
A120
Upper Dovercourt
Harwich
Dovercourt *i*
Landguard Point

Mile End
High Woods
Ardleigh
8
Burnt Heath
Little Bromley
Horsleycross Street
Wix
B1352
Bradfield Heath
Little Oakley
M

Fox Street
Parson's Heath
Crockleford Heath
Bromley Cross
Horsley Cross
19
Goose Green
Wix Green
Great Oakley
B1414

A134
A1232
Great Bromley
Tendring Heath
Tendring Green
Stones Green

COLCHESTER
A120
A120
Little Bentley
Goose Green
Beaumont
Horsey Island
Pennyhole Bay

AA
A133
Greenstead
Elmstead Market
Hare Green
Tendring
17
ESBJERG GÖTEBORG HAMBURG HOEK VAN HOLLAND

Old Heath
New Quay
Wivenhoe Cross
Elmstead Heath
Frating Green
B1035
Thorpe Green
Horsey Island
The Naze
v

4
B1027
Beth Chatto
Elmstead Row
Frating
Weeley
A133
Thorpe-le-Soken
Kirby-le-Soken
Walton on the Naze

Wivenhoe
Alresford
Great Bentley
16
B1033
B1033
1034
Kirby Cross
B1035

Blackheath
Rowhedge
Fingringhoe
High Park Corner
Tenpenny Heath
Aingers Green
Weeley Heath
B147
Great Holland
Frinton-on-sea

Malting Green
South Green
Thorrington
Little Clacton
Cook's Green
B1032

Abberton
Samson's Corner
B1442
Holland-on-Sea

Langenhoe
Abberton Reservoir
Peldon
B1029
Hurst Green
B1027
Great Clacton
TM

B1025
Brightlingsea
Cudmore Grove
St Osyth
Rush Green
A133
Holland-on-Sea

Great Wigborough
MERSEA ISLAND
Point Clear
CLACTON-ON-SEA *i*

West Mersea
East Mersea
Jaywick

Colne Point

Shinglehead Point

Sales Point
Bradwell Waterside
R. Colne

B1021
Bradwell-on-Sea

Tillingham

Dengie

Asheldham

Southminster

Holliwell Point

Burnham-on-Crouch

Foulness Point

0   1   2   3   4   5 miles
0 1 2 3 4 5 6 7 kilometres

Courtsend

Churchend

FOULNESS ISLAND

TR

29

v
VLISSINGEN (FLUSHING)
2
3
0   1

C A R D I G A N

B A Y

56

| 0 | 1 | 2 | 3 | 4 | 5 miles |

| 0 | 1 | 2 | 3 | 4 | 5 | 6 | 7 kilometres |

SN

9

8

7

Llansantf
Llan

A487

Aberarth

Aberaeron

Monachty

Ffos-y-ffin

Llyswen

Cilc

New Quay

Llanina

Llwyncelyn

Maen-y-groes

Gilfachrheda

B4342

Oakford

6

Cross
Inn

A487

Llanarth

Ceredigion
Heritage Coast

Nanternis

Caerwedros

Dihewyd

B4339

B4342

Ynys-Lochtyn

Llwyndafydd

Pentre'rbryn

Mydroilyn

Llangranog

Synod Inn

Pontgarreg

Ffynonddewi

Morfa

Plwmp

Penbryn

Ceredigion
Heritage Coast

311

15

Pentregat

Cardigan Island

Parcllyn

Aberporth

Sarnau

Talgarreg

Gorsgoch

B4338

Cardigan Island Coastal
Farm Park

Traethsaith

Brynhoffnant

324

Y Ferwig

Felinwynt
Rainforest &
Butterflies
Centre

Blaenannerch

Tan-y-groes

Capel Cynon

Bwlchyfadfa

5

Gwbert on Sea

A487

Glynarthen

B4459

Penparc

Tremain

Blaenporth

Bettws Evan

Rhydlewis

Cwrt-newydd

Cardigan

Beulah

Hawen

Ffostrasol

Pontshaen

Cwmsychbant

St Dogmaels

Llangoedmor

Brongest

Penrhiw-pal

Tre-groes

Llanwenog

Drefac

Moylgrove

Bridgend

Ponthirwaun

Troedyraur

Coed-y-bryn

Maesllyn

Rhydowen

Lli

Monington

A487

Llechryd

Llandygwydd

Llangynllo

Croe

Pren-gwyn

Pen-y-bryn

2

Cilgerran
Castle NT

31

3

4

Gorrin

Rhyddlan

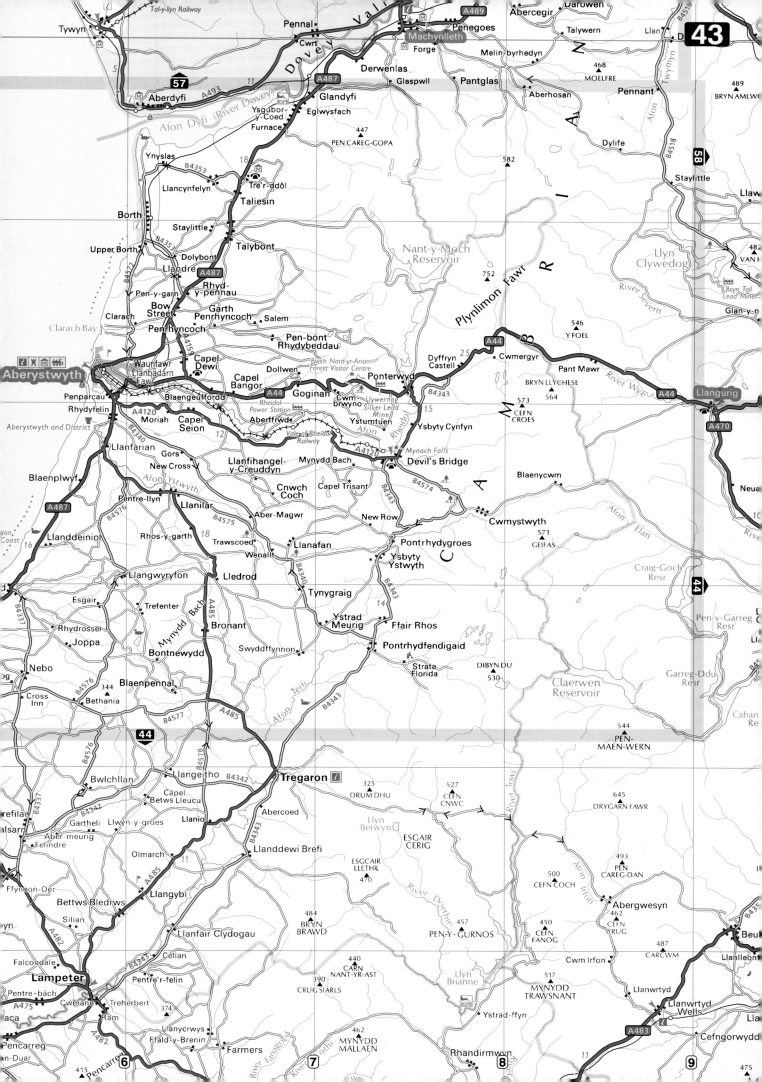

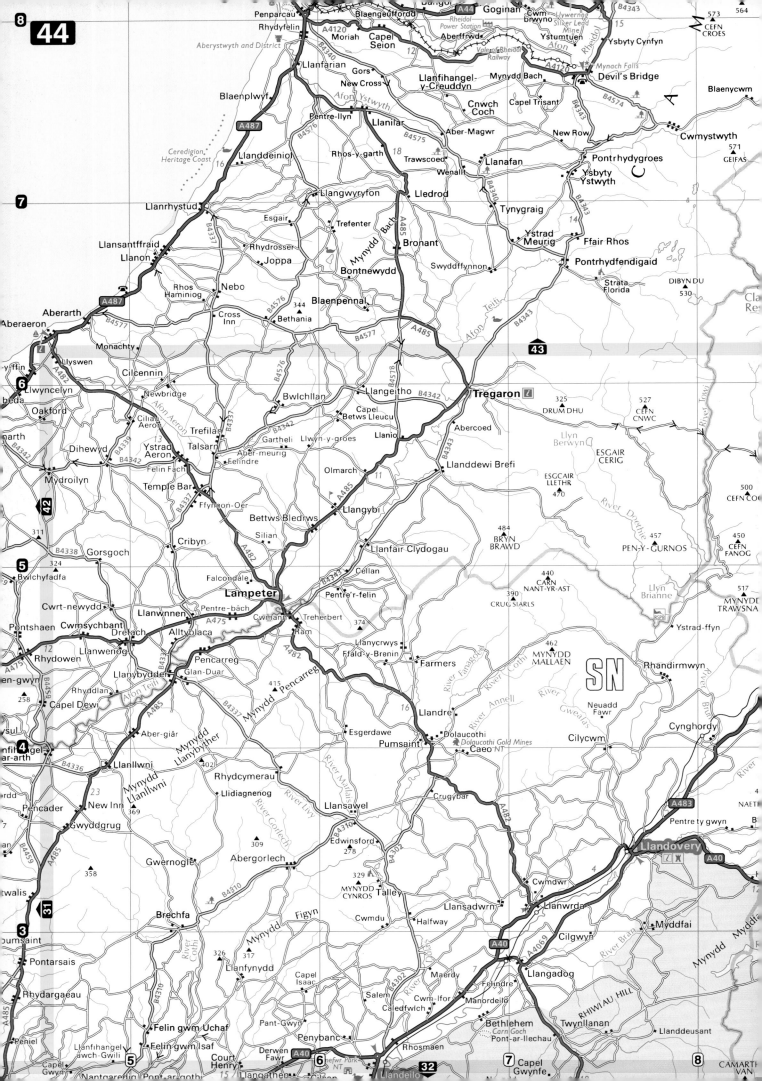

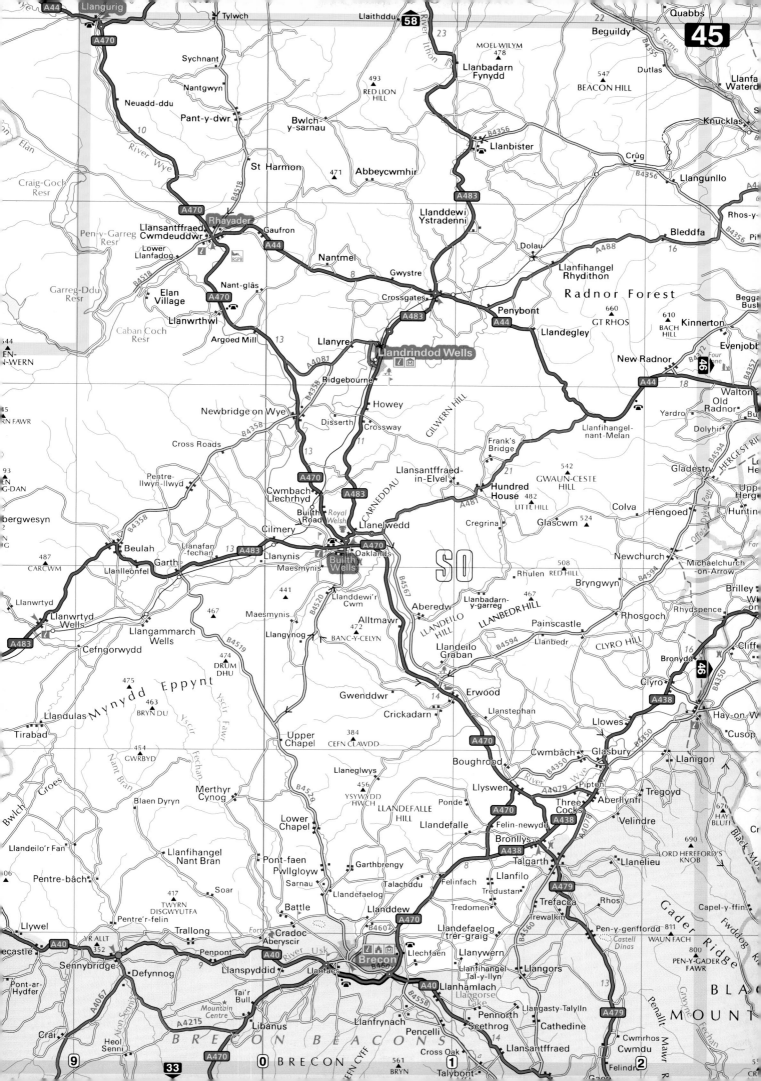

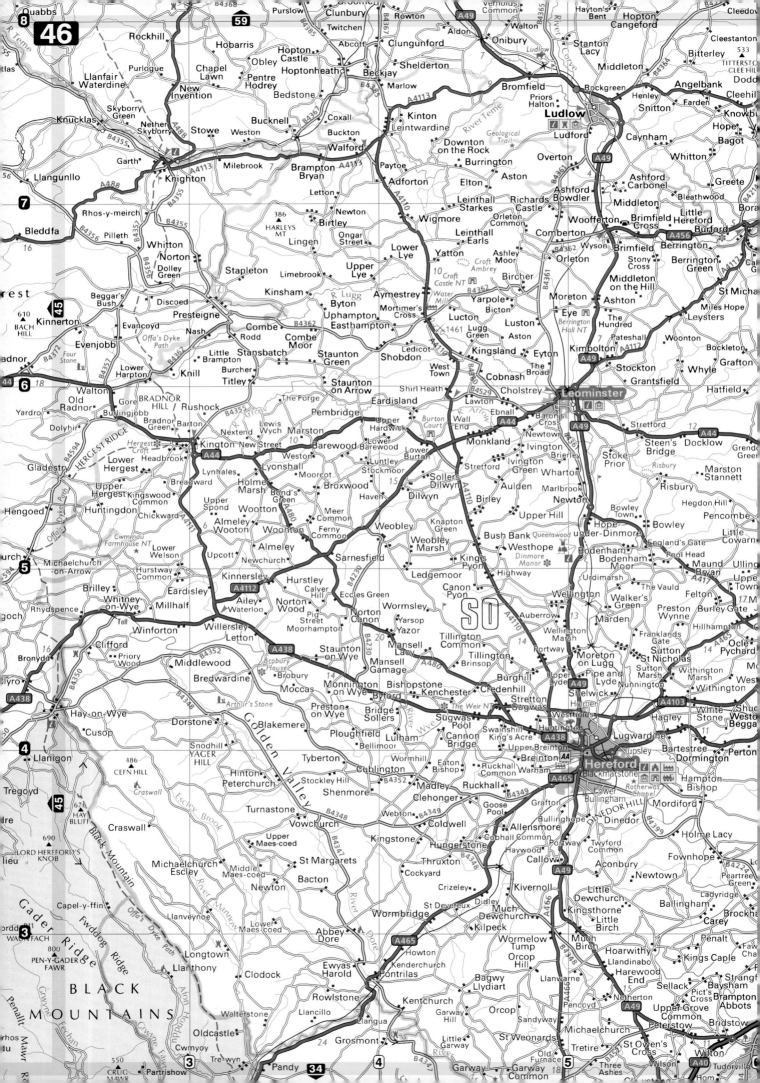

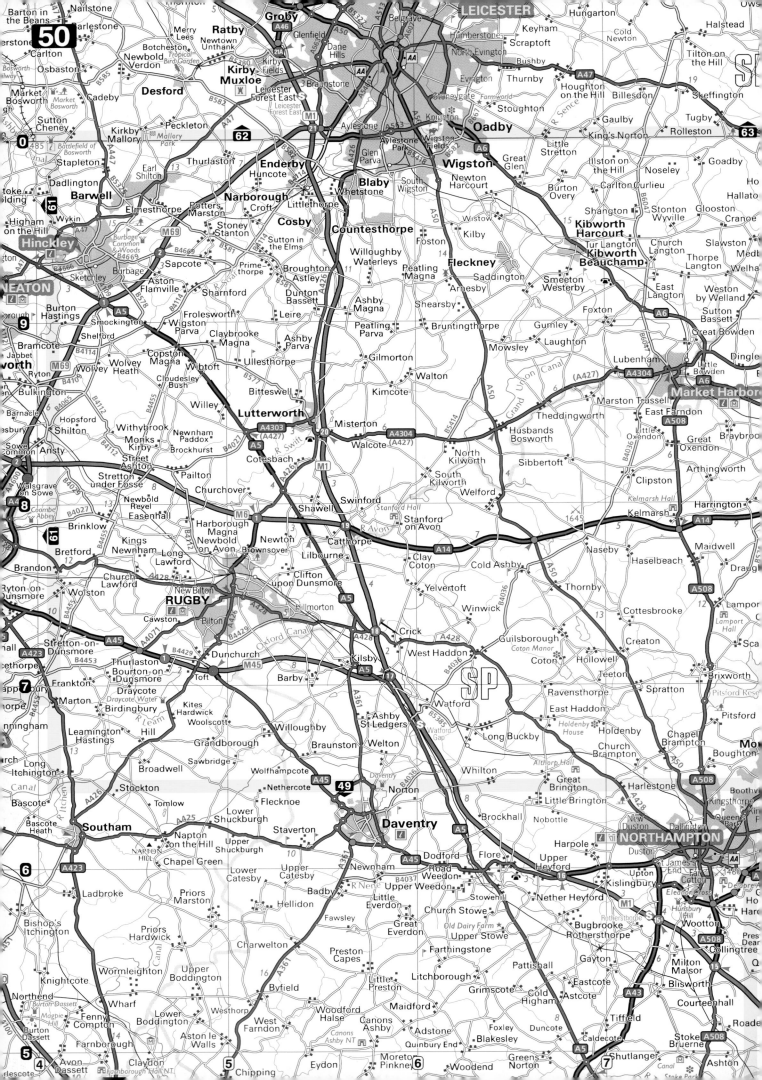

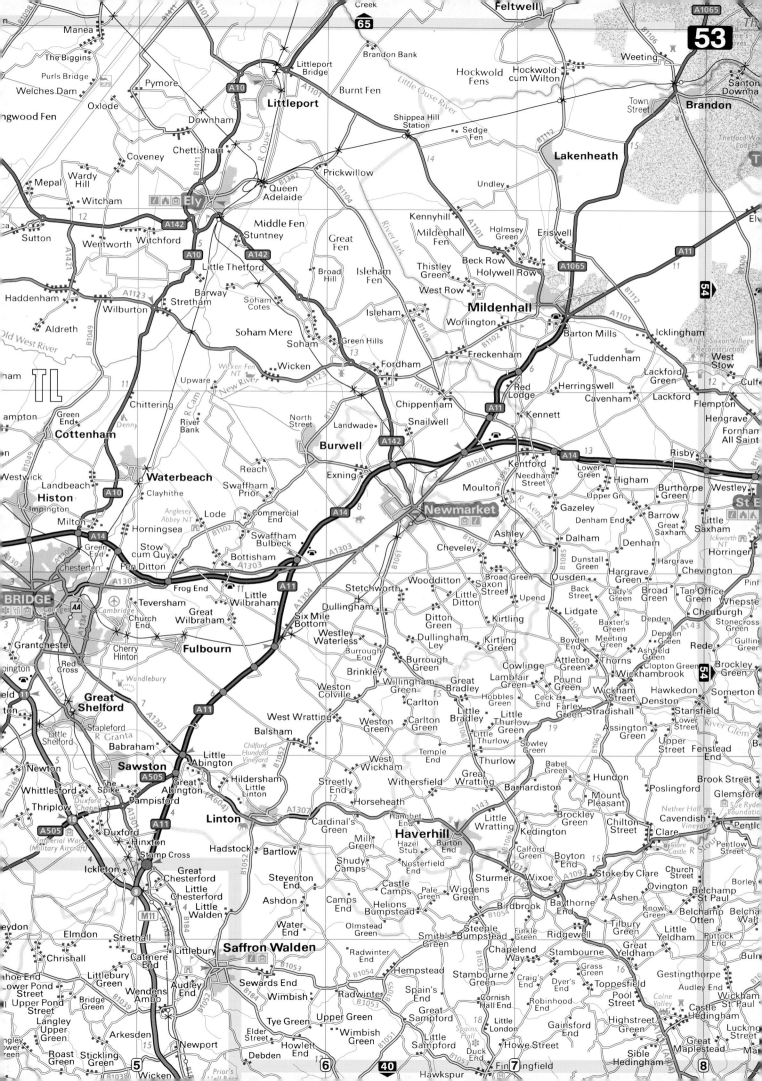

5

4

3

2

1

0

68

42

Aberdesach
Llanllyfn
Nebo
Clynnog-fawr
Capeluchaf
Nasareth
Gyrn-goch
Pant-gl
522
Y GYRN-DDU
19
Trevor
A499
Upper
Clynnog
Tre'r
Ceiri
Bryn
564
Llanaelhaearn
A487
Trwyn y
Grolech
YR EIFL
Glan-Dwyfach
20
P
Llithfaen
E
N
21
B4411
Carreg Ddu
Pistyll
B4417
I
N
St Cybi's Well
Afon
Porth
Nefyn
Llwyndyrys
Pencaenewydd
S
Rhoslan
Morfa Nefyn
Llangybi
Nefyn
U
Fron
B4354
Porth Dinllaen
Y Ffor
Llanarmon
Groesffordd
Edern
Rhos
Chwilog
Llanystumdwy
Rhos-y-llan
Bodfuan
fawr
B4354
A497
13
Porth Ysgaden
A497
L
Penarth Fawr
M
Llandudwen
Llannor
Abererch
Tudweiliog
L
A499
Rhyd-
Efailnewydd
Porth Colman
E
y-clafdy
Dinas
Denio
Pen-ychain
Bryn
371
Y
mawr
Garn
Llangwnnadl
14
Llaniestyn
Penrhos
7
Pen-y-graig
Meyllteyrn
Pwllheli
N
Botwnnog
Lleyn Heritage Coast
B4415
B4413
Sarn
17
Mynytho
Llanbedrog
Porthoer
Bryncroes
Nanhoron
B4413
Rhydlios
Rhoshirwaun
Llandegwning
A499
Trwyn Llanbedrog
Llangian
St Tudwal's
Anelog
B4413
Penycaerau
Road
Y Rhiw
Plas-Yn-Rhiw NT
Abersoch
Llanfaelrhys
Llanengan
Uwchmynydd
Porth
Ysgo
Porth Neigwl
Sarn-bâch
Marchros
St Tudwal's
Aberdaron
Bwlchtocyn
Island East
Aberdaron
Bay
St Tudwal's
Island West
Porth
Ceiriad
Bardsey Sound
St Mary's
BARDSEY
ISLAND

SH

C A R D I G A N

B A Y

0   1   2   3   4   5 miles
0 1 2 3 4 5 6 7 kilometres

1   2   3   4

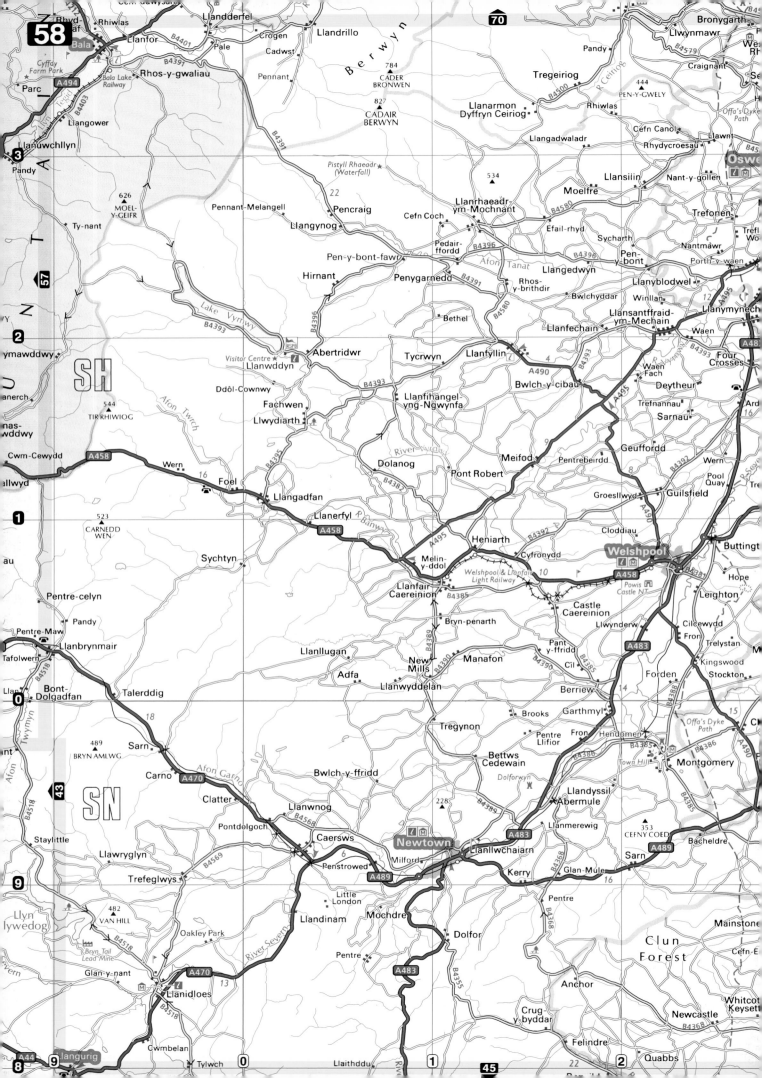

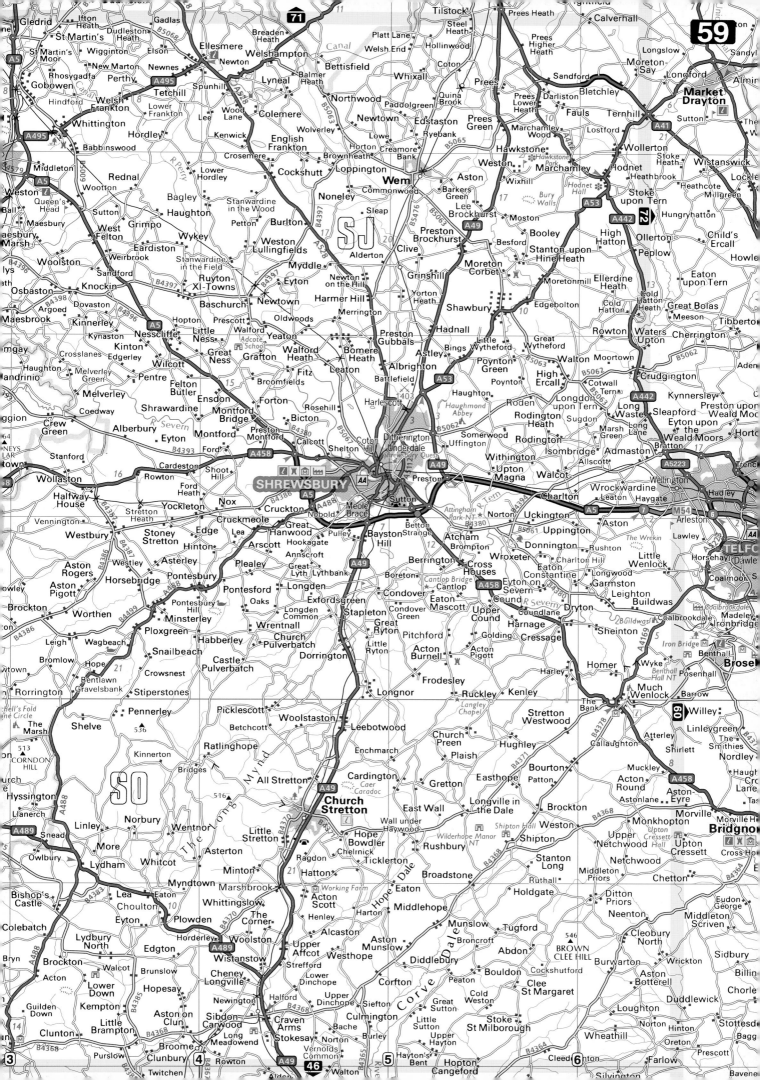

Scolt Head Island · · · Holkam Bay · North Norfolk Heritage Coast · Blakeney Point · Norfolk Coast Path · **Sheringham**

Burnham Deepdale
Burnham Overy Staithe
Holkham
Wells-next-the-Sea
Morston
Cley next the Sea A149
A149
Brancaster Staithe
Burnham Norton
Burnham Overy
Burnham Norton Friary
Stiffkey
Warham All Saints
Cockthorpe
Blakeney
Wiveton
Morston Marshes
Newgate
Salthouse
Weybourne
Burnham Market
Burnham Thorpe
Holkham Hall
Warham St Mary
Wighton
Westgate
Langham
Glandford
Kelling
Upper Sheringham
Bodham
A148
Docking
New Holkham
Wells & Walsingham Light Railway
Copy's Green
Binham
Lower Green
Saxlingham
Field Dalling
Sharrington
Little Thornage
Holt
North Norfolk Railway
West Beckham
Gresham
Baconsthorpe
Stanhoe
North Creake
South Creake
Waterden
Little Walsingham
North Barsham
Hindringham
Houghton St Giles
Great Walsingham
Bale
Brinton
Thornage
Stody Hunworth
Edgefield
Edgefield Green
Plumstead
Plumstead Green
Matlask
Bircham Newton
Barmer
Syderstone
Southgate
West Barsham
East Barsham
Great Snoring
Thursford
Barney
Croxton
Swanton Novers
Melton Constable
Briston
Briningham
Little Barningham
Bessingham
Bircham Tofts
Sculthorpe
Little Snoring
Kettlestone
Fulmodestone
Craymere Beck
Mannington Hall
Saxthorpe
Ittering
Calth
65
Tattersett
Coxford
Shereford
Dunton
Penthorpe Waterfowl Park
Fakenham
A1067
Stibbard
Hindolveston
Thurning
Norton Corner
Oulton
Oulton Street
Blick
3
Houghton Hall
New Houghton
West Rudham
Broomsthorpe
Hempton
Little Ryburgh
Wood Norton
Guestwick
Wood Dalling
Salle
Heydon
Ayl
East Rudham
Tatterford
Toftrees
Great Ryburgh
Guist
Foulsham
Southgate
A148
Harpley
Helhoughton
East Raynham
Colkirk
Gateley
Themelthorpe
Cawston
Reepham
Eastgate
Brandiston
West
17
West Raynham
Oxwick
Hamrow
Horningtoft
Twyford
Bintree
Broom Green
Foxley
Whitwell Street
Great Witchingham
A1065
Great Massingham
South Raynham
Weasenham St Peter
Whissonsett
Potthorpe
Saxon Cathedral
Billingford
Bawdeswell
Sparham
Alderford
Swannington
Felthorpe
Upgate
2
Weasenham All Saints
Wellingham
Tittleshall
North Elmham
Brisley
Sparhamill
Lenwade
B1145
Rougham
Stanfield
East Bilney
Beetley
Worthing
A1067
Morton
Attlebridge
T F
Mileham
Litcham
Gressenhall
Bittering
Hoe
Mill Street
Mill Street
Elsing
Lyng
West Acre
Castle Acre
West Lexham
East Lexham
Beeston
Longham
Gressenhall Green
Gressenhall
Swanton Morley
Woodgate
Peaseland Green
Greensgate
Weston Longville
Ta
Newton
Bailey Gate
Woodgate
Crane's Corner
Sparrow Green
Northall Green
Etling Green
Primrose Gn
Ringland
14
South Acre
Great Dunham
Little Dunham
Great Fransham
Wendling
Scarning
Toftwood
B1141
North Tuddenham
A47
Hockering
Honingham
Costes
1
Swaffham
A1065
Sporle
Little Fransham
Hulver Street
Daffy Green
Westfield
Yaxham
East Dereham
Mattishall
Burgh
Mattishall
Clint Green
South Green
East Tuddenham
Colton
Easton
A47
Col
Necton
Ivy Todd
West End
East Bradenham
Whinburgh
Runhall
Welborne
Brandon Parva
Barford
Marlingford
Royal Norfolk
65
North Pickenham
Holme Hale
West Bradenham
Shipdham
Garvestone
Thuxton
Coston
Barnham Broom
Wramplingham
High Green
Lynch Green
Hethersett
Cockley Cley
South Pickenham
Ashill
Crowshill
High Common
Reymerston
Danemoor Green
Kimberley
Carleton Forehoe
Bawburgh
Great Melton
Col
0
Saham Hills
Ovington
Cranworth
Southburgh
Hardingham
Hackford
Crownthorpe
Kidd's Moor
East Carlet
Great Cressingham
Saham Toney
Carbrooke
Woodrising
Hingham
Wicklewood
B1172
Beckett End
Bodney
Watton
Watton Green
Scoulton
Little Ellingham
Deopham
Morley St Botolph
Deopham Green
Wymondham
B1135
Little Cressingham
Merton
Griston
Northacre
Rockland St Peter
Bow Street
Great Ellingham
Spooner Row
Ashwellthorpe
Wreningham
Ickburgh
Peddars Way
Thompson
Caston
Rockland All Saints
Fen Street
Tropical Butterfly Gardens
Besthorpe
Fundenhall
Low
T L
Cranwich
Breckles
Lower Stow Bedon
Stow Bedon
Shropham
Mount Pleasant
Great Hockham
30
Black Car
Bunwell Street
Forncett End
Tacolneston
For
Mundford
Great Hockham
North End
Snetterton
Eccles Road
Attleborough
Carleton Rode
Bunwell
New Buckenham
Pottergate
St Mar
A1065
East Wretham
Stonebridge
South End
Puddledock
A11
Old Buckenham
Upgate Street
Hargate
Asclacton
9
8
Thetford
9
54
0
1
Tibenham

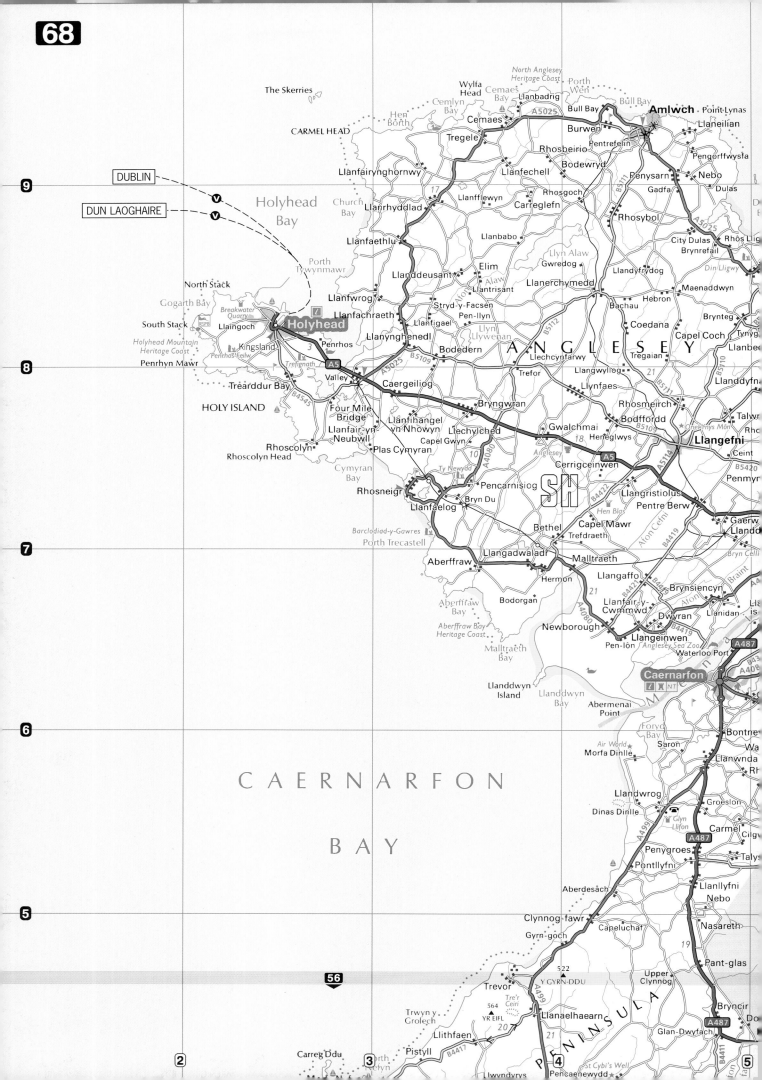

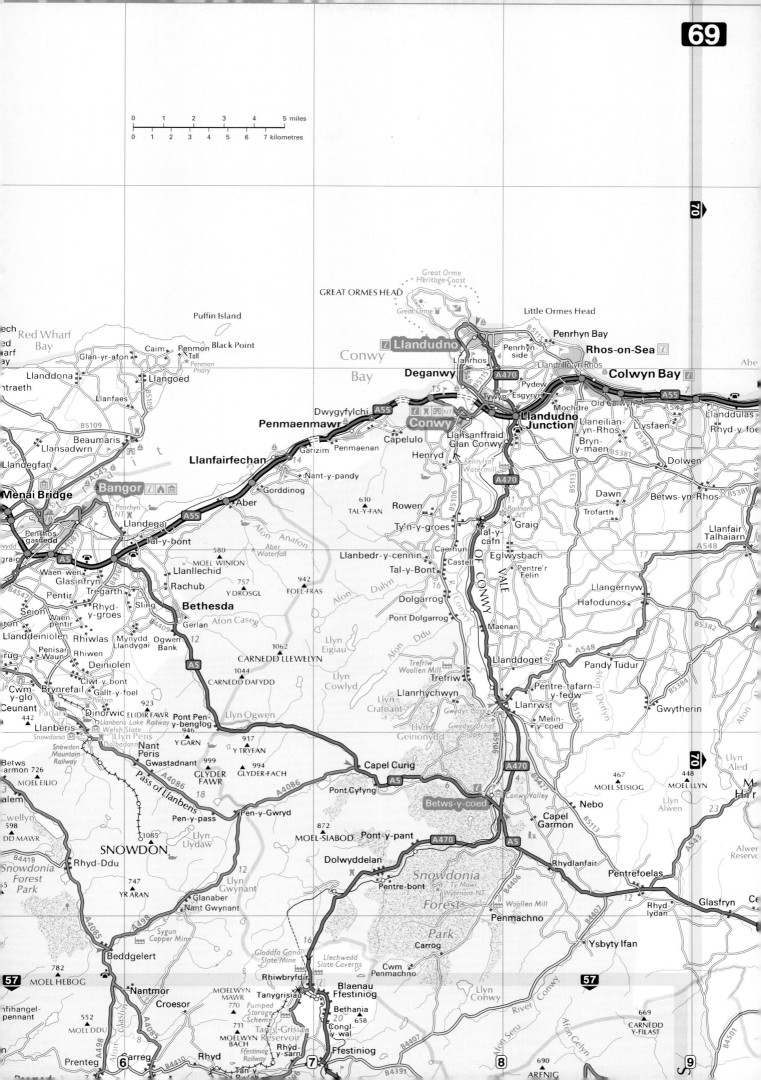

70

70

57

57

Great Orme
Heritage Coast

GREAT ORMES HEAD

Great Orme

Little Ormes Head

Puffin Island

Penrhyn Bay

Black Point

Penmon
Toll

Caim

Penrhyn-
side

Rhos-on-Sea

Penmon
Priory

Glan-yr-afon

Llangoed

Conwy

Llandudno

Llanrhos

Bay

Pydew

Llandrillo-yn Rhos

Colwyn Bay

Llanddona

Llanfaes

Deganwy

15

Tywyn

Esgyryn

Old Colwyn

Llandegfan

Llanrhos

Mochdre

A55

Llanddulas

Beaumaris

Llansadwrn

Dwygyfylchi

A55

Conwy

Llansanffraid
Glan Conwy

Bryn-
y-maen

Llaneilian-
yn-Rhos

Rhyd-y-foe

Penmaenmawr

Garizim

Penmaenan

Capelulo

Dawn

Betws-yn Rhos

Penrhyn
NT

Llanfairfechan

14

Nant-y-pandy

Henryd

Felinisaf
Watermill

A470

Dolwen

Llanfair
Talhaiarn

A548

Menai Bridge

Bangor

Gorddinog

Trofarth

Graig

Aber

610

Rowen

Badnant
NT

11

Llandegai

Tal-y-bont

TAL-Y-FAN

Ty'n-y-groes

Tal-y-
cafn

Eglwysbach

Pentre'r
Felin

Penrhos
garnedd

580

Aber
Waterfall

Caerhun

Llangernyw

A5

Bethesda

MOEL WINION

Afon Anafon

Llanbedr-y-cennin

Castell

Hafodunos

Waen-wen

Gerlan

Llanllechid

757

Tal-y-Bont

16

Glasinfryn

Rhiwlas

Rachub

Y DROSGL

FOEL-FRAS

VALE

B5382

Pentir

Afon Caseg

942

Dolgarrog

A548

Seion

Waen-
pentir

Rhyd-
y-groes

Sling

Ogwen
Bank

Afon Dulyn

Pont Dolgarrog

Maenan

OF CONWY

Pandy Tudur

Llanddeiniolen

Mynydd
Llandygai

CARNEDD LLEWELYN

Llyn
Eigiau

Afon Ddu

A5

1062

Rhiwen

Deiniolen

1044

Llyn
Cowlyd

Trefriw
Woollen Mill

Llanddoget

Gwytherin

Clwt-y-bont

CARNEDD DAFYDD

Trefriw

B5113

Cwm-
y-glo

Brynrefail

Gallt-y-foel

Llanrhychwyn

Llanrwst

Pentre-tafarn-
y-fedw

Ceunant

442

923

Llyn
Crafnant

Gwydir Castle

Melin-
y-coed

B5384

Llanberis

Llanberis Lake Railway

Llyn Peris

ELIDIR FAWR

Pont Pen-
y-benglog

Gwydyr Uchaf
Chapel

Welsh Slate

Dolbadarn

946

Llyn Ogwen

Llyn
Geirionydd

Llanrwst

Snowdonia

Snowdon
Mountain
Railway

Nant
Peris

Y GARN

12

B5106

Betws
Garmon 726

Gwastadnant

917

Y TRYFAN

A470

MOEL SEISIOG

467

MOEL LLYN

448

Llyn
Aled

MOEL EILIO

999

994

Capel Curig

B5427

Pass of Llanberis

A4086

GLYDER
FAWR

GLYDER-FACH

A5

6

Conwy Valley

Nebo

Llyn
Alwen

MOEL
Hir

Pen-y-pass

A4086

Pont Cyfyng

Betws-y-coed

Capel
Garmon

B5113

A543

Cwellyn
598

Pen-y-Gwryd

872

Pont-y-pant

A5

Rhydlanfair

Pentrefoelas

Alwen
Reservoir

DD MAWR

SNOWDON

18

Llyn
Llydaw

MOEL-SIABOD

Dolwyddelan

A470

A5

B4406

Rhyd-Ddu

12

Snowdonia

Pentrefoelas

Rhyd
lydan

Glasfryn

Snowdonia

747

Llyn
Gwynant

Pentre-bont

Forest

12

B4407

Forest

YR ARAN

Glanaber

Ty Mawr
Wybrnant-NT

Ce

Park

Nant Gwynant

Park

Woollen Mill

Beddgelert

Sygun
Copper Mine

Carrog

Penmachno

Ysbyty Ifan

6

782

MOEL HEBOG

16

Gloddfa Ganol
Slate Mine

Llechwedd
Slate Caverns

Cwm
Penmachno

River Conwy

Afon Serw

9

Nantmor

Rhiwbryfdir

Afon Celyn

Croesor

MOELWYN
MAWR

Tanygrisiau

**Blaenau
Ffestiniog**

Llyn
Conwy

669

nfihangel-
pennant

770

Pumped
Storage
Scheme

Bethania

CARNEDD
Y-FILAST

552

MOEL DDU

711

20

658

Prenteg

MOELWYN
BACH

Tan-y-Grisiau
Reservoir

Congl-
y-wal

6

Carreg

Ffestiniog
Railway

Rhyd-
y-sarn

Ffestiniog

B4391

7

Tan-y-

8

690

ARENIG

9

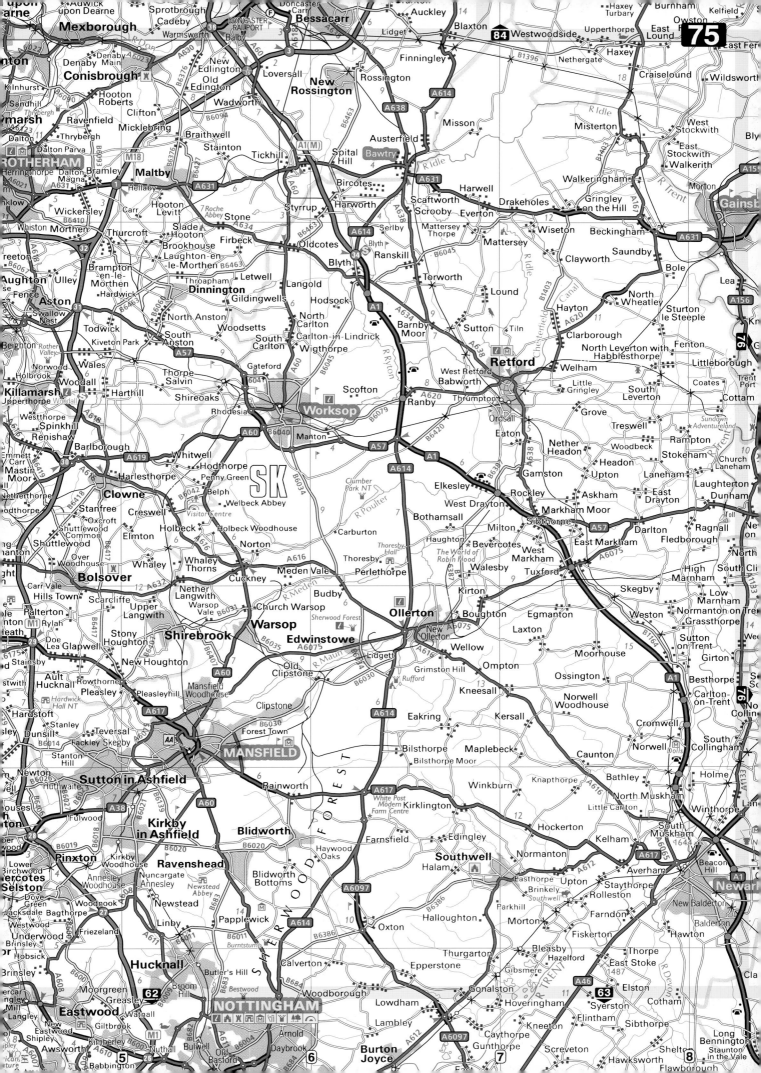

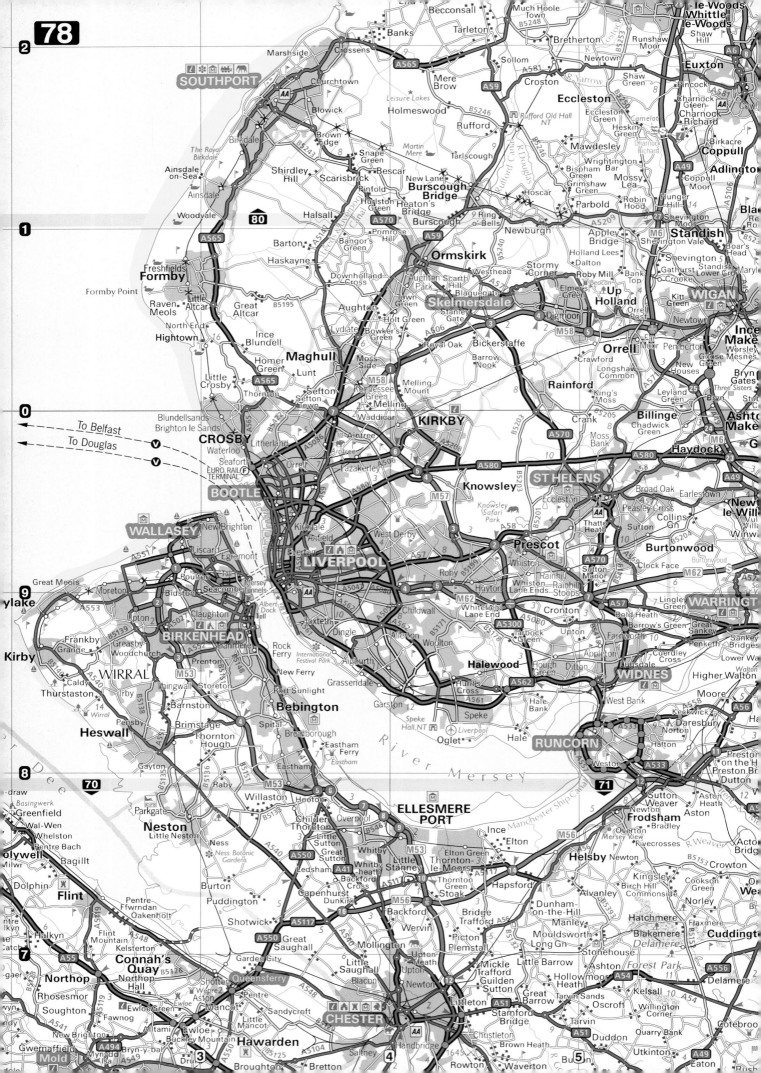

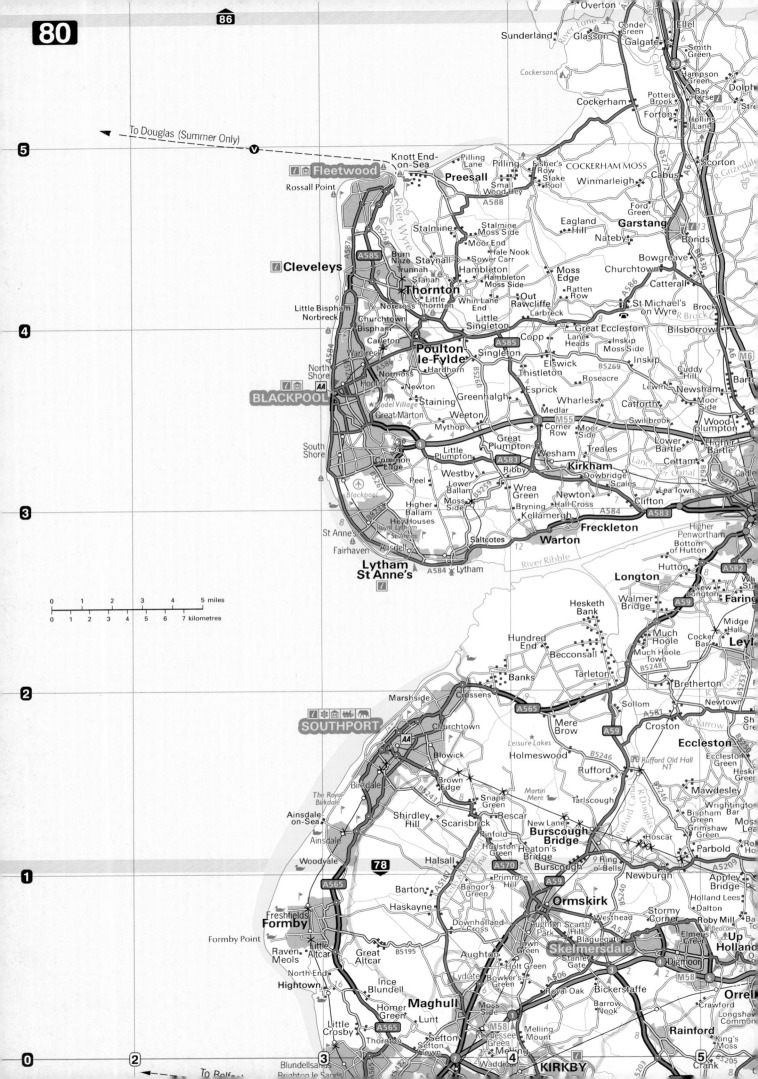

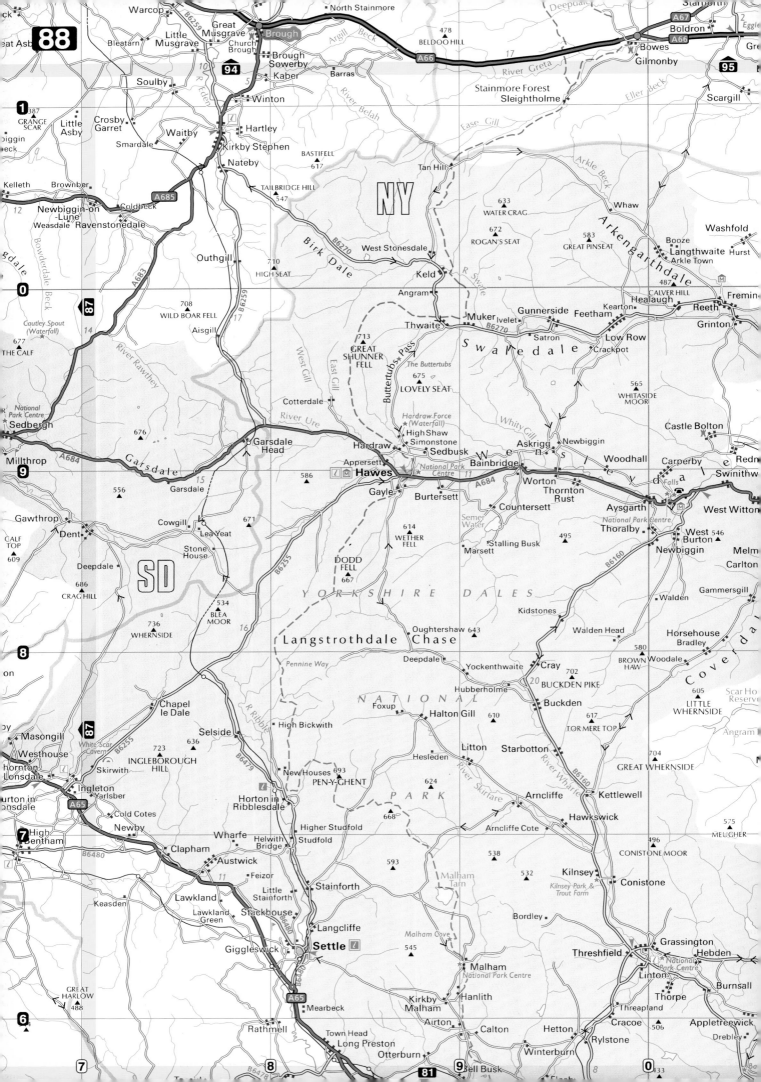

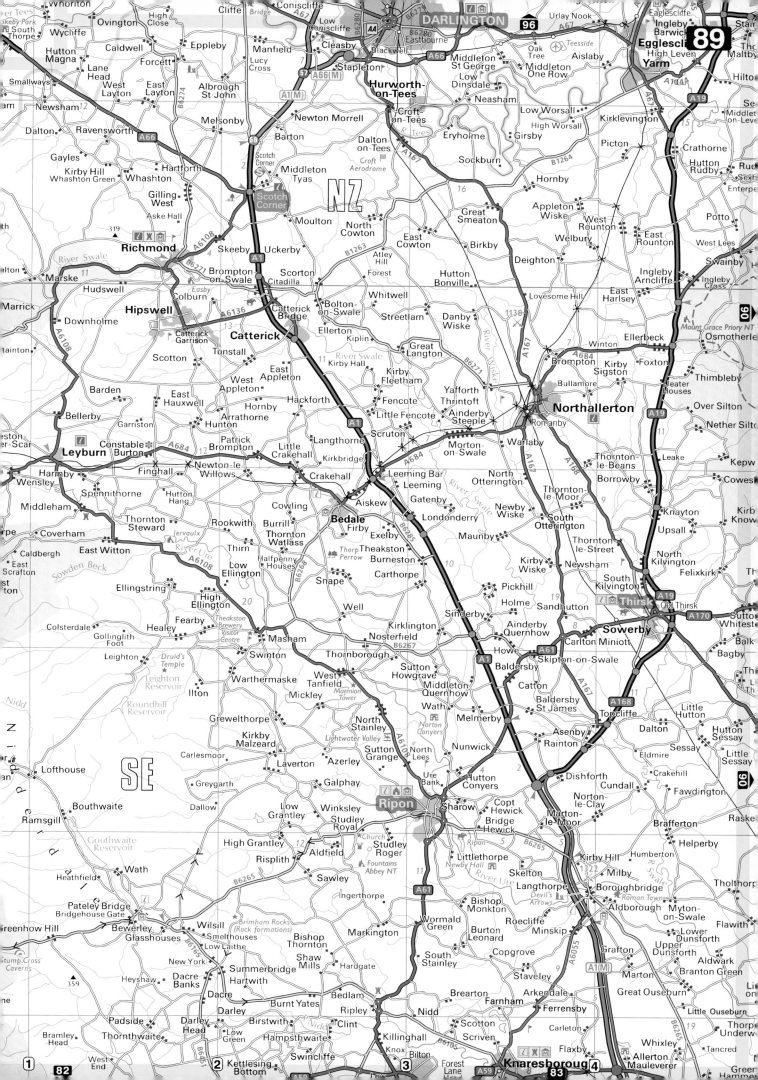

Wyke
▲ **Whitby** 🅘 🏛
Saltwick Bay
Stainsacre
Sneaton   High Hawsker
ebarnby Low
        Hawsker
neatonthorpe Raw   Ness Point or
                North Cheek
          Robin Hood's Bay
Fylingthorpe   *Robin Hood's*
                Bay
                Old Peak or
                South Cheek

Ravenscar

20
A171   Staintondale
            Hayburn Wyke
Harwood Dale   Cloughton
                Newlands
                Cloughton Wyke
Bickley Silpho   Cloughton
    Broxa   Burniston   Cromer Point
Langdale   Suffield   *Cleveland Way*
End   Hackness
Wrench Green   Scalby   Newby
        Everley
Forest Park   **Scarborough** 🅘 🏛
            Falsgrave
Bee Dale
Sawdon   Hutton   Oliver's Mount
    Buscel   East
West   Ayton
Ayton   Irton   Osgodby   *Cayton Bay*
Ebberston Ruston   Crossgates High Killerby   *The Wyke*   **TA**
    Wykeham   Seamer   Cayton
A170 Brompton   Lebberston   Filey Brigg
Snainton   Gristhorpe   *A1039*
Snainton   A64   Muston   **Filey** 🅘
Yedingham *R. Hertford*   Folkton
        Willerby   West   *Filey Bay*
A1039 Staxton Flixton Flotmanby
Sherburn   Ganton   Muston
16 A64   Hunmanby
East Heslerton   Potter   A165
West   Brompton   Reighton
Heslerton   Fordon   Speeton
                        RSPB   *Thornwick Bay*
        Foxholes Wold   Buckton
ringham   Newton   Burton   Bempton   *Flamborough Headland*
                Fleming   *Heritage Coast*
    Butterwick   North Landing
Weaverthorpe   Thwing   Grindale   *Selwicks Bay*
Helperthorpe   Octon   11   Marton   **FLAMBOROUGH**
                                HEAD
West East Lutton   Flamborough
Lutton
Kirby   Langtoft   B1253   Boynton   Sewerby
Grindalythe   Rudston *Monolith*   *Bondville*   **BRIDLINGTON**
Low   *Model Village*
owthorpe Sledmere   Cottam   Bessingby   **Bridlington** 🅘 🏛
                        Carnaby   Hilderthorpe   *BAY*
    B1252   Kilham Haisthorpe
        Burton   Thornholme
        Agnes *Norman*   A165
            Manor House   Fraisthorpe
B1251   Ruston Parva 12
A166   Lowthorpe Harpham
    Garton-on-   Nafferton Little Gransmoor
    the-Wolds   Kelk Great
Wetwang Elmswell   **Driffield** Kelk Lissett Barmston
9 A166 (A166) A614   **85**   Ulrome 2
0   B1248 Dri✝eld   Gembling B1242

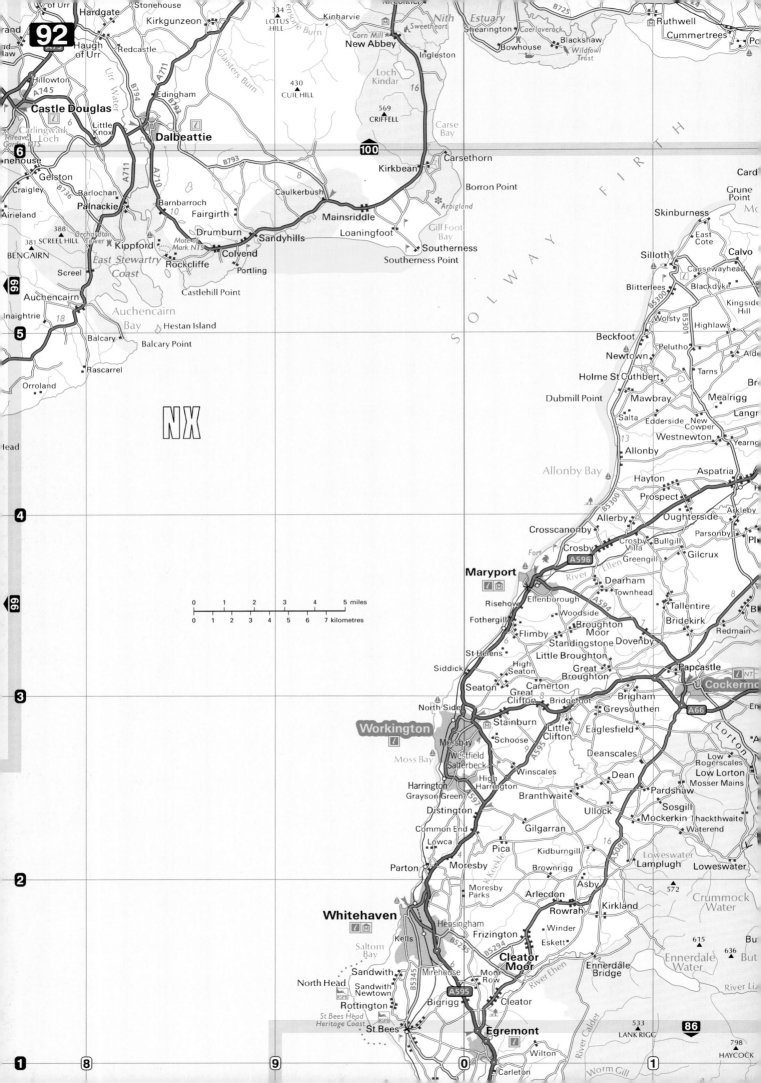

BERGEN
STAVANGER

GÖTEBORG
Summer Only

HAMBURG
Summer Only

AMSTERDAM
Summer Only

...ND

| 0 | 1 | 2 | 3 | 4 | 5 miles |

| 0 | 1 | 2 | 3 | 4 | 5 | 6 | 7 kilometres |

NZ

...gton
...ery

...rlee

...len

Blackhall Colliery
Blackhall Rocks
Blackhall

Hart
Station

...n Hart

High
Throston

Elwick

Historic
Quay
Middleton

HARTLEPOOL

AA

Dalton
Piercy

Hartlepool Bay

Brierton

Seaton Carew

Greatham

A689

Tees Bay

Newton
Bewley

Graythorpe

Hartlepool Power
Station Visitor
Centre

Billingham

Seal Sands

Coatham

Warrenby

Redcar

Cowpen
Bewley

Haverton Hill
Port
Clarence

Teesport

River Tees

Teesside

Marske-by-the-Sea

Kirkleatham

Saltburn-by-the-Sea

Toll

Grangetown

Lazenby

Yearby

Wilton

New
Brotton

Hummersea Scar

MIDDLESBROUGH

AA

North
Ormesby

South
Bank

A1085

Eston

A174

New Marske

Upleatham

Skelton

Brotton

Skinningrove

Street
Houses

Boulby

Teesside Park

Acklam

Normanby

Ormesby

Dunsdale

New
Skelton

North
Skelton

Kilton

Carlin
How

Kilton
Thorpe

Loftus

Easington

Dalehouse

Staithes

Port Mulgrave

Marton

Ormesby Hall NT

Tocketts

Boosbeck

Lingdale

Liverton
Mines

Roxby

Hinderwell

Stainton

Nunthorpe

Margrove
Park

Stanghow

Handale

Borrowby

Newton
Mulgrave

Runswick
Bay

Runswick

North York
...

Hemlington

5

Pinchinthorpe

A173

6

Guisborough

Liverton

90

7

8

Goldsb...

Newton

Hutton

Hutton
Hall

Moorsholm

Scaling

...llerby

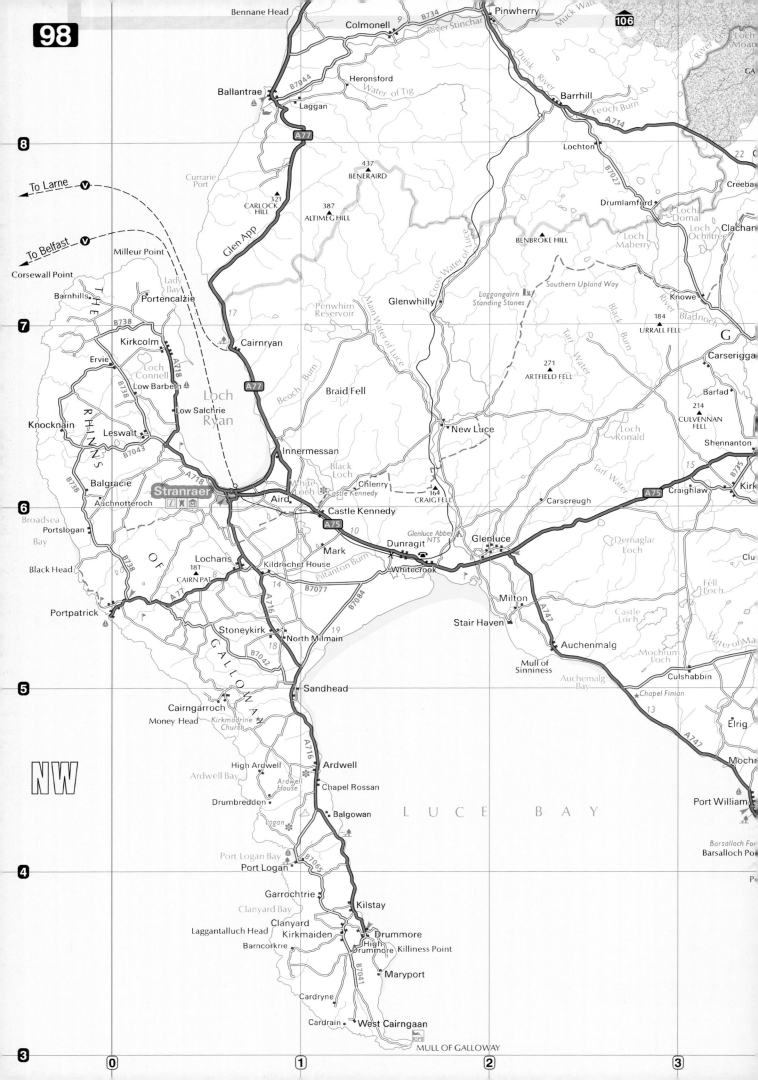

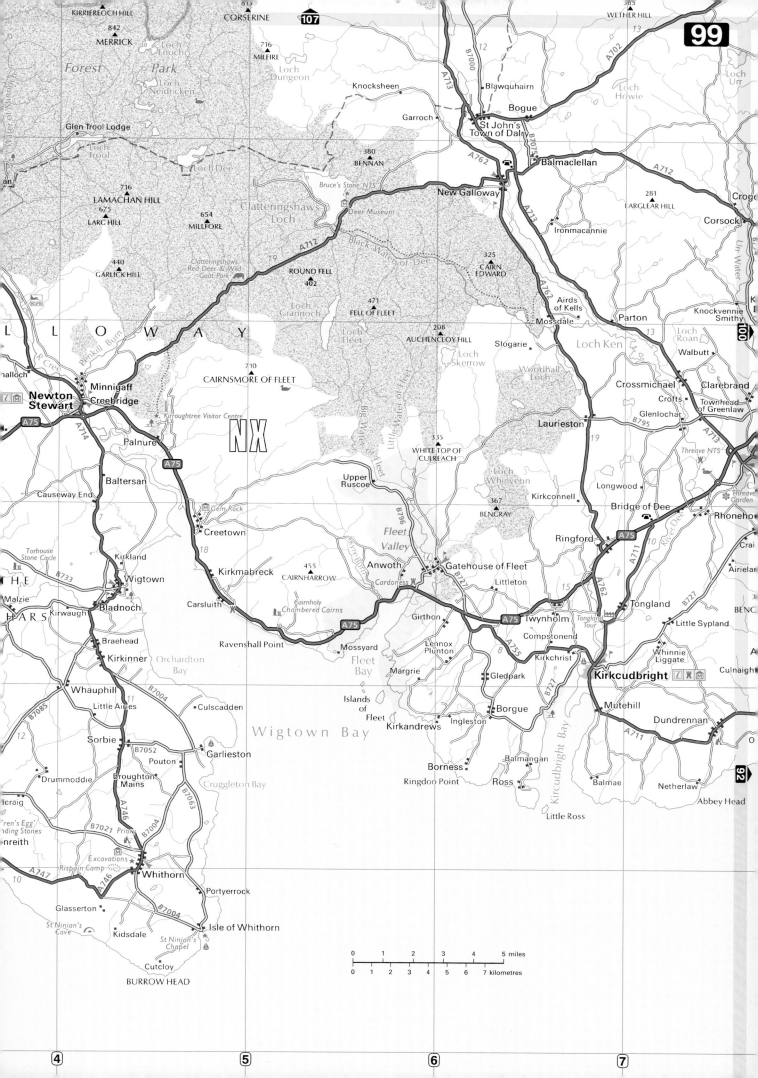

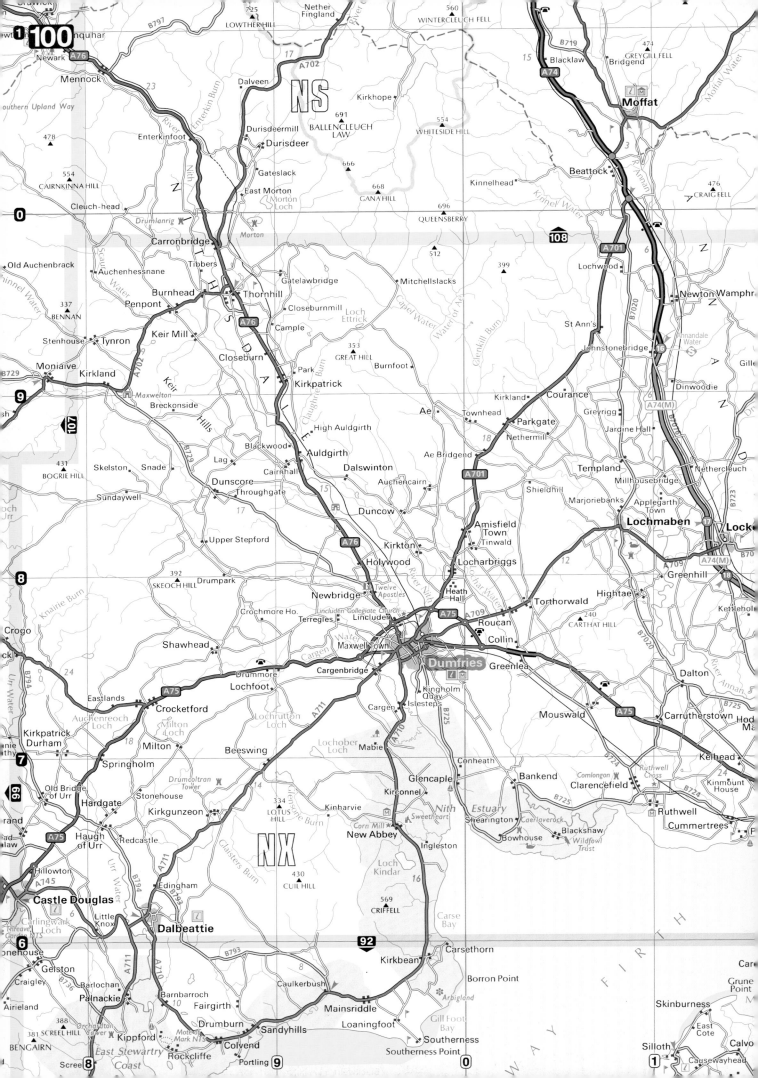

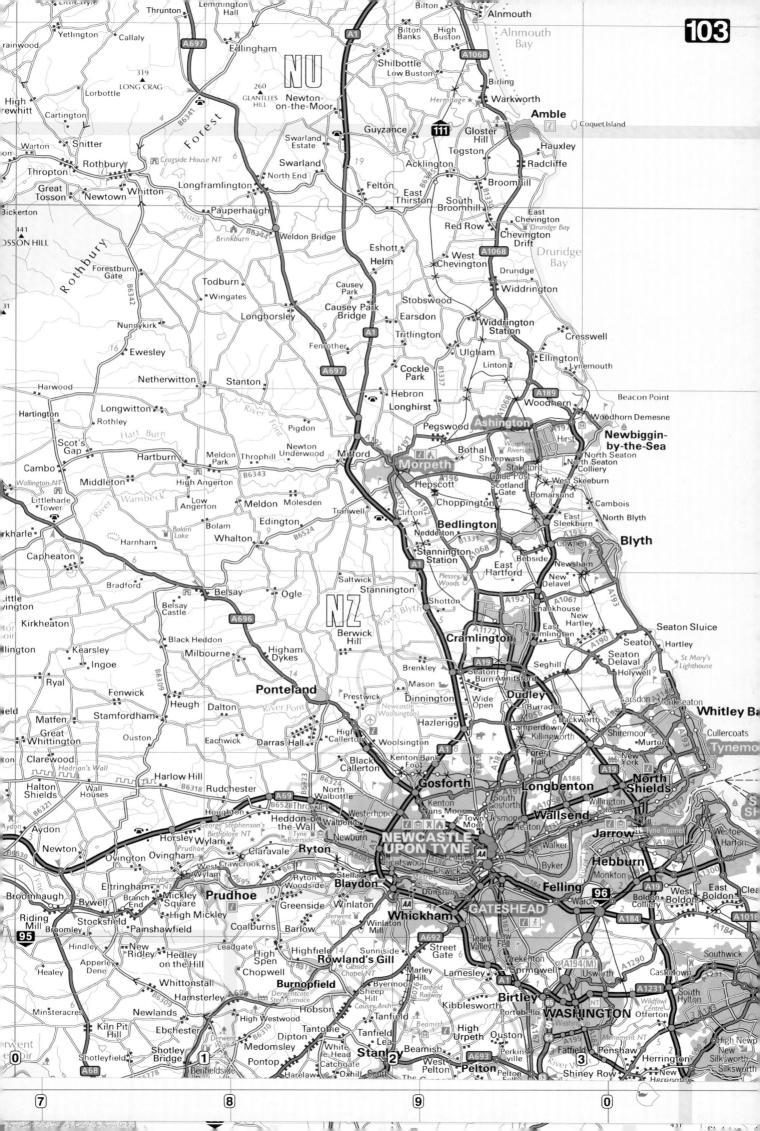

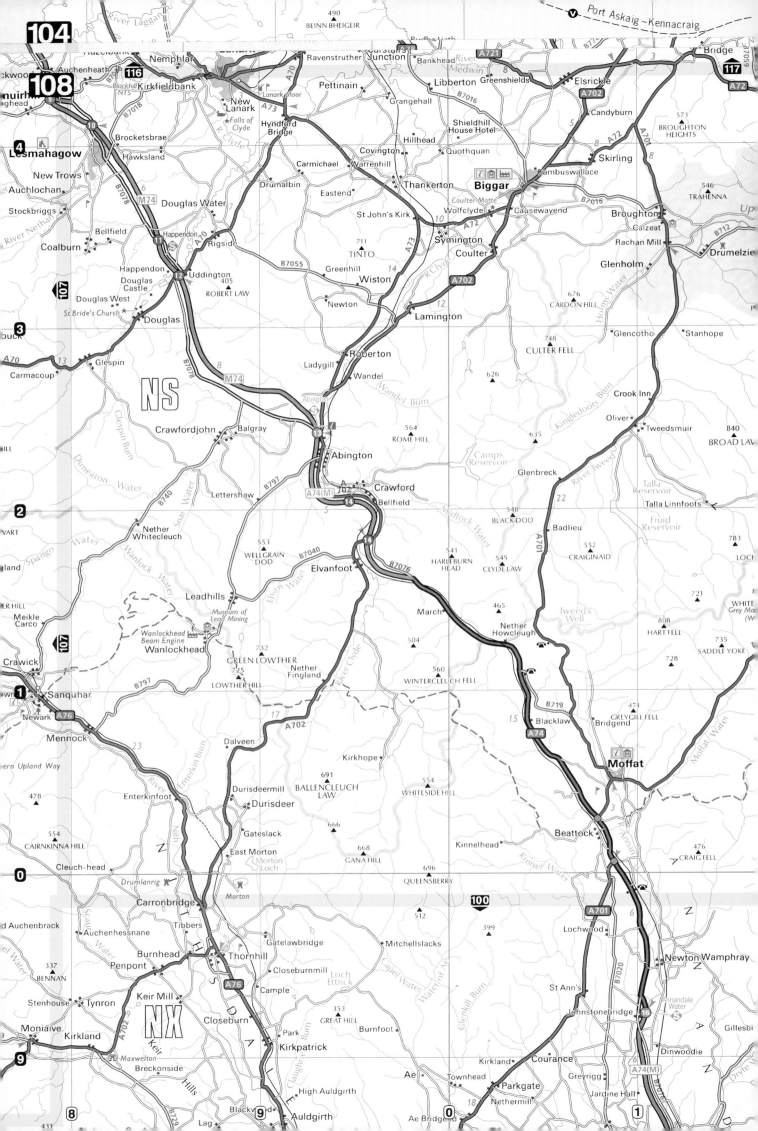

Port Askaig – Kennacraig

Port Ellen – Kennacraig

River Laggan

Duich R

BEINN BHEIGEIR
490

Rudha Liath

BEINN URAIRAIDH
454

Ardtalla

Loch Uraraidh

Claggain Bay

Laggan

A846

B8016

11

Glenegedale

Kintour

Bay

Islay
(Port Ellen)

Ardmore Point

Tarbert

Ardail

112

GIGHA

346

Kildalton Cross

BEINN SHOLUM

113

Eilean
a'Chuirn

Ardminish

Rudha Mòr

Achamore

165
MAOL BUIDHE

Lagavulin

A846

Ardbeg

Rudha na
Gainmhich

The   Oa

Laphroaig

Port
Ellen

Cara

Lower
Killeyan

Risabus

Kilnaughton Bay

Kinnabus

Texa

American
Monument

Loch
Kinnabus

OF OA

Rudha nan
Leacan

Glenacardoch Po

Bellochantuy

0	1	2	3	4	5 miles

0	1	2	3	4	5	6	7 kilometres

NR

Machrihanish
Bay

Machrihanish

Drumle

Earadale Point

385
THE STATE

446
CNOC MOY

Dalsmeran

Glen Brea

BEINN NA LICE

Strone Glen

428

Carskey

MULL OF
KINTYRE

Borgadelmo
Point

Sound of Bute

West

Clachan
Ronachan Point
A83
Ronachan
Loch Ciaran
Ballochroy

Claonaig
Skipness   Skipness Point

Crossaig
Cour Bay
Cour
Cock of Arran
Lochranza
Catacol
Glen Chalmadale
114

247
CRUACH MHIC GOUGAIN
264
CNOC-AN T-SAMHLAIDH
B842

Rhunahaorine
38

Tayinloan

354
CRUACH NAN GABHAR
39

Grogport
Barmollack
Pirnmill
Penrioch
North Arran
834
CAISTEAL ABHAIL
Sannox

A841
17
Whitefarland
715
BEINN BHARRAIN
Corrie
874
GOATFELL
A841

Glen Catacol
Glen Iorsa
Loch Tanna

Imachar
Balliekine
792
BEINN NUIS
Glen Rosa
Brodick NTS
6
Merkland Point
106
Brodick Bay

Arnicle
Barr Water
nbarr
Macalister Clan Visitor Centre
Carradale
B879
Dippen
Carradale House
Torrisdale Square
Carradale Point
Carradale Bay

Dougarie
A R R A N
Auchagallon Stone Circle
Machrie
B880
Glenloig
11
512
A'CHRUACH
Brodick
Strathwhillan
Corriegills
4
Clauchlan

Machrie Bay
Tormore
Machrie Moor
Moss Farm Road Stone Circle
503
BEINN BHREAC
Ballymichael
Shiskine
Birchburn
Lamlash
Lamlash Bay
Holy Is
Margnaheglish
Gordon
A841
4

454
BEINN AN TUIRC
319
408
BORD MOR
Saddell
Saddell Bay

Torbeg
Blackwaterfoot
Drumadoon Bay
Kilpatrick
Kilpatrick Dun
Brown Head
Glen Scorrodale
Cairn Ban
Kilmory Water
Auchencairn
Knockenkelly
Whiting Bay
Whiting Bay
Kingscross
Glen Ashdale
Largymore
Largybeg
Dippen
Dippen Head

396
SGREADAN HILL
Ugadale
Glen Lussa
Peninver
Ardnacross Bay
B842
Kilmichael
A83

Corriecravie
Torr a' Chaisteal Fort
Sliddery
Lagg
Kilmory
16
Cairn
Bennan
Levencorroch
Kildonan
Bennan Head
Pladda

Campbeltown
B842
Campbeltown Loch
Island Davaar

K
352
BEINN GHUILEAN
Kildalloig
Achinhoan
10
Conie Glen
B842
Glen Kerran
Ru Stafnish

Macharioch
Polliwilline Bay
Southend
Dunaverty
Sanda Sound
Sheep Island
Sanda Island

106

K I L B R A N N A N   S O U N D

S O U N D

Ailsa Craig

Corri

4

A841
6
Brodick NTS

Merkland Point

Brodick Bay

Strathwhillan

odick

Corriegills

4

105

Clauchlands Point

Lamlash

3
Margnaheglish

Lamlash Bay

Cordon

Holy Island

A841
4

Auchencairn

Kingscross

Knockenkelly

Whiting Bay

Whiting Bay

Glen Ashdale

Largymore

Largybeg

Dippen

ncorroch

Dippen Head

Kildonan

2
Pladda

105

0
Ailsa Craig

9

FIRTH

OF

CLYDE

Brodick-Ardrossan

V

Horse Isle

Ardrossan

Saltcoats

Irvine Bay

0

| 0 | 1 | 2 | 3 | 4 | 5 miles |

| 0 | 1 | 2 | 3 | 4 | 5 | 6 | 7 kilometres |

Heads of Ayr
Farm Park

Fisherton

Dunure

Drumshang

Croy Brae (Electric Brae)

Knoweside

Culzean Bay

Culzean Castle NTS

22 A719

Maidenhead Bay

1

Maidens

Pennyglen

Whitefaulds

Turnberry

12

Kirkoswald

Souter Johnnie's Cottage NTS

Turnberry

A77

Turnberry Bay

Crossraguel

Dipple

Roan of Craigoch

Wallacetown

Kilgrammie

Old Dailly

Dailly

Water of Girvan

B741

Penkill

0

Girvan

Dounepark

B734

Woodland

Pinminnoch

Tormitchell

C

Pinmore

297
GREY HILL

A714

8

13

A77

Lendalfoot

Bennane Head

9

1

Colmonell

9

B734

Pinwherry

2

River Stinchar

Muck Water

98

A78
Kilwinning

Fergushill

Torranyard

Montgreenan

A736

Eglinton

Cunninghamhead

Kilmaur

B785

Stevenston

Girdle Toll

Berceton

A78

Ardeer

Bankhead

Springside

Kr

Irvine

Maritime

Dreghorn

B7081

Crosshous

Fullarton

A71

A759

Drybridge

Gateheed

Gailes

A

Kinfold

A759

Dundonald

B7036

Barassie

12

Loans

Symington

He

A759

Helento

Troon

A78

12

Royal Troon

Monkton

A77

Prestwick

A719

A79

Prestwick

Mossblo

New Prestwick

Whitletts

St Quivox

Annban

B743

Ayr Bay

A719

Ayr

Wallacetown

River Ayr

B744

Ga

Belmont

A719

6

Doonfoot

Alloway

Burns Monument

A77

Doonholm

B7024

A713

Ma

Burns Cottage

Culroy

Minishant

9

B7034

Dalrymple

B7034

Ho

B742

Grimmet

Guiltreehill

Maybole

Kirkmichael

B7023

B7045

Threave

B7023

Crosshill

B741

Straito

NX

429
GARLEFFIN FELL

Linfern Loch

Dalquhairn

River Stinchar

Knockeen

Balloch

A

Barr

R

R

I

549
POLMADDIE HILL

SHALLOCH

Balligmorrie

3

4

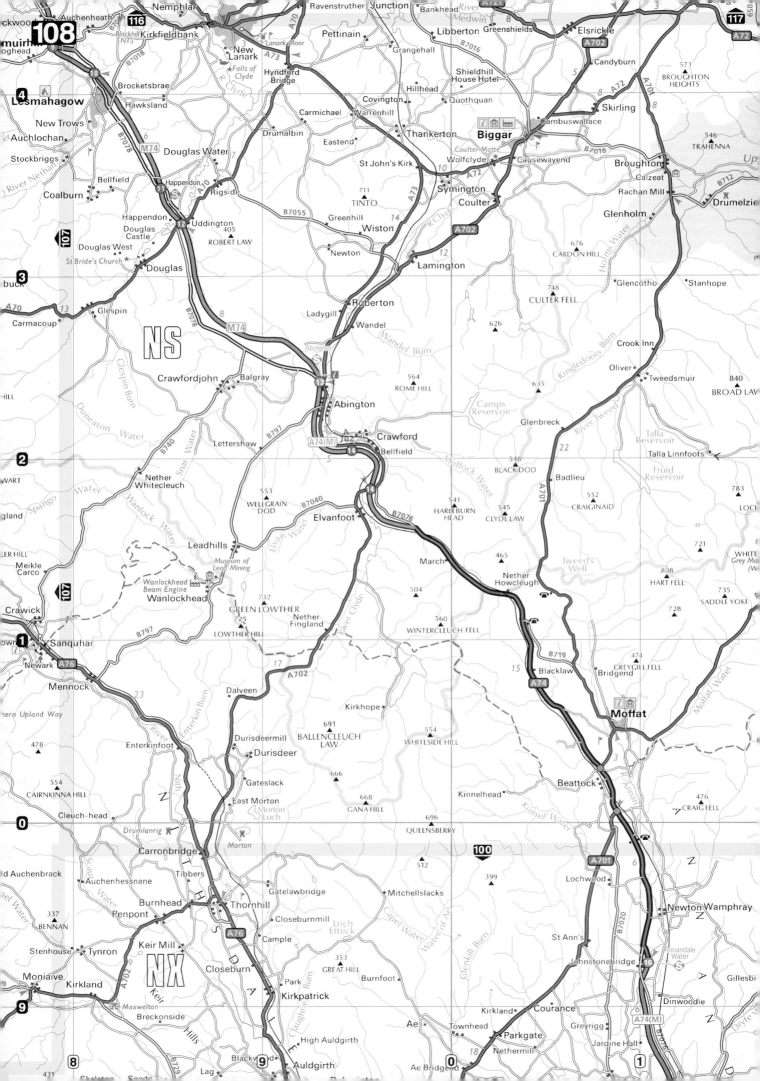

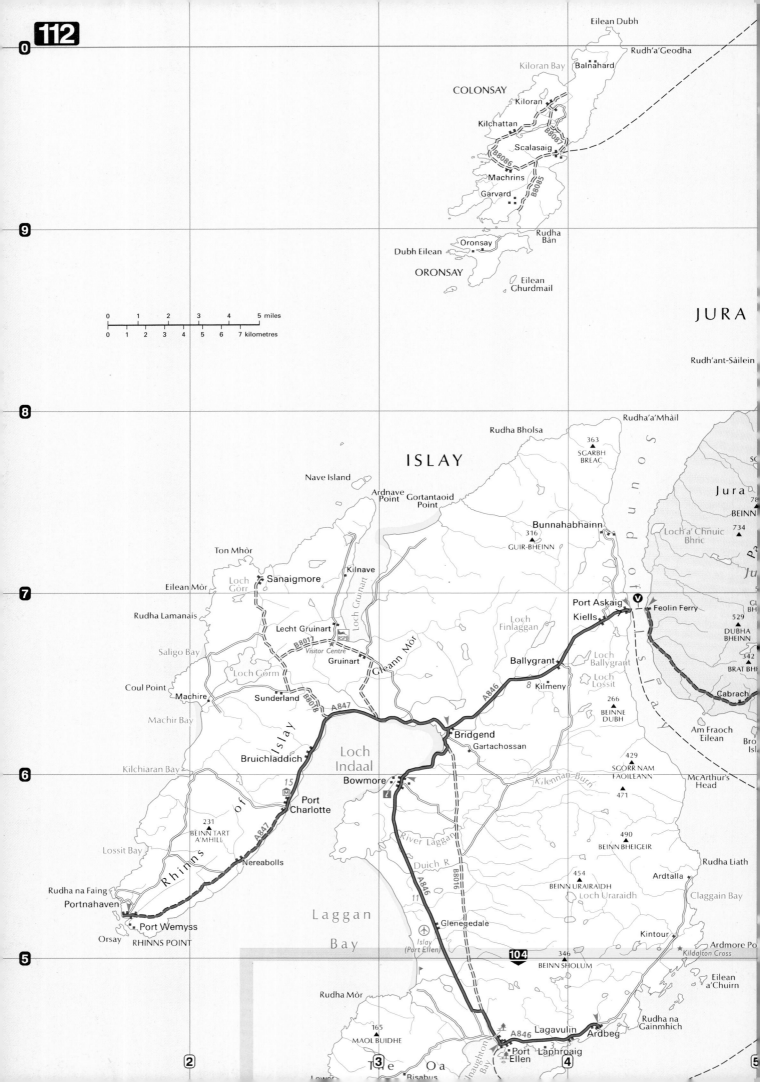

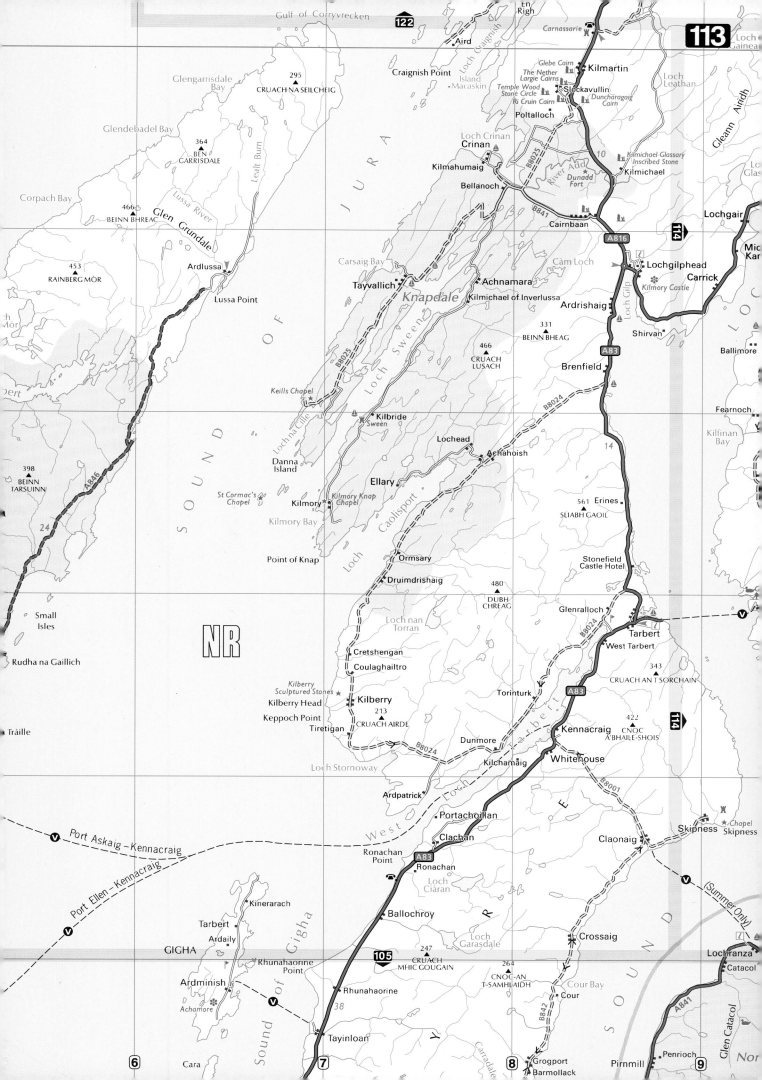

Gulf of Corryvrecken

En
Righ

Loch Craignish

Carnassarie

Aird

Loch
Caineal

Craignish Point

Island
Macaskin

Glebe Cairn
The Nether
Largie Cairns
Temple Wood
Stone Circle
Ri Cruin Cairn

Kilmartin

Slockavullin
Duncharagaig
Cairn

Poltalloch

Loch
Leathan

Glengarrisdale
Bay

295
CRUACH NA SEILCHEIG

Glendebadel Bay

364
BEN
GARRISDALE

Loch Crinan

Crinan

Kilmahumaig

Bellanoch

River Add

Dunadd
Fort

B8025

10

Kilmichael Glassary
Inscribed Stone

Kilmichael

Gleann Airidh

Loch
Glas

Corpach Bay

Lussa River

466
BEINN BHREAC

Glen Grundale

Ardlussa

B841

Cairnbaan

A816

114

Lochgair

453
RAINBERG MÒR

Lussa Point

Càm Loch

Lochgilphead

Carrick

Mic
Kar

Carsaig Bay

Tayvallich

Knapdale

Achnamara

Kilmichael of Inverlussa

Ardrishaig

Kilmory Castle

B8025

Loch Sween

331
BEINN BHEAG

Loch Gilp

A83

Shirvan

Ballimore

398
BEINN
TARSUINN

24

A846

Keills Chapel

Kilbride
Sween

Lochead

Achahoish

Brenfield

B8024

14

Fearnoch

Kilfinan
Bay

Danna
Island

Ellary

St Cormac's
Chapel

Kilmory Knap
Chapel

Caolisport

561 Erines
SLIABH GAOIL

Kilmory

Kilmory Bay

Ormsary

Stonefield
Castle Hotel

NR

Point of Knap

Druimdrishaig

480
DUBH
CHREAG

Glenralloch

B8024

Small
Isles

Loch nan
Torran

Tarbert

West Tarbert

343
CRUACH AN T SORCHAIN

Rudha na Gaillich

Cretshengan

Coulaghailtro

Torinturk

114

Kilberry
Sculptured Stones
Kilberry Head
Keppoch Point
Tiretigan

Kilberry

213
CRUACH AIRDE

A83

Dunmore

Kennacraig

422
CNOC
A'BHAILE-SHOIS

Tràille

B8024

Kilchamaig

Whitehouse

Loch Stornoway

Loch Tarbert

Ardpatrick

West

Port Askaig – Kennacraig

Portachoillan

Clachan

B8001

Skipness

Chapel
Skipness

Ronachan
Point

A83

Ronachan

Claonaig

Port Ellen – Kennacraig

Loch
Cìaran

(Summer Only)

Kinerarach

Ballochroy

Loch
Garasdale

Crossaig

Lochranza

Tarbert

Ardaily

GIGHA

Rhunahaorine
Point

105

247
CRUACH
MHIC GOUGAIN

264
CNOC-AN
T-SAMHLAIDH

Cour Bay

Catacol

Ardminish

Achamore

Sound of Gigha

Rhunahaorine

38

A83

Cour

B842

A841

Glen Catacol

Nor

6

Cara

7

Tayinloan

8

Grogport

Barmollack

Pirnmill

Penrioch

9

Sound

Of Loch

Of Jura

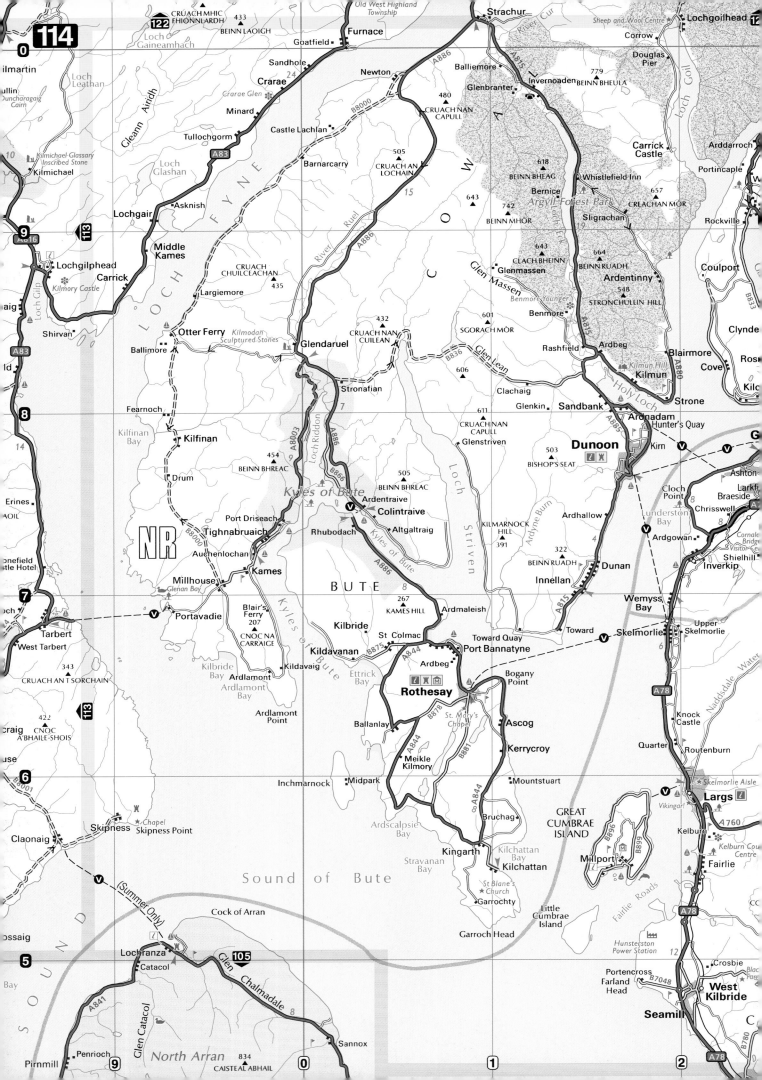

0   1   2   3   4   5 miles
0   1   2   3   4   5   6   7 kilometres

NU

ar

oxburn
650   Barns Ness
        East Barns
            Chapel Point
        Skateraw
12   Torness Power Station
        Thorntonloch
Innerwick   Crowhill
                    Reed Point
319   Dunglass   Cove   Pease
COCKLAW HILL   Collegiate   Bay   Siccar Point   Fast Castle Head
Oldhamstocks   Church
                Cockburnspath
391   St ABB'S HEAD
HEART LAW   196
            Ecclaw   BROWN RIG   St Abbs
                Southern
                Upland Way   Coldingham Bay
            Grantshouse   Coldingham
                                                            Eyemouth
        Butterdean   21   Houndwood   22
        Quixwood   Heugh Head   Cairncross
                            262
Abbey St Bathans   Edin's   HORSELEY HILL   B6438   Reston
                    Hall Broch   14   Ayton   A1
Ellemford   Auchencrow   Burnmouth
            325
chester   COCKBURN
E R M I R   LAW   Marygold
            B6355   Marshall Meadows Bay
Primrosehill   Lintlaw   B6437   Lamberton   North Northumberland
            Preston   Chirnside   B6355   Heritage Coast
        Cumledge   A1
TON   Duns Castle   Edrom   15   Foulden   Tithe Barn   1333
LAW   Church   Chirnsidebridge   Whiteadder   A6105
            Manderston   Broadhaugh   Edington   Water   Barracks
        Duns   Allanton   Hutton   Town Ramparts
Gavinton   Blackadder   Paxton   B6461   Berwick-upon-Tweed
B6456   Sinclair's   Blackadder   Sunwick   Fishwick   Paxton   Tweedmouth
        Nisbet   Hill   Whitsome   Hilton   Loanend   East   Spittal
Polwarth   Hill   13   Ord   Huds Head
110   Fogo   Scremerston
7   6   B6461   Horndean   Murton   111   Unthank
Greenlaw   Charterhall   Ladykirk   Norham   Thornton
A6105   Forgorig   Swinton   Upsettlington   West Allerdean   Cheswick
        Simprim   Ladykirk   Shoreswood   Ancroft   Goswick
11   Ho.   Grindon   0   A1
8   9   Shellacres   Felkington   Haggerston
10   Leitholm

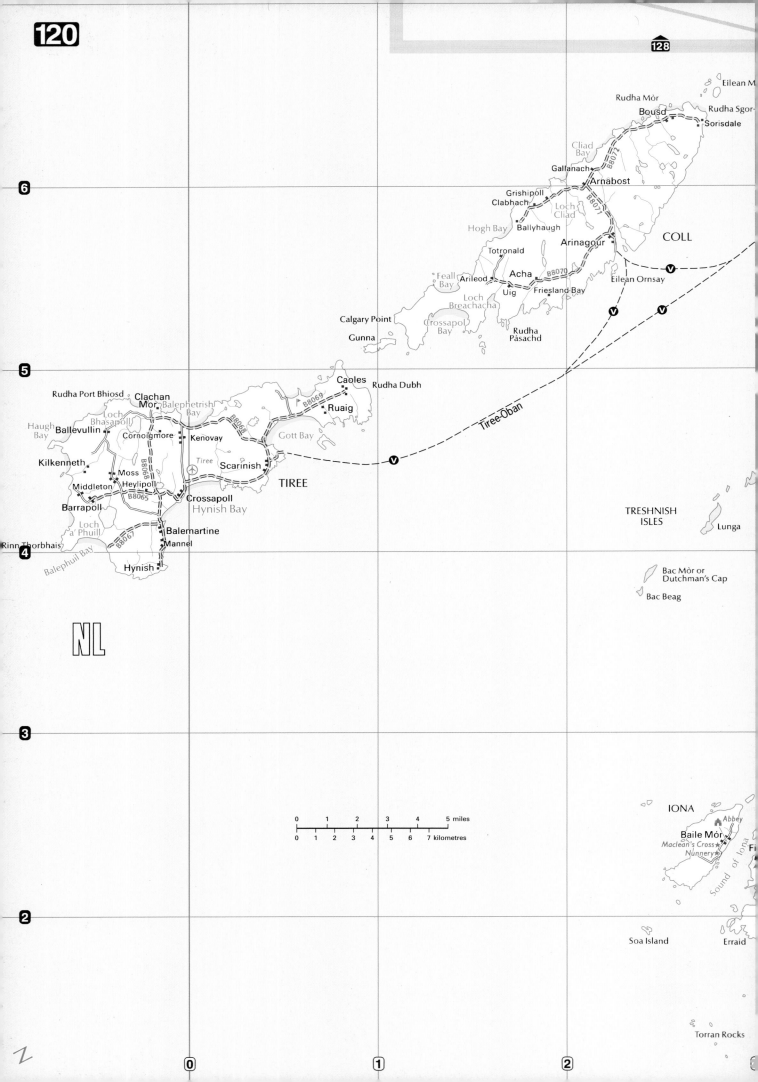

128

Eilean M
Rudha Mòr
Bousd
Rudha Sgor-
Sorisdale
Cliad
Bay
Gallanach
Arnabost
COLL
Grishipoll
Clabhach
Loch
Cliad
Hogh Bay
Ballyhaugh
Arinagour
Totronald
Acha
B8070
Arileod
Uig
Friesland Bay
Eilean Ornsay
Feall
Bay
Loch
Breachacha
Calgary Point
Crossapol
Bay
Rudha
Pàsachd
Gunna

Caoles
Rudha Dubh
Rudha Port Bhiosd
Clachan
Mòr
Balephetrish
Bay
B8069
Ruaig
Loch
Bhasapoll
B8068
Tiree-Oban
Haugh
Bay
Ballevullin
Cornaigmore
Kenovay
Gott Bay
Kilkenneth
Tiree
Scarinish
TIREE
TRESHNISH
ISLES
B8068
Moss
Lunga
Middleton
Heylipoll
Crossapoll
B8065
Barrapoll
Hynish Bay

Loch
a' Phuill
Balemartine
Bac Mòr or
Dutchman's Cap
Rinn Thorbhais
B8067
Mannel
Bac Beag
Balephuil Bay
Hynish

NL

IONA
Abbey
Baile Mòr
Maclean's Cross
Nunnery
Sound of Iona
Fi

0   1   2   3   4   5 miles
0 1 2 3 4 5 6 7 kilometres

Soa Island
Erraid

Torran Rocks

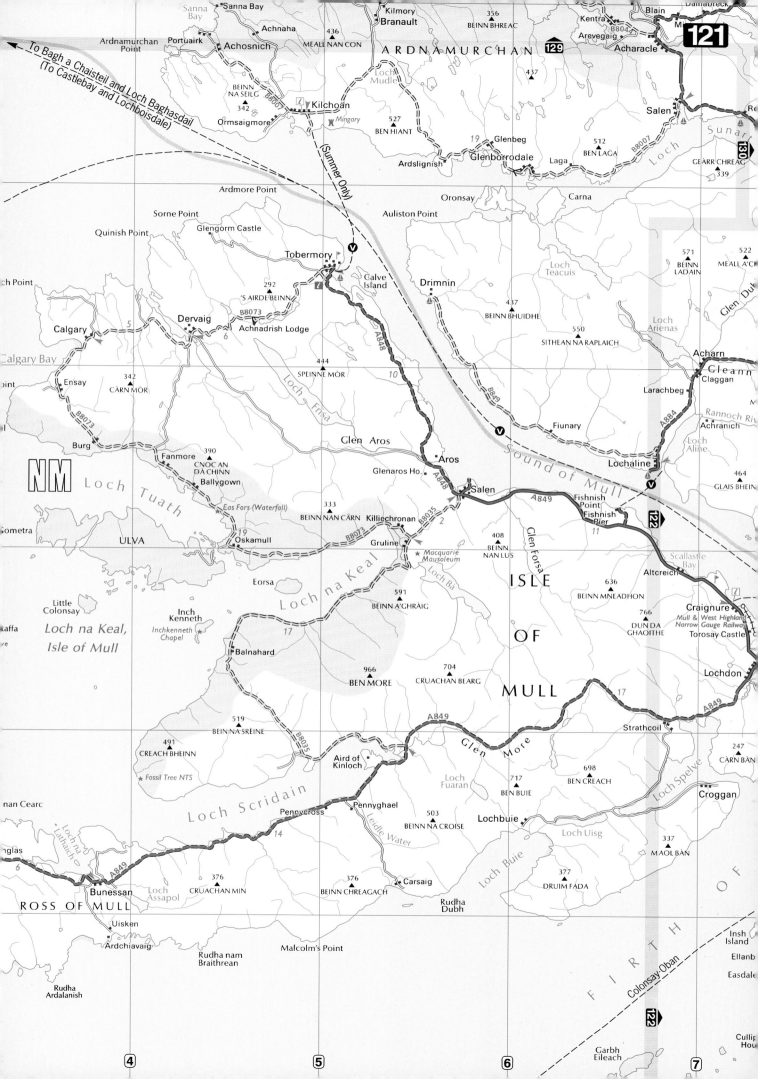

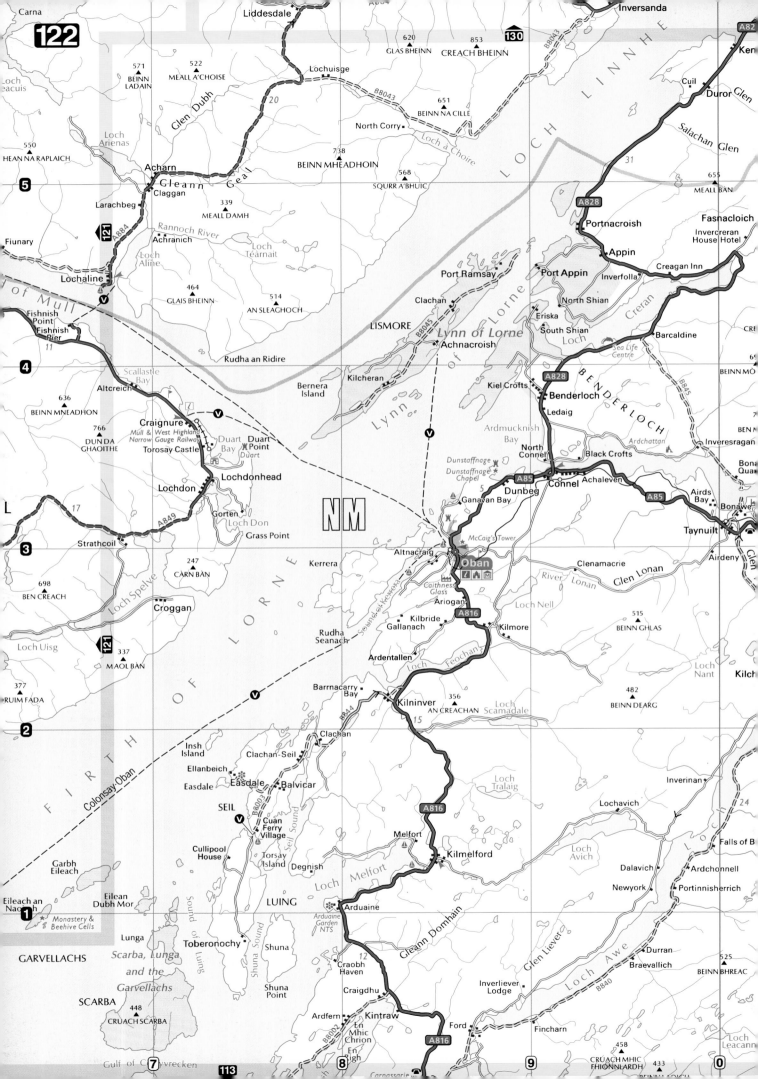

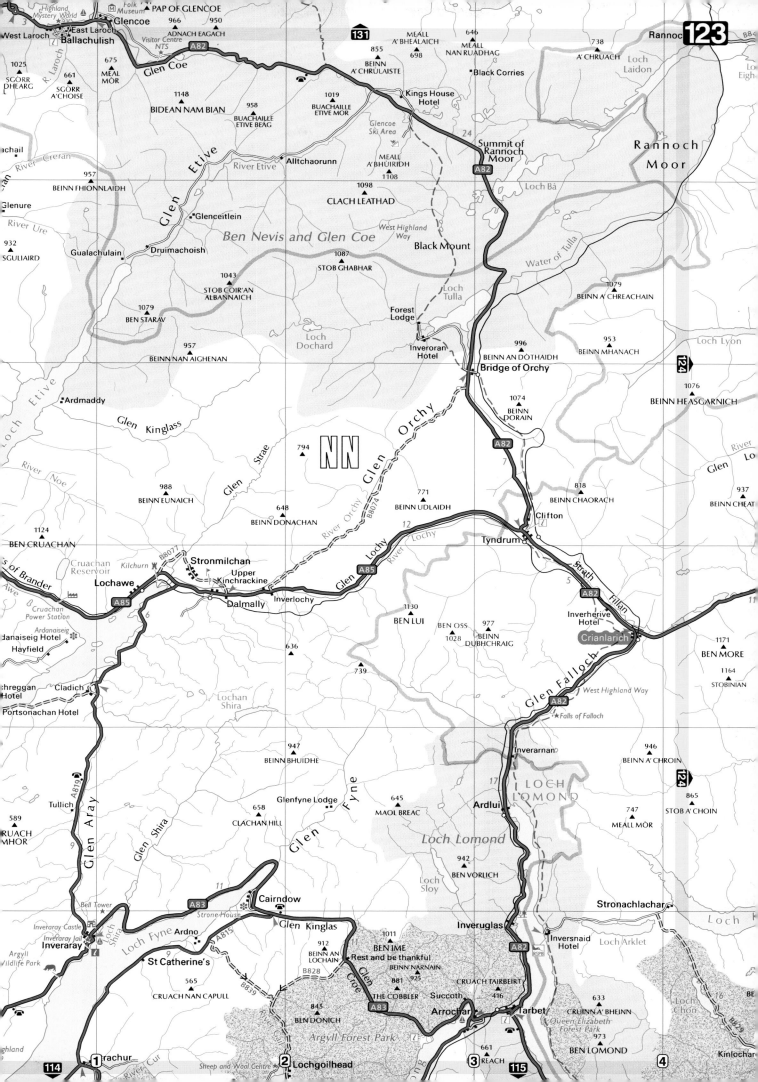

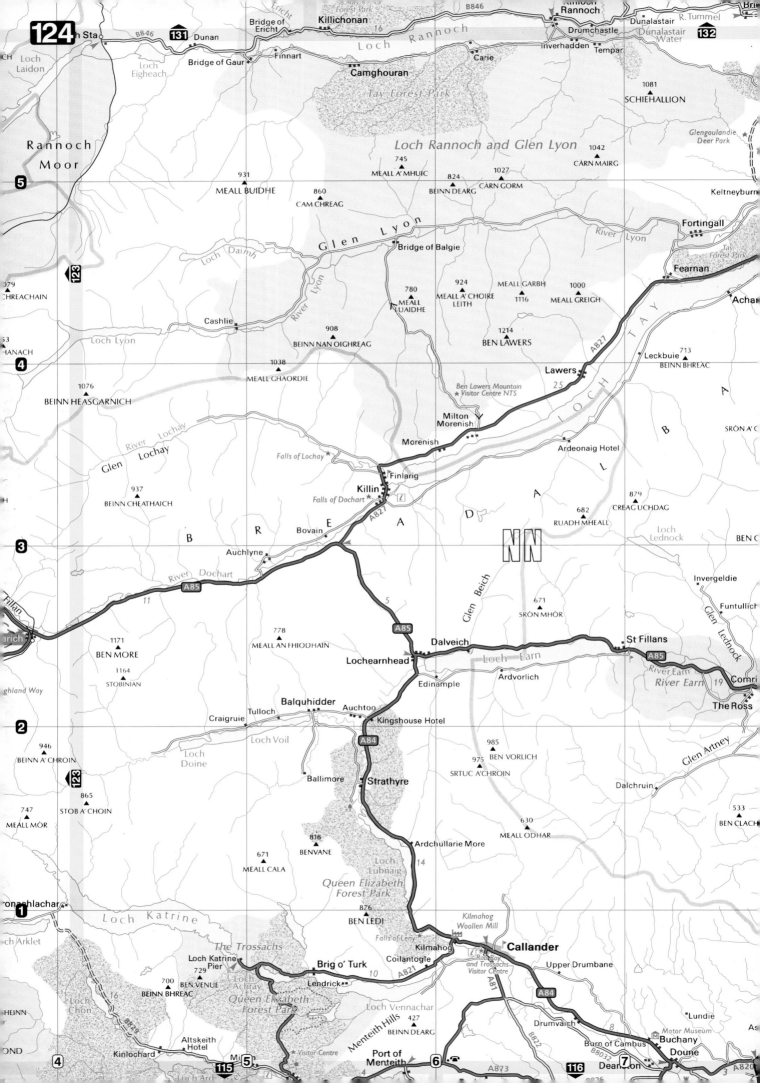

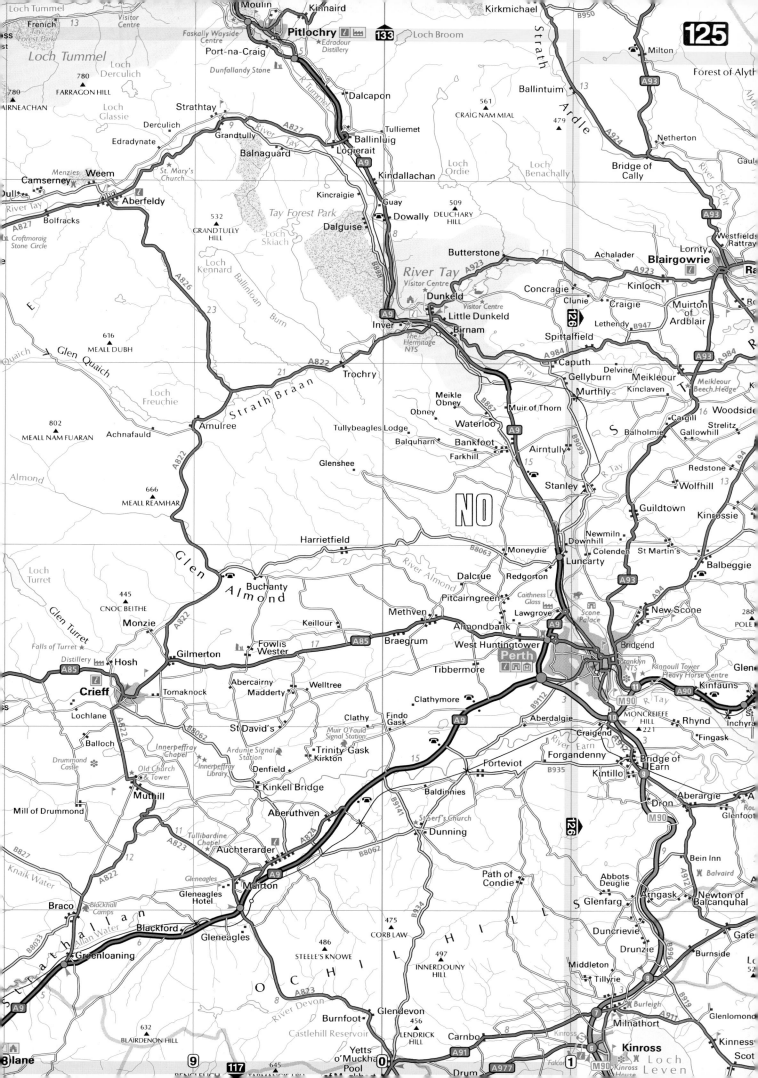

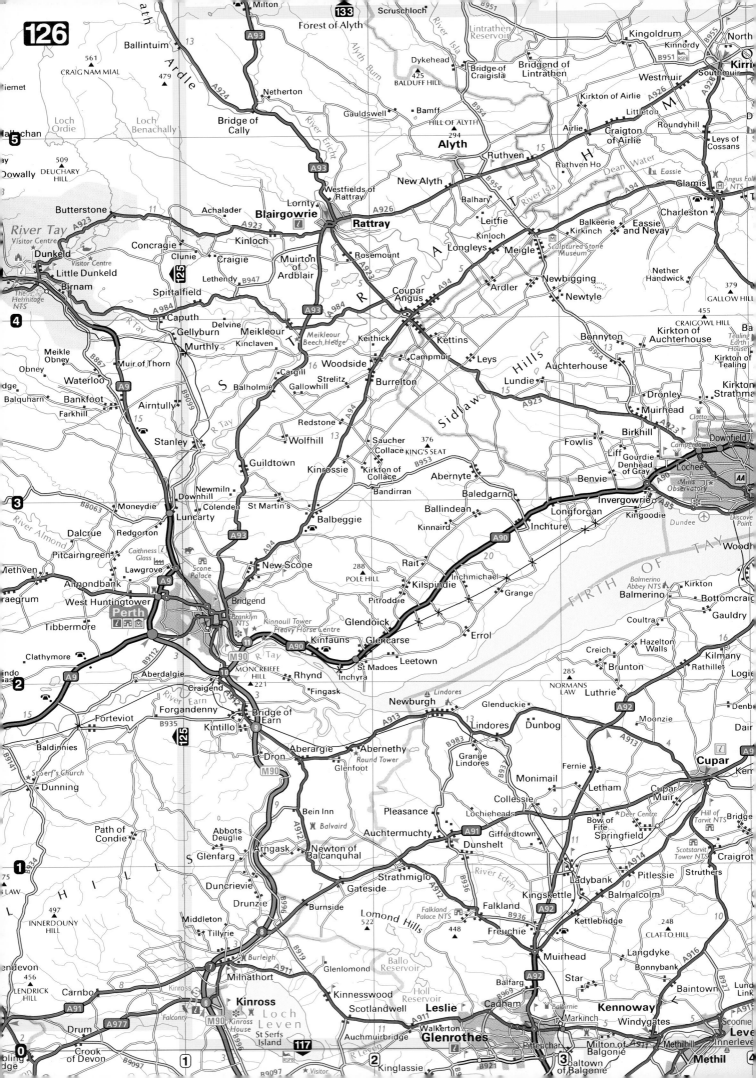

2

Loch Eynort

The Cuillin Hills

974 ▲
SGÙRR A' GHEADAIDH

434 ▲
AN CRUACHIN

Cuillin Hills

Glenbrittle
House

Bualintur

92
BLA

SGÙRR ALASDAIR
1009 ▲

Loch
Coruisk

Loch
Creithe

Cama

Loch Brittle

894 ▲
GARS BHEINN

225 ▲
CEANN NA BEINNE

Rudh'an Dùnain

Soay
Sound

Loch
Scavaig

BEN

Soay Sound

139 ▲
BEINN BHREAC

Mol-chlach

SOAY

Rudh' Aonghais

1

CUILLIN

NG

CANNA

210 ▲
CÀRN A' GHAILL

A'Chill

Garrisdale Point

Canna Harbour

Sanday

Sound of Canna

Rudha Shamhnan
Insir

SOUND

0

Oigh-sgeir

A Bhrideanach

570 ▲
ORVAL

302 ▲
MULLACH MÒR

Kinloch

Rudha na Roinne

Loch
Scresort

810 ▲
ASKIVAL

RUM

763 ▲
SGÙRR NAN
GILLEAN

The Small Isles

Rudha nam Meirleach

Sound of Rum

9

Bay of
Laig

Cleadale

EIGG

Rudha an
Fhasaidh

Laig

299 ▲
AN
CRUACHAN

Sandavore

393 ▲
AN SGÙRR

Kildonnan

Galmisdale

Eilean
Chathastail

Sound of Eigg

Eilean
nan Each

MUCK

Port Mor

0 1 2 3 4 5 miles

0 1 2 3 4 5 6 7 kilometres

8

7

Sanna Point

Sanna
Bay

Sanna Bay

Ock

Achnaha

Portuairk

436 ▲
MEALL NAN CON

B

Ardnamurchan
Point

Achosnich

Lo
Mu

To Bagh a Chaisteil
(To Castleb–

Eilean Mòr

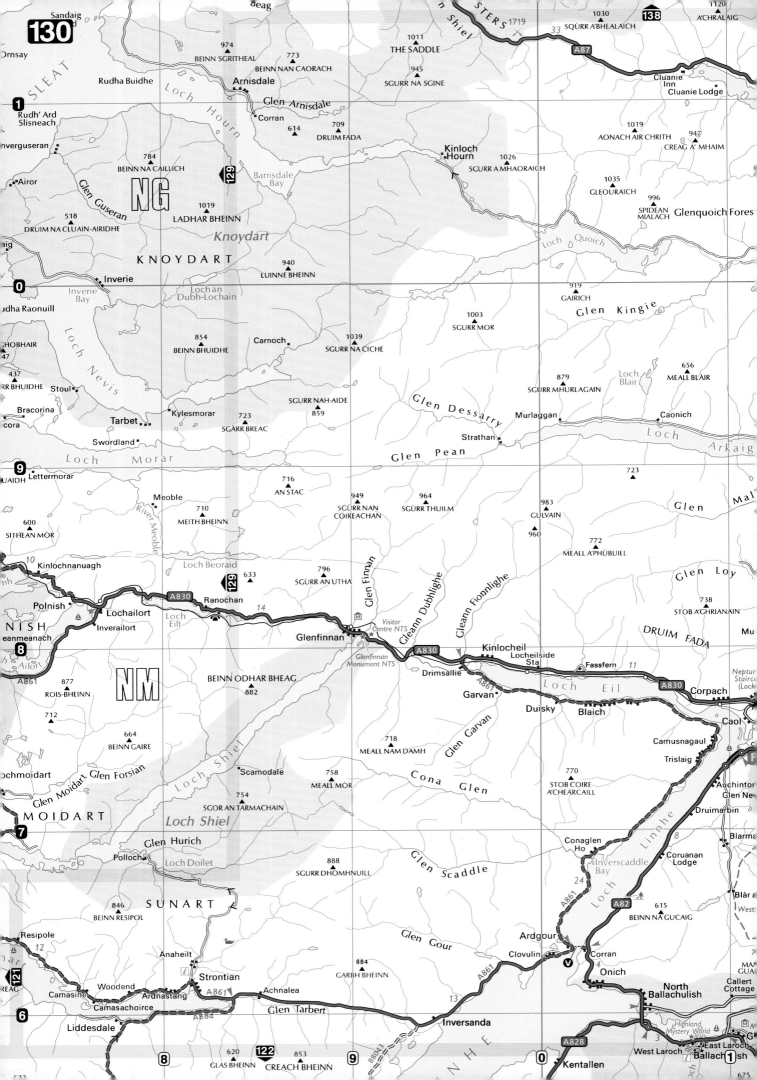

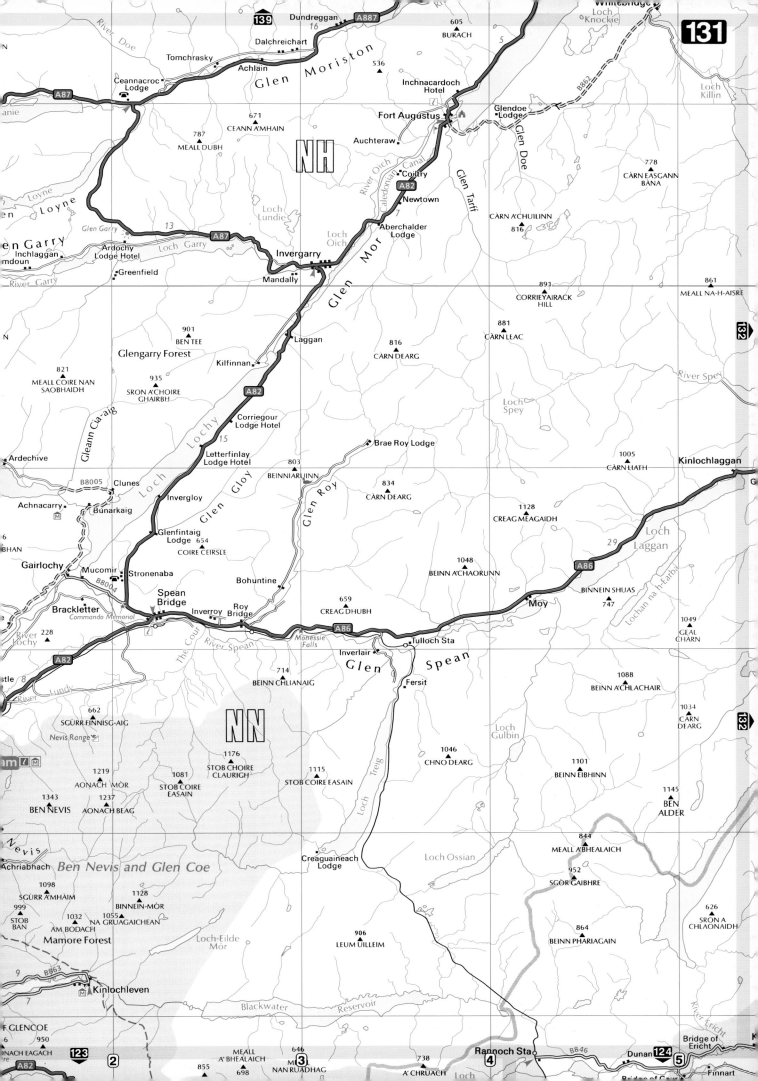

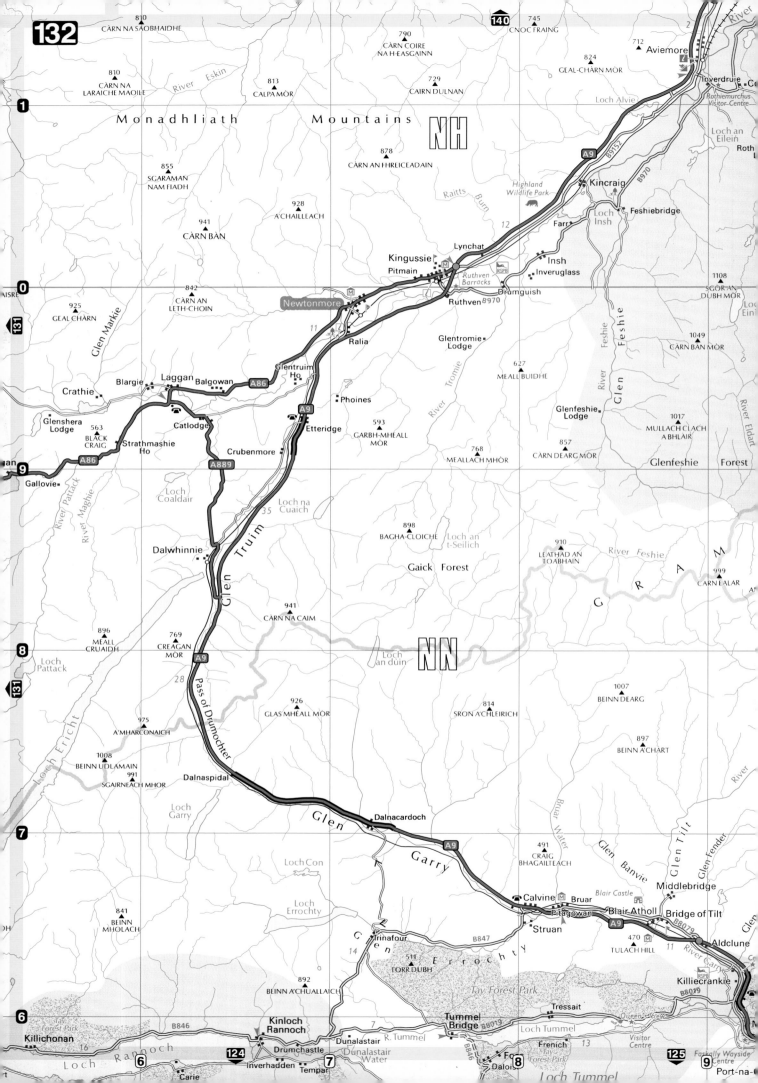

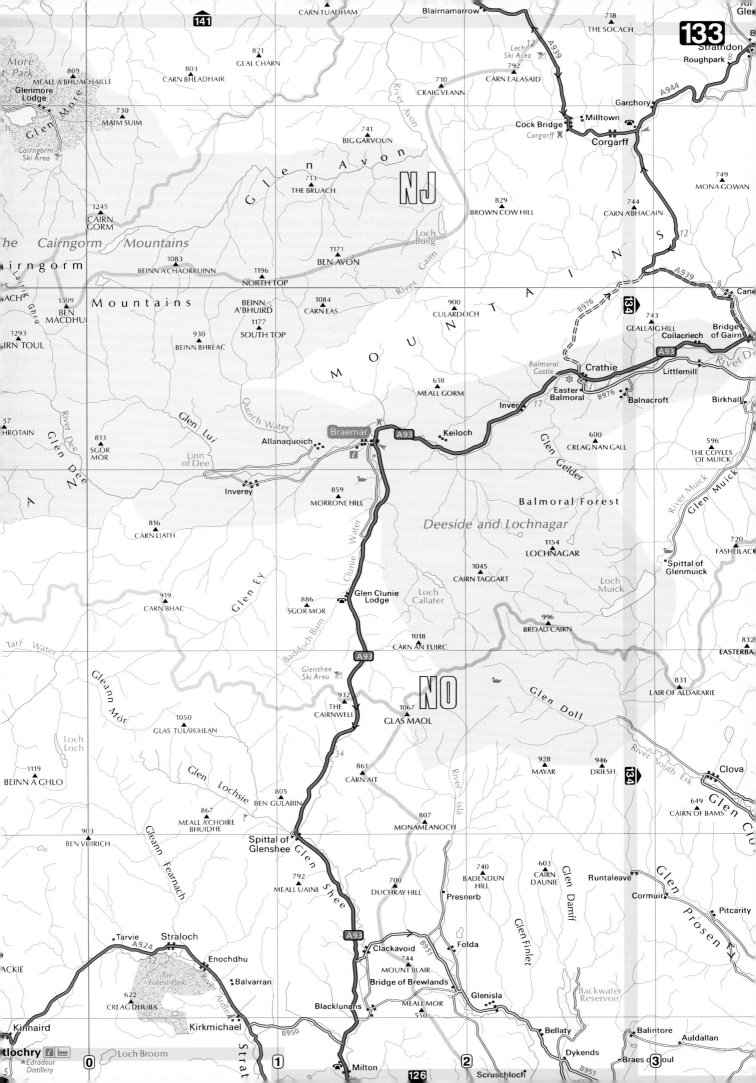

CÀRN TUADHAM
Blairnamarrow
718
THE SOCACH
Strathdon
Roughpark
8

A939

821
GEAL CHARN
803
CARN BHEADHAIR

Lecht
Ski Area
792
710
CARN EALASAID
CRAIG VEANN

Garchory
A944
Milltown
Cock Bridge
Corgarff
Corgarff

749
MONA GOWAN

More
t· Park
MEALL A'BHUACHAILLE
809
Glenmore
Lodge
730
MAIM SUIM

741
BIG GARVOUN

Glen Avon

NJ

A939

744
CARN A'BHACAIN

Cairngorm
Ski Area

713
THE BRUACH

829
BROWN COW HILL

1245
CAIRN
GORM

Loch
Builg

The Cairngorm Mountains

River
Cairn

B976
134

743
GEALLAIG HILL
Coilacriech
Bridge
of Gairn
Can

Mountains

1083
BEINN A'CHAORRUINN
1196
NORTH TOP

1171
BEN AVON

River

900
CULARDOCH

A93

Littlemill

River D

1309
BEN
MACDHUI

BEINN
A'BHUIRD
1084
CÀRN EAS

M
O
U
N
T
A
I
N
S

Balmoral
Castle
Crathie

IRN TOUL
1293

930
BEINN BHREAC
1177
SOUTH TOP

618
MEALL GORM

Easter
Balmoral
B976
Balnacroft
Birkhall

57
HROTAIN

Inver
17

Glen Dee

813
SGOR
MÒR

Quoich Water

Braemar
A93
Keiloch

Glen Gelder

600
CREAG NAN GALL

596
THE COYLES
OF MUICK

Glen Lui

Allanaquoich

River Muick

Glen Muick

Linn
of Dee

859
MORRONE HILL

Balmoral Forest

River Dee

Inverey

Deeside and Lochnagar

720
FASHEILAC

816
CÀRN LIATH

1154
LOCHNAGAR

Spittal of
Glenmuick

919
CARN BHAC

886
SGOR MOR

Glen Clunie
Lodge

Loch
Callater

1045
CAIRN TAGGART

Loch
Muick

Glen Ey

Clunie Water

996
BROAD CAIRN

832
EASTERBA

Tarf Water

Badenloch Burn

1018
CÀRN AN TUIRC

831
LAIR OF ALDARARIE

Gleann Mòr

Glenshee
Ski Area
A93

NO

Glen Doll

Loch
Loch

1050
GLAS TULAICHEAN

932
THE
CAIRNWELL

1067
GLAS MAOL

River South Esk

134

1119
BEINN A GHLO

Glen Lochsie

861
CÀRN AIT

928
MAYAR

946
DRIESH

Clova

867
MEALL A'CHOIRE
BHUIDHE

805
BEN GULABIN

River Isla

649
CAIRN OF BAMS

903
BEN VUIRICH

807
MONAMEANOCH

Glen Clo

Gleann Fearnach

Spittal of
Glenshee

740
BADENDUN
HILL

603
CAIRN
DAUNIE

Runtaleave

Glen Prosen

Glen Damff

Glen Shee

Glen Finlet

Cormuir

Tarvie
A924
Straloch
Enochdhu

792
MEALL UAINE

700
DUCHRAY HILL

Presnerb

Pitcarity

ACKIE

Tay
Forest
Park

River Ardle

River Ardle

A93

Clackavoid
B951
Folda

744
MOUNT BLAIR

Glenisla

Backwater
Reservoir

Balintore
Auldallan

622
CREAG DHUBA

Balvarran

Bridge of Brewlands

MEALL MOR

Bellaty

Kinnaird

Kirkmichael

Blacklunans

550

Dykends

Braes of oul

tlochry
Edradour
Distillery

Loch Broom

B950

Milton

126

Scruschloch

B951

0
1
2
3

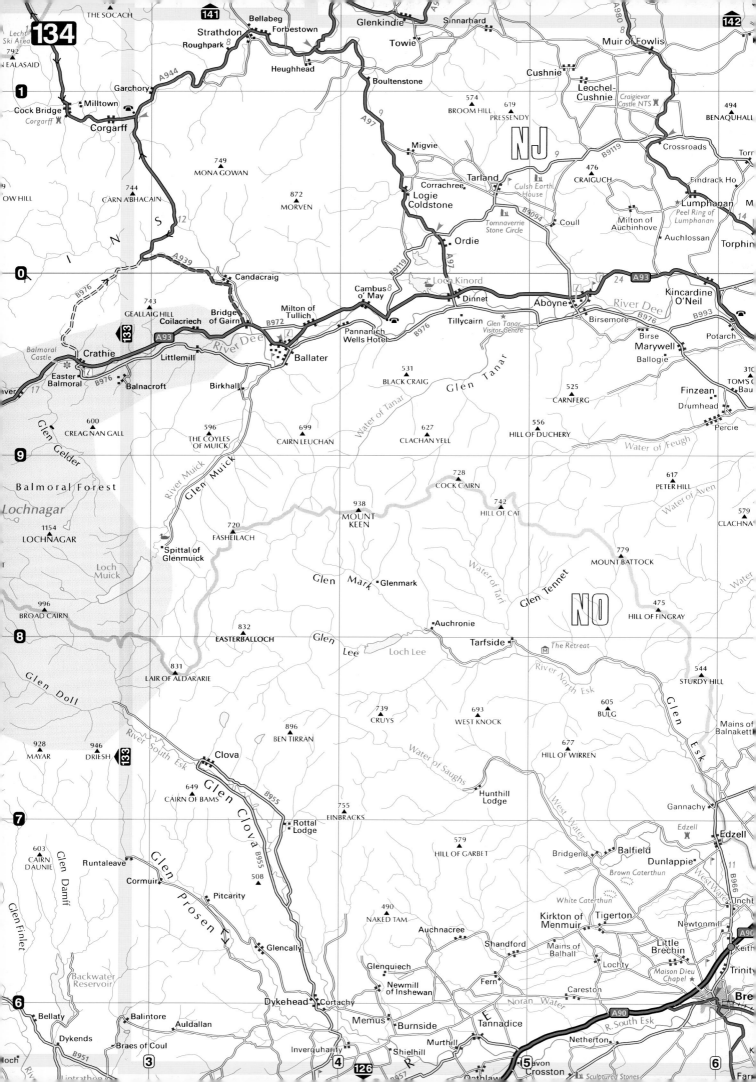

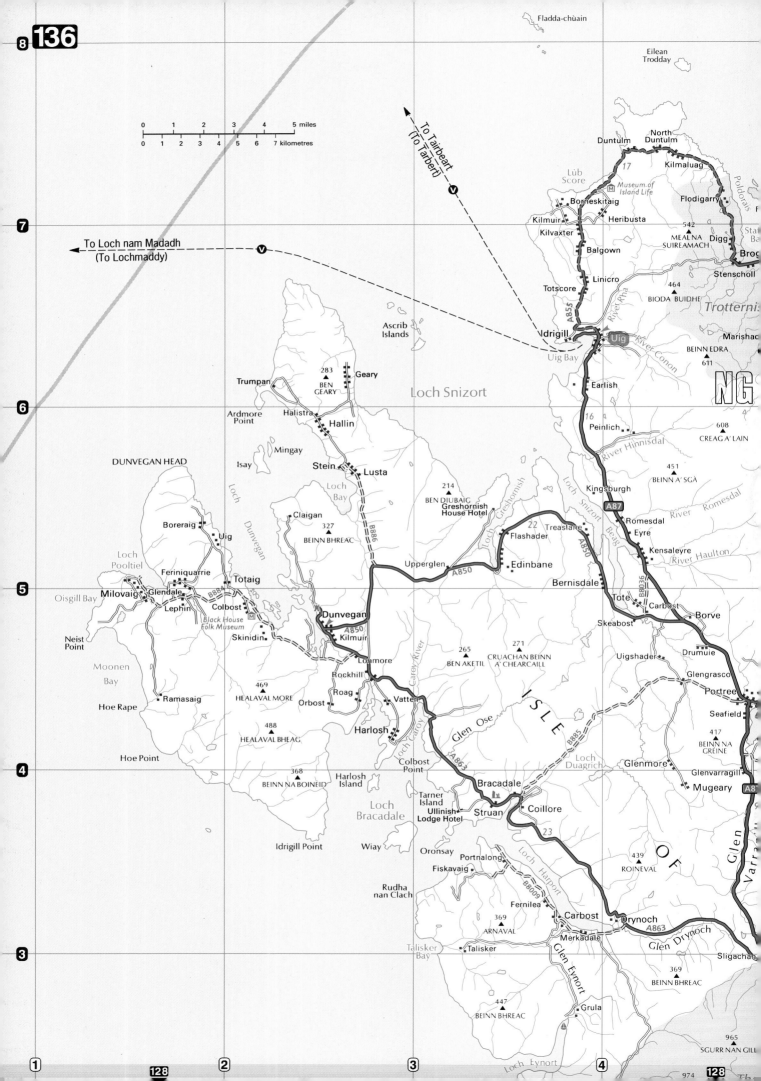

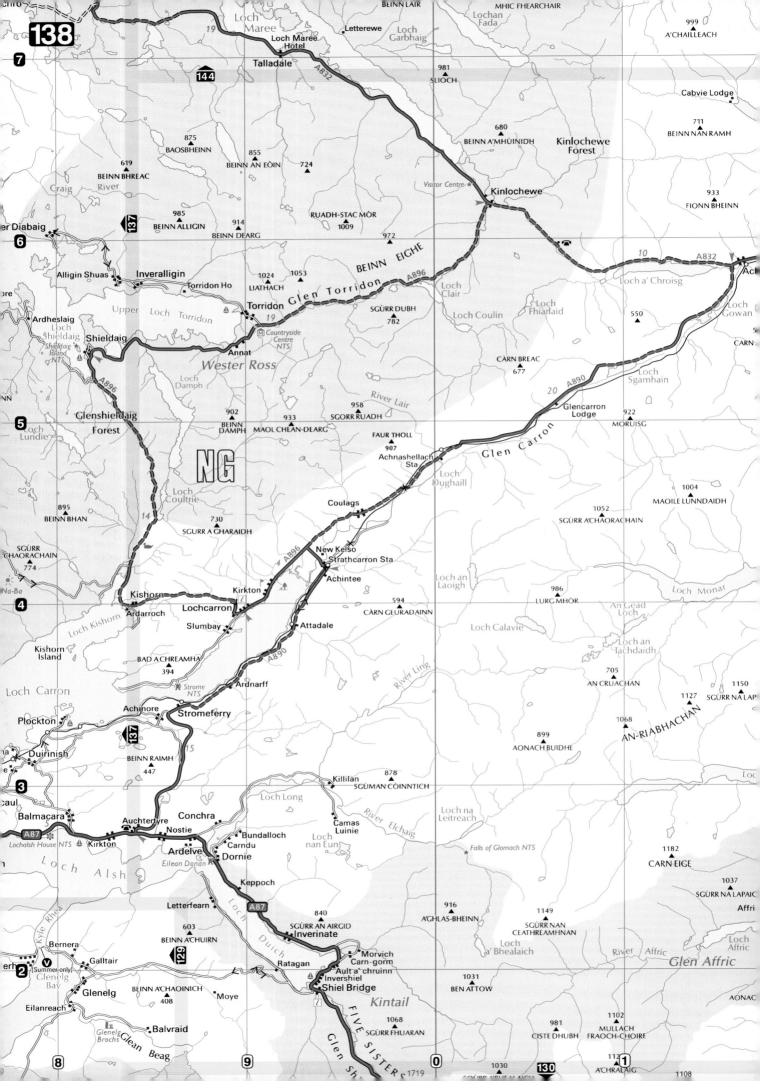

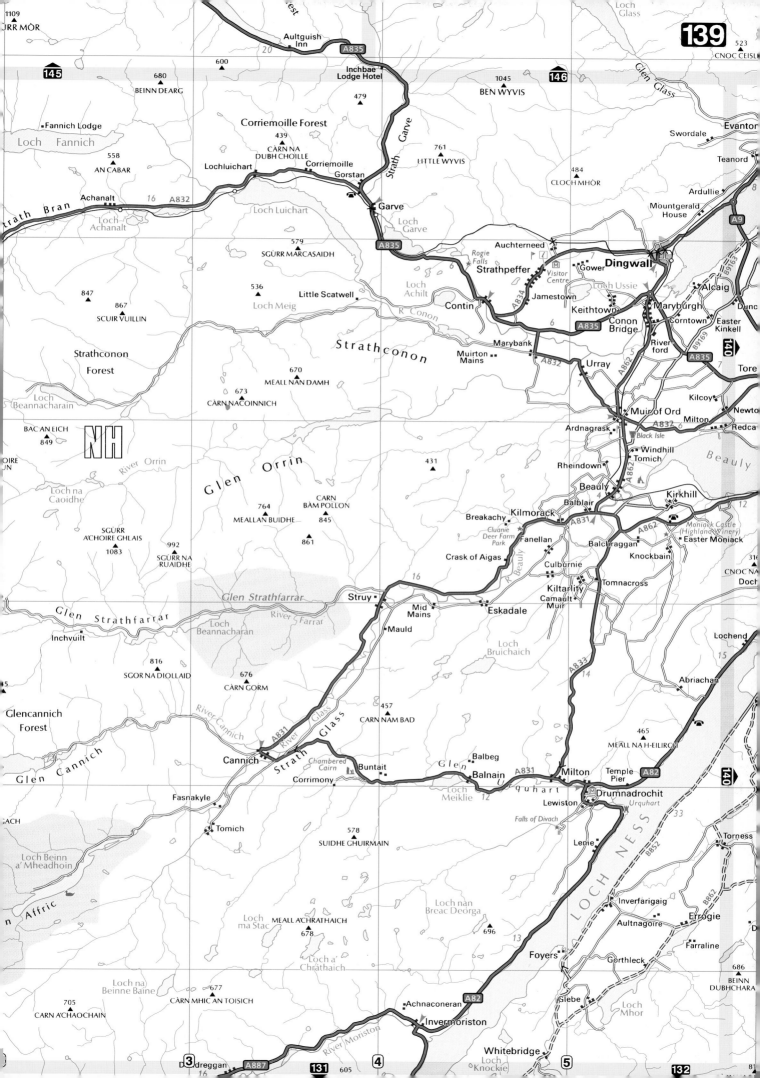

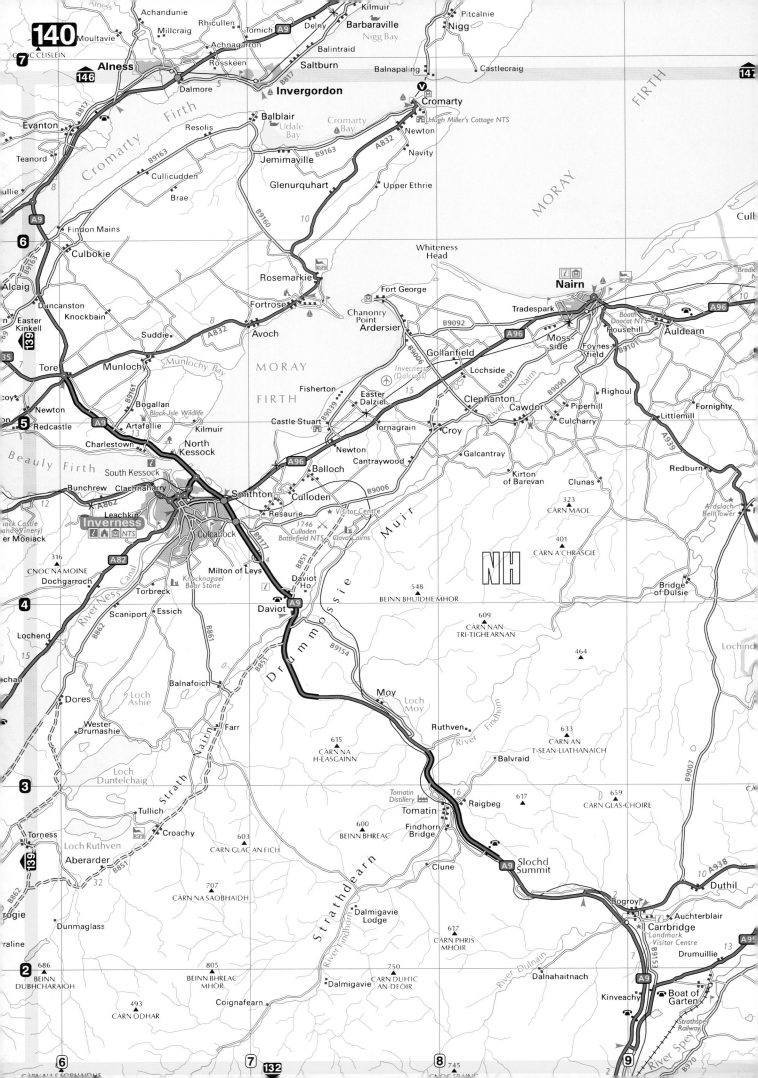

7

Portknockie
Findochty
Portessie
Buckie
Buckpool
Rathven
Cullen
Gullen Bay
Sandend
Sandend Bay
Portsoy
Whitehills
Banff
Banff Bay
Macduff
A98
B9139
Boyndie
Boyndie Bay
Inver-boyndie
A97
Duff House
A947
B9031
Silverfo
Longmanhill
Portgordon
A98
B1990
A98
Lintmill
Tochieneal
Birkenbog
Fordyce
Milton
Deskford
Deskford Church
Berryhillock
Windsele
6
B9022
Ord
Ella
Alvah
9
Gorrachie
Danshillock
11
River Deveron
Cairnfield Ho.
Drybridge
Broadley
Farnachty
Clochan
321 BIN OF CULLEN
272 ADDIE HILL
Craibstone
12
B9018
313 LURG HILL
Cornhill
B9025
B9121
Muirden
Fintr
6
141
264
WHITEASH HILL
Braes of Enzie
301 MILLSTONE HILL
429 KNOCK HILL
Glenbarry
271 WETHER HILL
20
Gordonstown
Lootcherbrae
Aberchirder
B9023
B9025
Turriff
Grange Crossroads
Berryhillock
Bracobrae
Knock
Drumnagorrach
Clunie
Carnousie
8
B9016
Forgie
Aultmore
Forgieside
Newmill
Davoch of Grange
Farmtown
A95
Strath Isla
Bridge of Marnoch
River Deveron
Auchininna
Muiresk
Darra
B9170
How
B9017
Rumbach
5
Strathisla Distillery
Fife Keith
Keith
A92
365 MEIKLE BALLOCH
B9022
Rothiemay
B9117
River Isla
Yonder Bognie
Inverkeithny
Muresk
Darra
osarie
B9014
338 LL OF TOWIE
11
Newtack
Ruthven
Bogniebrae
Forgue
Fortrie
Carlincraig
Pitglassie
Dykeside
B992
Auchterless
Drummuir
B9115
Cairnie
A96
River Deveron
B9001
12
Glendronach Distillery
Drumblair Ho
Balgaveny
NJ
A947
4
20
Invermarkie
Haugh of Glass
A920
Affleck
Drumblade
Drumblair Ho
Gordonstown
17
Fy
Huntly
A97
Brideswell
Badenscoth
Rothiebrisbane
Ythanwells
B992
Bridgend
Thomastown
Newtongarry Croft
Bainshole
Rothienorman
Fisherford
St Kat
Kirkstile
A96
Glens of Foudland
Culsalmond
Rothmaise
Newseat
Folla Rule
Cross o
Jackston
Culdrain
419 WICHACH HILL
466 HILL OF FOUDLAND
Colpy
21
Tocher
A920
Meikle Wartle
525
Gartly
Kirkney
440 CRANSMILL HILL
Largie
Picardy Symbol Stone
Kirkton of Rayne
Loanhead Stone Circle
Davio
Bridgend
18
Leith Hall NTS
564 TAP O'NOTH
A941
Kennethmont
B9002
23
Dunnideer
Pitmachie
Insch
Old Rayne
Hillhead of Durno
Whiteford
B9001
3
Cabrach
Belhinnie
Rhynie
Cottown
Clatt
Duncanstone
Kirkton
20
Oyne
Pitcaple
Pitodrie House Hotel
Maiden Stone
Chapel of Garioch
A96
Port
Elphinsto
141
B9002
722 THE BUCK
St Mary's Kirk
5
Knockespock Ho
Leslie
Auchleven
493 BENNACHIE
518 Mither Tap
Brandsbutt Symbol Stone
Lumsden
484
CORREEN HILLS
475 BRUX HILL
Lethenty
East Aquhorthies Stone Circle
2
632 CREAG AN EUNAN
Mossat
A944
6
Tullynessle
Scotsmill
Keig
River Don
Burnhervie
Pictillum
Kildrummy
Kildrummy
Milltown
Bridge of Alford
Montgarrie
Haughton House
B992
Pitfichie
Monymusk
Kemnay
B994
Belnacraig
Glenbuchat
Alford
Alford Valley Railway
Pitmunie
Whitehouse
Craigearn
Cottow
4
Glenkindie
Sinnarhard
A97
5
134
A980
A944
6
Whitehouse
7

Troup Head
Cullykhan Bay
Crovie
21
Pennan
Aberdour Bay
Protsthonhill
New Aberdour
Netherbrae
BRACKLAMORE HILL
221
New Pitsligo
A98
10
B9031
Boyndlie
Mid Ardlaw
Coburby
Percyhorner
Craigiefold
Peathill
Pittulie
Rosehearty
Sandhaven
Lighthouse
Kinnaird
Fraserburgh
Fraserburgh Bay
Kirktown
Pitblae
Memsie
Memsie Cairn
A90
Rathen
Newburgh
12
WAUGHTON HILL
234
Cairnbulg
Whitelinks Bay
Inverallochy
St Combs
B9033
Crofts of Savoch
Lonmay
Crimonmogate
Crimond
Loch of Strathbeg
RSPB
Rattray Head
Blackhill
18
New Byth
Bonnykelly
B9027
New Deer
mond
estown
13
B9030
Strichen
B9032
A981
A950
5
A981
B9093
New Leeds
Denhead
Leys
Fetterangus
(A92)
Backfolds
Rora
Kirktown
St Fergus
A90
(A952)
B9170
Maud
B9106
Deer Abbey
Dunshillock
Mintlaw
River Ugie
Longside
Inverugie
A950
Buchanhaven
Peterhead
New Deer
A948
Blackhill of Clackriach
Drymuir
Bulwark
Old Deer
Aden Visitor Centre
Stuartfield
B9029
Inverquhomery
Nether Kinmundy
Hillhead of Cocklaw
Peterhead Bay
Maryhill
Slacks of Cairnbanno
Nethermuir
Millbreck
Little Dens
A90
Burnhaven
Millbrex
Knaven
B9030
Kinnadie
Clola
Blackhill
Stirling
Boddam
Buchan Ness
Kirkton
Cottown of Gight
Cairnorrie
Brownhill
Auchnagatt
Inkhorn
12
Kinknockie
Blackhill
Lendrum Terrace
B9005
nty
ead
Haddo
Methlick
Coldwells
Muirtack
14
Hatton
Auchiries
Longhaven
Bullers of Buchan
A852
North Haven
Slains
Haddo House NTS
14
B9005
R Ythan
Ythanbank
Arthrath
A948
A952
(A92)
17
Bogbrae
Cruden Bay
Bartho! Chapel
Earlsford
Auchedly
Wedderlairs
Altar Tomb of William Forbes
Ythsie
Kinharrachie
Birness
Artrochie
Chapel Hill
A975
Whinnyfold
The Skares
Bay of Cruden
Tulloch
Tarves
B9170
Craigdam
Ellon
Esslemont
Kirkton of Logie Buchan
Collieston
Kirktown of Slains
Tolquhon
Pitmedden Garden NTS
A920
Pitmedden
B9000
32
rum
ktown Bourtie
Carnbrogie
Udny Green
Logierieve
Housieside
(A92)
Newburgh
Udny Station
B999
A90
Whiterashes
Woodland
Pettymuk
Cultercullen
Foveran
A947
Nether Crimond
Tillygreig
ie
B993
Straloch
Reisque
Causeyend
Delfrigs
17
Kinmuck
Church
Newmachar
A90
Balmedie
B979
Whitecairns
Belhelvie
Kinmundy
B977
Hatton of Fintray
18
B977
Dyce Symbol Stones
B997
Parkhill
Overton
Potterton
B999
Blackdog
135
9
0
1
Dyce

0 1 2 3 4 5 miles
0 1 2 3 4 5 6 7 kilometres

NK

2

1

0

9

8

7

NB

NG

To Steornabhagh (Stornoway)

Rhu Coigach

Rhu More
Reiff
Achnahaird

Eilean
Mullagrach

Altandhu

Isle Ristol

Polbai

Glas-leac Mòr

SUMMER ISLES

Tanera
Beg

Badentarb
Bay

Tanera More

Horse
Island

Glas-leac
Beag

Eilean
Dubh

Priest
Island

Greenstone Point

Cailleach Head

Rudha Beag

Mellon
Udrigle

Stattic Point

Scoraig

Gruinard
Island

Badluachrach

Little

Foura

Mellon
Charles

Laide

Gruinard Bay

A832

Rudha
Reidh

Cove

Ormiscaig

Badca

B8057

Aultbea

Gruinard

A832

Badca

296
AN CUAIDH

Little Gruinard River

Gruinard River

Gàir

Melvaig

Isle of Ewe

347
CREAG-MHEAL BEAG

Aultgrishin

Loch Ewe

Loch
Fada

293
CNOC BREAC

Inverasdale

Naast

250
MEALL NA MEINE

681
BEINN A'
CHAISGEIN BEAG

Inverewe
Garden NTS

13

North Erradale

Londubh

B8021

Poolewe

Wester Ross

Big Sand

A832

Fionn
Loch

Dubh
Loch

Longa Island

Strath
Smithstown

791
BEINN
AIRIDH CHARR

Lonemore

Heritage
Museum

Loch
Gairloch

Gairloch

Auchtercairn

421
MEALL AN DOIREIN

Eilean
Horrisdale

Charlestown

859
BEINN LÀIR

Port
Henderson

137

B8056

Badachro

Loch
Maree

Letterewe

Loch
Garbhaig

Opinan

19

South Erradale

Loch Maree
Hotel

Redpoint

Talladale

A832

981
SLIOCH

Red Point

875

7

8

9

0

0   1   2   3   4   5 miles
0 1 2 3 4 5 6 7 kilometres

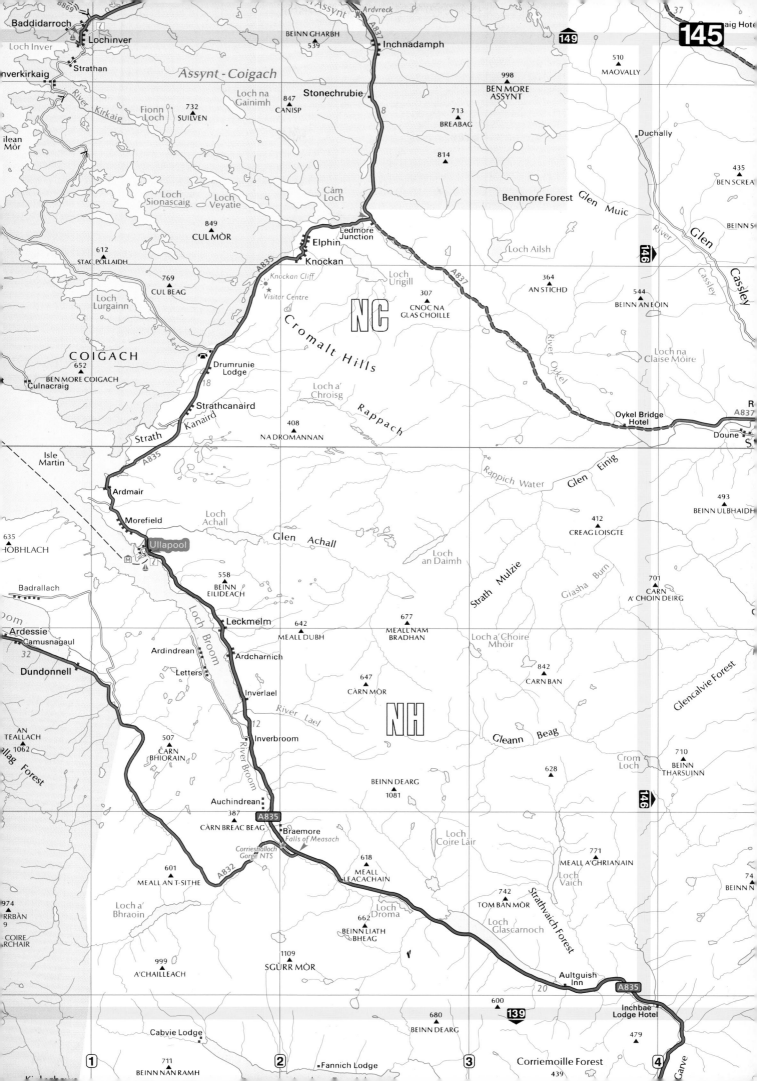

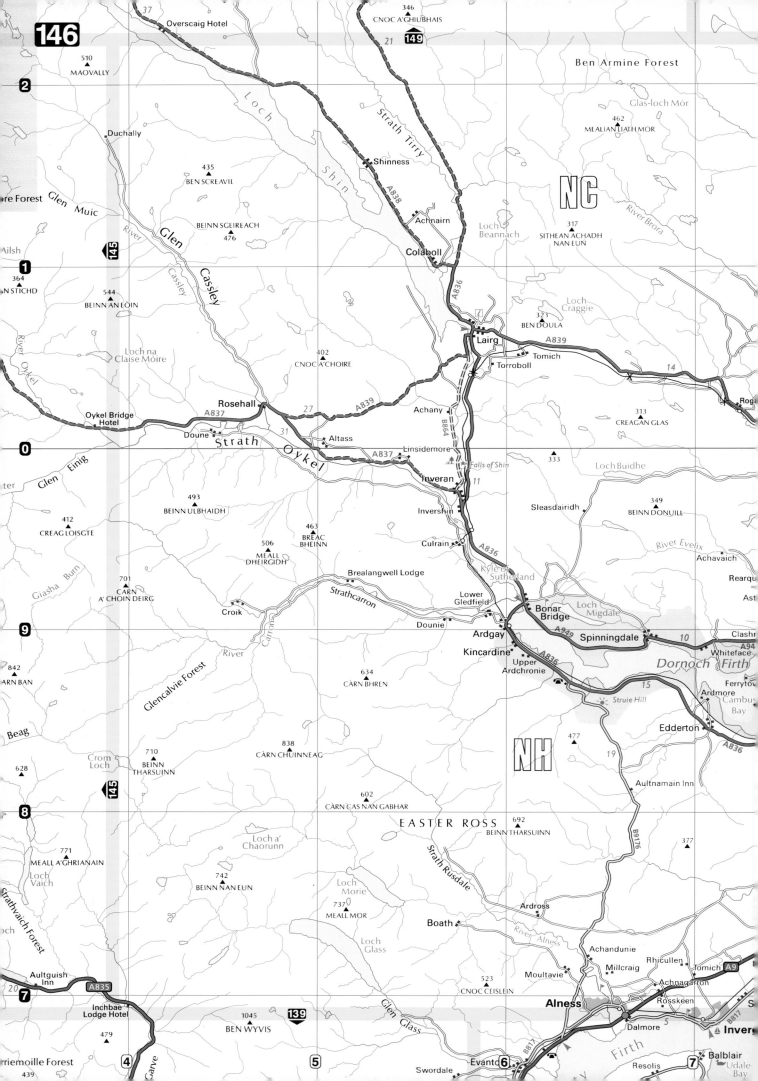

NC

NH

EASTER ROSS

Ben Armine Forest

CNOC A'GHIUBHAIS 346

Overscaig Hotel

510 ▲ MAOVALLY

Duchally

Loch Shin

Strath Tirry

Glas-loch Mòr

462 ▲ MEALLAN LIATH MOR

River Brora

Glen Muic

re Forest

Glen

River Cassley

435 ▲ BEN SCREAVIL

BEINN SGEIREACH 476 ▲

Shinness

A838

Achnairn

Colaboll

Loch Beannach

317 ▲ SITHEAN ACHADH NAN EUN

Ailsh

145

Cassley

Loch Craggie

364 ▲ N STICHD

544 ▲ BEINN AN EÒIN

Loch na Claise Mòire

CNOC A'CHOIRE 402 ▲

A836

Lairg

323 ▲ BEN DOULA

A839

Tomich

14

River Oykel

Oykel Bridge Hotel

A837

Rosehall

27

A839

Torroboll

Rog

Doune

31

Altass

A837

Achany

B864

Linsidemore

313 ▲ CREAGAN GLAS

Strath Oykel

Falls of Shin

Loch Buidhe

Inveran

11

333 ▲

Glen Einig

Glen

493 ▲ BEINN ULBHAIDH

Invershin

Sleasdairidh

349 ▲ BEINN DONUILL

412 ▲ CREAG LOISGTE

463 ▲ BREAC BHEINN

506 ▲ MEALL DHEIRGIDH

Culrain

A836

River Evelix

Achavaich

Giasha Burn

701 ▲ CARN A' CHOIN DEIRG

Brealangwell Lodge

Kyle of Sutherland

Rearqu

Ast

Strathcarron

Lower Gledfield

Bonar Bridge

Loch Migdale

9

Croik

Dounie

Ardgay

A949

Spinningdale

10

Clashr

A94

ARN BAN 842 ▲

River Carron

Kincardine

A836

Upper Ardchronie

Dornoch Firth

Whiteface

Ferrytow

Beag

634 ▲ CÀRN BHREN

Struie Hill

15

Ardmore

Cambus Bay

Glencalvie Forest

Edderton

A836

Crom Loch

710 ▲ BEINN THARSUINN

838 ▲ CÀRN CHUINNEAG

477 ▲

19

628 ▲

145

602 ▲ CÀRN CAS NAN GABHAR

Aultnamain Inn

8

692 ▲ BEINN THARSUINN

377 ▲

771 ▲ MEALL A'GHRIANAIN

Loch a' Chaorunn

Strath Rusdale

B9176

Loch Vaich

742 ▲ BEINN NAN EUN

Loch Morie

Ardross

Strathvaich Forest

737 ▲ MEALL MOR

Boath

River Alness

Achandunie

Rhicullen

Tomich A9

Millcraig

Achnagarron

20

Aultguish Inn

A835

7

523 ▲ CNOC CEISLEIN

Alness

Rosskeen

Inchbae Lodge Hotel

1045 ▲ BEN WYVIS

139

Glen Glass

Dalmore

B817

Inver

479 ▲

rriemoille Forest

4

Garve

5

6

Swordale

Evanto

Firth

7

Resolis

Balblair

Udale Bay

439

CNOC NA
BREUN-CHOILLE
388
CREAG NAM FIADH
Cairns, Stone Rows
& Stone Circle
CREAG SCALABSDALE
554

150

Kildonan
Lodge

Kildonan
BEINN DUBHAIN
416

401
CNOC NA MAOILE

17

404
Ord of Caithness

A897
River Helmsdale
Torrish

A9

337
CNOC NA
H-INNSE MOIRE

421
CNOC NAN
CRUBAG MOR

624
BEINN DHORAIN

591
BEINN NA MEILICH

Timespan
West
Helmsdale
Navidale House
Hotel
East Helmsdale
Helmsdale
Gartymore
Portgower

ND

Glen Loth

Balnacoil Lodge

539
COL-BHEINN

Lothmore

Lothbeg

Strath Brora

A9
21

River Brora

avoch Lodge

Loch
Brora

520
BEN HORN

Loch
Horn

378
CAGAR FEOSAIG

Dalchalm

Brora

Doll

446
BEINN LUNDIE

Backies

Golspie Burn

Rhives

Cairn Liath
Dunrobin Castle

Golspie

A9

Loch
Fleet

Skelbo

Skelbo Street

Fourpenny

0   1   2   3   4   5 miles

0   1   2   3   4   5   6   7 kilometres

Embo

Embo Street

Pitgrudy

B9168

A949

Camore

Dornoch

NJ

Tarbat Ness

Dornoch Firth

Innis Mhor

Wilkhaven

Brucefield

Portmahomack

Rockfield

Inver
Arboll

B9165

Toulvaddie

Loch
Eye

Rhynie

Fearn

A9
B9165

Balmuchy

11

Hill of Fearn

Newfield

Tullich

Hilton of Cadboll Chapel

Hilton

Arabella

B9166

Balintore

B9175

Milton
Ankerville

Shandwick

Shandwick Bay

Pitcalnie

raville

Nigg

gg Bay

Hopeman
Burghead Well

Balnapaling

140

Burghead

141

FIRTH

V
M
Cromarty

Burghead
Bay

Cummingston

h Miller's Cottage NTS

Roseisle
College of

Newton

8

9

0

1

B90

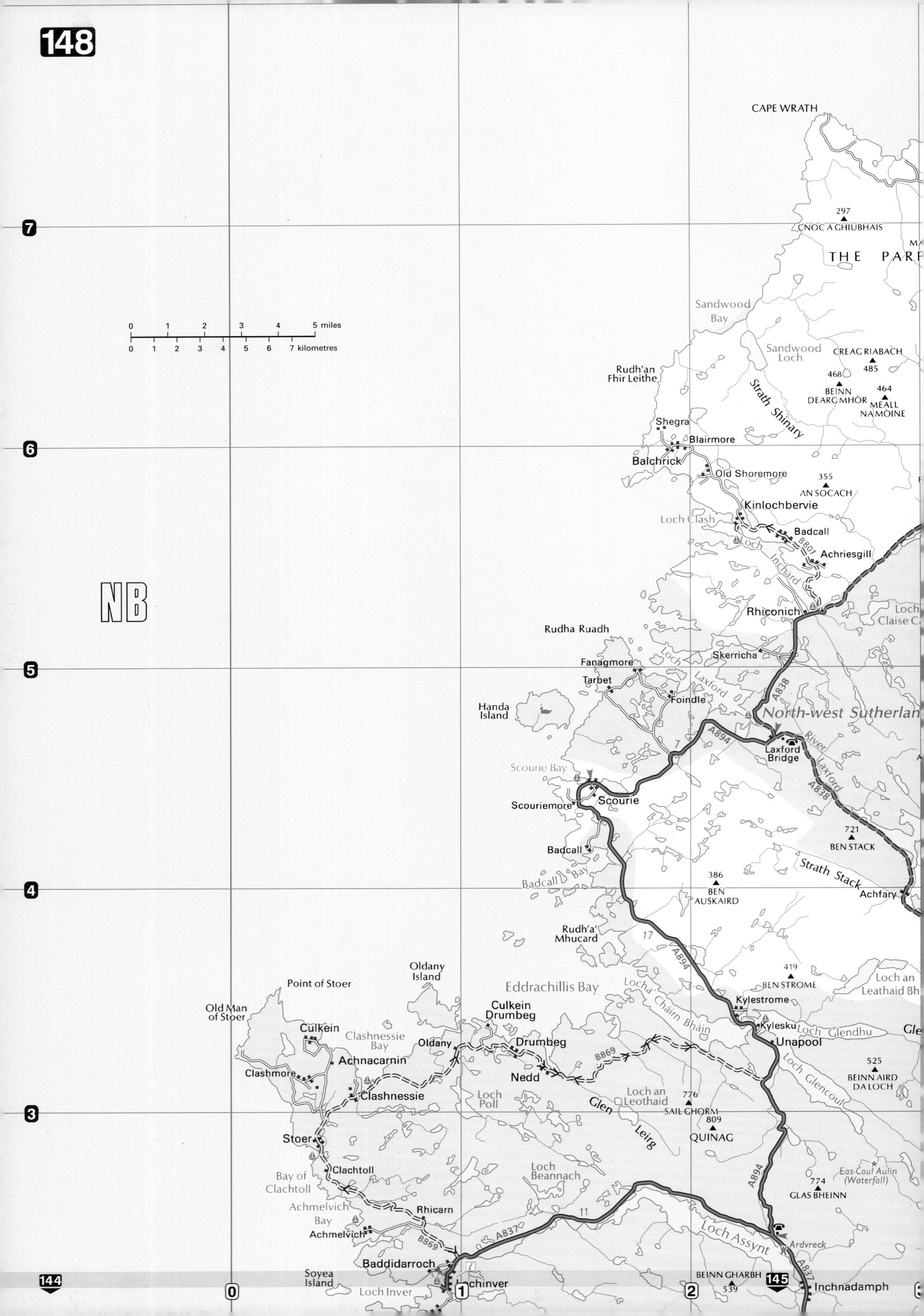

NB

CAPE WRATH

THE PAR[

297
CNOC A GHIUBHAIS ▲

Sandwood
Bay

Sandwood
Loch

CREAG RIABACH ▲
468 ▲   485 ▲

Rudh'an
Fhir Leithe

Strath Shinary

BEINN
DEARG MHOR ▲   464 ▲
MEALL
NA MOINE

Shegra ■
■■ Blairmore
Balchrick

Old Shoremore ■   355 ▲
AN SOCACH ▲

Loch Clash   Kinlochbervie

Badcall
B801
Achriesgill

Loch Inchard

Rhiconich   Loch
Claise C[

Rudha Ruadh

Skerricha

Loch Laxford

Fanagmore ■
Tarbet ■
Foindle ■

A838

North-west Sutherlan[

Handa
Island

7   A894

River
Laxford

Laxford
Bridge

A838

Scourie Bay

721 ▲
BEN STACK

Scouriemore   Scourie

Strath Stack

Badcall

386 ▲
BEN
AUSKAIRD

Achfary

Badcall Bay

Rudh'a'
Mhucard

17   A894

419 ▲
BEN STROME

Loch an
Leathaid Bh[

Point of Stoer

Oldany
Island

Eddrachillis Bay

Locha Chàirn Bhàin

Kylestrome

Kylesku   Loch Glendhu   Gle[

Old Man
of Stoer

Culkein
Drumbeg

Unapool

525 ▲
BEINN AIRD
DA LOCH

Culkein

Clashnessie
Bay

Oldany

Drumbeg

B869

Loch Glencoul

Achnacarnin

Nedd

Loch an
Leathaid

776 ▲
SAIL GHORM

Clashmore

Clashnessie

Loch
Poll

Glen   809 ▲
QUINAG

Leirg

Eas Coul Aulin
(Waterfall) ★

Stoer

Loch
Beannach

774 ▲
GLAS BHEINN

Clachtoll

Bay of
Clachtoll

A894

Achmelvich
Bay

Rhicarn

11

A837

Loch Assynt

Ardvreck

Achmelvich

B869

Baddidarroch

Soyea
Island

Loch Inver   Lochinver

A837

2   BEINN GHARBH
539 ▲

Inchnadamph

0   1   2   3   4   5 miles
0 1 2 3 4 5 6 7 kilometres

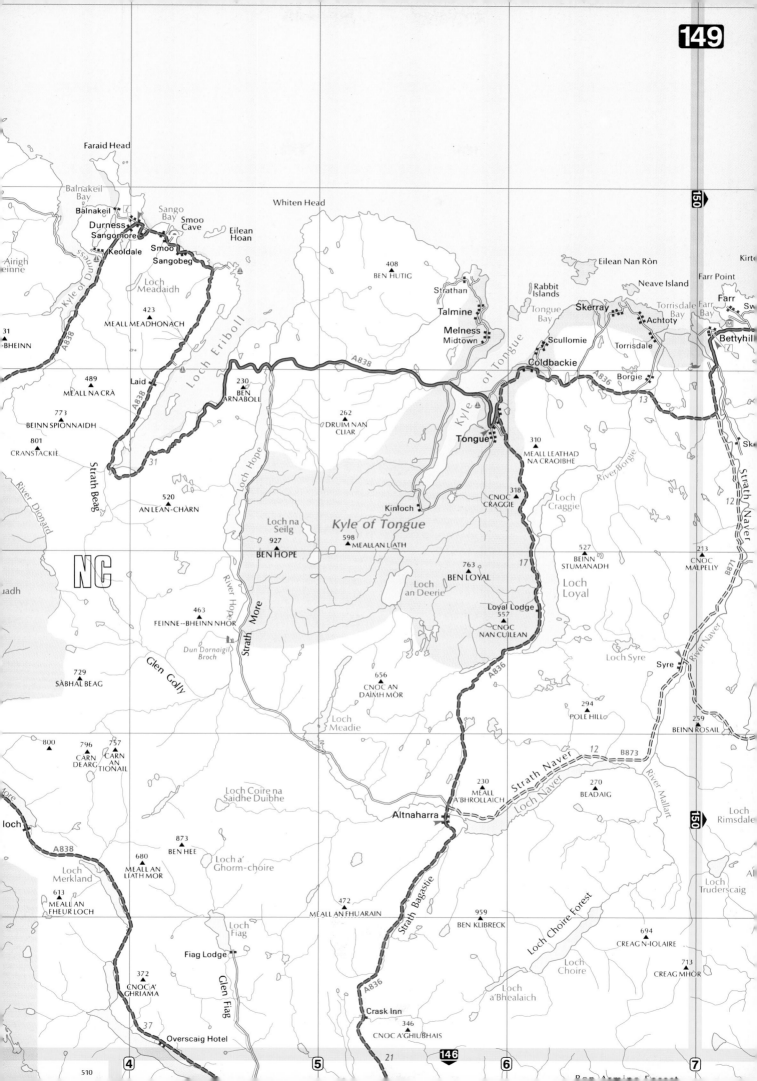

Faraid Head

Balnakeil
Bay
Balnakeil
Durness
Sangomore
Keoldale
Smoo
Cave
Eilean
Hoan
Sango
Bay
Smoo
Sangobeg

Whiten Head

31
-BHEINN

423
MEALL MEADHONACH

Loch
Meadaidh

A838

Kyle of Durness

489
MEALL NA CRÀ

773
BEINN SPIONNAIDH

801
CRANSTACKIE

Strath Beag

A838

Laid

31

Loch Eriboll

A838

230
BEN
ARNABOLL

262
DRUIM NAN
CLIAR

Loch Hope

520
AN LEAN-CHÀRN

NC

Loch na
Seilg

927
BEN HOPE

598
MEALLAN LIATH

Kyle of Tongue

Kinloch

River Hope

463
FEINNE--BHEINN NHOR

Strath More

Dun Dornaigil
Broch

Glen Golly

729
SÀBHAL BEAG

River Dionard

uadh

Airigh
einne

BEN HUTIG
408

Strathan

Talmine

Melness
Midtown

Rabbit
Islands

Tongue
Bay

Eilean Nan Ròn

Neave Island

Skerray

Scullomie

Torrisdale

Coldbackie

Kyle of Tongue

Tongue

310
MEALL LEATHAD
NA CRAOIBHE

318
CNOC
CRAGGIE

Loch
Craggie

River Borgie

A836

Borgie

13

763
BEN LOYAL

Loch
an Deerie

Loyal Lodge
557
CNOC
NAN CUILEAN

527
BEINN
STUMANADH

Loch
Loyal

17

A836

Farr Point

Farr

Torrisdale
Bay

Bettyhill

Farr
Sw

Sk

Strath Naver

12

213
CNOC
MALPELLY

B871

Loch Syre

Syre

River Naver

259
BEINN ROSAIL

656
CNOC AN
DAIMH MÒR

Loch
Meadie

294
POLE HILL

800

796
CÀRN
DEARG

757
CARN
AN
TIONAIL

Loch Coire na
Saidhe Duibhe

230
MEALL
A'BHROLLAICH

Strath Naver

Loch Naver

12

270
BEADAIG

B873

River Mallart

150

Loch
Rimsdale

Al

Altnaharra

A838

Loch
Merkland

613
MEALL AN
FHEUR LOCH

ore

och

873
BEN HEE

680
MEALL AN
LIATH MOR

Loch a'
Ghorm-choire

472
MEALL AN FHUARAIN

Loch
Fiag

Fiag Lodge

Glen Fiag

372
CNOC A'
CHRIAMA

37

Overscaig Hotel

510

Strath Bagastie

959
BEN KLIBRECK

694
CREAG N-IOLAIRE

Loch
a'Bhealaich

Loch
Choire

Loch Choire Forest

713
CREAG MHOR

Loch
Truderscaig

A836

Crask Inn

346
CNOC A'GHIUBHAIS

21

146

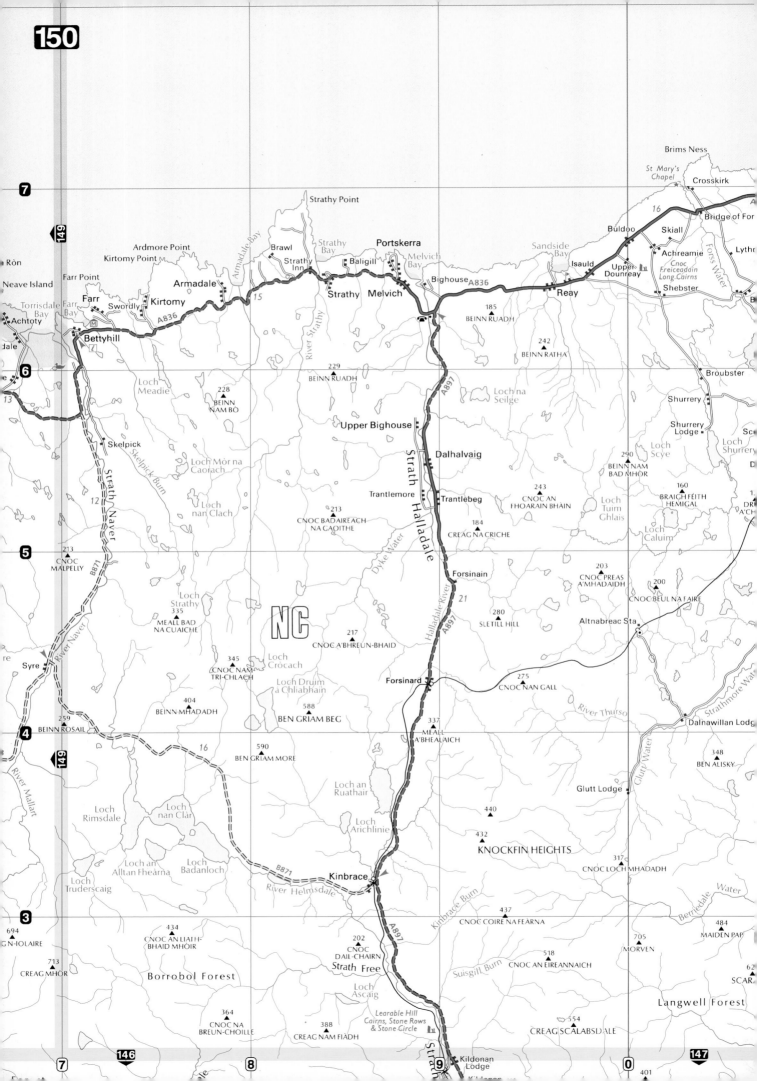

NC

Brims Ness
St Mary's Chapel
Crosskirk
Bridge of For
16
Buldoo
Skiall
Achreamie
Lythr
Sandside Bay
Cnoc Freiceadain Long Cairns
Isauld
Upper Dounreay
Shebster
B
Reay
Broubster
Shurrery
Shurrery Lodge
Loch Scye
Sc
Loch Shurrery
D
BEINN NAM BAD MHOR 290
160 BRAIGH FÉITH HEMIGAL
1.
DR A'CH

Strathy Point
Brawl
Strathy Bay
Portskerra
Melvich Bay
Ardmore Point
Kirtomy Point
Strathy Inn
Baligill
Strathy
Melvich
Bighouse A836
Armadale
Farr Point
Ròn
Neave Island
Farr
Swordly
Kirtomy
Bettyhill
A836
15

185 BEINN RUADH

242 BEINN RATHA

Loch na Seilge

A897

229 BEINN RUADH

Upper Bighouse

Dalhalvaig

Strath Halladale

Trantlemore
Trantlebeg

243 CNOC AN FHOARAIN BHÀIN

184 CREAG NA CRICHE

203 CNOC PREAS A'MHADAIDH

200 CNOC BEUL NA FAIRE

Forsinain

21

280 SLE TILL HILL

Altnabreac Sta.

228 BEINN NAM BO

Loch Meadie

Skelpick

Skelpick Burn

Loch Mòr na Caorach

Loch nan Clach

213 CNOC BADAIREACH NA GAOITHE

Dyke Water

Halladale River

A897

275 CNOC NAN GALL

River Thurso

Strathmore Wat

Dalnawillan Lodg

Torrisdale Bay
Farr Bay
Achtoty
13

Strath Naver

12

B871

213 CNOC MALPELLY

335 Loch Strathy

MEALL BAD NA CUAICHE

345 CNOC NAM TRI-CHLACH

Loch Cròcach

217 CNOC A'BHREUN-BHAID

Forsinard

348 BEN ALISKY

Glutt Lodge

Clubb Water

River Naver

Syre

259 BEINN ROSAIL

404 BEINN-MHADADH

 BEN GRIAM BEG 588

337 MEALL A'BHEALAICH

KNOCKFIN HEIGHTS

River Mallart

149

16

590 BEN GRIAM MORE

Loch an Ruathair

440

432

317 CNOC LOCH MHADADH

Loch Rimsdale

Loch nan Clàr

Loch Arichlinie

Loch an Alltan Fheàrna

Loch Badanloch

B871

Kinbrace

River Helmsdale

437 CNOC COIRE NA FEARNA

Kinbrace Burn

Berriedale Water

Loch Truderscaig

694 N-IOLAIRE

434 CNOC AN LIATH-BHAID MHÒIR

202 CNOC DAIL-CHAIRN

Strath Free

A897

518 CNOC AN EIREANNAICH

705 MORVEN

484 MAIDEN PAP

713 CREAG MHOR

Borrobol Forest

364 CNOC NA BREUN-CHOILLE

388 CREAG NAM FIADH

Learable Hill Cairns, Stone Rows & Stone Circle

554 CREAG SCALABSDALE

Langwell Forest

62 SCAR

Suisgill Burn

Kildonan Lodge
Strath

401

7
149
6
5
4
3

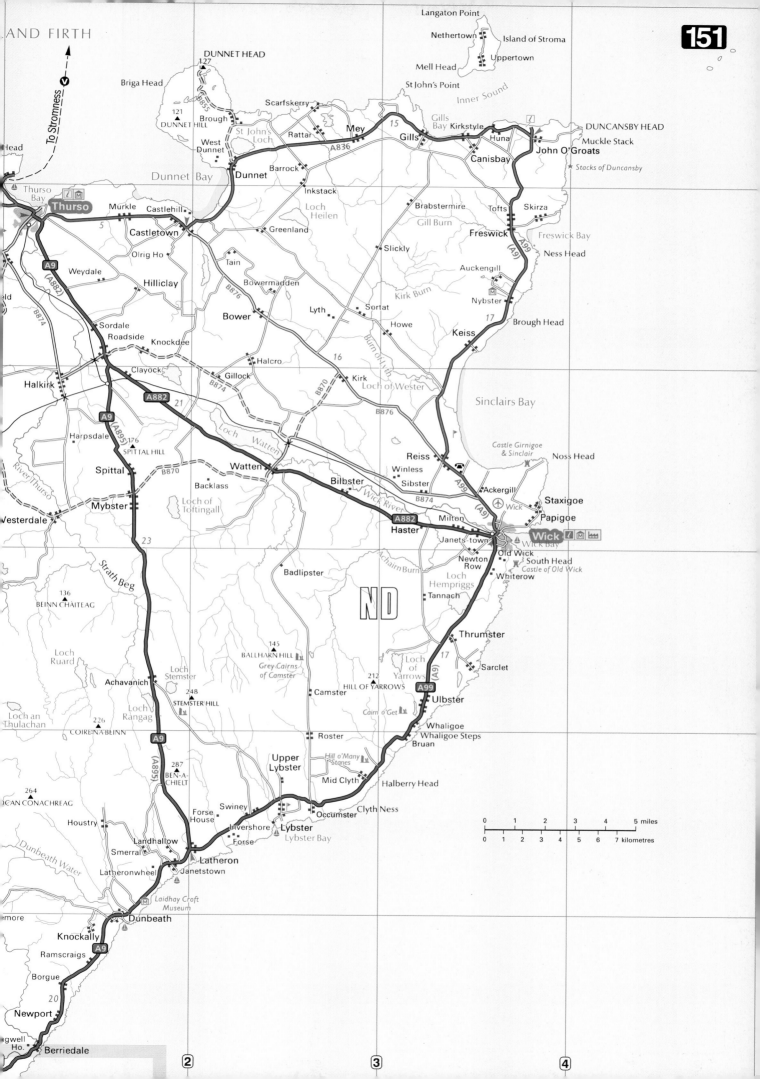

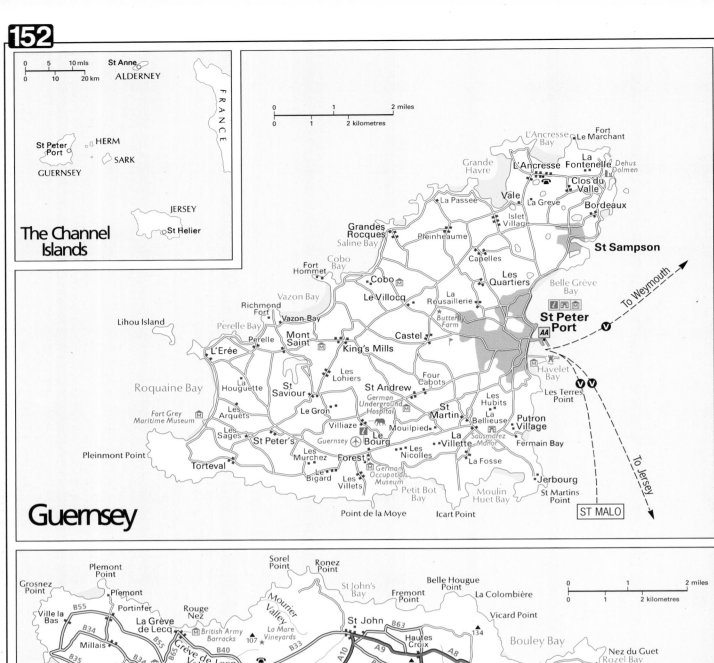

The Channel Islands

St Anne
ALDERNEY

St Peter Port
HERM
SARK
GUERNSEY

JERSEY
St Helier

FRANCE

Guernsey

To Weymouth
To Jersey
ST MALO

L'Ancresse Bay
Le Marchant
Fort
La Fontenelle
Dehus Dolmen
Grande Havre
L'Ancresse
Vale
Clos du Valle
La Grève
Bordeaux
La Passée
Islet Village
Grandes Rocques
Pleinheaume
Capelles
St Sampson
Saline Bay
Cobo Bay
Les Quartiers
Belle Grève Bay
Cobo
La Rousaillerie
Le Villocq
Vazon Bay
Butterfly Farm
St Peter Port
Richmond Fort
Castel
Vazon Bay
Mont Saint
King's Mills
Four Cabots
Havelet Bay
Perelle Bay
Perelle
Les Lohiers
St Andrew
Les Hubits
Les Terres Point
L'Erée
St Saviour
Le Gron
German Underground Hospital
La Bellieuse
Putron Village
Roquaine Bay
La Houguette
Villiaze
St Martin
Fermain Bay
Fort Grey Maritime Museum
Les Arquêts
Moulpied
La Villette
Les Sages
Le Bourg
La Fosse
Les Murchez
St Peter's
Guernsey
Les Nicolles
St Martins Point
Pleinmont Point
Forest
German Occupation Museum
Jerbourg
Torteval
Le Bigard
Les Villets
Petit Bot Bay
Moulin Huet Bay
Point de la Moye
Icart Point
Sausmarez Manor

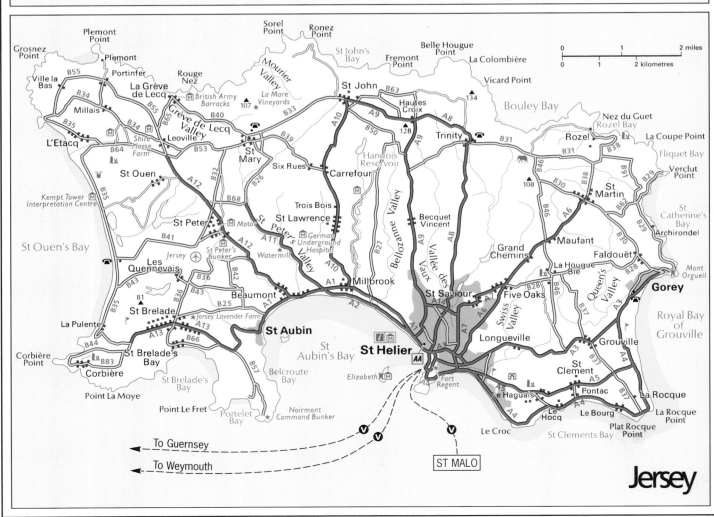

Jersey

To Guernsey
To Weymouth
ST MALO

Plemont Point
Grosnez Point
Sorel Point
Ronez Point
St John's Bay
Belle Hougue Point
La Colombière
Plemont
Fremont Point
Portinfer
Rouge Nez
Vicard Point
Ville la Bas
La Grève de Lecq
Mourier Valley
St John
Bouley Bay
Millais
British Army Barracks
La Mare Vineyards
Hautes Croix
Nez du Guet
Rozel Bay
Crève de Lecq Valley
107
134
Rozel
La Coupe Point
L'Etacq
Leoville
St Mary
128
Trinity
Fliquet Bay
Shire Horse Farm
Six Rues
Verclut Point
St Ouen
Carrefour
Handois Reservoir
108
St Martin
Kempt Tower Interpretation Centre
Trois Bois
St Catherine's Bay
St Peter
St Lawrence
Becquet Vincent
Archirondel
St Ouen's Bay
German Underground Hospital
Maufant
St Peter's Bunker
Vallée des Vaux
Grand Chemins
La Hougue Bie
Faldouët
Jersey
Watermill
Bellozanne Valley
Mont Orgueil
Les Quennevais
St Saviour
Queen's Valley
Beaumont
Millbrook
Five Oaks
Gorey
La Pulente
Jersey Lavender Farm
Swiss Valley
Grouville
St Brelade
St Aubin
St Helier
Longueville
Royal Bay of Grouville
Corbière Point
St Brelade's Bay
St Aubin's Bay
Elizabeth
St Clement
Corbière
Belcroute Bay
Fort Regent
Pontac
La Rocque
Point La Moye
St Brelade's Bay
Le Haguais
Le Bourg
Le Hocq
La Rocque Point
Point Le Fret
Portelet Bay
Noirmont Command Bunker
Le Croc
St Clements Bay
Plat Rocque Point

The Isle of Man

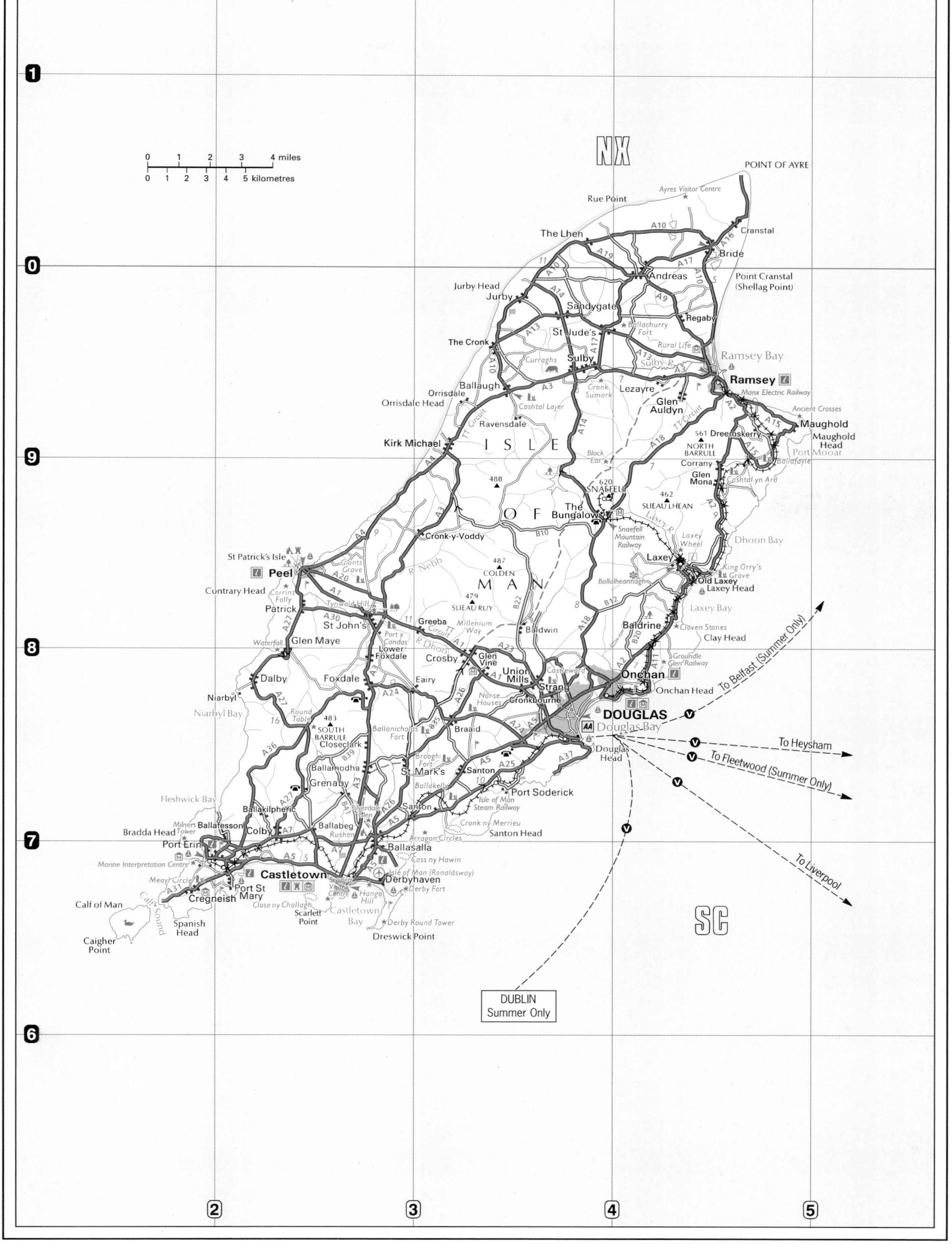

NX

0 1 2 3 4 miles
0 1 2 3 4 5 kilometres

POINT OF AYRE

Ayres Visitor Centre
Rue Point
The Lhen
Cranstal
A10
A16
A17
Bride
Point Cranstal
(Shellag Point)
Andreas
A9
Jurby Head
Jurby
Sandygate
A14
St Jude's
Regaby
Ballachurry Fort
Rural Life
The Cronk
A13
Sulby
A17
Ramsey Bay
Curraghs
Sulby R.
A3
A7
Ballaugh
Lezayre
Ramsey
Orrisdale
Cronk Sumark
Glen Auldyn
Manx Electric Railway
Orrisdale Head
Ravensdale
Cashtal Lajer
A18
Ancient Crosses
Kirk Michael
A14
A2
Maughold
561 Dreemskerry
TT Circuit
NORTH BARRULE
Maughold Head
ISLE
488
A1
Corrany
Port Mooar
Block Eary
620 SNAEFELL
Glen Mona
Ballafayle
Cashtal yn Ard
462 SLIEAU LHEAN
Cronk-y-Voddy
OF
The Bungalow
Snaefell Mountain Railway
Dhoon Bay
B10
Laxey
Laxey Wheel
St Patrick's Isle
Giants Grave
MAN
487 COLDEN
Ballaleannagh
King Orry's Grave
Peel
A20
Old Laxey
A3
Laxey Head
Contrary Head
Corrins Folly
479 SLIEAU RUY
B22
B12
Laxey Bay
Patrick
Tynwald Hill
A27
A1
Greeba
Baldrine
To Belfast (Summer Only)
Glen Maye
St John's
Port y Candas
Millenium Way
B20
Cloven Stones
A30
11 TT Circuit
Crosby
Baldwin
Groudle Glen Railway
Waterfall
Lower Foxdale
Glen Vine
A18
Onchan
Dalby
Foxdale
Union Mills
A23
Strang
Onchan Head
Eairy
Castleward
A24
A1
Cronkbourne
DOUGLAS
Niarbyl
A26
Norse Houses
AA
V
Niarbyl Bay
Round Table
Braaid
Douglas Bay
To Heysham
16
483 SOUTH BARRULE
Ballanicholas Fort
Douglas Head
To Fleetwood (Summer Only)
Closeclark
B39
Brough Fort
A25
A37
V
Ballamodha
St Mark's
Santon
V
Grenaby
A5
Port Soderick
Fleshwick Bay
A27
Ballakelly
Isle of Man Steam Railway
V
Ballakilpheric
Santon
Cronk ny Merriew
To Liverpool
Bradda Head
A36
Riverdale Glen
Santon Head
Ballafesson
Colby
A7
Ballabeg
A5
Arragon Circles
Milners Tower
Rushen
V
Port Erin
A31
Cass ny Hawin
Ballasalla
Isle of Man (Ronaldsway)
SC
Marine Interpretation Centre
Castletown
Cregneish
Port St Mary
Derbyhaven
Meayl Circle
Derby Fort
Calf of Man
Close ny Chollagh
Hango Hill
Castletown Bay
Derby Round Tower
Spanish Head
Scarlett Point
Dreswick Point
Caigher Point

DUBLIN
Summer Only

Western Isles

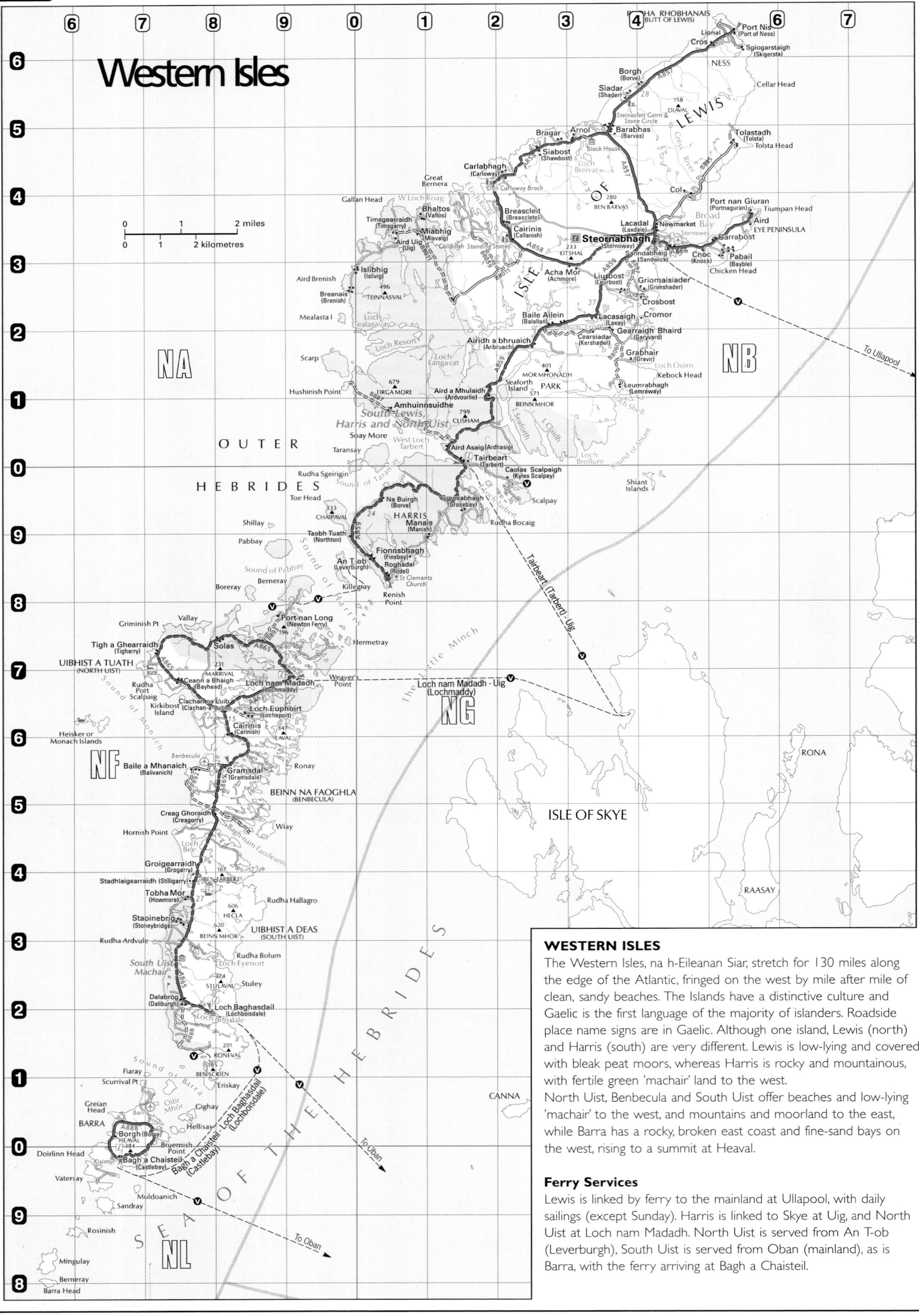

WESTERN ISLES

The Western Isles, na h-Eileanan Siar, stretch for 130 miles along the edge of the Atlantic, fringed on the west by mile after mile of clean, sandy beaches. The Islands have a distinctive culture and Gaelic is the first language of the majority of islanders. Roadside place name signs are in Gaelic. Although one island, Lewis (north) and Harris (south) are very different. Lewis is low-lying and covered with bleak peat moors, whereas Harris is rocky and mountainous, with fertile green 'machair' land to the west.

North Uist, Benbecula and South Uist offer beaches and low-lying 'machair' to the west, and mountains and moorland to the east, while Barra has a rocky, broken east coast and fine-sand bays on the west, rising to a summit at Heaval.

Ferry Services

Lewis is linked by ferry to the mainland at Ullapool, with daily sailings (except Sunday). Harris is linked to Skye at Uig, and North Uist at Loch nam Madadh. North Uist is served from An T-ob (Leverburgh), South Uist is served from Oban (mainland), as is Barra, with the ferry arriving at Bagh a Chaisteil.

OUTER HEBRIDES

NA   NB   NG   NF   NL

LEWIS

HARRIS

UIBHIST A TUATH (NORTH UIST)

BEINN NA FAOGHLA (BENBECULA)

UIBHIST A DEAS (SOUTH UIST)

BARRA

ISLE OF SKYE

SEA OF THE HEBRIDES

To Ullapool

To Oban

0   1   2 miles
0   1   2 kilometres

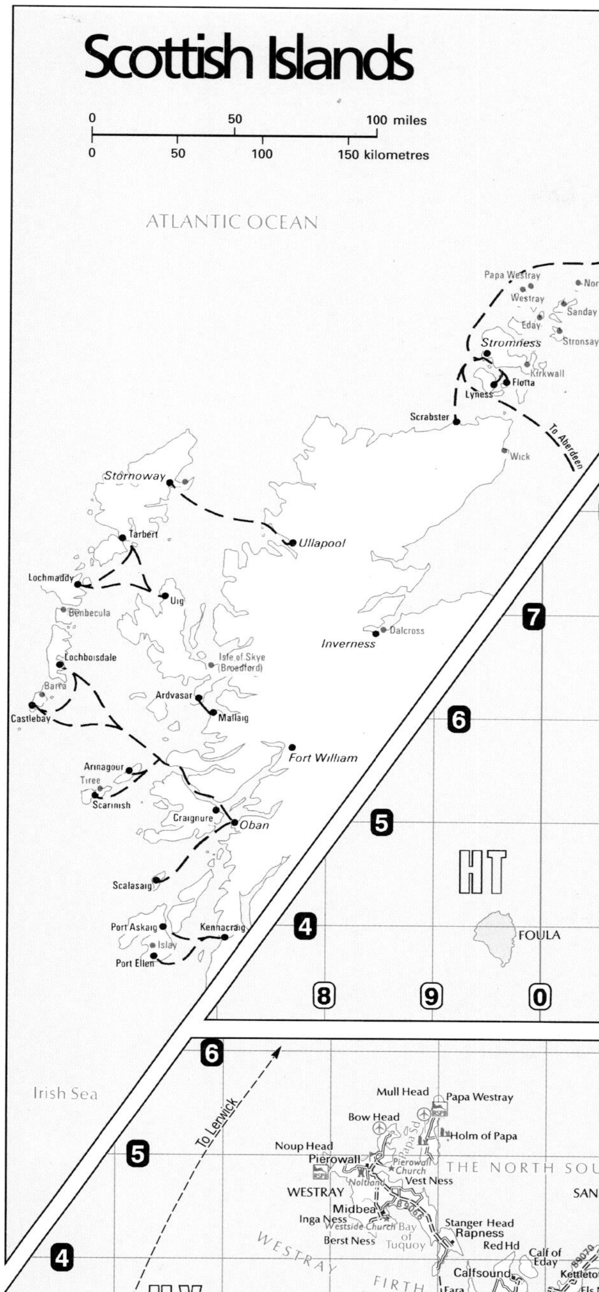

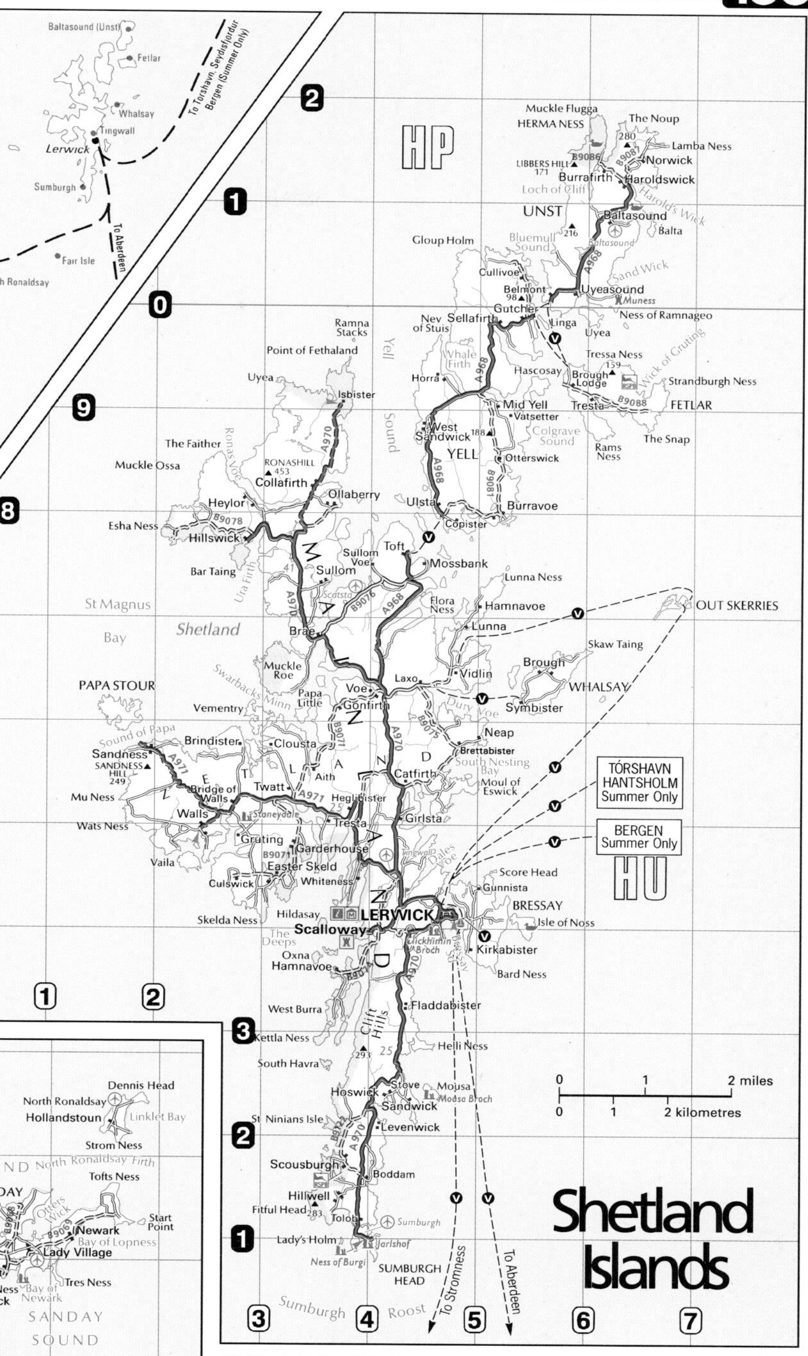

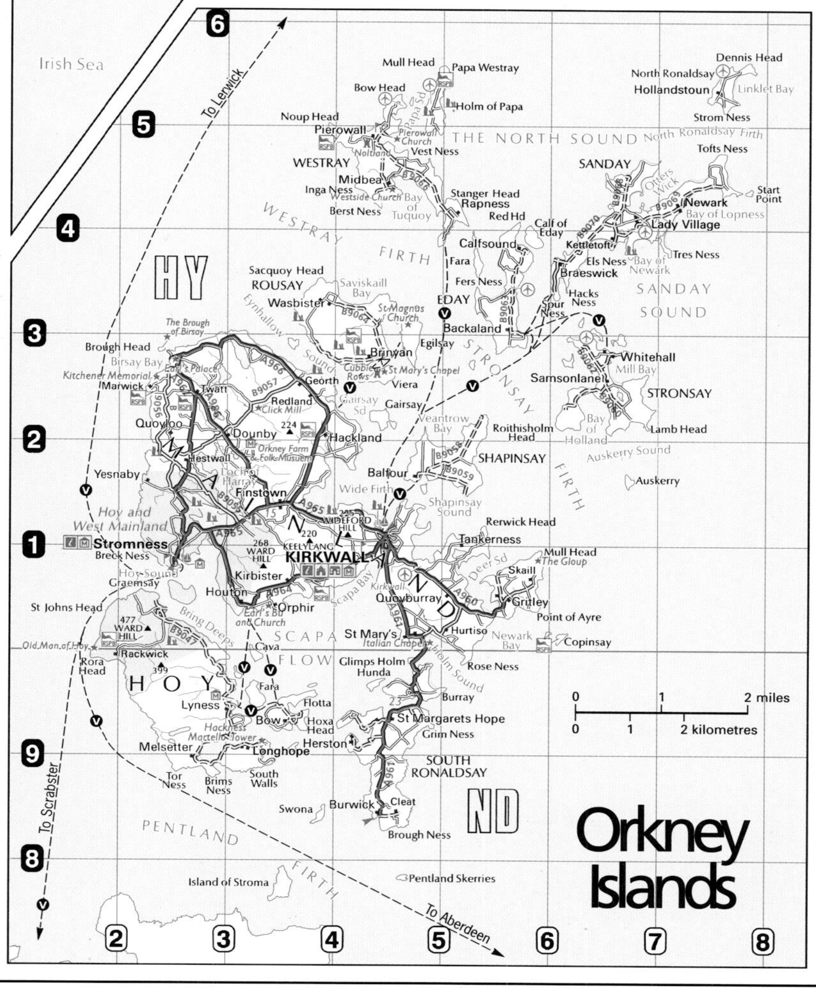

Scottish Islands

ATLANTIC OCEAN

HP

HT

HU

HY

ND

Shetland Islands

Orkney Islands

SHETLAND ISLANDS

The most northerly of all Britain's islands, this group numbers 100, though only 15 are inhabited. Most people live on the largest island, Mainland, on which Lerwick is the only town of importance. The scenery is magnificent, with unspoiled views, and the islands' northerly position means summer days have little or no darkness.

Ferry Services

The main service from the mainland is from Aberdeen to the island port of Lerwick. A service from Stromness (Orkney) to Lerwick is also available. During the summer months there are also services linking Shetland with Norway. Shetland Islands Council operates an inter-island service.

ORKNEY ISLANDS

Lying 20 miles north of the Scottish mainland, Orkney comprises 70 islands, of which 18 are inhabited, Mainland being the largest. Apart from Hoy, Orkney is generally green and flat, with few trees. The islands abound with prehistoric antiquities and rare birds. The climate is one of even temperatures and 'twilight' summer nights, but with violent winds at times.

Ferry Services

The main service is from Scrabster on the Caithness coast to the island port of Stromness. A service from Aberdeen to Stromness provides a link to Shetland at Lerwick. Inter-island services are also operated (advance reservations recommended).

Ireland

Abbeydorney G2
Abbeyfeale G2
Abbeyleix G4
Adamstown G4
Adare G2
Adrigole H2
Ahascragh F3
Ahoghill D5
Allihies H1
Anascaul H1
Annalong E5
Annestown H4
Antrim D5
Ardagh G2
Ardara D3
Ardcath F5
Ardee E4
Ardfert G2
Ardfinnan G3
Ardglass E5
Ardgroom H1
Arklow G5
Arless G4
Armagh D4
Armoy C5
Arthurstown H4
Arvagh E4
Ashbourne F5
Ashford F5
Askeaton G2
Athboy F4
Athea G2
Athenry F3
Athleague F3
Athlone F3
Athy F4
Augher D4
Aughnacloy D4
Aughrim G5
Avoca G5

Bagenalstown G4
(Muine Bheag)
Bailieborough E4
Balbriggan F5
Balla E2
Ballacolla G4
Ballaghaderreen E3
Ballina F3
Ballina E2
Ballinafad E3
Ballinagh E4
Ballinakill G4
Ballinalee E3
Ballinamallard D4
Ballinamore E3
Ballinascarty H2
Ballinasloe F3
Ballindine E2
Ballineen H2
Ballingarry G3
Ballingarry G2
Ballingeary H2
(Béal Átha an Ghaorthaidh)
Ballinhassig H2
Ballinlough E3
Ballinrobe E2
Ballinspittle H2
Ballintober E3
Ballintra D3
Ballivor F4
Ballon G4
Ballybaun F3
Ballybay E4
Ballybofey D3
Ballybunion G2
Ballycanew G5
Ballycarry D5
Ballycastle D2
Ballycastle C5
Ballyclare D5
Ballyconneely F1
Ballycotton H3
Ballycumber F3
Ballydehob J2
Ballydesmond H2
Ballyduff H3
Ballyduff G2
Ballygar F3
Ballygalley D5
Ballygawley D4
Ballygowan D5
Ballyhaise E4
Ballyhale G4
Ballyhaunis E3
Ballyhean E2
Ballyheige G2
Ballyjamesduff E4
Ballykeeran F3
Ballylanders G3
Ballylongford G2
Ballylooby G4
Ballylynan G4
Ballymahon F3
Ballymakeery H2
Ballymaloe H3
Ballymena D5
Ballymoe E3
Ballymoney C4
Ballymore F3
Ballymore Eustace F4
Ballymote E3
Ballynahinch D5

Ballynure D5
Ballyragget G4
Ballyroan F4
Ballyronan D4
Ballysadare E3
Ballyshannon D3
Ballyvaughan F2
Ballywalter D5
Balrothery F5
Baltimore J2
Baltinglass G4
Banagher F3
Banbridge D5
Bandon H2
Bangor D5
Bangor Erris E2
Bansha G3
Banteer H2
Bantry H2
Barryporeen G3
Beaufort H2
Belcoo D3
Belfast D5
Belgooly H3
Bellaghy D4
Belleek D3
Belmullet D2
(Béal an Mhuirhead)
Belturbet E4
Benburb D4
Bennettsbridge G4
Beragh D4
Birr F3
Blacklion D3
Blackwater G5
Blarney H3
Blessington F4
Boherbue H3
Borris G4
Borris-in-Ossory F3
Borrisokane F3
Borrisoleigh G3
Boyle E3
Bracknagh F4
Bray F5
Bridgetown H4
Brittas F4
Broadford G3
Broadford G2
Broughshane D5
Bruff G3
Bruree G3
Bunclody G4
Buncrana C4
Bundoran D3
Bunmahon H4
Bunnahowen D2
Bunnyconnellan E2
Bushmills C4
Butler's Bridge E4
Buttevant H2

Cadamstown F3
Caherconlish G3
Caherdaniel H1
Cahersiveen H1
Cahir G3
Caledon D4
Callan G4
Caltra F3
Camolin G4
Camp G1
Cappagh White G3
Cappamore G3
Cappoquin H3
Carlanstown E4
Carlingford E5
Carlow G4
Carndonagh C4
Carnew G4
Carnlough C5
Carracastle E3
Carrick D3
(An Charraig)
Carrickfergus D5
Carrickmacross E4
Carrickmore D4
Carrick-on-Shannon E3
Carrick-on-Suir G4
Carrigahorig F3
Carrigaline H3
Carrigallen E3
Carriganimmy H2
Carrigans C4
Carrigtohill H3
Carrowkeel C4
Carryduff D5
Cashel G3
Castlebar E2
Castlebellingham E5
Castleblayney E4
Castlebridge G4
Castlecomer G4
Castle Cove H1
Castlederg D3
Castledermot G4
Castleisland G2
Castlemaine H2
Castlemartyr H3
Castleplunkett E3
Castlepollard E4
Castlerea E3
Castlerock C4
Castleshane E4
Castletown F4

Castletownbere H1
Castletownroche H3
Castletownshend J2
Castlewellan E5
Causeway G2
Cavan E4
Celbridge F4
Charlestown E3
Charleville G2
(Rath Luirc)
Clady E4
Clane F4
Clara F3
Clarecastle G2
Claremorris E2
Clarinbridge F2
Clashmore H3
Claudy C4
Clifden F1
Cliffony D3
Clogh G4
Cloghan F3
Clogheen H3
Clogher D4
Clohamon G4
Clonakilty H2
Clonard F4
Clonaslee F4
Clonbulloge F4
Clonbur (An Fhairche) E2
Clondalkin F5
Clones E4
Clonmany C4
Clonmel G3
Clonmellon E4
Clonmore G3
Clonony F3
Clonoulty G3
Clonroche G4
Clontibret E4
Cloonbannin H2
Cloondara E3
Cloonkeen H2
Clough D5
Cloughjordan F3
Cloyne H3
Coagh D4
Coalisland D4
Cobh H3
Coleraine C4
Collinstown E4
Collon E4
Collooney E3
Comber D5
Conna H3
Cookstown D4
Coole E4
Cooraclare G2
Cootehill E4
Cork H3
Cornamona E2
Corofin F2
Courtmacsherry H2
Courtown Harbour G5
Craigavon D5
Craughwell F3
Creggs F3
Cresslough C3
Croagh G2
Crolly (Croithlí) C3
Crookedwood E4
Crookhaven J1
Crookstown H2
Croom G2
Crossakeel E4
Cross Barry H2
Crosshaven H3
Crossmaglen E4
Crossmolina E2
Crumlin D5
Crusheen F2
Culdaff C4
Culleybackey D5
Curracloe G4
Curraghboy F3
Curry E3
Cushendall C5

Drumconrath E4
Drumkeeran E3
Drumlish E3
Drumod E3
Drumquin D3
Drumshanbo E3
Drumsna E3
Duagh G2
Dublin F5
Duleek E5
Dunboyne F4
Duncormick H4
Dundalk E5
Dunderrow H3
Dundrum E5
Dunfanaghy C3
Dungannon D4
Dungarvan H3
Dungarvan G4
Dungiven D4
Dungloe C3
Dungourney H3
Dunkineely D3
Dun Laoghaire F5
Dunlavin F4
Dunleer E5
Dunloy C5
Dunmanway H2
Dunmore E3
Dunmore East H4
Dunmurry D5
Dunshaughlin F4
Durrow G4
Durrus H2

Easky D3
Edenderry F4
Edgeworthstown E4
Eglinton C4
Elphin E3
Emyvale D4
Enfield F4
Ennis G2
Enniscorthy G4
Enniscrone D2
Enniskean H2
Enniskillen D4
Ennistymon F2
Eyrecourt F3

Farnaght E3
Farranfore H2
Feakle F3
Fenagh E3
Fermoy H3
Ferns G4
Fethard H3
Fethard G3
Finnea E4
Fintona D4
Fivemiletown D4
Fontstown F4
Foulkesmills H4
Foxford E2
Foynes G2
Freemount G2
Frenchpark E3
Freshford G4
Fuerty E3

Goleen J2
Goresbridge G4
Gorey G5
Gort F2
Gortin D4
Gowran G4
Graiguenamanagh G4
Grallagh E3
Granard E4
Grange D3
Greencastle E5
Greyabbey D5
Greystones F5
Gulladuff D4

Hacketstown G4
Headford F2
Herbertstown G3
Hillsborough D5
Hilltown E5
Hospital G3
Holycross G3
Holywood D5
Howth F5

Inch H1
Inchigeelagh H2
Inishannon H2
Irvinestown D4

Johnstown G3

Kanturk H2
Keadue E3
Keady E4
Keel E1
Keenagh E3
Kells E4
Kenmare H2
Kesh D3
Kilbeggan F4
Kilberry E4
Kilbrittain H2
Kilcar D3
(Cill Charthaigh)
Kilcock F4
Kilcolgan F2
Kilconnell F3
Kilcoole F5
Kilcormac F3
Kilcullen F4
Kilcurry E5
Kildavin G4
Kildorrery H3
Kildress D4
Kilfenora F2
Kilfinnane G3
Kilgarvan H2
Kilkee G2
Kilkeel E5
Kilkelly E3
Kilkenny G4
Kilkieran F2
(Cill Ciaráin)
Kilkinlea G2
Kill H4
Killadysert G2
Killala D2
Killaloe G3
Killarney H2
Killashandra E4
Killashee E3
Killeagh H3
Killeigh F4
Killenaule G3
Killimer G2
Killimor F3
Killiney F5
Killinick H4
Killorglin H2
Killough E5
Killucan F4
Killybegs D3
Killyleagh D5
Kilmacanogue F5
Kilmacrenan C3
Kilmacthomas H4
Kilmaganny G4
Kilmaine E2
Kilmallock G3

Kilmanagh G4
Kilmanahan G3
Kilmeaden H4
Kilmeage F4
Kilmeedy G2
Kilmichael H2
Kilmore Quay H4
Kilnaleck E4
Kilrea C4
Kilrush G2
Kilsheelan G3
Kiltealy G4
Kiltegan G4
Kiltimagh E2
Kiltoom F3
Kingscourt E4
Kinlough D3
Kinnegad F4
Kinnitty F3
Kinsale H3
Kinvarra F2
Kircubbin D5

Lahinch F2
Lanesborough E3
Laragh F5
Larne D5
Lauragh H1
Laurencetown F3
Leap J2
Leenane E2
Leighlinbridge G4
Leitrim E3
Leixlip F4
Lemybrien H3
Letterfrack C4
Letterkenny C4
Lifford D4
Limavady C4
Limerick G3
Lisbellaw D4
Lisburn D5
Liscarroll G2
Lisdoonvarna F2
Lismore H3
Lisnaskea D4
Lisryan E4
Listowel G2
Loghill G2
Londonderry C4
Longford E3
Loughbrickland D5
Loughall D4
Loughglinn E3
Loughrea F3
Louisburgh E2
Lucan F4
Lurgan D5
Lusk F5

Macroom H2
Maghera E5
Maghera D4
Magherafelt D4
Maguiresbridge D4
Malahide F5
Malin C4
Malin More D3
Mallow H2
Manorhamilton D3
Markethill D4
Maynooth F4
Mazetown D5
Middletown D4
Midleton H3
Milford C4
Millstreet H2
Milltown H2
Milltown Malbay G2
Mitchelstown H3
Moate F3
Mohill E3
Molls Gap H2
Monaghan E4
Monasterevin F4
Moneygall G3
Moneymore D4
Monivea F3

Mooncoin H4
Moorfields D5
Mount Bellew F3
Mount Charles D3
Mountmellick F4
Mountrath F4
Mountshannon F3
Mourne Abbey H3
Moville C4
Moy D4
Moylett E4
Moynalty E4
Moyvore F3
Muckross H2
Muff C4
Mullabohy E4
Mullagh F4
Mullinavat G4
Mullingar F4
Mulrany E2
Myshall G4

Naas F4
Nad H2
Naul F5
Navan E4
Neale E2
Nenagh G3
Newbliss E4
Newbridge F4
(Droichead Nua)
Newcastle E5
Newcastle West G2
Newinn G3
Newmarket H2
Newmarket-on Fergus G2
Newport E2
Newport G2
New Ross G4
Newtown G4
Newtownabbey D5
Newtownards D5
Newtownbutler E4
Newtownmountkennedy F5
Newtownhamilton D4
Newtownstewart D4
Newtown Butler E4
Newtown Forbes E3
Nobber E4

Oilgate G4
Oldcastle E4
Omagh D4
Omeath E5
Oola G3
Oranmore F2
Oughterard F2
Ovens H3

Pallas Green G3
Parknasilla H1
Partry E2
Passage East H4
Passage West H3
Patrickswell G2
Paulstown G4
Pettigo D3
Plumbridge D4
Pomeroy D4
Portadown D5
Portaferry D5
Portarlington F4
Portavogie D5
Portglenone D5
Portlaoise F4
Portmarnock F5
Portrane F5
Portroe G3
Portrush C4
Portstewart C4
Portumna F3
Poyntzpass D5

Raharney F4
Randalstown D5
Rasharkin C5
Rathangan F4
Rathcoole F4
Rathcormack H3
Rathdowney G3
Rathdrum G5
Rathfriland E5

Rathkeale G2
Rathmelton C4
Rathmolyon F4
Rathmore H2
Rathmullan C4
Rathnew F5
Rathowen E4
Rathvilty G4
Ratoath F4
Ray C4
Ring H3
(An Rinn)
Ringaskiddy H3
Riverstown F3
Rockcorry E4
Roosky E3
Rosapenna C3
Rosbercon G4
Roscommon E3
Roscrea F3
Ross Carbery J2
Rosscor D3
Rosses Point D3
Rosslare Harbour H4
Roslea E4
Rostrevor E5
Roundstone F2
Roundwood F5
Rush F5

St Johnstown C4
Saintfield D5
Sallins F4
Scarriff G3
Scartaglen H2
Scarva D5
Scramoge E3
Schull J2
Scribbagh D3
Seskinore D4
Shanagolden G2
Shannonbridge F3
Shercock E4
Shillelagh G4
Shinrone F3
Shrule F2
Silvermines G3
Sion Mills D4
Sixmilebridge G2
Skerries F5
Skibbereen J2
Slane E4
Sligo D3
Smithborough E4
Sneem H1
Spiddal F2
(An Spideal)
Stewartstown D4
Stonyford G4
Strabane D4
Stradbally F4
Stradone E4
Strandhill D3
Strangford D5
Stranorlar D3
Stratford F4
Strokestown E3
Summerhill F4
Swanlinbar D3
Swatragh D4
Swinford E2
Swords F5

Taghmon G4
Tagoat H4
Tahilla H1
Tallaght F5
Tallow H3
Tallowbridge H3
Tandragee D5
Tang F3
Tarbert G2
Templemore G3
Templepatrick D5
Templetouhy G3
Termonfeckin E5
Thomas Street F3
Thomastown G4
Thurles G3
Timahoe G4
Timoleague H2
Tinahely G4
Tipperary G3
Tobercurry E3
Tobermore D4
Togher F3
Toomyvara G3
Toormore J2
Tralee G2
Tramore H4
Trim F4
Tuam F2
Tuamgraney G3
Tulla G3
Tullamore F4
Tullow G4
Tulsk E3
Turlough E2
Tyholland D4
Tyrrellspass F4

Urlingford G3

Virginia E4

Waddington H4
Warrenpoint E5
Waterford H4
Watergrasshill H3
Waterville H1
Westport E2
Wexford G4
Whitegate H3
Whitehead D5
Wicklow G5
Woodenbridge G5
Woodford F3

Youghal H3

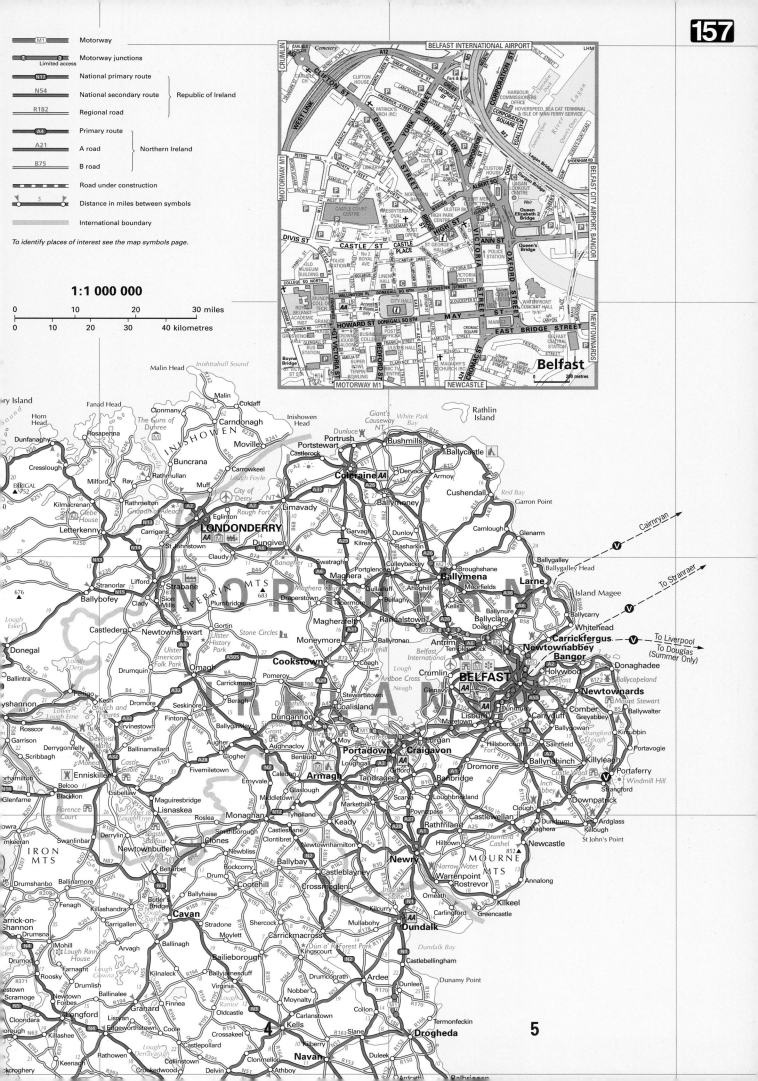

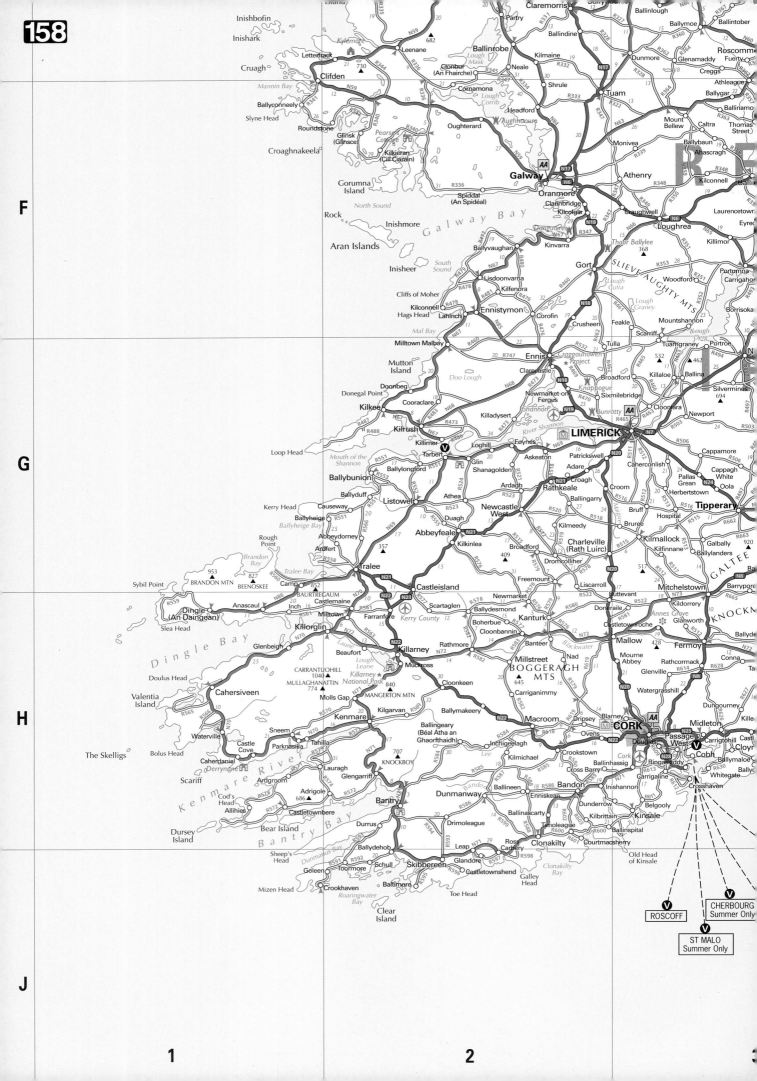

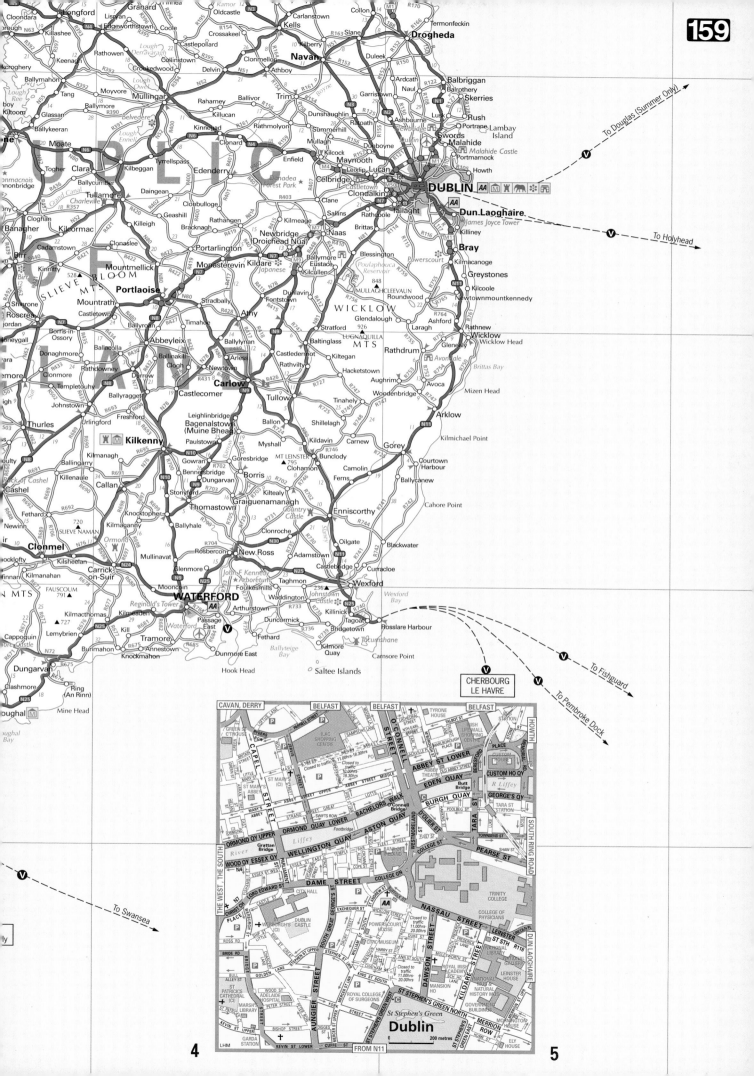

ports and airports

The following pages detail the major airports and seaports which help to provide a comprehensive domestic and international communications network. The maps indicate the approach roads into each complex and provide information on parking. Telephone numbers are provided for obtaining details on cost of parking and other travel information.

London Gatwick and London Heathrow are two of the busiest airports in the world, and many of the smaller airports listed below are constantly improving and expanding available services and destinations. The name of the airline concerned, or the flight number, must be known before aircraft arrivals and departures can be checked. Generally, no contact may be made with the passengers after they have cleared Customs on departure or before they have done so on arrival.

Always use the designated car parks. Your vehicle is liable to be removed if left unattended even for very short periods on any roads near the airport terminals. Facilities for travellers with disabilities are provided at the listed air and seaports, and in some cases parking concessions are available for Orange Badge holders. If special assistance is required the relevant airline or shipping company should be contacted.

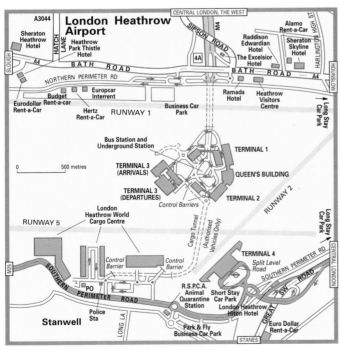

London Heathrow Airport – 16 miles west of London

Telephone: 0181 759 4321
Parking: Short-stay, long-stay and business parking available. For charge details tel: 0181 745 7160
Public Transport: Coach, bus and London Underground
There are several 4-star and 3-star hotels within easy reach of the airport, and car hire facilities are available

London Gatwick Airport – 35 miles south of London

Telephone: 01293 535353
Parking: Short-stay and long-stay parking available at both the North and South terminals. For charge details tel: 01293 502390 (short-stay) and either 0800 128128 or 01293 569222 (long-stay)
Public Transport: Coach, bus and rail. There are several 4-star and 3-star hotels within easy reach of the airport, and car hire facilities are available

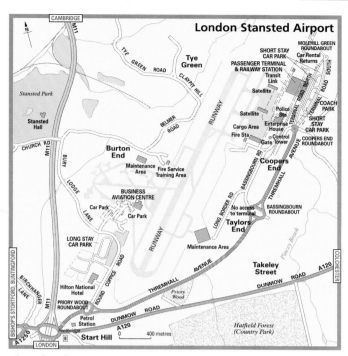

London Stansted Airport – 38 miles north-east of London

Telephone: 01279 680500
Parking: Short-stay and long-stay open-air parking available. For charge details tel: 01279 662373
Public Transport: Coach, bus and a direct rail link to London on the 'Stansted Express'
There are several 4-star and 3-star hotels within easy reach of the airport, and car hire facilities are available

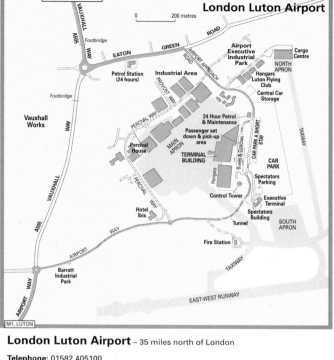

London Luton Airport – 35 miles north of London

Telephone: 01582 405100
Parking: Short-stay and long-stay open air parking available
Public Transport: Coach, bus and rail
There is one 2-star hotel at the airport and several 3-star hotels within easy reach of the airport. Car hire facilities are available

London City Airport – 7 miles east of London

Telephone: 0171 474 5555
Parking: Short-stay and long-stay parking available
Public Transport: 'Shuttlebus' service into London. Easy access to rail network and London Underground
There is a 4-star and 2-star hotel within easy reach of the airport, and car hire facilities are available

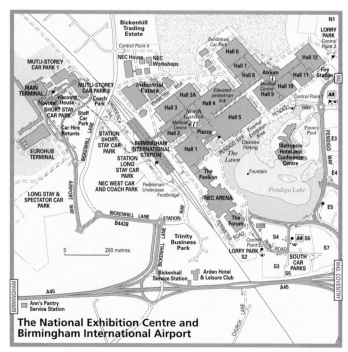

Birmingham International Airport – 8 miles east of of Birmingham

Telephone: 0121 767 5511 (Main Terminal), 0121 767 7502 (Eurohub Terminal)
Parking: Short-stay and long-stay parking available
For charge details tel: 0121 767 7861
Public Transport: Bus service and shuttle-bus service to Birmingham International railway station and the NEC.
There are several 3-star hotels within easy reach of the airport, and car hire facilities are available

major airports

East Midlands Airport
15 miles southwest of Nottingham. Next to the M1 at junctions 23A and 24

Telephone: 01332 852852
Parking: Short-stay and long-stay parking available. For charge details tel:0800 128128
Public Transport: Bus and coach services to major towns and cities in the East Midlands
There are several 3-star hotels within easy reach of the airport, and car hire facilities are available

Manchester Airport – 10 miles south of Manchester

Telephone: 0161 489 3000
Parking: Short-stay and long-stay parking available.
Public Transport: Bus, coach and rail. Manchester airport railway station connects with the Rail network
There are several 4-star and 3-star hotels within easy reach of the airport, and car hire facilities are available

Edinburgh Airport – 7 miles west of Edinburgh

Telephone: 0131 333 1000
Parking: Open-air parking is available. For charge details tel: 0131 344 3197
Public Transport: Regular coach services operate between central Edinburgh and Glasgow
There is one 4-star are several 3-star hotels within easy reach of the airport, and car hire facilities are available

Glasgow Airport – 8 miles west of Glasgow

Telephone: 0141 887 1111
Parking: Short-stay and long-stay parking is available, mostly open-air. For charge details tel: 0141 889 2751
Public Transport: Regular coach services operate between central Glasgow and Edinburgh
There are several 3-star hotels within easy reach of the airport, and car hire facilities are available

major ports

Dover

Pay-and-display parking available at the Dover Eastern Docks and at the Hoverport Terminal: for further information tel: 01304 240400
Other long-stay parking facilities are available with collection and delivery service: for charge details tel: 01304 203777, 208041 or 201227

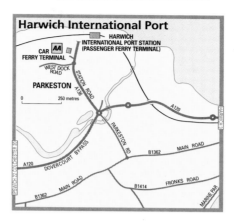

Harwich International Port

Open-air parking available at the terminal: for charge details tel: 01255 242000. Further parking 5 miles from Harwich International Port with collection and delivery service: for charge details tel: 01255 870217

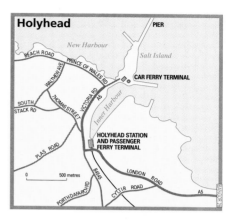

Holyhead

Open-air pay-and-display parking available close to the Passenger Terminal: for charge details tel: 01407 762304

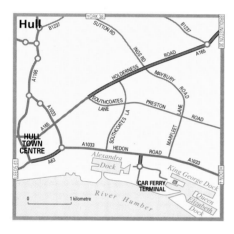

Hull

Free open-air parking at King George Dock (left at owners risk): tel: 01482 795141. Undercover parking available: for charge details tel: 01482 781021

Newhaven

Open and limited parking within harbour complex: for charge details tel: 01273 514131

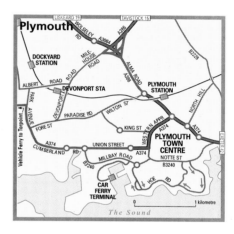

Plymouth

Free open-air parking available outside the terminal building: tel: 01752 252200 or 0990 360360

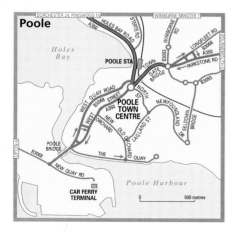

Poole

Free open-air parking for 300 vehicles available adjacent to ferry terminal: tel: 01202 685311

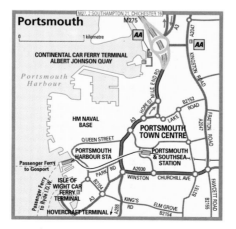

Portsmouth

Lock-up parking spaces available at Albert Johnson Quay: for charge details tel: 01705 751261
Pay-and-display parking available opposite the Hovercraft Terminal. Mutli-storey parking is also available close to the Isle of Wight Passenger Ferry Terminal: for charge details tel: 01705 823153 or 812071

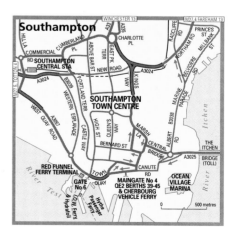

Southampton

Covered or fenced compound parking for 1,600 vehicles within the Western Docks with a collection and delivery service: for charge details tel: 01703 228001/2/3

the Channel Tunnel

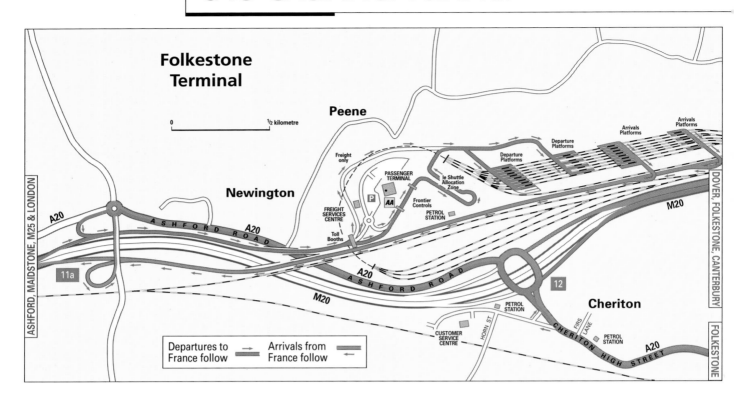

Folkestone Terminal

Peene

Newington

Cheriton

Departures to France follow →
Arrivals from France follow ←

Services to Europe

The Le Shuttle service for cars, motorcycles, coaches, cars towing caravans and trailers, and HGV vehicles runs between terminals at Folkestone and Calais.

It takes just over one hour to travel from the M20 motorway in Kent, via the Channel tunnel to the A16 autoroute in France.

The high number of trains running every day means travellers are not required to make advance reservations - just turn up and go. Call Le Shuttle Customer Services Centre (tel: 0990 353535) for further information.

Trains run at 15-minute intervals at peak times with the journey in the tunnel from platform to platform taking just 35 minutes.

Travellers pass through British and French frontier controls on departure, saving time on the other side of the channel. Each terminal has tax-and-duty free shops, bureau de change, restaurants and a variety of shops. In Calais, the Cité de l'Europe contains further shops, restaurants, hotels and a hypermarket.

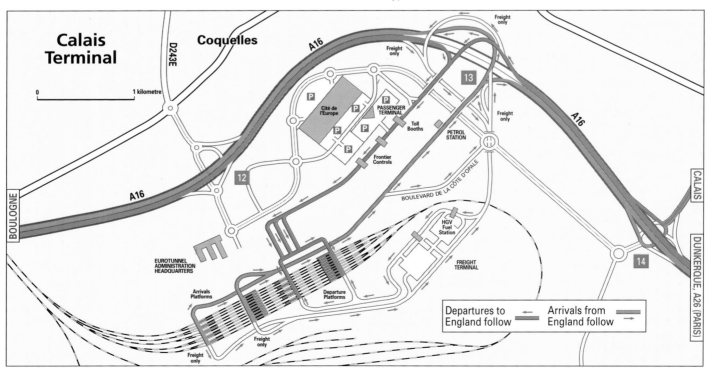

Calais Terminal

Coquelles

Departures to England follow ←
Arrivals from England follow →

ferry routes

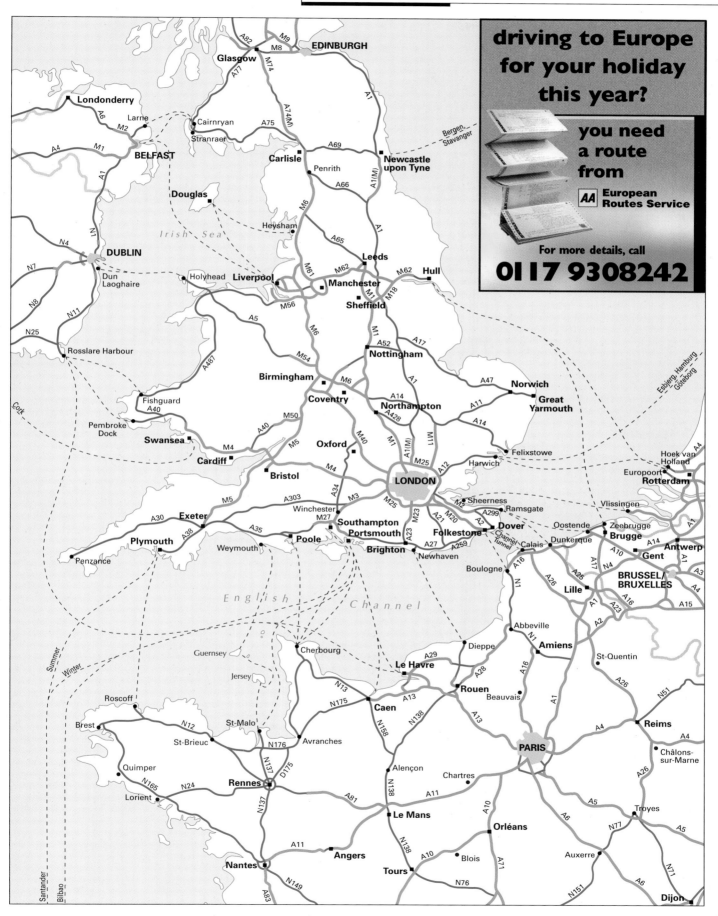

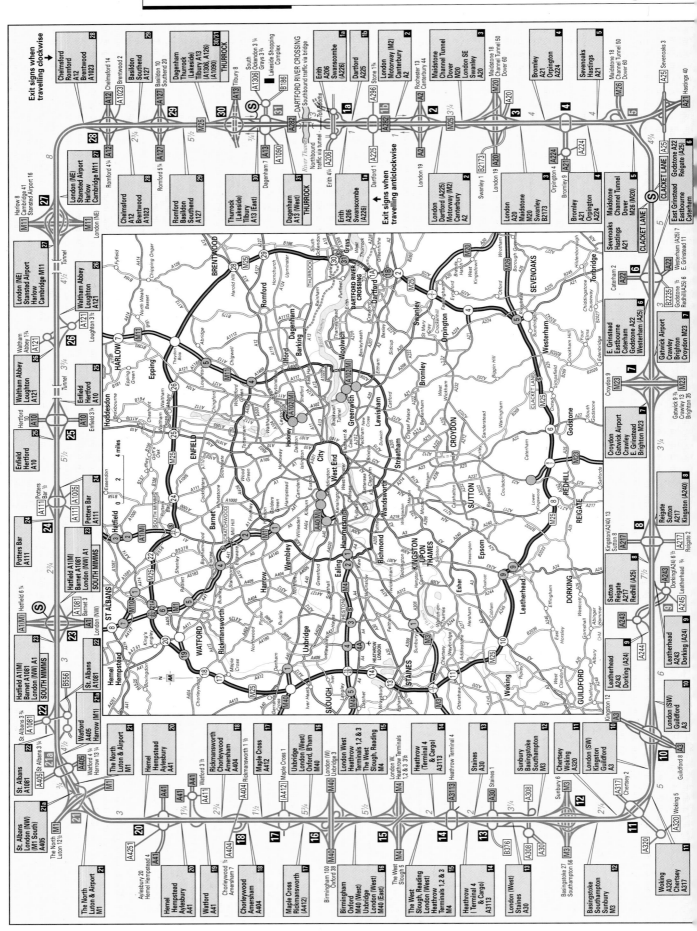

town plans

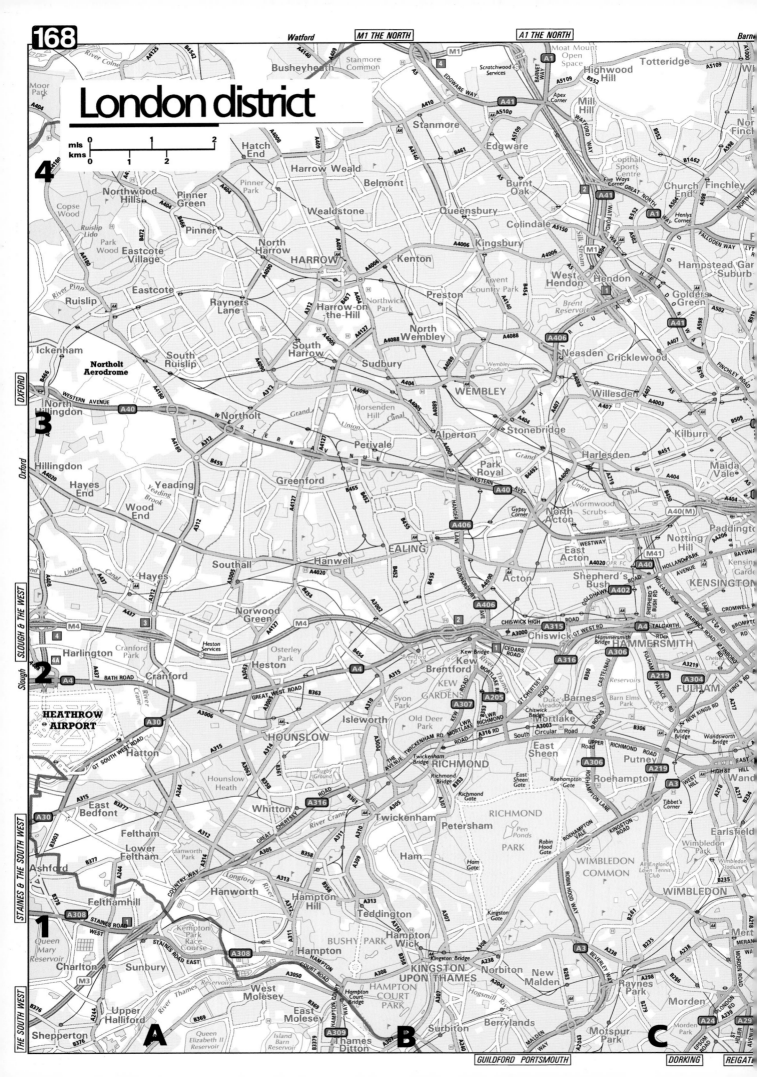

London

171 172 173
178 179
180

St Pancras | Finsbury
Bloomsbury
Paddington | Whitechapel | Stepney
Marylebone | Holborn
Soho | City
Mayfair | Strand
Hyde Park | Rotherhithe
Knightsbridge | Bermondsey
South Kensington | Lambeth | Southwark | Isle of Dogs
Westminster | Millwall
Newington | Greenwich
Chelsea | Vauxhall

174 175 176 177

Scale: 1:10,000
approx 6 inches to 1 mile

0   250   500   750 metres

Symbol	Description
	Motorway
	Primary route single/dual
	Other A road single/dual
	B road single/dual
	Unclassified road single/dual
	Unclassified road wide/narrow
	Road under construction
	Road tunnel wide/narrow
	Restricted road (access only/private)*
	Footpath
	Track
	Pedestrian street
	Railway line/in tunnel
←	One-way street
	Compulsory turn
	Banned turn
	Banned turn (restricted periods only)
•	Mini-roundabout
	Barrier
	British Rail station
	London Regional Transport station
	Docklands Light Railway station
P	Parking
PO	Post Office
POL	Police station
	Steps
✝	Church
AA	AA shop
i	Tourist Information Centre
i	Tourist Information Centre (summer only)

Royal Parks (Opening and closing times for traffic)

Green Park — Constitution Hill is always open except Sundays when it is closed 08.00–dusk

Hyde Park — 05.00–midnight

Regent's Park — 05.00–dusk

St James's Park — The Mall is always open except on Sundays when it is closed 08.00–dusk

New traffic regulations in the City of London include security checkpoints and restrict the number of entry and exit points. Changes may occur.

* Note: Oxford Street is closed to through traffic (except buses & taxis) 07.00-19.00 hrs, Monday-Saturday

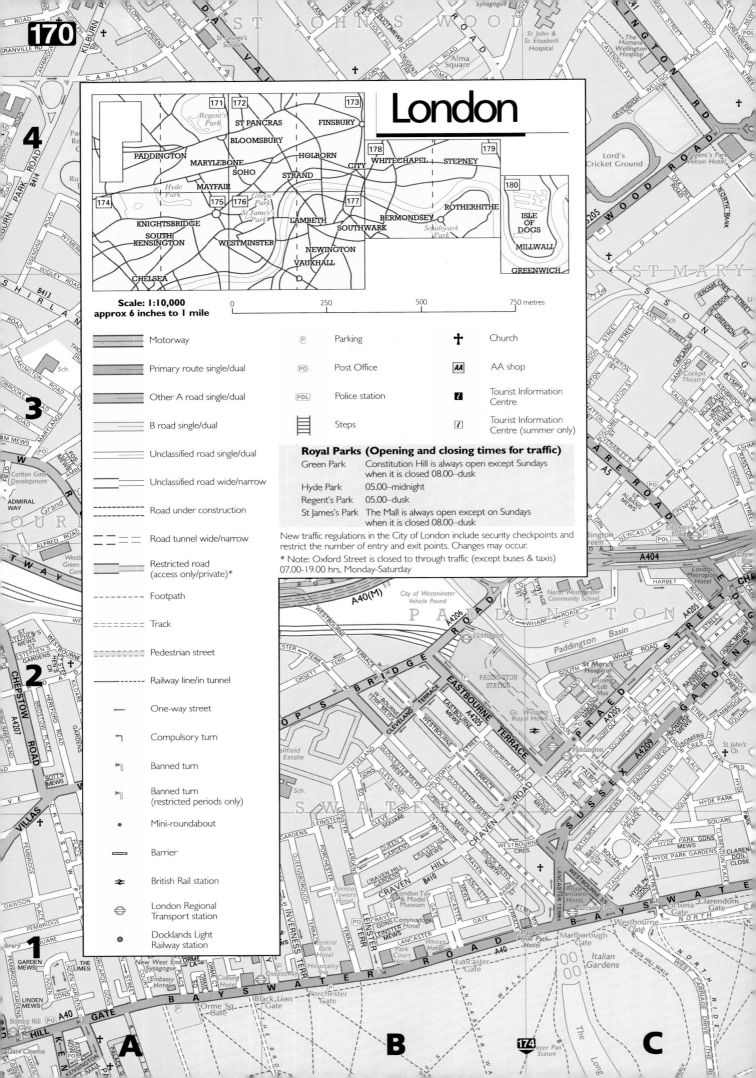

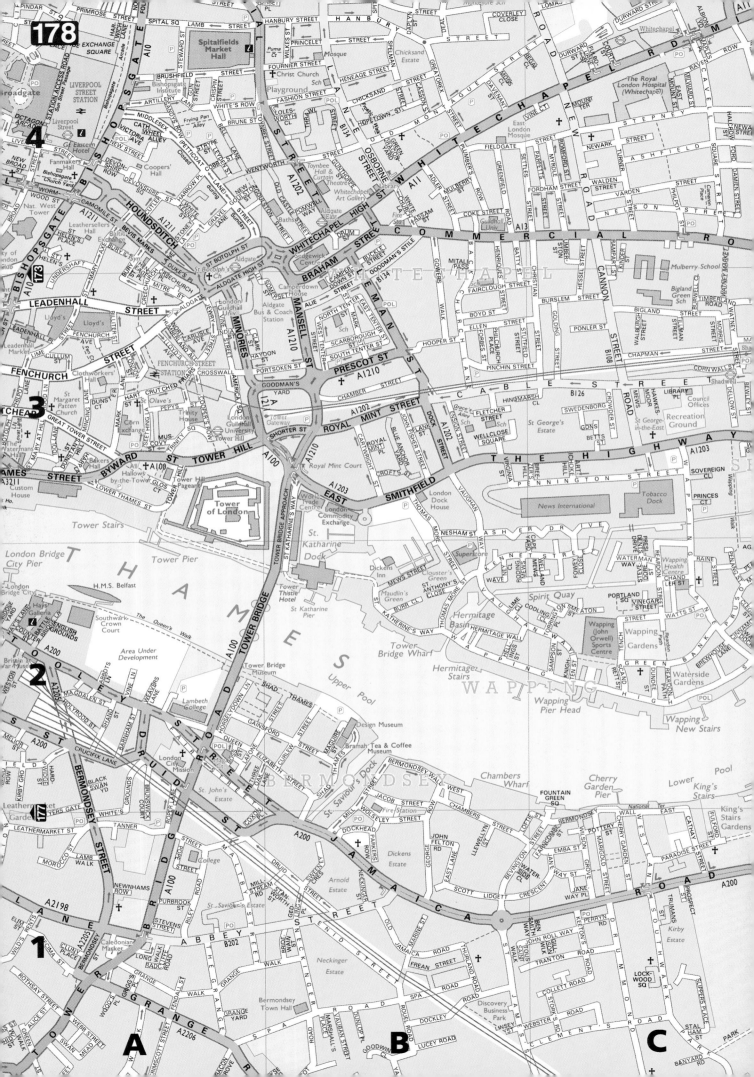

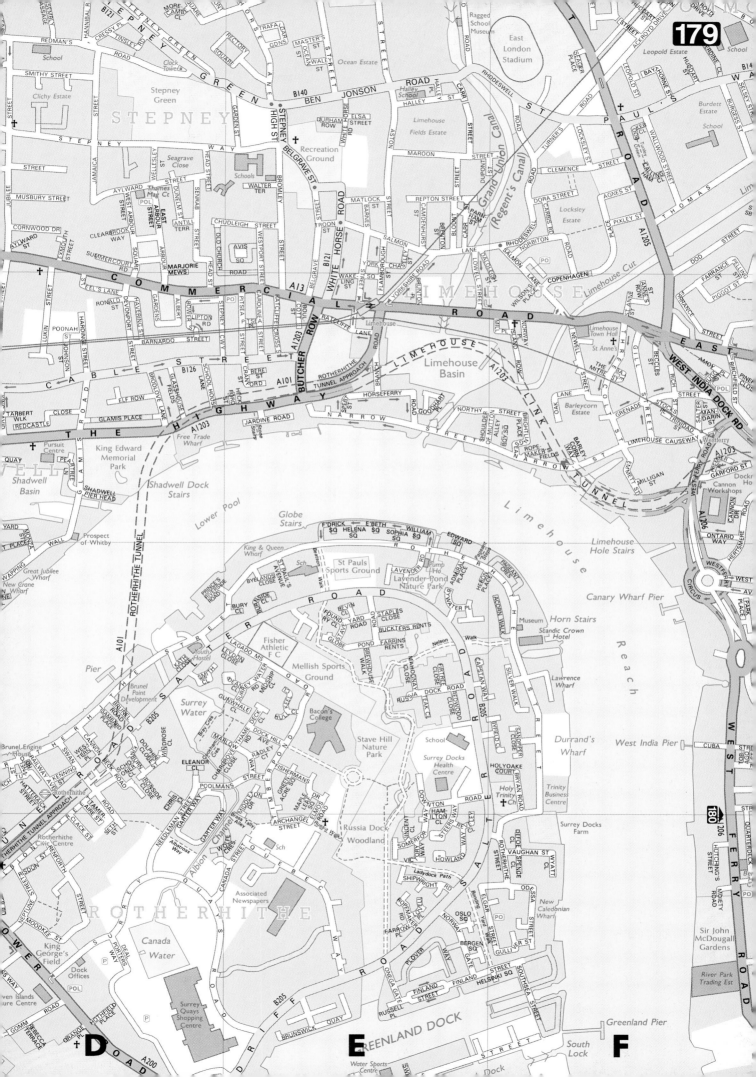

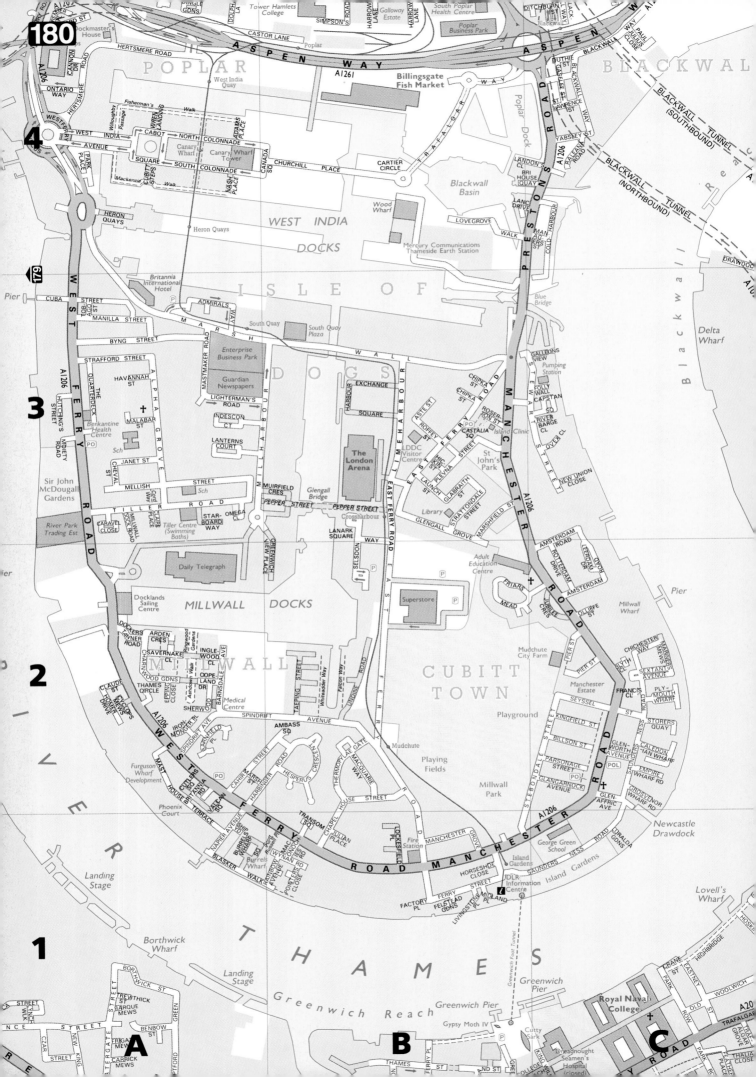

London street index

In the index the street names are listed in alphabetical order and written in full, but may be abbreviated on the map. Postal codes are listed where information is available. Each entry is followed by its map page number in bold type, and an arbitrary letter and grid reference number. For example, for Exhibition Road SW7 **174** C3, turn to page '**174**'. The letter 'C' refers to the grid square located at the bottom of the page; the figure '3' refers to the grid square located at the left-hand side of the page. Exhibition Road is found within the intersecting square. SW7 is the postcode. A proportion of street names and their references are also followed by the name of another street in italics. These entries do not appear on the map due to insufficient space but can be located adjacent to the name of the road in italics.

A

Abbey Orchard Street SW1...	176	B3
Abbey Street SE1	178	A1
Abbots Gardens W8	174	A3
St Mary's Place		
Abbots Lane SE1	178	A2
Abbots Walk W8	174	A3
St Mary's Place		
Abchurch Lane EC4	173	F1
Aberdour Street SE1	177	F2
Abingdon Road W8	174	A3
Abingdon Street SW1	176	B3
Abingdon Villas W8	174	A3
Achilles Way W1	175	E4
Ackroyd Drive E3	179	F4
Acorn Walk SE16	179	F2
Acton Street WC1	172	C4
Adam And Eve Court W1	171	E1
Oxford Street		
Adam And Eve Mews W8	174	A3
Adam Street WC2	172	B1
Adam's Row W1	171	E1
Adams Place E14	180	A4
Addington Street SE1	176	C3
Addle Hill EC4	173	E1
Addle Street EC2	173	E2
Adelaide Street WC2	172	B1
William IV Street		
Adelina Grove E1	178	D4
Adeline Place WC1	172	B2
Adelphi Terrace WC2	172	B1
Adams Street		
Adler Street E1	178	B4
Admiral Place SE16	179	E2
Admiral Way W9	170	A4
Admirals Way E14	180	A3
Adpar Street W2	170	C3
Adrian Mews SW10	174	A1
Agar Street WC2	172	B1
Agatha Close E1	178	C2
Agdon Street EC1	173	D3
Agnes Street E14	179	F4
Ainstey Street SE16	179	D1
Brunel Road		
Air Street W1	172	A1
Alaska Street SE1	176	C4
Albany Mews SE5	177	E1
Albany Road SE5	177	E1
Albany Street NW1	171	F4
Albatross Way SE16	179	D1
Albemarle Street W1	171	F1
Albemarle Way EC1	172	C3
Clerkenwell Road		
Albert Court SW7	174	C3
Albert Embankment SE1	176	B1
Albert Gardens E1	179	D3
Albert Hall Mansions SW7	174	C3
Albert Mews W8	174	B3
Albert Place W8	174	B3
Alberta Street SE17	177	D1
Albion Close W2	171	D1
Albion Mews W2	171	D1
Albion Place EC1	173	D3
Albion Street SE16	179	D1
Albion Street W2	171	D1
Albion Way EC1	173	E2
Albion Yard E1	178	C4
Aldburgh Mews W1	171	E2
Marylebone Lane		
Aldenham Street NW1	172	A4
Aldermanbury EC2	173	E2
Aldermanbury Square EC2	173	E2
Aldermanbury		
Alderney Street SW1	175	F2
Aldersgate Street EC1	173	E3
Aldford Street W1	171	E1
Aldgate EC3	178	A3
Aldgate High Street EC3	178	A3
Aldwych WC2	172	C1
Alexander Place SW7	174	C2
Alexander Square SW3	174	C2
Alford Place N1	173	E4
Alfred Mews W1	172	A3
Alfred Place WC1	172	A3
Alice Street SE1	177	F3
Alie Street E1	178	B3
All Hallows Lane EC4	173	F1
All Soul's Place W1	171	F2
Langham Street		
Allen Street W8	174	A3
Allington Street SW1	175	F3
Allsop Place NW1	171	D3
Alpha Grove E14	180	A3
Alpha Place SW3	175	D1
Alsace Road SE17	177	F1
Alscot Road SE1	178	B1
Alvey Street SE17	177	F2
Ambassador Square E14	180	B2
Ambergate Street SE17	177	D1
Ambrosden Avenue SW1	176	A3
Amelia Street SE17	177	E2
Amen Corner EC4	173	D2
Amen Court EC4	173	D2
America Square EC3	178	A3

America Street SE1	177	E4
Amoy Place E14	179	F3
Ampton Place WC1	172	C4
Ampton Street WC1	172	C4
Amsterdam Road E14	180	C2
Amwell Street EC1	172	C4
Anderson Street SW3	175	D2
Andrew Borde Street WC2	172	B2
Charing Cross Road		
Angel Court EC2	173	F2
Angel Court SW1	176	A4
King Street		
Angel Passage EC4	173	F1
Angel Place SE1	177	E4
Angel Street EC1	173	E2
Ann Moss Way SE16	179	D1
Ansdell Street W8	174	A3
Antill Terrace E1	179	D4
Apothecary Street EC4	173	D2
New Bridge Street		
Apple Tree Yard SW1	172	A1
Appold Street EC2	173	F3
Aquinas Street SE1	177	D4
Arbour Square E1	179	D4
Archangel Street SE16	179	E1
Archer Street W1	172	A1
Arden Crescent E14	180	A2
Argent Street SE1	177	E4
Loman Street		
Argyle Square WC1	172	B4
Argyle Street WC1	172	B4
Argyle Walk WC1	172	B4
Argyll Road W8	174	A3
Argyll Street W1	171	F2
Arlington Street SW1	175	F4
Arlington Way EC1	173	D4
Arne Street WC2	172	B2
Arneway Street SW1	176	A2
Arnside Street SE17	177	E1
Arthur Street EC4	173	F1
Artichoke Hill E1	178	C3
Artillery Lane E1	178	A4
Artillery Passage E1	178	A4
Artillery Lane		
Artillery Row SW1	176	A3
Artizan Street E1	178	A4
Harrow Place		
Arundel Street WC2	172	C1
Ashbridge Street NW8	170	C3
Ashburn Gardens SW7	174	B2
Ashburn Mews SW7	174	B2
Ashburn Place SW7	174	B2
Ashby Street EC1	173	D4
Ashdown Walk E14	180	A2
Asher Drive E1	178	B3
Ashfield Street E1	178	C4
Ashland Place W1	170	A3
Ashley Place SW1	175	F3
Ashmill Street NW1	170	C3
Aske Street N1	173	F4
Asolando Drive SE17	177	E2
King & Queen Street		
Aspen Way E14	180	B4
Assam Street E1	178	B4
Assembly Passage E1	179	D4
Aste Street E14	180	B3
Astell Street SW3	175	D2
Aston Street E14	179	E4
Astwood Mews SW7	174	B2
Atherstone Mews SW7	174	B2
Atterbury Street SW1	176	B2
Attneave Street WC1	172	C4
Auckland Street SE11	176	C1
Augustus Street NW1	171	F4
Aulton Place SE11	177	D1
Austin Friars EC2	173	F2
Austin Friars Square EC2	173	F2
Austin Friars		
Austral Street SE11	177	D2
Ave Maria Lane EC4	173	E2
Aveline Street SE11	176	C1
Avery Row W1	171	F1
Avis Square E1	179	E4
Avon Place SE1	177	E3
Avonmouth Street SE1	177	E3
Aybrook Street W1	171	E2
Aylesbury Road SE17	177	F1
Aylesbury Street EC1	173	D3
Aylesford Street SW1	176	A1
Aylward Street E1	179	D4
Ayres Street SE1	177	E4

B

Babmaes Street SW1	176	A4
Jermyn Street		
Bacchus Walk N1	173	F4
Bache's Street N1	173	F4
Back Church Lane E1	178	B4
Back Hill EC1	173	D3
Bacon Grove SE1	178	A1
Bainbridge Street WC1	172	B2
Baker Street W1 & NW1	171	D3
Baker's Mews W1	171	E2

Baker's Row EC1	173	F3
Baker's Yard EC1	173	D3
Baker's Row		
Bakers Hall Court EC3	178	A3
Harp Lane		
Balcombe Street NW1	171	D3
Balderton Street W1	171	E1
Baldwin Street EC1	173	F4
Baldwin's Gardens EC1	172	C3
Balfe Street N1	172	B4
Balfour Mews W1	171	E1
Balfour Place W1	171	E1
Balfour Street SE17	177	F2
Ballast Quay SE10	180	C1
Balneil Gate SW1	176	A1
Baltic Street EC1	173	E3
Balvaird Place SW1	176	B2
Bancroft Road E1	176	C1
Bank End SE1	177	E4
Bankside Jetty SE1	173	E1
Banner Street EC1	173	E3
Banyard Road SE16	178	C1
Barbon Close WC1	172	C3
Barge House Street SE1	173	D1
Barkston Gardens SW5	174	A2
Barleycorn Way E14	179	F3
Barlow Place W1	171	F1
Barlow Street SE17	177	F2
Barnaby Place SW7	174	C2
Barnardo Street E1	179	D3
Barnby Street NW1	172	A4
Barnes Street E14	179	E4
Barnfield Place E14	180	A2
Barnham Street SE1	178	A2
Barnsdale Avenue E14	180	A2
Baron's Place SE1	177	D3
Barque Mews SE8	180	A1
Barrett Street W1	171	E2
Barrie Street W2	170	B1
Barrow Hill Road NW8	170	C4
St Johns Wood High Street		
Barter Street WC1	172	B2
Barth Lane EC2	173	F2
Bartholomew Close EC1	173	E2
Bartholomew Square EC1	173	E3
Bartholomew Street SE1	177	F2
Barton Street SW1	176	B3
Basil Street SW3	175	D3
Basinghall Avenue EC2	173	E2
Basinghall Street EC2	173	E2
Bastwick Street EC1	173	E3
Bate Street E14	179	F3
Bateman Street W1	172	A2
Bateman's Buildings W1	172	A2
Bath Court EC1	172	C3
Warner Street		
Bath Place N1	173	F4
Bath Street EC1	173	E4
Bath Terrace SE1	177	E3
Bathurst Mews W2	170	C1
Bathurst Street W2	170	C1
Battle Bridge Lane SE1	177	F4
Batty Street E1	178	B4
Bayley Street WC1	172	A2
Baylis Road SE1	176	C3
Bayswater Road W2	170	A1
Baythorne Street E3	179	F4
Beaconsfield Road SE17	177	F1
Beak Street W1	172	A1
Bear Gardens SE1	173	E1
Bear Lane SE1	177	D4
Bear Street WC2	172	B1
Cranbourn Street		
Beatrice Place W8	174	A2
Beauchamp Place SW3	175	D3
Beauchamp Street EC1	173	D3
Brooke Street		
Beaufort Gardens SW3	175	D3
Beaufort Street SW3	174	B1
Beaumont Mews W1	171	E2
Beaumont Place W1	172	A3
Beaumont Street W1	171	E3
Beccles Street E14	179	F3
Beckway Street SE17	177	F2
Bedale Street SE1	177	E3
Borough High Street		
Bedford Avenue WC1	172	B2
Bedford Court WC2	172	B1
Bedford Gardens W8	174	A4
Bedford Place WC1	172	B3
Bedford Row WC1	172	C3
Bedford Square WC1	172	B2
Bedford Street WC2	172	B1
Bedford Way WC1	172	B3
Bedfordbury WC2	172	B1
Bedser Close SE11	176	C1
Beech Street EC2	173	E3
Beeston Place SW1	175	F3
Bekesbourne Street E14	171	E2
Marylebone Lane		
Belgrave Mews North SW1...	175	E3
Belgrave Mews South SW1...	175	E3
Belgrave Mews West SW1	175	E3
Belgrave Place SW1	175	E3
Belgrave Road SW1	175	F2
Belgrave Square SW1	175	E3
Belgrave Street E1	179	E3
Belgrove Street WC1	172	B4
Bell Lane E1	178	A4

London district index

District names are listed in alphabetical order and are referenced to the London district map on pages 168–169. Each entry is followed by its map page number, in bold type, plus a grid reference.

189

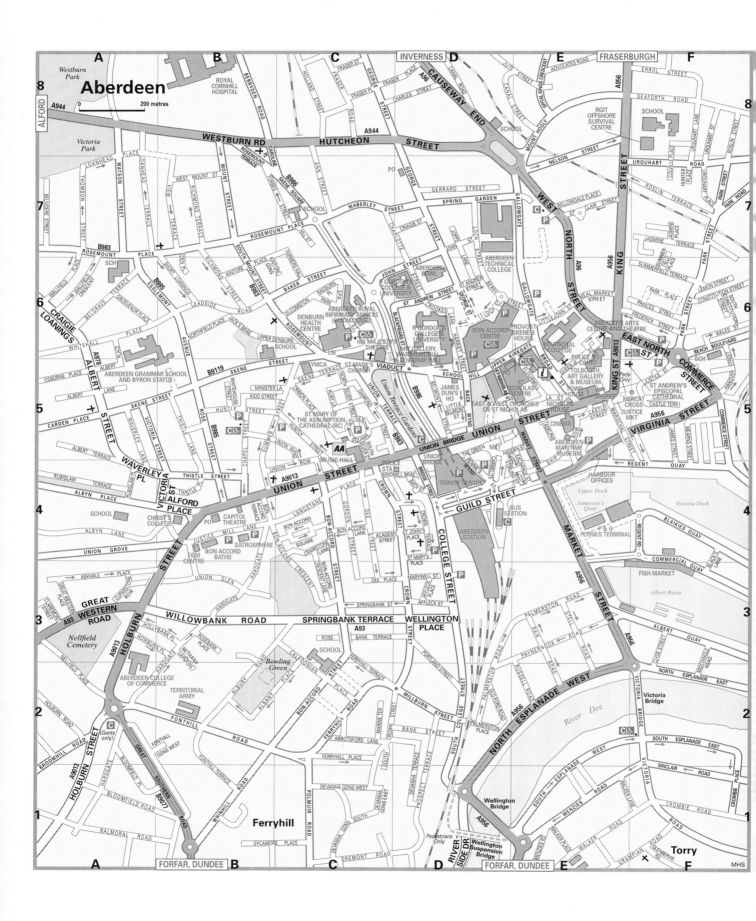

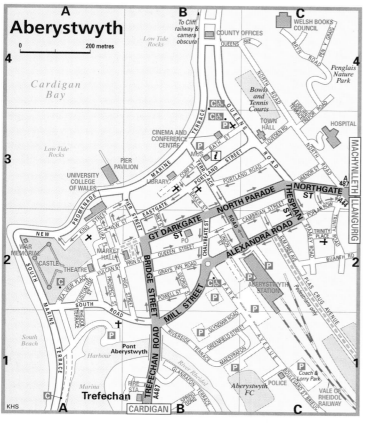

Aberystwyth

Aberystwyth is found on atlas page **43**,
grid reference SN**58**81

Baker Street	B3	Riverside Terrace	B1
Bath Steet	B3	Sea View Place	A2
Boulevard St Brieuc	C1	South Marine Terrace	A1-A2
Bridge Street	B1-B2	South Road	A2-B1
Bryn Road	C4	Spring Gardens	B1
Buarth Road	C2	Stanley Road	C2
Cambrian Street	C2-C3	Terrace Road	B3-C2
Chalybeate Street	B2	Thespian Street	C2-C3
Corporation Street	B3	Trefechan Road	B1
Custom House Street	A2	Trefor Road	C3-C4
Eastgate	B2-B3	Trinity Place	C2
Elmtree Avenue	C2	Trinity Road	C2-C3
George Street	B2	Union Street	B2
Glanrafon Terrace	B1	Vaenor Road	C3
Glyndwr Road	B1	Vulcan Street	A2
Grays Inn Road	B2		
Great Darkgate Street	B2		
Greenfield Street	B1-C1		
High Street	A2-B2		
King Street	A2-A3		
Laura Place	A2		
Lisburn Terrace	C3-C4		
Loveden Road	C3		
Maesyrafon	B1-C1		
Marine Terrace	B4-B3		
Market Street	B2		
Mill Street	B1-B2		
New Promenade	A2-B3		
New Street	A2-B2		
North Parade	B2-C3		
North Road	C3-C4		
Northgate Street	C3		
Park Avenue	B2-C1		
Pen y Graig	C4		
Pier Street	B2-B3		
Plas Crug Avenue	C1-C2		
Poplar Row	C2-C3		
Portland Road	B3-C3		
Portland Street	B3-C3		
Powell Street	B2		
Princess Street	B2		
Prospect Street	A2		
Queen Street	B2		
Queens Avenue	B4-C4		
Queens Road	B4-C3		
Rheidol Terrace	A1		

Aberdeen

Aberdeen is found on atlas page **135**,
grid reference NJ**93**06

Abbotsford Lane	C2	Broomhill Road	A1-A2
Academy Street	C4-D4	Caledonian Lane	C2
Advocates Road	E8	Caledonian Place	C3-C2
Affleck Place	D3	Canal Road	D8
Affleck Street	D3	Canal Street	D8-E8
Albany Place	B2-C2	Carden Place	A5
Albert Lane	A5	Carmelite Street	D4-D5
Albert Quay	F3-E3	Caroline Place	B7-B8-C7
Albert Place	A5-A6	Castle Street	E5
Albert Street	A5-A6	Castle Terrace	F5
Albert Terrace	A5	Causewayend	D8
Albury Road	B2-B3-C3	Chapel Street	B5-B4
Albyn Lane	A4-B4	Charles Street	C8-D8
Albyn Place	A4	Charlotte Street	D7-C7-D6
Alford Place	A4	Claremont Street	A3
Ann Street	C7-C8	Clyde Street	F2-F3
Ashvale Place	A3-B3	College Street	D4-D3
Back Wynd	D5	Colville Place	F7-F8
Baker Street	C6	Commerce Street	F5
Balmoral Road	A1-B1	Commercial Quay	F3-F4
Bank Street	D2	Constitution Street	F6
Bath Street	D4	Craibstone Lane	C4
Beach Boulevard	F6	Craigie Loanings	A6
Belgrave Terrace	A6	Craigie Street	D7
Belmont Street	D5	Crimon Place	C5
Belvidere Street	A7	Crombie Place	F1-F2
Berry Street	D6-E6	Crombie Road	F1
Berryden Road	B8	Crooked Lane	D6
Bethany Gardens	B2-B3	Crown Street	C4-D4-D3-D2
Blackfriars Street	D5-D6	Crown Terrace	D4
Black's Lane	F3-F4	Cuparstone Row	A3
Blaikies Quay	F4	Dee Place	C3-D3
Bloomfield Place	A2-A1-B1	Dee Street	C4-C3
Bloomfield Road	A1-B1	Deemont Road	C1-D1
Bon-Accord Crescent	B4-C4-C3	Devanha Gardens East	C1
Bon-Accord Crescent Lane	C3-C4	Devanha Gardens South	C1
Bon-Accord Lane	C4	Devanha Gardens West	C1
Bon-Accord Square	C4	Devanha Terrace	D1-D2
Bon-Accord Street	B2-C2-C3-C4	Diamond Street	C5
Bon-Accord Terrace	B4	Duff Street	F7
Bridge Street	D4	East North Street	E6-F6
Broad Street	E5	Eden Place	B6-B7

Erroll Street	F8	Justice Street	F5
Esslemont Avenue	A6-B6-B5	Justice Mill Lane	B4
Exchange Street	E5-E4	Jute Street	D8-E8
Farmers Hall	C7-C6	Kidd Street	B5-C5
Ferryhill Place	C2	King Street	E5-E6-E7-E8
Ferryhill Road	C2-D2	Kintore Gardens	B6-C6
Ferryhill Terrace	C3-C2	Kintore Place	B6-B7-C7
Flourmill Lane	E5	Langstane Place	C4
Fonthill Gardens West	A2-B2	Leadside Road	B6
Fonthill Road	A2-B2-C2	Lemon Street	F6
Fonthill Terrace	B1-B2	Little Belmont Street	D5
Forbes Street	B7-C7	Little John Street	E6
Fraser Place	C8-D8	Loanhead Place	A7
Fraser Road	C8	Loanhead Terrace	A7
Fraser Street	C8	Loch Street	D7-D6
Frederick Street	E6	Maberley Street	C7-D7
Gallowgate	E7-E6	Marischal Street	E5-F5-F4
George Street	C8-D8-D7-D6	Market Street	E5-E4-E3
Gerrard Street	D7	Marine Terrace	C2
Gilcomston Park	C6	Marywell Street	D3
Glenbervie Road	F1	Meal Market Street	E6
Golden Square	C5	Mearns Street	F5-F4
Gordon Street	C4-C3	Menzies Road	E1-F1-F2
Grampian Road	E1-F1	Midchingle Road	F2-F3
Great Southern Road	A1-A2-B1	Millburn Street	D2
Great Western Place	A3	Minister Lane	B5-C5
Great Western Road	A3	Mount Holly	E8
Grosvenor Place	A6	Mount Street	B7
Guild Street	D4-E4	Nellfield Place	A2-A3
Hadden Street	D5-E5	Nelson Street	E7-E8
Hanover Street	F6-F5	North Esplanade East	F2
Hardgate	A1-A2-B2-B3-B4	North Esplanade West	D1-E3
Harriet Street	D5-D6	North Silver Street	C5
Hill Street	C7	Northfield Place	B6
Holburn Road	A2	Old Ford Road	D2
Holburn Street	A1-A2-A3-B3-B4	Osborne Place	A5
Holland Street	C8	Oscar Road	F1
Hollybank Place	A3-B3	Palmerston Place	D2
Howburn Place	A3-B3	Palmerston Road	D2-D3-E3
Hunter Place	F7	Park Place	F6
Huntly Street	B5-C5-C4	Park Road	F7
Hutcheon Street	C8-D8	Park Street	F6-F7
Irvine Place	A2	Polmuir Road	C1-C2
Jack's Brae	B6	Portland Street	D3-D2
James Street	F5	Poynernook Road	D2-E2-E3
Jasmine Place	F7	Princes Street	F6
Jasmine Terrace	F7	Prospect Terrace	D1-D2
John Street	C6-D6-D7	Queen Street	E5-E6
Jopp's Lane	D7-D6	Raeburn Place	C6

Raik Road	E3-E2	Sycamore Place	B1-C1
Regent Road	F4	The Green	D5
Regent Quay	E4-F4	Thistle Lane	B5-B4
Rennies Wynd	D4	Thistle Place	B4
Richmond Street	B6-B7	Thistle Street	B4
Richmond Terrace	B7	Thomson Street	A7
Riverside Drive	D1	Union Bridge	D4-D5
Rose Street	B5-B4	Union Glen	B3
Rosebank Place	B3	Union Grove	A4-B4
Rosebank Terrace	C3-D3	Union Row	B4-C4
Rosemount Place	A7-B7-C7	Union Street	B4-C4-D4-D5-E5
Rosemount Terrace	B8-B7	Union Terrace	C5-D5
Rosemount Viaduct	B6-C6-C5	Union Wynd	B5-C5-C4
Roslin Street	F7-F8	Upper Denburn	B6-C6
Roslin Terrace	F7	Upper Kirkgate	D5-D6-E6
Rubislaw Place	A4	Urquhart Lane	F7-F8
Rubislaw Terrace	A4	Urquhart Place	F7
Ruby Lane	C5	Urquhart Road	F7
Russell Road	E2-E3	Urquhart Street	F8-F7
St Andrew Street	D6	Victoria Bridge	F2
St Clair Street	E7	Victoria Road	F2-F1
St John's Place	D4	Victoria Street	A5-B5-B4
St Mary's Place	D4	View Terrace	B7
St Nicholas Street	D5-E5	Virginia Street	E5-F5
School Hill	D5	Wales Street	F6
Seaforth Road	F8	Walker Lane	E1-F1
Ship Row	E4-E5	Walker Place	E1
Short Loanings	B6	Walker Road	E1-F1
Sinclair Road	F1-F2	Wallfield Crescent	A6
Skene Square	C6-C5	Wallfield Place	A6
Skene Street	A5-B5-C5	Watson Street	A7-A8
Skene Terrace	C5	Waverley Lane	A5-A4
South College Street	D3-D2-D1	Waverley Place	A4-B4
South Constitution Street	F6	Wellington Place	D3
South Crown Street	C1-C2-D2	Wellington Road	E1
South Esplanade East	F2	West Mount Street	B7
South Esplanade West	F2-F1-E2	West North Street	E7-E6
South Mount Street	B7-B6	Westburn Road	A8-B8
South Silver Street	C5	Whinhill Road	B1-B2
Spa Street	C6	Whitehall Place	A6-B6
Spital Kings Crescent	E8	Whitehouse Street	B5
Spring Garden	D7	Willowbank Road	B3-C3
Springbank Street	C3-D3	Willowdale Place	E7
Springbank Terrace	C3-D3	Windmill Brae	C4-D4
Stell Road	E3		
Stirling Street	D4-E4		
Summerfield Place	F6-F7	AA shop	C5
Summerfield Terrace	F6	19-20 Golden Square	
Summer Street	B4-B5-C5	Aberdeen AB9 1JN	

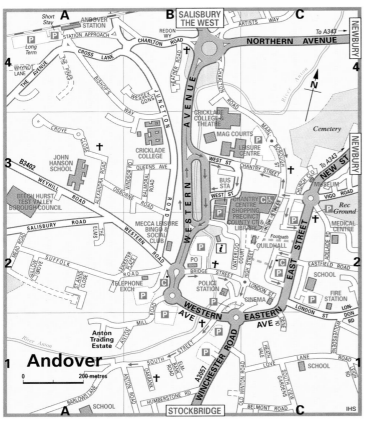

Andover

Andover is found on atlas page **23**, grid reference SU**3645**

Adelaide Road	C2-C3	The Elms	A2
Alexandra Road	A3	The Pines	A4
Anton Mill Road	A1-B1-B2	Vigo Road	C3
Anton Road	B1	Waterloo Court	B2
Artists Way	B4-C4	Wessex Gardens	B4
Balmoral Road	B3	Western Avenue	B1-B2-B3
Barlows Lane	A1	Western Road	A2-B2
Belmont Road	B1-C1	West Street	B2-B3
Bishop's Way	A4-B4-B3	Weyhill Road	A3
Bridge Street	B2	Whynot Lane	A4
Chantry Street	B3-C3	Winchester Road	B1
Charlton Road	B4-B3-C3	Windsor Road	B3
Church Close	C3	Willow Grove	A2
Cross Lane	A4	Wolversdene Road	C1
Croye Close	A3		
Dene Road	C1		
Eastfield Road	C2		
East Street	C2-C3		
Eastern Avenue	C1-C2		
Elmbank Road	B1		
Heath Vale	C1		
Heather Drive	B4		
High Street	B2-C2-C3		
Humberstone Road	B1		
Junction Road	B2-B3-B4		
Leicester Place	B2		
Leigh Road	C1		
London Road	C1		
London Street	C1		
Love Lane	C1-C2		
Marlborough Street	C3		
Mead Road	A2		
New Street	C3		
Northern Avenue	B4-C4		
Oak Bank Road	B1		
Old Winton Road	B1-C1		
Osborne Road	A3-B3		
Queens Avenue	B3		
Redon Way	B4		
St Anns Close	A2		
Salisbury Road	A2		
South Street	B1-B2		
Southview Gardens	C1		
Station Approach	A4		
Suffolk Road	A2-B2		
The Avenue	A4		

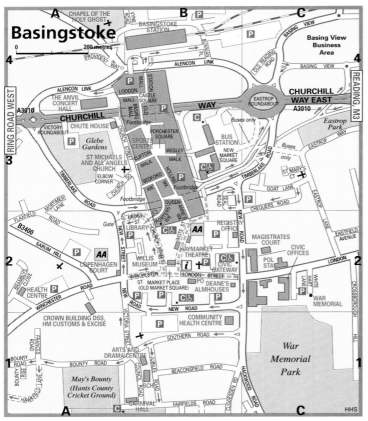

Basingstoke

Basingstoke is found on atlas page **24**, grid reference SU**6352**

Alencon Link	A4-C4
Basing View	C4
Beaconsfield Road	B1
Bounty Rise	A1
Bounty Road	A1
Bramblys Close	A2
Bunnian Place	B4
Chequers Road	B2-C3
Church Square	A2-B2
Church Street	A2-B2
Churchill Way	A3-B4
Churchill Way East	C4
Cliddesden Road	B1
Council Road	B1
Cross Street	A2-B2
Crossborough Hill	C1-C2
Eastrop Lane	C2-C3
Eastrop Way	C3
Elbow Corner	A3
Fairfields Road	B1
Flaxfield Road	B2
Frances Road	A1
Goat Lane	C3
Hackwood Road	B1-C1
Hawkfield Lane	A1
Jubilee Road	B1
London Road	C2
London Street	B2
Mortimer Lane	A2-A3
New Road	A2-B3
New Street	A2
Old Reading Road	C3
Provident Way	A4
Sarum Hill	A2
Seal Road	B1-B2
Southern Road	B1
St Mary's Court	C3
Timberlake Road	A3-C3
Victoria Street	A2-B1
Vyne Road	A4-B4
White Hart Lane	C2
Winchester Road	A2
Winchester Street	B2
Wote Street	B2

AA shop
21-23 Wote Street
Basingstoke RG21 1NE

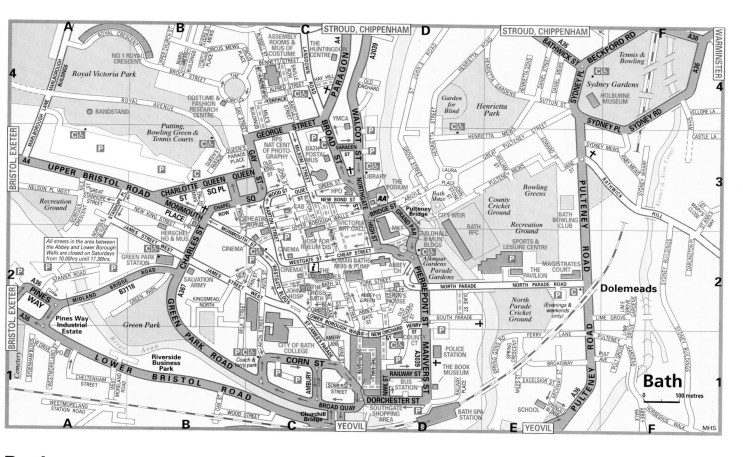

Bath

Bath is found on atlas page **22**,
grid reference ST**7464**

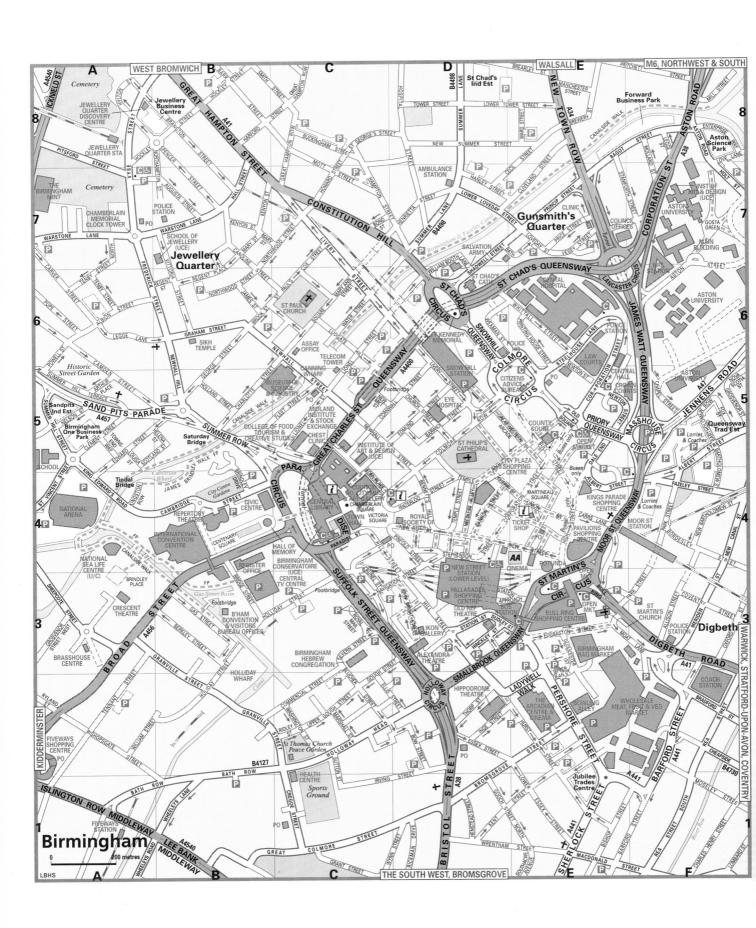

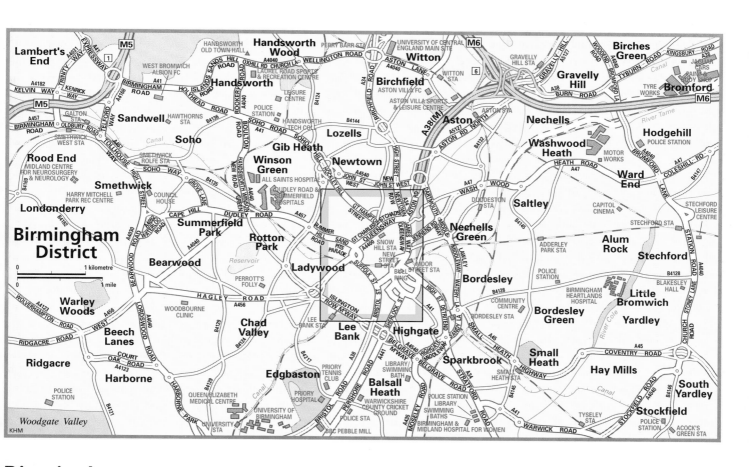

Birmingham

Birmingham is found on atlas page **61**,
grid reference **SP0786**

Albert St	E4-F4-F5	Cannon Street	D4	Gosta Green	F7	King Edwards Road	A5-A4	Old Square	E5	Summer Hill Terrace	A5
Albion Street	A6	Caroline Street	B7-B6-C6	Gough Street	C2-C3-D3	Kingston Row	A4	Oxford Street	F3	Summer Lane	D7-D8
Allison Street	F3-F4	Carrs Lane	E4	Graham Street	B6	Ladywell Walk	D2-E2-E3	Paradise Circus	B4-C4-C5-B5	Summer Row	B5
Arthur Place	A5	Carver Street	A7-A6	Grant Street	C1	Lancaster Circus	E7-E6-F6-F7	Paradise Street	C4	Sutton Street	C2-C1
Aston Road	F8-F7	Cecil Street	D7-E7-E8	Granville Street	A3-B3-B2-C2	Lee Bank Middleway	B1	Park Street	E3-F3-F4	Temple Row	D5-D4-E5
Aston Street	F6-F7	Chamberlain Square	C4	Great Charles Street	C5	Legge Street	A6-B6	Pershore Street	E2	Temple Street	D4
Augusta Street	B7	Chapel Street	F5	Great Colmore Street	B1-C1-C2	Lionel Street	C5-C6-D6	Pinfold Street	C4-D4	Tenby Street	A7
Bagot Street	E7-E8-F8	Charles Henry Street	F1	Great Hampton Row	C7-C8	Livery Street	C7-C6-D6-D5	Pitsford Street	A7-A8	Tenby Street North	A6-A7
Barford Street	F2-F1-E1	Charlotte Street	B5-C6	Great Hampton Street	B8-B7	Louisa Street	A5	Pope Street	A7	Tennant Street	A1-A2-A3
Barr Street	B8-C8	Cherry Street	D4-E4	Great Western Arcade	D5-E5	Love Lane	F7-F8	Powell Street	A6	Thorp Street	D2
Bartholomew Row	F5	Church Street	D5	Grosvenor Street	F5	Loveday Street	E7	Price Street	E7	Tower Street	D8
Bartholomew Street	F4-F5	Clement Street	A5	Grosvenor Street West	A3	Lower Essex Street	D2-E2-E1	Princip Street	E7	Townsend Way	A5
Barwick Street	D5	Cliveland Street	D7-E7-E8	Hall Street	B7-B8	Lower Loveday Street	D7-E7	Printing House Street	E6	Union Street	E4
Bath Row	A1-B1-B2-C2	Coleshill Street	F5-F6	Hampton Street	D7-C7-C8	Lower Tower Street	D8-E8	Priory Queensway	E5	Upper Dean Street	E2-E3
Bath Street	D7-E7	Colmore Circus	D5-D6-E6-E5	Hanley Street	D7	Ludgate Hill	C6-C5	Pritchett Street	E8-F8	Upper Gough Street	C2
Bennett's Hill	D4	Colmore Row	C4-D4-D5	Harford Street	B8-C8	Macdonald Street	E1-F1	Queensway	C5-D6	Vesey Street	E7
Berkley Street	B3	Commercial Street	B2-C2-C3	Helena Street	A5-B5	Manchester Street	E8	Rea Street	F1-F2	Vittoria Street	B7-B6
Birchall Street	F1	Constitution Hill	C7-D7-D6	Henrietta Street	C7-D7	Marshall Street	C2	Rea Street South	F1	Vyse Street	A7-A8-B8
Bishop Street	E1	Cornwall Street	C5-D5-D6	Henstead Street	D1	Mary Ann Street	C6	Regent Place	B7-B6	Ward Street	E8
Bishopsgate Street	A2-A1-B1	Corporation Street	D4-E5-E6-F7	High Street	E4	Mary Street	B7-C7	Rickman Drive	D1	Warstone Lane	A7-B7
Blucher Street	C3-C2	Coventry Street	F3	Hill Street	C4-D3	Masshouse Circus	E5-F5	Ridley Street	C2	Washington Street	C2
Bond Street	C7	Cox Street	C6-C7	Hinckley Street	D3	Meriden Street	F3	Royal Mail Street	C3	Water Street	C6
Bordesley Street	F4	Cregoe Street	C1	Hockley Street	A8-B8	Mill Street	F8	St Chad's Circus	D6	Waterloo Street	C4-D4
Bow Street	D2	Dale End	E4-E5	Holland Street	B5	Moat Lane	E3-F3	St Chad's Queensway	D6-E6-E7	Weaman Street	E6-D6
Bradford Street	F2	Digbeth Road	F3	Holliday Street	A2-B2-B3-C3	Molland Street	F8-F7	St Martin's Circus	E4-E5	Wheeleys Lane	A1-B1
Branston Street	A8-B8-B7	Dudley Street	D3	Holloway Circus	D2	Moor Street Queensway	E4-F4	St Paul's Square	B6-C6	Wheeleys Road	A1
Brearley Street	D8-E8	Eden Place	C5-C4	Holloway Head	C2-D2	Moseley Street	F2-F1	St Vincent Street	A4-A5	Whittall Street	D6-E6
Brewery Street	E8	Edgbaston Street	E3	Hospital Street	D8-D7	Mott Street	C8-C7	Sand Pits Parade	A5-B5	William Booth Lane	D6-D7
Bridge Street	B3-B4	Edmund Street	C5-D5	Howard Street	C7-C8-D8	Navigation Street	C3-D3-D4	Severn Street	C3	William Street	A2-B2
Brindley Drive	B4-B5	Edward Street	A4-A5	Hurst Street	D2-E2-E1	Needless Alley	D4	Shadwell Street	D6-D7-E7	Wrentham Street	D1-E1
Brindley Place	A4	Ellis Street	C2-D2	Hylton Street	A8	Nelson Street	A5	Sheepcote Street	A4-A3	Wynn Street	C1-D1
Bristol Street	D1-D2	Enterprise Way	F8	Icknield Street	A8	New Bartholomew Street	F4	Sherlock Street	E1	
Broad Street	A2-A3-B3-B4-C4	Essex Street	D2	Inge Street	D2	New Canal Street	F4	Smallbrook Queensway	D2-D3-E3	
Bromsgrove Street	D1-E2-E2	Fazeley Street	F4	Irving Street	C1-D1-D2	New Street	C4-D4-E4	Smith Street	B8-C8	
Brook Street	B6	Fleet Street	B5-C5	Islington Row Middleway	A1	New Summer Street	D8-E8	Snowhill Queensway	D6	
Brunel Street	C3	Fox Street	F5	James Brindley Walk	A4-B4-B5	New Town Row	E8-E7	Spencer Street	B8-B7	
Buckingham Street	C8	Frederick Street	A7-A6-B6	James Street	B6	Newhall Hill	B6-B5	Staniforth Street	E8-E7-F7	
Bull Ring	E3-F3	Gas Street	B3	James Watt Queensway	F5-F6-E6	Newhall Street	B6-C6-C5-D5	Station Street	D3	
Bull Street	E5-E4	George Road	A1	Jennens Road	F5-F6	Newton Street	E5-E6	Steelhouse Lane	E5-E6	
Cambridge Street	A4-B4	George Street	B6-B5	John Bright Street	D3	Northampton Street	A8-B8-B7	Stephenson Street	D4	
Camden Street	A6-A5	Gloucester Street	E3	Kent Street	D1-E1	Northwood Street	B6-B7-C7	Suffolk Street Queensway	C4-D2	
Canalside Walk	B3-A4-A5-B5-C5	Gooch Street North	D1-E1	Kenyon Street	B7	Nova Scotia Street	F5	Summer Hill Street	A5	
								AA shop	D4	
								134 New Street		
								Birmingham B2 4NP		

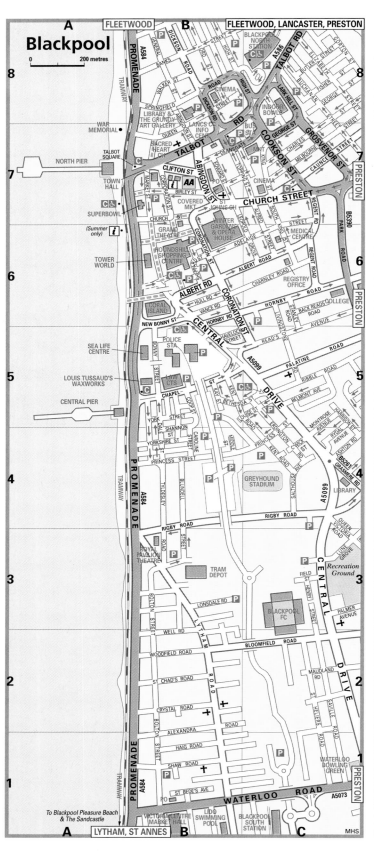

Blackpool

Blackpool is found on atlas page **80**,
grid reference SD**3036**

Abingdon Street	B7-B8	Walker Street	B8
Adelaide Street	B6-C7	Waterloo Road	B1-C1
Albert Road	B6-C6	Well Road	B2-B3
Alexandra Road	B1-B2	Woodfield Road	B2
Alfred Street	C6-C7	York Street	B5
Ashton Road	C4	Yorkshire Street	B4
Back Reads Road	C6		
Banks Street	B8		
Belmont Avenue	C5		
Bethesda Street	B5-C5		
Birley Street	B7		
Bloomfield Road	B2-C3		
Blundell Street	B3-B4		
Bolton Street	B1-B3		
Bonny Street	B5		
Buchanan Street	C7-C8		
Butler Street	C8		
Caroline Street	B4		
Caunce Street	C7		
Central Drive	B6-C1		
Chadwick Street	C4		
Chapel Street	B5		
Charles Street	C7-C8		
Charnley Road	B6-C6		
Church Street	B7-C8		
Clifton Street	B7		
Cocker Street	B8		
Cookson Street	C7-C8		
Coop Street	B5		
Coronation Street	B7-C5		
Corporation Street	B7		
Crystal Road	B2		
Dale Street	B4-B5		
Deansgate	B7-C8		
Dickson Road	B7-B8		
Edward Street	B7		
Elizabeth Street	C8		
Erdington Road	C4-C5		
Field Street	C3		
Fisher Street	C8		
General Street	B8		
George Street	C7-C8		
Gorton Street	C8		
Grasmere Road	C4		
Haig Road	B1		
Harrison Street	C4-C5		
Havelock Street	B5		
Henry Street	C2-C3		
High Street	B8-C8		
Hornby Road	B6-C6		
Hull Street	B6		
Kay Street	B5		
Kent Road	B5-C4		
Keswick Road	C4		
King Street	C7		
Lark Hill Street	C8		
Leamington Road	C7		
Leopold Grove	B7-C6		
Livingstone Road	C5-C6		
Lonsdale Road	B3		
Lord Street	B8		
Louise Street	B5-C5		
Lune Grove	C3		
Lytham Road	B1-B3		
Market Street	B7		
Maudland Road	C2		
Middle Street	B4		
Milbourne Street	C7-C8		
Montrose Avenue	C4-C5		
New Bonny Street	B6		
North Promenade	B6-B8		
Palatine Road	C5		
Palmer Avenue	C3		
Park Road	C5-C7		
Peter Street	C7		
Princess Street	B4-C5		
Promenade	A1-B6		
Queen Street	B7-B8		
Queen Victoria Road	C4		
Read's Avenue	B5-C6		
Regent Road	C6-C7		
Ribble Road	C5		
Rigby Road	B3-C4		
Rydal Avenue	C4-C5		
Salthouse Avenue	C4		
Saville Road	C1-C2		
Shannon Street	B4-B5		
Shaw Road	B1		
Sheppard Street	B6		
South King Street	C6-C7		
Springfield Road	B8		
St Bede's Avenue	B1		
St Chad's Road	B2		
St Heliers Road	C1-C2		
Stanley Road	C5-C6		
Talbot Road	B7-B8		
Topping Street	B7-C7	AA shop	B7
Tyldesley Road	B3-B4	13 Clifton Street	
Vance Road	B6	Blackpool FY1 1JD	

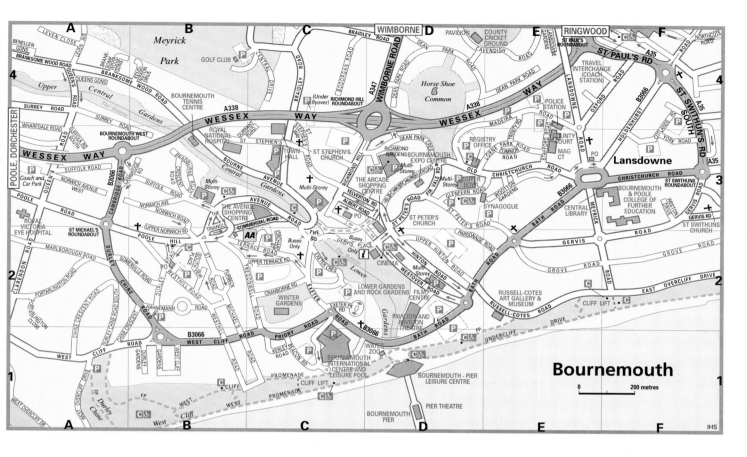

Bournemouth

Bournemouth is found on atlas page 12,
grid reference SZ0809

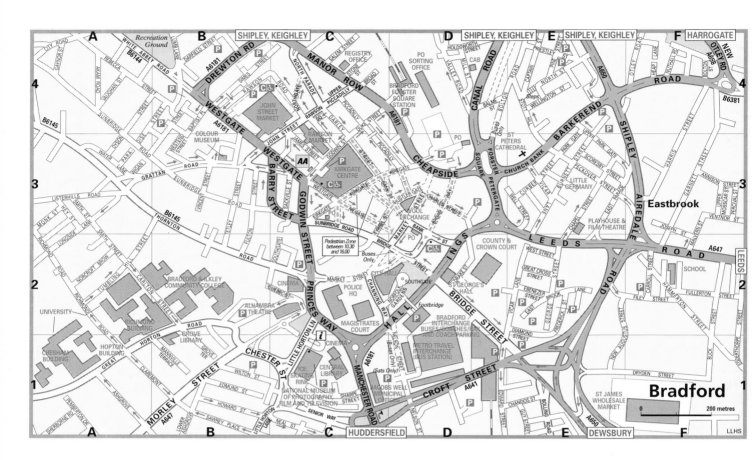

Bradford

Bradford is found on atlas page **82**,
grid reference SE1632

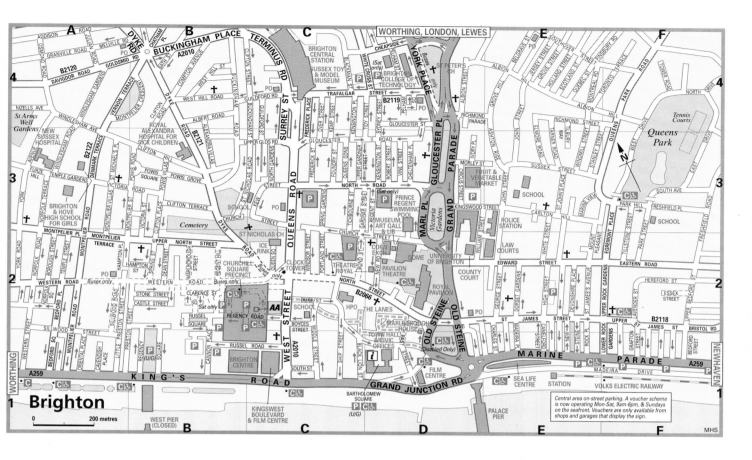

Brighton

Brighton is found on atlas page **15**,
grid reference TQ3104

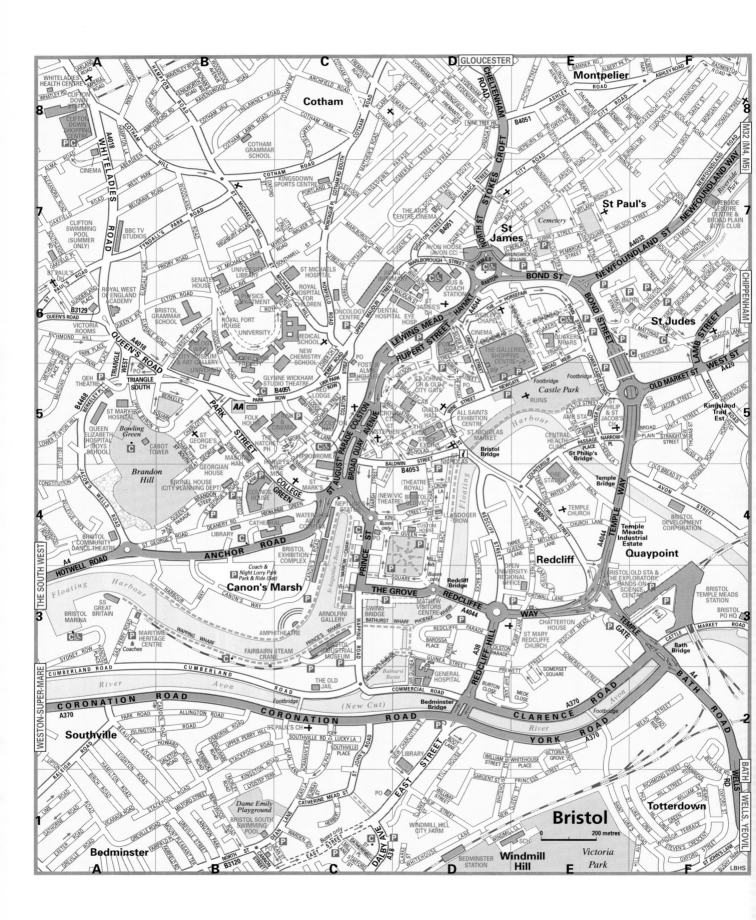

Bristol

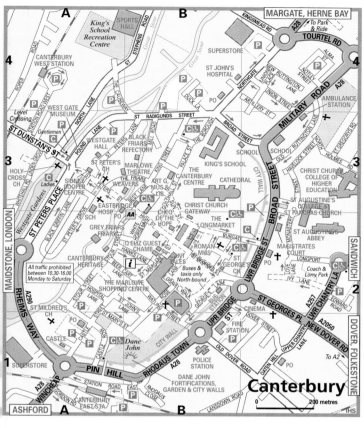

Canterbury

Canterbury is found on atlas page **29**,
grid reference TR1457

Alma Street	C4	Lower Bridge Street	C2	St Georges Place	C1-C2
Artillery Street	B4-C3	Lower Chantry Lane	C1-C2	St Georges Street	B2
Beer Cart Lane	A2-B2	Military Road	C3-C4	St Gregory's Road	C3
Best Lane	B3	Mill Road	B3	St Margaret's Street	B2
Black Griffin Lane	A2-A3	Monastery Street	C2-C3	St Mary's Street	A2-B1
Broad Street	B3-C3-C2	New Dover Road	C1	St Peter's Grove	A2-A3
Burgate	B2-C2	New Ruttington Lane	C4	St Peters Lane	A3-B3
Castle Row	A1-A2	North Holmes Road	C3	St Peters Place	A2-A3
Castle Street	A1-A2	North Lane	A3-A4	St Peters Street	A3-B3
Dover Street	B2-C1	Northgate	B4-C4	St Radigunds Street	B3
Duck Lane	B4	Notley Street	C4	St Stephen's Road	A4-B4
Edward Road	C2	Oaten Hill	C1	Station Road East	A1-B1
Gordon Road	A1	Old Dover Road	B1-C1	Station Road West	A3-A4
Gravel Walk	B2	Old Ruttington Lane	C3-C4	Stour Street	A2-B2
Guildhall Street	B2-B3	Palace Street	B3	Sun Street	B2-B3
Havelock Street	C3	Pin Hill	A1-B1	The Borough	B3
Hawks Lane	A2-B2	Pound Lane	A3	The Causeway	A4-B4
High Street	B2-B3	Rheims Way	A1-A2	The Friars	A3-B3
Hospital Lane	A2	Rhodaus Close	B1	Tourtel Road	C4
Ivy Lane	C2	Rhodaus Town	B1	Union Place	C4
King Street	B3	Roper Road	A4	Upper Bridge Street	B1-B2
Kingsmead Road	B4-C4	Rose Lane	B1-B2	Upper Chantry Lane	C1
Lansdown Road	B1	Simmonds Road	A1	Watling Street	B1-B2
Linden Grove	A3	St Dunstan's Street	A3	White Horse Lane	B2
Love Lane	C2	St George's Lane	B1-B2	Whitehall Road	A2-A3
				Wincheap	A1
				AA shop	B3
				13 Best Lane	
				Canterbury CT1 2JB	

Bristol

Bristol is found on atlas page **34**,
grid reference ST5972

Abbotsford Road	A8-B8	Campbell Street	E8	Denbigh Street	E8	Horfield Road	C6-C7	Park Road	A2	Stokes Croft	D7-D8
Aberdeen Road	A7-A8-B8	Cannon Street	B1	Denmark Street	C5-C4	Horton Road	F5	Park Row	B5-C5	Straight Street	F5
Acraman's Road	C2	Canon's Road	C3-C4	Dighton Street	D7	Hotwell Road	A3-A4	Park Street	B5	Stratton Street	E6
Albert Park	F8	Canon's Way	B3	Dove Lane	F7	Houlton Street	F6-F7	Passage Place	E5	Sunderland Place	A6
Albert Park Place	E8	Canynge Street	E3	Dove Street	C7-D7-D8	Howard Road	A2-B2	Pembroke Road	B2	Surrey Street	E7
Alexandra Road	A7	Castle Street	E5	Dove Street South	D7-D8	Imperial Road	A8	Pembroke Street	E7	Sydenham Hill	D8
Alfred Hill	C7-C6	Catherine Mead Street	C1	Drummond Road	E8	Islington Road	A2-B2	Penn Street	E6	Sydenham Lane	D8
Alfred Place	D3	Cattle Market Road	F3	East Street	C1-D1-D2	Jacob Street	F5	Pennywell Road	F6	Sydenham Road	D8
Allington Road	B2	Charles Street	D7	Edgeware Road	B2	Jacob's Wells Road	A4-A5	Perry Road	C5-C6	Sydney Row	A3
Alma Road	A7-A8	Charlotte Street	B5	Elmdale Road	A7-A6-B6	Jamaica Street	D7	Philip Street	D1	Temple Back	E4-E5
Alpha Road	C1-C2	Charlotte Street South	B5	Elton Road	A6-B6	Jubilee Street	F5	Picton Street	E8	Temple Gate	E3
Anchor Road	A4-B4-C4	Cheese Lane	E5	Eugene Street	C7-D7	Kingsmead Parade	C7-C8-D8	Pipe Lane	C5	Temple Street	E4
Archfield Road	C8	Cheltenham Road	D8	Eugene Street	F6	Kings Square	D7	Portland Square	E7	Temple Way	E3-E4-E5
Argyle Road	E7-E8	Church Lane	E4	Exeter Road	A1	King Street	C4-D4	Portland Street	C7	Terrell Street	C6-C7
Armada Place	D8	City Road	D7-E7-E4-F8	Fairfax Street	D5	Kingston Road	B1-B2	Portwall Lane	D3-E3	The Grove	C3-D3
Ashley Road	E8-F8	Clare Road	C8-D8	Fairfield Place	A1-B1	Lamb Street	F5-F6	Prewett Street	D2-E3	The Horsefair	D6-E6
Avon Street	E4-F4	Clarence Road	D2-E2-F3	Fairfield Road	A1	Langton Park	B1	Prince Street	C3-C4	The Pithay	D5
Backfields	D7-E7	Clarke Street	D1	Franklyn Street	F8	Leighton Road	A1-A2	Princess Street	D1-E1-E2	Thomas Street	F8
Badminton Road	F8	Clement Street	F7	Frederick Place	A6	Lewins Mead	C6-D6	Princes Street	E7	Three Queens Lane	D4-E4
Baldwin Street	C5-D5	Clevedon Terrace	C7	Fremantle Road	C8-D8	Lime Road	A1	Priory Road	A6-B7	Tower Hill	E5
Banner Road	E8	College Green	B4-C4-B4-B5	Fremantle Square	D8	Little Ann Street	F6	Pritchard Street	E7-E6	Trelawney Road	B8-C8
Barossa Place	D3	College Street	B4	Frog Lane	B4	Little George Street	F6	Pump Lane	D3-E3	Trenchard Street	C5
Barton Road	F4-F5	Colston Avenue	C5	Frogmore Street	C5	Little Paul Street	B7-C7	Pyle Hill Crescent	F1	Triangle South	A5
Bath Road	F2	Colston Parade	D3	Gas Ferry Road	A3	Lodge Street	C5	Quakers Friars	E6	Triangle West	A6
Bathurst Parade	C2-C3	Colston Street	C5-C6	Gathorpe Road	A1	Lower Castle Street	E5-E6	Queen Charlotte Street	D4	Tyndall Avenue	B6
Beauley Road	A2-B1	Commercial Road	C2-D2	Gloucester Street	E7-E6	Lower Church Lane	C5-C6	Queen's Avenue	A6	Tyndall's Park Road	A7-B7
Belgrave Road	A7-B7	Corn Street	C5-D5	Great Ann Street	F6	Lower Clifton Hill	A5	Queen's Parade	B4	Union Street	D5-D6
Bellevue	A4-A5	Coronation Road	A2-B2-C2-D2	Great George Street	B4-B5	Lower Guinea Street	D2-D3	Queen's Road	A6-B6-B5	Unity Street	F5
Bellevue Crescent	A4	Cotham Grove	C8	Green Street	F1	Lower Maudlin Street	D6	Queen Square	C3-C4-D4-E3	University Road	B6
Bellevue Road	F2	Cotham Hill	A8-B7	Greville Road	A1	Lower Park Row	C5	Queen Street	E5	Upper Byron Place	A5
Berkeley Place	A5	Cotham Lawn Road	B8	Greville Street	B1	Lucky Lane	C2	Raleigh Road	A1-A2	Upper Maudlin Street	C6
Berkeley Square	A5-B5	Cotham Park	C8	Grosvenor Road	E8-F8	Ludlow Close	F8	Ravenswood Road	B8	Upper Perry Hill	B2
Birch Road	A1-A2	Cotham Road	B7-C7-C8	Guinea Street	D2-D3	Lydstep Terrace	B1-B2	Redcliff Backs	D4-D3	Upper York Street	D7-E7
Bishop Street	E7	Cotham Road South	C7-C8	Gwyn Street	E8	Marlborough Hill	C7	Redcliffe Parade	D3	Upton Road	A1-A2
Bond Street	D6-E6	Cotham Side	C8-D8	Halston Drive	F7-F8	Marlborough Street	D6-D7	Redcliffe Way	D3-E3	Vicarage Road	A1
Boot Lane	D2	Cotham Vale	B8	Hamilton Road	A1-A2	Marsh Street	C4	Redcliff Hill	D2-D3	Victoria Grove	E2
Bragg's Lane	F6	Cottage Place	C7	Hampton Lane	A8	Mead Rise	F2	Redcliff Mead Lane	E3	Victoria Road	E4
Brandon Steep	B4	Countership	E4-E5	Hampton Park	A8	Mead Street	E2-F2	Redcliff Street	D3-D4	Victoria Walk	D8
Brighton Street	E8	Crow Lane	D4	Hampton Road	B8	Mede Close	E2	Redcross Street	F6	Wade Street	F6
Brigstocke Road	E7-E8	Cumberland Road	A2-B2-C2	Hanover Place	A3	Merchant Street	D6-E6-E5	Richmond Hill	A6	Walker Street	C7
Broadmead	D6-E6	Cumberland Street	D7-E7	Harbour Way	A3-B3	Meridian Place	A5-A6	Richmond Street	F1-F2	Wapping Road	C3
Broad Plain	F5	Dalby Avenue	C1	Hatfield Avenue	C8	Merrywood Road	B1	River Street	F6	Warden Road	C1
Broad Quay	C4-C5	Dale Street	F6	Haymarket	D6	Midland Road	F5	Royal Fort Road	B6-C6	Warwick Road	A8
Broad Street	C5-D5	Dalston Road	B2	Henry Street	F1	Milford Street	B1	Rupert Street	C6-D6	Water Lane	E4
Broad Weir	E5-E6	Dalrymple Road	E8	Hepburn Road	D8-E8	Mill Avenue	D4	Russ Street	F5	Waterloo Road	F5
Brunswick Street	E7	Davey Street	F8	Herbert Street	C1	Mill Lane	C1	St Augustine's Parade	C4-C5	Waterloo Street	F5-F6
Burnell Drive	E8-F8	David Street	F5	Highbury Villas	B7	Mitchell Court	E4	St Catherines Place	C1	Wellington Avenue	E8
Burton Close	D2	Deanery Road	B4	High Street	D5	Mitchell Lane	E4	St George's Road	A4-B4	Wellington Road	E6-F6-F7
Bushy Park	F1	Dean Lane	B1-C1-C2	Hiill Avenue	F1	Montague Place	C7	St James' Barton	D6	Wells Road	F1
Cambridge Street	F1	Dean Street	B1	Hill Street	B5	Moon Street	D7	St John's Lane	F1	Welsh Back	D3-D4-D5
Camden Road	A2	Dean Street	E7	Hill Street	F1	Morgan Street	F8	St John's Road	C1-C2	West Park	A7
						Morley Road	B1	St Luke's Crescent	E1-F1	West Street	F5-F6
						Mount Pleasant Terrace	B1	St Luke's Road	E2-E1-F1	Whatley Road	A8
						Murray Street	C1	St Matthew's Road	C7-C8	Whitehouse Lane	C1-D1
						Myrtle Road	B7-C7	St Matthias Park	E6-F6	Whitehouse Place	D2-E2
						Narrow Place	E5	St Michael's Hill	B7-B6-C6	Whitehouse Street	D1-D2
						Narrow Quay	C3-C4	St Michael's Park	B6-B7	Whiteladies Road	A6-A7-A8
						Nelson Street	C5-D5-D6	St Nicholas Road	F8	Whitson Street	D6
						New Charlotte Street	C2-D2	St Nicholas Street	C5-D5	Wilder Street	D7-E7
						Newfoundland Road	F7-F8	St Paul's Road	A6-A7	William Street	D2
						Newfoundland Street	E6-E7-F7	St Paul's Street	E7	William Street	E8-F8
						Newfoundland Way	F8	St Thomas Street	D4-E4-E3	William Street	F1
						Newgate	D5-E5	Sargent Street	D1	Willway Street	D1
						New Kingsley Road	F4-F5	Ship Lane	D2	Wilson Place	F7
						New Queen Street	D1	Silver Street	D6	Wilson Street	E7-F7
						New Street	F6	Small Street	C5-D5	Windmill Close	D1
						New Thomas Street	F5	Somerset Square	E2-E3	Windsor Terrace	F1
						Nine Tree Hill	D8	Somerset Street	E2-E3	Wine Street	D5
						North Street	B1	Somerset Street	C7-D7-D8	Woodland Road	B5-B6-B7
						North Street	D7	Southleigh Road	A7	York Place	A7
						Nugent Hill	D8	Southville Place	C2	York Road	D2-E2-F2
						Oakfield Place	A6-A7	Southville Road	C2	York Street	E6-E7
						Oakfield Road	A7	Southwell Street	B6-C7		
						Old Bread Street	F4	Springfield Road	D8		
						Old Market Street	E6	Spring Street	E2		
						Osborne Road	B2	Stackpool Road	A1-A2-B2	AA shop	B5
						Oxford Place	F1	Stafford Street	C1	Fanum House	
						Oxford Street	B7	Steven's Crescent	F1	26-32 Park Row	
						Park Place	A6	Stillhouse Lane	D1-D2	Bristol BS1 5LY	

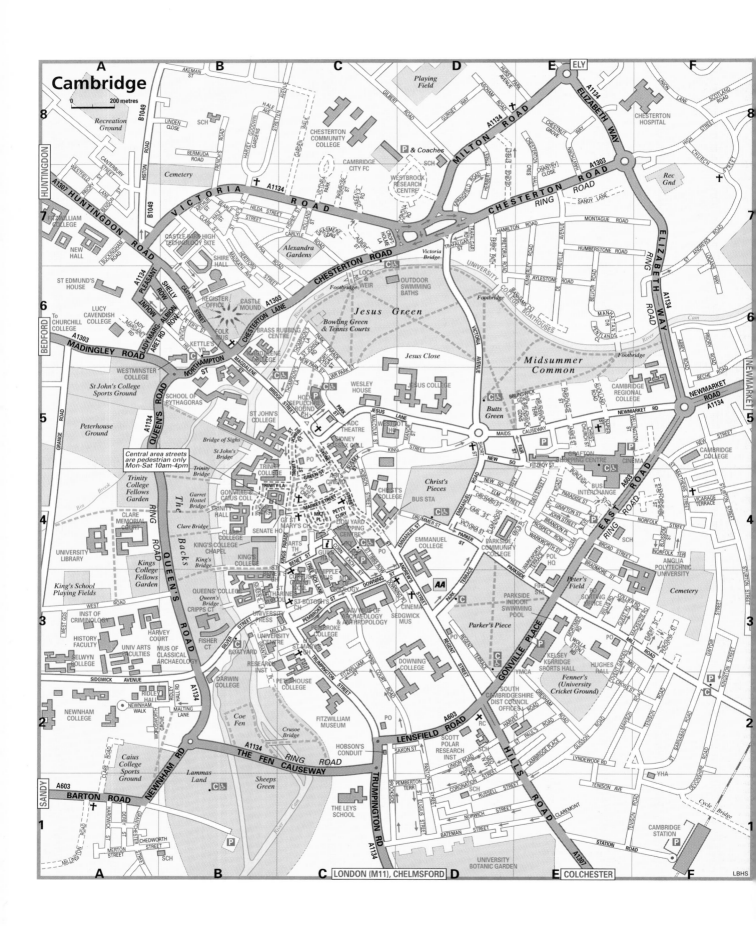

Cambridge

Central area streets are pedestrian only Mon-Sat 10am-4pm

Cheltenham

Cheltenham is found on atlas page **35**,
grid reference SO**9422**

Albert Place	C4	Monson Avenue	B4	Suffolk Road	A1
Albert Road	C4	Montpellier Drive	A2-B1	Suffolk Square	A1
Albion Street	B3-C3	Montpellier Grove	A1	Swindon Road	A4-B4
All Saints Road	C3-C4	Montpellier Parade	A1-A2	Sydenham Villas Road	C2
Ambrose Street	A4	Montpellier Spa Road	A2	Trafalgar Street	A2-B2
Argyll Road	C1	Montpellier Street	A2-A3	Victoria Place	C3
Avenalls Parade	C1	Montpellier Terrace	A1-B1	Victoria Walk	A2-B2
Bath Parade	B2	Montpellier Walk	A2-A3	Wellington Road	C4
Bath Road	A1-B3	New Street	A4	Wellington Street	B2
Bath Street	B2-B3	North Place	B4	Winchcombe Street	B3-B4
Bayshill Road	A2-A3	North Street	B3-B4		
Bennington Street	B3-B4	Old Bath Road	C1		
Berkeley Street	C2-C3	Oriel Road	A2-B2		
Brighton Road	C3	Orrisdale Terrace	B1		
Brunswick Street	A4	Oxford Street	C2		
Cambray Place	B2-B3	Pitville Circus	C4		
Carlton Street	C2-C3	Pitville Circus Road	C4		
Christowe Lane	C1	Poole Way	A4		
Clarence Road	B4	Portland Street	B3-B4		
Clarence Street	A3-B3	Prestbury Road	C4		
College Baths Road	C1	Prince's Street	C2		
College Lawn	B1	Priory Place	C2		
College Road	B1-C2	Priory Street	C2		
Corpus Street	C2	Promenade	A3-B3		
Devonshire Street	A4	Regent Street	A3-B3		
Duke Street	C2-C3	Rodney Road	B2-B3		
Dunalley Street	B4	Royal Crescent	A3		
Evesham Road	B4	Royal Well Road	A3		
Fairview Road	B4-C3	Sandford Mill Road	C1		
Gloucester Place	B3	Sandford Road	B1-C1		
Great Norwood Street	A1	Selkirk Close	C4		
Grosvenor Street	B2-C3	Selkirk Gardens	C4		
Grove Street	A4	Selkirk Street	C4		
Henrietta Street	A4	Sherborne Place	B3-C3		
Hewlett Road	C2-C3	Sherborne Street	C3-C4		
High Street	A4-B3-B2	St George's Place	A3		
Imperial Square	A2	St George's Road	A3		
Jersey Avenue	C3	St George's Street	A4		
Jessop Avenue	A3	St James's Square	A3-A4		
Keynsham Road	B1-C2	St James's Street	B2-C3		
Keynshambury Road	C1-C2	St John's Avenue	C3		
King Street	A4	St Luke's Road	B1-B2		
Knapp Road	A4	St Margarets Road	B4		
Leighton Road	C3	St Paul's Road	B4	AA shop	B3
London Road	C1-C2	St Paul's Street South	A4	90 High Street	
Milsom Street	A4	Suffolk Parade	A1	Cheltenham GL50 1EG	

Cambridge

Cambridge is found on atlas page **53**,
grid reference TL**4558**

Abbey Road	F5-F6	Clare Road	A1-A2	Green Street	C4-C5	Malcolm Street	C5	Pound Hill	B6	The Fen Causeway	B2-C2
Adam and Eve Street	E4	Clare Street	B7	Green's Road	C7	Malting Lane	B2	Pretoria Road	D6-D7	Thomson's Lane	C5-C6
Akeman Street	B8	Claremont	E1	Gresham Road	E2	Manhattan Drive	E6	Primrose Street	C7	Trafalgar Road	D7
Albert Street	C7	Clarendon Street	D4-E4	Guest Road	E3	Manor Street	D5	Priory Road	F5-F6	Trafalgar Street	D7
Albion Row	B6	Collier Road	E3-F3	Gurney Way	D8	Market Place	C4	Priory Street	A7	Trinity Lane	B4-C4
Alpha Road	B7-B6-C6	Corn Exchange Street	C3-C4	Gwydir Street	F2-F3	Market Street	C4	Prospect Row	E4	Trinity Street	C4-C5
Arthur Street	B7	Corona Road	D7	Hale Avenue	B8	Mawson Road	E2-F2-F3	Queen's Lane	B3	Trumpington Street	C2-C3
Ascham Road	D8	Coronation Street	D1-D2	Hale Street	B7	Melbourne Place	D4-E4	Queens Road	B2-B4-A4-B5	Trumpington Road	C1-C2
Auckland Road	E5	Covent Garden	E2-E3	Hamilton Road	D7-E7	Merton Street	A1	Regent Street	D2-D3	Union Lane	F8
Aylestone Road	D6-E6	Cross Street	E2-F2	Hardwick Street	A1	Mill Lane	B3-C3	Regent Terrace	D2-D3	Union Road	D2
Banhams Close	D6-E6	De Freville Avenue	E6-E7	Harvey Goodwin Gardens	B7-B8	Mill Road	F2-F3-E3	Ridley Hall Road	B2	Vicarage Terrace	F4
Barton Road	A1	Derby Street	A1	Harvey Road	D2-E2	Mill Street	E3-F3-F2	Rose Crescent	C4	Victoria Avenue	D5-D6-D7
Bateman Street	C1-D1-E1	Devonshire Road	F1-F2	Hawthorn Way	E7-E8	Millington Road	A1	Russell Street	D1-E1	Victoria Park	C7-C8
Beche Road	F5-F6	Downing Place	C3-D3	Herbert Street	D7-D8	Milton Road	D7-D8-E8	Sandy Lane	E7	Victoria Road	A7-B7-C7-D7
Belvoir Road	E6-E7	Downing Street	C3-D3	Hertford Street	B7-B6-C6	Montague Road	E7-F7	Saxon Street	C2-D2	Victoria Street	D4
Benet Street	C4	Drummer Street	D4	High Street	F8	Mortimer Road	E3	Scotland Road	F8	Warkworth Strreet	E4
Benson Street	A7	Earl Street	D4	Hilda Street	B7-C7	Mount Pleasant	A6	Searle Street	B7-C7	Warkworth Terrrace	E3-E4
Bermuda Road	B8	East Road	E3-E4-F4-F5	Hills Road	E1-D2	Napier Street	E5	Shelly Row	A6-B6	Wellington Street	E5-F5
Blossom Street	F4	Eden Street	E4	Histon Road	A7-A8	New Park Street	C5-C6	Short Street	D5	West Gardens	A3
Bradmore Street	E3-E4	Elizabeth Way	E8-E7-F7-F6-F5	Hobson Street	C4-C5	New Square	D5-D4	Sidgwick Avenue	A2-B2	West Road	A3-B3
Brandon Place	E4	Elm Street	D4-E4	Holland Street	C7	New Street	F5	Silver Street	B3-C3	Westfield Lane	A7
Brentwick Street	D1-D2	Emerey Street	F3	Humberstone Road	E7-F7	Newmarket Road	E5-F5	Springfield Road	D7	Willis Road	E3
Bridge Street	B5-C5	Emmanuel Road	D4-D5	Huntington Road	A7	Newnham Road	A1-B1-B2	St Andrew's Street	D3-D4-C4	Wollaston Road	E3
Broad Street	E4-F4	Emmanuel Street	D4	Hurst Park Avenue	D8-E8	Newnham Walk	A2-B2	St Andrews Road	F6-F7	Wordworth Grove	A2
Brookside	C1-C2	Fair Street	E5	James Street	E5	Norfolk Street	E4-F4	St Barnabas Road	F2		
Brunswick Gardens	E5	Ferry Path	D6-D7	Jesus Lane	C5-D5	Norfolk Terrace	F4	St Eligius Street	D1		
Brunswick Terrace	E5	Fisher Street	C7	John Street	E4	Northampton Street	B5-B6	St John's Road	C6		
Buckingham Road	A7	Fitzroy Street	E5	Kimberley Road	E6-E7	Norwich Street	D1-E1	St John's Street	C5		
Burleigh Street	E4-E5	Fitzwilliam Street	C2-C3	King Street	D5-E5	Orchard Street	D4-E4	St Luke's Street	B7		
Cambridge Place	E2	Free School Lane	C3-C4	Kings Parade	C4	Panton Street	D1-D2	St Matthews Street	F4-F5		
Canterbury Street	A7-A8	French Road	B7-B8	Kingston Street	F2-F3	Paradise Street	E4	St Paul's Road	D2-E2		
Carlyle Road	B7-C7	Garden Walk	C7-C8	Lady Margaret Road	A6	Park Parade	C6	St Peter's Street	B6		
Castle Street	B6	George IV Street	D2	Lenfield Road	C2-D2	Park Street	C5	St Tibbs Row	C3-C4		
Chantry Close	E7	George Street	D7-D8	Linden Close	A8-B8	Park Terrace	D3-D4	Staffordshire Street	F4		
Chedworth Street	A1-B1	Gilbert Road	C8-D8	Logans Way	F6-F7	Parker Street	D4	Station Road	E1-F1		
Chesterton Hall Crescent	E7-E8	Glisson Road	E1-E2	Lower Park Street	C5-C6	Parkside	E3-D3-D4	Stretten Avenue	B7-B8-C8		
Chesterton Lane	B6-C6	Gonville Place	D2-D3-E3	Lyndewode Road	E2	Parsonage Street	E5	Sturton Street	F3-F4-F5		
Chesterton Road	E7-D7-C7-C6	Grafton Street	E3-F3	Mackenzie Road	E4	Pemberton Terrace	C1-D1	Sussex Street	C4-C5		
Chestnut Grove	E8	Grange Road	A3-A4-A5-A6	Madingley Road	A6-B6-B5	Pembroke Street	C3	Sydney Street	C4-C5		
Christchurch Street	E5	Granta Place	B2-B3	Magdalene Street	B5-B6	Pentlands Close	E6	Tenison Avenue	E1	AA shop	D3
Church Street	F7-F8	Grantchester Street	A1	Magrath Avenue	B7-B6	Perowne Street	F3	Tenison Road	E1-F1-E2-F2	Janus House	
City Road	E4	Grasmere Gardens	C7	Maids Causeway	D5-E5	Portugal Street	C6	Tennis Court Road	C3-C2-D2	46-48 St Andrew's Street	
										Cambridge CB2 3BH

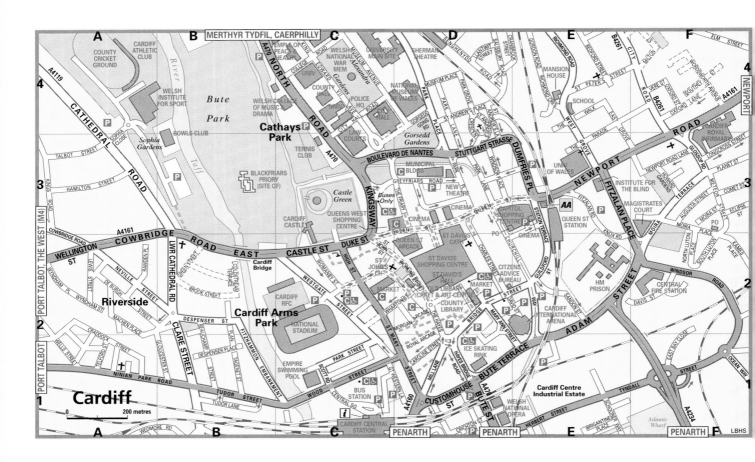

Cardiff

Cardiff is found on atlas page **33**,
grid reference ST1876

Adam Street	E1-E2-F2	Glossop Road	F3	Park Grove	D4	Wharton Street	C2-D2
Augusta Street	F3	Gloucester Street	B1	Park Lane	D4-D3	Windsor Place	D3
Bedford Street	E4	Gordon Road	E4	Park Place	D4-D3	Windsor Road	F2
Beauchamp Street	B1-B2	Gorsedd Gardens Road	D4	Park Street	C1	Wood Street	C1-D1
Boulevard de Nantes	C3-D3	Great Western Lane	D1-C1	Planet Street	F3	Wordsworth Avenue	F4
Bridge Street	D1-D2-E2	Green Street	B2	Plantagenet Street	B1-B2	Working Street	D2
Brigantine Place	E1	Greyfrairs Road	D3	Queen Street	C2-C3-D3-E3	Womanby Street	C2
Brook Street	B2	Guildford Street	E2	Rawden Place	A2	Wyndham Place	A2
Bute Street	D1	Hamilton Street	A3	Richmond Crescent	E4	Wyndham Street	A2
Bute Terrace	D1-E1	Hayes Bridge Road	D1	Richmond Road	E4		
Caroline Street	D1	Herbert Street	E1	Royal Arcade	D1-D2		
Castle Street	C2	High Street	C2	St Andrew's Crescent	D3-D4		
Cathedral Street	A4-A3-B3	Howard Gardens	F3	St Andrew's Lane	D4		
Central Square	C1	Kames Place	F2	St Andrew's Place	D4		
Charles Street	D2-E2	King Edward VII Avenue	C3-C4	St John Street	C2		
Churchill Way	E2-E3	King's Road	A2-A3	St Marys Street	D1-C2		
City Hall Road	C3-C4	Kingsway	C3	St Peter's Street	E4-F4		
City Road	E4-F4	Knox Road	E2-E3	Salisbury Road	D4		
Clare Street	B1-B2	Lewis Street	A2	Sandon Street	E2		
Coldstream Terrace	B2	Llanwit Street	D4	Schooner Way	E1		
College Road	C4	Longcross Street	F3-F4	Scott Road	C1		
Comet Street	F3	Lower Cathedral Road	B1	Senghenydd Road	D4		
Cowbridge Road	A2-A3	Machen Place	A1-A2	Sophia Close	A3-A4		
Cowbridge Road East	A2-B2-C2	Mary Ann Street	D1-D2-E1-E2	Southey Street	F4		
Craddock Street	A1-A2	Meteor Street	F3	South Luton Place	F2		
Cranbrook Street	E4	Mill Lane	D1	Station Terrace	E2-E3		
Crichton Street	D1	Milton Street	F4	Stuttgart Strasse	D3-E3		
Customhouse Street	D1	Morgan Arcade	D2	The Friary	D3		
David Street	D2-E2	Moira Place	F3	The Hayes	D2		
Davis Street	F2	Moira Terrace	F2-F3	The Parade	E3-E4-F4		
De Burgh Street	A2-B1	Museum Avenue	C4-D4	The Walk	E4		
Despenser Place	B1	Museum Place	D4	Talbot Street	A3		
Despenser Street	B2	Neville Street	A2-B2	Telford Street	A1		
Duke Street	C2	Newport Road	E3-F3-F4	Tresillian Way	D1		
Dumfries Place	E3	Newport Road Lane	F3	Tudor Lane	B1		
East Bay Close	F1-F2	Ninian Park Road	A1-B1	Tudor Street	B1-C1		
East Grove	E3-F3-E4	North Luton Place	F2-F3	Tyndall Street	E1-F1		
Eclipse Street	F3	North Road	B4-C4-C3	Vere Street	F4		
Elm Street	F4	Ocean Way	F1	Wellington Street	A2	AA shop	E3
Fitzalan Place	F2-F3-E3	Oxford Lane	F4	Wells Street	A1-A2	Fanum House	
Fitzalan Road	E3	Oxford Street	F4	Westgate Street	C1-C2	140 Queen Street	
Fitzhamon Embankment	B2-B1-C1			West Grove	E4-E3	Cardiff CF1 1YF	

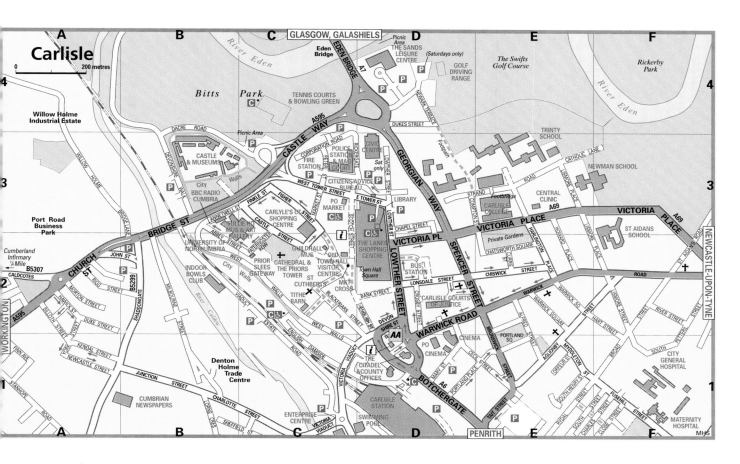

Carlisle

Carlisle is found on atlas page **93**,
grid reference NY**3956**

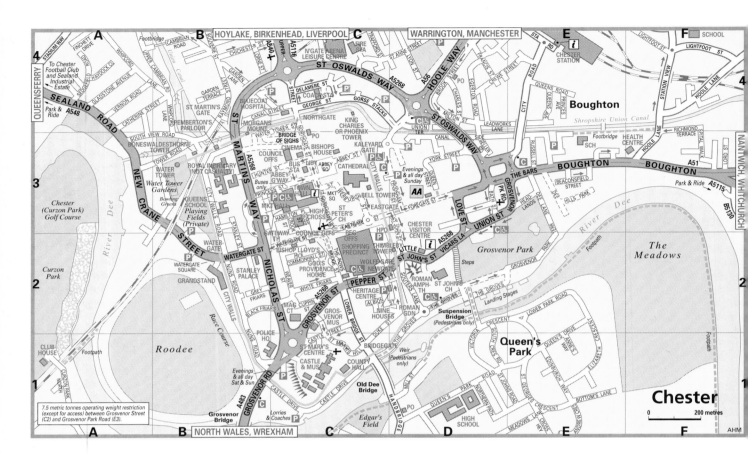

Chester

Chester is found on atlas page **71**,
grid reference SJ**4066**

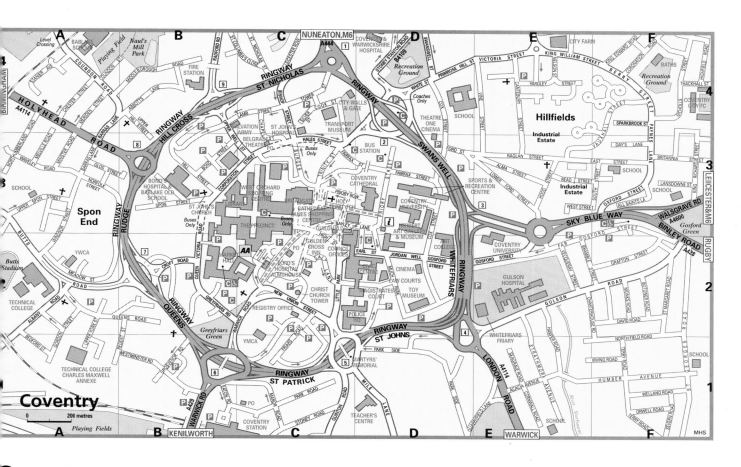

Coventry

oventry is found on atlas page **61**,
rid reference SP**3378**

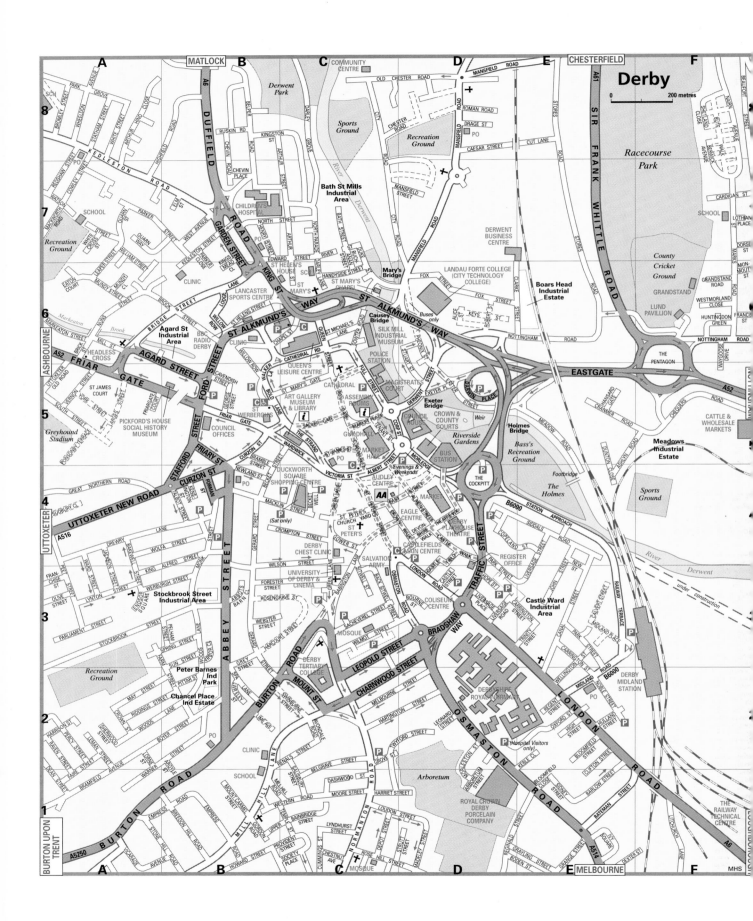

Derby

0   200 metres

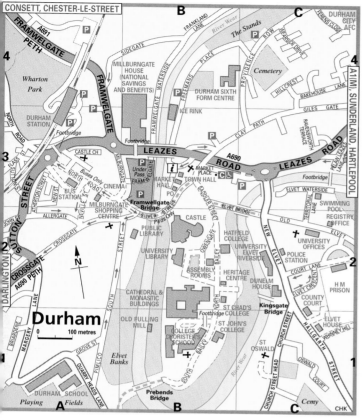

Durham

Durham is found on atlas page **96**,
grid reference NZ2742

Allergate	A2	Old Elvet	C2
Atherton Street	A2-A3	Oswald Court	C1
Bakehouse Lane	C4	Owengate	B2
Briardene	A1	Pelaw Leazes Lane	C3
Castle Church	A3	Pimlico South Street	A1-A2-B2
Church Street	C1	Providence Row	C3-C4
Church Street Head	C1	Quarry Heads Lane	A1
Clay Path	B3-C3	Ravensworth Terrace	C3
Court Lane	C2	Saddler Street	B2-B3
Crossgate	A2	Sidegate	A4-B4
Elvet Bridge	B3-C3-C2	Silver Street	B2-B3
Elvet Crescent	C2	South Bailey	B1
Elvet Waterside	C3	Sutton Street	A2-A3
Ferens Close	C4	Sutton Street	A3
Framwelgate	A3-A4	Territorial Lane	C2-C3
Framwelgate Peth	A4	Wearside Drive	C4
Framwelgate Waterside	B3-B4	Whinney Hill	C1
Frankland Lane	B4		
Freemans Place	B3-B4-C4		
Giles Gate	C3-C4		
Grove Street	A1		
Halgarth Street	C1		
Hilcrest	C4		
John Street	A2		
Leazes Road	B3-C3		
Margery Lane	A1-A2		
Milburngate	A3-B3		
Neville Street	A2-A3		
New Elvet	C2-C3		
New Street	A3		
North Bailey	B1-B2		
North Road	A3		

Derby

Derby is found on atlas page **62**,
grid reference SK3536

Abbey Street	B2-B3-B4	Bute Walk	F8-F7	Dorset Street	F7
Abbots Barn Close	B3	Caesar Street	D8	Drage Street	D8
Abingdon Street	A6-B6-B5	Calvert Street	E3	Drewry Lane	A4-B4
Albert Street	C4-C5-D5	Canal Street	E3-E4	Duke Street	C7-C6
Albion Street	D4	Cardigan Street	A5	Duffield Road	B8-B7
Alice Street	D6	Carrington Street	D3-E3	Dunton Close	E5-E4
Arbor Close	B3	Castle Field	D3-D4	Eastgate	E5
Arboretum Street	D1-D2	Castle Street	D3	East Street	C4-D4
Argyle Street	B2	Castle Walk	D4	Eaton Court	A6
Arthur Hind Close	A7-A8	Cathedral Road	B5-B6-C5-C6	Edward Street	B7-C7
Arthur Street	B8-C8-C7-C6	Cavendish Street	B5	Elm Street	B7
Ashlyn Road	E4-E5-F5	Chancel Street	B2	Empress Road	A1-B1
Avondale Road	C2	Chapel Street	C6	Endsor Square	A3
Babington Lane	C3-C4	Charnwood Street	C2-D2-D3	Exeter Place	D5
Back Sitwell Street	C3	Chester Road	C8-D8	Exeter Street	D5
Bainbridge Street	C1	Chequers Road	F5	Faire Street	A1-A2
Bakewell Street	A4-A3	Chestnut Avenue	C1	Farm Street	A3-B3-B2
Barlow Street	E1-E2	Chevin Place	B7	Ford Street	B5-B6
Bateman Street	E1	Chevin Road	B8-B7	Forester Street	B3-C3
Bath Street	C7	City Road	C8-C7-D7-D6	Forman Street	B4
Beaufort Street	F8-F7	Clarke Street	D6-E6	Fox Street	D6
Becket Street	B4-B5-C5	Clifton Street	E1-E2	Franchise Street	A3
Becket Well	C4	Copeland Street	D4-E4	Francis Street	F6
Belgrave Street	C1-C2	Corn Market	C5	Friar Gate	A6-A5-B5
Belper Road	B8-B7	Corporation Street	D5	Friargate Court	A5
Berwick Avenue	F8-F7	Cowley Street	A7-A8	Friary Street	B5
Bloomfield Close	E1	Cranmer Road	E5-F5	Full Street	C6-C5
Bloomfield Street	E2	Crompton Street	B4-C4	Garden Street	B6-B7
Boden Street	D1-E1	Crown Street	A2	George Street	B5
Bold Lane	B5-C5	Crown Walk	C4-D4	Gerard Street	B2-B3-B4
Bourne Street	D3	Cummings Street	C1	Gordon Road	B1
Bowyer Street	A2-B2	Curzon Street	B4-B5	Gower Street	C4
Bradshaw Way	D3	Cut Lane	E8	Grandstand Road	A6
Bramble Street	B5	Darley Grove	C8-C7	Grange Street	E1
Bramfield Avenue	A1-A2	Darley Lane	C6-C7	Grayling Street	D1-E1
Breedon Hill Road	B1	Darwin Place	D5	Great Northern Road	A4
Brick Street	A6	Dashwood Street	C1	Green Lane	C3-C4
Bridge Street	A5-A6-B6	Dean Street	A2-A1	Grey Street	B3
Bromley Street	A8	Depot Street	C1	Grove Street	C2-D2
Brook Street	A6-B6	Derwent Street	D5-D6	Handyside Street	C6
Buchanan Street	C6-C7	Devonshire Walk	D4	Hansard Gate	E5
Burton Road	A1-B1-B2-C2-C3	Dexter Street	E1-F1	Harcourt Street	B3-C3

Harriet Street	C1-D1	Mundy Close	A6	Sowter Road	C6
Harrison Street	A2	Mundy Street	A6	Spa Lane	B2
Hartington Street	C2-D2	Nairn Avenue	F7-F8	Spring Street	B3
Henry Street	B7	New Street	E4	Stafford Street	B4-B5
Highfield Road	A7-A8-B8	Newland Street	B4	Statham Street	A8
High Street	E2	Noble Street	E2	Station Approach	D4-E4
Hope Street	D3	Normanton Road	C1-C2-C3	Stockbrook Street	A2-A3-B3
Howard Street	B1	North Parade	C7	Stone Hill Road	A1-B1
Hulland Street	E2	North Street	B7-C7	Stores Road	E6-E7-E8
Huntingdon Green	F6	Nottingham Road	D6-E6-F6	Strutt Street	D1
Iron Gate	C5	Nuns Street	A6	Stuart Street	D5-D6
Ivy Square	E1	Old Chester Road	C8-D8	Sudbury Close	A4
Jackson Street	A3-A4	Olive Street	A3	Sun Street	B3
John Street	E3-E4	Osmaston Road	E1-C4	Swinburne Street	C2
Keble Close	E2	Otter Street	C7-C8	Talbot Street	B4
Kedleston Road	A8-A7-B7	Oxford Street	E2	Temple Street	C1
Kedleston Street	B7	Parker Close	B6-B7	Tenant Street	C5
Kensington Street	B4	Parker Street	A7-B7	Theatre Walk	D4
Keys Street	D6	Park Grove	A8	The Cockpitt	D4
King Alfred Street	A3-B3-B4	Park Street	D4-D3-E3	The Pentagon	F5-F6
Kings Mead Close	B6	Parliament Street	A3	The Strand	C5
Kingston Street	B8-C8	Peet Street	A3-A4	Traffic Street	D3-D4
King Street	B6-C6	Pelham Street	B3	Trinity Street	E3
Kirk Street	D8	Percy Street	A2	Twyford Street	C2-D2
Larges Street	A5	Phoenix Street	D6	Upper Bainbridge Street	B1-C1
Leaper Street	A6-A7	Pittar Street	B2	Uttoxeter New Road	A4-B4
Leman Street	A2	Ponsonby Terrace	A5	Uttoxeter Old Road	A5
Leonard Street	D2	Provident Street	C1	Vicarage Avenue	A1-B1
Leopold Street	C2-C3-D3	Quarn Street	A7	Victoria Street	C4
Lime Avenue	B2-C2	Quarn Way	A7	Vernon Street	A5
Litchurch Lane	F1	Queen Street	C5-C6	Ward Street	A3-A4
Liversage Place	D3	Railway Terrace	E3-E4	Warner Street	A1-A2-B2
Liversage Road	D3	Raven Street	A1-A2	Wardwick	B5-C5-C4
Liversage Street	D3	Redshaw Street	A7-A8	Watson Street	A7
Lodge Lane	B6	Regent Street	E2	Waygoose Drive	F5-F6
London Road	D4-D3-E3-E2-F2-F1	Reginald Street	D1-E1	Webster Street	B3-C3
Lorne Street	A2	Renals Street	B2-C2	Wellington Street	E2-E3
Lothian Place	F7	Riddings Street	A2	Werburgh Street	A3-B3
Loudon Street	F1-D1	River Street	C7	West Avenue	B7
Lower Eley Street	B2	Robert Street	D6	Western Road	B1-C1
Lyndhurst Street	C1	Roman Road	D8	Westmorland Close	F6
Lynton Street	A3	Rose Hill Street	C1-D1	Wheeldon Avenue	A8
Macklin Street	B4-C4	Rosengrave Street	B3-C3	White Street	A8
Mackworth Road	A7	Ruskin Road	B8	Whitecross Street	A7
Madeley Street	D1	St Alkmund's Way	B6-D5	William Street	A6-A7
Mansfield Road	D6-D7-D8-E8	St Helens Street	B6	Willow Row	B5-B6
Mansfield Street	C7-D7	St James Court	A5	Wilmot Street	C3-D3
May Street	A2	St James Street	C5	Wilson Street	B3-B4-C4
Markeaton Street	A6	St Marks Road	F6-F7	Wolfa Street	A4-B4
Market Place	C5	St Mary's Gate	B5-C5	Woods Lane	A2-B2-B3
Meadow Road	E5	St Michael's Lane	C6	Wood Street	D6
Melbourne Street	C2-D2	St Peter's Church Yard	C4	York Street	A5
Midland Place	E3	St Peter's Street	C4		
Midland Road	E2-E3	Sacheverel Street	C3		
Mill Hill Lane	B1-B2-C2	Sadler Gate	C5		
Mill Hill Road	B1-C1	Salisbury Street	C1-C2		
Mill Street	A6	Sherwood Street	A2		
Monk Street	B3-B4	Shetland Close	F8		
Monmouth Street	F6	Siddals Road	D4-E4		
Moore Street	C1	Sidney Street	E1		
Morledge	D4-D5	Sir Frank Whittle Road	F6-E6-E8		
Morleston Street	D1-D2	Sitwell Street	C3		
Mount Street	C2	Society Place	C1	AA shop	D4
Mount Carmel Street	B1	South Street	A5	22 East Street	
				Derby DE1 2AF	

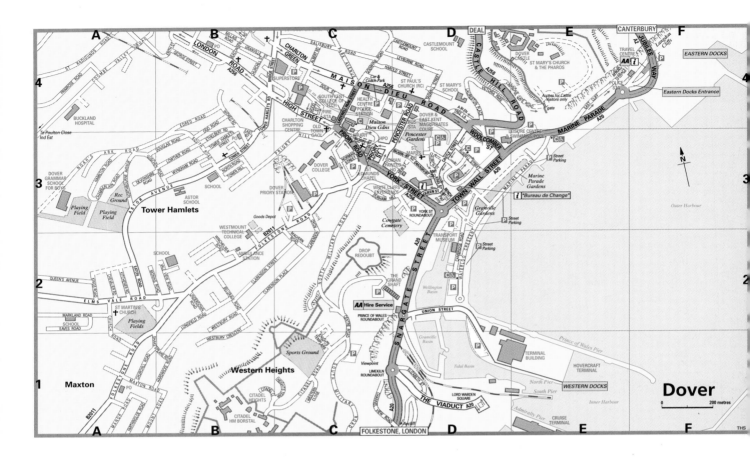

Dover

Dover is found on atlas page **29**,
grid reference TR**3241**

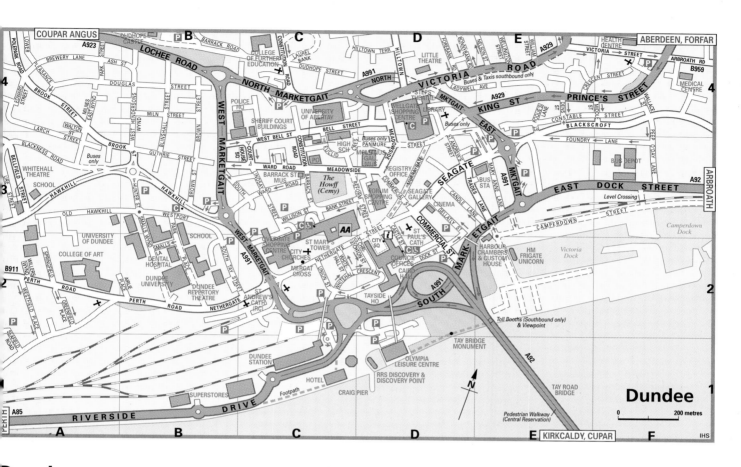

Dundee

Dundee is found on atlas page **126**,
grid reference NO**4030**

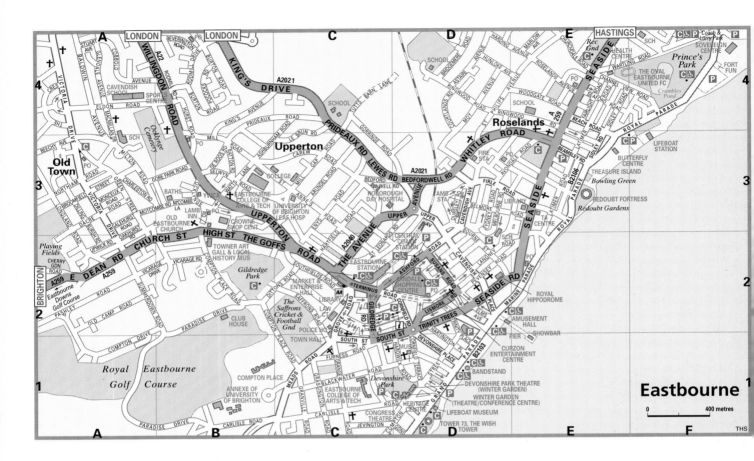

Eastbourne

Eastbourne is found on atlas page **16**,
grid reference TV**6199**

Arundel Road	C3	Enys Road	C2-C3	Northiam Road	A3	Victoria Drive	A2-A3-A4
Ashburnham Road	B3-C3	Fairlight Road	E4	Oakhurst Road	A2-A3	Wartling Road	E4-F4
Ashford Road	C2-D2	Firle Road	D3-E3	Ocklynge Road	B3	Watts Lane	B3
Astaire Avenue	D4	Furness Road	C1	Old Camp Road	A2	Whitley Road	D3-E3
Avondale Road	D3-E3	Gildredge Road	C1-C2	Paradise Drive	A1-B1-B2	Willingdon Road	A4-B4-B3
Baldwin Avenue	A3-A4	Glendale Avenue	A4	Pashley Road	A2	Winchelsea Road	E4
Beach Road	E3-E4	Gore Park Road	A3-B3	Pevensey Road	D2-E2	Woodgate Road	E4
Beamsley Road	E3	Gorringe Road	C4-C3-D3	Pococks Road	B3-B4		
Bedfordwell Road	C3-D3	Grand Parade	D1	Prideaux Avenue	B3-C3-C4		
Beechy Avenue	A3	Grange Road	C1	Prideaux Road	C3-C4		
Belmore Road	D3-E3	Granville Road	C1	Ringwood Road	D4-E4		
Beverington Road	B4	Grassington Road	C1	Rodmill Drive	B4		
Blackwater Road	C1-D1	Green Street	A2-A3	Rodmill Road	B4		
Bourne Street	D2	Grove Road	C1-C2	Roselands Avenue	E4		
Bridgemere Road	D4	Harding Avenue	D4-E4	Royal Parade	E2-E3-F3-F4		
Broomfield Street	A3	Hardwick Road	D1	St Anne's Road	B3-C3-C2		
Burton Road	B4	Hartfield Road	C2-C3	St Leonards Road	C2-D2		
Carew Road	B3-C3	Hartington Place	D1	St Philips Avenue	D3-D4-E4		
Carlisle Road	B1-C1-D1	High Street	B2	Saffrons Road	C2-C1		
Cavendish Avenue	D3	Hunloke Avenue	D4-E4	Salehurst Road	A3		
Cavendish Place	D2	Hurst Road	B3-B4	Seaford Road	E3		
Central Avenue	A4	Jevington Gardens	C1-D1	Seaside	E2-E3-E4		
Channel View Road	E3-E4-F4	King's Avenue	B3-B4	Seaside Road	D2-E2		
Charleston Road	A3	King's Drive	B4-C4	Selwyn Road	B3-C3		
Churchdale Road	E4	Langney Road	D2-E2	Sidley Road	E3-E4		
Church Street	A2-B2	Latimer Road	E3-E4	South Street	C1-D1		
Cobbold Avenue	A4	Le Brun Road	C3-C4	Southfields Road	C2		
Compton Drive	A1-A2	Lewes Road	C3-D3	Stuart Avenue	A4		
Compton Place Road	B2-C2-C1	Lismore Road	D2	Summerdown Road	A1-B2		
Compton Street	D1	Longland Road	A2-A3	Susans Road	D2		
Cornfield Road	D2	Macmillan Drive	A3-A4	Sydney Road	D3		
Cornfield Terrace	D1	Marine Parade	D2-E2	Terminus Road	C2-D2		
Courtlands Road	D4	Marlow Avenue	E4	The Avenue	C2-C3		
Dacre Road	A2-A3	Meads Road	C1	The Crescent	A4		
De Roos Road	B3	Melbourne Road	D2-D3	The Goffs	B2-C2		
Devonshire Place	D1	Mill Gap Road	C3	Trinity Trees	D2		
Dillingburgh Road	A2-A3	Mill Road	B3	Tutts Barn Lane	C4		
Dittons Road	B2-C2	Milton Road	A3	Upper Avenue	C3-D3		
Dursley Road	D3	Monceux Road	A3	Upperton Road	B3-C3-C2		
East Dean Road	A2	Motcombe Lane	B3	Upwick Road	A2	AA shop	C2
Eldon Road	A4-B4	Motcombe Road	A3-B3	Vicarage Drive	A2-B2	2 Terminus Building	
Elms Avenue	D2	Moy Avenue	D3-D4	Vicarage Road	B2	Upperton Road	
						Eastbourne BN21 1BE	

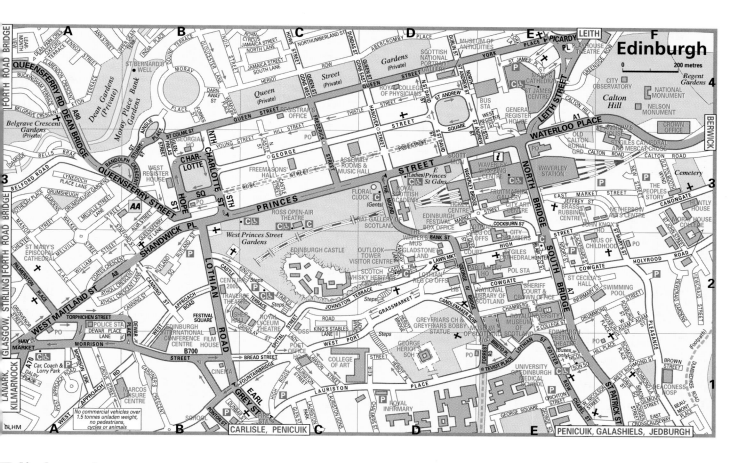

Edinburgh

Edinburgh is found on atlas page 117,
grid reference NT2573

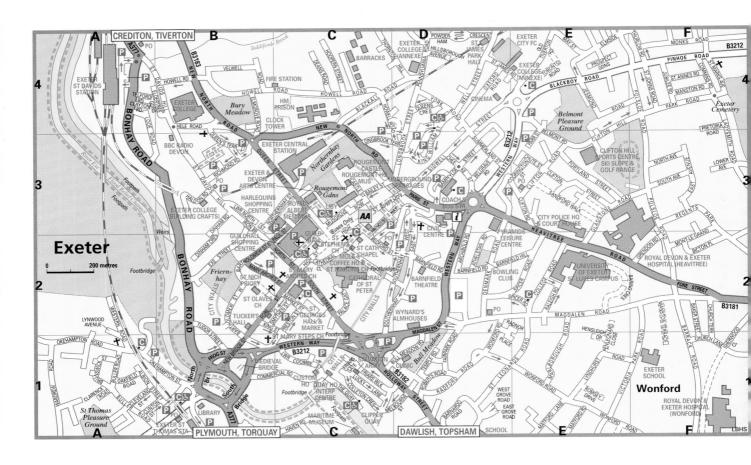

Exeter

Exeter is found on atlas page **9**,
grid reference SX**9292**

Albion Street	A1-B1	Denmark Road	D2-D3	Magdalen Street	D1-D2	Radnor Place	D1-D2
Archibold Road	D2-D3	Dinham Crescent	B2-B3	Manston Road	F4	Raleigh Road	E2
Athelstan Road	D2-D3	Dinham Road	B3	Manston Terrace	F1-F2	Regents Park	F2-F3
Bailey Street	C3	East Avenue	F3	Market Street	C2	Richmond Road	B3
Baker Street	F1-F2	East Grove Road	D1	Marlborough Road	E1-E2	Roberts Road	D1
Bampflyde Street	D3	Eldertree Gardens	A4-B4	Mary Arches Street	B2-C2	Romsey Drive	E1
Baring Crescent	E2	Elmgrove Road	B3-B4	Matford Lane	E1	Sandford Walk	E3
Barnardo Road	D1	Elmside	E4	Matford Road	E1	Sherwood Close	F1-F2
Barnfield Hill	D2-E2	Exe Street	B2-B3	May Street	E4	Sidwell Street	D3-D4
Barnfield Road	D2	Fairpark Road	D1-D2	Melbourne Street	C1-D1	Smythen Street	B2-C2
Barrack Road	F1-F2	Fore Street	B2-C2	Monks Road	F4	South Avenue	F3
Bartholomew Street East	B2	Fore Street	F2	Mont-Le-Grand	F2-F3	South Street	C2
Bartholomew Street West	B1-B2	Friars Gate	C1	Musgrove Row	C3	Southernhay East	C2-D3
Bedford Street	C3-D2	Friars Walk	C1	New Bridge Street	B1-B2	Southernhay West	C2-D3
Belgrave Road	D3	Frog Street	B1	New North Road	B3-C3	Spicer Road	D2-E2
Belmont Road	E3-E4	Gladstone Road	E2-F3	North Avenue	F3	St Annes Road	F4
Bicton Place	F2	Grendon Road	F2	North Street	B2-C2	St Davids Hill	A4-B3
Blackall Road	C4-D4	Haldon Road	B3	Northernhay Street	B3-C3	St James Road	D4-D5
Blackboy Road	E4	Heavitree Road	D3-E2	Oakfield Road	A1	St Johns Road	F4
Bonhay Road	A4-B1	Hele Road	B4	Okehampton Road	A1	St Leonards Road	D1-E2
Brunswick Street	A1	Hensleigh Drive	E1	Okehampton Street	A1-B1	St Marks Avenue	F4
Bull Meadow Road	C1-D1	High Street	C2-D3	Old Tiverton Road	E4	Summerland Street	D3-D4
Buller Road	A1	Hillsborough Avenue	D4	Oxford Road	D4	Telford Road	A4
Castle Street	C3	Holloway Street	C1-D1	Palace Gate	C2	Temple Road	D1
Cathedral Close	C2	Hoopern Street	C4	Paris Street	D3	The Quay	C1
Cheeke Street	D3	Howell Road	B4-D3	Park Road	F4	Thornton Hill	C4-D4
Church Lane	F1	Iron Bridge	B2-B3	Parr Street	E3-E4	Thurlow Road	E4-F4
Church Terrace	F1-F2	Jesmond Road	E4-F4	Paul Street	B2-C3	Toronto Road	E4
Chute Street	E3	Jubilee Road	F4	Penleonard Close	E1-E2	Tudor Street	B1-B2
Clarence Road	A1	King Street	B2-C1	Pennsylvania Road	D4	Velwell Road	B4
Clayton Road	A4	King William Street	D3-D4	Pinhoe Road	F4	Victoria Road	E1-F2
Cleveland Street	A1	Ladysmith Road	F3-F4	Polsloe Road	E4-F2	Wardrew Road	A1
Clifton Hill	E3-F4	Longbrook Street	C3-D4	Portland Street	E3	Well Street	D4
Clifton Road	E3	Longbrook Terrace	C3-D3	Powderham Crescent	D4	West Grove Road	D1
Clifton Street	E3	Looe Road	A3-A4	Preston Street	C2	Western Road	A1-A2
Clinton Street	A1-B1	Lower Avenue	F3	Pretoria Road	F3-F4	Western Way	B1-C1
Codrington Street	D3-E3	Lower Coombe Street	C1	Princess Way	C2-D3	Western Way	D2-E4
College Road	E2	Lower North Street	B3	Prospect Gardens	E4	Wonford Road	D2-F1
Colleton Crescent	C1	Lucky Lane	C1	Queen Street	B3-C3	York Road	D4
Commercial Road	B1-C1	Lyndhurst Road	E1	Queen's Terrace	B3-B4		
Commins Road	F4	Lynwood Avenue	A1-A2	Queens Crescent	D4		
Deans Road	C4	Magdalen Road	D2-F2	Radford Road	D1		

AA shop   C2
1-5 Princeshay
Exeter EX1 1NQ

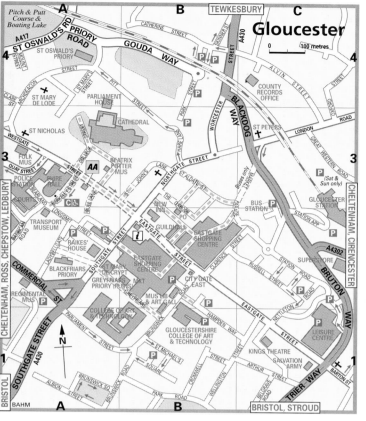

Gloucester

Gloucester is found on atlas page **35**,
grid reference SO**8318**

Albion Street	AI	St Michael's Square	BI
Alvin Street	C3-C4	St Oswald's Road	A4
Archdeacon Street	A3-A4	Station Approach	C2
Arthur Street	CI	Station Road	C2
Barbican Road	A2	The Oxbode	B2-B3
Barton Street	CI	Trier Way	CI
Bearland	A3	Wellington Street	BI-CI
Belgrave Road	CI	Westgate Street	A3-B3
Berkeley Street	A3	Worcester Street	B3-B4
Blackdog Way	B4-C3		
Brunswick Road	AI-B2		
Brunswick Square	AI		
Bruton Way	CI-C3		
Bull Lane	A2-A3		
Catherine Street	B4		
Clare Street	A4		
Clarence Street	B2-C2		
College Street	A3		
Commercial Street	A2		
Cromwell Street	BI		
Eastgate Street	B2-CI		
Gouda Way	A4-B4		
Great Western Road	C3		
Greyfriars	A2-BI		
Hampden Way	B2-CI		
Hare Lane	B3		
Ladybellgate	A2		
London Road	C3		
Longsmit Street	A2-A3		
Market Parade	B2-C3		
Mount Street	A4		
Nettleton Road	CI-C2		
Northgate Street	B3		
Oxford Street	C3-C4		
Park Road	BI		
Park Street	B3-B4		
Parliament Street	AI-BI		
Pitt Street	A4-B3		
Priory Road	A4		
Quay Street	A3		
Russell Street	B2-C2		
Skinner Street	B4		
Southgate Street	AI-B2		
St Aldate Street	B3	AA shop	A3
St John's Lane	B3	51 Westgate Street	
St Mary's Street	A4	Glouscester GL1 2NW	

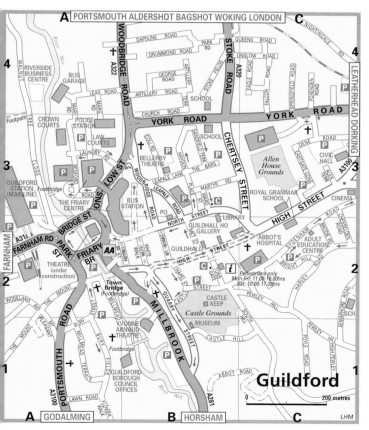

Guildford

Guildford is found on atlas page **25**,
grid reference SU**9949**

Abbot Road	BI-CI	Nightingale Road	C4
Alex Terrace	C3	North Street	A2-B3
Artillery Road	B4	Onslow Road	B4-C4
Artillery Terrace	B4	Onslow Street	A3-B4
Bedford Road	A3	Park Road	B4
Bridge Street	A2-A3	Park Street	A2
Bright Hill	C2	Pewley Hill	B2-CI
Brodie Road	C2	Portsmouth Road	AI-A2
Bury Fields	AI	Poyle Road	CI
Bury Street	AI-A2	Quarry Street	A2-BI
Castle Hill	BI-CI	Queens Road	B4-C4
Castle Street	B2-C2	Sandfield Terrace	B3
Chapel Street	B2	Semaphore Road	CI-C2
Chertsey Street	B3-C2	South Hill	B2-CI
Chesselden Road	C2-C3	Springfield Road	C4
Church Road	B3-B4	Stoke Fields	B4
College Road	B3	Stoke Road	B4
Dapdune Road	B4	Swan Lane	B2
Dene Road	C3	Sydenham Road	C2-C3
Drummond Road	B4	The Bars	B3
Eagle Road	C4	The Mount	AI-A2
Eastgate Gardens	C3	Tunsgate	B2
Falcon Road	C4	Walnut Tree Close	A2-A4
Farnham Road	A2	Ward Street	B3
Flower Walk	AI	Whitelion Walk	B2
Foxenden Road	C4	Wodeland Ave	A2
Friary Bridge	A2	Woodbridge Road	B2-B3-B4-A4
Friary Street	A2-B2	York Road	B3-C4
George Road	B4		
Harvey Road	C2		
Haydon Place	B3		
High Pewley	CI		
High Street	B2-C3		
Laundry Road	A3		
Lawn Road	AI		
Leapale Lane	B3		
Leapale Road	B3		
Leas Road	A4		
Margaret Road	A3-A4		
Market Street	B2		
Martyr Road	B3		
Mary Road	A3-A4		
Millbrook	A2-BI		
Millmead	A2-BI	AA shop	A2
Millmead Terrace	AI	22 Friary Street	
Mount Pleasant	AI-A2	Guildford GU1 4EH	

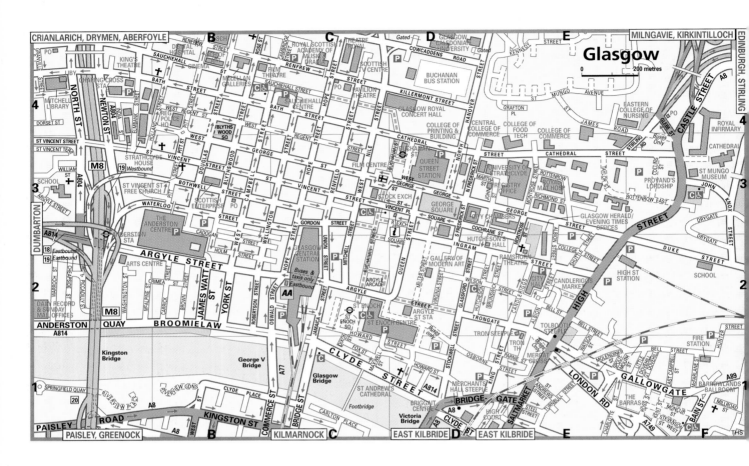

Glasgow

Glasgow is found on atlas page **115**,
grid reference NS**5865**

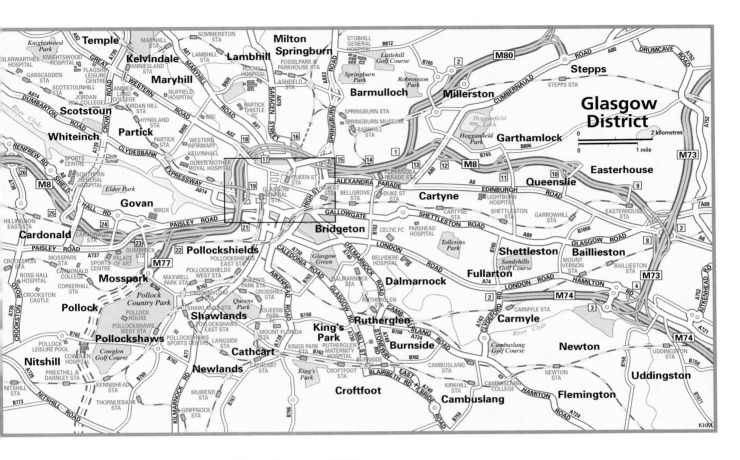

Hanley

Hanley is found on atlas page **72**,
grid reference SJ**8847**

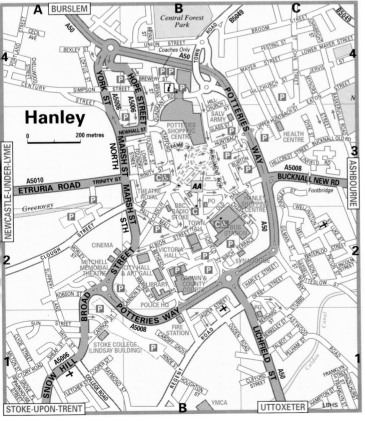

Albion Street	B2	Hillcrest Street	C3	Stafford Street		B3
Baskerville Road	C3-C4	Hinde Street	B1	Stubbs Lane		C1-C2
Berkeley Street	C1	Hope Street	B3-B4	Sun Street		A1
Bernard Street	C1-C2	Hordley Street	C3	Talbot Street		C1
Bethesda Street	B2	Houghton Street	B1	Town Road		B4
Bexley Street	A4	Huntbach Street	B3-C3	Trinity Street		A3-B3
Birch Terrace	B2-C2	Jasper Street	B1-B2	Union Street		B4
Botteslow Street	C2	Jervis Street	C4	Upper Huntbach Street		C3-C4
Brewery Street	B4	Johnbright Street	C4	Warner Street		B2
Broad Street	A1-B2	Lamb Street	B3	Waterloo Street		C2
Broom Street	B4-C4	Lichfield Street	B2-C1	Well Street		C2
Bryan Street	B4	Lincoln Street	C2	Wellington Street		C2-C3
Bucknall New Road	C3	Linfield Road	C3	Yates Street		A1
Bucknall Old Road	C3	Loftus Street	A4	York Street		A3-A4
Bucknall Road	C3	Lower Foundry Street	B3			
Burton Place	B3-C3	Lower Mayer Street	C4			
Cannon Street	A1-B2	Marsh Street North	A3-B3			
Cardiff Grove	B1	Marsh Street South	B2-B3			
Cecil Avenue	A4	Mayer Street	B4-C4			
Century Street	A3-A4	Milton Street	A1			
Charter Street	B3-C2	Morley Street	A2			
Chellwood Street	A4	Mynors Street	C3-C4			
Clifford Street	C1	Nelson Place	C2			
Clough Street	A2-B3	Newhall Street	A3-B3			
Clyde Street	A1	Ogden Street	B1-C1			
College Street	A1	Old Hall Street	B2-C3			
Cooper Street	A1	Pall Mall	B2-B3			
Derby Street	C2	Parkhouse Street	A1			
Dyke Street	C3	Parliament Row	B3			
Eastwood Road	C1	Pelham Street	C1			
Eaton Street	C4	Piccadilly	B2-B3			
Etruria Road	A3	Picton Street	C2			
Festing Street	C4	Portland Street	A4			
Fletcher Street	A1	Potteris Way	A2-A4			
Foundry Street	B3	Quadrant Road	B3-B4			
Franklyn Street	C1	Raymond Street	A1-B1			
Gilman Street	C2	Rectory Road	A1			
Glass Street	B3	Regent Street	B1-C2			
Grove Place	A1	Robson Street	A2			
Hampton Street	C1	Sheaf Street	A1			
Harley Street	C2	Simpson Street	A4-B4			
Hassell Street	C2	Slippery Lane	A1-A2			
Hazelhurst Street	C1	Snow Hill	A1	AA shop		B3
Hillchurch Street	B3-B4	St John Street	C4	32-38 Stafford Street		
Hillchurch Street	C4	St Luke Street	C2	Hanley ST1 1JP		

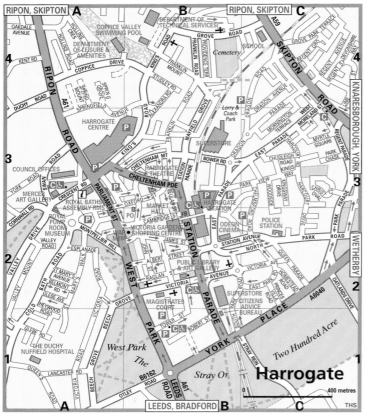

Harrogate

Harrogate is found on atlas page **82**, grid reference SE**3054**

Albert Street	B2	Montpellier Hill	A2
Alexandra Road	B3-B4	Mornington Terrace	C3-C4
Beech Grove	A1-B2	Myrtle Square	C3
Belmont Road	A1	North Park Road	B2-C2
Beulah Street	B3	Oakdale Avenue	A4
Bower Road	B3	Oatlands Drive	C1-C2
Cambridge Street	B2	Otley Road	A1-B1
Chelmsford Road	C3-C4	Oxford Street	A3-B3
Cheltenham Mount	B3	Park Chase	C3
Cheltenham Parade	A3-B3	Park Parade	C2-C3
Christchurch Oval	C3	Park View Way	B3-C3
Chudleigh Road	C3	Parliament Street	A2-A3
Cold Bath Road	A1-A2	Princes Villa Road	C2
Coppice Drive	A4	Providence Terrace	B4
Cornwall Road	A2-A3	Queen Parade	C2
Crescent Road	A3	Queen's Road	A1
Devonshire Way	C4	Raglan Street	B2
Dragon Avenue	C3-C4	Regent Avenue	C4
Dragon Parade	C3-C4	Regent Grove	C4
Dragon Road	B3-C4	Regent Parade	C3
Duchy Road	A3-A4	Regent Street	C4
East Parade	B2-C3	Ripon Road	A3-A4
East Park Road	B2-C2	Robert Street	B1
Esplanade	A2	Skipton Road	C3-C4
Franklin Mount	B4	South Park Road	B1-B2
Franklin Road	B3-B4	Spring Grove	A4
Glebe Avenue	A2	Spring Mount	A4
Glebe Road	A1	Springfield Avenue	A3-B4
Grove Park Terrace	C4	St Mary's Avenue	A2
Grove Road	B4-C4	Station Avenue	B2-C2
Harcourt Drive	C2-C3	Station Parade	B1-B2-B3
Harcourt Road	C3	Stray Rein	B1-C1
Heywood Road	A1-A2	St Mary's Walk	A1-A2
Hollins Crescent	A4	Studley Road	B4
Hollins Road	A4	Swan Road	A3
Homestead Road	C2	Tower Street	B1-B2
James Street	B2	Valley Drive	A2
John Street	B2	Valley Mount	A1-A2
Kent Road	A4	Valley Road	A2
King's Road	A3-B4	Victoria Avenue	B2-C2
Kings Way	C3	Victoria Road	A1-A2
Kingsway Drive	C3	West Park	A2-B1
Lancaster Road	A1	Westmoreland Street	C3-C4
Leeds Road	B1	Woodside	C2-C3
Lime Street	C4	York Place	B1-C2
Mayfield Grove	B3-B4	York Road	A3

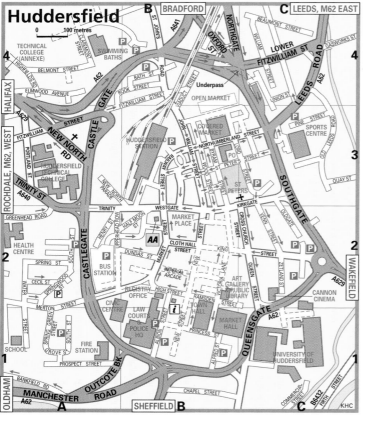

Huddersfield

Huddersfield is found on atlas page **82**, grid reference SE**1416**

Albion Street	B1-B2	Pine Street	C3
Alfred Street	B1	Portland Street	A3
Bankfield Road	A1	Princess Street	B1
Bath Street	B4	Prospect Street	A1
Beaumont Street	C4	Quay Street	C3
Belmont Street	A4	Queen Street	C2
Byram Street	B3	Queensgate	B1-C2
Castlegate	B1-B4	Railway Street	B3
Cecil Street	A2	Ramsden Street	B2-C2
Chapel Street	B1	Rook Street	A4-B4
Claremont Street	A4	South Street	A1-A2
Cloth Hall Street	B2	Southgate	B4-C2
Commercial Street	C1	Spring Green Street	A1
Cross Church Street	C2	Spring Street	A2
Dundas Street	B2	Springwood Street	A2
Elmwood Avenue	A4	St John's Road	B4
Firth Street	C1	St Peter's Street	B3-C3
Fitzwilliam Street	A3-B4	Trinity Street	A2-A3
Gasworks Street	C4	Trinity Westgate	A2-B2
Greenhead Road	A2	Union Street	C4
Grove Street	A1	Upperhead Row	A2
Half Moon Street	B2	Venn Street	C2-C3
Henry Street	A2	Viaduct Street	B4
High Street	B2	Victoria Lane	B1-B2
Highfields Road	A4	Water Street	A1-A2
Imperial Arcade	B2	William Street	C4
John William Street	B3-B4	Wood Street	B3
King Street	B2-C2	Zetland Street	C2
Kirkgate	B2-C3		
Leeds Road	C3-C4		
Lord Street	B3-C3		
Lower Fitzwilliam Street	C4		
Manchester Road	A1-B1		
Market Street	A2-B2		
Merton Street	B1		
New North Parade	A3-B3		
New North Road	A3-A4		
New Street	B1-B2		
Northgate	B4-C4		
Northumberland Street	B3-C3		
Old Leeds Road	C3-C4		
Oldgate	C2-C3	AA shop	B2
Outcote Bridge	A1-B1	7 Cherry Tree Centre	
Oxford Street	B4	Market Street	
Park Drive South	A3	Huddersfield HD1 2ET	

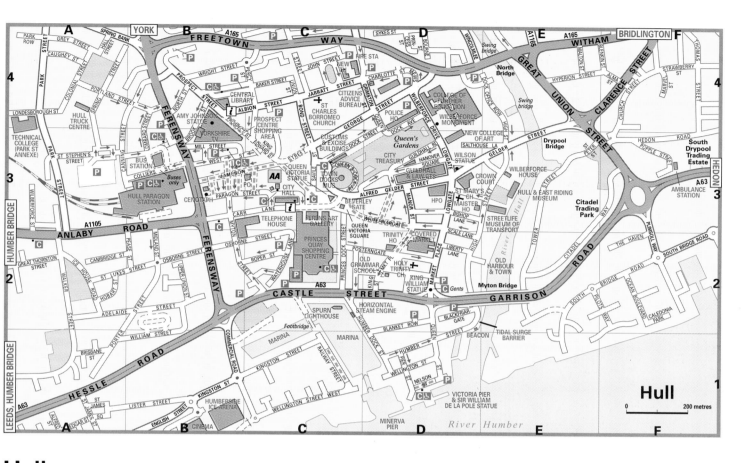

Hull

Hull is found on atlas page **85**,
grid reference TA**0829**

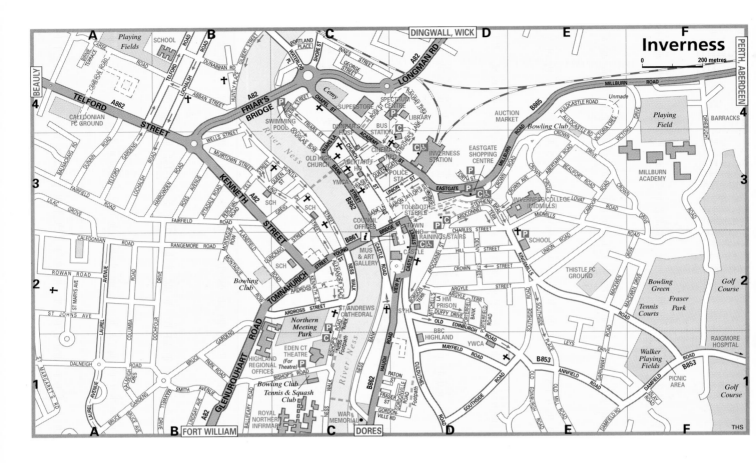

Inverness

Inverness is found on atlas page **140**,
grid reference NH**6645**

Abban Street	B4	Dalneigh Road	A1-B1	Longman Road	C4-D4
Abertarff Road	E3	Damfield Road	E1-F1	Lovat Road	E3-F3
Academy Street	C4-D3	Darnaway Road	E1-E2	Macewen Drive	E2-F2
Alexander Place	C2	Denny Street	D2	Maxwell Drive	B1
Annfield Road	E1-F1	Diriebught Road	F1-F4	Mayfield Road	D1
Ardconnel Street	D2	Dochfour Drive	A1-B3	Midmills Road	E3-F2
Ardconnel Terrace	D3	Douglas Row	C3-C4	Millburn Road	D3-F4
Ardross Place	C2	Duffy Drive	D2	Mitchell's Lane	D2
Ardross Street	B2-C2	Dunabban Road	B4	Montague Row	B2-B3
Argyle Street	D2-E2	Dunain Road	A3-A4	Muirtown Street	B3
Argyle Terrace	D2	Duncraig Street	B2-C3	Ness Bank	C1-C2
Attadale Road	B3	Eastgate	D3	Ness Walk	C1-C2
Auldcastle Road	E3-F4	Eriskay Road	F1	Old Edinburgh Road	D2-E1
Ballifeary Road	B1	Fairfield Road	A3-B3	Old Mill Road	E1
Balnacraig Road	A3-A4	Forth Street	D3	Park Road	B1
Bank Lane	C3	Fraser Street	C1-D1	Paton Street	C1-D1
Bank Street	C3	Fraser Street	C3	Perceval Road	B3
Baron Taylor's Street	D3	Friar's Bridge	B4-C4	Planefield Road	B3-C2
Beaufort Road	E3	Friars Lane	C3-C4	Porterfield Bank	D2
Birnie Terrace	A4	Friars Street	C3-C4	Portland Place	C4
Bishop's Road	B1-C2	George Street	C4	Queen Street	B3-C3
Bordon Terrace	D2	Gilbert Street	B4	Queensgate	C3-D3
Bridge Street	C2-D3	Glebe Street	C4	Railway Terrace	D4
Bruce Avenue	A1	Glenurquhart Road	B1-B2	Rangemore Road	B2
Bruce Gardens	A1-B2	Gordonville Road	C1-D1	Rose Street	C4
Caledonian Road	A3-B2	Greig Street	B3-C3	Ross Avenue	B3
Cameron Road	A4	Harrowden Road	A3-B3	Rowan Road	A2
Carse Road	A4-B4	Haugh Road	C1-D2	Shore Street	C4
Castle Road	C2	Hill Street	D2-E2	Smith Avenue	B1
Castle Street	D2-D3	Huntly Place	B4	Southside Place	E1-D2
Cawdor Road	E3	Huntly Street	B4-C2	Southside Road	D1-E2
Celt Street	B3	Inglis Street	D3	St Johns Avenue	A2
Chapel Street	C4	Innes Street	C4-D4	St Margaret's Road	A1-A2
Charles Street	D3	Islay Road	F1	St Marys Avenue	A2
Church Street	C3-D3	Kenneth Street	B3-C2	Stephens Brae	D3
Columba Road	A1-A2	King Street	B3-C2	Strother's Lane	D3-D4
Crown Avenue	D3-E3	Kingsmills Road	D3-F1	Telford Gardens	A3-A4
Crown Circus	E3	Laurel Avenue	A1-A2	Telford Road	A4-B4
Crown Road	D3-F2	Leys Drive	E1-F1	Telford Street	A4-B3
Crown Street	D2-E2	Lilac Grove	A3	Tomnahurich Street	B2-C2
Culduthel Road	D1-D2	Lindsay Avenue	B1	Union Road	E2-E3
Dalneigh Crescent	A1	Lochalsh Road	A3-B4	Union Street	C3-D3

Victoria Crescent	E3-F4
Victoria Drive	E3-F4
View Place	D2
Waterloo Place	C4
Wells Street	B3-B4
Young Street	C2

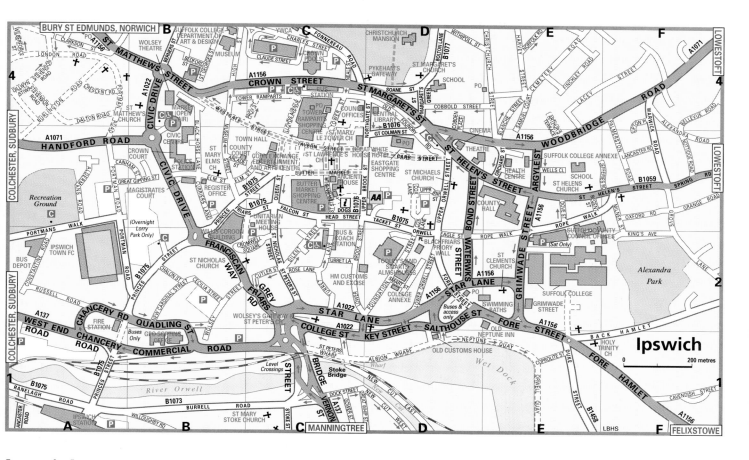

Ipswich

Ipswich is found on atlas page **54**,
grid reference **TM1644**

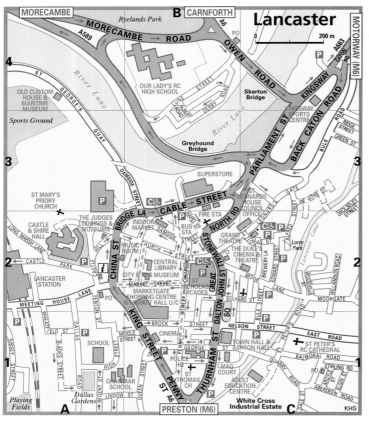

Lancaster

Lancaster is found on atlas page **87**, grid reference SD**476I**

Aberdeen Road	CI	Moorgate	C2
Albert Road	B3-B4	Morecambe Road	A4-B4
Alfred Street	C2-C3	Nelson Street	BI-CI
Argyle Street	CI	North Road	B2-B3
Back Caton Road	C3-C4	Owen Road	B4-C4
Balmoral Road	CI	Parliament Street	C3-C4
Blades Street	AI	Penny Street	BI-B2
Brewery Lane	C2	Quarry Road	CI
Bridge Lane	A2-B2	Queen Street	BI
Brock Street	B2	Regent Street	AI
Bulk Road	C3-C4	Ridge Street	C3
Bulk Street	CI-C2	Sibsey Street	AI
Cable Street	B2-B3	St George's Quay	A3-A4
Castle Hill	A2	St Leonard's Gate	B2-C3
Castle Park	A2	St Peter's Road	CI-C2
Caton Road	C4	Stirling Road	CI
Chapel Street	B2	Stonewall	B2
Cheapside	B2	Sulyard Street	B2-C2
China Street	A2	Thurnham Street	BI
Church Street	B2	Wheatfield Street	AI-A2
Dale Street	CI	Williamson Road	C2
Dallas Road	AI-A2	Wolseley Street	C2-C3
Dalton Square	BI-B2	Woodville Street	C2
Damside Street	A3-B3-B2		
De Vitre Street	C3		
Derby Road	B3-B4		
East Road	CI		
Edward Street	C2		
Elgin Street	CI		
Fenton Street	AI-A2		
George Street	BI-CI		
Great John Street	B2		
Green Street	C3		
High Street	AI		
King Street	AI-A2		
Kingsway	C4		
Lindow Street	AI-A2		
Lodge Street	C2		
Long Marsh Lane	A2		
Lune Street	B3-B4		
Main Way	C4		
Market Street	B2		
Meeting House Lane	A2		
Middle Street	AI-BI		
Moor Lane	B2-C2		

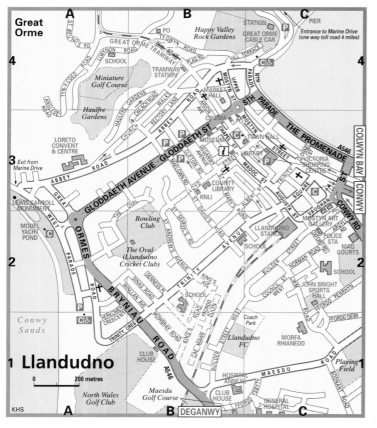

Llandudno

Llandudno is found on atlas page **69**, grid reference SH**7882**

Abbey Road	A3-C4	Rectory Lane	B3-B4
Albert Street	B2-C3	South Parade	B4-C3
Anglesey Road	A3-A4	St Andrew's Avenue	B2-B3
Argyll Road	C2	St Beuno's Road	A4
Arvon Avenue	B3-B4	St David's Road	B2-B3
Augusta Street	C2-C3	St Mary's Road	B3-C2
Bodnant Road	CI	St Seirol's Road	B2-B3
Bryniau Road	A2-BI	The Oval	A2-B3
Builder Street	C2	The Parade	C3
Builder Street West	BI-C2	Trinity Avenue	BI-C3
Cae Mawr	BI	Trinity Crescent	AI-BI
Chapel Street	B3	Trinity Square	C3
Church Walks	A3-B4	Ty-Gwyn Road	B4
Clifton Road	B3	Tyn-y-Coed Road	A4
Clonnel Street	C3	Upper Mostyn Street	B4
Conwy Road	C2-C3	Vaughan Street	C2-C3
Council Street West	C2	West Parade	A2-A3
Cwlach Road	B3-B4	Winllan Avenue	A2-B2
Cwm Road	CI-C2		
Deganwy Avenue	B3		
Denness Place	B2		
Dinas Road	B2		
Ffordd Dulyn	BI-B2		
Ffordd Dewi	CI		
Ffordd Penrhyn	CI-C2		
Ffordd Ysbyty	BI-CI		
Gloddaeth Avenue	A2-B3		
Gloddaeth Street	B3		
Great Ormes Road	AI-A3		
Haulfre Gardens	A3-B4		
Herkomer Crescent	AI-A2		
Hill Terrace	B4-C4		
King's Avenue	B2		
King's Road	BI-B2		
Lloyd Street	B3-C3		
Llwynon Road	A4-B4		
Madoc Street	B3-C3		
Maelgwn Road	B3		
Maesdu Road	BI-CI		
Mostyn Street	B3-C3		
Mowbray Road	BI		
Norman Road	C2		
North Parade	C3		
Oxford Road	C2		
Plas Road	B4		

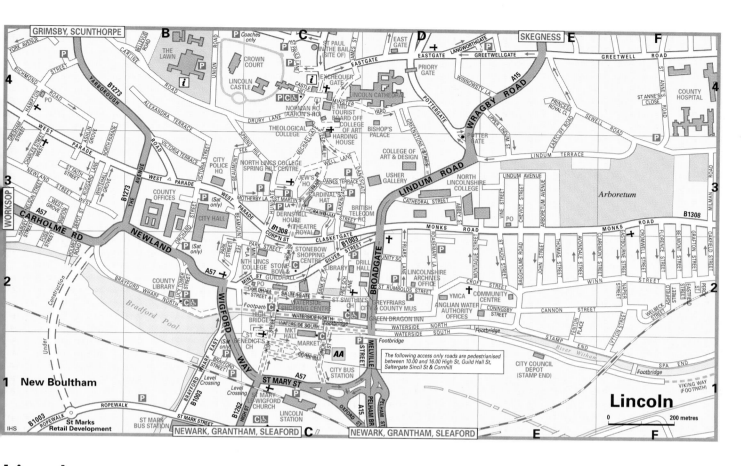

Lincoln

Lincoln is found on atlas page **76**,
grid reference SK**977**1

Abbey Street	D3	Grafton Street	F2-F3	Princess Royal Close	E4	Wragby Road	D3-E4
Alexandra Terrace	B3-B4	Grantham Street	C3-D3	Richmond Road	A4	Yarborough Road	A4-B3
Arboretum Avenue	E3	Greenstone Stairs	D3-D4	Ropewalk	A1-B1	York Avenue	A4
Ashfield Street	F2	Greetwell Road	F4	Rosemary Lane	D2		
Ashlin Grove	A3-A4	Greetwellgate	D4-E4	Ross Street	A2-A3		
Avondale Street	E2	Gresham Street	A3-A4	Rudgard Lane	A3		
Bagholme Road	E2	Guildhall Street	C2	Saltergate	C2		
Bank Street	C2	Hampton Street	A4	Sewell Road	E4-F3		
Beaumont Fee	B2-C3	Harvey Street	A2-A3	Silver Street	C2-D2		
Bellevue Road	B4	High Street	B1-C3	Sincil Street	C1-C2		
Belmont Street	F2-F3	Holmes Road	A2	Spa End	F1		
Brayford Street	B1	Hungate	C2-C3	Spring Hill	B4-C3		
Brayford Wharf East	B1-B2	James Street	C4	St Anne's Close	F4		
Brayford Wharf North	A2-B2	John Street	E2	St Anne's Road	F3-F4		
Broadgate	D2-D3	Langworthgate	D4-E4	St Faith Street	A3		
Cannon Street	E2-F2	Lindum Avenue	E3	St Hugh Street	E2		
Carholme Road	A2-A3	Lindum Road	D3	St Mark Street	B1		
Carline Road	A4-B4	Lindum Terrace	D3-F3	St Martin's Lane	C3		
Castle Hill	C4	Lucy Tower Street	B2	St Mary Street	C1		
Cathedral Street	D3	Lytton Street	F1-F2	St Pauls Lane	C4		
Charles Street West	A3	Melville Street	D1	St Rumbolds Street	D2		
Cheviot Street	E3	Michaelgate	C3-C4	Stamp End	E1-E2		
Claremont Street	F2-F3	Milman Road	F3	Steep Hill	C3-C4		
Clasketgate	C2-D4	Minster Yard	C4-D4	The Avenue	A3-B3		
Coningsby Street	E2	Mint Lane	C2	The Strait	C3		
Cornhill	C1	Mint Street	B2-C2	Thomas Street	E2		
Corporation Street	C2-C3	Monks Road	D3-F3	Union Road	B4		
Croft Street	D2-E2	Montague Street	D2	Unity Square	D2		
Cromwell Street	F2-F3	Motherby Lane	B3-C3	Upper Lindum Street	E3-E4		
Danes Terrace	C3	Napier Street	F2	Victoria Street	B3		
Danesgate	C3-D3	Nelson Street	A3	Victoria Terrace	B3		
Depot Street	A3	Newland	B2-B3	Vine Street	E3		
Drury Lane	B4-C4	Newland Street West	A3	Waterside North	C2-E2		
Eastbourne Street	F2-F3	North Parade	A3-A4	Waterside South	C2-F1		
Eastcliff Road	E3-E4	Oakfield Street	F2-F3	Welbeck Street	F2		
Eastfield Street	F2	Orchard Street	B2-B3	Well Lane	C3		
Eastgate	C4-D4	Oxford Street	C1-D1	West Parade	A4-C3		
Fenton Place	E1-E2	Park Street	B2-C2	Westbourne Grove	A3		
Flaxengate	C2-C3	Pelham Bridge	D1	Whitehall Grove	A3		
Florence Street	F2-F3	Pelham Street	D1	Wigford Way	B2-C1	AA shop	C1
Free School Lane	C2	Percy Street	F2	Winn Street	E2-F2	33 Sincil Street	
Friars Lane	D2-D3	Pottergate	D3-D4	Winnowsty Lane	D4-E4	Lincoln LN5 7ET	

IHS

223

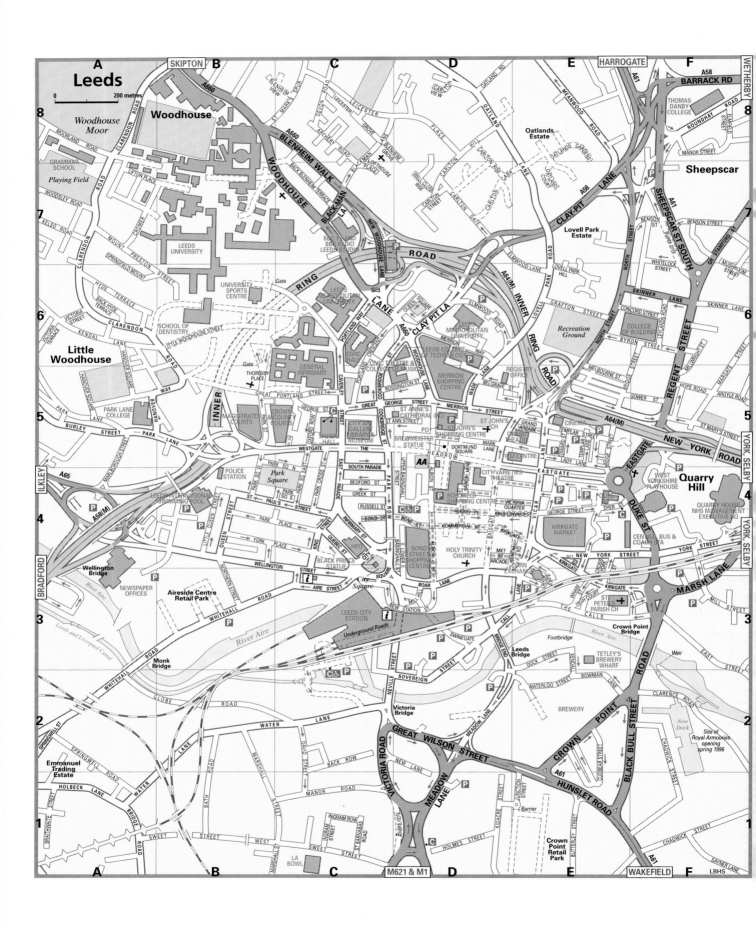

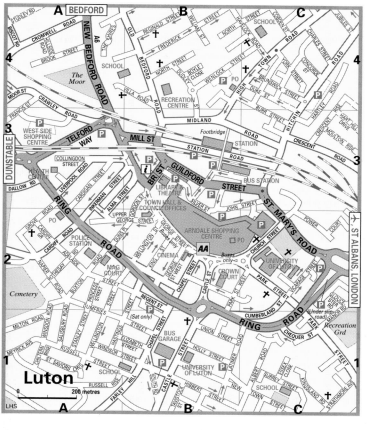

Luton

Luton is found on atlas page **38**,
grid reference TL0921

Adelaide Street	A2-B2	Hartley Road	C3-C4	Tavistock Street	B1
Albert Road	B1-C1	Hastings Street	A1-B2	Telford Way	A3
Alma Street	A2-B3	Havelock Road	B4-C4	The Shires	A4
Biscot Road	A4	Hibbert Street	B1	Union Street	B1
Boyle Close	B4	High Town Road	B3-C4	Upper George Street	A2-B2
Bridge Street	B3	Hillside Road	A4	Vicarage Street	C2
Brook Street	A4	Hitchin Road	C3-C4	Villa Road	A4-B4
Brunswick Street	C4	Holly Street	B1	Wellington Street	A1-B2
Burr Street	C3-C4	Inkerman Street	A2-A3	Wenlock Street	B4-C4
Buxton Road	A2	John Street	B2-C3	William Street	B4
Cardiff Grove	A2	Jubilee Street	C4	Windsor Street	A1-B1
Cardiff Road	A2	King Street	B2	Winsdon Road	A1-A2
Cardigan Street	A3	Kingsland Road	C1	York Street	C4
Castle Street	B1-B2	Latimer Road	B1-C1		
Chapel Street	B1-B2	Liverpool Road	A3		
Charles Street	C4	Manor Road	C1-C2		
Chequer Street	C1	Meyrick Avenue	A2		
Chiltern Rise	A1	Midland Road	D3-C3		
Church Street	B2-C2	Mill Street	B3		
Cobden Street	C4	Milton Road	A1		
Collingdon Street	A3	Moor Street	A4		
Concorde Street	C4	Moulton Rise	C3		
Crawley Green Road	C2	Napier Road	A2		
Crawley Road	A3-A4	New Bedford Street	A4-B3		
Crescent Rise	C3-C4	New Town Street	B1-C1		
Crescent Road	C3	North Street	B4-C4		
Cromwell Road	A4	Old Bedford Road	A4-B3		
Cumberland Street	C1-C2	Park Street	C1-C2		
Dallow Road	A3	Park Street West	B2-C2		
Dudley Street	B3-B4	Power Court	C2		
Duke Street	C3-C4	Princess Street	A2		
Dumfries Street	A2-B1	Regent Street	B1-B2		
Duns Place	A2-B2	Reginald Street	B4		
Dunstable Road	A4-C2	Rothesay Road	A2		
Elizabeth Street	A1-B1	Russell Rise	A1		
Essex Close	C1	Russell Street	A1-B1		
Farley Hill	A1-B1	Salisbury Road	A1-A2		
Francis Street	A3-A4	Silver Street	B3		
Frederick Street	B4	South Road	B1		
George Street	B2	St Mary's Road	C2-C3		
George Street West	B2	St Saviours Crescent	A1		
Gloucester Road	C2	Stanley Street	A1-A2		
Gordon Street	B2-B3	Station Road	B3-C3		
Grove Road	A2-A3	Strathmore Avenue	C1	AA shop	B2
Guildford Street	B3-C3	Studley Road	A4	45 George Street	
Hart Hill Drive	C3	Surrey Street	C1	Luton LU1 2AQ	

Leeds

Leeds is found on atlas page **82**,
grid reference SE2932

Aire Street	C3	Clay Pit Lane	D6-E7	Infirmary Street	C4	Mushroom Street	F6-F7	St Mary's Street	F5
Albion Place	D4	Commercial Street	D4	Ingram Row	C1	Neville Street	C2-D3	St Paul's Street	B4-C4
Albion Street	D3-D5	Concord Street	E6-F6	Ingram Street	C1	New Lane	C2-D1	Sweet Street	C1
Archery Road	C8	Cookridge Street	C5-D6	Inner Ring Road	B5-E5	New Station Street	C3-D3	Sweet Street West	A1-B1
Argyle Road	F5	Cromer Terrace	A7-B7	Junction Street	E1	New Woodhouse Lane	C6-C7	Swinegate	D3
Back Blenheim Terrace	C7-C8	Cross York Street	E3-E4	Kelso Road	A7	New York Road	E5-F5	Templar Lane	E5
Back Row	C1-C2	Crown Point Road	E2-F3	Kendal Lane	A6	New York Street	E4-F4	Templar Street	E5
Barrack Road	F8	Crown Street	E3	Kendal Street	E2-E3	North Street	E5-E7	The Calls	E3-F3
Bath Road	B1-B2	Cudbear Street	E1-E2	Kidacre Street	D1	Northern Street	B3-B4	The Headrow	C5-D4
Bedford Street	C4	David Street	C1-C2	King Edward Street	D4-E4	Oatland Court	E7	Thoresby Place	B5-B6
Belgrave Street	D4-E4	Devon Road	C8	King Street	C4	Oatland Lane	D8-E7	Upper Basinghall Street	D4-D5
Benson Street	F7	Dewsbury Road	D1	Kirkgate	D4-F3	Oatland Road	D8	Vicar Lane	E4-E5
Black Bull Street	E1-F2	Dock Street	E3	Lady Lane	E4-E5	Oatlands Gardens	E8	Victoria Quarter	D4-E4
Black Hyde Terrace	A6	Dortmund Square	D5	Lands Lane	D4	Oxford Row	C5	Victoria Road	C1-C2
Blackman Lane	C7-C8	Duke Street	E4-F3	Leicester Grove	C8	Park Cross Street	C4-C5	Victoria Street	A6
Blenheim Grove	C8-D8	Dyer Street	E4	Leicester Place	C8-D8	Park Lane	A5-B5	Victoria Terrace	A6
Blenheim View	B8-C8	East Parade	C4-C5	Leylands Road	F6	Park Place	B4-C4	Wade Lane	D5
Blenheim Walk	B8-D7	East Street	F2-F3	Lifton Place	A7-B7	Park Road	C4-C5	Water Lane	A1-C2
Boar Lane	D3-E4	Eastgate	E4-F5	Little Queen Street	B4	Park Square East	C4-C5	Waterloo Street	E2
Bond Street	C4-D4	Edward Street	E5	Little Woodhouse Street	B6	Park Square North	B5-C4	Well Close Rise	D7-D8
Bowman Lane	E2	Elmfield Street	F8	Lofthouse Place	C7	Park Square South	C4	Wellington Street	A4-C3
Braithwaite Street	A1	Elmwood Lane	D7-E6	Lovell Park Hill	E6	Park Square West	B4-B5	Westgate	B5-C5
Bridge End	D3	Elmwood Road	D6	Lovell Park Road	D6-E7	Park Street	B5	Wharf Street	E3
Bridge Road	A1	George Street	C5	Lower Basinghall Street	D3-D4	Portland Crescent	C5-C6	Whitehall Road	A2-C3
Bridge Street	E4-E5-F6	George Street	E4	Manor Road	C1	Portland Way	C6	Whitelock Street	F6-F7
Briggate	D3-D5	Globe Road	A2-C2	Manor Street	F8	Quebec Street	C4	Woodhouse Lane	B8-D5
Burley Street	A5	Gower Street	E5-F5	Margate Street	F5-F6	Queen Square	D6	Woodsley Road	A7
Butterley Street	E1	Grafton Street	E6	Mark Lane	D5-E5	Queen Street	B4	York Place	B4-C4
Byron Street	E6-F6	Grand Arcade	E5	Market Street Arcade	D4	Regent Street	F5-F6	York Street	F4
Call Lane	D3-E3	Great George Street	C5-D5	Marlborough Street	A4-A5	Rossington Street	C5-D5		
Carlton Carr	D7-E8	Great Portland Street	B5-C5	Marsh Lane	F3-F4	Rossville Road	F7		
Carlton Gate	D7	Great Stamford Street	F6-F7	Marshall Street	B1-B2	Roundhay Road	F8		
Carlton Hill	D7-D8	Great Wilson Street	D2	Meadow Lane	D1-D2	Russell Street	C4		
Carlton Rise	D7-D8	Greek Street	C4	Meanwood Road	E7-E8	Sheepscar Street South	F6-F8		
Carlton Street	D7	Hanover Square	A5-A6	Melbourne Street	E5	Skinner Lane	E6-F6		
Carlton View	D8	Hanover Way	A5-B5	Merrion Street	D5-E5	South Parade	C4		
Caverley Street	B6-C5	High Court	E3	Merrion Way	D6	Sovereign Street	C2-D3		
Central Road	D3-E4	Holbeck Lane	A1	Mill Hill	D3	Springfield Mount	A7-B6		
Chadwick Street	F1-F2	Holmes Street	D1	Mill Street	F3-F4	Springwell Road	A1-A2		
City Square	C3-C4	Hope Road	F5	Millwright Street	F5-F6	St Ann Street	C5-D5	AA shop	B2
Clarence Road	F2	Hunslet Road	E1-F1	Moorland Road	A8-B7	St Barnabas Road	C1	95 The Headrow	
Clarendon Road	B5-B8	Hyde Terrace	A6	Mount Preston Street	A7-B6	St Mark's Spur	B8-C8	Leeds LS1 6LU	

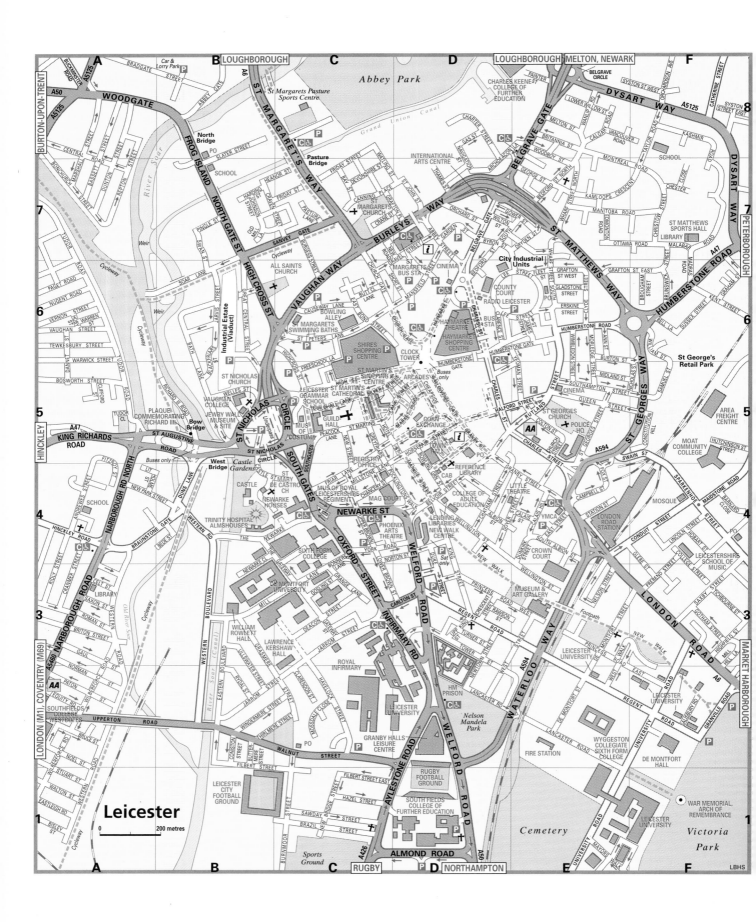

Leicester

0   200 metres

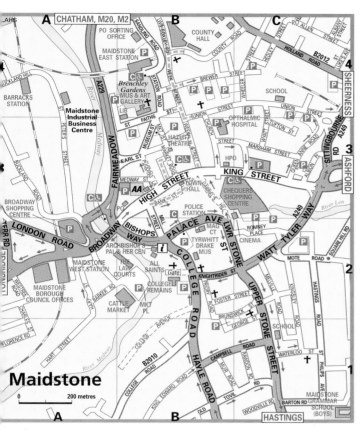

Maidstone

Maidstone

Maidstone is found on atlas page **28**,
grid reference TQ**7555**

Albany Street	C4	Knightrider Street	B2-C2	Week Street	B3-B4
Albion Place	C3	London Road	A2-A3	Westree Road	A2
Allen Street	C4	Lower Boxley Road	B4	Wheeler Street	C4
Bank Street	B3	Market Buildings	B3	Woodville Road	C1
Barker Road	A2	Market Street	B3	Wyatt Street	C3-C4
Barker Road	A2	Marsham Street	C3		
Barton Road	C1	Medway Street	B3		
Bishops Way	B2	Melville Road	C1-C2		
Brewer Street	B4-C4	Mill Street	B2-B3		
Broadway	A2-B2	Mote Road	C2		
Brunswick Street	B2-C2	Muir Road	B1-C1		
Buckland Hill	A4	Museum Street	B3		
Buckland Road	A3	Old Tovil Road	B1-C1		
Campbell Road	B1-C1	Palace Avenue	B2-B3		
Charles Street	A1-A2	Priory Road	B2		
Church Street	B3-C3	Pudding Lane	B3		
College Avenue	B1-B2	Queen Anne Road	C3		
College Road	B1-B2	Rawdon Road	C1		
County Road	B4-C4	Romney Place	C2		
Earl Street	B3	Sandling Road	B4		
Fairmeadow	A3-A4	Sittingbourne Road	C3-C4		
Florence Road	A1	Square Hill Road	C2		
Foster Street	B2-C2	St Faiths Street	B3-B4		
Gabriel's Hill	B3	St Luke's Avenue	C4		
George Street	B1-C2	St Peter's Street	A3-A4		
Hart Street	A1-A2	St Philips Avenue	C1		
Hastings Road	C1-C2	Station Road	B4		
Hayle Road	B1	Terrace Road	A2		
Hedley Street	C4	Tonbridge Road	A2		
High Street	B3	Tufton Street	C3		
Holland Road	C4	Union Street	B3-C4		
Kingsley Road	C1-C2	Upper Stone Street	C1-C2	AA shop	B3
King Edward Road	B1	Waterloo Street	C1	26-27 High Street	
King Street	B3-B4	Watt Tyler Way	C2-C3	Maidstone ME14 1JF	

Abbey Gate	B8	Calais Street	E4	Dunkirk Street	E4	Greyfriars	C5	Newarke Street	C4-D4	Southgates	C4-C5
Abbey Street	D7	Calgary Road	E8	Duns Lane	B4-B5	Guildhall Lane	C5	Newbridge Street	C1	Sparkenhoe Street	F4-F5
All Saints Road	D4	Campbell Street	E4	Dunton Street	A7-A8	Halford Street	D5-E5	New Park Street	A4-B4	Station Street	E4
All Saints Road	B7	Cank Street	C5-D5	Dysart Way	F7-F8-E8	Harding Street	B7	New Road	C7-D7	Stuart Street	A2
Andrewes Street	A4-A5	Canning Place	C7	East Bond Street	C6-D6	Havelock Street	C2-C3	New Street	C4-C5	Sussex Street	F6
Archdeacon Lane	D7-D8-E8	Carlton Street	C3-D3	East Street	E4	Haymarket	D6	Newtown Street	D2-D3	Swain Street	E5-F5
Aylestone Road	C1-D2	Castle Street	B4-C4	Eastern Boulevard	B2-B3	Hazel Street	C1	New Walk	D4-E4-E3-F3	Swan Street	B6-B7
Barnard Close	F4	Catherine Street	F8	Eastleigh Road	A1	Heanor Street	B7-C7	Nicholas Street	E5-F5	Syston Street East	F8
Baron Street	E5-E6	Causeway Lane	C6	Edmonton Road	E7	High Cross Street	C5-B6-C6	Noel Street	A1-A2	Syston Street West	E8-F8
Bassett Street	A7-A8	Celt Street	A3	Equity Road	A2	Highfield Street	F3	Northgate Street	B7	The Newarke	B4-C4
Bath Lane	B5-B6	Central Road	A7-A8	Erskine Street	E6	High Street	C5-D5	Norman Street	A2-A3	Taylor Road	F7-F8
Bay Street	C7	Chancery Street	C4	Filbert Street	B1-C1-B2-C2	Hinckley Road	A4	Norton Street	C4-D4	Tewkesbury Street	A6
Bede Street	A4-B4	Charles Street	E4-D6-D5-E5	Filbert Street East	C1	Hobart Street	F4	Nugent Street	A6	The Gateway	B4-C3
Belgrave Circle	E8	Charlton Street	C3-D3	Fitzroy Street	A4-A5	Hoby Street	A6	Old Mill Lane	B7	Thames Street	D7
Belgrave Gate	D7-D8-E8	Charter Street	D8	Fleet Street	E4	Horsefair Street	C5-D5	Orchardson Avenue	F8	Thirlemere Street	B2-C3
Bell Lane	F6	Chatham Street	D4-D5	Fosse Road	A8	Hotel Street	C5	Orchard Street	D7	Tichbourne Street	F3
Belvoir Street	D4	Cheapside	D5	Fox Street	E4	Humberstone Gate	D5-D6-E6	Ottawa Road	E7-F7	Tower Street	D2-D3
Bisley Street	A1	Chester Close	F7	Freeschool Lane	C5-C6	Humberstone Road	F6-E6	Oxford Street	C3-C4	Tudor Close	A5
Blackfriars Street	B5-B6	Christow Street	F7	Friar Lane	C5-C4	Hutchinson Street	F5	Paget Road	A7	Tudor Road	A5-A6-A7
Bonchurch Street	A7-A8	Church Gate	C7-C6-D6	Friday Street	B7-C7-C8	Infirmary Road	C3-C2-D3	Painter Street	E8	Turner Street	D3
Bonners Lane	C4	Church Street	E5	Frog Island	B7-B8	Jarrom Street	B2-C2-C3	Paton Street	A2	Ullswater Street	B3-B8
Bosworth Street	A5	Clarence Street	D6	Gallowtree Gate	D5	Jarvis Street	B6	Peacock Lane	C5	University Road	E1-E2-F2-F3
Bowling Green Street	D5-D4	Clarendon Street	C2	Garden Street	D7	Johnson Street	B7	Pingle Street	B7	Upper Brown Street	C4
Bradgate Street	A8-B8	Clifford Street	A5	Gas Street	D8	Kamloops Crescent	E7-F7	Pocklingtons Walk	C4-D4	Upper King Street	D3
Braunstone Gate	A4-B4	Clyde Street	E6	Gateway Street	B4-C4-C3	Kashmir Road	F8-F7	Prebend Street	F3-F4	Upperton Road	A2-B2
Brazil Street	C1	College Street	F4-F5	Gaul Street	A3-A2	Kent Street	F6	Princess Road East	E3-F3-F2	Vancouver Road	E8-F8
Britannia Street	E8	Colton Street	E5	George Street	E7	King Richards Road	A5	Princess Road West	D3-E3	Vaughan Way	C6-C7
Briton Street	A3	Conduit Street	E4-F4	Gladstone Street	E6	King Street	D3-D4	Queen Street	E5	Vaughan Street	A6
Brougham Street	F6	Coniston Street	B2	Glebe Street	F3-F4	Lancaster Road	D3-E3-E2	Rawson Street	D3-E3	Vernon Street	A6
Bruce Street	A2	Constitution Hill	F5	Gosling Street	C3	Latimer Street	A3-A4	Regent Road	D3-E3-E2-F2	Walnut Street	B2-C2-D2
Brunswick Street	F6-F7	Crafton Street	E6-F6	Gotham Street	F3	Lee Street	E6-D6	Repton Street	A7-A8	Walton Street	A1
Burgess Street	C6-C7	Crane Street	C7	Gower Street	E7-D7	Lincoln Street	F4	Richard III Road	B5	Wanlip Road	E8
Burleys Way	C7-D1	Cranmer Street	A3-A4	Grafton Place	C7-D7	Little Holme Street	A4-B4	Ridley Street	A3-A4	Warren Street	A6
Burnmoor Street	C1	Craven Street	B7-C7	Grafton Street East	E6-F6	London Road	E4-F3-E3-F2	Roman Street	A3	Warwick Street	A5-A6
Burton Street	E6	Crescent Street	D3	Grafton Street West	E7	Lower Brown Street	C3-C4-D3	Rutland Street	D5-E5-E6	Waterloo Way	E2-E3-D2-E4
Butt Close Lane	C6	Dannet Street	A5-A6	Graham Street	F6	Lower Willow Street	E8	Rydal Street	B2	Watling Street	C7-C8
Buttermere Street	B2	Deacon Street	C3	Granby Street	D4-D5-E4	Madras Road	F6-F7	St Augustine Road	A5-B5	Welford Road	D1-D2-D3-D4
Byron Street	D6-D7-E6-E7	De Montfort Street	E2-E3-F3	Grange Lane	C3	Maidstone Road	F4-F5	St George Street	E5	Welles Street	B5
Calais Hill	E4	Devonshire Street	C7	Granville Road	F2-F3	Malabar Road	F7	St Georges Way	E5-F5-F6	Wellington Street	D4-E3-E4
		Dover Street	D4-E4	Grasmere Street	B2-B3-C2-C1	Manitoba Road	E7-F7	St James Street	E6	Western Boulevard	D2-D3-E3
		Dryden Street	D7-E7	Gravel Street	C6-D7	Mansfield Street	D6-D7	St John Street	D8	Western Road	A1-A2-A3-A4-B4
		Duke Street	D4-D3	Great Central Street	B6	Mantle Road	A6-A7	St Margaret's Way	B8-C8-C7	West Street	D2-D3-E3
						Market Place	C5-D5	St Martins	C5	Wharf Street North	E7-E8
						Market Street	D4-D5	St Matthews Way	E6-E7	Wharf Street South	E6-E7
						Marshall Street	A7-A8	St Nicholas Circle	B5-C5	Wilberforce Road	A1-A2-A3
						Mayors Walk	E1	St Peters Lane	C6	William Street	F6
						Melton Street	E8	Salisbury Road	F2	Wilton Street	D7
						Midland Street	E5	Samuel Street	F5	Wimbledon Street	E5-E6
						Mill Hill Lane	F3	Sanvey Gate	B7-C7	Windermere Street	B2-C2
						Mill Lane	B3-C3	Sawday Street	C1	Woodboy Street	E8-E7
						Millstone Lane	C4	Saxby Street	F3-F4	Woodgate	A8-B8
						Morledge Street	E5-E6	Saxon Street	A3	Yeoman Street	D6-E5-E6
						Montreal Road	E7-E8-F7	Severn Street	F4	York Road	C4-D4
						Mossdale Close	C2	Short Street	C6-D6		
						Narborough Road	A2-A3-A4	Silver Street	C5-D5		
						Narborough Road North	A3-A5	Slater Street	B8		
						Navigation Street	D7-D8	Soar Lane	B6-B7	AA shop	E4
						Nelson Street	E3	South Albion Street	E4	132 Charles Street	
						Newarke Close	B3-B4	Southampton Street	E5	Leicester LE1 1NA	

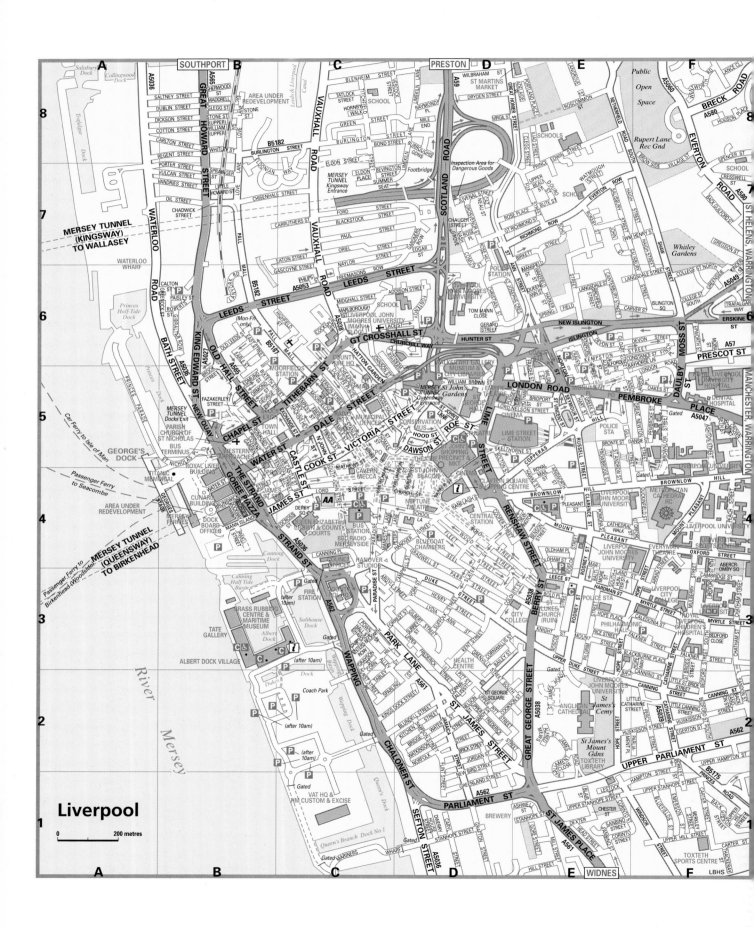

Liverpool

0   200 metres

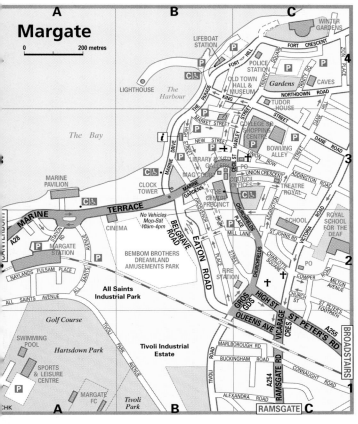

Margate

Margate is found on atlas page **29**, grid reference TR3571

Addington Road	C3	Fort Hill	B4-C4	Queens Avenue	C1
Addington Street	C2-C3	Fulsam Place	A2	Ramsgate Road	C1
Alexandra Road	B1-C1	Grosvenor Gardens	C2	St Johns Road	C2
All Saints Avenue	A2	Grosvenor Place	B2-B3	St Peter's Footpath	C1-C2
Belgrave Road	B2	Hawley Street	C3-C4	St Peter's Road	C1
Buckingham Road	B1-C1	High Street	B3-B2-C2	Station Road	A2
Cecil Street	C3	King Street	B4-C4-C3	The Parade	B4
Charlotte Square	C2	Marine Drive	B3	Tivoli Park Avenue	A2-A1-B1
Churchfields	C2	Marine Gardens	B3	Tivoli Road	B1
Churchfields Place	C2-C3	Marine Terrace	A2-A3-B3	Trinity Square	C4
Church Street	C2	Market Street	B3-C3	Union Crescent	C3
Connaught Road	C1	Marlborough Road	B1-C1	Union Row	C3
Cowper Road	C2	Mill Lane	B2-C2	Vicarage Crescent	C1
Dane Hill	C3-C4	Milton Avenue	C2	Victoria Road	C2-C3
Dane Road	C3	Naylands	A2	Zion Place	C4
Eaton Road	B2-B3	New Street	B3		
Fort Crescent	C4	Northdown Road	C4		

Liverpool

Liverpool is found on atlas page **78**, grid reference SJ3490

...ddison Street	C6-D6	Brunswick Street	B4	Craven Street	E5-E6	Gradwell Street	D3-D4	Mile End	D8	Seymour Street	E5
...delaide Place	E8	Burlington Street	B8-D8	Cresswell Street	F7	Grafton Street	D1	Mill Street	E1	Shaw Street	F6-F7
...insworth Street	E4-E5	Burroughs Gardens	D8	Cross Hall Street	C5-D5	Grayson Street	C3	Moira Street	F6	Shaws Alley	C3-D2
...lfred Mews	E2	Bute Street	E7	Crown Street	F5	Great Crosshall Street	C6-D6	Monument Place	E5	Sherwood Street	B8
...nson Place	F5	Caledonia Street	F3	Cunliffe Place	C5	Great George Street	E1-E3	Moorfields	C5	Simpson Street	D2
...olton Street	E5	Calton Street	B6	Dale Street	C5-D5	Great Homer Street	D7-D8	Moss Street	F6	Skelthorne Street	D5-E5
...rgyle Street	C3-D3	Cambridge Street	F3	Dansie Street	E5-F5	Great Howard Street	B6-B8	Mount Pleasant	F4	Slater Street	D3-D4
...rrad Street	F3-F4	Campbell Street	D3-D4	Daulby Street	F5	Great Newton Street	F4-F5	Mount Pleasant Street	E4-F4	Soho Street	E7
...shton Street	F4-F5	Canning Place	C4	Dawson Street	D5	Great Orford Street	F4	Mount Street	E3	South Hunter Street	E3
...shwell Street	E1	Canning Street	E2-F2	Devon Street	E6-F6	Greek Street	E5	Mulberry Street	F3-F4	South John Street	C4-C5
...udley Street	E5-E6	Canterbury Street	E6	Dexter Street	E1	Green Street	C8-D8	Myrtle Street	F3	Sparling Street	C2-D2-D3
...ack Canning Street	F2-F3	Carlton Street	A8-B8	Dickson Street	A8-B8	Greenland Street	D1-E2	Nash Grove	D7	Spencer Street	F8
...ack Gibson Street	F1	Carpenters Row	C3	Douro Street	E7	Greenock Street	B6	Naylor Street	C6-D7	Spranger Street	B7
...ack Guildford Street	F7	Carruthers Street	B7-C7	Dryden Street	D8	Greenside	F6	Nelson Street	D2	Springfield Street	E6-E7
...ack Sandon Street	F2	Carter Street	F1	Dublin Street	A8-B8	Gregson Street	F7	Netherfield Road South	E8-F7	St Andrew Street	E4-E5
...ailey Street	D2-E3	Carver Street	E6-F6	Duckinfield Street	F4	Grenville Street South	D3-E2	New Bird Street	D1-D2	St Ann Street	D7-E6
...altimore Street	E3-E4	Caryl Street	D1	Duke Street	C3-E3	Grosvenor Street	D7	New Islington	E6-F6	St Brides Street	F2-F3
...ath Street	A6-B5	Castle Street	C4-C5	Dwerry House Street	D1	Hackins Hey	C5	New Quay	B5	St James Place	E1
...aton Street	B7-C7	Catharine Street	F2-F3	Earle Street	B5-B6	Haigh Street	E7-F6	Newington	E4	St James Road	E1-E2
...ayhorse Lane	E5-F6	Cathedral Walk	E4	East Street	B6	Hampton Street	E1-F2	Norfolk Street	D2	St James Street	D2-E2
...eckwith Street	C3	Cazneau Street	D7	Eberle Street	C5	Hanover Street	C3-D4	North John Street	C5	St John's Lane	D5
...edford Close	F3	Chadwick Street	B7	Edgar Street	D7	Hardman Street	E3	Norton Street	E5-E6	St Josephs Crescent	D6-E6
...edford Street North	F3-F4	Chaloner Street	C2-D1	Edmund Street	B5	Harker Street	E6	Oakes Street	F5	St Nicholas Place	B5
...edford Street South	F2-F3	Chapel Street	B5	Egerton Street	F2	Hart Street	E5	Oil Street	A7-B7	St Thomas Street	C5-D5
...enson Street	E4	Chatham Street	F3	Eldon Place	C7	Hatton Garden	C5-C6	Old Hall Street	B5-B6	St Vincent Street	E5
...erkley Street	F1-F2	Chaucer Street	D7	Eldon Street	C7-C8	Hawke Street	E4-E5	Old Leeds Street	B6	Stafford Street	E5-E6
...erry Street	E3	Cheapside	C5-C6	Eldonian Way	B8-C8	Head Street	E1	Oldham Place	E4	Stanhope Street	D1-E1
...evington Street	C7-D7	Chester Street	E1	Elizabeth Street	F5	Henry Street	D3	Oldham Street	E4	Stanley Street	C4-C5
...rchfield Street	E6	Chisenhale Street	B7-C7	Emerson Street	F1	Highfield Street	B6-c6	Oriel Street	C7-D7	Stone Street	B8
...rkett Street	E7	Christian Street	D6	Epworth Street	F6	Hill Street	E1	Ormond Street	B5	Strand Street	B4-C4
...xteth Street	B5-C5	Church Street	C4-D4	Erskine Street	F6	Hodson Place	F8	Oxford Street	F4	Suffolk Street	D3
...ackburne Place	E3-F3	Churchill Way	C6-D6	Everton Road	F7-F8	Hood Street	D5	Paisley Street	B6	Summer Seat	C7-D7
...ackstock Street	C7-D7	Clarence Street	E4	Everton Row	E7	Hope Place	E3	Pall Mall	B7-C5	Tabley Street	C2-D3
...lair Street	E1	Clegg Street	E7-E8	Exchange Street East	C5	Hope Street	E2-F4	Paradise Street	C3-C4	Tarleton Street	D4-D5
...lenheim Street	C8-D8	Cockspur Street	C6	Falkner Street	E3-F3	Hopeway	F3	Park Lane	C3-D2	Tatlock Street	C8
...luefields Street	F1	College Street North	F6	Fazakerley Street	B5	Hornby Walk	C8	Parker Street	D4	Tempest Hey	C5
...lundell Street	C2-D2	College Street South	F6	Fenwick Street	B5-C4	Hotham Street	E5	Parliament Close	E1-D2	Temple Street	C5
...old Place	E3	Colquitt Street	D3-E3	Finch Place	F6	Hunter Street	D6	Parliament Place	F2	Thackeray Street	F1
...old Street	D4-E3	Comus Street	D6-D7	Fleet Street	D3-D4	Hurst Street	C2-C3	Parliament Street	D1-E1	The Strand	B4
...olton Street	D4-D5	Constance Street	E6-F6	Flint Street	D1-D2	Huskisson Street	E2-F2	Parr Street	D3	Titchfield Street	C7-C8
...ond Street	C8-D8	Cook Street	C4-C5	Fontenoy Street	D6	Ilford Street	E5	Paul Street	C7-D7	Tithebarn Street	C5-C6
...reck Road	F8	Cookson Street	D2-E2	Ford Street	C7-D7	Iliad Street	E8	Peach Street	F4	Tom Mann Close	D6
...rick Street	D2	Cooper Street	D4-E4	Forrest Street	C3-D3	Irwell Street	B4	Pembroke Place	E5-F5	Trafalgar Way	F6
...ridgewater Street	D2	Copperas Hill	D4-E5	Fox Street	D8-E7	Islington	E6	Pembroke Street	F5	Trowbridge Street	E4-E5
...ridport Street	E5	Corinto Street	E1-F1	Fraser Street	E5-E6	Islington Square	E7	Percy Street	F2	Upper Beau Street	E7
...ronte Street	E5	Corn Hill	C3	Freemasons Row	C6-D7	Jamaica Street	D1-D2	Peter's Lane	C4-D4	Upper Duke Street	E2-E3
...rook Street	B5	Cornwall Street	D2	Gardners Row	D7	James Street	B4-C4	Philips Street	C6	Upper Frederick Street	C3-D2-E2
...row Side	F7-F8	Corwallis Street	D3-E3	Gascoyne Street	B7-C6	John Street	E7	Pilgrim Street	E3	Upper Hampton Street	F2
...rownlow Hill	D4-F4	Cotton Street	A8-B8	George Street	B5	Johnson Street	C5-C6	Pitt Street	D2-D3	Upper Hill Street	F1
...rownlow Street	F4-F5	Covent Garden	B5	George's Dockway	B4	Jordan Street	D2	Pleasant Street	E4	Upper Parliament Street	E1-F2
				Gerard Street	D6	Juvenal Street	D7	Pomonia Street	E4	Upper Richmond Street	D7-E7
				Gibraltar Row	B6	Kempson Street	E6-F6	Porter Street	A7-B7	Upper Stanhope Street	E1-F1
				Gilbert Street	D3	Kent Street	D3	Portland Place	E8	Upper Stone Street	B8
				Gildart Street	E5-E6	Kinder Street	F6-F7	Pownhall Street	C3	Upper William Street	B8
				Gill Street	E5-F4	King Edward Street	B5-B6	Prescot Street	F6	Vandries Street	A7-B7
				Glegg Street	B8	Kings Dock Street	C2-D2	Prince Edwin Street	E7-E8	Vauxhall Road	C6-C8
				Gore Street	E1	Kitchen Street	D2	Princes Parade	A5-A6	Vernon Street	C5
				Goree Piazza	B4	Knight Street	E3	Princes Road	F1-F2	Vescock Street	C8-D8
						Lace Street	C6-D6	Princes Street	C5	Victoria Street	C5-D5
						Lance Close	F8	Pudsey Street	D5-E5	Village Street	F7-F8
						Langrove Street	E8	Queen Ann Street	E6	Virgil Street	D8
						Langsdale Street	E6-F6	Ranelagh Street	D4	Vulcan Street	A7-B7
						Lanyork Road	B6	Raymond Place	D8	Wakefield Street	E6
						Leece Street	E3	Redcross Street	B4-C4	Wapping	C2-C3
						Leeds Street	B6-D6	Regent Street	A8-B8	Water Street	B4-B5-C5
						Lestock Street	E1	Renshaw Street	D4-E4	Waterloo Road	A6-A8
						Lime Street	D4-D6	Rice Street	E3	Watkinson Street	D2
						Limekiln Lane	D7-D8	Richmond Row	D7-E7	Watmough Street	E7
						Little Canning Street	F2	Roberts Street	B6	Webster Street	C6-D6
						Little Catharine Street	F2	Rodney Street	E3-E4	Wentworth Road	F8
						Little Howard Street	B7	Roe Street	D5	Whitechapel	C4-D5
						Little St Brides Street	F2	Rokeby Street	E7	Whitley Street	B8
						London Road	D5-E5-F5-F6	Roscoe Street	E3-E4	Wilbraham Street	D8
						Lord Nelson Street	D5-E5	Roscommon Street	E8	Wilde Street	E5
						Lord Street	C4	Rose Hill	D6-D7	William Brown Street	D5
						Love Lane	B7-B8	Rose Place	D7-E7	Williamson Street	C4-D5
						Lower Castle Street	C4-C5	Royal Mail Street	E4-E5	Windsor Street	E1-F1
						Lydia Ann Street	D3	Rumford Street	B5	Wood Street	D3-D4
						Maddrell Street	B8	Russell Street	E3	York Street	D3
						Manesty's Lane	C4	Salisbury Street	E7-F6		
						Mann Island	B4	Saltney Street	A8-B8		
						Mansfield Street	E6-E7	Sanbino Street	E1		
						Mariners Wharf	C1-D1	Sandon Street	F2-F3		
						Marlborough Street	C6	School Lane	C4-D4	AA shop	C4
						Maryland Street	E4-E3-F3	Scotland Road	D6-D8	Derby Square	
						Matthews Street	C4-C5	Seel Street	D4-E3	Liverpool L2 1UF	
						Midghall Street	C6	Sefton Street	D1		

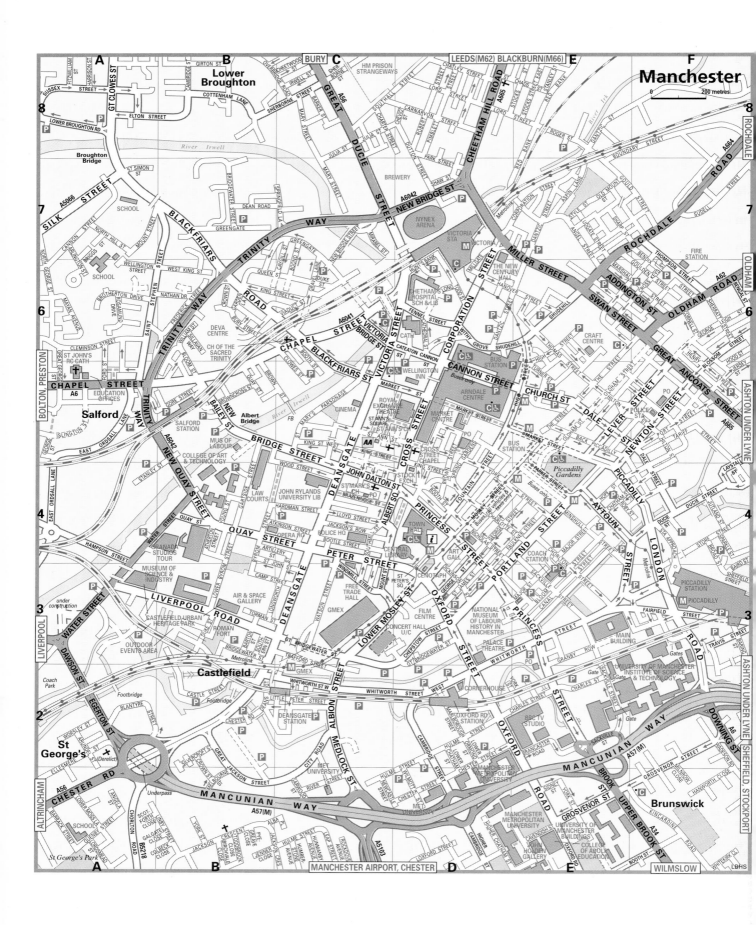

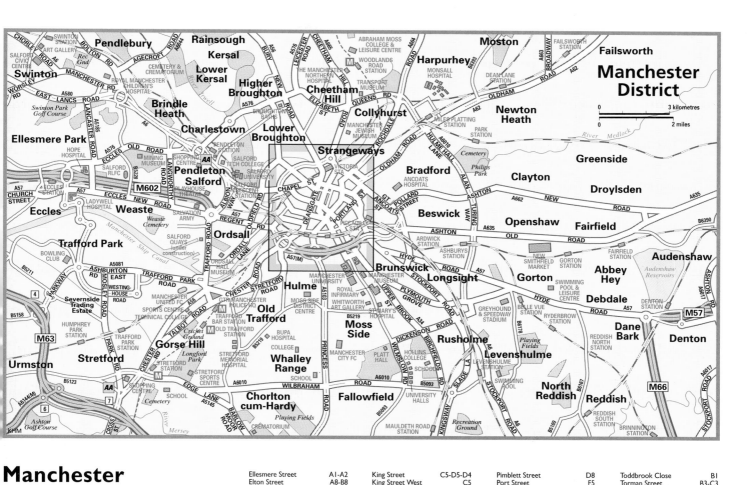

Manchester

Manchester is found on atlas page **79**,
grid reference SJ**8497**

Addington Street	E6-F6	Camp Street	B3-C3	Ellesmere Street	A1-A2	King Street	C5-D5-D4	Pimblett Street	D8	Toddbrook Close	B1
Alba Place	B1-C1	Canal Street	E3-E4	Elton Street	A8-B8	King Street West	C5	Port Street	F5	Torman Street	B3-C3
Albert Square	C4-D4	Cannon Street	D5-D6	Fairfield Street	E3-F3	Laystall Street	F4-F5	Portland Street	D3-E4	Trafford Street	C2-C3
Albion Street	C2-C3	Carnarvon Street	C8-D8	Faulkner Street	D4-E4	Leap Street	C1	Princess Street	D4-E2	Travis Street	F3
Angel Street	E6-E7	Castle Street	B2-B3	Fennel Street	D6	Lever Street	E5-F5	Pyegreave Close	B1	Trinity Way	A5-C7
Angela Street	A1	Cateaton Street	D6	Fitzwilliam Street	A8	Linby Street	A1-B1	Quay Street	B4-C4	Turner Street	E5
Arlington Street	A6-A7	Cathedral Street	D6	Ford Street	A5-A6	Little Peter Street	B2-C2	Quay Street	B5	Upper Brook Street	E1-F1
Artillery Street	B4-C4	Cavendish Street	E1	Fountain Street	D4-D5	Liverpool Road	A3-B3	Queen Street	B6-C6	Viaduct Street	C6
Arundel Street	A1-A2	Caygill Street	B6-C7	Frederick Street	B6	Livesey Street	F8	Quenby Street	A1	Victoria Bridge Street	C6
Aspin Lane	E7	Chapel Street	A5-D6	Galgate Close	A1-B1	Lloyd Street	C4	Red Bank	D7-E8	Victoria Street	C5-D6
Atherton Street	B4	Charles Street	D2-E2	Garden Lane	B6	London Road	F2-F4	River Street	C1	Wadeson Road	F1-F2
Atkinson Street	B4-C4	Charlotte Street	D4-E4	Gartside Street	B4-B5	Long Millgate	D6-D7	Robert Street	D8	Watson Street	C3-C4
Aytoun Street	E3-E4	Charter Street	C8-D8	Garwood Street	C1	Longworth Street	B3-C4	Roby Street	E4-F4	Wellington Street	A6
Back Piccadilly	E5	Chatham Street	E4	George Leigh Street	F6	Lord Street	D8-E8	Rochdale Road	E6-F7	West King Street	B6
Baird Street	F3-F4	Chatley Street	D8	George Street	A5	Lordsmead Street	A1	Rockdove Avenue	C1	Whitekirk Close	F1
Baring Street	F3	Cheetham Hill Road	D7-D8	George Street	D3-D4-E4	Lower Broughton Road	A8	Roger Street	E8	Whitworth Street	D2-E3
Barker Street	C8	Cheetwood Street	B8-C8	Girton Street	B8	Lower Byrom Street	B3-B4	Rosamund Drive	A6	Whitworth Street West	C2-D2
Barrack Street	A1	Chepstow Street	D3	Gore Street	A5-B5	Lower Chatham Street	D1-D2	Sackville Street	E2-E4	William Street	B6
Barton Street	B3	Chester Road	B2	Gould Street	E8-F7	Lower Mosley Street	C3-D3	Saint Stephen Street	A5-B7	Wilmott Street	D1
Bendix Street	F6-F7	Chester Road	A1	Goulden Street	E7-F6	Lower Moss Lane	A1	Scotford Close	A1	Windmill Street	C3
Bengal Street	F6	Chester Street	D1-D2	Granby Row	E3	Lower Ormond Street	D2	Sharp Street	D7	Withy Grove	D6
Birchvale Close	B1	Cheviot Street	D8	Gravel Lane	C6-C7	Loxford Street	D1	Shaw Street	D7	Wood Street	B5-C4
Blackfriars Road	A8-C6	Chorlton Road	A1	Great Ancoats Street	F5-F6	Ludgate Street	E7	Sheffield Street	F3	Worsley Street	A2
Blackfriars Street	C5-C6	Chorlton Street	E3-E4	Great Bridge Street	C3-D3	Major Street	D3-E4	Sherborne Street	B8-C8	York Street	B1
Blantyre Street	A2-B2	Church Street	E5	Great Ducie Street	C8-D6	Mancunian Way	B1-F2	Sherratt Street	F6	York Street	D2-E2
Bloom Street	B5-B6	City Road	C1-C2	Great George Street	A5-A6	Market Street	C5-E4	Shudehill	D6-E6	York Street	D5-E4
Bloom Street	E3-E4	Cleminson Street	A6	Great Gower Street	A8	Marlborough Street	D2	Sidney Street	E1	York Street	E1
Blossom Street	F5-F6	Clowes Street	C5-C6	Great Jackson Street	B1-B2	Marshall Street	E6-F6	Silk Street	A7	Young Street	B4
Boond Street	C6-C7	Colbeck Close	A1-B1	Greengate	B7-C7-C6	Mary Street	C7-C8	Sillavan Way	B6		
Booth Street	C5-C6	Cornell Street	F6	Grosvenor Street	E1-F2	Mayan Avenue	A6	Silvercroft Street	B1-B2		
Booth Street	D4	Corporation Street	D5-E7	Hanover Street	D6-E6	Medlock Street	C1-C2	Southall Street	C8-D8		
Booth Street	E1-F1	Cottenham Lane	B8	Hanworth Close	F1	Melbourne Street	B1	Southern Street	B3		
Bootle Street	C4	Cross Keys Street	E6-F6	Hardman Street	B4-C4	Miller Street	D7-E6	Southmill Street	C4		
Boundary Street	E8-F8	Cross Street	D4-D5	Harrison Street	A8	Milnrow Close	F1-F2	Sparkle Street	E4		
Brancaster Road	E2	Crown Street	B1-B2	Henry Street	F5-F6	Minchull Street	E4	Spring Gardens	D4-D5		
Brazenose Street	C4	Crown Street	B6	High Street	D5-E6	Mirabel Street	C7	Springfield Lane	B7-C7		
Bridge Street	B5-C4	Dale Street	E5-F4	Higher Cambridge Street	D1	Mosley Street	D4	St Ann Street	C5-D5		
Bridgewater Street	B3	Dantzic Street	D6-E7-E8	Higher Chatham Street	D1-E1	Mount Street	A7	St Chads Street	D8-E8		
Bridgewater Street	B7-B8	Dawson Street	A2-A3	Hilton Street	E5-F5	Mount Street	C3	St James Street	D3-D4		
Briggs Street	A6-A7	Dean Road	B7	Hood Street	F5-F6	Nathan Drive	B6	St John Street	B4-C3		
Broad Street	F3-F4	Deans Gate	B2	Hope Street	E4	New Bailey Street	B5	St Mary's Parsonage	C5		
Brook Street	E1-E2	Deansgate	B3-C5	Hulme Street	C1	New Bridge Street	C6-C7-D7	St Simon Street	A7		
Brotherton Drive	A6	Dickinson Street	D3-D4	Hulme Street	C1-D2	New Quay Street	A5-B4	Stanley Street	E8		
Brown Street	B5-C5	Downing Street	F2	Humberstone Avenue	C1	Newcastle Street	C1-D1	Stanley Street	A4-B5		
Brown Street	D4-D5	Duke Street	B3	Hunmanby Avenue	C1	Newton Street	E4-F5	Station Approach	F3-F4		
Browncross Street	B5	Duke Street	C6	Hunt's Bank	D6-D7	Nicholas Street	D4	Stocks Street	D8-E8		
Bury Street	B6-C6	Ducie Street	F4	Irwell Street	C8	North George Street	A6-A7	Stocks Street East	E8		
Byrom Street	B3-C4	Dutton Street	D7-D8	Islington Street	A5	North Hill Street	A7	Store Street	F3-F4		
Cambridge Street	B8	East Ordsall Lane	A4-A5	Jackson Crescent	B1-C1	North West Street	E7	Style Street	E7		
Cambridge Street	D1-D2	Egerton Street	A2	Jackson's Row	C4	Oldham Road	F6	Sudell Street	F7		
				Jenner Close	B1	Oldham Street	E5-F7	Sussex Street	A8		
				Jersey Street	F5-F6	Overbridge Street	B8-C8	Swan Street	E6-F6		
				John Dalton Street	C4-D4	Oxford Street	D3-E1	Tariff Street	F5		
				Julia Street	C7-C8	Park Street	D7-D8	The Street	E5-F6		
				Jutland Street	F4	Parker Street	E4	Thomas Street	E5-E6	AA shop	C5
				Kincardine Road	F1	Peter Street	C4-D3	Thompson Street	F6-F7	St Ann's House	
				King Street	B6-C6	Piccadilly	E4-F4	Todd Street	D6-D7	St Ann's Place	
										Manchester M2 7LP	

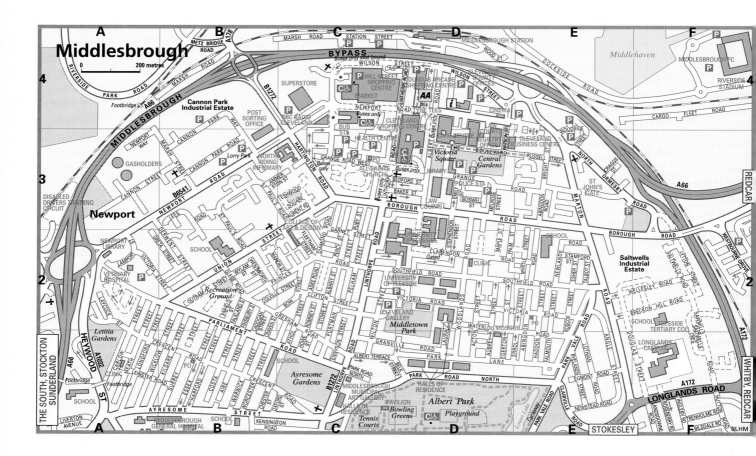

Middlesbrough

Middlesbrough is found on atlas page **97**,
grid reference NZ**4919**

AA shop — D4
17 Corporation Road
Middlesbrough TS1 1LS

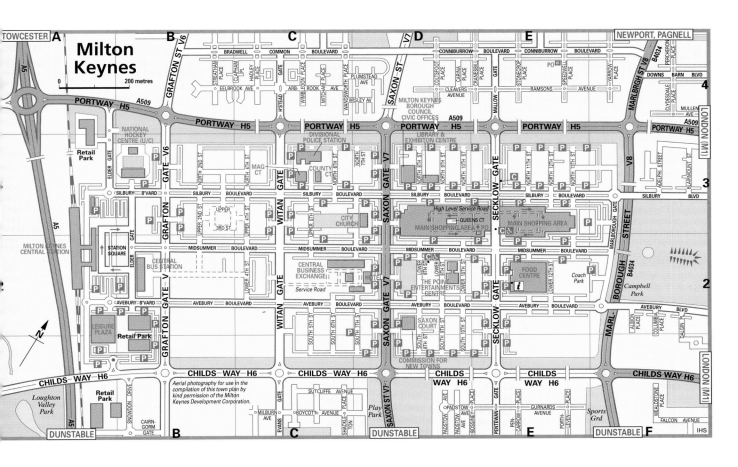

Milton Keynes

Milton Keynes is found on atlas page **38**,
grid reference SP**8537**

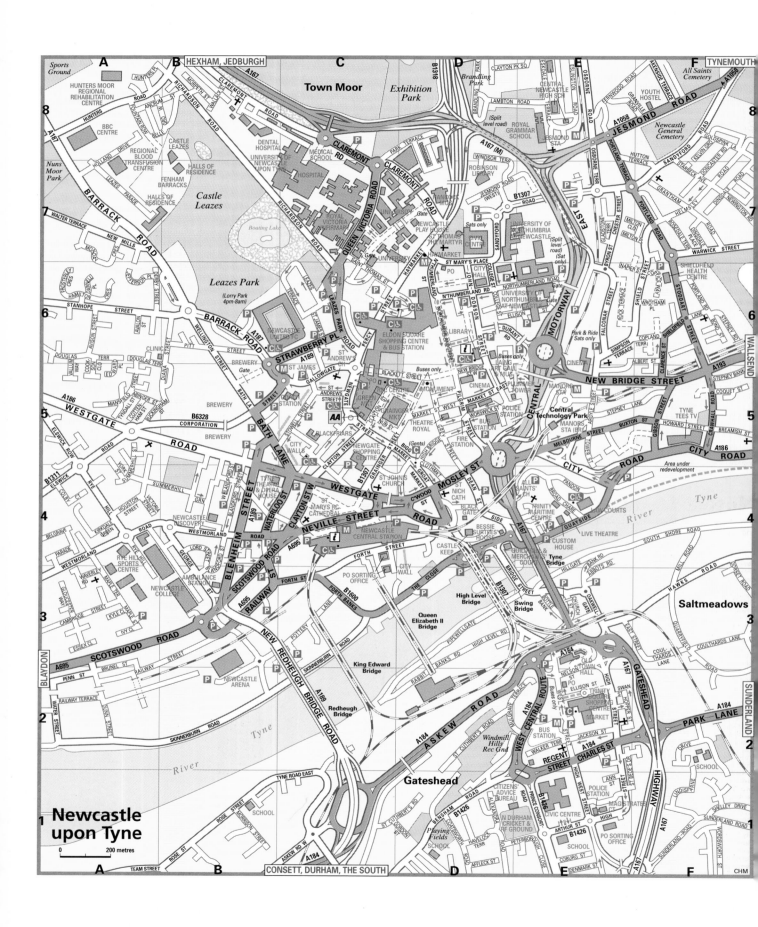

Newcastle upon Tyne

Northampton

Northampton is found on atlas page **49**, grid reference SP**75**60

Abington Square	C3	Horseshoe Street	A1-A2
Abington Street	B2-B3-C3	Hunter Street	C4
Albion Place	B1-B2	Kingswell	A1-A2
Alcombe Road	C4	Lady's Lane	A3-B3-C3
Alexandra Road	C2-C3	Lower Mounts	C3
Angel Street	B2	Margaret Street	B4
Arundel Street	A4	Market Square	B2
Ash Street	B4	Mayor Hold	A3
Bailiff Street	B4	Mercer's Row	B2
Barrack Road	A4-B4	Newlands	B3
Bath Street	A3	Oak Street	B4
Bedford Road	C1	Overstone Road	C3-C4
Billing Road	C2	Priory Street	A4
Bridge Street	A1-A2	Quorn Way	A4
Broad Street	A3-A4	Regent Street	A4
Campbell Street	A4-B4	Robert Street	B4
Castle Street	A3	Sheep Street	A3-A4
Cattlemarket Road	B1	Silver Street	A3
Charles Street	B4-C4	Somerset Street	C4
Cheyne Walk	C1-C2	Spencer Parade	C2
Church Lane	A3-B3-B4	Spring Gardens	C2
Clare Street	C4	St Andrew's Street	A3-A4
Cloutsham Street	C4	St Giles Square	B2
College Street	A2	St Giles Street	B2-C2
Commercial Street	A1	St Giles Terrace	C2-C3
Connaught Street	B4	St James Street	A1
Cranstoun Street	B4-C4	St John's Street	B1
Craven Street	B4-C4	St Katherine Street	A2
Crispin Street	A3	St Mary's Street	A2
Derngate	C1-C2-B2	St Michael's Road	C3
Duke Street	B4-C4	St Peter's Way	A1
Dunster Street	C3-C4	Swan Street	B1-B2
Earl Street	B3-C4	The Drapery	A2-B2
Fetter Street	B1-B2	The Riding	B2-C2
Foundry Street	A1	Upper Mounts	B3-B4
George Row	B2	Victoria Gardens	B1
Georges Street	A4	Victoria Promenade	B1-C1
Gold Street	A2	Victoria Street	B3-B4
Grafton Street	A4	Wellington Street	B3-C3
Great Russell Street	C4	Woolmonger Street	A2
Grey Friars	A3-B3-C3	York Road	C2-C3
Guildhall Road	B1-B2		
Harding Street	A4		
Hazelwood Road	C2		
Herbert Street	A3		
Horsemarket	A2-A3		

Newcastle upon Tyne

Newcastle upon Tyne is found on atlas page **103**, grid reference NZ**24**64

Abbots Road	E3-E4	Clothmarket	D4-D5	George Street	B3-B4	Market Street East	D5	Queen Victoria Road	C7	Tower Street	E4-E5
Abinger Street	A5	Coatsworth Road	D1	Gibson Street	F5	Market Street West	D5	Rabbit Banks Road	C2-D3	Tyndall Street	A5
Akenside Terrace	F8	Coburg Street	E1	Gloucester Way	A3	Melbourne Street	E5	Railway Street	A2-B4	Tyne Road East	C1
Alexandra Road	D1	Colby Court	A4	Goldspink Lane	F8	Milk Market	E4	Railway Terrace	A2	Tyneside Road	A2
Ancrum Street	A8-B8	College Street	D6	Gordon Street	C1-D1	Mill Road	F2-F4	Regent Street	E1-E2	Vallum Way	A5-A6
Ann Street	E1	Collingwood Street	D4	Grainger Street	C4-D5	Milton Place	E7-F7	Richardson Road	A8-C6	Victoria Street	A4
Argyle Street	E5	Cookson Close	A5-A6	Grantham Road	F7	Mitford Street	A2-B2	Rock Terrace	E6	Walker Terrace	E2
Arthur Street	E1	Copland Terrace	F6	Granville Road	E8-F8	Monday Crescent	A6-A7	Rose Street	B1	Wallace Street	B8
Askew Road	C1-E3	Coppice Way	F6	Grey Street	D4-D5	Morpeth Street	B8	Rosedale Terrace	F7	Walter Terrace	A7
Askew Road West	B1-C1	Coquet Street	F5	Groat Market	D4-D4	Morrison Street	B1	Rye Hill	A3-A4	Water Street	A2
Avison Street	A6	Corporation Street	A5-C5	Hamilton Crescent	A6	Moseley Street	D4-D5	Saint Thomas Street	C6-C7	Waterloo Street	B4-C4
Bank Road	E3-E4	Cottenham Street	A5	Havelock Terrace	D1	Mulgrave Terrace	D2-E2	Sandgate	E4	Warwick Street	F7
Barrack Road	A8-B6	Coulthards Lane	F3	Hawks Road	E3-F4	Napier Street	E6-F6	Sandyford Road	D7-F8	Waverley Road	A3
Bath Lane	B5-C4	Crawhall Road	F5	Haymarket	D6-D7	Nelson Street	E2-E3	Scotswood Road	A1-C4	Wellington Street	B5-B6
Belle Grove West	A8-B8	Dean Street	D4	Helmsley Road	F7-F8	Neville Street	C4	Shelley Drive	F1	West Blandford Street	B4
Belgrave Parade	A4	Denmark Street	E1	High Bridge	D5	New Bridge Street	E5-F6	Shield Street	E6-F7	West Central Route	E2-E3
Bensham Road	C1-D1	Derby Street	A6	High Level Road	D3	New Bridge Street West	D5	Shieldfield Lane	F6	West Street	E2
Bigg Market	C5-D5	Diana Street	B5-B6	High Street	E1-E3	New Mills	A7	Side	D4-E4	Westgate Road	A5-D4
Blackett Street	C5-D5	Dinsdale Place	F7	High Street West	E1-E2	New Redheugh Bridge Rd	B3-C1	Simpson Terrace	E6	Westmorland Road	A3-B4
Blackgate	D4	Dinsdale Road	F7	Hillgate	E3-E4	Newgate Street	C5	Skinnerburn Road	A2-C3	Windsor Terrace	D7-D8
Blandford Street	B3-B4	Doncaster Road	F7-F8	Holland Drive	A7-A8	Newington Road	F7	South Shore Road	E4-F4	Wordsworth Street	F1
Blenheim Street	B3-B5	Dorset Road	F3-F4	Hopper Street	E2	Northumberland Road	D6-E6	St Andrews Street	C5	Worswick Street	D5-E5
Bottle Bank	E3	Douglas Terrace	A5-A6	Houston Street	A4	Northumberland Street	D5-D7	St Ann's Street	F4-F5	Wrotham Place	F6
Brandling Park	D8	Dunn Street	A2	Howard Street	F5	Nun Street	C5	St Bede's Drive	E1-E2	York Street	A4-A5
Breamish Street	F5	Durant Road	D6-E6	Hunters Road	A8-B8	Oakwellgate	E3	St Cuthbert's Road	C1-D1-D2		
Bridge Street	D4-E3	East Street	E3-F3	Hutton Terrace	E8-F7	Osborne Road	E8	St James Street	C6		
Broad Chare	E4	Edward Place	A5-A6	Ivy Close	A3	Osborne Terrace	E7-E8	St Mary's Place	D6-D7		
Brunel Street	A2-A3	Ellison Street	D6-E6	Jackson Street	E2	Oystershell Lane	B5	St Mary's Street	F4		
Buckingham Street	A5-B5	Ellison Street	E2	Jefferson Place	A6	Pandon	E4	Stanhope Street	A6-B6		
Buxton Street	E5-F5	Elswick Road	A4-A5	Jesmond Road (West)	D7-E7	Park Lane	F2	Starbeck Avenue	F7-F8		
Byron Street	E6-E7	Elswick Row	A4-A5	Jesmond Road	E7-F8	Park Terrace	C8-D8	Stepney Bank	F5		
Cambridge Street	A3	Elswick Street	A5	John Dobson Street	D5-D6	Penn Street	A2	Stepney Lane	E5-F5		
Central Motorway East	D5-E7	Eskdale Terrace	E8	Kelvin Grove	F8	Percy Street	C6	Stepney Road	F6		
Charles Street	E2	Eslington Road	E8	Kirkdale Green	A4	Peterborough Street	D1-E1	Stoddart Street	F5-F6		
Chester Street	E7	Essex Close	A3	Kyle Close	A3	Pilgrim Street	D5	Stowell Street	C5		
Church Street	E3	Falconar Street	E6	Lambton Road	D8-E8	Pipewellgate	D3-E3	Strawberry Place	B6-C6		
City Road	E5-F5	Fenwood Road	E8-F8	Leazes Park Road	C6	Pitt Street	B6	Summerhill Green	A4-B5		
Claremont Road	B8-D7	Forth Banks	C3	Leazes Terrace	C6	Portland Road	E8-F7-F6	Summerhill Street	A4-A5		
Clarence Street	F5-F6	Forth Street	C3-D4	Lindisfarne Drive	F1-F2	Portland Terrace	E7-E8	Sunderland Road	F1		
Clayton Park Square	D8-E8	Fountain Row	A8	Mansfield Street	A5	Pottery Lane	C3	Swan Street	E2		
Clayton Street	C4-C5	Gallowgate	C5	Maple Street	A3	Prince Consort Road	E1	Team Street	A1-B1		
Clayton Street West	C4	Gateshead Highway	E3-F1	Maple Terrace	A3-A4	Quayside	E4-F4	The Close	C3-D4		

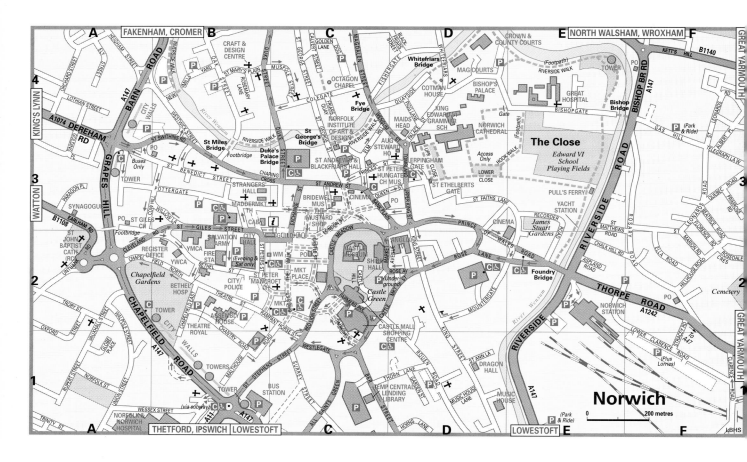

Norwich

Norwich is found on atlas page **67**,
grid reference TG**2308**

AA shop
Fanum House
126 Thorpe Road
Norwich NR1 1RL

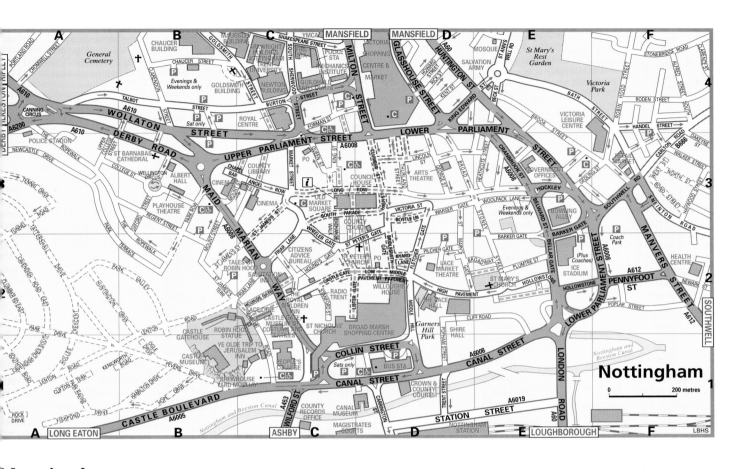

Nottingham

Nottingham is found on atlas page **62**,
grid reference SK**5739**

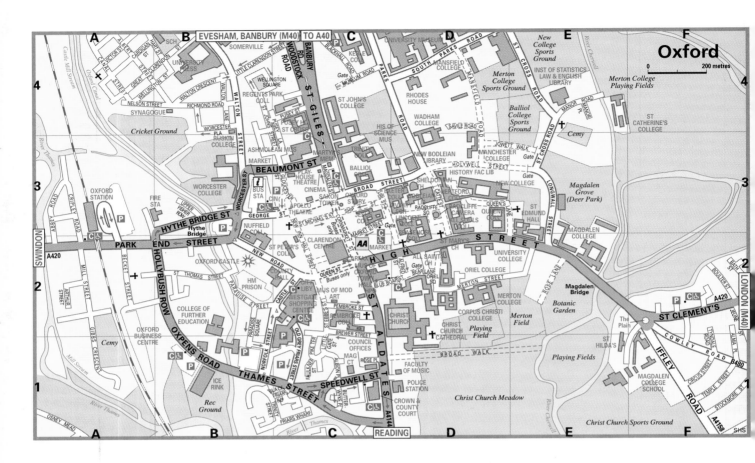

Oxford

Oxford is found on atlas page **37**,
grid reference SP**5**1**06**

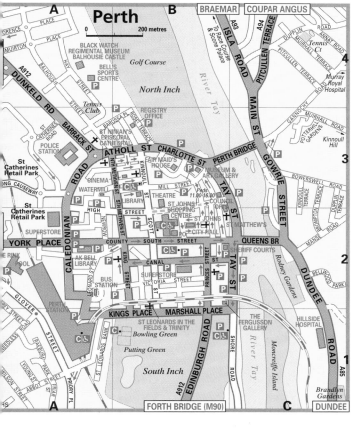

Perth

Perth is found on atlas page **126**,
grid reference NO**1123**

Abbot Street	A1	Princes Street	B2
Annat Road	C4	Priory Place	A1
Atholl Street	A3-B3	Queen's Bridge	C2
Balhousie Street	A3-A4	Raeburn Park	A1
Barossa Place	A3-B3	Rose Terrace	B3
Barrack Street	A3	Scott Street	B2
Bellwood Park	C2	Shore Road	B1
Bowerswell Road	C3	South Methven Street	B2-B3
Brompton Terrace	C2-C3	St Catherines Road	A3
Caledonian Road	A2-A3	St Leonards Bank	A1
Canal Street	B2	Tay Street	B1-B3
Charlotte Street	B3	Victoria Street	B2
County South Street	A2-B2	Wilson Street	A1
Dundee Road	C1-C2	York Place	A2
Dunkeld Street	A3-A4	Young Street	A1
Dupplin Road	C4		
Dupplin Terrace	C2-C3		
Edinburgh Road	B1		
Florence Place	A4		
Friar Street	A1		
Gannochy Road	C3-C4		
Glover Street	A1-A2		
Gowrie Street	C2-C3		
Grey Street	A1-A2		
Hay Street	A3-A4		
High Street	A2-B2		
Isla Road	B4-C4		
King Street	B2		
Kings Place	A1-B1		
Kinnoull Street	B3		
Kinnoull Terrace	C2-C3		
Leonard Street	A2		
Long Causeway	A3		
Main Street	C3-C4		
Manse Road	C2		
Marshall Place	B1		
Mill Street	B3		
Muirhall Road	C3		
Muirhall Terrace	C4		
Muirton Place	A4		
Needless Road	A1		
Newrow	A2		
North Methven Street	A3-B3		
Perth Bridge	B3-C3		
Pitcullen Terrace	C4		
Potterhill Gardens	C3		

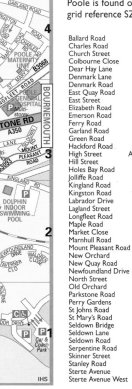

Poole

Poole is found on atlas page **11**,
grid reference SZ**0090**

Ballard Road	B1-C1	Sterte Close	B3
Charles Road	C4	Sterte Esplande	B4-B3
Church Street	A1-A2	Sterte Road	B4-B3
Colbourne Close	C2-C1	Strand Street	A1-B1
Dear Hay Lane	A2-B2	Taverner Close	C2
Denmark Lane	C3-C4	Thames Street	A1
Denmark Road	C3	The Quay	A1-B1
East Quay Road	B1	Towngate Bridge	B3
East Street	B2-B1	Vallis Close	C1
Elizabeth Road	C3-C4	Waldren Close	C2
Emerson Road	B2-C2	West Quay Road	A1-A2-B2-B3
Ferry Road	A1	West Street	A1-A2-B2
Garland Road	C4	West View Road	B4
Green Road	B2-C1	Wimborne Road	C4-C3
Hackford Road	C4		
High Street	A1-B1-B2-B3		
Hill Street	B2		
Holes Bay Road	B3-B4-A4		
Jolliffe Road	C4		
Kingland Road	B2-B3-C3		
Kingston Road	C4		
Labrador Drive	B1		
Lagland Street	B1-B2		
Longfleet Road	C3-C4		
Maple Road	C3-C4		
Market Close	B2		
Marnhull Road	C4		
Mount Pleasant Road	C3		
New Orchard	A2-B2		
New Quay Road	A1		
Newfoundland Drive	B2-C2-C1		
North Street	B2		
Old Orchard	B2-B1		
Parkstone Road	C3		
Perry Gardens	B1		
St Johns Road	C4		
St Mary's Road	C3-C4		
Seldown Bridge	C1-C2		
Seldown Lane	C3		
Seldown Road	C3		
Serpentine Road	B3-C3		
Skinner Street	B1-B2		
Stanley Road	B1-C1		
Sterte Avenue	A4-B4	AA shop	B3
Sterte Avenue West	A4	10 Falkland Square	
		Poole BH15 1ER	

239

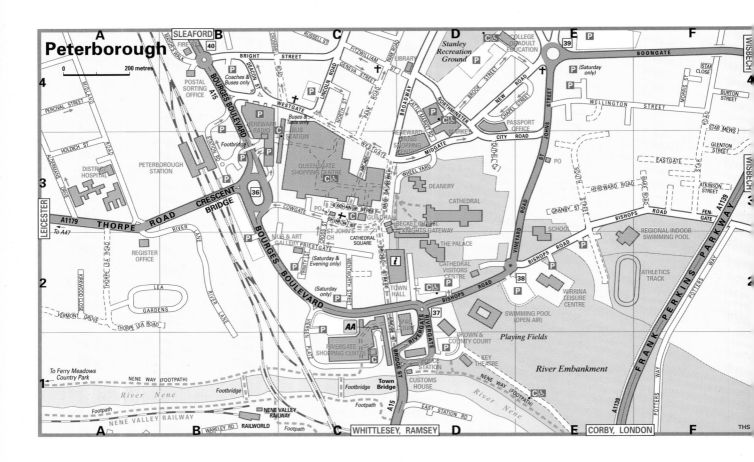

Peterborough

Peterborough is found on atlas page **64**,
grid reference TL**1998**

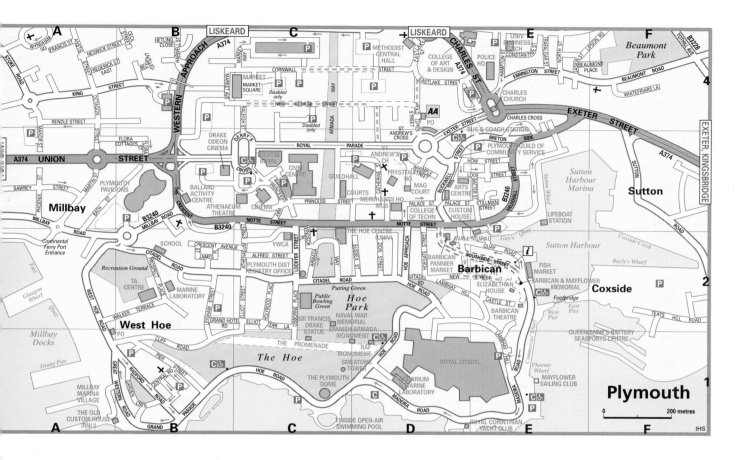

lymouth

ymouth is found on atlas page **6**,
id reference SX**4754**

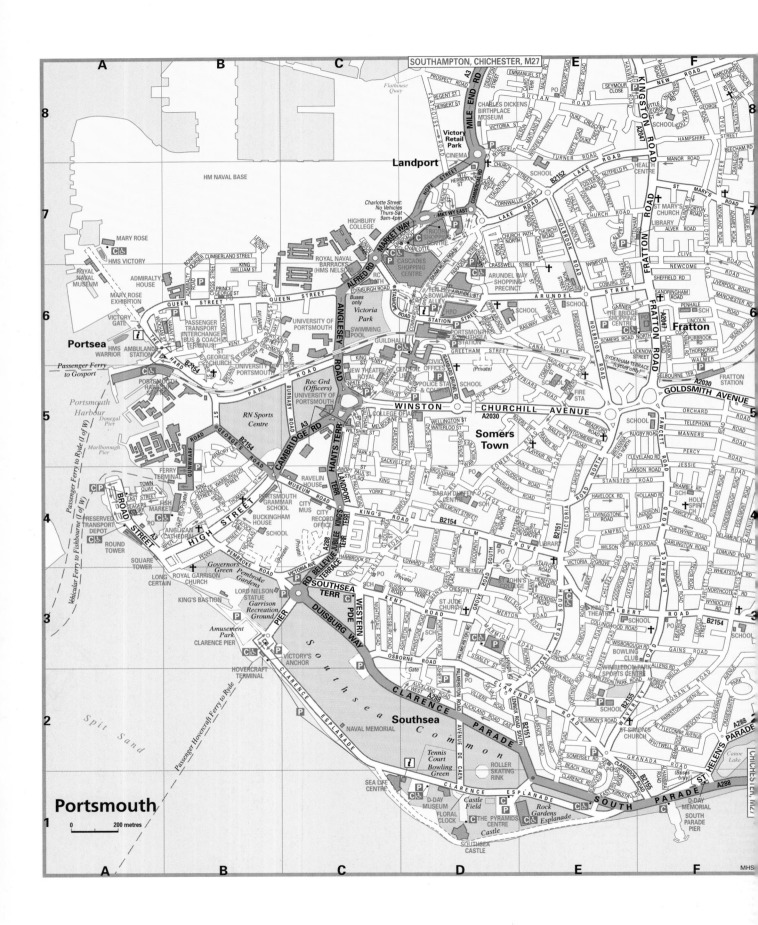

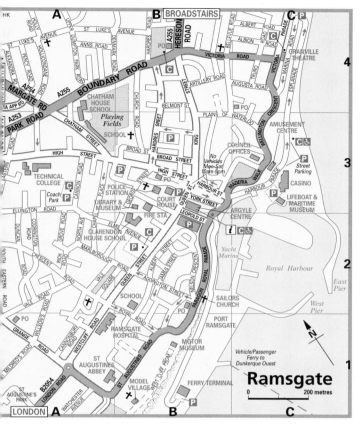

Ramsgate

Ramsgate

Ramsgate is found on atlas page **29**,
grid reference TR**3865**

Addington Street	B2	High Street	A3-B3	Watchester Avenue	A1
Albert Road	C4	Hollicondane Road	A4	Wellington Crescent	C3-C4
Albert Street	B2	Holly Road	A4	West Cliff Promenade	B1
Albion Road	B4-C4	James Street	B2	Westcliff Road	A1-A2
Alexandra Road	A4	King Street	B3-B4	Willson's Road	A1-A2
Anns Road	A4	Leopold Street	B2-B3	York Street	B3
Artillery Road	B4	London Road	A1		
Augusta Road	B4-C4	Madeira Walk	B3-C3		
Bellevue Road	B4	Margate Road	A4		
Belmont Street	B4	Marina Road	C4		
Boundary Road	A4-B4	Marlborough Road	A2-B2		
Broad Street	B3	Nelson Crescent	B2		
Cannonbury Road	A1	North Avenue	A2		
Canon Road	A3	Paragon Royal Parade	B1-B2		
Chapel Place	A2-A3	Park Road	A3		
Chatham Street	A3	Percy Road	A4		
Church Road	B3-B4	Plains of Waterloo	B3-C3		
Codrington Road	A2	Queen Street	A2-B2-B3		
Crescent Road	A2	Richmond Road	A2		
Denmark Road	A4-B4	Royal Road	A2-B2-B1		
Duncan Road	A2	South Eastern Road	A2-A3		
Ellington Road	A2-A3	St Augustine's Park	A1		
Elms Avenue	A2-B2	St Augustines Road	A1-B1		
Esplanade	C3-C4	St Luke's Avenue	A4-B4		
George Street	B3	St Mildred's Road	A1		
Grange Road	A1	Station Approach Road	A4		
Grove Road	A2	Truro Road	A4		
Harbour Parade	B3-C3	Upper Dumpton Park Road	A4		
Harbour Street	B3	Vale Road	A1-A2		
Hardres Road	B4	Vale Square	A2-B2		
Hardres Street	B3-B4	Victoria Parade	C4		
Hereson Road	B4	Victoria Road	B4-C4		

Ramsgate

0   200 metres

Portsmouth

Portsmouth is found on atlas page **13**,
grid reference SU**6400**

James Road	F7	Campbell Road	E4-F4	Edmund Road	F4	Hereford Road	E3
ddison Road	F4	Canal Walk	E5-E6	Eldon Street	D4-D5	High Street	B4
dmiralty Road	B6	Cascades Approach	C7-D7	Elm Grove	D4-E4	Highbury Street	B4
incourt Road	E8	Castle Road	C3-D4	Elphinstone Road	D3	Holbrook Road	E5-E7
bany Road	E3-E4	Cavendish Road	E3	Emmanuel Street	D8-E8	Holland Road	F4
bert Grove	E3-E4	Cecil Place	C3-C4	Ernest Road	F7-F8	Hope Street	D7
bert Road	E5-F3	Charles Street	E6-E7	Esslemont Road	F4	Hudson Road	D4-E4
ec Rose Lane	D5	Charlotte Street	D7	Ewart Road	F8	Hyde Park Road	D5
exandra Road	E7	Chelsea Road	E3-E4	Exmouth Road	E3	Inglis Road	E4-F4
fred Road	C6	Chetwynd Road	F4	Fawcett Road	F3-F5	Inverness Road	F8
hambra Road	F1-F2	Church Path North	D7-E7	Fitzherbert Street	D7	Isambard Brunel Road	D5-D6
Saints Street	D7	Church Road	E7	Flathouse Road	D7-D8	Jacob's Street	D6-D7
lens Street	F3	Church Street	D7-E7	Florence Road	E1-E2	Jessie Road	F4
ver Road	F7	Claredon Street	E7	Forge Street	F8	Jubilee Terrace	C4
glesey Road	C5-C6	Claremont Road	F5-F6	Forton Road	F7	Kent Road	C3-D3
moury Lane	B5	Clarence Esplanade	B3-E1	Foster Road	E7	Kent Street	B6
undel Street	D6-F6	Clarence Parade	C2-E1	Francis Avenue	F3-F4	King Albert Street	E7
shby Place	D2-D3	Clarence Road	E1-E2	Fraser Road	E5	King Charles Street	B4
shurton Road	C3-D3	Clarence Street	D7	Fratton Road	F5-F7	King Henry Street	C5-C6
ckland Road East	D2	Clarendon Road	D2-F1	Fulham Road	D4	King Street	C4-D4
ckland Road West	D2	Cleveland Road	E4-F5	Gains Road	F3	King William Street	B6-B7
enue De Caen	D1-D2	Clifton Street	E6-F6	Garnier Street	E6-F6	King's Road	C4-D4
lward Street	B6	Clive Road	F6-F7	Goldsmith Avenue	F5	King's Terrace	C4
iley's Road	E5	Coburg Street	E6	Goodwood Road	E3-E4	Kingston Road	F7-F8
liou Road	F8	Collingwood Road	E3-F3	Grafton Street	D8	Kirkstall Road	E1-F1
ach Road	E1-E2	Commercial Road	D6-D7	Granada Road	E2-F1	Lake Road	D7-E8
atrice Road	F3	Cornwall Road	F6	Great Southsea Road	C4	Landport Street	C4
echam Road	F8	Cornwallis Crescent	D7-E7	Green Road	D4	Landport Street	E6
llevue Terrace	C3-C4	Cottage Road	D4-E4	Greetham Street	D6-E6	Landport Terrace	C4
mont Street	D4	Cottage View	E6	Grosvenor Street	D4-D5	Langford Road	F8
mbridge Crescent	F2	Craneswater Avenue	F2-F3	Grove Road North	D4	Lawrence Road	F3-F4
ackfriars Road	D6-E5	Craneswater Park	F2	Grove Road South	D3-D4	Lawson Road	E4-F4
nfire Corner	B6-B7	Cranleigh Road	F7-F8	Guildford Road	F6-F7	Lennox Road North	D2-D3
ulton Road	F3-F4	Craswell Street	D6-E6	Guildhall Walk	C5	Lennox Road South	D2-E2
adford Road	E5	Cressy Road	C5	Gunwharf Road	B4-B5	Lennox Row	B7
amble Road	F4	Cross Street	B6-B7	Hale Street South	E7	Leopold Street	F3
andon Road	E2	Cumberland Street	B7	Hambrook Street	C4	Lincoln Road	F6
idgeside Close	E6	Curzon Howe Road	B6	Hamilton Road	E2-E3	Little George Street	F8
idport Street	D6	Darlington Road	F4	Hampshire Street	F8	Liverpool Road	F6
itain Street	B5	Daulston Road	F8	Hampshire Terrace	C4-C5	Livingstone Road	E4
tannia Road North	E5	Delamere Road	F8	Hanway Road	E8-F8	Lombard Street	B4
oad Street	A4	Duisburg Way	C2-C3	Harcourt Road	F8	Londesborough Road	F4
ougham Street	D4	Duke Crescent	E8	Harold Road	F3-F4	Lords Street	E7
rgoyne Road	E1-E2	Duncan Road	E3	Havant Street	B6	Lucknow Street	E6-F6
rnaby Road	C5-C6	Earlsdon Street	C4-D5	Havelock Road	E4	Maitland Street	E8
tcher Street	B5-B6	East Street	A4	Hay Street	B6	Mallins Road	E8
iro Terrace	E8	Eastern Villas Road	E1-E2	Herbert Road	F2	Malvern Road	E2
mbridge Road	B4-C5	Edinburgh Road	C6	Herbert Street	D8	Manchester Road	F6

		Manners Road	F5	
		Manor Road	F7-F8	
		Margate Road	D4-E4	
		Market Way	C7-D7	
		Market Way East	D7	
		Marmion Road	D3-E3	
		Melbourne Place	C5-D5	
		Merton Road	D3-E3	
		Middle Street	D5	
		Mile End Road	D8	
		Montgomerie Road	E5	
		Moorland Road	F7	
		Museum Road	C4	
		Napier Road	E2-E3	
		Nelson Road	D3-E3	
		Nelson Road	E8	
		Nettlecombe Avenue	F2	
		New Road	F8	
		Newcome Road	F6	
		Nightingale Road	C3	
		Norfolk Street	C4-D4	
		North Street	B6	

Northam Street	E6	St Ursula Grove	E4				
Northcote Road	F3	St Vincent Road	E3				
Nuttfield Place	E7	Stafford Road	E3-E4				
Olinda Street	F7	Stanhope Road	C6-D6				
Omega Street	E5	Stanley Street	D3-E2				
Orchard Road	F5	Stansted Road	E4-F4				
Osborne Road	C3-D3	Station Street	D6				
Outram Road	E4	Staunton Street	D7				
Oxford Road	E3-F4	Sultan Road	D8-E8				
Pain's Road	E4	Sussex Road	C3-D3				
Palmerston Road	D2-D3	Sussex Terrace	D3				
Paradise Street	D6-D7	Sutherland Road	F4				
Park Road	B5-C6	Swan Street	C5				
Park Street	C5	Sydenham Terrace	E6-F5				
Parkstone Road	F2	Talbot Road	F4-F5				
Peacock Lane	B4	Taswell Road	E2				
Pembroke Road	B4-C3	Telephone Road	F5				
Penhale Road	F6	The Hard	A6-B5				
Penny Street	B3-B4	The Retreat	D3				
Percy Road	F4-F5	The Vale	D2				
Pier Road	B3-C3	Thorncroft Road	F6				
Playfair Road	E4-E5	Tottenham Road	E7-F7				
Portland Road	D3	Town Quay	A4				
Portland Street	B6-C6	Trevor Road	F3-F4				
Prince George Street	B6	Turner Road	E8				
Prospect Road	D8	Union Place	E7				
Purbrook Road	F6	Union Road	C7				
Queen Street	A6-C6	Upper Arundel Street	D6				
Queen's Crescent	D3	Victoria Avenue	B3-C4				
Queen's Place	D3	Victoria Grove	E4				
Raglan Street	E5-E6	Victoria Road North	E4-E5				
Railway View	D6-E6	Victoria Road South	E2-E4				
Regent Road	D8	Victoria Street	D8-E8				
Renny Road	F6	Villiers Road	D2				
Richmond Place	B6	Walmer Road	F5-F6				
Richmond Road	E2-E3	Waltham Street	C5				
Rivers Street	D5-E5	Warblington Street	B4				
Rugby Road	E5-F5	Warwick Crescent	D4-D5				
Sackville Street	C5-D4	Waterloo Street	D5				
Samuel Road	F7	Watts Road	E8				
Sandringham Road	F6	Waverley Road	E2-F3				
Seagers Court	A4	Welch Road	F2-F3				
Selbourne Terrace	F5	Wellington Street	D5				
Seymour Close	E8	Western Parade	C3				
Shaftesbury Road	C3	Wheatstone Road	F3				
Shearer Road	F7-F8	White Hart Road	B4				
Sheffield Road	F6	White Swan Road	C5				
Somers Road	D4-E5	Whitwell Road	F2				
Somers Road North	E6-F6	Wickham Street	A6-B6				
Somerset Road	E2	Wilson Grove	E4				
South Parade	E1-F1	Wiltshire Street	C5				
South Road	F8	Wimbledon Park Road	E2				
Southsea Terrace	C3	Wimpole Street	E6				
St Andrew's Road	E4-E5	Wingfield Street	D8-E8				
St David's Road	E4-E5	Winston Churchill Avenue	C5-E5				
St Edward's Road	C4-D3	Wisborough Road	E3-F3				
St Faith's Road	D7	Woodpath	D3-D4				
St George's Road	B4-B5	Worthing Road	E2				
St George's Way	B6	Wyndcliffe Road	F3				
St Helen's Parade	F1-F2	Yarborough Road	D4				
St James's Road	D4-D5	Yorke Street	C4-D4				
St James's Street	B6						
St Mary's Road	F7	AA shop					
St Nicholas Street	B4	12 London Road					
St Paul's Road	C4-C5	Portsmouth PO1 1NL					
St Paul's Square	C4						
St Peter's Grove	E4	AA Port shop					
St Ronan's Road	F2	Wharf Road View					
St Simon's Road	E2	Portsmouth PO2 8HB					
St Thomas's Street	B4						

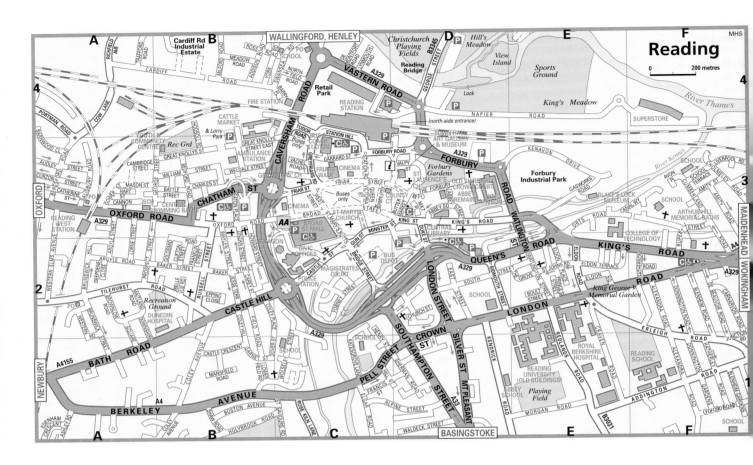

Reading

Reading is found on atlas page **24**,
grid reference SU**7**1**73**

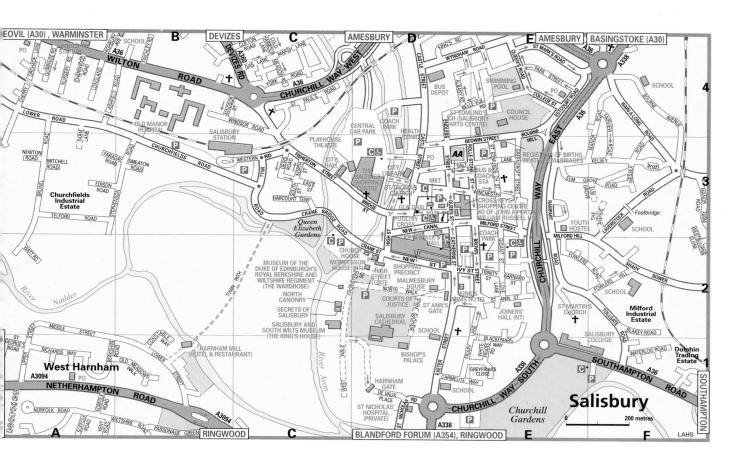

alisbury

alisbury is found on atlas page **23**,
id reference SU1429

bany Road	D4	Faraday Road	A3-B3	Nursery Road	A4	
hfield Road	A4-B4	Farm Lane	A3-A4	Old Meadows Walk	A1-B1	
rnard Street	E2	Finchley Road	B4	Park Street	E4	
dwin Street	D3-E3	Fisherton Street	C3-C4	Parsonage Green	B1	
lle Vue Road	D4-E4	Fowlers Hill	F2	Queen Street	D3	
rkshire Road	A1	Fowlers Road	E2-F2	Queen's Road	E4	
shops Walk	D2	Friary Lane	D1-E2	Rampart Road	E2-E3	
ackfriars Way	E1-E2	Gas Lane	C4	Richards Way	A1	
akey Road	F2	Gigant Street	E2-E3	Salt Lane	D3-E3	
urne Avenue	F3-F4	Gorringe Road	A4	Shady Bower	F2	
urne Hill	E3-E4	Greencroft Street	E3	Smeaton Road	B3	
idge Street	D3	Greyfriars Close	E1	South Street	C3	
own Street	E2-E3	Hamilton Road	D4	South Western Road	B3-C3	
unel Road	A2-A4	Harcourt Terrace	C3	Southampton Road	E1-F1	
rmelite Way	D1-E1	High Street	D2-D3	St Ann Street	E2	
rrion Pond Drive	A1	Highbury Avenue	A4	St Edmund's Church Street	E3	
stle Street	D3-D4	Ivy Street	D2-E2	St George's Road	A1	
therine Street	D2	Kelsey Road	E3-F3	St Mark's Road	E4	
arnwood Road	A4	Kent Road	A1	St Nicholas Road	D1	
erry Orchard Lane	A3-A4	King's Road	D4	St Paul's Road	C4	
oristers Square	C2-D2	Laverstock Road	F3	Stephenson Road	A3-B4	
urchfields Road	B4-C3	Longland	A4	Suffolk Road	A1	
urchill Way East	E2-F4	Love Lane	E2	Telford Road	A3	
urchill Way South	D1-E1	Lower Road	A4	The Avenue	F3	
urchill Way West	C4-D4	Lower Street	B1	Tollgate Road	E2-F1	
fton Road	C4	Manor Farm Road	F3	Trinity Street	E2	
oldharbour Lane	C4	Manor Road	E3-F4	Upper Street	A1-A2	
ollege Street	E4	Marlborough Road	D4	Wain-A-Long Road	F3-F4	
nstable Way	B1-B2	Marsh Lane	C4	Waterloo Road	F1	
ane Bridge Road	C3	Meadow Road	C4	Watt Road	A2	
ane Street	D2	Middle Street	A2-B1	Wessex Road	F3	
e Vaux Place	D1	Milford Hill	E2-E3	West Walk	C1-C2	
evizes Road	B4-C4	Milford Street	D3-E3	Westbourne Close	F2-F3	
ews Road	C3	Mill Road	C3	Whitefriars Road	E1	
st Street	C3	Mitchell Road	A3	Wilton Road	A4-C4	
ison Road	A3-B3	Netherhampton Road	A1-B1	Wiltshire Road	A1-B1	
n Grove	F3	New Canal	D3	Winchester Street	D3-E3	
n Grove Road	E3-F3	New Street	D2	Windsor Road	B4-C4	
dless Street	D3-D4	Newton Road	A3	Windsor Street	B4	
court Road	E4	Norfolk Road	A1	Wyndham Road	D4-E4	
eter Street	D1-D2	North Street	C3	York Road	C4	AA shop	D3
rview Road	F3-F4	North Walk	D2			1 Winchester Street	
						Salisbury SP1 1HB	

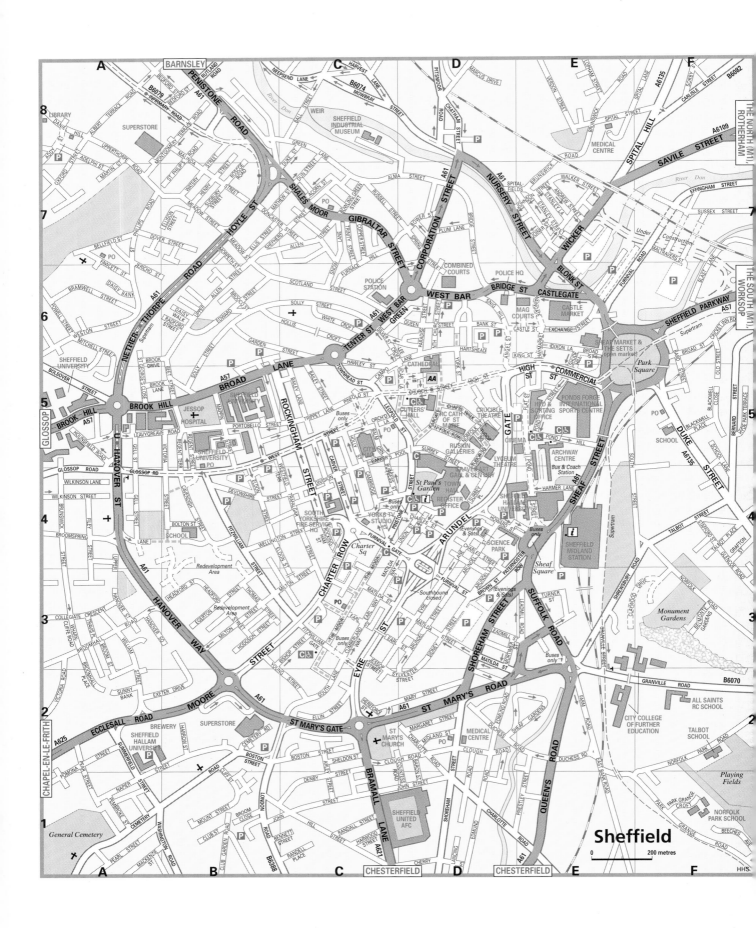

Sheffield

0   200 metres

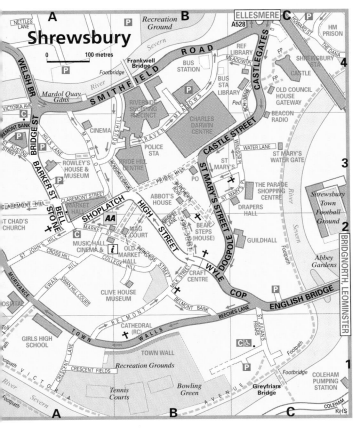

Shrewsbury

Shrewsbury is found on atlas page **59**,
grid reference SJ**4912**

Barker Street	A3	Roushill Bank	B3
Beeches Lane	B1-C2	School Gardens	C3-C4
Belmont	A1-B2	Shoplatch	A2-B3
Belmont Bank	B2	Smithfield Road	A4-C4
Bellstone	A2-A3	St Austins Street	A3
Bridge Street	A3	St John's Hill	A2
Butcher's Row	B3	St Julian's Friars	C1-C2
Castle Street	B3-C3	St Mary's Place	B3-C3
Castlegates	C4	St Mary's Street	B2-B3
Claremont Bank	A3	Swan Hill	A2
Claremont Hill	A3	Swan Hill Court	A2
Claremont Street	A3	The Dana	C4
Coleham	C1	Town Walls	A2-B1
College Hill	A2-B2	Victoria Avenue	A4
Crescent Fields	A1-B1	Water Lane	C3
Crescent Lane	A1	Welsh Bridge	A4
Cross Hill	A2	Windsor Place	C3
Dogpole	B2	Wyle Cop	B2-C2
English Bridge	C2		
Fish Street	B2-B3		
Grope Lane	B2-B3		
High Street	B2-B3		
Hills Lane	A3		
Howard Street	C4		
Mardol	A3-A4		
Market Street	A2		
Meadow Place	B4-C4		
Milk Street	B2		
Murivance	A2		
Nettles Lane	A4		
Pride Hill	B3		
Princess Street	B2	AA shop	A2
Raven Meadows	B3-B4	6 Market Street	
Roushill	A3-B4	Shrewsbury SY1 1LE	

Harmer Lane	E4	Nursery Street	D7-E7-E6	Spring Street	D6-E7
Harrow Street	B2	Old Street	F6-F5	Stafford Street	F4
Hartshead	D6	Orchard Lane	C5	Stanley Lane	E7
Harvest Lane	C8	Oxford Street	A7-A8	Stanley Street	E7
Harwood Street	C1	Paradise Street	D6	Sudbury Street	F7
Hawley Street	C6-C5	Park Grange Croft	F1	Suffolk Road	E3
Haymarket	E6	Park Grange Road	E1-F1	Summerfield Street	A2-A1
Headford Street	B3	Park Square	E5-E6-F6-F5	Sunny Bank	A2
Henry Street	B7	Paternoster Row	D3-D4-E4	Surrey Place	D4
Hereford Street	C2	Pear Street	A1-A2	Surrey Street	D5
High Street	D5-E5	Pearl Street	A1	Sussex Street	F7
Hill Street	B1-C1	Pembroke Street	A1	Sylvester Street	C2-D2
Hodgson Street	B3	Penistone Road	B7-B8	Talbot Place	F4
Hollis Croft	B6-C6	Pinfold Street	C5	Talbot Street	F4
Holly Street	C4-C5	Pinstone Street	C4-D4-D5	Tenter Street	C6
Hounsfield Road	A5	Pitsmoor Road	D8	The Moor	C3-C4
Howard Street	D4-E4	Plum Lane	D7	Thomas Street	B3
Hoyle Street	B7	Pomona Street	A1-A2	Townhead Street	C5
Hyde Park Terrace	F5	Pond Hill	E5	Trippet Lane	C5
Infirmary Road	A8-B8	Pond Street	E5	Trafalgar Street	C3-C4
Jericho Street	A6-A7	Portobello Street	B5-C5	Travis Place	A3
Jessop Street	C2-C3	Powell Street	A3	Trinity Street	C7
John Street	B1-C1-D1	Priestley Street	D1-E1-E2	Tudor Street	D4-D5
Johnson Street	D7-E7	Queen Street	C6-D6	Turner Street	E3
Joiner Street	E7	Queen's Road	E1-E2	Union Street	C4-D4
King Street	D5-E5	Radford Street	B6	Upper Allen Street	B6
Lancing Road	D1	Randall Street	C1	Upper Hanover Street	A3-A4-A5
Leadmill Road	D3	Randell Place	C1	Upperthorpe Road	A7-A8
Leadmill Street	E3	Regent Street	B4-B5	Verdon Street	E8
Leavygreave Road	A5-B5	Regent Terrace	B4-B5	Vicar Lane	C5-D5
Lee Croft	C6	Rockingham Street	B5-C5-C4	Victoria Road	A2-A3
Leopold Street	C5-C6	Roscoe Road	B7	Victoria Street	B4-B5
London Road	B1-B2-C2	Russell Street	C7	Waingate	E6
Lopham Street	E8	Rutland Road	B8	Walker Street	E7
Mackenie Street	A1	St Georges Close	A5-A6	Washington Road	A1-B1
Maltravers Street	F6-F7	St Mary's Gate	C2	Watery Street	B7-B8
Mappin Street	B5	St Mary's Road	C2-D2-E2	Wellington Street	B4-C4
Marcus Drive	D8	St Philip's Road	A6-A7-B7-B8	West Bar	D6
Margaret Street	D2	Savile Street	E7-F7-F8	West Bar Green	C6-D6
Martin Street	A7-A8	School Lane	F5	West Street	B4-B5-C5
Mary Street	C2-D2	Scotland Street	B6-C6	Westfield Terrace	B4-C5
Mathew Street	B7-C7	Shales Moor	B7-C7	Weston Street	A5-A6
Matilda Street	C3-D3-D2	Sheaf Gardens	D2-E2	Wharncliffe Road	A3
Matilda Way	C3-C4	Sheaf Street	E4-E5	White Croft	C6
Meadow Street	B6-B7	Sheffield Parkway	F6	Wicker	E6-E7
Milton Street	B3-C3	Shepherd Street	B6-B7-C7	Wilkinson Lane	A4
Mitchell Street	A5-A6	Shoreham Street	D1-D2-E3	Wilkinson Street	A4
Montgomery Terrace Road		Shrewsbury Road	E3-E4-F3-F4	William Street	A2-A3
	A7-B8-A8	Shude Hill	E5-E6	York Street	D5-D6
Moore Street	B2-B3-C3	Sidney Street	D3	Young Street	B3-C2
Morpeth Street	B6-B7	Silver Street	C6		
Mount Street	B1	Snig Hill	D6		
Mowbray Street	C8-D8	Snow Lane	C6-C7		
Napier Street	A2-A1-B2	Solly Street	B5-B6-C6		
Neepsend Lane	B8-C8	Sorby Street	F8		
Netherthorpe Road	A5-A6-B6-B7	South Lane	C2		
Norfolk Park Road	E1-E2-F2	South Street	E4-E5	AA shop	D5
Norfolk Road	F3-F4	Spitalfields	D7-E7	5 St James Row,	
Norfolk Row	D5	Spital Hill	E7-E8-F8	Sheffield S1 1AY	
Norfolk Street	D5	Spital Lane	F8		
North Church Street	D6	Spital Street	E8-F8		

Sheffield

Sheffield is found on atlas page **74**,
grid reference SK**3587**

Acorn Street	C7	Brook Lane	A5-B5	Doncaster Street	B7-C7
Adelphi Street	A7 -A8	Broom Close	C1-B1	Dover Street	A7-B7
Addy Street	A8	Broom Street	A3-A2	Duchess Road	D2-E2
Albert Terrace Road	A8	Broomhall Place	A2-A3	Duke Lane	C8
Allen Street	C7	Broomhall Road	A3	Duke Street	F4-F5
Andrew Street	E7	Broomspring Lane	A4-B4	Earl Street	C3-D3
Angel Street	D5-D6	Brown Street	D3	Earl Way	C3
Arundel Street	C1-C2	Brunswick Street	A3-A4	East Bank Road	E1-E2
Arundel Gate	D4-D5	Brunswick Road	E7-E8	Ecclesall Road	A2-B2
Arundel Street	D3-D4	Burgess Street	C4-C5	Edmund Road	D1-D2
Bailey Lane	C5	Cambridge Street	C4	Edward Street	B6
Bailey Street	C5	Campo Lane	C5-D5-D6	Effingham Street	F7
Ball Street	C8	Carlisle Street	F8	Egerton Street	B3
Balm Green	C5	Carver Street	C4-C5	Eldon Street	B4-C4
Bank Street	D6	Castle Street	D6-E6	Ellin Street	C2
Bard Street	F5-F6	Castlegate	B4	Ellis Street	B7
Barker's Pool	C4-C5-D5	Cavendish Street	B4	Ellison Street	B7
Baron Street	D1-D2	Cemetery Road	A1-B1-B2	Eyre Street	C2-C3-D3-D4
Bedford Street	B8	Chapel Walk	D5	Exchange Street	E6
Beeches Avenue	F1	Charles Street	D4	Exeter Drive	A2-B2
Beet Street	B5-B6	Charlotte Road	D2-D1-E1	Eyre Lane	C3-D3
Belmonte Gardens	F3	Charter Row	C3-C4	Fargate	D5
Bennet Street	B1-C1	Chatham Street	D7-D8	Farm Road	E2
Bernard Street	F4-F5-F6	Cherry Street	D1	Fawcett Street	A6-A7
Bishop Street	B2-C2	Church Street	C5-D5	Filey Street	A3-A4
Blackwell Close	F5	Claywood Drive	E3-F3	Fitzwilliam Gate	C3
Blackwell Place	F5	Cliff Street	B1	Fitzwilliam Street	B4-B3-C3
Blast Lane	F6-F7	Clough Road	C2-D2	Flat Street	E5
Blonk Street	E6	Club Garden Road	B1	Furnace Hill	C6-C7
Bolton Street	B4	Club Street	B1	Furnival Gate	C4-D4
Bolsover Street	A5	Collegiate Crescent	A3	Furnival Road	E6-F6-F7
Boston Street	B2-C2	Commercial Street	E5	Furnival Street	D3
Bower Street	C7-D7	Copper Street	C7	Garden Street	B6-C6
Bowling Green Street	C7	Corporation Street	D6-D7	Gell Street	A4-A5
Bramall Lane	C1-C2	Countess Road	D1-D2	Gibraltar Street	D7-C7-D6
Bramwell Street	A6	Cricket Inn Road	F6	Glencoe Road	F3-F4
Bridge Street	D7-D6-E6	Cumberland Way	C3	Glossop Road	A4-B4
Broad Lane	B5-C5-C6	Daisy Bank	A6	Grafton Street	F4
Broad Street	F6	Daisy Walk	B6	Granville Road	E2-F2
Brocco Street	B6	Daniel Hill	A8	Granville Street	E3-E4
Brook Drive	A6-B6	Denby Street	C1	Green Lane	B8-C8-C7
Brook Hill	A5-B5	Devonshire Street	B4-C4	Hanover Square	A3
		Division Street	C4	Hanover Way	A3-B3-B2

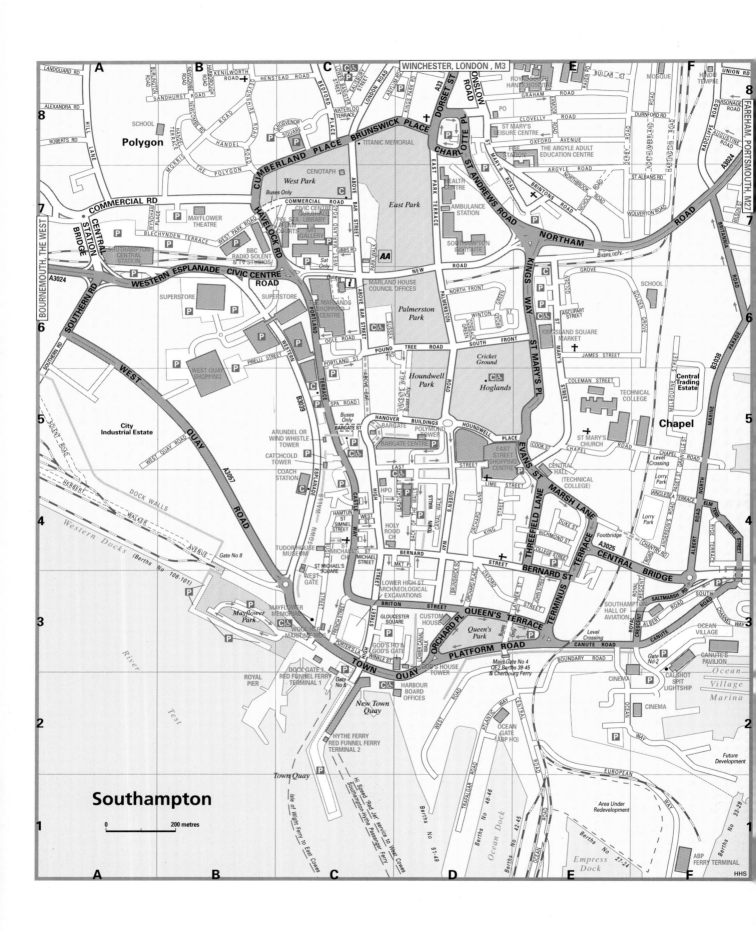

Southampton

0   200 metres

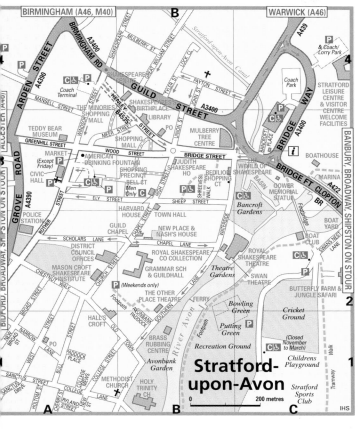

Stratford-upon-Avon

Stratford-upon-Avon is found on atlas page **48**, grid reference SP20**55**

Arden Street	A4
Avonbank Paddock	B1-B2
Bancroft Place	C3
Birmingham Road	A4
Brewery Street	A4
Bridge Foot	C3
Bridge Street	B3
Bridge Way	C3-C4
Broad Street	A1-A2
Bull Street	A1-A2
Chapel Lane	B2-B3
Cherry Street	A1
Chestnut Walk	A2
Church Street	A2-B2
Clopton Bridge	C2-C3
College Lane	A1-B1
College Mews	A1
College Street	A1-B1
Ely Street	A3-B3
Great William Street	B4
Greenhill Street	A3
Grove Road	A2-A3
Guild Street	A4-B3
Henley Street	A4-B3
High Street	B3
Holtom Street	A1
Lock Close	B4
Mansell Street	A3-A4
Meer Street	A3-B3
Mulberry Street	B4
Narrow Lane	A1
New Broad Street	A1
New Street	A1
Old Town	A2-B1
Paddock Place	A1
Payton Street	B4-C4
Rother Street	A2-A3
Ryland Street	A1
Sanctus Drive	A1
Sanctus Street	A1
Scholars Lane	A2-B2
Shakespeare Street	A4-B4
Sheep Street	B3
Shreeves Walk	B3
Southern Lane	B1-B2
Swans Nest Lane	C2
Tyler Street	B4
Union Street	B3
Waterside	B2-B3
Wenlock Road	C4
West Street	A1-A2
Windsor Street	A3-A4
Wood Street	A3-B3

Southampton

Southampton is found on atlas page **13**, grid reference SU4**112**

Above Bar Street	C5-C6-C7-C8	Cumberland Place	B7 -C7-C8
Albert Road North	F4	Derby Road	E7-E8-F8
Albert Road South	F3	Devonshire Road	B8
Alexandra Road	A8	Dorset Street	D8
Atlantic Way	D2-E2	Duke Street	E4
Anderson's Road	F4	Dunford Road	F8
Anglesea Terrace	F4	East Gate Street	D4
Argyle Road	E7	East Park Terrace	D7-D8
Ascupart Street	E6	East Street	C4-D4-D5
Asylum Road	C8-D8	Elm Terrace	F4
Augustine Road	F8	Endle Street	F4
Back of the Walls	D3-D4	European Way	F1-E1-E2
Bargate Street	C5	Evans Street	E4-E5
Bedford Place	C8	Exmoor Road	E8
Bernard Street	C4-D4-D3-E3	French Street	C3
Blechynden Terrace	A7-B7	Gibbs Road	C7
Boundary Road	E2-E3	Gloucester Square	C3-D3
Brintons Road	E7-D7-D8	Golden Grove	E6-F6
Britannia Road	F6-F7	Graham Road	D8-E8
Briton Street	C3-D3	Granville Street	F4-F5
Broad Green	D6	Grosvenor Square	C8
Brunswick Place	C8-D8	Hamtun Street	C4
Brunswick Square	D3-D4	Handel Road	B7-B8
Bugle Street	C3-C4	Handel Terrace	B8
Bullar Street	E8	Hanover Buildings	C5-D5
Burlington Road	A8-B8	Harborough Road	B8
Canal Walk	D4	Hartington Road	F7-F8
Canute Road	E3-F3	Havelock Road	B7-C7
Castle Way	C4-C3	Henstead Road	B8-C8
Central Bridge	E4-F4-F3	Herbert Walker Avenue	A4-B3
Central Road	E2	High Street	C3-C4-C5
Central Station Bridge	A6-A7	Hill Lane	A7-A8
Channel Way	F3	Houndwell Place	D5-E5
Chantry Road	F4	James Street	E6-F6
Chapel Road	E5-F5	John Street	E3
Charlotte Place	D8	Kenilworth Road	B8
Civic Centre Road	B6-C6	King Street	D4
Clovelly Road	D8-E8	Kings Park Road	D8
Coleman Street	E5	Kings Way	E6-E7
College Street	E4	Languard Road	A8
Commercial Road	A7-B7-C7	Latimer Street	E3
Cook Street	E5	Lime Street	D4-E4
Cossack Green	D6	London Road	C8

Lower Banister Street	C8	Saltmarsh Road	F3
Lower Canal Walk	D3	Sandhurst Road	A8-B8
Marine Parade	F5-F6	Simnel Street	C4
Market Place	D4	Solent Road	A4-A5
Marsh Lane	E4	South Front	D6-E6
Melbourne Street	F5-F6	Southern Road	A5-A6
Michael Street	C4	Spa Road	C5
Morris Road	B7-B8	St Albans Road	F7
New Road	C7-D6-D7-E7	St Andrews Road	E7-D7-D8
Newcombe Road	B8	St Mary's Place	E5-E6
Nichols Road	E7	St Mary's Road	E7-D7-D8
North Front	D6	St Mary's Street	E5-E6-E7
Northam Road	E7-F7	St Michael's Square	C4
Northbrook Road	E7	Sussex Road	C6-D6
Northumberland Road	F7-F8	Terminus Terrace	E3-E4
Ocean Road	E1	The Polygon	B7-B8
Ocean Way	F1-F2-E2-E3	Threefield Lane	E4
Ogle Street	C6	Town Quay	C3-C2-D2
Onslow Road	D8	Trafalgar Road	D1-D2
Orchard Lane	D4	Union Road	F8
Orchard Place	D3-D4	Vincents Walk	D5-D6
Oxford Avenue	D8-E8	Waterloo Terrace	C8
Oxford Street	E3-D3-D4	West Marland Road	B6-B7
Page Street	F4	West Park Road	B6
Palmerston Road	D5-D6	West Quay Road	A6-C3
Park Walk	C6-C7	West Road	D1-D2-D3
Pasonage Road	F8	West Street	C4
Pirelli Street	B6-E6	Western Esplanade	A6-C3
Platform Road	D3-E3	Wilson Street	F7
Porter's Lane	C3	Winkle Street	C3
Portland Street	C6	Winton Street	D6-E6
Portland Terrace	C6-C5	Wolverton Road	E7-F7
Pound Tree Road	C6-D6	Wyndham Place	A7
Queen's Terrace	D3-E3		
Queens Way	D3-D4-D5		
Radcliffe Road	F7-F8		
Raven Road	E8		
Richmond Street	E4		
Roberts Road	A8		
Royal Cresent	F3		
Royal Cresent Road	F3-F4	AA shop	C7
Ryde Terrace	F4	126 Above Bar Street	
Salisbury Street	C8	Southampton SO9 1GY	

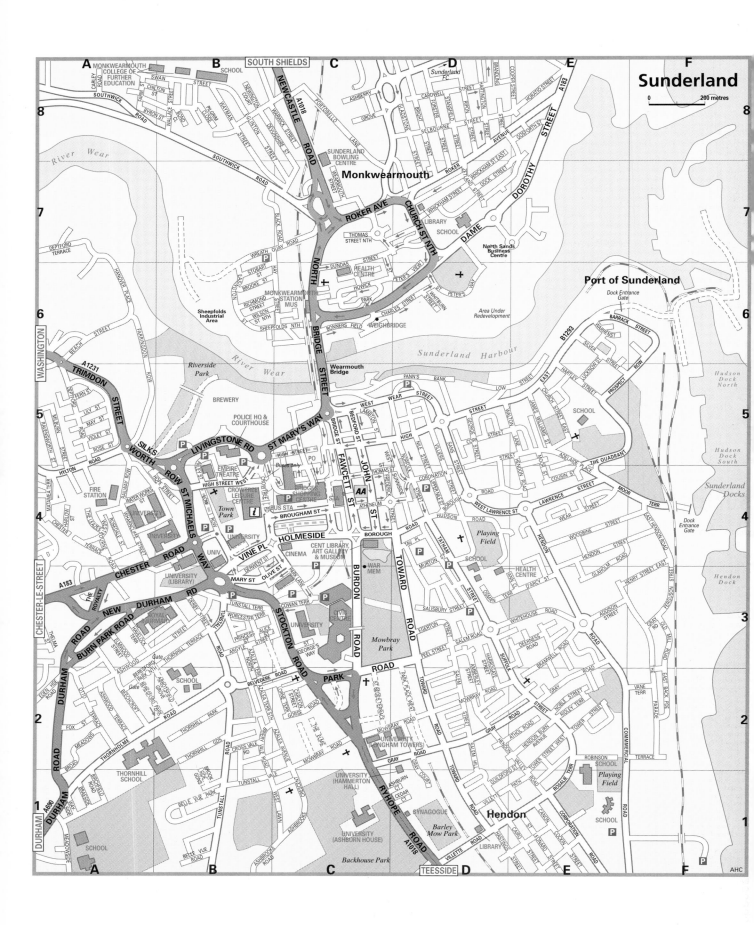

Sunderland

0   200 metres

AHC

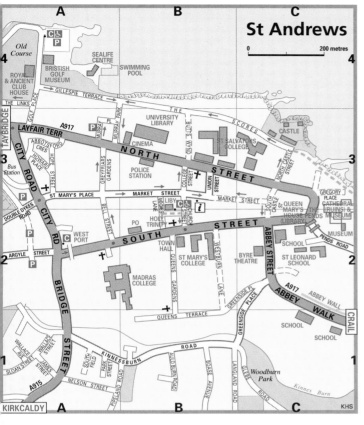

St Andrews

St Andrews is found on atlas page **127**, grid reference NO**5116**

Abbey Street	C2
Abbey Walk	C1-C2
Abbotsford Crescent	A3
Argyle Street	A2
Auld Burn Road	B1
Bell Street	A2-A3
Boase Avenue	B1
Bridge Street	A1-A2
Butts Wynd	B3
Church Street	B2-B3
City Road	A2-A3
College Street	B3
Double Dykes Road	A2-A3
Gillespie Terrace	A4
Glebe Road	C1
Golf Place	A3-A4
Greenside Place	C1-C2
Gregory Place	C3
Greyfriars Gardens	A3
Hope Street	A3
Howard Place	A3
James Street	A1
Kinnessburn Road	A1-B1
Langland Road	C1
Layfair Terrace	A3
Logies Lane	B2-B3
Market Street	B3-C3
Murray Park	A3-B4
Murray Place	A3
Nelson Street	A1
North Castle Street	C3
North Street	A3-C3
Park Street	A1
Pends Road	C2
Pipeland Road	A1-B1
Queens Gardens	B1-B2
Queens Terrace	B1
Sloan Street	A1
South Castle Street	C2-C3
South Street	A2-C2
Southfield	A1
St Mary's Place	A3
The Links	A4
The Scores	B4-C3
Union Street	B3
Wallace Avenue	A1
Wallace Street	A1
Westburn Lane	B2

Sunderland

Sunderland is found on atlas page **96**, grid reference NZ**3957**

Abbotsfield Grove	B2	Cedar Court	D1	Guildford Street	D1-E2	Old Mill Road	F3	The Elms	C2
Addison Street	E3	Charles Street	C6-D6	Gunton Street	B8-C7	Olive Street	B3-C4	The Leazes	A4
Adelaide Place	E4-E5	Chester Road	A3-B4	Hanover Place	A6-A7	Osman Terrace	D3-E3	The Parade	E3-F2
Alice Street	B3	Chester Terrace	A4	Hartington Street	D8	Otto Terrace	A2	The Quadrant	E5
Amberley Street	D2-D3	Chilton Street	A8-B8	Harlow Street	A4	Paley Street	B4-B5	The Royalty	A3
Ann Close	D3-E3	Church Street East	E5	Harrogate Street	D2-D3	Pann's Bank	C5-D5	Thelma Street	A3
Argyle Street	B3-C3	Commercial Road	E1-E2	Hartley Street	E5-E6	Park Lane	C3-C4	Thomas Street North	C7
Ashberry Grove	C8	Cooper Street	E8	Hastings Road	D1-E1	Park Place West	D2	Thornhill Gardens	B2
Ashbrooke Crescent	C1	Cork Street	D5-E5	Havelock Terrace	A3	Park Road	C2-D3	Thornhill Park	B2
Ashbrooke Road	B1-C1	Coronation Street	D4-E5	Hay Street	C6-C7	Peel Street	D3	Thornhill Terrace	B3
Ashburn Court	C1-C2	Corporation Road	E1	Hendon Burn Avenue	D2-E2	Pilgrim Close	B8	Thornholme Road	A1-B2
Ashwood Street	A2-B3	Cousin Street	E4	Hendon Road	E2-E5	Portobello Lane	C7-C8	Toward Road	D1-D4
Ashwood Terrace	A2	Cowan Terrace	C3	Hendon Street	E4-F4	Princess Street	B3	Tower Street	E2
Atheneum	C4-D4	Cross Vale Road	B2	Hendon Valley Road	D2-E1	Prospect Row	E5-F6	Tower Street West	E2
Athol Road	D2-E2	Crowtree Road	B4	Henry Street East	E3-F4	Railway Row	A4-A5	Trimdon Street	A5-A6
Azalea Avenue	C2	D'Arcy Street	E3	High Street	B5-D5	Ravensworth Street	A4-A5	Tunstall Road	B1-B3
Azalea Terrace North	B2-B3	Dame Dorothy Street	D6-E8	High Street West	B4	Richmond Street	B6	Tunstall Terrace	B3
Azalea Terrace South	B2	Deerness Road	E3	Holmside	C4	Ridley Terrace	E2	Tunstall Vale	B1-C2
Beach Street	A6	Deptford Road	A5	Hope Street	A4-B4	Ripon Street	D8	Upper Nile Street	D4
Bedford Street	C5	Deptford Terrace	A7	Horatio Street	E8	Robinson Terrace	E2-F2	Vane Terrace	F2
Beechcroft	A2	Derby Street	B3	Howick Park	C6	Roker Avenue	C7-E8	Villette Path	D1-E1
Belle Vue Park	B1	Derwent Street	B3-C3	Hudson Street	D4	Rosalie Terrace	E1-E2	Villette Road	D1-E1
Belvedere Road	B2-C3	Devonshire Street	B8-C7	Hylton Road	A4-A5	Rose Street	A5	Villiers Street	D4-D5
Beresford Park North	A2-B3	Dock Street	D7-E8	James Williams Street	E5	Rosedale Street	A4	Vine Place	B3-B4
Beresford Road	A2-B2	Dundas Street	C6-C7	John Street	C4-C5	Ryhope Road	C2-D1	Violet Street	A5
Birchfield Road	A1	Durham Road	A1-A3	Lambton Street	C5	Salem Hill	D2	Wallace Street	B8
Black Road	B7-C7	Easington Street	B6	Lawrence Street	E4	Salem Road	D3	Walton Lane	D5-E5
Bond Close	B8	East Back Poe	F2	Lily Street	A5	Salem Street	D2-D3	Warren Street	E6
Bonners Field	C6	East Barrack Street	D5-F6	Livingstone Road	B5	Salisbury Street	D3	Warwick Street	B8-C8
Borough Road	C4-E4	East Hendon Road	F4	Lorne Terrace	C2	Sans Street	D4-D5	Waterworks Street	A4
Braeside	A1	Eden House Road	A2	Low Row	B4	Selbourne Street	D8	Wayman Street	B8-C7
Bramwell Road	E2-E3	Egerton Street	D3	Low Street	D5-E6	Sheepfolds North	B6-C6	Wayside	A1
Brandling Street	D8	Elmwood Street	A3	Lucknow Street	E5-E6	Silksworth Row	A5-B4	Wear Street	E4
Bridge Street	C5	Farm Street	A8	Mary Street	B3	Silver Street	E5-E6	Wearmouth Street	C7
Briery Vale Road	B1-B2	Farringdon Row	A5-A6	Matamba Terrace	A4	Southwick Road	A8-C7	West Lawn	B1-C1
Bright Street	D7-D8	Fawcett Street	C4-C5	May Street	A5	St Bedes Terrace	C2	West Lawrence Street	D4-E4
Broad Meadows	A1-A2	Ferguson Street	F3	Meadowside	A1	St George's Way	C3	West Sunniside	C5-D4
Brooke Street	B6	Fern Street	A5	Milburn Street	A5	St Leonard Street	E1	West Wear Street	C5-D5
Brookside Gardens	B1-B2	Forster Street	D7-D8	Moor Street	E4-E5	St Mary's Way	B5-C5	Westbourne Road	A3-A4
Brougham Street	B4-C4	Fox Street	A2	Moor Terrace	E4-F4	St Michael's Way	B3-B4	Wharncliffe Street	A4
Burdon Road	C2-C4	Frederick Street	C4-D4	Mowbray Road	C2-E2	St Peter's View	C7-D7	Whickham Street	D7-D8
Burn Park Road	A3	George Street	D5	Murton Street	D3-D4	St Peter's Way	D6-D7	Whitburn Street	D6
Byron Street	A8-B8	Gladstone Street	D7-D8	New Durham Road	A3-B3	St Thomas Street	C4-D4	Whitehouse Road	D3-E3
Cairo Street	E1	Glaholm Road	E3-E4	Newington Court	B8	Stansfield Street	D7-D8	Wilson Street North	B6
Canon Cockin Street	E1	Gorse Road	C2	Nile Street	D4-D5	Stobart Street	B6-B7	Woodbine Street	E4-F4
Cardwell Street	D8	Gosforth Street	E8	Noble Street	E2	Stockton Road	B3-C2	Worcester Terrace	B3
Carley Road	A8	Gray Court	D1-D2	Norfolk Street	D4-D5	Swan Street	A8-B8	Wreath Quay Road	B6-C7
Carlyon Street	C2	Gray Road	C2-E3-F3	North Bridge Street	C5-C7	Tavistock Place	D4	Zetland Street	D7

AA shop	C4
49 Fawett Street	
Sunderland SR1 1RR	

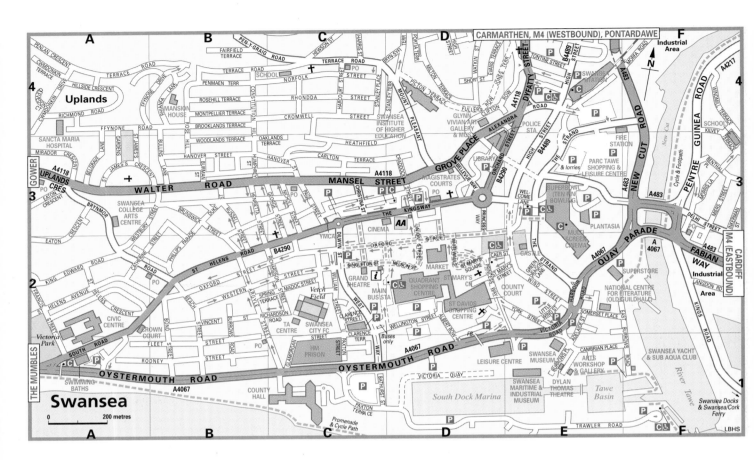

Swansea

Swansea is found on atlas page **32**,
grid reference SS**6592**

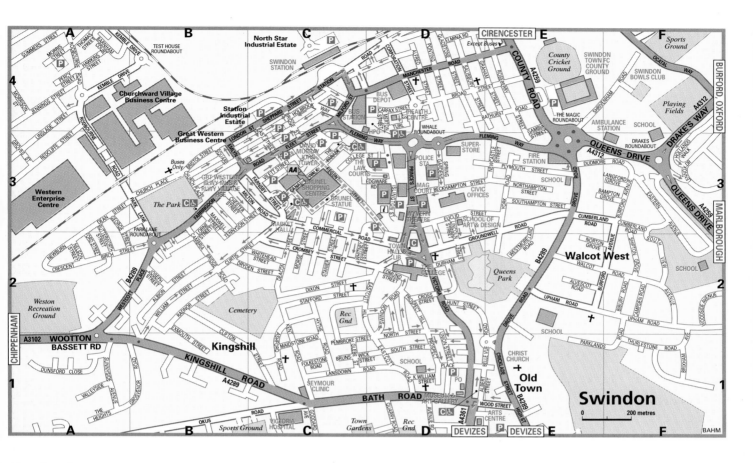

Swindon

Swindon is found on atlas page **36**,
grid reference SU1484

Albert Street	D1	Drove Road	E2-E3	King William Street	D1	Shipton Grove	F2
Albion Street	B2	Dryden Street	B2-C2	Langford Grove	F3	Shrivenham Road	E4-F4
Alfred Street	D4	Dudmore Road	E3-F3	Lansdown Road	C1-D1	South Street	D1
Alvescot Road	E2	Dunsford Close	A1	Lennox Drive	F3	South View Avenue	F2-F3
Ashford Road	C1-C2	Durham Street	D2	Linslade Street	A3-A4	Southampton Street	E3
Avenue Road	D1	East Street	C3-C4	Lincoln Street	D2-D3	Spring Gardens	D3
Bampton Grove	E3-F3	Eastcott Hill	D2-D3	London Street	B3-C4	Stafford Street	C2
Barnham Court	A4	Eastcott Road	D1	Lorne Street	B2-B3	Stanier Street	C2
Bath Road	C1-D1	Eastern Avenue	F2-F3	Maidstone Road	C1	Station Road	C4-D4
Bathurst Road	D4-E4	Edgware Road	C3-D3	Manchester Road	C4-E4	Summers Street	A4
Beckhampton Street	D3	Edmund Street	D2	Maxwell Street	B2-B3	Sunnyside Avenue	A1
Bellevue Road	D1-E2	Elmina Road	D4	Merton Street	D4	Swindon Road	D2
Bibury Road	F2	Emlyn Square	B3	Milford Street	C4	Tennyson Street	B2-C3
Birch Street	2-B2	Euclid Street	D3-E3	Milton Road	B3-C3	The Heights	A1
Bradford Road	D1	Exmouth Street	B1-B2	Morris Street	A4	The Parade	C3
Bridge Street	C3-C4	Farnsby Street	C3	Morrison Street	A4	Thomas Street	A4
Bristol Street	B3	Farringdon Road	B2-C3	Morse Street	C2-C2	Thurlestone Road	F1
Brixham Avenue	F1	Fleet Street	C3-C4	Nelson Street	A2	Turl Street	D4
Broad Street	D4-E4	Fleming Way	C4-E3	Newburn Crescent	A2	Union Street	D1
Brunswick Street	C1-D1	Folkestone Road	C1	Newcastle Street	E3	Upham Road	E2-F2
Burford Avenue	E2-F3	Ford Street	A2	North Street	D1	Valleyside	A1
Butterworth Street	A2-A3	Gambia Street	E3-E4	Northampton Street	E3	Victoria Road	D1-D2
Cambria Bridge Road	B2-B3	George Street	A2-A3	Norton Grove	E2-F2	Vilett Street	C3
Campden Road	F2	Gladstone Street	D4	Octal Way	F4	Walcot Road	E2-F2
Canal Walk	C3	Glebe Street	C1	Okus Road	B1-C1	Westcott Place	A2-B2
Carfax Street	D4	Goddard Avenue	C1	Park Lane	A3-B3	Westmoreland Road	E2-E3
Chester Street	B3	Graham Street	D4-E4	Parklands Road	E1-F2	Whitehead Street	B2-C2
Church Place	B3	Grosvenor Road	A1-B1	Pembroke Street	C1-D1	Whitney Street	C2-D3
Clifton Street	B2-C1	Groundwell Road	D2-E3	Percy Street	A4	William Street	B1-B2
College Street	C3-D3	Groves Street	A3	Plymouth Street	D3-E3	Wood Street	D1-E1
Commercial Road	C3-D2	Hawkins Street	A4	Ponting Street	D4	Woodside Avenue	F2
Corporation Street	D4	High Street	E1	Princes Street	D3	Wootton Bassett Road	A1
County Road	E4	Holbrook Way	C4	Prospect Hill	D1-D2	York Road	E2-E3
Cricklade Street	E1	Hollands Walk	F3-F4	Prospect Place	D1		
Crombey Street	C2-D2	Hunt Street	D2	Queens Drive	E3-F2		
Cross Street	D2	Hythe Road	C1-C2	Radnor Street	B1-B2		
Cumberland Road	E3-F2	Islington Street	D3	Redcliffe Street	A3-A4		
Curtis Street	B2-C3	Jennings Street	A4	Regent Street	C3-D3	AA shop	C3
Deacon Street	C2-C3	Joseph Street	B2	Rodbourne Road	A3-A4	22 Canal Walk	
Dean Street	A2-A3	Kemble Drive	A4-B4	Roseberry Street	E3-E4	Brunel Shopping Centre	
Dixon Street	C2-D2	Kent Road	C1-C2	Salisbury Street	D4-E4	Swindon SN1 1LD	
Drakes Drive	F3-F4	Kingshill Road	B1-C1	Sheppard Street	C4		

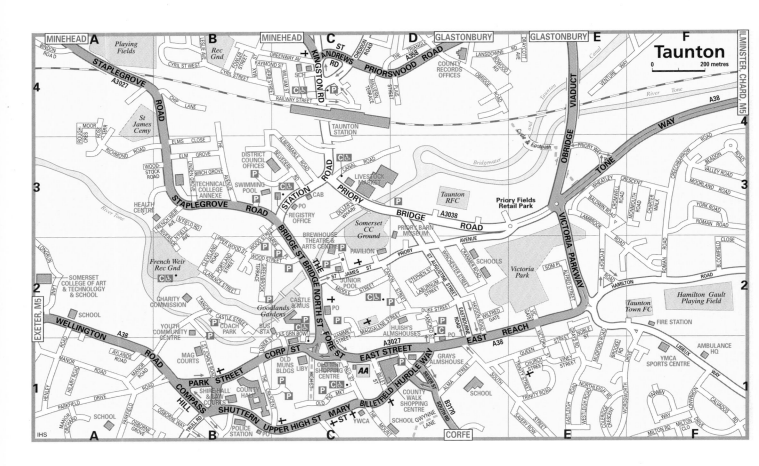

Taunton

Taunton is found on atlas page **20**,
grid reference ST**2224**

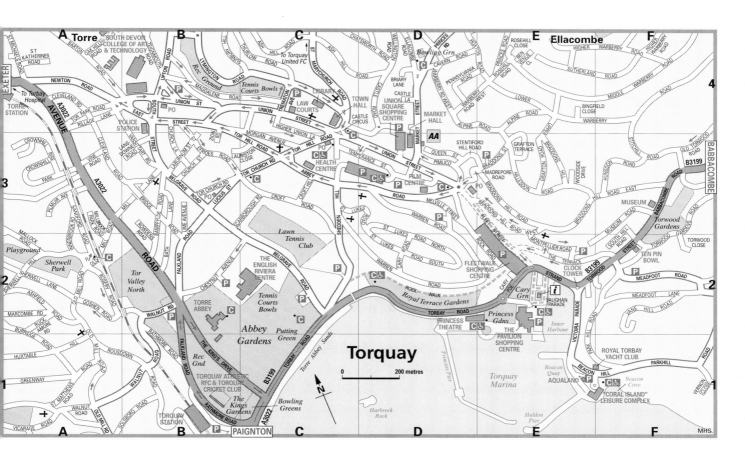

Torquay

Torquay is found on atlas page **7**,
grid reference SX**9**1**6**4

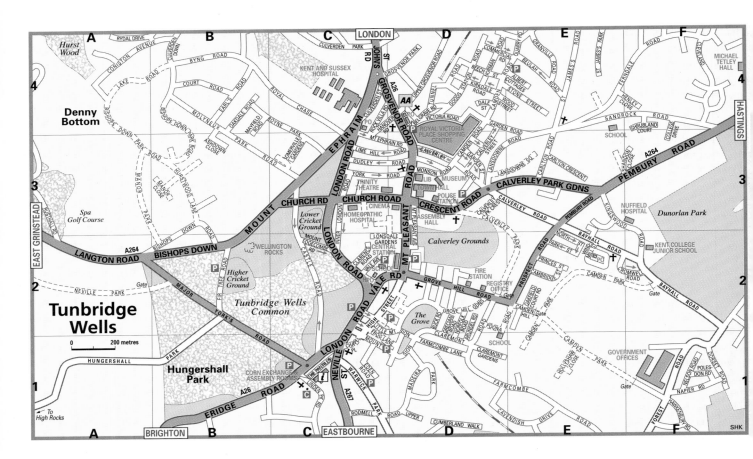

Tunbridge Wells

Tunbridge Wells is found on atlas page **16**,
grid reference TQ**5839**

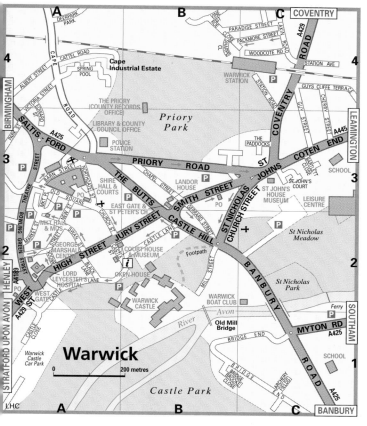

Warwick

Warwick is found on atlas page **48**, grid reference SP**2865**

Albert Street	A4	St John's Court	C3
Archery Fields	C1	St Johns	C3
Banbury Road	B2-C1	St Nicholas Church St	B2-C3
Barn Street	A3	Station Avenue	C4
Bartlett Close	C3	Station Road	C4
Black Lane	A2	Swan Street	A2
Bowling Green Street	A2	The Butts	A3-B2
Bridge Brooke Close	B1-C1	The Paddocks	C3
Bridge End	B1-C1	Theatre Street	A3
Brook Street	A2	Victoria Street	A3-A4
Cape Road	A3-A4	Vine Street	B4
Castle Close	A1	West Street	A1-A2
Castle Hill	B2	Woodcote Road	C4
Castle Lane	A2-B2		
Castle Street	A2-B2		
Cattel Road	A4		
Chapel Street	B3		
Cherry Street	C3-C4		
Church Street	A2		
Coten End	C3		
Coventry Road	C3-C4		
Deerpark Park	A4		
Edward Street	A3-A4		
Gerrard Street	B2-B3		
Guy Street	C3-C4		
Guys Cliffe Terrace	C4		
High Street	A2		
Jury Street	A2-B2		
Lakin Road	C4		
Market Place	A3		
Market Street	A2		
Mill Street	B2		
Myton Road	C1		
New Street	A2-A3		
Northgate Street	A3		
Old Square	A3		
Packmore Street	B4-C4		
Paradise Street	B4-C4		
Park Street	A3		
Priory Road	A3-C3		
Roe Close	B4		
Saltisford	A3-A4		
Sharpe Close	B4		
Smith Street	B2-C3		
Spring Pool	A4		

Windsor

Windsor is found on atlas page **26**, grid reference SU**9576**

Adelaide Square	B2-C2	Royal Mews	C3
Albany Road	B2	Royal Ward	B3
Albert Road	C1	Russell Street	B2
Albert Street	A3	Sheet Street	C2-C3
Alexandra Road	B1-B3	Springfield Road	A1-A2
Alma Road	B1-B3	St Albans Street	C3
Arthur Road	A3-B3	St Leonard's Road	A1-B3
Balmoral Gardens	B1	St Mark's Road	A2-B2
Barry Avenue	A4-B4	Stovell Road	A4
Beaumont Road	B2	Temple Road	B2
Bexley Street	A3	Thames Street	B3-C4
Bolton Avenue	B1	The Long Walk	C1-C3
Bolton Crescent	B1	Trinity Place	B2-B3
Brocas Street	B4	Vansittart Road	A2-A4
Brook Street	C2	Victoria Street	B3-C3
Bulkeley Avenue	A1	York Avenue	A1-A2
Castle Hill	C3	York Road	A2
Charles Street	B3		
Clarence Crescent	B3		
Clarence Road	A3-B3		
College Crescent	A1-A2		
Dagmar Road	B2		
Datchet Road	B4-C4		
Devereaux Road	B2		
Dorset Road	B2-B3		
Duke Street	A3-A4		
Elm Road	A1		
Fountain Gardens	B1-C1		
Frances Road	B1-C2		
Frogmore Drive	C2-C3		
Goslar Way	A2		
Goswell Road	B3-B4		
Green Lane	A2		
Grove Road	B2		
High Street	B4		
High Street	C3		
King's Road	C1-C2		
Maidenhead Road	A3		
Meadow Lane	A4-B4		
Osborne Road	A2-C1		
Oxford Road	A3		
Park Street	C3		
Peascod Street	B3		
Princess Avenue	A1		
Queen's Road	A2-B2		
River Street	B4		

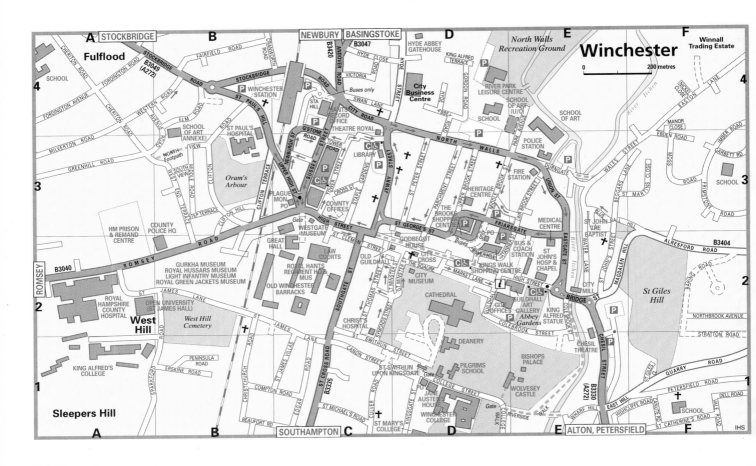

Winchester

Winchester is found on atlas page **24**,
grid reference SU**48**29

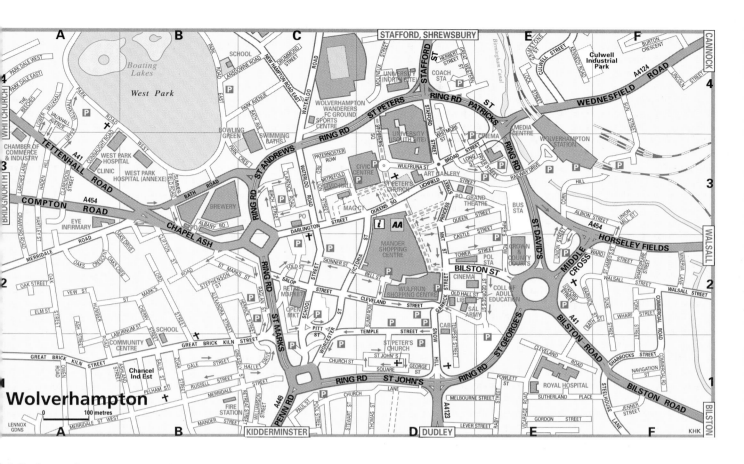

Wolverhampton

Wolverhampton is found on atlas page **60**,
grid reference SO**9198**

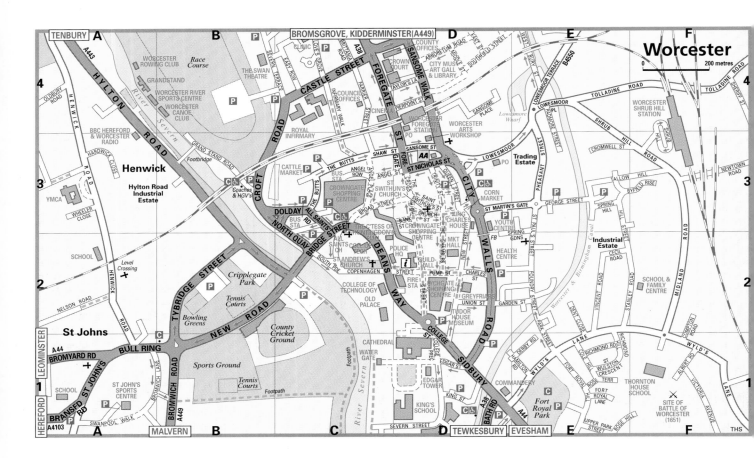

Worcester

Worcester is found on atlas page **47**,
grid reference SO**8554**

Albert Road	F1	Garden Street	D2-E2	Southfield Street	D4
All Saints Road	C3	George Street	E3	Spring Gardens	C2-C3-D2-D3
Angel Place	C3	Grand Stand Road	B3	Spring Hill	E3
Angel Row	C3	Hamilton Road	D1-E1	St Martin's Gate	D3-E3
Angel Street	C3-D3	Hardwick Close	A3	St Nicholas Street	D3
Arboretum Road	D4	Henwick Road	A1-A2-A3-A4	St Paul's Street	E2-E3
Bank Street	D3	High Street	D2-D3	St Swithun's Street	D3
Bath Road	D1	Hill Street	E3-E2	St Wulston Crescent	E1
Bransfield Road	A1	King Street	D1	Stanley Road	E2-F2
Bridge Street	C2-C3	Love's Grove	C4	Swanpool Walk	A1
Brittania Road	C4	Lowesmoor	D3-D4-E4	Tallow Hill	E3-F3
Broad Street	C2-D2	Lowesmoor Place	E4	Taylor's Lane	C4-D4
Bromwich Lane	A1-B1	Lowesmoor Terrace	E4	The Butts	C3
Bromwich Road	B1	Middle Street	D4	The Cross	D3
Bromyard Road	A1	Midland Road	F1-F2-F3	The Shambles	D2-D3
Bull Ring	A1-B1	Nelson Road	A2	Tolladine Road	E4-F4
Byfield Rise	E3-F3	New Road	B1-B2-C2	Trinity Street	D3
Castle Street	C4	New Street	D2-D3	Tybridge Street	B1-B2
Cecil Road	F3	Newtown Road	F2	Union Street	D2
Charles Street	D2	North Quay	C2-C3-B3	Upper Park Street	E1
Church Street	D3	Oldbury Road	A4	Victoria Avenue	F1
City Walls Road	D1-D2-D3	Padmore Street	E3-E4	Vincent Road	E2
Cole Hill	E1	Park Street	E1-E2	Westbury Street	E4
College Precinct	D1	Pheasant Street	E3-E4	Wheeler Close	A3
College Street	D1-D2	Pierpoint Street	D4	Wyld's Lane	D1-E1-E2-F2-F1
Compton Road	F1-F2	Pump Street	D2		
Copenhagen Street	C2-D2	Queen Street	D3		
Croft Road	B3-C3-C4	Richmond Hill	E1		
Cromwell Street	E3	Richmond Road	E1		
Deans Way	C3-C2-D2	Rose Hill	E1-F1		
Dent Close	E2	Rose Terrace	E1		
Derby Road	E1	Sansome Place	D4		
Dolday	B3-C3	Sansome Street	D3		
East Street	D4	Sansome Walk	D3-D4		
Easy Row	C4	Severn Street	C1-D1		
Edgar Street	D1	Severn Terrace	B4-C4		
Farrier Street	C3-C4	Shaw Street	C3-D3		
Foregate Street	C4-D4-D3	Sheriff Street	F4	AA shop	D3
Fort Royal Hill	E1	Shrub Hill	F3-F4	Unit 5, Haswell House	
Fort Royal Lane	E1	Shrub Hill Road	E4-E3-F3	St Nicholas Street	
Foundary Street	E2	South Parade	C2	Worcester WR1 1UW	

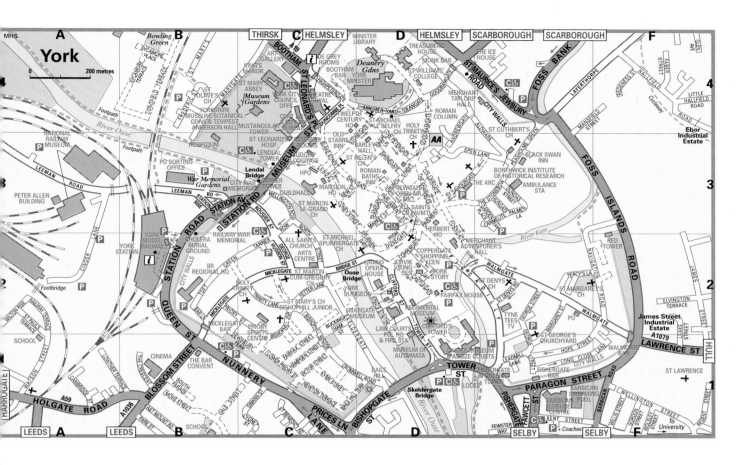

York

York is found on atlas page **83**,
grid reference SE**60**5I

Each place name entry in this index is identified by its County, County Borough or Council Area name. These are shown in *italics*.

A list of the abbreviated forms used is shown on the left.

To locate a place name in the atlas turn to the map page indicated in bold type in the index and use the 4-figure grid reference.

For example, **Hythe** *Kent* **29** **TR1634** is found on page 29.

The two letters 'TR' refer to the National Grid.

To pinpoint our example the first bold figure **'1'** is found along the bottom edge of the page.

The following figure '6' indicates how many imaginary tenths to move east of the line **'1'**.

The next bold figure **'3'** is found up the left-hand side of the page.

The last figure '4' shows how many imaginary tenths to move north of the line **'3'**. You will locate Hythe where these two lines intersect.

England

7	*Beds*	**Bedfordshire**
8	*Berks*	**Berkshire**
12	*Bristl*	**Bristol**
13	*Bucks*	**Buckinghamshire**
15	*Cambs*	**Cambridgeshire**
19	*Ches*	**Cheshire**
23	*Cnwll*	**Cornwall**
24	*Cumb*	**Cumbria**
26	*Derbys*	**Derbyshire**
27	*Devon*	**Devon**
28	*Dorset*	**Dorset**
32	*Dur*	**Durham**
37	*E R Yk*	**East Riding of Yorkshire**
38	*E Susx*	**East Sussex**
39	*Essex*	**Essex**
43	*Gloucs*	**Gloucestershire**
44	*Gt Lon*	**Greater London**
45	*Gt Man*	**Greater Manchester**
46	*Guern*	**Guernsey**
48	*Hants*	**Hampshire**
49	*H & W*	**Hereford & Worcester**
50	*Herts*	**Hertfordshire**
53	*IOM*	**Isle of Man**
54	*IOW*	**Isle of Wight**
55	*IOS*	**Isles of Scilly**
56	*Jersey*	**Jersey**
57	*Kent*	**Kent**
58	*Lancs*	**Lancashire**
59	*Leics*	**Leicestershire**
60	*Lincs*	**Lincolnshire**
61	*Mersyd*	**Merseyside**
68	*Norfk*	**Norfolk**
71	*N York*	**North Yorkshire**
72	*Nhants*	**Northampton-shire**
73	*Nthumb*	**Northumberland**
74	*Notts*	**Nottinghamshire**
76	*Oxon*	**Oxfordshire**
82	*Rutlnd*	**Rutland**
84	*Shrops*	**Shropshire**
85	*Somset*	**Somerset**
88	*S York*	**South Yorkshire**
89	*Staffs*	**Staffordshire**
91	*Suffk*	**Suffolk**
92	*Surrey*	**Surrey**
95	*T & W*	**Tyne & Wear**
97	*Warwks*	**Warwickshire**
100	*W Mids*	**West Midlands**
101	*W Susx*	**West Sussex**
102	*W York*	**West Yorkshire**
103	*Wilts*	**Wiltshire**

Scotland

2	*Aber C*	**Aberdeen City**
3	*Abers*	**Aberdeenshire**
5	*Angus*	**Angus**
6	*Ag & B*	**Argyll & Bute**
10	*Border*	**Borders (Scottish)**
20	*C Edin*	**City of Edinburgh**
21	*C Glas*	**City of Glasgow**
22	*Clacks*	**Clackmannan-shire**
29	*D & Cb*	**Dumbarton & Clydebank**
30	*D & G*	**Dumfries & Galloway**
31	*Dund C*	**Dundee City**
33	*E Ayrs*	**East Ayrshire**
34	*E Duns*	**East Dunbartonshire**
35	*E Loth*	**East Lothian**
36	*E Rens*	**East Renfrewshire**
40	*Falk*	**Falkirk**
41	*Fife*	**Fife**
51	*Highld*	**Highland**
52	*Inver*	**Inverclyde**
63	*Mdloth*	**Midlothian**
65	*Moray*	**Moray**
69	*N Ayrs*	**North Ayrshire**
70	*N Lans*	**North Lanarkshire**
75	*Ork*	**Orkney Islands**
78	*P & K*	**Perthshire & Kinross**
80	*Rens*	**Renfrewshire**
83	*Shet*	**Shetland Islands**
86	*S Ayrs*	**South Ayrshire**
87	*S Lans*	**South Lanarkshire**
90	*Stirlg*	**Stirling**
98	*W Isls*	**Western Isles**
99	*W Loth*	**West Lothian**

Wales

1	*A & C*	**Aberconwy & Colwyn**
4	*Angles*	**Anglesey**
9	*Blae G*	**Blaenau Gwent**
11	*Brdgnd*	**Bridgend**
14	*Caerph*	**Caerphilly**
16	*Cardif*	**Cardiff**
17	*Cardgn*	**Cardiganshire**
18	*Carmth*	**Carmarthenshire**
25	*Denbgs*	**Denbighshire**
42	*Flints*	**Flintshire**
47	*Gwynd*	**Gwynedd**
62	*Myr Td*	**Merthyr Tydfil**
64	*Mons*	**Monmouthshire**
66	*Neath*	**Neath & Port Talbot**
67	*Newpt*	**Newport**
77	*Pembks*	**Pembrokeshire**
79	*Powys*	**Powys**
81	*Rhondd*	**Rhondda Cynon Taff**
93	*Swans*	**Swansea**
94	*Torfn*	**Torfaen**
96	*V Glam*	**Vale of Glamorgan**
104	*Wrexhm*	**Wrexham**

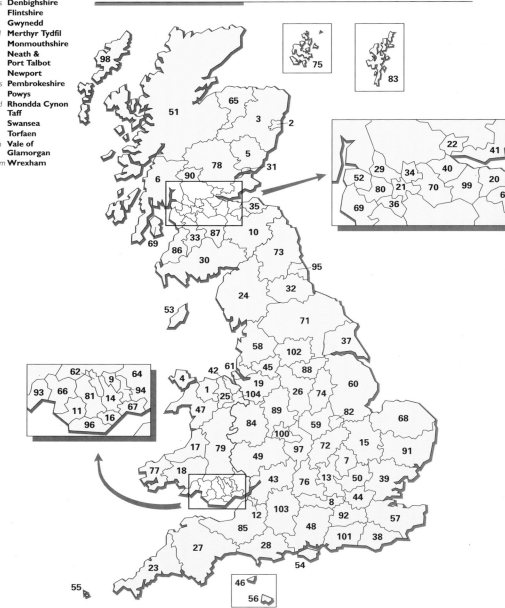

A

A'Chill *Highld*	128	NG2705
Ab Kettleby *Leics*	63	SK7223
Ab Lench *H & W*	47	SP0151
Abbas Combe *Somset*	22	ST7022
Abberley *H & W*	47	SO7567
Abberley Common *H & W*	47	SO7467
Abberton *Essex*	41	TM0019
Abberton *H & W*	47	SO9953
Abberwick *Nthumb*	111	NU1313
Abbess Roding *Essex*	40	TL5711
Abbey *Devon*	9	ST1410
Abbey Dore *H & W*	46	SO3830
Abbey Green *Staffs*	72	SJ9757
Abbey Hill *Somset*	10	ST2718
Abbey St Bathans *Border*	119	NT7661
Abbey Town *Cumb*	93	NY1750
Abbey Village *Lancs*	81	SD6422
Abbey Wood *Gt Lon*	27	TQ4779
Abbeycwmhir *Powys*	45	SO0571
Abbeydale *S York*	74	SK3281
Abbeystead *Lancs*	81	SD5654
Abbot's Chair *Derbys*	74	SK0290
Abbot's Salford *Warwks*	48	SP0650
Abbotrule *Border*	110	NT6113
Abbots Bickington *Devon*	18	SS3813
Abbots Bromley *Staffs*	73	SK0724
Abbots Deuglie *P & K*	126	NO1111
Abbots Langley *Herts*	26	TL0901
Abbots Leigh *Somset*	34	ST5474
Abbots Morton *H & W*	48	SP0255
Abbots Ripton *Cambs*	52	TL2377
Abbots Worthy *Hants*	24	SU4932
Abbotsbury *Dorset*	10	SY5785
Abbotsford *Border*	109	NT5034
Abbotsham *Devon*	18	SS4226
Abbotskerswell *Devon*	7	SX8568
Abbotsleigh *Devon*	7	SX8048
Abbotsley *Cambs*	52	TL2256
Abbotstone *Hants*	24	SU5634
Abbotswood *Hants*	23	SU3623
Abbott Street *Dorset*	11	ST9800
Abbotts Ann *Hants*	23	SU3243
Abcott *Shrops*	46	SO3978
Abdon *Shrops*	59	SO5786
Abenhall *Gloucs*	35	SO6717
Aber *Gwynd*	69	SH6572
Aber Clydach *Powys*	33	SO1021
Aber-arad *Carmth*	31	SN3140
Aber-banc *Cardgn*	31	SN3541
Aber-giar *Carmth*	44	SN5040
Aber-Magwr *Cardgn*	43	SN6673
Aber-meurig *Cardgn*	44	SN5656
Aber-nant *Rhondd*	33	SO0103
Aberaeron *Cardgn*	42	SN4562
Aberaman *Rhondd*	33	SO0100
Aberangell *Gwynd*	57	SH8410
Aberarder *Highld*	140	NH6225
Aberargie *P & K*	126	NO1615
Aberarth *Cardgn*	42	SN4763
Aberavon *Neath*	32	SS7489
Aberbargoed *Caerph*	33	SO1500
Aberbeeg *Blae G*	33	SO2002
Abercairny *P & K*	125	NN9222
Abercanaid *Myr Td*	33	SO0503
Abercarn *Caerph*	33	ST2194
Abercastle *Pembks*	30	SM8533
Abercegir *Powys*	57	SH8001
Aberchalder Lodge *Highld*	131	NH3403
Aberchirder *Abers*	142	NJ6252
Abercoed *Cardgn*	44	SN6757
Abercraf *Powys*	33	SN8212
Abercregan *Neath*	33	SS8496
Abercwmboi *Rhondd*	33	ST0299
Abercych *Pembks*	31	SN2441
Abercynon *Rhondd*	33	ST0794
Aberdalgie *P & K*	125	NO0720
Aberdare *Rhondd*	33	SO0002
Aberdaron *Gwynd*	56	SH1726
Aberdeen *Aber C*	135	NJ9306
Aberdesach *Gwynd*	68	SH4251
Aberdour *Fife*	117	NT1985
Aberdulais *Neath*	32	SS7799
Aberdyfi *Gwynd*	43	SN6196
Aberedw *Powys*	45	SO0847
Abereiddy *Pembks*	30	SM7931
Abererch *Gwynd*	56	SH3936
Aberfan *Myr Td*	33	SO0700
Aberfeldy *P & K*	125	NN8549
Aberffraw *Angles*	68	SH3569
Aberffrwd *Cardgn*	43	SN6878
Aberford *W York*	83	SE4337
Aberfoyle *Stirlg*	115	NN5200
Abergarw *Brdgnd*	33	SS9184
Abergarwed *Neath*	33	SN8102
Abergavenny *Mons*	34	SO2914
Abergele *A & C*	70	SH9477
Abergorlech *Carmth*	44	SN5833
Abergwesyn *Powys*	45	SN8552
Abergwili *Carmth*	31	SN4320
Abergwydol *Powys*	57	SH7903
Abergwynfi *Neath*	33	SS8995
Abergynolwyn *Gwynd*	57	SH6806
Aberhosan *Powys*	43	SN8197
Aberkenfig *Brdgnd*	33	SS8984
Aberlady *E Loth*	118	NT4679
Aberlemno *Angus*	127	NO5255
Aberllefenni *Powys*	57	SH7609
Aberllynfi *Powys*	45	SO1737
Aberlour *Moray*	141	NJ2642
Abermorddu *Flints*	71	SJ3056
Abermule *Powys*	58	SO1694
Abernant *Carmth*	31	SN3323
Abernethy *P & K*	126	NO1816
Abernyte *P & K*	126	NO2531
Aberporth *Cardgn*	42	SN2651
Abersoch *Gwynd*	56	SH3127
Abersychan *Torfn*	34	SO2603
Aberthin *V Glam*	33	ST0074
Abertillery *Blae G*	33	SO2104
Abertridwr *Caerph*	33	ST1289
Abertridwr *Powys*	58	SJ0319
Abertysswg *Caerph*	33	SO1305
Aberuthven *P & K*	125	NN9615
Aberyscir *Powys*	45	SN9929
Aberystwyth *Cardgn*	43	SN5881
Abingdon *Oxon*	37	SU4997
Abinger *Surrey*	14	TQ1145
Abinger Hammer *Surrey*	14	TQ0947
Abington *Nhants*	50	SP7861
Abington *S Lans*	108	NS9323
Abington Pigotts *Cambs*	39	TL3044
Ablington *Gloucs*	36	SP1007
Ablington *Wilts*	23	SU1546
Abney *Derbys*	74	SK1980
Above Church *Staffs*	73	SK0150
Aboyne *Abers*	134	NO5298
Abram *Gt Man*	78	SD6001
Abriachan *Highld*	139	NH5535
Abridge *Essex*	27	TQ4696
Abson *Gloucs*	35	ST7074
Abthorpe *Nhants*	49	SP6446
Aby *Lincs*	77	TF4078
Acaster Malbis *N York*	83	SE5845
Acaster Selby *N York*	83	SE5741
Accott *Devon*	19	SS6432
Accrington *Lancs*	81	SD7628
Acha *Ag & B*	120	NM1854
Acha Mor *W Isls*	154	NB3029
Achahoish *Ag & B*	113	NR7877
Achalader *P & K*	126	NO1245
Achaleven *Ag & B*	122	NM9233
Achanalt *Highld*	139	NH2661
Achandunie *Highld*	146	NH6472
Achany *Highld*	146	NC5602
Acharacle *Highld*	121	NM6767
Acharn *Highld*	122	NM7050
Acharn *P & K*	124	NN7543
Achavanich *Highld*	151	ND1842
Achduart *Highld*	145	NC0403
Achfary *Highld*	148	NC2939
Achiltibuie *Highld*	144	NC0208
Achinhoan *Ag & B*	105	NR7516
Achintee *Highld*	138	NG9441
Achlain *Highld*	131	NH2812
Achmelvich *Highld*	148	NC0524
Achmore *Highld*	138	NG8533
Achmore *W Isls*	154	NB3029
Achnacarnin *Highld*	148	NC0432
Achnacarry *Highld*	131	NN1787
Achnacloich *Highld*	129	NG5908
Achnaconeran *Highld*	139	NH4118
Achnacroish *Ag & B*	122	NM8541
Achnadrish Lodge *Ag & B*	121	NM4652
Achnafauld *P & K*	125	NN8736
Achnagarron *Highld*	146	NH6870
Achnaha *Highld*	128	NM4668
Achnahaird *Highld*	144	NC0013
Achnairn *Highld*	146	NC5512
Achnalea *Highld*	130	NM8561
Achnamara *Ag & B*	113	NR7887
Achnasheen *Highld*	138	NH1658
Achnashellach Station *Highld*	138	NH0048
Achnastank *Moray*	141	NJ2733
Achosnich *Highld*	121	NM4467
Achranich *Highld*	122	NM7047
Achreamie *Highld*	150	ND0166
Achriabhach *Highld*	131	NN1468
Achriesgill *Highld*	148	NC2554
Achtoty *Highld*	149	NC6762
Achurch *Nhants*	51	TL0283
Achvaich *Highld*	146	NH7194
Ackergill *Highld*	151	ND3553
Acklam *N York*	97	NZ4817
Acklam *N York*	90	SE7861
Ackleton *Shrops*	60	SO7698
Acklington *Nthumb*	103	NU2301
Ackton *W York*	83	SE4121
Ackworth Moor Top *W York*	83	SE4316
Acle *Norfk*	67	TG4010
Acock's Green *W Mids*	61	SP1283
Acol *Kent*	29	TR3067
Acomb *N York*	83	SE5651
Acomb *Nthumb*	102	NY9366
Acombe *Somset*	9	ST1914
Aconbury *H & W*	46	SO5133
Acre *Lancs*	81	SD7924
Acrefair *Wrexhm*	70	SJ2743
Acresford *Derbys*	61	SK2913
Acton *Ches*	71	SJ6352
Acton *Dorset*	11	SY9978
Acton *Gt Lon*	26	TQ2080
Acton *H & W*	47	SO8467
Acton *Shrops*	59	SO3185
Acton *Staffs*	72	SJ8241
Acton *Suffk*	54	TL8945
Acton Beauchamp *H & W*	47	SO6850
Acton Bridge *Ches*	71	SJ6075
Acton Burnell *Shrops*	59	SJ5302
Acton Green *H & W*	47	SO6950
Acton Park *Wrexhm*	71	SJ3451
Acton Pigott *Shrops*	59	SJ5402
Acton Round *Shrops*	59	SO6395
Acton Scott *Shrops*	59	SO4589
Acton Trussell *Staffs*	72	SJ9318
Acton Turville *Gloucs*	35	ST8080
Adbaston *Staffs*	72	SJ7627
Adber *Dorset*	21	ST5920
Adbolton *Notts*	62	SK5938
Adderbury *Oxon*	49	SP4735
Adderley *Shrops*	72	SJ6640
Adderstone *Nthumb*	111	NU1330
Addiewell *W Loth*	117	NS9962
Addingham *W York*	82	SE0749
Addington *Bucks*	49	SP7428
Addington *Gt Lon*	27	TQ3664
Addington *Kent*	28	TQ6559
Addiscombe *Gt Lon*	27	TQ3366
Addlestone *Surrey*	26	TQ0564
Addlestonemoor *Surrey*	26	TQ0565
Addlethorpe *Lincs*	77	TF5468
Adeney *Shrops*	72	SJ6918
Adeyfield *Herts*	38	TL0708
Adfa *Powys*	58	SJ0601
Adforton *H & W*	46	SO4071
Adisham *Kent*	29	TR2253
Adlestrop *Gloucs*	48	SP2426
Adlingfleet *E R Yk*	84	SE8421
Adlington *Ches*	79	SJ9180
Adlington *Lancs*	81	SD6013
Admaston *Shrops*	59	SJ6313
Admaston *Staffs*	73	SK0423
Admington *Warwks*	48	SP2045
Adsborough *Somset*	20	ST2729
Adscombe *Somset*	20	ST1837
Adstock *Bucks*	49	SP7329
Adstone *Nhants*	49	SP5951
Adswood *Gt Man*	79	SJ8888
Adversane *W Susx*	14	TQ0723
Advie *Highld*	141	NJ1234
Adwalton *W York*	82	SE2328
Adwell *Oxon*	37	SU6999
Adwick Le Street *S York*	83	SE5308
Adwick upon Dearne *S York*	83	SE4701
Ae *D & G*	100	NX9889
Ae Bridgend *D & G*	100	NY0186
Affetside *Gt Man*	81	SD7513
Affleck *Abers*	142	NJ5540
Affpuddle *Dorset*	11	SY8093
Affric Lodge *Highld*	138	NH1822
Afon-wen *Flints*	70	SJ1371
Afton *Devon*	7	SX8462
Afton *IOW*	12	SZ3486
Afton Bridgend *E Ayrs*	107	NS6213
Agglethorpe *N York*	89	SE0885
Aigburth *Mersyd*	78	SJ3886
Aike *E R Yk*	84	TA0446
Aiketgate *Cumb*	94	NY4846
Aikhead *Cumb*	93	NY2349
Aikton *Cumb*	93	NY2753
Ailby *Lincs*	77	TF4376
Ailey *H & W*	46	SO3348
Ailsworth *Cambs*	64	TL1198
Ainderby Quernhow *N York*	89	SE3480
Ainderby Steeple *N York*	89	SE3392
Aingers Green *Essex*	41	TM1120
Ainsdale *Mersyd*	80	SD3112
Ainsdale-on-Sea *Mersyd*	80	SD2912
Ainstable *Cumb*	94	NY5246
Ainsworth *Gt Man*	79	SD7610
Ainthorpe *N York*	90	NZ7007
Aintree *Mersyd*	78	SJ3898
Ainville *W Loth*	117	NT1063
Aird *Ag & B*	113	NM7600
Aird *D & G*	98	NX0960
Aird *W Isls*	154	NB5635
Aird a Mhulaidh *W Isls*	154	NB1810
Aird Asaig *W Isls*	154	NB1202
Aird of Kinloch *Ag & B*	121	NM5228
Aird of Sleat *Highld*	129	NG5900
Aird Uig *W Isls*	154	NB0533
Airdeny *Ag & B*	122	NM9929
Airdrie *N Lans*	116	NS7565
Airdriehill *N Lans*	116	NS7867
Airds Bay *Ag & B*	122	NM9932
Airds of Kells *D & G*	99	NX6770
Airidh a bhruaich *W Isls*	154	NB2417
Airieland *D & G*	99	NX7556
Airlie *Angus*	126	NO3150
Airmyn *E R Yk*	84	SE7224
Airntully *P & K*	125	NO0935
Airor *Highld*	129	NG7205
Airth *Falk*	116	NS9087
Airton *N York*	88	SD9059
Aisby *Lincs*	76	SK8692
Aisby *Lincs*	64	TF0138
Aisgill *Cumb*	88	SD7797
Aish *Devon*	7	SX6960
Aish *Devon*	7	SX8458
Aisholt *Somset*	20	ST1935
Aiskew *N York*	89	SE2788
Aislaby *Dur*	89	NZ4012
Aislaby *N York*	90	NZ8608
Aislaby *N York*	90	SE7785
Aisthorpe *Lincs*	76	SK9480
Aith *Shet*	155	HU3455
Akeld *Nthumb*	111	NT9529
Akeley *Bucks*	49	SP7037
Akenham *Suffk*	54	TM1449
Albaston *Devon*	6	SX4270
Alberbury *Shrops*	59	SJ3614
Albourne *W Susx*	15	TQ2516
Albourne Green *W Susx*	15	TQ2616
Albrighton *Shrops*	59	SJ4918
Albrighton(Wolverhampton) *Shrops*	60	SJ8004
Alburgh *Norfk*	55	TM2687
Albury *Herts*	39	TL4324
Albury *Oxon*	37	SP6505
Albury *Surrey*	14	TQ0447
Albury End *Herts*	39	TL4223
Albury Heath *Surrey*	14	TQ0646
Alby Hill *Norfk*	67	TG1934
Alcaig *Highld*	139	NH5657
Alcaston *Shrops*	59	SO4587
Alcester *Warwks*	48	SP0857
Alcester Lane End *W Mids*	61	SP0780
Alciston *E Susx*	16	TQ5005
Alcombe *Wilts*	35	ST8169
Alconbury *Cambs*	52	TL1875
Alconbury Weston *Cambs*	52	TL1777
Aldborough *N York*	89	SE4066
Aldborough *Norfk*	66	TG1834
Aldbourne *Wilts*	36	SU2676
Aldbrough *E R Yk*	85	TA2438
Aldbrough St John *N York*	89	NZ2011
Aldbury *Herts*	38	SP9612
Aldcliffe *Lancs*	87	SD4660
Aldclune *P & K*	132	NN8964
Aldeburgh *Suffk*	55	TM4656
Aldeby *Norfk*	67	TM4493
Aldenham *Herts*	26	TQ1498
Alder Moor *Staffs*	73	SK2226
Alderbury *Wilts*	23	SU1827
Aldercar *Derbys*	62	SK4447
Alderford *Norfk*	66	TG1218
Alderholt *Dorset*	12	SU1212
Alderley *Gloucs*	35	ST7690
Alderley Edge *Ches*	79	SJ8478
Aldermans Green *W Mids*	61	SP3683
Aldermaston *Berks*	24	SU5965
Alderminster *Warwks*	48	SP2348
Aldershot *Hants*	25	SU8650
Alderton *Gloucs*	47	SP0033
Alderton *Nhants*	49	SP7446
Alderton *Shrops*	59	SJ4924
Alderton *Suffk*	55	TM3441
Alderton *Wilts*	35	ST8482
Alderwasley *Derbys*	73	SK3053
Aldfield *N York*	89	SE2669
Aldford *Ches*	71	SJ4159
Aldgate *Rutlnd*	63	SK9804
Aldham *Essex*	40	TL9126
Aldham *Suffk*	54	TM0545
Aldingbourne *W Susx*	14	SU9205
Aldingham *Cumb*	86	SD2870
Aldington *H & W*	48	SP0644
Aldington *Kent*	29	TR0736
Aldington Corner *Kent*	29	TR0636
Aldivalloch *Moray*	141	NJ3526
Aldochlay *Ag & B*	115	NS3591
Aldon *Shrops*	46	SO4379
Aldoth *Cumb*	92	NY1448
Aldreth *Cambs*	53	TL4473
Aldridge *W Mids*	61	SK0500
Aldringham *Suffk*	55	TM4461
Aldro *N York*	90	SE8162
Aldsworth *Gloucs*	36	SP1509
Aldsworth *W Susx*	14	SU7608
Aldunie *Moray*	141	NJ3626
Aldwark *Derbys*	74	SK2257
Aldwark *N York*	89	SE4663
Aldwick *W Susx*	14	SZ9198
Aldwincle *Nhants*	51	TL0081
Aldworth *Berks*	37	SU5579
Alexandria *D & Cb*	115	NS3979
Aley *Somset*	20	ST1838
Alfardisworthy *Devon*	18	SS2911
Alfington *Devon*	9	SY1197
Alfold *Surrey*	14	TQ0333
Alfold Bars *W Susx*	14	TQ0333
Alfold Crossways *Surrey*	14	TQ0335
Alford *Abers*	142	NJ5715
Alford *Lincs*	77	TF4575
Alford *Somset*	21	ST6032
Alfreton *Derbys*	74	SK4155
Alfrick *H & W*	47	SO7453
Alfrick Pound *H & W*	47	SO7452
Alfriston *E Susx*	16	TQ5103
Algarkirk *Lincs*	64	TF2935
Alhampton *Somset*	21	ST6234
Alkborough *Lincs*	84	SE8821
Alkerton *Gloucs*	35	SO7705
Alkerton *Oxon*	48	SP3743
Alkham *Kent*	29	TR2542
Alkington *Shrops*	71	SJ5339
Alkmonton *Derbys*	73	SK1838
All Cannings *Wilts*	23	SU0661
All Saints South Elmham *Suffk*	55	TM3482
All Stretton *Shrops*	59	SO4595
Allaleigh *Devon*	7	SX8053
Allanaquoich *Abers*	133	NO1291
Allanbank *N Lans*	116	NS8458
Allanton *Border*	119	NT8654
Allanton *N Lans*	116	NS8457
Allanton *S Lans*	116	NS7454
Allaston *Gloucs*	35	SO6304
Allbrook *Hants*	13	SU4521
Allen End *Warwks*	61	SP1696
Allen's Green *Herts*	39	TL4516
Allendale *Nthumb*	95	NY8355
Allenheads *Nthumb*	95	NY8645
Allensford *Dur*	95	NZ0750
Allensmore *H & W*	46	SO4635
Allenton *Derbys*	62	SK3732
Aller *Devon*	19	SS7625
Aller *Somset*	21	ST4029
Allerby *Cumb*	92	NY0839
Allercombe *Devon*	9	SY0494
Allerford *Somset*	20	SS9046
Allerston *N York*	90	SE8782
Allerthorpe *E R Yk*	84	SE7847
Allerton *Mersyd*	78	SJ3987
Allerton *W York*	82	SE1234
Allerton Bywater *W York*	83	SE4227
Allerton Mauleverer *N York*	89	SE4157
Allesley *W Mids*	61	SP3080
Allestree *Derbys*	62	SK3439
Allet Common *Cnwll*	3	SW7948
Allexton *Leics*	51	SK8100
Allgreave *Ches*	72	SJ9767
Allhallows *Kent*	28	TQ8377
Allhallows-on-Sea *Kent*	40	TQ8478
Alligin Shuas *Highld*	137	NG8357
Allimore Green *Staffs*	72	SJ8519
Allington *Dorset*	10	SY4693
Allington *Kent*	28	TQ7557
Allington *Lincs*	63	SK8540
Allington *Wilts*	35	ST8975
Allington *Wilts*	23	SU0663
Allington *Wilts*	23	SU2039
Allithwaite *Cumb*	87	SD3876
Alloa *Clacks*	116	NS8892
Allonby *Cumb*	92	NY0842
Allostock *Ches*	79	SJ7471
Alloway *S Ayrs*	106	NS3318
Allowenshay *Somset*	10	ST3913
Allscott *Shrops*	59	SJ6113
Allscott *Shrops*	60	SO7396
Alltami *Flints*	70	SJ2665
Alltchaorunn *Highld*	123	NN1951
Alltmawr *Powys*	45	SO0746
Alltwalis *Carmth*	31	SN4431
Alltwen *Neath*	32	SN7303
Alltyblaca *Cardgn*	44	SN5245
Allweston *Dorset*	11	ST6614
Allwood Green *Suffk*	54	TM0472
Almeley *H & W*	46	SO3351
Almeley Wooton *H & W*	46	SO3352
Almer *Dorset*	11	SY9199
Almholme *S York*	83	SE5808
Almington *Staffs*	72	SJ7034
Almodington *W Susx*	14	SZ8297
Almondbank *P & K*	125	NO0625
Almondbury *W York*	82	SE1614
Almondsbury *Gloucs*	34	ST6084
Alne *N York*	90	SE4965
Alnesbourn Priory *Suffk*	55	TM1940
Alness *Highld*	146	NH6569
Alnham *Nthumb*	111	NT9810
Alnmouth *Nthumb*	111	NU2410
Alnwick *Nthumb*	111	NU1813
Alperton *Gt Lon*	26	TQ1883
Alphamstone *Essex*	54	TL8735
Alpheton *Suffk*	54	TL8750
Alphington *Devon*	9	SX9190
Alpington *Norfk*	67	TG2901
Alport *Derbys*	74	SK2264
Alpraham *Ches*	71	SJ5859
Alresford *Essex*	41	TM0621
Alrewas *Staffs*	61	SK1614
Alsager *Ches*	72	SJ7955
Alsagers Bank *Staffs*	72	SJ7948
Alsop en le Dale *Derbys*	73	SK1554
Alston *Cumb*	94	NY7146
Alston *Devon*	10	ST3002
Alston Sutton *Somset*	21	ST4151
Alstone *Gloucs*	47	SO9832
Alstone *Somset*	21	ST3146
Alstone Green *Staffs*	72	SJ8518
Alstonefield *Staffs*	73	SK1355
Alswear *Devon*	19	SS7222
Alt *Gt Man*	79	SD9403
Altandhu *Highld*	144	NB9812
Altarnun *Cnwll*	5	SX2281
Altass *Highld*	146	NC5000
Altcreich *Ag & B*	122	NM6938
Altgaltraig *Ag & B*	114	NS0473
Altham *Lancs*	81	SD7732
Althorne *Essex*	40	TQ9198
Althorpe *Lincs*	84	SE8309
Altnabreac Station *Highld*	150	ND0045
Altnacraig *Ag & B*	122	NM8429
Altnaharra *Highld*	149	NC5635
Altofts *W York*	83	SE3823
Alton *Derbys*	74	SK3664
Alton *Hants*	24	SU7139
Alton *Staffs*	73	SK0741
Alton *Wilts*	23	SU1546
Alton Barnes *Wilts*	23	SU1062
Alton Pancras *Dorset*	11	ST7002
Alton Priors *Wilts*	23	SU1162
Altrincham *Gt Man*	79	SJ7687
Altskeith Hotel *Stirlg*	124	NN4602
Alva *Clacks*	116	NS8897
Alvah *Abers*	142	NJ6760
Alvanley *Ches*	71	SJ4974
Alvaston *Derbys*	62	SK3833
Alvechurch *H & W*	60	SP0272
Alvecote *Warwks*	61	SK2404
Alvediston *Wilts*	22	ST9723
Alveley *Shrops*	60	SO7584
Alverdiscott *Devon*	19	SS5225
Alverstoke *Hants*	13	SZ6098
Alverstone *IOW*	13	SZ5785
Alverthorpe *W York*	82	SE3121
Alverton *Notts*	63	SK7942
Alves *Moray*	141	NJ1362
Alvescot *Oxon*	36	SP2704
Alveston *Gloucs*	35	ST6388
Alveston *Warwks*	48	SP2356
Alvingham *Lincs*	77	TF3691
Alvington *Gloucs*	34	SO6000
Alwalton *Cambs*	64	TL1396
Alwinton *Nthumb*	110	NT9106
Alwoodley *W York*	82	SE2840
Alwoodley Gates *W York*	82	SE3140

Astwith

Barkston

Astwith *Derbys* 75 SK4464
Astwood *Bucks* 38 SP9547
Astwood *H & W* 47 SO9365
Astwood Bank *H & W* 48 SP0462
Aswarby *Lincs* 64 TF0639
Aswardby *Lincs* 77 TF3770
Atch Lench *H & W* 48 SP0350
Atcham *Shrops* 59 SJ5409
Athelhampton *Dorset* 11 SY7694
Athelington *Suffk* 55 TM2171
Athelney *Somset* 21 ST3428
Athelstaneford *E Loth* 118 NT5377
Atherfield Green *IOW* 13 SZ4679
Atherington *Devon* 19 SS5922
Atherington *W Susx* 14 TQ0000
Atherstone *Somset* 10 ST3816
Atherstone *Warwks* 61 SP3097
Atherstone on Stour *Warwks* 48 SP2051
Atherton *Gt Man* 79 SD6703
Atley Hill *N York* 89 NZ2802
Atlow *Derbys* 73 SK2248
Attadale *Highld* 138 NG9238
Attenborough *Notts* 62 SK5034
Atterby *Lincs* 76 SK9792
Attercliffe *S York* 74 SK3788
Atterley *Shrops* 59 SO6397
Atterton *Leics* 61 SP3598
Attleborough *Norfk* 66 TM0495
Attleborough *Warwks* 61 SP3790
Attlebridge *Norfk* 66 TG1216
Attleton Green *Suffk* 53 TL7454
Atwick *E R Yk* 85 TA1850
Atworth *Wilts* 22 ST8565
Auberrow *H & W* 46 SO4947
Aubourn *Lincs* 76 SK9262
Auchedly *Abers* 143 NJ8933
Auchenblae *Abers* 135 NO7279
Auchenbowie *Stirlg* 116 NS7987
Auchencairn *D & G* 92 NX7951
Auchencairn *D & G* 100 NX9884
Auchencairn *N Ayrs* 105 NS0427
Auchencrow *Border* 119 NT8560
Auchendinny *Mdloth* 117 NT2561
Auchengray *S Lans* 117 NS9954
Auchenhalrig *Moray* 141 NJ3761
Auchenheath *S Lans* 108 NS8043
Auchenhessnane *D & G* 100 NX8096
Auchenlochan *Ag & B* 114 NR9772
Auchenmade *N Ayrs* 115 NS3548
Auchenmalg *D & G* 98 NX2352
Auchentibber *S Lans* 116 NS6755
Auchentiber *N Ayrs* 115 NS3647
Auchentroig *Stirlg* 115 NS5493
Auchindrean *Highld* 145 NH1980
Auchininna *Abers* 142 NJ6546
Auchinleck *E Ayrs* 107 NS5521
Auchinloch *N Lans* 116 NS6570
Auchinstarry *N Lans* 116 NS7176
Auchintore *Highld* 130 NN0972
Auchiries *Abers* 143 NK0737
Auchlee *Abers* 135 NO8996
Auchleven *Abers* 142 NJ6224
Auchlochan *S Lans* 107 NS7937
Auchlossan *Abers* 134 NJ5601
Auchlyne *Stirlg* 124 NN5129
Auchmillan *E Ayrs* 107 NS5129
Auchmithie *Angus* 127 NO6743
Auchmuirbridge *Fife* 126 NO2101
Auchnacree *Angus* 134 NO4663
Auchnagatt *Abers* 143 NJ9241
Auchnarrow *Moray* 141 NJ2023
Auchnotteroch *D & G* 98 NW9960
Auchroisk *Moray* 141 NJ3351
Auchronie *Angus* 134 NO4480
Auchterarder *P & K* 125 NN9412
Auchteraw *Highld* 131 NH3507
Auchterblair *Highld* 140 NH9222
Auchtercairn *Highld* 144 NG8077
Auchterderran *Fife* 117 NT2195
Auchterhouse *Angus* 126 NO3337
Auchterless *Abers* 142 NJ7141
Auchtermuchty *Fife* 126 NO2311
Auchterneed *Highld* 139 NH4959
Auchtertool *Fife* 117 NT2190
Auchtertyre *Highld* 138 NG8427
Auchtoo *Stirlg* 124 NN5520
Auckengill *Highld* 151 ND3663
Auckley *S York* 75 SE6400
Audenshaw *Gt Man* 79 SJ9197
Audlem *Ches* 72 SJ6543
Audley *Staffs* 72 SJ7950
Audley End *Essex* 39 TL5337
Audley End *Essex* 54 TL8137
Audley End *Suffk* 54 TL8553
Audmore *Staffs* 72 SJ8321
Audnam *W Mids* 60 SO8986
Aughertree *Cumb* 93 NY2538
Aughton *Lancs* 78 SD3905
Aughton *Lancs* 87 SD5567
Aughton *E R Yk* 84 SE7038
Aughton *S York* 75 SK4586
Aughton *Wilts* 23 SU2356
Aughton Park *Lancs* 78 SD4006
Auldallan *Angus* 134 NO3158
Auldearn *Highld* 140 NH9255
Aulden *H & W* 46 SO4654
Auldgirth *D & G* 100 NX9186
Auldhouse *S Lans* 116 NS6250
Ault a' chruinn *Highld* 138 NG9420
Ault Hucknall *Derbys* 75 SK4665
Aultbea *Highld* 144 NG8789
Aultgrishin *Highld* 144 NG7485
Aultguish Inn *Highld* 145 NH3570
Aultmore *Moray* 142 NJ4053
Aultnagoire *Highld* 139 NH5423
Aultnamain Inn *Highld* 146 NH6681
Aunby *Lincs* 64 TF0214
Aunk *Devon* 9 ST0400
Aunsby *Lincs* 64 TF0438
Aust *Gloucs* 34 ST5788
Austendike *Lincs* 64 TF2821
Austerfield *S York* 75 SK6694
Austerlands *Gt Man* 79 SD9505
Austhorpe *W York* 83 SE3733
Austonley *W York* 82 SE1107
Austrey *Warwks* 61 SK2906
Austwick *N York* 88 SD7668
Authorpe *Lincs* 77 TF3980
Authorpe Row *Lincs* 77 TF5373
Avebury *Wilts* 36 SU1069
Avebury Trusloe *Wilts* 36 SU0969
Aveley *Essex* 27 TQ5680
Avening *Gloucs* 35 ST8898
Averham *Notts* 75 SK7654
Aveton Gifford *Devon* 7 SX6947
Aviemore *Highld* 132 NH8913
Avington *Berks* 23 SU3767
Avoch *Highld* 140 NH7055
Avon *Dorset* 12 SZ1498
Avon Dassett *Warwks* 49 SP4150
Avonbridge *Falk* 116 NS9172
Avonmouth *Bristl* 34 ST5178
Avonwick *Devon* 7 SX7158
Awbridge *Hants* 12 SU3224
Awkley *Gloucs* 34 ST5985
Awliscombe *Devon* 9 ST1301
Awre *Gloucs* 35 SO7008
Awsworth *Notts* 62 SK4844
Axborough *H & W* 60 SO8579
Axbridge *Somset* 21 ST4354
Axford *Hants* 24 SU6043
Axford *Wilts* 36 SU2370
Axminster *Devon* 10 SY2998
Axmouth *Devon* 10 SY2591
Axton *Flints* 70 SJ1080
Aycliffe *Dur* 96 NZ2822
Aydon *Nthumb* 103 NZ0065
Aylburton *Gloucs* 34 SO6101
Ayle *Cumb* 94 NY7149
Aylebridge *Cnwll* 18 SS2103
Aylesbeare *Devon* 9 SY0392
Aylesbury *Bucks* 38 SP8213
Aylesby *Lincs* 85 TA2007
Aylesford *Kent* 28 TQ7359
Aylesham *Kent* 29 TR2452
Aylestone *Leics* 50 SK5700
Aylestone Park *Leics* 50 SK5800
Aylmerton *Norfk* 66 TG1839
Aylsham *Norfk* 67 TG1926
Aylton *Gloucs* 47 SO6537
Aylworth *Gloucs* 36 SP1021
Aymestrey *H & W* 46 SO4265
Aynho *Nhants* 49 SP5133
Ayot Green *Herts* 39 TL2214
Ayot St Lawrence *Herts* 39 TL1916
Ayot St Peter *Herts* 39 TL2115
Ayr *S Ayrs* 106 NS3321
Aysgarth *N York* 88 SE0088
Ayshford *Devon* 9 ST0415
Ayside *Cumb* 87 SD3983
Ayston *Rutlnd* 51 SK8600
Aythorpe Roding *Essex* 40 TL5815
Ayton *Border* 119 NT9260
Azerley *N York* 89 SE2574

B

Babbacombe *Devon* 7 SX9265
Babbington *Notts* 62 SK4943
Babbinswood *Shrops* 59 SJ3329
Babbs Green *Herts* 39 TL3916
Babcary *Somset* 21 ST5628
Babel *Carmth* 44 SN8235
Babel Green *Suffk* 53 TL7348
Babell *Flints* 70 SJ1573
Babeny *Devon* 7 SX6775
Babington *Somset* 22 ST7051
Bablock Hythe *Oxon* 36 SP4304
Babraham *Cambs* 53 TL5150
Babworth *Notts* 75 SK6880
Bachau *Angles* 68 SH4383
Bache *Shrops* 59 SO4681
Bacheldre *Powys* 58 SO2492
Bachelor's Bump *E Susx* 17 TQ8412
Back o' th' Brook *Staffs* 73 SK0751
Back of Keppoch *Highld* 129 NM6587
Back Street *Suffk* 53 TL7458
Backaland *Ork* 155 HY5630
Backbarrow *Cumb* 87 SD3584
Backe *Carmth* 31 SN2615
Backfolds *Abers* 143 NK0252
Backford *Ches* 71 SJ3971
Backford Cross *Ches* 71 SJ3873
Backies *Highld* 147 NC8302
Backlass *Highld* 151 ND2053
Backwell *Somset* 21 ST4968
Backworth *T & W* 103 NZ3072
Bacon's End *W Mids* 61 SP1888
Baconsthorpe *Norfk* 66 TG1236
Bacton *H & W* 46 SO3732
Bacton *Norfk* 67 TG3433
Bacton *Suffk* 54 TM0567
Bacton Green *Suffk* 54 TM0365
Bacup *Lancs* 81 SD8622
Badachro *Highld* 137 NG7873
Badbury *Wilts* 36 SU1980
Badby *Nhants* 49 SP5658
Badcall *Highld* 148 NC1541
Badcall *Highld* 148 NC2455
Badcaul *Highld* 144 NH0291
Baddeley Edge *Staffs* 72 SJ9150
Baddeley Green *Staffs* 72 SJ9151
Baddesley Clinton *Warwks* 61 SP2070
Baddesley Ensor *Warwks* 61 SP2798
Baddidarroch *Highld* 145 NC0822
Baddinsgill *Border* 117 NT1254
Badenscoth *Abers* 142 NJ6938
Badenyon *Abers* 141 NJ3319
Badgall *Cnwll* 5 SX2486
Badgeney *Cambs* 65 TL4397
Badger *Shrops* 60 SO7699
Badger's Cross *Cnwll* 2 SW4833
Badgers Mount *Kent* 27 TQ4962
Badgeworth *Gloucs* 35 SO9019
Badgworth *Somset* 21 ST3952
Badharlick *Cnwll* 5 SX2686
Badicaul *Highld* 137 NG7529
Badingham *Suffk* 55 TM3068
Badlesmere *Kent* 28 TR0153
Badlieu *Border* 108 NT0518
Badlipster *Highld* 151 ND2448
Badluachrach *Highld* 144 NG9994
Badninish *Highld* 147 NH7594
Badrallach *Highld* 145 NH0691
Badsey *H & W* 48 SP0743
Badshot Lea *Surrey* 25 SU8648
Badsworth *W York* 83 SE4614
Badwell Ash *Suffk* 54 TL9868
Badwell Green *Suffk* 54 TM0169
Bag Enderby *Lincs* 77 TF3571
Bagber *Dorset* 11 ST7513
Bagby *N York* 89 SE4680
Bagendon *Gloucs* 35 SP0106
Bagginswood *Shrops* 60 SO6881
Baggrow *Cumb* 93 NY1741
Bagh a Chaisteil *W Isls* 154 NL6698
Bagham *Kent* 29 TR0753
Bagillt *Flints* 70 SJ2175
Baginton *Warwks* 61 SP3474
Baglan *Neath* 32 SS7492
Bagley *Shrops* 59 SJ4027
Bagley *Somset* 21 ST4645
Bagley *W York* 82 SE2235
Bagmore *Hants* 24 SU6544
Bagnall *Staffs* 72 SJ9250
Bagnor *Berks* 24 SU4569
Bagot *Shrops* 46 SO5873
Bagshot *Surrey* 25 SU9063
Bagshot *Wilts* 23 SU3165
Bagstone *Gloucs* 35 ST6987
Bagthorpe *Notts* 75 SK4651
Bagworth *Leics* 62 SK4408
Bagwy Llydiart *H & W* 46 SO4426
Baildon *W York* 82 SE1539
Baildon Green *W York* 82 SE1439
Baile a Mhanaich *W Isls* 154 NF7755
Baile Ailein *W Isls* 154 NB2920
Baile Mor *Ag & B* 120 NM2824
Bailey Green *Hants* 13 SU6627
Baileyhead *Cumb* 101 NY5179
Bailiff Bridge *W York* 82 SE1425
Baillieston *C Glas* 116 NS6764
Bailrigg *Lancs* 87 SD4858
Bainbridge *N York* 88 SD9390
Bainshole *Abers* 142 NJ6035
Bainton *Cambs* 64 TF0906
Bainton *E R Yk* 84 SE9652
Bainton *Oxon* 49 SP5827
Baintown *Fife* 126 NO3503
Bairnkine *Border* 110 NT6515
Baker Street *Essex* 40 TQ6381
Baker's End *Herts* 39 TL3917
Bakewell *Derbys* 74 SK2168
Bala *Gwynd* 58 SH9235
Balallan *W Isls* 154 NB2920
Balbeg *Highld* 139 NH4431
Balbeggie *P & K* 126 NO1629
Balblair *Highld* 139 NH5145
Balblair *Highld* 140 NH7066
Balby *S York* 75 SE5600
Balcary *D & G* 92 NX8149
Balchraggan *Highld* 139 NH5343
Balchrick *Highld* 148 NC1960
Balcombe *W Susx* 15 TQ3130
Balcombe Lane *W Susx* 15 TQ3132
Balcomie Links *Fife* 127 NO6209
Baldersby *N York* 89 SE3578
Baldersby St James *N York* 89 SE3676
Balderstone *Gt Man* 79 SD9010
Balderstone *Lancs* 81 SD6332
Balderton *Notts* 75 SK8151
Baldhu *Cnwll* 3 SW7743
Baldinnie *Fife* 127 NO4211
Baldinnies *P & K* 125 NO0216
Baldock *Herts* 39 TL2434
Baldovie *Dund C* 127 NO4533
Baldrine *IOM* 153 SC4281
Baldslow *E Susx* 17 TQ8013
Baldwin *IOM* 153 SC3581
Baldwin's Gate *Staffs* 72 SJ7939
Baldwin's Hill *Surrey* 15 TQ3839
Baldwinholme *Cumb* 93 NY3351
Bale *Norfk* 66 TG0136
Baledgarno *P & K* 126 NO2730
Balemartine *Ag & B* 120 NL9841
Balerno *C Edin* 117 NT1666
Balfarg *Fife* 126 NO2803
Balfield *Angus* 134 NO5468
Balfour *Ork* 155 HY4716
Balfron *Stirlg* 115 NS5489
Balgaveny *Abers* 142 NJ6540
Balgavies *Angus* 127 NO5451
Balgonar *Fife* 117 NT0293
Balgowan *D & G* 98 NX1142
Balgowan *Highld* 132 NN6494
Balgown *Highld* 136 NG3868
Balgracie *D & G* 98 NW9860
Balgray *Angus* 126 NO4038
Balgray *S Lans* 108 NS8824
Balham *Gt Lon* 27 TQ2873
Balhary *P & K* 126 NO2646
Balholmie *P & K* 126 NO1436
Baligill *Highld* 150 NC8565
Balintore *Angus* 133 NO2859
Balintore *Highld* 147 NH8675
Balintraid *Highld* 146 NH7370
Balivanich *W Isls* 154 NF7755
Balk *N York* 89 SE4780
Balkeerie *Angus* 126 NO3244
Balkholme *E R Yk* 84 SE7828
Ball *Shrops* 59 SJ3026
Ball Green *Staffs* 72 SJ8952
Ball Haye Green *Staffs* 72 SJ9856
Ball Hill *Hants* 24 SU4163
Ball's Green *Gloucs* 35 ST8699
Ballabeg *IOM* 153 SC2570
Ballachulish *Highld* 130 NN0858
Ballafesson *IOM* 153 SC2070
Ballakilpheric *IOM* 153 SC2271
Ballamodha *IOM* 153 SC2773
Ballanlay *Ag & B* 114 NS0462
Ballantrae *S Ayrs* 98 NX0882
Ballards Gore *Essex* 40 TQ9092
Ballards Green *Warwks* 61 SP2791
Ballasalla *IOM* 153 SC2870
Ballater *Abers* 134 NO3695
Ballaugh *IOM* 153 SC3493
Ballchraggan *Highld* 147 NH7675
Ballechin *P & K* 125 NN9353
Ballencrieff *E Loth* 118 NT4878
Ballevullin *Ag & B* 120 NL9546
Ballidon *Derbys* 73 SK2054
Balliekine *N Ayrs* 105 NR8739
Balliemore *Ag & B* 114 NS1099
Balligmorrie *S Ayrs* 106 NX2290
Ballimore *Ag & B* 114 NR9283
Ballimore *Stirlg* 124 NN5317
Ballindalloch *Moray* 141 NJ1636
Ballindean *P & K* 126 NO2529
Ballingdon *Essex* 54 TL8640
Ballinger Common *Bucks* 38 SP9103
Ballingham *H & W* 46 SO5731
Ballingry *Fife* 117 NT1797
Ballinluig *P & K* 125 NN9752
Ballinshoe *Angus* 126 NO4153
Ballintuim *P & K* 126 NO1055
Balloch *D & Cb* 115 NS3982
Balloch *Highld* 140 NH7247
Balloch *N Lans* 116 NS7374
Balloch *P & K* 125 NN8419
Balloch *S Ayrs* 106 NX3295
Ballochroy *Ag & B* 113 NR7352
Ballogie *Abers* 134 NO5795
Balls Cross *W Susx* 14 SU9826
Balls Green *E Susx* 16 TQ4936
Ballygown *Ag & B* 121 NM4343
Ballygrant *Ag & B* 112 NR3966
Ballyhaugh *Ag & B* 120 NM1758
Ballymenoch *Ag & B* 115 NS3086
Ballymichael *N Ayrs* 105 NR9231
Balmacara *Highld* 137 NG8028
Balmaclellan *D & G* 99 NX6579
Balmae *D & G* 99 NX6844
Balmaha *Stirlg* 115 NS4290
Balmalcolm *Fife* 126 NO3208
Balmangan *D & G* 99 NX6445
Balmedie *Abers* 143 NJ9618
Balmer Heath *Shrops* 59 SJ4434
Balmerino *Fife* 126 NO3524
Balmerlawn *Hants* 12 SU3003
Balmore *E Duns* 115 NS5973
Balmuchy *Highld* 147 NH8678
Balmuir *Angus* 127 NO5648
Balmule *Fife* 117 NT2088
Balmullo *Fife* 127 NO4220
Balnacoil Lodge *Highld* 147 NC8011
Balnacroft *Abers* 133 NO2894
Balnafoich *Highld* 140 NH6835
Balnaguard *P & K* 125 NN9451
Balnahard *Ag & B* 121 NM4534
Balnahard *Ag & B* 112 NR4199
Balnain *Highld* 139 NH4430
Balnakeil *Highld* 149 NC3968
Balnapaling *Highld* 147 NH7969
Balne *N York* 83 SE5918
Balquharn *P & K* 125 NO0235
Balquhidder *Stirlg* 124 NN5320
Balsall Common *W Mids* 61 SP2376
Balsall Heath *W Mids* 61 SP0784
Balsall Street *W Mids* 61 SP2276
Balscote *Oxon* 48 SP3942
Balsham *Cambs* 53 TL5850
Baltasound *Shet* 155 HP6208
Balterley *Staffs* 72 SJ7650
Balterley Green *Staffs* 72 SJ7650
Baltersan *D & G* 99 NX4261
Baltonsborough *Somset* 21 ST5434
Balvarran *P & K* 133 NO0761
Balvicar *Ag & B* 122 NM7616
Balvraid *Highld* 129 NG8416
Balvraid *Highld* 140 NH8231
Balwest *Cnwll* 2 SW5930
Bamber Bridge *Lancs* 81 SD5625
Bamber's Green *Essex* 40 TL5722
Bamburgh *Nthumb* 111 NU1734
Bamff *P & K* 126 NO2251
Bamford *Derbys* 74 SK2083
Bamford *Gt Man* 81 SD8612
Bampton *Cumb* 94 NY5118
Bampton *Devon* 20 SS9522
Bampton *Oxon* 36 SP3103
Bampton Grange *Cumb* 94 NY5218
Banavie *Highld* 130 NN1177
Banbury *Oxon* 49 SP4540
Banc-y-ffordd *Carmth* 31 SN4037
Bancffosfelem *Carmth* 32 SN4811
Banchory *Abers* 135 NO6995
Banchory-Devenick *Abers* 135 NJ9002
Bancycapel *Carmth* 31 SN4214
Bancyfelin *Carmth* 31 SN3218
Bandirran *P & K* 126 NO2030
Bandrake Head *Cumb* 86 SD3187
Banff *Abers* 142 NJ6863
Bangor *Gwynd* 69 SH5772
Bangor's Green *Lancs* 78 SD3709
Bangor-is-y-coed *Wrexhm* 71 SJ3845
Bangors *Cnwll* 18 SX2099
Bangrove *Suffk* 54 TL9372
Banham *Norfk* 54 TM0687
Bank *Hants* 12 SU2807
Bank Ground *Cumb* 86 SD3196
Bank Newton *N York* 81 SD9053
Bank Street *H & W* 47 SO6362
Bank Top *Lancs* 78 SD5207
Bank Top *W York* 82 SE1024
Bankend *D & G* 100 NY0268
Bankfoot *P & K* 125 NO0635
Bankglen *E Ayrs* 107 NS5912
Bankhead *Aber C* 135 NJ9009
Bankhead *N Ayrs* 106 NS3739
Bankhead *S Lans* 116 NS9844
Banknock *Falk* 116 NS7779
Banks *Cumb* 101 NY5664
Banks *Lancs* 80 SD3920
Banks Green *H & W* 47 SO9967
Bankshill *D & G* 101 NY1982
Banningham *Norfk* 67 TG2129
Bannister Green *Essex* 40 TL6920
Bannockburn *Stirlg* 116 NS8190
Banstead *Surrey* 27 TQ2559
Bantham *Devon* 7 SX6643
Banton *N Lans* 116 NS7480
Banwell *Somset* 21 ST3959
Bapchild *Kent* 28 TQ9263
Bapton *Wilts* 22 ST9938
Bar Hill *Cambs* 52 TL3863
Barabhas *W Isls* 154 NB3649
Barassie *S Ayrs* 106 NS3232
Barbaraville *Highld* 146 NH7472
Barber Booth *Derbys* 74 SK1184
Barber Green *Cumb* 87 SD3982
Barbieston *S Ayrs* 107 NS4317
Barbon *Cumb* 87 SD6282
Barbridge *Ches* 71 SJ6156
Barbrook *Devon* 19 SS7147
Barby *Nhants* 50 SP5470
Barcaldine *Ag & B* 122 NM9641
Barcheston *Warwks* 48 SP2639
Barclose *Cumb* 101 NY4462
Barcombe *E Susx* 15 TQ4114
Barcombe Cross *E Susx* 15 TQ4115
Barcroft *W York* 82 SE0437
Barden *N York* 89 SE1493
Barden Park *Kent* 16 TQ5746
Bardfield End Green *Essex* 40 TL6231
Bardfield Saling *Essex* 40 TL6826
Bardney *Lincs* 76 TF1269
Bardon *Leics* 62 SK4412
Bardon Mill *Nthumb* 102 NY7764
Bardowie *E Duns* 115 NS5873
Bardown *E Susx* 16 TQ6629
Bardrainney *Inver* 115 NS3373
Bardsea *Cumb* 86 SD3074
Bardsey *W York* 83 SE3643
Bardsley *Gt Man* 79 SD9201
Bardwell *Suffk* 54 TL9473
Bare *Lancs* 87 SD4564
Bareppa *Cnwll* 3 SW7729
Barewood *H & W* 46 SO3856
Barfad *D & G* 98 NX3266
Barford *Norfk* 66 TG1107
Barford *Warwks* 48 SP2760
Barford St John *Oxon* 49 SP4433
Barford St Martin *Wilts* 23 SU0531
Barford St Michael *Oxon* 49 SP4332
Barfrestone *Kent* 29 TR2650
Bargate *Derbys* 62 SK3546
Bargeddie *N Lans* 116 NS6964
Bargoed *Caerph* 33 ST1599
Bargrennan *D & G* 98 NX3577
Barham *Cambs* 52 TL1375
Barham *Kent* 29 TR2050
Barham *Suffk* 54 TM1451
Barholm *Lincs* 64 TF0810
Barkby *Leics* 63 SK6309
Barkby Thorpe *Leics* 63 SK6309
Barkers Green *Shrops* 59 SJ5228
Barkestone-le-Vale *Leics* 63 SK7734
Barkham *Berks* 25 SU7766
Barking *Gt Lon* 27 TQ4484
Barking *Suffk* 54 TM0753
Barking Tye *Suffk* 54 TM0652
Barkingside *Gt Lon* 27 TQ4489
Barkisland *W York* 82 SE0519
Barkla Shop *Cnwll* 3 SW7350
Barkston *Lincs* 63 SK9341

Berkley
Blanefield

Berkley *Somset*	22	ST8049
Berkswell *W Mids*	61	SP2479
Bermondsey *Gt Lon*	27	TQ3479
Bernera *Highld*	129	NG8020
Bernice *Ag & B*	114	NS1391
Bernisdale *Highld*	136	NG4050
Berrick Prior *Oxon*	37	SU6294
Berrick Salome *Oxon*	37	SU6293
Berriedale *Highld*	147	ND1222
Berrier *Cumb*	93	NY3929
Berriew *Powys*	58	SJ1801
Berrington *H & W*	46	SO5767
Berrington *Nthumb*	111	NU0043
Berrington *Shrops*	59	SJ5206
Berrington Green *H & W*	46	SO5766
Berrow *H & W*	47	SO7934
Berrow *Somset*	20	ST2951
Berrow Green *H & W*	47	SO7458
Berry Brow *W York*	82	SE1314
Berry Cross *Devon*	18	SS4714
Berry Down Cross *Devon*	19	SS5743
Berry Hill *Gloucs*	34	SO5712
Berry Hill *Pembks*	30	SN0640
Berry Pomeroy *Devon*	7	SX8261
Berry's Green *Gt Lon*	27	TQ4359
Berryhillock *Moray*	142	NJ5054
Berryhillock *Moray*	142	NJ5060
Berrynarbor *Devon*	19	SS5646
Bersham *Wrexhm*	71	SJ3049
Berthengam *Flints*	70	SJ1179
Berwick *E Susx*	16	TQ5105
Berwick Bassett *Wilts*	36	SU0973
Berwick Hill *Nthumb*	103	NZ1775
Berwick St James *Wilts*	23	SU0739
Berwick St John *Wilts*	22	ST9422
Berwick St Leonard *Wilts*	22	ST9233
Berwick-upon-Tweed *Nthumb*	119	NT9953
Bescaby *Leics*	63	SK8126
Bescar *Cumb*	80	SD3913
Besford *H & W*	47	SO9144
Besford *Shrops*	59	SJ5525
Besom Hill *Gt Man*	79	SD9508
Bessacarr *S York*	75	SE6100
Bessels Leigh *Oxon*	37	SP4501
Besses o' th' Barn *Gt Man*	79	SD8005
Bessingby *E R Yk*	91	TA1566
Bessingham *Norfk*	66	TG1636
Bestbeech Hill *E Susx*	16	TQ6231
Besthorpe *Norfk*	66	TM0595
Besthorpe *Notts*	75	SK8264
Beswick *E R Yk*	84	TA0147
Betchcott *Shrops*	59	SO4398
Betchworth *Surrey*	26	TQ2150
Bethania *Cardgn*	43	SN5763
Bethania *Gwynd*	57	SH7044
Bethel *Angles*	68	SH3970
Bethel *Gwynd*	68	SH5265
Bethel *Gwynd*	70	SH9839
Bethel *Powys*	58	SJ1021
Bethersden *Kent*	28	TQ9240
Bethesda *Gwynd*	69	SH6266
Bethesda *Pembks*	31	SN0918
Bethlehem *Carmth*	44	SN6825
Bethnal Green *Gt Lon*	27	TQ3482
Betley *Staffs*	72	SJ7548
Betsham *Kent*	27	TQ6071
Betteshanger *Kent*	29	TR3152
Bettiscombe *Dorset*	10	ST3900
Bettisfield *Wrexhm*	59	SJ4635
Betton *Shrops*	72	SJ6936
Betton Strange *Shrops*	59	SJ5009
Bettws *Newpt*	34	ST2890
Bettws Bledrws *Cardgn*	44	SN5952
Bettws Cedewain *Powys*	58	SO1296
Bettws Evan *Cardgn*	42	SN3047
Bettws-Newydd *Mons*	34	SO3606
Bettyhill *Highld*	150	NC7061
Betws *Brdgnd*	33	SS9086
Betws *Carmth*	32	SN6311
Betws Garmon *Gwynd*	69	SH5357
Betws Gwerfil Goch *Denbgs*	70	SJ0346
Betws-y-coed *A & C*	69	SH7956
Betws-yn-Rhos *A & C*	69	SH9073
Beulah *Cardgn*	42	SN2846
Beulah *Powys*	45	SN9251
Bevendean *E Susx*	15	TQ3306
Bevercotes *Notts*	75	SK6972
Beverley *E R Yk*	84	TA0339
Beverstone *Gloucs*	35	ST8694
Bevington *Gloucs*	35	ST6596
Bewaldeth *Cumb*	93	NY2034
Bewcastle *Cumb*	101	NY5674
Bewdley *H & W*	60	SO7875
Bewerley *N York*	89	SE1565
Bewholme *E R Yk*	85	TA1649
Bewlbridge *Kent*	16	TQ6834
Bexhill *E Susx*	17	TQ7407
Bexley *Gt Lon*	27	TQ4973
Bexleyheath *Gt Lon*	27	TQ4875
Bexleyhill *W Susx*	14	SU9125
Bexon *Kent*	28	TQ8959
Bexwell *Norfk*	65	TF6303
Beyton *Suffk*	54	TL9363
Beyton Green *Suffk*	54	TL9363
Bhaltos *W Isls*	154	NB0936
Bibstone *Gloucs*	35	ST6991
Bibury *Gloucs*	36	SP1106
Bicester *Oxon*	49	SP5823
Bickenhill *W Mids*	61	SP1882
Bicker *Lincs*	64	TF2237
Bicker Bar *Lincs*	64	TF2438
Bicker Gauntlet *Lincs*	64	TF2139
Bickershaw *Gt Man*	79	SD6201
Bickerstaffe *Lancs*	78	SD4404
Bickerton *Ches*	71	SJ5052
Bickerton *Devon*	7	SX8139
Bickerton *N York*	83	SE4550
Bickerton *Nthumb*	103	NT9900
Bickford *Staffs*	60	SJ8814
Bickington *Devon*	19	SS5332
Bickington *Devon*	7	SX8072
Bickleigh *Devon*	9	SS9407
Bickleigh *Devon*	6	SX5262
Bickleton *Devon*	19	SS5030
Bickley *Ches*	71	SJ5348
Bickley *Gt Lon*	27	TQ4268
Bickley *H & W*	47	SO6371
Bickley *N York*	91	SE9191
Bickley Moss *Ches*	71	SJ5448
Bicknacre *Essex*	40	TL7802
Bicknoller *Somset*	20	ST1139
Bicknor *Kent*	28	TQ8658
Bickton *Hants*	12	SU1412
Bicton *H & W*	46	SO4764
Bicton *Shrops*	59	SJ4415
Bicton *Shrops*	59	SO2983
Bidborough *Kent*	16	TQ5643
Bidden *Hants*	24	SU7049
Biddenden *Kent*	28	TQ8538
Biddenden Green *Kent*	28	TQ8842
Biddenham *Beds*	38	TL0250
Biddestone *Wilts*	35	ST8673
Biddisham *Somset*	21	ST3853
Biddlesden *Bucks*	49	SP6340
Biddlestone *Nthumb*	111	NT9508
Biddulph *Staffs*	72	SJ8858
Biddulph Moor *Staffs*	72	SJ9058
Bideford *Devon*	18	SS4526
Bidford-on-Avon *Warwks*	48	SP1052
Bidston *Mersyd*	78	SJ2890
Bielby *E R Yk*	84	SE7843
Bieldside *Aber C*	135	NJ8702
Bierley *IOW*	13	SZ5078
Bierton *Bucks*	38	SP8415
Big Balcraig *D & G*	99	NX3843
Big Carlae *D & G*	107	NX6597
Big Sand *Highld*	144	NG7578
Bigbury *Devon*	7	SX6646
Bigbury-on-Sea *Devon*	7	SX6544
Bigby *Lincs*	84	TA0507
Biggar *Cumb*	86	SD1966
Biggar *S Lans*	108	NT0437
Biggin *Derbys*	74	SK1559
Biggin *Derbys*	73	SK2549
Biggin *N York*	83	SE5434
Biggin Hill *Gt Lon*	27	TQ4159
Biggleswade *Beds*	39	TL1944
Bigholms *D & G*	101	NY3180
Bighouse *Highld*	150	NC8964
Bighton *Hants*	24	SU6134
Bigland Hall *Cumb*	87	SD3583
Biglands *Cumb*	93	NY2553
Bignor *W Susx*	14	SU9814
Bigrigg *Cumb*	92	NY0013
Bilborough *Notts*	62	SK5241
Bilbrook *Somset*	20	ST0341
Bilbrook *Staffs*	60	SJ8703
Bilbrough *N York*	83	SE5346
Bilbster *Highld*	151	ND2853
Bildershaw *Dur*	96	NZ2024
Bildeston *Suffk*	54	TL9949
Billacott *Cnwll*	5	SX2690
Billericay *Essex*	40	TQ6794
Billesdon *Leics*	63	SK7202
Billesley *Warwks*	48	SP1456
Billingborough *Lincs*	64	TF1133
Billinge *Mersyd*	78	SD5200
Billingford *Norfk*	66	TG0120
Billingford *Norfk*	54	TM1678
Billingham *Dur*	97	NZ4624
Billinghay *Lincs*	76	TF1554
Billingley *S York*	83	SE4304
Billingshurst *W Susx*	14	TQ0825
Billingsley *Shrops*	60	SO7085
Billington *Beds*	38	SP9422
Billington *Lancs*	81	SD7235
Billington *Staffs*	72	SJ8820
Billockby *Norfk*	67	TG4313
Billy Row *Dur*	96	NZ1637
Bilsborrow *Lancs*	80	SD5139
Bilsby *Lincs*	77	TF4776
Bilsham *W Susx*	14	SU9702
Bilsington *Kent*	17	TR0434
Bilsthorpe *Notts*	75	SK6460
Bilsthorpe Moor *Notts*	75	SK6560
Bilston *Mdloth*	117	NT2664
Bilston *W Mids*	60	SO9596
Bilstone *Leics*	62	SK3605
Bilting *Kent*	28	TR0549
Bilton *E R Yk*	85	TA1632
Bilton *N York*	83	SE4749
Bilton *N York*	89	SE3157
Bilton *Nthumb*	111	NU2210
Bilton *Warwks*	50	SP4873
Bilton Banks *Nthumb*	111	NU2010
Binbrook *Lincs*	76	TF2093
Binchester Blocks *Dur*	96	NZ2232
Bincombe *Dorset*	11	SY6884
Binegar *Somset*	21	ST6149
Bines Green *W Susx*	15	TQ1817
Binfield *Berks*	25	SU8471
Binfield Heath *Oxon*	37	SU7477
Bingfield *Nthumb*	102	NY9772
Bingham *Notts*	63	SK7039
Bingham's Melcombe *Dorset*	11	ST7702
Bingley *W York*	82	SE1039
Bings *Shrops*	59	SJ5318
Binham *Norfk*	66	TF9839
Binley *Hants*	24	SU4253
Binley *W Mids*	61	SP3778
Binnegar *Dorset*	11	SY8887
Binniehill *Falk*	116	NS8572
Binns Farm *Moray*	141	NJ3164
Binscombe *Surrey*	25	SU9645
Binsey *Oxon*	37	SP4907
Binstead *Hants*	25	SU7740
Binstead *IOW*	13	SZ5892
Binsted *W Susx*	14	SU9806
Binton *Warwks*	48	SP1454
Bintree *Norfk*	66	TG0123
Binweston *Shrops*	59	SJ3004
Birch *Essex*	40	TL9419
Birch *Gt Man*	79	SD8507
Birch Close *Dorset*	11	ST8803
Birch Cross *Staffs*	73	SK1230
Birch Green *Essex*	40	TL9418
Birch Green *H & W*	47	SO8645
Birch Green *Herts*	39	TL2911
Birch Heath *Ches*	71	SJ5461
Birch Hill *Ches*	71	SJ5173
Birch Vale *Derbys*	74	SK0286
Birch Wood *Somset*	9	ST2414
Bircham Newton *Norfk*	65	TF7733
Bircham Tofts *Norfk*	65	TF7732
Birchanger *Essex*	39	TL5122
Birchburn *N Ayrs*	105	NR9129
Birchencliffe *W York*	82	SE1218
Bircher *H & W*	46	SO4765
Birchfield *W Mids*	61	SP0790
Birchgrove *Cardif*	33	ST1679
Birchgrove *E Susx*	15	TQ4029
Birchgrove *Swans*	32	SS7098
Birchington *Kent*	29	TR3069
Birchley Heath *Warwks*	61	SP2894
Birchmoor Green *Beds*	38	SP9534
Birchover *Derbys*	74	SK2362
Birchyfield *H & W*	47	SO6453
Bircotes *Notts*	75	SK6391
Bird End *W Mids*	60	SP0194
Bird Street *Suffk*	54	TM0052
Birdbrook *Essex*	53	TL7041
Birdforth *N York*	90	SE4875
Birdham *W Susx*	14	SU8200
Birdingbury *Warwks*	50	SP4368
Birdlip *Gloucs*	35	SO9214
Birdoswald *Cumb*	102	NY6166
Birds Edge *W York*	82	SE2007
Birds Green *Essex*	40	TL5808
Birdsall *N York*	90	SE8165
Birdsgreen *Shrops*	60	SO7785
Birdsmoorgate *Dorset*	10	ST3900
Birdwell *S York*	83	SE3401
Birdwood *Gloucs*	35	SO7418
Birgham *Border*	110	NT7939
Birichin *Highld*	147	NH7592
Birkacre *Lancs*	81	SD5714
Birkby *N York*	89	NZ3202
Birkdale *Mersyd*	80	SD3214
Birkenbog *Abers*	142	NJ5365
Birkenhead *Mersyd*	78	SJ3288
Birkenhills *Abers*	142	NJ7445
Birkenshaw *W York*	82	SE2028
Birkhall *Abers*	134	NO3493
Birkhill *Angus*	126	NO3534
Birkhill *D & G*	109	NT2015
Birkholme *Lincs*	63	SK9623
Birkin *N York*	83	SE5326
Birks *W York*	82	SE2626
Birkshaw *Nthumb*	102	NY7765
Birley *H & W*	46	SO4553
Birley Carr *S York*	74	SK3392
Birling *Kent*	28	TQ6860
Birling *Nthumb*	111	NU2406
Birling Gap *E Susx*	16	TV5596
Birlingham *H & W*	47	SO9343
Birmingham *W Mids*	61	SP0786
Birnam *P & K*	125	NO0341
Birness *Abers*	143	NJ9933
Birse *Abers*	134	NO5697
Birsemore *Abers*	134	NO5297
Birstall *Leics*	62	SK5909
Birstall *W York*	82	SE2225
Birstwith *N York*	89	SE2359
Birthorpe *Lincs*	64	TF1033
Birtley *H & W*	46	SO3669
Birtley *Nthumb*	102	NY8778
Birtley *T & W*	96	NZ2756
Birts Street *H & W*	47	SO7836
Bisbrooke *Rutlnd*	51	SP8899
Biscathorpe *Lincs*	76	TF2284
Biscovey *Cnwll*	3	SX0552
Bish Mill *Devon*	19	SS7425
Bisham *Berks*	26	SU8485
Bishampton *H & W*	47	SO9951
Bishop Auckland *Dur*	96	NZ2028
Bishop Burton *E R Yk*	84	SE9839
Bishop Middleham *Dur*	96	NZ3231
Bishop Monkton *N York*	89	SE3266
Bishop Norton *Lincs*	76	SK9892
Bishop Sutton *Somset*	21	ST5859
Bishop Thornton *N York*	89	SE2563
Bishop Wilton *E R Yk*	84	SE7955
Bishop's Castle *Shrops*	59	SO3288
Bishop's Cleeve *Gloucs*	47	SO9627
Bishop's Frome *H & W*	47	SO6648
Bishop's Green *Essex*	40	TL6217
Bishop's Green *Hants*	24	SU5063
Bishop's Itchington *Warwks*	48	SP3857
Bishop's Norton *Gloucs*	47	SO8424
Bishop's Nympton *Devon*	19	SS7523
Bishop's Offley *Staffs*	72	SJ7729
Bishop's Stortford *Herts*	39	TL4821
Bishop's Sutton *Hants*	24	SU6032
Bishop's Tachbrook *Warwks*	48	SP3161
Bishop's Tawton *Devon*	19	SS5729
Bishop's Waltham *Hants*	13	SU5517
Bishop's Wood *Staffs*	60	SJ8309
Bishop`s Caundle *Dorset*	11	ST6913
Bishopbridge *Lincs*	76	TF0391
Bishopbriggs *E Duns*	116	NS6070
Bishopmill *Moray*	141	NJ2163
Bishops Cannings *Wilts*	23	SU0364
Bishops Gate *Surrey*	25	SU9871
Bishops Hull *Somset*	20	ST2024
Bishops Lydeard *Somset*	20	ST1729
Bishopsbourne *Kent*	29	TR1852
Bishopsteignton *Devon*	7	SX9073
Bishopstoke *Hants*	13	SU4619
Bishopston *Swans*	32	SS5789
Bishopstone *Bucks*	38	SP8010
Bishopstone *E Susx*	16	TQ4701
Bishopstone *H & W*	46	SO4143
Bishopstone *Kent*	26	TQ2068
Bishopstone *Wilts*	23	SU0625
Bishopstone *Wilts*	36	SU2483
Bishopstrow *Wilts*	22	ST8943
Bishopswood *Somset*	10	ST2612
Bishopsworth *Bristl*	21	ST5768
Bishopthorpe *N York*	83	SE5947
Bishopton *Dur*	96	NZ3621
Bishopton *Rens*	115	NS4371
Bishopton *Warwks*	48	SP1956
Bishton *Newpt*	34	ST3887
Bishton *Staffs*	73	SK0220
Bisley *Gloucs*	35	SO9005
Bisley *Surrey*	25	SU9559
Bisley Camp *Surrey*	25	SU9357
Bispham *Lancs*	80	SD3140
Bispham Green *Lancs*	80	SD4813
Bissoe *Cnwll*	3	SW7741
Bisterne *Hants*	12	SU1401
Bitchet Green *Kent*	27	TQ5654
Bitchfield *Lincs*	63	SK9828
Bittadon *Devon*	19	SS5441
Bittaford *Devon*	7	SX6656
Bittering *Norfk*	66	TF9417
Bitterley *Shrops*	46	SO5677
Bitterne *Hants*	13	SU4513
Bitteswell *Leics*	50	SP5385
Bitton *Gloucs*	35	ST6869
Bix *Oxon*	37	SU7284
Blaby *Leics*	50	SP5697
Black Bourton *Oxon*	36	SP2804
Black Callerton *T & W*	103	NZ1769
Black Car *Norfk*	66	TM0995
Black Corner *W Susx*	15	TQ2939
Black Corries *Highld*	123	NN2956
Black Crofts *Ag & B*	122	NM9234
Black Cross *Cnwll*	4	SW9060
Black Dog *Devon*	19	SS8009
Black Heddon *Nthumb*	103	NZ0775
Black Lane *Gt Man*	79	SD7708
Black Lane Ends *Lancs*	81	SD9243
Black Moor *W York*	82	SE2939
Black Notley *Essex*	40	TL7620
Black Street *Suffk*	55	TM5186
Black Tar *Pembks*	30	SM9909
Black Torrington *Devon*	18	SS4605
Blackadder *Border*	119	NT8452
Blackawton *Devon*	7	SX8051
Blackbank *Warwks*	61	SP3586
Blackbeck *Cumb*	86	NY0207
Blackborough *Devon*	9	ST0909
Blackborough End *Norfk*	65	TF6615
Blackboys *E Susx*	16	TQ5220
Blackbrook *Derbys*	62	SK3347
Blackbrook *Staffs*	72	SJ7638
Blackbrook *Surrey*	15	TQ1846
Blackburn *Abers*	135	NJ8212
Blackburn *Lancs*	81	SD6827
Blackburn *W Loth*	117	NS9865
Blackcraig *E Ayrs*	107	NS6308
Blackden Heath *Ches*	79	SJ7871
Blackdog *Abers*	135	NJ9513
Blackdown *Devon*	5	SX5079
Blackdown *Dorset*	10	ST3903
Blackdyke *Cumb*	92	NY1452
Blackenall Heath *W Mids*	60	SK0002
Blacker *S York*	83	SE3309
Blacker Hill *S York*	83	SE3602
Blackfen *Gt Lon*	27	TQ4674
Blackfield *Hants*	13	SU4402
Blackford *Cumb*	101	NY3961
Blackford *P & K*	125	NN8908
Blackford *Somset*	21	ST4147
Blackford *Somset*	21	ST6526
Blackford Bridge *Gt Man*	79	SD8007
Blackfordby *Leics*	62	SK3217
Blackgang *IOW*	13	SZ4876
Blackhall *C Edin*	117	NT1975
Blackhall *Dur*	97	NZ4638
Blackhall Colliery *Dur*	97	NZ4539
Blackhaugh *Border*	109	NT4238
Blackheath *Essex*	40	TM0021
Blackheath *Gt Lon*	27	TQ3876
Blackheath *Suffk*	55	TM4274
Blackheath *Surrey*	14	TQ0346
Blackheath *W Mids*	60	SO9786
Blackhill *Abers*	143	NK0039
Blackhill *Abers*	143	NK0755
Blackhill *Abers*	143	NK0843
Blackhill *Dur*	95	NZ0851
Blackhill of Clackriach *Abers*	143	NJ9246
Blackhorse *Devon*	9	SX9893
Blackhorse Hill *E Susx*	17	TQ7714
Blackjack *Lincs*	64	TF2639
Blackland *Somset*	19	SS8336
Blackland *Wilts*	22	SU0168
Blacklaw *D & G*	108	NT0408
Blackley *Gt Man*	79	SD8502
Blacklunans *P & K*	133	NO1460
Blackmarstone *H & W*	46	SO5038
Blackmill *Brdgnd*	33	SS9386
Blackmoor *Hants*	14	SU7733
Blackmoor *Somset*	21	ST4661
Blackmoorfoot *W York*	82	SE0913
Blackmore *Essex*	40	TL6001
Blackmore End *Essex*	40	TL7430
Blackmore End *Herts*	39	TL1716
Blackness *Falk*	117	NT0579
Blacknest *Berks*	25	SU9568
Blacknest *Hants*	25	SU7941
Blacko *Lancs*	81	SD8541
Blackpill *Swans*	32	SS6190
Blackpool *Devon*	7	SX8547
Blackpool *Devon*	7	SX8174
Blackpool *Lancs*	80	SD3036
Blackpool Gate *Cumb*	101	NY5377
Blackridge *W Loth*	116	NS8967
Blackrock *Cnwll*	2	SW6534
Blackrock *Mons*	33	SO2112
Blackrock *Mons*	34	ST5188
Blackrod *Gt Man*	78	SD6110
Blacksboat *Moray*	141	NJ1838
Blackshaw *D & G*	100	NY0465
Blackshaw Head *W York*	82	SD9527
Blacksmith's Green *Suffk*	54	TM1465
Blacksnape *Lancs*	81	SD7121
Blackstone *W Susx*	15	TQ2316
Blackthorn *Oxon*	37	SP6219
Blackthorpe *Suffk*	54	TL9063
Blacktoft *E R Yk*	84	SE8324
Blacktop *Aber C*	135	NJ8604
Blackwall *Derbys*	73	SK2548
Blackwater *Cnwll*	3	SW7346
Blackwater *Hants*	25	SU8459
Blackwater *IOW*	13	SZ5086
Blackwater *Somset*	10	ST2615
Blackwaterfoot *N Ayrs*	105	NR9028
Blackwell *Cumb*	93	NY4053
Blackwell *Derbys*	74	SK1272
Blackwell *Derbys*	75	SK4458
Blackwell *Dur*	89	NZ2713
Blackwell *H & W*	60	SO9972
Blackwell *Warwks*	48	SP2443
Blackwellsend Green *Gloucs*	47	SO7825
Blackwood *Caerph*	33	ST1797
Blackwood *D & G*	100	NX9087
Blackwood *S Lans*	116	NS7844
Blackwood Hill *Staffs*	72	SJ9255
Blacon *Ches*	71	SJ3868
Bladbean *Kent*	29	TR1847
Bladnoch *D & G*	99	NX4254
Bladon *Oxon*	37	SP4514
Bladon *Somset*	21	ST4220
Blaen Dyryn *Powys*	45	SN9336
Blaen-y-Coed *Carmth*	31	SN3427
Blaen-y-cwm *Blae G*	33	SO1311
Blaen-y-cwm *Rhondd*	33	SS9298
Blaenannerch *Cardgn*	42	SN2448
Blaenau Ffestiniog *Gwynd*	57	SH7045
Blaenavon *Torfn*	34	SO2508
Blaenffos *Pembks*	31	SN1937
Blaengarw *Brdgnd*	33	SS9092
Blaengeuffardd *Cardgn*	43	SN6480
Blaengwrach *Neath*	33	SN8605
Blaengwynfi *Neath*	33	SS8996
Blaenllechau *Rhondd*	33	ST0097
Blaenpennal *Cardgn*	43	SN6264
Blaenplwyf *Cardgn*	43	SN5775
Blaenporth *Cardgn*	42	SN2648
Blaenrhondda *Rhondd*	33	SS9299
Blaenwaun *Carmth*	31	SN2327
Blaenycwm *Cardgn*	43	SN8275
Blagdon *Devon*	7	SX8561
Blagdon *Somset*	20	ST2118
Blagdon *Somset*	21	ST5059
Blagdon Hill *Somset*	9	ST2117
Blagill *Cumb*	94	NY7347
Blaguegate *Lancs*	78	SD4506
Blaich *Highld*	130	NN0376
Blain *Highld*	129	NM6769
Blaina *Blae G*	33	SO2008
Blair Atholl *P & K*	132	NN8665
Blair Drummond *Stirlg*	116	NS7399
Blairgowrie *P & K*	126	NO1745
Blairingone *P & K*	117	NS9896
Blairlogie *Stirlg*	116	NS8396
Blairmore *Ag & B*	114	NS1983
Blairmore *Highld*	148	NC1959
Blairnamarrow *Moray*	141	NJ2015
Blairs Ferry *Ag & B*	114	NR9869
Blaisdon *Gloucs*	35	SO7017
Blake End *Essex*	40	TL7023
Blakebrook *H & W*	60	SO8276
Blakedown *H & W*	60	SO8878
Blakeley Lane *Staffs*	72	SJ9746
Blakemere *Ches*	71	SJ5571
Blakemere *H & W*	46	SO3641
Blakemore *Devon*	7	SX7660
Blakeney *Gloucs*	35	SO6707
Blakeney *Norfk*	66	TG0243
Blakenhall *Ches*	72	SJ7247
Blakenhall *W Mids*	60	SO9197
Blakeshall *H & W*	60	SO8381
Blakesley *Nhants*	49	SP6250
Blanchland *Nthumb*	95	NY9650
Bland Hill *N York*	82	SE2053
Blandford Camp *Dorset*	11	ST9107
Blandford Forum *Dorset*	11	ST8806
Blandford St Mary *Dorset*	11	ST8805
Blanefield *Stirlg*	115	NS5479

Blankney Bradley Green

Blankney *Lincs* 76 TF0660
Blantyre *S Lans* 116 NS6957
Blar a' Chaorainn *Highld* 130 NN1066
Blargie *Highld* 132 NN6094
Blarmachfoldach *Highld* 130 NN0969
Blashford *Hants* 12 SU1506
Blaston *Leics* 51 SP8095
Blatherwycke *Nhants* 51 SP9795
Blawith *Cumb* 86 SD2888
Blawquhairn *D & G* 99 NX6282
Blaxhall *Suffk* 55 TM3656
Blaxton *S York* 75 SE6700
Blaydon *T & W* 103 NZ1863
Bleadney *Somset* 21 ST4845
Bleadon *Somset* 21 ST3456
Bleak Street *Somset* 22 ST7631
Blean *Kent* 29 TR1260
Bleasby *Lincs* 76 TF1384
Bleasby *Notts* 75 SK7149
Bleasdale *Lancs* 81 SD5745
Bleatarn *Cumb* 94 NY7313
Bleathwood *H & W* 46 SO5570
Blebocraigs *Fife* 127 NO4214
Bleddfa *Powys* 45 SO2068
Bledington *Gloucs* 36 SP2422
Bledlow *Bucks* 37 SP7702
Bledlow Ridge *Bucks* 37 SU7997
Bleet *Wilts* 22 ST8958
Blegbie *E Loth* 118 NT4861
Blencarn *Cumb* 94 NY6331
Blencogo *Cumb* 93 NY1947
Blendworth *Hants* 13 SU7113
Blennerhasset *Cumb* 93 NY1741
Bletchingdon *Oxon* 37 SP5018
Bletchingley *Surrey* 27 TQ3250
Bletchley *Bucks* 38 SP8633
Bletchley *Shrops* 59 SJ6233
Bletherston *Pembks* 31 SN0721
Bletsoe *Beds* 51 TL0258
Blewbury *Oxon* 37 SU5385
Blickling *Norfk* 66 TG1728
Blidworth *Notts* 75 SK5956
Blidworth Bottoms *Notts* 75 SK5954
Blindburn *Nthumb* 110 NT8210
Blindcrake *Cumb* 92 NY1434
Blindley Heath *Surrey* 15 TQ3645
Blisland *Cnwll* 4 SX1073
Bliss Gate *H & W* 60 SO7472
Blissford *Hants* 12 SU1713
Blisworth *Nhants* 49 SP7253
Blithbury *Staffs* 73 SK0819
Blitterlees *Cumb* 92 NY1052
Blo Norton *Norfk* 54 TM0179
Blockley *Gloucs* 48 SP1634
Blofield *Norfk* 67 TG3309
Bloomfield *Border* 110 NT5824
Blore *Staffs* 72 SJ7234
Blore *Staffs* 73 SK1349
Blounts Green *Staffs* 73 SK0732
Blowick *Mersyd* 80 SD3516
Bloxham *Oxon* 49 SP4336
Bloxwith *W Mids* 60 SJ9902
Bloxworth *Dorset* 11 SY8894
Blubberhouses *N York* 82 SE1655
Blue Anchor *Cnwll* 4 SW9157
Blue Anchor *Somset* 20 ST0243
Blue Bell Hill *Kent* 28 TQ7462
Blundellsands *Mersyd* 78 SJ3099
Blundeston *Suffk* 67 TM5297
Blunham *Beds* 52 TL1551
Blunsdon St Andrew *Wilts* 36 SU1389
Bluntington *H & W* 60 SO9074
Bluntisham *Cambs* 52 TL3674
Blunts *Cnwll* 5 SX3463
Blunts Green *Warwks* 48 SP1468
Blurton *Staffs* 72 SJ8941
Blyborough *Lincs* 76 SK9394
Blyford *Suffk* 55 TM4276
Blymhill *Staffs* 60 SJ8112
Blymhill Lawn *Staffs* 60 SJ8211
Blyth *Notts* 75 SK6287
Blyth *Nthumb* 103 NZ3181
Blyth Bridge *Border* 117 NT1345
Blythburgh *Suffk* 55 TM4475
Blythe *Border* 110 NT5849
Blythe Bridge *Staffs* 72 SJ9541
Blythe End *Warwks* 61 SP2190
Blythe Marsh *Staffs* 72 SJ9640
Blyton *Lincs* 76 SK8594
Bo'Ness *Falk* 117 NT0081
Boar's Head *Gt Man* 78 SD5708
Boarhills *Fife* 127 NO5613
Boarhunt *Hants* 13 SU6008
Boarley *Kent* 28 TQ7659
Boars Hill *Oxon* 37 SP4902
Boarsgreave *Lancs* 81 SD8420
Boarshead *E Susx* 16 TQ5332
Boarstall *Bucks* 37 SP6214
Boasley Cross *Devon* 5 SX5093
Boat of Garten *Highld* 140 NH9319
Boath *Highld* 146 NH5774
Bobbing *Kent* 28 TQ8865
Bobbington *Staffs* 60 SO8090
Bobbingworth *Essex* 39 TL5305
Bocaddon *Cnwll* 4 SX1858
Bochym *Cnwll* 2 SW6920
Bocking *Essex* 40 TL7623
Bocking Churchstreet *Essex* 40 TL7525
Bockleton *H & W* 46 SO5961
Boconnoc *Cnwll* 4 SX1460
Boddam *Abers* 143 NK1342
Boddam *Shet* 155 HU3915
Boddington *Gloucs* 47 SO8925
Bodedern *Angles* 68 SH3380
Bodelwyddan *Denbgs* 70 SJ0075
Bodenham *H & W* 46 SO5350
Bodenham *Wilts* 23 SU1626
Bodenham Moor *H & W* 46 SO5450
Bodewryd *Angles* 68 SH4090
Bodfari *Denbgs* 70 SJ0970
Bodffordd *Angles* 68 SH4277
Bodfuan *Gwynd* 56 SH3237
Bodham *Norfk* 66 TG1240
Bodiam *E Susx* 17 TQ7825
Bodicote *Oxon* 49 SP4538
Bodieve *Cnwll* 4 SW9973
Bodinnick *Cnwll* 3 SX1352
Bodle Street Green *E Susx* 16 TQ6514
Bodmin *Cnwll* 4 SX0667
Bodney *Norfk* 66 TL8298
Bodorgan *Angles* 68 SH3867
Bodrean *Cnwll* 3 SW8448
Bodsham Green *Kent* 29 TR1045
Bodwen *Cnwll* 4 SX0360
Bodymoor Heath *Warwks* 61 SP1996
Bogallan *Highld* 140 NH6350
Bogbrae *Abers* 143 NK0335
Boghall *Mdloth* 117 NT2465
Boghall *W Loth* 117 NS9867
Boghead *S Lans* 107 NS7742
Boghead Farm *Moray* 141 NJ3559
Bogmoor *Moray* 141 NJ3563
Bogmuir *Abers* 135 NO6471
Bogniebrae *Abers* 142 NJ5945
Bognor Regis *W Susx* 14 SZ9399
Bogroy *Highld* 140 NH9022
Bogue *D & G* 99 NX6481
Bohetherick *Devon* 5 SX4167
Bohortha *Cnwll* 3 SW8532
Bohuntine *Highld* 131 NN2983
Bojewyan *Cnwll* 2 SW3934
Bokiddick *Cnwll* 4 SX0562
Bolam *Dur* 96 NZ1922
Bolam *Nthumb* 103 NZ1082
Bolberry *Devon* 7 SX6939
Bold Heath *Mersyd* 78 SJ5389
Boldmere *W Mids* 61 SP1194
Boldon Colliery *T & W* 96 NZ3462
Boldre *Hants* 12 SZ3198
Boldron *Dur* 95 NZ0314
Bole *Notts* 75 SK7987
Bole Hill *Derbys* 74 SK3374
Bolehill *Derbys* 73 SK2955
Bolenowe *Cnwll* 2 SW6738
Bolfracks *P & K* 125 NN8248
Bolham *Devon* 9 SS9515
Bolham Water *Devon* 9 ST1612
Bolingey *Cnwll* 3 SW7653
Bollington *Ches* 79 SJ9377
Bollington Cross *Ches* 79 SJ9277
Bollow *Gloucs* 35 SO7413
Bolney *W Susx* 15 TQ2622
Bolnhurst *Beds* 51 TL0859
Bolshan *Angus* 127 NO6252
Bolsover *Derbys* 75 SK4770
Bolster Moor *W York* 82 SE0815
Bolsterstone *S York* 74 SK2696
Boltby *N York* 90 SE4886
Boltenstone *Abers* 134 NJ4110
Bolter End *Bucks* 37 SU7992
Bolton *Cumb* 94 NY6323
Bolton *E Loth* 118 NT5070
Bolton *E R Yk* 84 SE7752
Bolton *Gt Man* 79 SD7108
Bolton *Nthumb* 111 NU1013
Bolton Abbey *N York* 82 SE0754
Bolton Bridge *N York* 82 SE0653
Bolton by Bowland *Lancs* 81 SD7849
Bolton Hall *N York* 88 SE0789
Bolton le Sands *Lancs* 87 SD4867
Bolton Low Houses *Cumb* 93 NY2344
Bolton New Houses *Cumb* 93 NY2444
Bolton Percy *N York* 83 SE5341
Bolton Town End *Lancs* 87 SD4867
Bolton Upon Dearne *S York* 83 SE4502
Bolton-on-Swale *N York* 89 SE2599
Boltonfellend *Cumb* 101 NY4768
Boltongate *Cumb* 93 NY2340
Bolventor *Cnwll* 4 SX1876
Bomarsund *Nthumb* 103 NZ2684
Bomere Heath *Shrops* 59 SJ4719
Bonar Bridge *Highld* 146 NH6191
Bonawe *Ag & B* 122 NN0131
Bonawe Quarries *Ag & B* 122 NN0033
Bonby *Lincs* 84 TA0015
Boncath *Pembks* 31 SN2038
Bonchester Bridge *Border* 110 NT5812
Bonchurch *IOW* 13 SZ5778
Bond's Green *H & W* 46 SO3554
Bondleigh *Devon* 8 SS6505
Bonds *Lancs* 80 SD4944
Bone *Cnwll* 2 SW4632
Bonehill *Staffs* 61 SK1902
Boney Hay *Staffs* 61 SK0410
Bonhill *D & Cb* 115 NS3979
Boningale *Shrops* 60 SJ8202
Bonjedward *Border* 110 NT6522
Bonkle *N Lans* 116 NS8457
Bonnington *Angus* 127 NO5739
Bonnington *C Edin* 117 NT1269
Bonnington *Kent* 17 TR0535
Bonnybank *Fife* 126 NO3503
Bonnybridge *Falk* 116 NS8279
Bonnykelly *Abers* 143 NJ8653
Bonnyrigg *Mdloth* 117 NT3065
Bonnyton *Angus* 126 NO3338
Bonsall *Derbys* 74 SK2758
Bonshaw Tower *D & G* 101 NY2472
Bont *Mons* 34 SO3819
Bont-Dolgadfan *Powys* 57 SH8800
Bontddu *Gwynd* 57 SH6718
Bonthorpe *Lincs* 77 TF4872
Bontnewydd *Cardgn* 43 SN6165
Bontnewydd *Gwynd* 68 SH4859
Bontuchel *Denbgs* 70 SJ0857
Bonvilston *V Glam* 33 ST0673
Bonwm *Denbgs* 70 SJ1042
Bonymaen *Swans* 32 SS6795
Boode *Devon* 19 SS5037
Boohay *Devon* 7 SX8952
Booker *Bucks* 37 SU8391
Booley *Shrops* 59 SJ5625
Boon *Border* 110 NT5745
Boon Hill *Staffs* 72 SJ8150
Boorley Green *Hants* 13 SU5014
Boosbeck *N York* 97 NZ6617
Boose's Green *Essex* 40 TL8431
Boot *Cnwll* 5 SX2697
Boot *Cumb* 86 NY1700
Boot Street *Suffk* 55 TM2248
Booth *E R Yk* 84 SE7326
Booth *W York* 82 SE0427
Booth Green *Ches* 79 SJ9280
Booth Town *W York* 82 SE0926
Boothby Graffoe *Lincs* 76 SK9859
Boothby Pagnell *Lincs* 63 SK9730
Boothstown *Gt Man* 79 SD7200
Boothville *Nhants* 50 SP7864
Bootle *Cumb* 86 SD1088
Bootle *Mersyd* 78 SJ3495
Boots Green *Ches* 79 SJ7572
Booze *N York* 88 NZ0102
Boraston *Shrops* 46 SO6169
Bordeaux *Guern* 152 GN0000
Borden *Kent* 28 TQ8862
Borden *W Susx* 14 SU8324
Border *Cumb* 92 NY1654
Bordley *N York* 88 SD9465
Bordon *Hants* 14 SU8035
Bordon Camp *Hants* 14 SU7936
Boreham *Essex* 40 TL7609
Boreham *Wilts* 22 ST8944
Boreham Street *E Susx* 16 TQ6611
Borehamwood *Herts* 26 TQ1996
Boreland *D & G* 100 NY1691
Boreraig *Highld* 136 NG1853
Boreston *Devon* 7 SX7653
Boreton *Ches* 59 SJ5106
Borgh *W Isls* 154 NB4055
Borgh *W Isls* 154 NF6501
Borgie *Highld* 149 NC6759
Borgue *D & G* 99 NX6248
Borgue *Highld* 151 ND1326
Borley *Essex* 54 TL8443
Borley Green *Essex* 54 TL8442
Borley Green *Suffk* 54 TL9960
Borneskitaig *Highld* 136 NG3770
Borness *D & G* 99 NX6145
Borough Green *Kent* 27 TQ6157
Boroughbridge *N York* 89 SE3966
Borras Head *Wrexhm* 71 SJ3653
Borrowash *Derbys* 62 SK4234
Borrowby *N York* 97 NZ7715
Borrowby *N York* 89 SE4289
Borrowdale *Cumb* 93 NY2514
Borrowstoun *Falk* 117 NS9980
Borstal *Kent* 28 TQ7366
Borth *Cardgn* 43 SN6090
Borth-y-Gest *Gwynd* 57 SH5637
Borthwick *Mdloth* 118 NT3659
Borthwickbrae *Border* 109 NT4113
Borthwickshiels *Border* 109 NT4315
Borve *Highld* 136 NG4448
Borve *W Isls* 154 NB4055
Borve *W Isls* 154 NF6501
Borve *W Isls* 154 NG0394
Borwick *Lancs* 87 SD5272
Borwick Lodge *Cumb* 87 SD3499
Borwick Rails *Cumb* 86 SD1879
Bosavern *Cnwll* 2 SW3730
Bosbury *H & W* 47 SO6943
Boscarne *Cnwll* 4 SX0367
Boscastle *Cnwll* 4 SX0990
Boscombe *Dorset* 12 SZ1191
Boscombe *Wilts* 23 SU2038
Boscoppa *Cnwll* 3 SX0353
Bosham *W Susx* 14 SU8003
Bosham Hoe *W Susx* 14 SU8102
Bosherston *Pembks* 30 SR9694
Boskednan *Cnwll* 2 SW4434
Boskenna *Cnwll* 2 SW4223
Bosley *Ches* 72 SJ9165
Bosoughan *Cnwll* 4 SW8760
Bossall *N York* 90 SE7160
Bossiney *Cnwll* 4 SX0688
Bossingham *Kent* 29 TR1548
Bossington *Somset* 19 SS8947
Bostock Green *Ches* 79 SJ6769
Boston *Lincs* 64 TF3343
Boston Spa *W York* 83 SE4245
Boswarthan *Cnwll* 2 SW4433
Boswinger *Cnwll* 3 SW9841
Botallack *Cnwll* 2 SW3732
Botany Bay *Gt Lon* 27 TQ2999
Botcheston *Leics* 62 SK4804
Botesdale *Suffk* 54 TM0475
Bothal *Nthumb* 103 NZ2386
Bothampstead *Berks* 37 SU5076
Bothamsall *Notts* 75 SK6773
Bothel *Cumb* 93 NY1838
Bothenhampton *Dorset* 10 SY4791
Bothwell *S Lans* 116 NS7058
Botley *Bucks* 26 SP9802
Botley *Hants* 13 SU5113
Botley *Oxon* 37 SP4806
Botolph Claydon *Bucks* 49 SP7324
Botolph's Bridge *Kent* 17 TR1233
Botolphs *W Susx* 15 TQ1909
Bottesford *Leics* 63 SK8038
Bottesford *Lincs* 84 SE8906
Bottisham *Cambs* 53 TL5460
Bottom o' th' Moor *Gt Man* 81 SD6511
Bottom of Hutton *Lancs* 80 SD4827
Bottomcraig *Fife* 126 NO3724
Bottoms *Cnwll* 2 SW3824
Bottoms *W York* 81 SD9321
Botts Green *Warwks* 61 SP2492
Botusfleming *Cnwll* 5 SX4061
Botwnnog *Gwynd* 56 SH2631
Bough Beech *Kent* 16 TQ4847
Boughrood *Powys* 45 SO1239
Boughspring *Gloucs* 34 ST5597
Boughton *Cambs* 52 TL1965
Boughton *Nhants* 50 SP7565
Boughton *Norfk* 65 TF7002
Boughton *Notts* 75 SK6768
Boughton Aluph *Kent* 28 TR0348
Boughton End *Beds* 38 SP9838
Boughton Green *Kent* 28 TQ7650
Boughton Lees *Kent* 28 TR0246
Boughton Malherbe *Kent* 28 TQ8849
Boughton Monchelsea *Kent* 28 TQ7650
Boughton Street *Kent* 28 TR0559
Boulby *N York* 97 NZ7618
Boulder Clough *W York* 82 SE0323
Bouldnor *IOW* 12 SZ3789
Bouldon *Shrops* 59 SO5485
Boulge *Suffk* 55 TM2552
Boulmer *Nthumb* 111 NU2614
Boulston *Pembks* 30 SM9712
Boultham *Lincs* 76 SK9669
Bourn *Cambs* 52 TL3256
Bourne *Lincs* 64 TF0920
Bourne End *Beds* 38 SP9644
Bourne End *Beds* 51 TL0160
Bourne End *Bucks* 26 SU8987
Bourne End *Herts* 38 TL0206
Bournebridge *Essex* 27 TQ5094
Bournebrook *W Mids* 61 SP0483
Bournemouth *Dorset* 12 SZ0890
Bournes Green *Essex* 40 TQ9186
Bournes Green *Gloucs* 35 SO9104
Bournheath *H & W* 60 SO9574
Bournmoor *Dur* 96 NZ3051
Bournstream *Gloucs* 35 ST7494
Bournville *W Mids* 61 SP0481
Bourton *Dorset* 22 ST7630
Bourton *Oxon* 36 SU2386
Bourton *Shrops* 59 SO5996
Bourton *Somset* 21 ST3864
Bourton *Wilts* 23 SU0464
Bourton on Dunsmore *Warwks* 50 SP4370
Bourton-on-the- Hill *Gloucs* 48 SP1732
Bourton-on-the-Water *Gloucs* 36 SP1620
Bousd *Ag & B* 120 NM2563
Boustead Hill *Cumb* 93 NY2959
Bouth *Cumb* 86 SD3285
Bouthwaite *N York* 89 SE1271
Bouts *H & W* 48 SP0359
Bovain *Stirlg* 124 NN5430
Boveney *Berks* 26 SU9377
Boveridge *Dorset* 12 SU0514
Bovey Tracey *Devon* 8 SX8178
Bovingdon *Herts* 38 TL0103
Bovingdon Green *Bucks* 37 SU8386
Bovinger *Essex* 39 TL5205
Bovington Camp *Dorset* 11 SY8389
Bow *Cumb* 93 NY3356
Bow *Devon* 8 SS7201
Bow *Devon* 7 SX8156
Bow *Gt Lon* 27 TQ3683
Bow *Ork* 155 ND3693
Bow Brickhill *Bucks* 38 SP9034
Bow of Fife *Fife* 126 NO3212
Bow Street *Cardgn* 43 SN6285
Bow Street *Norfk* 66 TM0198
Bowbank *Dur* 95 NY9423
Bowbridge *Gloucs* 35 SO8505
Bowburn *Dur* 96 NZ3037
Bowcombe *IOW* 13 SZ4786
Bowd *Devon* 9 SY1090
Bowden *Border* 109 NT5530
Bowden *Devon* 7 SX8449
Bowden Hill *Wilts* 22 ST9367
Bowdon *Gt Man* 79 SJ7686
Bower *Highld* 151 ND2362
Bower Ashton *Bristl* 34 ST5671
Bower Hinton *Somset* 10 ST4517
Bower House Tye *Suffk* 54 TL9840
Bower's Row *W York* 83 SE4028
Bowerchalke *Wilts* 23 SU0223
Bowerhill *Wilts* 22 ST9162
Bowermadden *Highld* 151 ND2464
Bowers *Staffs* 72 SJ8135
Bowers Gifford *Essex* 40 TQ7588
Bowershall *Fife* 117 NT0991
Bowes *Dur* 95 NY9913
Bowgreave *Lancs* 80 SD4943
Bowhouse *D & G* 100 NY0165
Bowithick *Cnwll* 4 SX1882
Bowker's Green *Lancs* 78 SD4004
Bowland *Border* 109 NT4540
Bowland Bridge *Cumb* 87 SD4189
Bowlee *Gt Man* 79 SD8406
Bowley *H & W* 46 SO5452
Bowley Town *H & W* 46 SO5352
Bowlhead Green *Surrey* 25 SU9138
Bowling *D & Cb* 115 NS4373
Bowling *W York* 82 SE1731
Bowling Bank *Wrexhm* 71 SJ3948
Bowling Green *H & W* 47 SO8251
Bowmanstead *Cumb* 86 SD3096
Bowmore *Ag & B* 112 NR3159
Bowness-on-Solway *Cumb* 101 NY2262
Bowness-on-Windermere *Cumb* 87 SD4097
Bowriefauld *Angus* 127 NO5147
Bowscale *Cumb* 93 NY3531
Bowsden *Nthumb* 111 NT9941
Bowthorpe *Norfk* 66 TG1709
Box *Gloucs* 35 SO8600
Box *Wilts* 22 ST8268
Box End *Beds* 38 TL0049
Box Hill *Surrey* 26 TQ1951
Box's Shop *Cnwll* 18 SS2101
Boxbush *Gloucs* 35 SO6720
Boxbush *Gloucs* 35 SO7413
Boxford *Berks* 24 SU4271
Boxford *Suffk* 54 TL9640
Boxgrove *W Susx* 14 SU9007
Boxholm *Lincs* 76 TF0653
Boxley *Kent* 28 TQ7758
Boxmoor *Herts* 38 TL0406
Boxted *Essex* 41 TL9933
Boxted *Suffk* 54 TL8251
Boxted Cross *Essex* 41 TM0032
Boxted Heath *Essex* 41 TM0031
Boxwell *Gloucs* 35 ST8192
Boxworth *Cambs* 52 TL3464
Boxworth End *Cambs* 52 TL3667
Boyden End *Suffk* 53 TL7355
Boyden Gate *Kent* 29 TR2265
Boylestone *Derbys* 73 SK1835
Boyndie *Abers* 142 NJ6463
Boyndlie *Abers* 143 NJ9162
Boynton *E R Yk* 91 TA1367
Boys Hill *Dorset* 11 ST6710
Boysack *Angus* 127 NO6249
Boythorpe *Derbys* 74 SK3869
Boyton *Cnwll* 5 SX3292
Boyton *Suffk* 55 TM3747
Boyton *Wilts* 22 ST9539
Boyton Cross *Essex* 40 TL6409
Boyton End *Suffk* 53 TL7244
Bozeat *Nhants* 51 SP9058
Braaid *IOM* 153 SC3276
Brabling Green *Suffk* 55 TM2964
Brabourne *Kent* 29 TR1041
Brabourne Lees *Kent* 29 TR0840
Brabstermire *Highld* 151 ND3169
Bracadale *Highld* 136 NG3538
Braceborough *Lincs* 64 TF0713
Bracebridge Heath *Lincs* 76 SK9867
Bracebridge Low Fields *Lincs* 76 SK9666
Braceby *Lincs* 64 TF0135
Bracewell *Lancs* 81 SD8648
Brackenfield *Derbys* 74 SK3759
Brackenhurst *N Lans* 116 NS7468
Brackenthwaite *Cumb* 93 NY2946
Brackenthwaite *N York* 82 SE2851
Bracklesham *W Susx* 14 SZ8096
Brackletter *Highld* 131 NN1882
Brackley *Nhants* 49 SP5837
Brackley Hatch *Nhants* 49 SP6441
Bracknell *Berks* 25 SU8769
Braco *P & K* 125 NN8309
Bracobrae *Moray* 142 NJ5053
Bracon *Lincs* 84 SE7807
Bracon Ash *Norfk* 66 TM1899
Bracora *Highld* 129 NM7192
Bracorina *Highld* 129 NM7292
Bradaford *Devon* 5 SX3994
Bradbourne *Derbys* 73 SK2052
Bradbury *Dur* 96 NZ3128
Bradden *Nhants* 49 SP6448
Braddock *Cnwll* 4 SX1662
Bradeley *Staffs* 72 SJ8851
Bradenham *Bucks* 37 SU8297
Bradenstoke *Wilts* 35 SU0079
Bradfield *Berks* 24 SU6072
Bradfield *Devon* 9 ST0509
Bradfield *Essex* 41 TM1430
Bradfield *Norfk* 67 TG2733
Bradfield *S York* 74 SK2692
Bradfield Combust *Suffk* 54 TL8957
Bradfield Green *Ches* 72 SJ6859
Bradfield Heath *Essex* 41 TM1430
Bradfield St Clare *Suffk* 54 TL9057
Bradfield St George *Suffk* 54 TL9059
Bradford *Cnwll* 4 SX1175
Bradford *Devon* 18 SS4207
Bradford *Nthumb* 111 NU1532
Bradford *Nthumb* 103 NZ0679
Bradford *W York* 82 SE1632
Bradford Abbas *Dorset* 10 ST5813
Bradford Leigh *Wilts* 22 ST8362
Bradford Peverell *Dorset* 11 SY6593
Bradford-on-Avon *Wilts* 22 ST8261
Bradford-on-Tone *Somset* 20 ST1722
Bradiford *Devon* 19 SS5534
Brading *IOW* 13 SZ6087
Bradley *Ches* 71 SJ5377
Bradley *Derbys* 73 SK2246
Bradley *H & W* 47 SO9860
Bradley *Hants* 24 SU6341
Bradley *Lincs* 85 TA2406
Bradley *N York* 88 SE0380
Bradley *Staffs* 72 SJ8717
Bradley *W Mids* 60 SO9595
Bradley *W York* 82 SE1720
Bradley *Wrexhm* 71 SJ3253
Bradley Green *Ches* 71 SJ5045
Bradley Green *H & W* 47 SO9862

Bromborough
Burton

Bromborough Mersyd 78 SJ3582
Brome Suffk 54 TM1376
Brome Street Suffk 54 TM1576
Bromeswell Suffk 55 TM3050
Bromfield Cumb 93 NY1746
Bromfield Shrops 46 SO4876
Bromham Beds 38 TL0051
Bromham Wilts 22 ST9665
Bromley Gt Lon 27 TQ4069
Bromley S York 74 SK3298
Bromley Shrops 60 SO7395
Bromley W Mids 60 SO9088
Bromley Common Gt Lon 27 TQ4266
Bromley Cross Essex 41 TM0627
Bromlow Shrops 59 SJ3201
Brompton Kent 28 TQ7668
Brompton N York 89 SE3796
Brompton N York 91 SE9482
Brompton Shrops 59 SJ5408
Brompton Ralph Somset 20 ST0832
Brompton Regis Somset 20 SS9531
Brompton-on-Swale N York 89 SE2199
Bromsash H & W 47 SO6524
Bromsberrow Gloucs 47 SO7433
Bromsberrow Heath Gloucs 47 SO7333
Bromsgrove H & W 60 SO9670
Bromstead Heath Staffs 72 SJ7917
Bromyard H & W 47 SO6554
Bromyard Downs H & W 47 SO6655
Bronaber Gwynd 57 SH7131
Bronant Cardgn 43 SN6467
Broncroft Shrops 59 SO5486
Brongest Cardgn 42 SN3245
Bronington Wrexhm 71 SJ4839
Bronllys Powys 45 SO1434
Bronwydd Carmth 31 SN4123
Bronydd Powys 45 SO2245
Bronygarth Shrops 58 SJ2637
Brook Carmth 31 SN2609
Brook Hants 12 SU2714
Brook Hants 23 SU3429
Brook IOW 13 SZ3983
Brook Kent 29 TR0644
Brook Surrey 14 SU9237
Brook Surrey 14 TQ0546
Brook End Beds 51 TL0763
Brook End Beds 52 TL1547
Brook End Bucks 38 SP9244
Brook End Cambs 51 TL0773
Brook Hill Hants 12 SU2714
Brook House Denbgs 70 SJ0765
Brook Street Essex 27 TQ5793
Brook Street Kent 17 TQ9333
Brook Street Suffk 54 TL8248
Brook Street W Susx 15 TQ3026
Brooke Norfk 67 TM2899
Brooke Rutlnd 63 SK8405
Brookfield Rens 115 NS4164
Brookhampton Hants 13 SU7106
Brookhampton Oxon 37 SU6098
Brookhampton Somset 21 ST6327
Brookhouse Lancs 87 SD5464
Brookhouse S York 75 SK5188
Brookhouse Green Ches 72 SJ8161
Brookhouses Derbys 74 SK0388
Brookland Kent 17 TQ9926
Brooklands Gt Man 79 SJ7890
Brookmans Park Herts 39 TL2404
Brooks Powys 58 SO1499
Brooks End Kent 29 TR2967
Brooks Green W Susx 14 TQ1224
Brooksby Leics 63 SK6715
Brookthorpe Gloucs 35 SO8312
Brookville Norfk 65 TL7396
Brookwood Surrey 25 SU9557
Broom Beds 39 TL1742
Broom Dur 96 NZ2441
Broom S York 75 SK4491
Broom Warwks 48 SP0853
Broom Green Norfk 66 TF9823
Broom Hill Dorset 12 SU0302
Broom Hill H & W 60 SO9175
Broom Hill Notts 62 SK5447
Broom Hill S York 83 SE4102
Broom Street Kent 28 TR0462
Broom's Green Gloucs 47 SO7132
Broome H & W 60 SO9078
Broome Norfk 67 TM3591
Broome Shrops 59 SO4080
Broome Park Nthumb 111 NU1012
Broomedge Ches 79 SJ7085
Broomer's Corner W Susx 14 TQ1220
Broomershill W Susx 14 TQ0619
Broomfield Essex 40 TL7010
Broomfield Kent 28 TQ8452
Broomfield Kent 29 TR1966
Broomfield Somset 20 ST2232
Broomfields Shrops 59 SJ4217
Broomfleet E R Yk 84 SE8727
Broomhall Surrey 25 SU9566
Broomhaugh Nthumb 103 NZ0261
Broomhill Nthumb 103 NU2401
Broomhill Green Ches 71 SJ6247
Broomley Nthumb 103 NZ0360
Broomsthorpe Norfk 66 TF8428
Brora Highld 147 NC9103
Broseley Shrops 60 SJ6701
Brotherhouse Bar Lincs 64 TF2614
Brotherlee Dur 95 NY9237
Brothertoft Lincs 77 TF2746
Brotherton N York 83 SE4825
Brotton N York 97 NZ6819
Broubster Highld 150 ND0359
Brough Cumb 95 NY7914
Brough Derbys 74 SK1882
Brough E R Yk 84 SE9326
Brough Highld 151 ND2273
Brough Notts 76 SK8458
Brough Shet 155 HU5665
Brough Lodge Shet 155 HU5892
Brough Sowerby Cumb 95 NY7912
Broughall Shrops 71 SJ5741
Broughton Border 108 NT1136
Broughton Bucks 38 SP8413
Broughton Bucks 38 SP8939
Broughton Cambs 52 TL2878
Broughton Flints 71 SJ3363
Broughton Gt Man 79 SD8201
Broughton Hants 23 SU3033
Broughton Lancs 80 SD5234
Broughton Lincs 84 SE9608
Broughton N York 82 SD9451
Broughton N York 90 SE7673
Broughton Nhants 51 SP8375
Broughton Oxon 49 SP4138
Broughton Staffs 72 SJ7634
Broughton V Glam 33 SS9270
Broughton Astley Leics 50 SP5292
Broughton Beck Cumb 86 SD2882
Broughton Gifford Wilts 22 ST8763
Broughton Green H & W 47 SO9561
Broughton Hackett H & W 47 SO9254
Broughton Mains D & G 99 NX4545
Broughton Mills Cumb 86 SD2290
Broughton Moor Cumb 92 NY0533
Broughton Poggs Oxon 36 SP2303
Broughton Tower Cumb 86 SD2187
Broughton-in-Furness Cumb 86 SD2187
Broughty Ferry Dund C 127 NO4630
Brow End Cumb 86 SD2674
Brow-of-the-Hill Norfk 65 TF6819
Brown Candover Hants 24 SU5739
Brown Edge Lancs 80 SD3614
Brown Edge Staffs 72 SJ9053
Brown Heath Ches 71 SJ4564
Brown Lees Staffs 72 SJ8756
Brown Street Suffk 54 TM0663
Brown's Green W Mids 61 SP0591
Brownber Cumb 87 NY7005
Brownheath Shrops 59 SJ4629
Brownhill Abers 143 NJ8640
Brownhills Fife 127 NO5215
Brownhills W Mids 61 SK0405
Brownieside Nthumb 111 NU1623
Browninghill Green Hants 24 SU5859
Brownlow Heath Ches 72 SJ8360
Brownrigg Cumb 92 NY0420
Brownrigg Cumb 92 NY1652
Brownsham Devon 18 SS2826
Brownsover Warwks 50 SP5177
Brownston Devon 7 SX6952
Browston Green Norfk 67 TG4901
Broxa N York 91 SE9491
Broxbourne Herts 39 TL3606
Broxburn E Loth 119 NT6977
Broxburn W Loth 117 NT0872
Broxfield Nthumb 111 NU2016
Broxted Essex 40 TL5727
Broxton Ches 71 SJ4754
Broxwood H & W 46 SO3654
Broyle Side E Susx 16 TQ4513
Bruan Highld 151 ND3139
Bruar P & K 132 NN8265
Brucefield Highld 147 NH9386
Bruchag Ag & B 114 NS1157
Bruera Ches 71 SJ4360
Bruern Abbey Oxon 36 SP2620
Bruichladdich Ag & B 112 NR2661
Bruisyard Suffk 55 TM3266
Bruisyard Street Suffk 55 TM3365
Brumby Lincs 84 SE8909
Brund Staffs 74 SK1061
Brundall Norfk 67 TG3308
Brundish Suffk 55 TM2769
Brundish Street Suffk 55 TM2671
Brunnian Cnwll 2 SW5036
Brunslow Shrops 59 SO3684
Bruntcliffe W York 82 SE2526
Brunthwaite W York 82 SE0546
Bruntingthorpe Leics 50 SP6089
Brunton Fife 126 NO3220
Brunton Nthumb 111 NU2024
Brunton Wilts 23 SU2456
Brushford Somset 20 SS9225
Brushford Barton Devon 8 SS6707
Bruton Somset 22 ST6835
Bryan's Green H & W 47 SO8868
Bryanston Dorset 11 ST8607
Bryant's Bottom Bucks 26 SU8599
Brydekirk D & G 101 NY1870
Brymbo Wrexhm 71 SJ2953
Brympton Somset 10 ST5115
Bryn Ches 71 SJ6072
Bryn Gt Man 78 SD5600
Bryn Neath 33 SS8192
Bryn Shrops 59 SO2985
Bryn Du Angles 68 SH3472
Bryn Gates Lancs 78 SD5901
Bryn Golau Rhondd 33 ST0088
Bryn Saith Marchog Denbgs 70 SJ0750
Bryn-bwbach Gwynd 57 SH6236
Bryn-coch Neath 32 SS7499
Bryn-Eden Gwynd 57 SH7129
Bryn-henllan Pembks 30 SN0139
Bryn-mawr Gwynd 56 SH2433
Bryn-newydd Denbgs 70 SJ1842
Bryn-penarth Powys 58 SJ1004
Bryn-y-bal Flints 70 SJ2564
Bryn-y-maen A & C 69 SH8376
Bryn-yr-Eos Wrexhm 70 SJ2840
Brynaman Carmth 32 SN7114
Brynberian Pembks 31 SN1035
Brynbryddan Neath 32 SS7792
Bryncae Rhondd 33 SS9982
Bryncethin Brdgnd 33 SS9183
Bryncir Gwynd 56 SH4844
Bryncroes Gwynd 56 SH2231
Bryncrug Gwynd 57 SH6103
Bryneglwys Denbgs 70 SJ1447
Brynfields Wrexhm 71 SJ3044
Brynford Flints 70 SJ1774
Bryngwran Angles 68 SH3577
Bryngwyn Mons 34 SO3909
Bryngwyn Powys 45 SO1849
Brynhoffnant Cardgn 42 SN3351
Bryning Lancs 80 SD4029
Brynithel Blae G 33 SO2101
Brynmawr Blae G 33 SO1911
Brynmenyn Brdgnd 33 SS9084
Brynmill Swans 32 SS6392
Brynna Rhondd 33 SS9883
Brynrefail Angles 68 SH4886
Brynrefail Gwynd 69 SH5562
Brynsadler Rhondd 33 ST0280
Brynsiencyn Angles 68 SH4867
Brynteg Angles 68 SH4982
Bualintur Highld 128 NG4020
Buarth-draw Flints 70 SJ1779
Bubbenhall Warwks 61 SP3672
Bubwith E R Yk 84 SE7136
Buchanan Smithy Stirlg 115 NS4689
Buchanhaven Abers 143 NK1247
Buchanty P & K 125 NN9328
Buchany Stirlg 124 NN7102
Buchlyvie Stirlg 115 NS5793
Buck's Cross Devon 18 SS3522
Buck's Mills Devon 18 SS3523
Buckabank Cumb 93 NY3749
Buckden Cambs 52 TL1967
Buckden N York 88 SD9477
Buckenham Norfk 67 TG3505
Buckerell Devon 9 ST1200
Buckfast Devon 7 SX7467
Buckfastleigh Devon 7 SX7366
Buckhaven Fife 118 NT3598
Buckholm Border 109 NT4738
Buckholt Mons 34 SO5016
Buckhorn Weston Dorset 22 ST7524
Buckhurst Hill Essex 27 TQ4194
Buckie Moray 142 NJ4265
Buckingham Bucks 49 SP6933
Buckland Bucks 38 SP8812
Buckland Devon 7 SX6743
Buckland Gloucs 48 SP0835
Buckland Hants 12 SZ3196
Buckland Herts 39 TL3533
Buckland Kent 29 TR3042
Buckland Oxon 36 SU3498
Buckland Surrey 26 TQ2150
Buckland Brewer Devon 18 SS4220
Buckland Common Bucks 38 SP9207
Buckland Dinham Somset 22 ST7551
Buckland Filleigh Devon 18 SS4609
Buckland in the Moor Devon 7 SX7273
Buckland Monachorum Devon 6 SX4968
Buckland Newton Dorset 11 ST6805
Buckland Ripers Dorset 11 SY6582
Buckland St Mary Somset 10 ST2613
Buckland-Tout-Saints Devon 7 SX7645
Bucklebury Berks 24 SU5570
Bucklerheads Angus 127 NO4636
Bucklers Hard Hants 13 SU4000
Bucklesham Suffk 55 TM2441
Buckley Flints 70 SJ2763
Buckley Green Warwks 48 SP1567
Buckley Mountain Flints 70 SJ2765
Bucklow Hill Ches 79 SJ7383
Buckminster Leics 63 SK8722
Bucknall Lincs 76 TF1668
Bucknall Staffs 72 SJ9047
Bucknell Oxon 49 SP5625
Bucknell Shrops 46 SO3574
Buckpool Moray 142 NJ4165
Bucks Green W Susx 14 TQ0833
Bucks Hill Herts 26 TL0500
Bucks Horn Oak Hants 25 SU8041
Bucksburn Aber C 135 NJ8909
Buckshead Cnwll 3 SW8346
Buckton E R Yk 91 TA1872
Buckton H & W 46 SO3873
Buckton Nthumb 111 NU0838
Buckworth Cambs 52 TL1476
Budbrooke Warwks 48 SP2665
Budby Notts 75 SK6169
Budd's Titson Cnwll 18 SS2401
Buddileigh Staffs 72 SJ7449
Buddon Angus 127 NO5232
Bude Cnwll 18 SS2105
Budge's Shop Cnwll 5 SX3259
Budlake Devon 9 SS9800
Budle Nthumb 111 NU1535
Budleigh Salterton Devon 9 SY0682
Budlett's Common E Susx 16 TQ4723
Budock Water Cnwll 3 SW7831
Buerton Ches 72 SJ6843
Bugbrooke Nhants 49 SP6757
Bugford Devon 7 SX8350
Buglawton Ches 72 SJ8763
Bugle Cnwll 4 SX0158
Bugley Dorset 22 ST7824
Bugthorpe E R Yk 90 SE7757
Buildwas Shrops 59 SJ6204
Builth Road Powys 45 SO0353
Builth Wells Powys 45 SO0350
Bulbourne Herts 38 SP9313
Bulbridge Wilts 23 SU0830
Bulby Lincs 64 TF0526
Buldoo Highld 150 ND0067
Bulford Wilts 23 SU1643
Bulford Barracks Wilts 23 SU1843
Bulkeley Ches 71 SJ5354
Bulkington Warwks 61 SP3986
Bulkington Wilts 22 ST9458
Bulkworthy Devon 18 SS3914
Bull Bay Angles 68 SH4294
Bull's Green Herts 39 TL2717
Bull's Green Norfk 67 TM4194
Bullamore N York 89 SE3994
Bullbridge Derbys 74 SK3552
Bullbrook Berks 25 SU8869
Bullen's Green Herts 39 TL2105
Bulley Gloucs 35 SO7619
Bullgill Cumb 92 NY0938
Bullinghope H & W 46 SO5136
Bullington Hants 24 SU4541
Bullington Lincs 76 TF0877
Bullington End Bucks 38 SP8145
Bullockstone Kent 29 TR1665
Bulmer Essex 54 TL8440
Bulmer N York 90 SE6967
Bulmer Tye Essex 54 TL8438
Bulphan Essex 40 TQ6385
Bulstone Devon 9 SY1789
Bulstrode Herts 26 TL0302
Bulstrode Park Bucks 26 SU9888
Bulterley Heath Staffs 72 SJ7450
Bulverhythe E Susx 17 TQ7708
Bulwark Abers 143 NJ9345
Bulwell Notts 62 SK5343
Bulwick Nhants 51 SP9694
Bumble's Green Essex 39 TL4005
Bunacaimb Highld 129 NM6588
Bunarkaig Highld 131 NN1887
Bunbury Ches 71 SJ5657
Bunbury Heath Ches 71 SJ5558
Bunchrew Highld 140 NH6246
Buncton W Susx 15 TQ1413
Bundalloch Highld 138 NG8927
Bunessan Ag & B 121 NM3821
Bungay Suffk 55 TM3389
Bunker's Hill Lincs 77 TF2653
Bunnahabhainn Ag & B 112 NR4173
Bunny Notts 62 SK5829
Buntait Highld 139 NH4030
Buntingford Herts 39 TL3629
Bunwell Norfk 66 TM1292
Bunwell Street Norfk 66 TM1193
Bupton Derbys 73 SK2237
Burbage Derbys 74 SK0472
Burbage Leics 50 SP4492
Burbage Wilts 23 SU2261
Burcher H & W 46 SO3360
Burchett's Green Berks 37 SU8481
Burchett's Green E Susx 16 TQ6631
Burcombe Wilts 23 SU0730
Burcot H & W 60 SO9871
Burcot Oxon 37 SU5695
Burcote Shrops 60 SO7495
Burcott Bucks 38 SP8415
Burcott Bucks 38 SP8823
Burdale N York 90 SE8762
Bures Suffk 54 TL9034
Burford H & W 46 SO5868
Burford Oxon 36 SP2512
Burg Ag & B 121 NM3845
Burgates Hants 14 SU7728
Burge End Herts 38 TL1432
Burgess Hill W Susx 15 TQ3218
Burgh Suffk 55 TM2351
Burgh by Sands Cumb 93 NY3259
Burgh Castle Norfk 67 TG4805
Burgh Heath Surrey 26 TQ2457
Burgh Hill E Susx 17 TQ7226
Burgh Le Marsh Lincs 77 TF5065
Burgh next Aylsham Norfk 67 TG2125
Burgh on Bain Lincs 76 TF2186
Burgh St Margaret Norfk 67 TG4413
Burgh St Peter Norfk 67 TM4693
Burghclere Hants 24 SU4761
Burghead Moray 141 NJ1168
Burghfield Berks 24 SU6668
Burghfield Common Berks 24 SU6566
Burghill H & W 46 SO4844
Burghwallis S York 83 SE5311
Burham Kent 28 TQ7262
Buriton Hants 13 SU7419
Burland Ches 71 SJ6153
Burlawn Cnwll 4 SW9970
Burleigh Berks 25 SU9169
Burleigh Gloucs 35 SO8601
Burlescombe Devon 9 ST0716
Burleston Dorset 11 SY7794
Burlestone Devon 7 SX8248
Burley Hants 12 SU2102
Burley Rutlnd 63 SK8810
Burley Shrops 59 SO4881
Burley Gate H & W 46 SO5947
Burley in Wharfedale W York 82 SE1646
Burley Lawn Hants 12 SU2103
Burley Street Hants 12 SU2004
Burley Wood Head W York 82 SE1544
Burleydam Ches 71 SJ6042
Burlingham Green Norfk 67 TG3610
Burlingjobb Powys 46 SO2558
Burlington Shrops 60 SJ7711
Burlton Shrops 59 SJ4526
Burmarsh Kent 17 TR1032
Burmington Warwks 48 SP2637
Burn N York 83 SE5928
Burn Cross S York 74 SK3496
Burn Naze Lancs 80 SD3443
Burn of Cambus Stirlg 124 NN7102
Burnage Gt Man 79 SJ8692
Burnaston Derbys 73 SK2832
Burnbanks Cumb 94 NY5016
Burnbrae N Lans 116 NS8759
Burnby E R Yk 84 SE8346
Burndell W Susx 14 SU9802
Burnden Gt Man 79 SD7207
Burnedge Gt Man 79 SD9110
Burneside Cumb 87 SD5095
Burneston N York 89 SE3084
Burnett Somset 22 ST6665
Burnfoot Border 109 NT4113
Burnfoot Border 109 NT5116
Burnfoot D & G 100 NX9791
Burnfoot D & G 101 NY3388
Burnfoot D & G 101 NY3996
Burnfoot P & K 125 NN9904
Burnham Bucks 26 SU9282
Burnham Lincs 84 TA0516
Burnham Deepdale Norfk 66 TF8044
Burnham Green Herts 39 TL2616
Burnham Market Norfk 66 TF8342
Burnham Norton Norfk 66 TF8343
Burnham Overy Norfk 66 TF8442
Burnham Overy Staithe Norfk 66 TF8444
Burnham Thorpe Norfk 66 TF8541
Burnham-on-Crouch Essex 40 TQ9496
Burnham-on-Sea Somset 20 ST3049
Burnhaven Abers 143 NK1244
Burnhead D & G 100 NX8695
Burnhervie Abers 142 NJ7319
Burnhill Green Staffs 60 SJ7800
Burnhope Dur 96 NZ1948
Burnhouse N Ayrs 115 NS3850
Burniston N York 91 TA0193
Burnley Lancs 81 SD8432
Burnmouth Border 119 NT9560
Burnopfield Dur 96 NZ1757
Burnrigg Cumb 94 NY4856
Burnsall N York 88 SE0361
Burnside Angus 134 NO4259
Burnside Angus 127 NO5050
Burnside Fife 126 NO1608
Burnside Moray 147 NJ1769
Burnside W Loth 117 NT0575
Burnside of Duntrune Angus 127 NO4434
Burnt Heath Essex 41 TM0627
Burnt Hill Berks 24 SU5774
Burnt Houses Dur 96 NZ1223
Burnt Oak E Susx 16 TQ5126
Burnt Yates N York 89 SE2561
Burntcommon Surrey 26 TQ0354
Burntheath Derbys 73 SK2431
Burnthouse Cnwll 3 SW7636
Burntisland Fife 117 NT2385
Burntwood Staffs 61 SK0509
Burntwood Green Staffs 61 SK0608
Burnville Devon 5 SX4982
Burnworthy Somset 9 ST1915
Burpham Surrey 26 TQ0152
Burpham W Susx 14 TQ0308
Burradon Nthumb 111 NT9806
Burradon T & W 103 NZ2772
Burrafirth Shet 155 HP6113
Burras Cnwll 2 SW6734
Burraton Cnwll 5 SX4167
Burraton Devon 6 SX6153
Burravoe Shet 155 HU5180
Burrells Cumb 94 NY6718
Burrelton P & K 126 NO2037
Burridge Devon 19 SS5735
Burridge Devon 10 ST3106
Burridge Hants 13 SU5110
Burrill N York 89 SE2387
Burringham Lincs 84 SE8309
Burrington Devon 19 SS6416
Burrington H & W 46 SO4472
Burrington Somset 21 ST4859
Burrough End Cambs 53 TL6255
Burrough Green Cambs 53 TL6355
Burrough on the Hill Leics 63 SK7510
Burrow Lancs 87 SD6174
Burrow Somset 20 SS9342
Burrow Bridge Somset 21 ST3530
Burrowhill Surrey 25 SU9762
Burrows Cross Surrey 14 TQ0846
Burry Swans 32 SS4590
Burry Port Carmth 32 SN4400
Burrygreen Swans 32 SS4591
Burscough Lancs 78 SD4310
Burscough Bridge Lancs 80 SD4412
Bursea E R Yk 84 SE8033
Burshill E R Yk 85 TA0948
Bursledon Hants 13 SU4809
Burslem Staffs 72 SJ8649
Burstall Suffk 54 TM0944
Burstock Dorset 10 ST4202
Burston Norfk 54 TM1383
Burston Staffs 72 SJ9330
Burstow Surrey 15 TQ3141
Burstwick E R Yk 85 TA2227
Burtersett N York 88 SD8989
Burtholme Cumb 101 NY5463
Burthorpe Green Suffk 53 TL7764
Burthwaite Cumb 93 NY4149
Burthy Cnwll 3 SW9155
Burtle Hill Somset 21 ST3843
Burtoft Lincs 64 TF2635
Burton Ches 71 SJ3174
Burton Ches 71 SJ5063

Burton
Carnbo

Burton *Dorset* 11 SY6891
Burton *Dorset* 12 SZ1694
Burton *Lincs* 76 SK9574
Burton *Nthumb* 111 NU1833
Burton *Pembks* 30 SM9805
Burton *Somset* 20 ST1944
Burton *Somset* 10 ST5313
Burton *Wilts* 35 ST8179
Burton *Wilts* 22 ST8232
Burton Agnes *E R Yk* 91 TA1062
Burton Bradstock *Dorset* 10 SY4889
Burton Coggles *Lincs* 63 SK9725
Burton Dassett *Warwks* 48 SP3951
Burton End *Essex* 39 TL5323
Burton End *Suffk* 53 TL6645
Burton Fleming *E R Yk* 91 TA0871
Burton Green *Warwks* 61 SP2675
Burton Green *Wrexhm* 71 SJ3458
Burton Hastings *Warwks* 50 SP4189
Burton in Lonsdale *N York* 87 SD6572
Burton Joyce *Notts* 63 SK6443
Burton Latimer *Nhants* 51 SP9074
Burton Lazars *Leics* 63 SK7716
Burton Leonard *N York* 89 SE3263
Burton on the Wolds *Leics* 62 SK5821
Burton Overy *Leics* 50 SP6798
Burton Pedwardine *Lincs* 64 TF1142
Burton Pidsea *E R Yk* 85 TA2431
Burton Salmon *N York* 83 SE4927
Burton upon Stather *Lincs* 84 SE8717
Burton upon Trent *Staffs* 73 SK2323
Burton's Green *Essex* 40 TL8226
Burton-in-Kendal *Cumb* 87 SD5376
Burtonwood *Ches* 78 SJ5692
Burwardsley *Ches* 71 SJ5156
Burwarton *Shrops* 59 SO6185
Burwash *E Susx* 16 TQ6724
Burwash Common *E Susx* 16 TQ6323
Burwash Weald *E Susx* 16 TQ6523
Burwell *Cambs* 53 TL5866
Burwell *Lincs* 77 TF3579
Burwen *Angles* 68 SH4293
Burwick *Ork* 155 ND4484
Bury *Cambs* 52 TL2883
Bury *Gt Man* 81 SD8011
Bury *Somset* 20 SS9427
Bury *W Susx* 14 TQ0113
Bury End *Beds* 38 TL1235
Bury End *Bucks* 26 SU9697
Bury Green *Herts* 39 TL4521
Bury St Edmunds *Suffk* 54 TL8564
Burythorpe *N York* 90 SE7964
Busby *E Rens* 115 NS5756
Buscot *Wilts* 36 SU2298
Bush *Abers* 135 NO7565
Bush *Cnwll* 18 SS2307
Bush Bank *H & W* 46 SO4551
Bush Green *Norfk* 55 TM2187
Bush Green *Suffk* 54 TL9157
Bush Hill Park *Gt Lon* 27 TQ3395
Bushbury *W Mids* 60 SJ9202
Bushby *Leics* 63 SK6503
Bushey *Herts* 26 TQ1395
Bushey Heath *Herts* 26 TQ1494
Bushley *H & W* 47 SO8734
Bushley Green *H & W* 47 SO8634
Bushmead *Beds* 52 TL1160
Bushton *Wilts* 36 SU0677
Busk *Cumb* 94 NY6042
Buslingthorpe *Lincs* 76 TF0785
Bussage *Gloucs* 35 SO8803
Bussex *Somset* 21 ST3535
Butcher Hill *W York* 81 SD9322
Butcher's Cross *E Susx* 16 TQ5525
Butcher's Pasture *Essex* 40 TL6024
Butcombe *Somset* 21 ST5161
Butleigh *Somset* 21 ST5233
Butleigh Wootton *Somset* 21 ST5035
Butler's Cross *Bucks* 38 SP8407
Butler's Hill *Notts* 75 SK5448
Butlers Marston *Warwks* 48 SP3250
Butley *Suffk* 55 TM3650
Butley Corner *Suffk* 55 TM3849
Butt Green *Ches* 72 SJ6651
Butt Lane *Staffs* 72 SJ8254
Butt's Green *Essex* 40 TL7603
Buttercrambe *N York* 90 SE7358
Butterdean *Border* 119 NT7964
Butterknowle *Dur* 95 NZ1025
Butterleigh *Devon* 9 SS9708
Butterley *Derbys* 74 SK4051
Buttermere *Cumb* 93 NY1717
Buttermere *Wilts* 23 SU3461
Butters Green *Staffs* 72 SJ8150
Buttershaw *W York* 82 SE1329
Butterstone *P & K* 125 NO0645
Butterton *Staffs* 72 SJ8242
Butterton *Staffs* 73 SK0756
Butterwick *Dur* 96 NZ3830
Butterwick *Lincs* 64 TF3845
Butterwick *N York* 90 SE7277
Butterwick *N York* 91 SE9871
Buttington *Powys* 58 SJ2408
Buttonbridge *Shrops* 60 SO7379
Buttonoak *Shrops* 60 SO7578
Buttsash *Hants* 13 SU4206
Buttsbear Cross *Cnwll* 18 SS2604
Buxhall *Suffk* 54 TM0057
Buxhall Fen Street *Suffk* 54 TM0059
Buxted *E Susx* 16 TQ4923
Buxton *Derbys* 74 SK0572
Buxton *Norfk* 67 TG2322
Buxton Heath *Norfk* 66 TG1821
Bwlch *Powys* 33 SO1522
Bwlch-y-cibau *Powys* 58 SJ1717
Bwlch-y-ffridd *Powys* 58 SO0795
Bwlch-y-groes *Pembks* 31 SN2436
Bwlch-y-sarnau *Powys* 45 SO0374
Bwlchgwyn *Wrexhm* 70 SJ2653
Bwlchllan *Cardgn* 44 SN5758
Bwlchnewydd *Carmth* 31 SN3624
Bwlchtocyn *Gwynd* 56 SH3125
Bwlchyddar *Powys* 58 SJ1722
Bwlchyfadfa *Cardgn* 42 SN4349
Bwlchymyrdd *Swans* 32 SS5798
Byermoor *T & W* 96 NZ1857
Byers Garth *Dur* 96 NZ3140
Byers Green *Dur* 96 NZ2233
Byfield *Nhants* 49 SP5152
Byfleet *Surrey* 26 TQ0661
Byford *H & W* 46 SO3942
Byker *T & W* 103 NZ2764
Bylchau *A & C* 70 SH9762
Byley *Ches* 79 SJ7269
Bynea *Carmth* 32 SS5499
Byrewalls *Border* 110 NT6642
Byrness *Nthumb* 102 NT7602
Bystock *Devon* 9 SY0283
Bythorn *Cambs* 51 TL0575
Byton *H & W* 46 SO3764
Bywell *Nthumb* 103 NZ0461
Byworth *W Susx* 14 SU9821

C

Cabourne *Lincs* 85 TA1401
Cabrach *Ag & B* 112 NR4964
Cabrach *Moray* 141 NJ3826
Cabus *Lancs* 80 SD4948
Cabvie Lodge *Highld* 138 NH1567
Cackle Street *E Susx* 16 TQ4526
Cackle Street *E Susx* 16 TQ6919
Cackle Street *E Susx* 17 TQ8218
Cadbury *Devon* 9 SS9105
Cadbury Barton *Devon* 19 SS6917
Cadder *E Duns* 116 NS6072
Caddington *Beds* 38 TL0619
Caddonfoot *Border* 109 NT4535
Cade Street *E Susx* 16 TQ6020
Cadeby *Leics* 62 SK4202
Cadeby *S York* 75 SE5100
Cadeleigh *Devon* 9 SS9108
Cadgwith *Cnwll* 3 SW7214
Cadham *Fife* 126 NO2801
Cadishead *Gt Man* 79 SJ7091
Cadle *Swans* 32 SS6296
Cadley *Lancs* 80 SD5231
Cadley *Wilts* 23 SU2066
Cadley *Wilts* 23 SU2453
Cadmore End *Bucks* 37 SU7892
Cadnam *Hants* 12 SU3013
Cadney *Lincs* 84 TA0103
Cadole *Flints* 70 SJ2062
Cadoxton *V Glam* 20 ST1269
Cadoxton Juxta-Neath *Neath* 32 SS7598
Cadsden *Bucks* 38 SP8204
Cadwst *Denbgs* 58 SJ0235
Cae'r bryn *Carmth* 32 SN5913
Cae'r-bont *Powys* 32 SN8011
Caeathro *Gwynd* 68 SH5061
Caehopkin *Powys* 33 SN8212
Caenby *Lincs* 76 SK9989
Caenby Corner *Lincs* 76 SK9689
Caeo *Carmth* 44 SN6740
Caer Farchell *Pembks* 30 SM7927
Caerau *Brdgnd* 33 SS8694
Caerau *Cardif* 33 ST1375
Caerdeon *Gwynd* 57 SH6518
Caergeiliog *Angles* 68 SH3178
Caergwrle *Flints* 71 SJ3057
Caerhun *A & C* 69 SH7770
Caerlanrig *Border* 109 NT3904
Caerleon *Newpt* 34 ST3490
Caernarfon *Gwynd* 68 SH4862
Caerphilly *Caerph* 33 ST1587
Caersws *Powys* 58 SO0392
Caerwedros *Cardgn* 42 SN3755
Caerwent *Mons* 34 ST4790
Caerwys *Flints* 70 SJ1272
Caerynwch *Gwynd* 57 SH7617
Caggle Street *Mons* 34 SO3717
Caim *Angles* 69 SH6280
Cairinis *W Isls* 154 NF8260
Cairinis *W Isls* 154 NB2133
Cairnbaan *Ag & B* 113 NR8390
Cairnbrogie *Abers* 143 NJ8527
Cairnbulg *Abers* 143 NK0365
Cairncross *Border* 119 NT8963
Cairncurran *Inver* 115 NS3170
Cairndow *Ag & B* 123 NN1810
Cairneyhill *Fife* 117 NT0486
Cairnfield House *Moray* 142 NJ4162
Cairngarroch *D & G* 98 NX0549
Cairngrassie *Abers* 135 NO9095
Cairnhall *D & G* 100 NX9086
Cairnie *Abers* 142 NJ4844
Cairnorrie *Abers* 143 NJ8641
Cairnryan *D & G* 98 NX0668
Cairnty *Moray* 141 NJ3352
Caister-on-Sea *Norfk* 67 TG5112
Caistor *Lincs* 85 TA1101
Caistor St Edmund *Norfk* 67 TG2303
Cake Street *Norfk* 54 TM0690
Cakebole *H & W* 60 SO8772
Calais Street *Suffk* 54 TL9739
Calbourne *IOW* 13 SZ4286
Calceby *Lincs* 77 TF3875
Calcot *Berks* 24 SU6671
Calcot *Flints* 70 SJ1674
Calcot *Gloucs* 36 SP0810
Calcot Row *Berks* 24 SU6771
Calcots *Moray* 141 NJ2563
Calcott *Kent* 29 TR1762
Calcott *Shrops* 59 SJ4413
Calcutt *N York* 83 SE3455
Calcutt *Wilts* 36 SU1193
Caldbeck *Cumb* 93 NY3240
Caldbergh *N York* 89 SE0985
Caldecote *Cambs* 52 TL1488
Caldecote *Cambs* 52 TL3456
Caldecote *Herts* 39 TL2338
Caldecote *Nhants* 49 SP6851
Caldecote Highfields *Cambs* 52 TL3559
Caldecott *Nhants* 51 SP9868
Caldecott *Oxon* 37 SU4996
Caldecott *Rutlnd* 51 SP8693
Calder Bridge *Cumb* 86 NY0306
Calder Grove *W York* 82 SE3016
Calder Vale *Lancs* 80 SD5345
Calderbank *N Lans* 116 NS7663
Calderbrook *Gt Man* 82 SD9418
Caldercote *Bucks* 38 SP8935
Caldercruix *N Lans* 116 NS8167
Caldermill *S Lans* 107 NS6641
Caldermore *Gt Man* 81 SD9316
Caldicot *Mons* 34 ST4888
Caldwell *N York* 89 NZ1613
Caldy *Mersyd* 78 SJ2285
Caledfwlch *Carmth* 44 SN6525
Calendra *Cnwll* 3 SW9240
Calenick *Cnwll* 3 SW8243
Calford Green *Suffk* 53 TL7045
Calfsound *Ork* 155 HY5738
Calgary *Ag & B* 121 NM3751
Califer *Moray* 141 NJ0857
California *Derbys* 62 SK3335
California *Falk* 116 NS9076
California *Norfk* 67 TG5115
California *Suffk* 54 TM0641
California Cross *Devon* 7 SX7053
Calke *Derbys* 62 SK3721
Callakille *Highld* 137 NG6955
Callaly *Nthumb* 111 NU0509
Callander *Stirlg* 124 NN6207
Callanish *W Isls* 154 NB2133
Callaughton *Shrops* 59 SO6197
Callert Cottage *Highld* 130 NN1060
Callestick *Cnwll* 3 SW7750
Calligarry *Highld* 129 NG6203
Callington *Cnwll* 5 SX3669
Callingwood *Staffs* 73 SK1823
Callow *H & W* 46 SO4934
Callow End *H & W* 47 SO8350
Callow Hill *H & W* 60 SO7573
Callow Hill *H & W* 47 SP0164
Callow Hill *Wilts* 36 SU0384
Callows Grave *H & W* 46 SO5967
Calmore *Hants* 12 SU3414
Calmsden *Gloucs* 36 SP0508
Calne *Wilts* 35 ST9971
Calow *Derbys* 74 SK4071
Calshot *Hants* 13 SU4701
Calstock *Cnwll* 6 SX4368
Calstone Wellington *Wilts* 23 SU0268
Calthorpe *Norfk* 66 TG1831
Calthorpe Street *Norfk* 67 TG4025
Calthwaite *Cumb* 93 NY4640
Calton *N York* 88 SD9059
Calton *Staffs* 73 SK1049
Calton Green *Staffs* 73 SK1049
Calveley *Ches* 71 SJ5958
Calver *Derbys* 74 SK2374
Calver Hill *H & W* 46 SO3748
Calver Sough *Derbys* 74 SK2374
Calverhall *Shrops* 59 SJ6037
Calverleigh *Devon* 9 SS9214
Calverley *W York* 82 SE2036
Calvert *Bucks* 49 SP6824
Calverton *Bucks* 38 SP7939
Calverton *Notts* 75 SK6149
Calvine *P & K* 132 NN8065
Calvo *Cumb* 92 NY1453
Calzeat *Border* 108 NT1135
Cam *Gloucs* 35 ST7599
Camas Luinie *Highld* 138 NG9428
Camasachoirce *Highld* 130 NM7660
Camasine *Highld* 130 NM7561
Camastianavaig *Highld* 137 NG5039
Camasunary *Highld* 128 NG5118
Camault Muir *Highld* 139 NH5040
Camber *E Susx* 17 TQ9618
Camberley *Surrey* 25 SU8860
Camberwell *Gt Lon* 27 TQ3276
Camblesforth *N York* 83 SE6425
Cambo *Nthumb* 103 NZ0285
Cambois *Nthumb* 103 NZ3083
Camborne *Cnwll* 2 SW6440
Cambridge *Cambs* 53 TL4558
Cambridge *Gloucs* 35 SO7403
Cambrose *Cnwll* 2 SW6845
Cambus *Clacks* 116 NS8594
Cambus O' May *Abers* 134 NO4198
Cambusavie Platform *Highld* 147 NH7696
Cambusbarron *Stirlg* 116 NS7792
Cambuskenneth *Stirlg* 116 NS8094
Cambuslang *S Lans* 116 NS6460
Cambuswallace *S Lans* 108 NT0438
Camden Town *Gt Lon* 27 TQ2883
Cameley *Somset* 21 ST6157
Camelford *Cnwll* 4 SX1083
Camelon *Falk* 116 NS8680
Camer's Green *H & W* 47 SO7735
Camerory *Highld* 141 NJ0131
Camerton *Cumb* 92 NY0330
Camerton *Somset* 22 ST6857
Camghouran *P & K* 124 NN5556
Camieston *Border* 110 NT5730
Cammachmore *Abers* 135 NO9195
Cammeringham *Lincs* 76 SK9482
Camore *Highld* 147 NH7889
Camp The *Gloucs* 35 SO9109
Campbeltown *Ag & B* 105 NR7120
Camperdown *T & W* 103 NZ2772
Cample *D & G* 100 NX8993
Campmuir *Angus* 126 NO2137
Camps *W Loth* 117 NT0968
Camps End *Cambs* 53 TL6142
Campsall *S York* 83 SE5413
Campsie *E Duns* 116 NS6079
Campsie Ash *Suffk* 55 TM3356
Campton *Beds* 38 TL1238
Camptown *Border* 110 NT6813
Camrose *Pembks* 30 SM9220
Camserney *P & K* 125 NN8149
Camster *Highld* 151 ND2642
Camusnagaul *Highld* 145 NH0589
Camusnagaul *Highld* 130 NN0874
Camusteel *Highld* 137 NG7042
Camusterrach *Highld* 137 NG7141
Canada *Hants* 12 SU2818
Canal Foot *Cumb* 86 SD3177
Canaston Bridge *Pembks* 30 SN0615
Candacraig *Abers* 134 NO3499
Candle Street *Suffk* 54 TM0374
Candlesby *Lincs* 77 TF4567
Candover Green *Shrops* 59 SJ5005
Candyburn *Border* 108 NT0741
Cane End *Oxon* 37 SU6779
Canewdon *Essex* 40 TQ9094
Canfold Bottom *Dorset* 12 SU0305
Canford Cliffs *Dorset* 12 SZ0589
Canford Magna *Dorset* 12 SZ0398
Canhams Green *Suffk* 54 TM0565
Canisbay *Highld* 151 ND3472
Canklow *S York* 74 SK4291
Canley *W Mids* 61 SP3077
Cann *Dorset* 22 ST8721
Cannich *Highld* 139 NH3331
Canning Town *Gt Lon* 27 TQ4081
Cannington *Somset* 20 ST2539
Cannock *Staffs* 60 SJ9810
Cannock Wood *Staffs* 61 SK0412
Cannon Bridge *H & W* 46 SO4340
Canon Frome *H & W* 47 SO6443
Canon Pyon *H & W* 46 SO4548
Canonbie *D & G* 101 NY3976
Canons Ashby *Nhants* 49 SP5750
Canonstown *Cnwll* 2 SW5335
Canterbury *Kent* 29 TR1457
Cantley *Norfk* 67 TG3704
Cantley *S York* 83 SE6202
Cantlop *Shrops* 59 SJ5205
Canton *Cardif* 33 ST1676
Cantraywood *Highld* 140 NH7847
Cantsfield *Lancs* 87 SD6272
Canvey Island *Essex* 40 TQ7983
Canwick *Lincs* 76 SK9869
Canworthy Water *Cnwll* 5 SX2291
Caol *Highld* 130 NN1175
Caolas Scalpaigh *W Isls* 154 NG2198
Caoles *Ag & B* 120 NM0848
Caonich *Highld* 130 NM0692
Capel *Kent* 16 TQ6344
Capel *Surrey* 15 TQ1740
Capel Bangor *Cardgn* 43 SN6580
Capel Betws Lleucu *Cardgn* 44 SN6058
Capel Coch *Angles* 68 SH4682
Capel Curig *A & C* 69 SH7258
Capel Cynon *Cardgn* 42 SN3849
Capel Dewi *Cardgn* 31 SN4542
Capel Dewi *Carmth* 32 SN4720
Capel Garmon *A & C* 69 SH8155
Capel Green *Suffk* 55 TM3649
Capel Gwyn *Angles* 68 SH3475
Capel Gwyn *Carmth* 32 SN4622
Capel Gwynfe *Carmth* 32 SN7222
Capel Hendre *Carmth* 32 SN5911
Capel Isaac *Carmth* 44 SN5926
Capel Iwan *Carmth* 31 SN2936
Capel le Ferne *Kent* 29 TR2539
Capel Llanilltern *Cardif* 33 ST0979
Capel Mawr *Angles* 68 SH4171
Capel Seion *Cardgn* 43 SN6379
Capel St Andrew *Suffk* 55 TM3748
Capel St Mary *Suffk* 54 TM0838
Capel Trisant *Cardgn* 43 SN7175
Capel-Dewi *Cardgn* 43 SN6282
Capel-y-ffin *Powys* 46 SO2531
Capel-y-graig *Gwynd* 69 SH5469
Capelles *Guern* 152 GN0000
Capeluchaf *Gwynd* 68 SH4349
Capelulo *A & C* 69 SH7476
Capenhurst *Ches* 71 SJ3673
Capernwray *Lancs* 87 SD5371
Capheaton *Nthumb* 103 NZ0380
Caplaw *E Rens* 115 NS4458
Capon's Green *Suffk* 55 TM2867
Cappercleuch *Border* 109 NT2423
Capstone *Kent* 28 TQ7865
Capton *Devon* 7 SX8353
Capton *Somset* 20 ST0839
Caputh *P & K* 125 NO0840
Car Colston *Notts* 63 SK7142
Caradon Town *Cnwll* 5 SX2971
Carbeth Inn *Stirlg* 115 NS5279
Carbis *Cnwll* 4 SX0059
Carbis Bay *Cnwll* 2 SW5238
Carbost *Highld* 136 NG3731
Carbost *Highld* 136 NG4248
Carbrook *S York* 74 SK3889
Carbrooke *Norfk* 66 TF9402
Carburton *Notts* 75 SK6172
Carclaze *Cnwll* 3 SX0254
Carclew *Cnwll* 3 SW7838
Carcroft *S York* 83 SE5409
Cardenden *Fife* 117 NT2195
Cardeston *Shrops* 59 SJ3912
Cardewlees *Cumb* 93 NY3551
Cardhu *Moray* 141 NJ1943
Cardiff *Cardif* 33 ST1876
Cardigan *Cardgn* 42 SN1746
Cardinal's Green *Cambs* 53 TL6146
Cardington *Beds* 38 TL0847
Cardington *Shrops* 59 SO5095
Cardinham *Cnwll* 4 SX1268
Cardrain *D & G* 98 NX1231
Cardrona *Border* 109 NT3038
Cardross *Ag & B* 115 NS3477
Cardryne *D & G* 98 NX1132
Cardurnock *Cumb* 93 NY1758
Careby *Lincs* 64 TF0216
Careston *Angus* 134 NO5260
Carew *Pembks* 30 SN0403
Carew Cheriton *Pembks* 30 SN0402
Carew Newton *Pembks* 30 SN0404
Carey *H & W* 46 SO5730
Carfin *N Lans* 116 NS7759
Carfraemill *Border* 118 NT5053
Cargate Green *Norfk* 67 TG3912
Cargen *D & G* 100 NX9672
Cargenbridge *D & G* 100 NX9575
Cargill *P & K* 126 NO1536
Cargo *Cumb* 93 NY3659
Cargreen *Cnwll* 6 SX4362
Cargurrel *Cnwll* 3 SW8737
Carham *Nthumb* 110 NT7938
Carhampton *Somset* 20 ST0042
Carharrack *Cnwll* 3 SW7341
Carie *P & K* 124 NN6257
Carinish *W Isls* 154 NF8260
Carisbrooke *IOW* 13 SZ4888
Cark *Cumb* 87 SD3676
Carkeel *Cnwll* 5 SX4160
Carlabhagh *W Isls* 154 NB2043
Carland Cross *Cnwll* 3 SW8554
Carlbury *Dur* 96 NZ2115
Carlby *Lincs* 64 TF0413
Carlcroft *Nthumb* 110 NT8311
Carlecotes *S York* 82 SE1703
Carleen *Cnwll* 2 SW6130
Carlesmoor *N York* 89 SE2073
Carleton *Cumb* 93 NY4252
Carleton *Cumb* 94 NY5329
Carleton *Lancs* 80 SD3339
Carleton *N York* 82 SD9749
Carleton *N York* 89 SE3959
Carleton *W York* 83 SE4620
Carleton Forehoe *Norfk* 66 TG0905
Carleton Rode *Norfk* 66 TM1093
Carleton St Peter *Norfk* 67 TG3402
Carlidnack *Cnwll* 3 SW7729
Carlin How *N York* 97 NZ7019
Carlincraig *Abers* 142 NJ6743
Carlingcott *Somset* 22 ST6958
Carlisle *Cumb* 93 NY3956
Carloggas *Cnwll* 4 SW8765
Carlops *Border* 117 NT1656
Carloway *W Isls* 154 NB2043
Carlton *Beds* 51 SP9555
Carlton *Cambs* 53 TL6452
Carlton *Cumb* 86 NY0109
Carlton *Dur* 96 NZ3921
Carlton *Leics* 62 SK3904
Carlton *N York* 90 NZ5004
Carlton *N York* 88 SE0684
Carlton *N York* 90 SE6086
Carlton *N York* 83 SE6423
Carlton *Notts* 62 SK6041
Carlton *S York* 83 SE3610
Carlton *Suffk* 55 TM3764
Carlton *W York* 83 SE3327
Carlton Colville *Suffk* 55 TM5189
Carlton Curlieu *Leics* 50 SP6997
Carlton Green *Cambs* 53 TL6451
Carlton Husthwaite *N York* 90 SE4976
Carlton in Lindrick *Notts* 75 SK5883
Carlton Miniott *N York* 89 SE3981
Carlton Scroop *Lincs* 63 SK9445
Carlton-le-Moorland *Lincs* 76 SK9058
Carlton-on-Trent *Notts* 75 SK7963
Carluddon *Cnwll* 3 SX0255
Carluke *S Lans* 116 NS8450
Carlyon Bay *Cnwll* 3 SX0552
Carmacoup *S Lans* 107 NS7927
Carmarthen *Carmth* 31 SN4120
Carmel *Carmth* 32 SN5816
Carmel *Flints* 70 SJ1676
Carmel *Gwynd* 68 SH4954
Carmichael *S Lans* 108 NS9238
Carminowe *Cnwll* 2 SW6623
Carmunnock *C Glas* 115 NS5957
Carmyle *C Glas* 116 NS6462
Carmyllie *Angus* 127 NO5442
Carn Brea *Cnwll* 2 SW6841
Carn-gorm *Highld* 138 NG9520
Carnaby *E R Yk* 91 TA1465
Carnbee *Fife* 127 NO5206
Carnbo *P & K* 125 NO0503

Clopton
Corndon

Clopton *Suffk* 55 TM2253
Clopton Corner *Suffk* 55 TM2254
Clopton Green *Suffk* 53 TL7655
Clopton Green *Suffk* 54 TL9759
Clos du Valle *Guern* 152 GN0000
Closeburn *D & G* 100 NX8992
Closeburnmill *D & G* 100 NX9094
Closeclark *IOM* 153 SC2775
Closworth *Somset* 10 ST5610
Clothall *Herts* 39 TL2731
Clotton *Ches* 71 SJ5264
Cloudesley Bush *Warwks* 50 SP4686
Clough *Gt Man* 79 SD9408
Clough Foot *W York* 81 SD9123
Clough Head *N York* 82 SE0918
Cloughton *N York* 91 TA0194
Cloughton Newlands *N York* 91 TA0096
Clousta *Shet* 155 HU3057
Clova *Angus* 134 NO3273
Clovelly *Devon* 18 SS3124
Clovenfords *Border* 109 NT4536
Clovulin *Highld* 130 NN0063
Clow Bridge *Lancs* 81 SD8228
Clowne *Derbys* 75 SK4875
Clows Top *H & W* 60 SO7172
Cloy *Wrexhm* 71 SJ3943
Cluanie Inn *Highld* 130 NH0711
Cluanie Lodge *Highld* 130 NH0910
Clubworthy *Cnwll* 5 SX2792
Clugston *D & G* 98 NX3557
Clun *Shrops* 59 SO3080
Clunas *Highld* 140 NH8846
Clunbury *Shrops* 59 SO3780
Clune *Highld* 140 NH7925
Clunes *Highld* 131 NN1988
Clungunford *Shrops* 46 SO3978
Clunie *Abers* 142 NJ6350
Clunie *P & K* 126 NO1043
Clunton *Shrops* 59 SO3381
Clutton *Ches* 71 SJ4654
Clutton *Somset* 21 ST6259
Clutton Hill *Somset* 21 ST6359
Clwt-y-bont *Gwynd* 69 SH5762
Clydach *Mons* 34 SO2213
Clydach *Swans* 32 SN6800
Clydach Vale *Rhondd* 33 SS9792
Clydebank *D & Cb* 115 NS4970
Clydey *Pembks* 31 SN2535
Clyffe Pypard *Wilts* 36 SU0777
Clynder *Ag & B* 114 NS2484
Clynderwen *Carmth* 31 SN1219
Clyne *Neath* 32 SN8000
Clynnog-fawr *Gwynd* 68 SH4149
Clyro *Powys* 45 SO2143
Clyst Honiton *Devon* 9 SX9893
Clyst Hydon *Devon* 9 ST0301
Clyst St George *Devon* 9 SX9888
Clyst St Lawrence *Devon* 9 ST0200
Clyst St Mary *Devon* 9 SX9791
Cnoc *W Isls* 154 NB4931
Cnwch Coch *Cardgn* 43 SN6774
Coad's Green *Cnwll* 5 SX2976
Coal Aston *Derbys* 74 SK3679
Coal Pool *W Mids* 60 SP0199
Coal Street *Suffk* 55 TM2371
Coalbrookdale *Shrops* 60 SJ6604
Coalbrookvale *Blae G* 33 SO1909
Coalburn *S Lans* 108 NS8134
Coalburns *T & W* 96 NZ1260
Coalcleugh *Nthumb* 95 NY8045
Coaley *Gloucs* 35 SO7701
Coalfell *Cumb* 94 NY5959
Coalhill *Essex* 40 TQ7597
Coalmoor *Shrops* 60 SJ6607
Coalpit Heath *Gloucs* 35 ST6780
Coalpit Hill *Staffs* 72 SJ8253
Coalport *Shrops* 60 SJ6902
Coalsnaughton *Clacks* 116 NS9195
Coaltown of Balgonie *Fife* 117 NT2999
Coaltown of Wemyss *Fife* 118 NT3295
Coalville *Leics* 62 SK4214
Coanwood *Nthumb* 94 NY6859
Coat *Somset* 21 ST4520
Coatbridge *N Lans* 116 NS7365
Coatdyke *N Lans* 116 NS7465
Coate *Wilts* 23 SU0462
Coate *Wilts* 36 SU1882
Coates *Cambs* 64 TL3097
Coates *Gloucs* 35 SO9701
Coates *Lincs* 75 SK8181
Coates *Lincs* 76 SK9083
Coates *W Susx* 14 SU9917
Coatham *N York* 97 NZ5925
Coatham Mundeville *Dur* 96 NZ2820
Cobbaton *Devon* 19 SS6126
Coberley *Gloucs* 35 SO9616
Cobhall Common *H & W* 46 SO4535
Cobham *Kent* 28 TQ6768
Cobham *Surrey* 26 TQ1060
Coblers Green *Essex* 40 TL6819
Cobley *Dorset* 12 SU0220
Cobnash *H & W* 46 SO4560
Cobo *Guern* 152 GN0000
Cobridge *Staffs* 72 SJ8747
Coburby *Abers* 143 NJ9164
Cock Alley *Derbys* 74 SK4170
Cock Bank *Wrexhm* 71 SJ3545
Cock Bevington *Warwks* 48 SP0552
Cock Bridge *Abers* 133 NJ2509
Cock Clarks *Essex* 40 TL8102
Cock End *Suffk* 53 TL7253
Cock Green *Essex* 40 TL6919
Cock Marling *E Susx* 17 TQ8718
Cock Street *Kent* 28 TQ7850
Cockayne *N York* 90 SE6198
Cockayne Hatley *Beds* 52 TL2649
Cockburnspath *Border* 119 NT7770
Cockenzie and Port Seton *E Loth* 118 NT4075
Cocker Bar *Lancs* 80 SD5022
Cocker Brook *Lancs* 81 SD7425
Cockerdale *W York* 82 SE2329
Cockerham *Lancs* 80 SD4651
Cockermouth *Cumb* 92 NY1230
Cockernhoe Green *Herts* 38 TL1223
Cockett *Swans* 32 SS6394
Cockfield *Dur* 96 NZ1224
Cockfield *Suffk* 54 TL9054
Cockfosters *Gt Lon* 27 TQ2796
Cocking *W Susx* 14 SU8717
Cocking Causeway *W Susx* 14 SU8819
Cockington *Devon* 7 SX8963
Cocklake *Somset* 21 ST4449
Cockle Park *Nthumb* 103 NZ2091
Cockley Beck *Cumb* 86 NY2501
Cockley Cley *Norfk* 66 TF7904
Cockpole Green *Berks* 37 SU7981
Cocks *Cnwll* 3 SW7652
Cockshutford *Shrops* 59 SO5885
Cockshutt *Shrops* 59 SJ4328
Cockthorpe *Norfk* 66 TF9842
Cockwells *Cnwll* 2 SW5234
Cockwood *Devon* 9 SX9780
Cockwood *Somset* 20 ST2242
Cockyard *Derbys* 74 SK0479
Cockyard *H & W* 46 SO4133
Coddenham *Suffk* 54 TM1354
Coddington *Ches* 71 SJ4555
Coddington *H & W* 47 SO7142
Coddington *Notts* 76 SK8354
Codford St Mary *Wilts* 22 ST9739
Codford St Peter *Wilts* 22 ST9639
Codicote *Herts* 39 TL2118
Codmore Hill *W Susx* 14 TQ0520
Codnor *Derbys* 74 SK4149
Codrington *Gloucs* 35 ST7278
Codsall *Staffs* 60 SJ8603
Codsall Wood *Staffs* 60 SJ8404
Coed Morgan *Mons* 34 SO3511
Coed Talon *Flints* 70 SJ2659
Coed Ystumgwern *Gwynd* 57 SH5824
Coed-y-Bryn *Cardgn* 42 SN3545
Coed-y-caerau *Newpt* 34 ST3891
Coed-y-paen *Mons* 34 ST3398
Coed-yr-ynys *Powys* 33 SO1520
Coedana *Angles* 68 SH4382
Coedely *Rhondd* 33 ST0285
Coedkernew *Newpt* 34 ST2783
Coedpoeth *Wrexhm* 70 SJ2851
Coedway *Powys* 59 SJ3315
Coelbren *Powys* 33 SN8511
Coffinswell *Devon* 7 SX8968
Coffle End *Beds* 51 TL0159
Cofton Hackett *H & W* 60 SP0075
Cogan *V Glam* 33 ST1771
Cogenhoe *Nhants* 51 SP8260
Cogges *Oxon* 36 SP3609
Coggeshall *Essex* 40 TL8522
Coggin's Mill *E Susx* 16 TQ5927
Coignafearn *Highld* 140 NH7018
Coilacriech *Abers* 134 NO3296
Coilantogle *Stirlg* 124 NN5907
Coillore *Highld* 136 NG3537
Coiltry *Highld* 131 NH3506
Coity *Brdgnd* 33 SS9281
Col *W Isls* 154 NB4739
Colaboll *Highld* 146 NC5610
Colan *Cnwll* 4 SW8661
Colaton Raleigh *Devon* 9 SY0787
Colbost *Highld* 136 NG2148
Colburn *N York* 89 SE1999
Colbury *Hants* 12 SU3410
Colby *Cumb* 94 NY6620
Colby *IOM* 153 SC2370
Colby *Norfk* 67 TG2231
Colchester *Essex* 41 TL9925
Cold Ash *Berks* 24 SU5169
Cold Ashby *Nhants* 50 SP6576
Cold Ashton *Gloucs* 35 ST7572
Cold Aston *Gloucs* 36 SP1219
Cold Blow *Pembks* 31 SN1212
Cold Brayfield *Bucks* 38 SP9252
Cold Cotes *N York* 88 SD7171
Cold Green *H & W* 47 SO6842
Cold Hanworth *Lincs* 76 TF0383
Cold Harbour *Herts* 38 TL1415
Cold Harbour *Oxon* 37 SU6379
Cold Harbour *Wilts* 22 ST8645
Cold Hatton *Shrops* 59 SJ6221
Cold Hatton Heath *Shrops* 59 SJ6321
Cold Hesledon *Dur* 96 NZ4146
Cold Hiendley *W York* 83 SE3714
Cold Higham *Nhants* 49 SP6653
Cold Kirby *N York* 90 SE5384
Cold Newton *Leics* 63 SK7106
Cold Northcott *Cnwll* 5 SX2086
Cold Norton *Essex* 40 TL8500
Cold Overton *Leics* 63 SK8010
Cold Weston *Shrops* 59 SO5583
Coldbackie *Highld* 149 NC6160
Coldbeck *Cumb* 88 NY7204
Coldean *E Susx* 15 TQ3308
Coldeast *Devon* 7 SX8174
Colden *W York* 82 SD9628
Colden Common *Hants* 13 SU4822
Coldfair Green *Suffk* 55 TM4360
Coldham *Cambs* 65 TF4303
Coldharbour *Cnwll* 3 SW7548
Coldharbour *Devon* 9 ST0612
Coldharbour *Gloucs* 34 SO5503
Coldharbour *Surrey* 15 TQ1443
Coldingham *Border* 119 NT9065
Coldmeece *Staffs* 72 SJ8532
Coldred *Kent* 29 TR2747
Coldridge *Devon* 8 SS6907
Coldstream *Border* 110 NT8439
Coldwaltham *W Susx* 14 TQ0216
Coldwell *H & W* 46 SO4235
Cole *Somset* 22 ST6733
Cole End *Warwks* 61 SP2089
Cole Green *Herts* 39 TL2811
Cole Green *Herts* 39 TL4330
Cole Henley *Hants* 24 SU4651
Cole's Cross *Devon* 7 SX7746
Colebatch *Shrops* 59 SO3187
Colebrook *Devon* 9 ST0006
Colebrook *Devon* 6 SX5457
Colebrooke *Devon* 8 SX7699
Coleby *Lincs* 84 SE8919
Coleby *Lincs* 76 SK9760
Coleford *Devon* 8 SS7701
Coleford *Gloucs* 34 SO5710
Coleford *Somset* 22 ST6848
Coleford Water *Somset* 20 ST1133
Colegate End *Norfk* 55 TM1987
Colehill *Dorset* 12 SU0201
Coleman Green *Herts* 39 TL1812
Coleman's Hatch *E Susx* 16 TQ4433
Colemere *Shrops* 59 SJ4332
Colemore *Hants* 24 SU7030
Colemore Green *Shrops* 60 SO7197
Colenden *P & K* 126 NO1029
Coleorton *Leics* 62 SK4017
Colerne *Wilts* 35 ST8271
Coles Cross *Dorset* 10 ST3902
Coles Green *Suffk* 54 TM1041
Colesbourne *Gloucs* 35 SP0013
Colesden *Beds* 52 TL1255
Coleshill *Bucks* 26 SU9495
Coleshill *Oxon* 36 SU2393
Coleshill *Warwks* 61 SP2089
Colestocks *Devon* 9 ST0900
Coley *Somset* 21 ST5855
Colgate *W Susx* 15 TQ2332
Colgrain *Ag & B* 115 NS3280
Colinsburgh *Fife* 127 NO4703
Colinton *C Edin* 117 NT2168
Colintraive *Ag & B* 114 NS0374
Colkirk *Norfk* 66 TF9126
Collace *P & K* 126 NO2032
Collafirth *Shet* 155 HU3482
Collaton *Devon* 7 SX7139
Collaton *Devon* 7 SX7952
Collaton St Mary *Devon* 7 SX8660
College Green *Somset* 21 ST5736
College of Roseisle *Moray* 141 NJ1466
College Town *Berks* 25 SU8560
Collessie *Fife* 126 NO2813
Colleton Mills *Devon* 19 SS6615
Collier Row *Gt Lon* 27 TQ5091
Collier Street *Kent* 28 TQ7145
Collier's End *Herts* 39 TL3720
Collier's Green *Kent* 17 TQ7822
Colliers Green *Kent* 28 TQ7538
Colliery Row *T & W* 96 NZ3249
Collieston *Abers* 143 NK0328
Collin *D & G* 100 NY0276
Collingbourne Ducis *Wilts* 23 SU2453
Collingbourne Kingston *Wilts* 23 SU2355
Collingham *W York* 83 SE3945
Collington *H & W* 47 SO6460
Collingtree *Nhants* 49 SP7555
Collins Green *Ches* 78 SJ5594
Collins Green *H & W* 47 SO7457
Colliston *Angus* 127 NO6045
Colliton *Devon* 9 ST0804
Collyweston *Nhants* 63 SK9902
Colmonell *S Ayrs* 98 NX1485
Colmworth *Beds* 51 TL1058
Coln Rogers *Gloucs* 36 SP0809
Coln St Aldwyns *Gloucs* 36 SP1405
Coln St Dennis *Gloucs* 36 SP0810
Colnbrook *Berks* 26 TQ0277
Colne *Cambs* 52 TL3775
Colne *Lancs* 81 SD8939
Colne Bridge *W York* 82 SE1720
Colne Edge *Lancs* 81 SD8841
Colne Engaine *Essex* 40 TL8430
Colney *Norfk* 66 TG1807
Colney Heath *Herts* 39 TL2005
Colney Street *Herts* 26 TL1502
Colpy *Abers* 142 NJ6432
Colquhar *Border* 109 NT3341
Colquite *Cnwll* 4 SX0570
Colscott *Devon* 18 SS3614
Colsterdale *N York* 89 SE1381
Colsterworth *Lincs* 63 SK9324
Colston Bassett *Notts* 63 SK7033
Colt Hill *Hants* 24 SU7551
Colt's Hill *Kent* 16 TQ6443
Coltfield *Moray* 141 NJ1163
Coltishall *Norfk* 67 TG2719
Colton *Cumb* 86 SD3185
Colton *N York* 83 SE5444
Colton *Norfk* 66 TG1009
Colton *Staffs* 73 SK0420
Colton *W York* 83 SE3732
Columbjohn *Devon* 9 SX9699
Colva *Powys* 45 SO1952
Colvend *D & G* 92 NX8654
Colwall *H & W* 47 SO7542
Colwell *Nthumb* 102 NY9575
Colwich *Staffs* 73 SK0121
Colwick *Notts* 62 SK6140
Colwinston *V Glam* 33 SS9375
Colworth *W Susx* 14 SU9103
Colwyn Bay *A & C* 69 SH8578
Colyford *Devon* 10 SY2592
Colyton *Devon* 9 SY2494
Combe *Berks* 23 SU3760
Combe *Devon* 7 SX7238
Combe *Devon* 7 SX8448
Combe *H & W* 46 SO3463
Combe *Oxon* 36 SP4116
Combe Almer *Dorset* 11 SY9597
Combe Common *Surrey* 14 SU9436
Combe Fishacre *Devon* 7 SX8465
Combe Florey *Somset* 20 ST1531
Combe Hay *Somset* 22 ST7359
Combe Martin *Devon* 19 SS5846
Combe Moor *H & W* 46 SO3663
Combe Raleigh *Devon* 9 ST1502
Combe St Nicholas *Somset* 10 ST3011
Combeinteignhead *Devon* 7 SX9071
Comberbach *Ches* 79 SJ6477
Comberford *Staffs* 61 SK1907
Comberton *Cambs* 52 TL3856
Comberton *H & W* 46 SO4968
Combpyne *Devon* 10 SY2892
Combridge *Staffs* 73 SK0937
Combrook *Warwks* 48 SP3051
Combs *Derbys* 74 SK0478
Combs *Suffk* 54 TM0456
Combs Ford *Suffk* 54 TM0457
Combwich *Somset* 20 ST2542
Comers *Abers* 135 NJ6707
Comhampton *H & W* 47 SO8367
Commercial *Pembks* 31 SN1416
Commercial End *Cambs* 53 TL5563
Commins Coch *Powys* 57 SH8402
Common Edge *Lancs* 80 SD3232
Common End *Cumb* 92 NY0022
Common Moor *Cnwll* 5 SX2469
Common Platt *Wilts* 36 SU1186
Common Side *Derbys* 74 SK3375
Common The *Wilts* 23 SU2432
Commondale *N York* 90 NZ6610
Commonside *Ches* 71 SJ5473
Commonside *Derbys* 73 SK2441
Commonwood *Shrops* 59 SJ4828
Commonwood *Wrexhm* 71 SJ3753
Compass *Somset* 20 ST2934
Compstall *Gt Man* 79 SJ9690
Compstonend *D & G* 99 NX6652
Compton *Berks* 37 SU5280
Compton *Devon* 7 SX8664
Compton *Hants* 23 SU3529
Compton *Hants* 13 SU4625
Compton *Staffs* 60 SO8284
Compton *Surrey* 25 SU9546
Compton *W Susx* 14 SU7714
Compton *Wilts* 23 SU1351
Compton Abbas *Dorset* 22 ST8618
Compton Abdale *Gloucs* 36 SP0516
Compton Bassett *Wilts* 36 SU0372
Compton Beauchamp *Oxon* 36 SU2786
Compton Bishop *Somset* 21 ST3955
Compton Chamberlayne *Wilts* 23 SU0229
Compton Dando *Somset* 21 ST6464
Compton Dundon *Somset* 21 ST4932
Compton Durville *Somset* 10 ST4117
Compton Greenfield *Gloucs* 34 ST5681
Compton Martin *Somset* 21 ST5457
Compton Pauncefoot *Somset* 21 ST6426
Compton Valence *Dorset* 10 SY5993
Compton Verney *Warwks* 48 SP3152
Comrie *Fife* 117 NT0289
Comrie *P & K* 124 NN7722
Conaglen House *Highld* 130 NN0268
Conchra *Highld* 138 NG8827
Concraigie *P & K* 125 NO0944
Conder Green *Lancs* 80 SD4556
Conderton *H & W* 47 SO9637
Condicote *Gloucs* 48 SP1528
Condorrat *N Lans* 116 NS7373
Condover *Shrops* 59 SJ4905
Coney Hill *Gloucs* 35 SO8517
Coney Weston *Suffk* 54 TL9578
Coneyhurst Common *W Susx* 14 TQ1023
Coneysthorpe *N York* 90 SE7171
Conford *Hants* 14 SU8233
Congdon's Shop *Cnwll* 5 SX2878
Congerstone *Leics* 62 SK3605
Congham *Norfk* 65 TF7123
Conghurst *Kent* 17 TQ7628
Congl-y-wal *Gwynd* 57 SH7044
Congleton *Ches* 72 SJ8562
Congresbury *Somset* 21 ST4363
Congreve *Staffs* 60 SJ9013
Conheath *D & G* 100 NX9969
Conicavel *Moray* 140 NH9853
Coningsby *Lincs* 76 TF2257
Conington *Cambs* 52 TL1885
Conington *Cambs* 52 TL3266
Conisbrough *S York* 75 SK5098
Conisholme *Lincs* 77 TF4095
Coniston *Cumb* 86 SD3097
Coniston *E R Yk* 85 TA1535
Coniston Cold *N York* 81 SD9054
Conistone *N York* 88 SD9867
Connah's Quay *Flints* 71 SJ2969
Connel *Ag & B* 122 NM9134
Connel Park *E Ayrs* 107 NS6012
Connor Downs *Cnwll* 2 SW5939
Conon Bridge *Highld* 139 NH5455
Cononley *N York* 82 SD9846
Consall *Staffs* 72 SJ9848
Consett *Dur* 95 NZ1051
Constable Burton *N York* 89 SE1690
Constable Lee *Lancs* 81 SD8123
Constantine *Cnwll* 3 SW7329
Constantine Bay *Cnwll* 4 SW8774
Contin *Highld* 139 NH4556
Conwy *A & C* 69 SH7877
Conyer *Kent* 28 TQ9664
Conyer's Green *Suffk* 54 TL8867
Cooden *E Susx* 17 TQ7107
Cook's Green *Essex* 41 TM1818
Cookbury *Devon* 18 SS4006
Cookbury Wick *Devon* 18 SS3905
Cookham *Berks* 26 SU8985
Cookham Dean *Berks* 26 SU8685
Cookham Rise *Berks* 26 SU8885
Cookhill *Warwks* 48 SP0558
Cookley *H & W* 60 SO8480
Cookley *Suffk* 55 TM3475
Cookley Green *Oxon* 37 SU6990
Cookney *Abers* 135 NO8693
Cooks Green *Suffk* 54 TL9753
Cooksbridge *E Susx* 15 TQ4013
Cooksey Green *H & W* 47 SO9069
Cookshill *Staffs* 72 SJ9443
Cooksland *Cnwll* 4 SX0867
Cooksmill Green *Essex* 40 TL6306
Cookson Green *Ches* 71 SJ5774
Cookson's Green *Dur* 96 NZ2933
Coolham *W Susx* 14 TQ1122
Cooling *Kent* 28 TQ7575
Cooling Street *Kent* 28 TQ7474
Coombe *Cnwll* 2 SW6242
Coombe *Cnwll* 3 SW8340
Coombe *Devon* 8 SX8384
Coombe *Devon* 7 SX9373
Coombe *Devon* 9 SY1091
Coombe *Gloucs* 35 ST7694
Coombe *Hants* 13 SU6620
Coombe *Wilts* 23 SU1450
Coombe Bissett *Wilts* 23 SU1026
Coombe Cellars *Devon* 7 SX9072
Coombe Cross *Hants* 13 SU6620
Coombe End *Somset* 20 ST0329
Coombe Hill *Gloucs* 47 SO8826
Coombe Keynes *Dorset* 11 SY8484
Coombe Pafford *Devon* 7 SX9166
Coombe Street *Somset* 22 ST7631
Coombes *W Susx* 15 TQ1808
Coombeswood *W Mids* 60 SO9785
Cooper Street *Kent* 29 TR3060
Cooper Turning *Gt Man* 79 SD6308
Cooper's Corner *Kent* 16 TQ4849
Cooperhill *Moray* 141 NH9953
Coopers Green *E Susx* 16 TQ4723
Coopers Green *Herts* 39 TL1909
Coopersale Common *Essex* 27 TL4702
Coopersale Street *Essex* 27 TL4701
Cootham *W Susx* 14 TQ0714
Cop Street *Kent* 27 TQ2959
Copdock *Suffk* 54 TM1242
Copford Green *Essex* 40 TL9222
Copgrove *N York* 89 SE3463
Copister *Shet* 155 HU4879
Cople *Beds* 38 TL1048
Copley *Dur* 95 NZ0825
Copley *Gt Man* 79 SJ9798
Copley *W York* 82 SE0822
Coplow Dale *Derbys* 74 SK1679
Copmanthorpe *N York* 83 SE5646
Copmere End *Staffs* 72 SJ8029
Copp *Lancs* 80 SD4239
Coppathorne *Cnwll* 18 SS2000
Coppenhall *Staffs* 72 SJ9019
Coppenhall Moss *Ches* 72 SJ7058
Copperhouse *Cnwll* 2 SW5637
Coppicegate *Shrops* 60 SO7379
Coppingford *Cambs* 52 TL1679
Coppins Corner *Kent* 28 TQ9448
Copplestone *Devon* 8 SS7702
Coppull *Lancs* 81 SD5614
Coppull Moor *Lancs* 81 SD5512
Copsale *W Susx* 15 TQ1724
Copster Green *Lancs* 81 SD6733
Copston Magna *Warwks* 50 SP4588
Copt Heath *W Mids* 61 SP1777
Copt Hewick *N York* 89 SE3471
Copthall Green *Essex* 27 TL4201
Copthorne *Cnwll* 5 SX2692
Copthorne *W Susx* 15 TQ3139
Copy's Green *Norfk* 66 TF9439
Copythorne *Hants* 12 SU3014
Coram Street *Suffk* 54 TM0042
Corbets Tey *Gt Lon* 27 TQ5685
Corbiere *Jersey* 152 JS0000
Corbridge *Nthumb* 103 NY9964
Corby *Nhants* 51 SP8988
Corby Glen *Lincs* 63 TF0024
Corby Hill *Cumb* 94 NY4857
Cordon *N Ayrs* 105 NS0230
Cordwell *Derbys* 74 SK3176
Coreley *Shrops* 46 SO6173
Cores End *Bucks* 26 SU9087
Corfe *Somset* 20 ST2319
Corfe Castle *Dorset* 11 SY9681
Corfe Mullen *Dorset* 11 SY9896
Corfton *Shrops* 59 SO4985
Corgarff *Abers* 133 NJ2708
Corhampton *Hants* 13 SU6120
Corks Pond *Kent* 28 TQ6540
Corley *Warwks* 61 SP3085
Corley Ash *Warwks* 61 SP2986
Corley Moor *Warwks* 61 SP2884
Cormuir *Angus* 134 NO3066
Cornard Tye *Suffk* 54 TL9041
Corndon *Devon* 8 SX6985

D

Drumfearn

East Pennar

Drumfearn Highld	129	NG6716
Drumfrennie Abers	135	NO7298
Drumguish Highld	132	NH7900
Drumhead Abers	134	NO6092
Drumin Moray	141	NJ1830
Drumjohn D & G	107	NX5297
Drumlamford S Ayrs	98	NX2876
Drumlasie Abers	135	NJ6405
Drumleaning Cumb	93	NY2751
Drumlemble Ag & B	104	NR6619
Drumlithie Abers	135	NO7880
Drummoddie D & G	99	NX3845
Drummore D & G	98	NX1336
Drummore D & G	100	NX9074
Drummuir Moray	141	NJ3843
Drumnadrochit Highld	139	NH5030
Drumnagorrach Moray	142	NJ5252
Drumpark D & G	100	NX8779
Drumrunie Lodge Highld	145	NC1604
Drumshang S Ayrs	106	NS2514
Drumuie Highld	136	NG4546
Drumuillie Highld	140	NH9420
Drumvaich Stirlg	124	NN6704
Drunzie P & K	126	NO1308
Druridge Nthumb	103	NZ2796
Drury Flints	71	SJ2964
Dry Doddington Lincs	63	SK8546
Dry Drayton Cambs	52	TL3861
Dry Sandford Oxon	37	SP4600
Dry Street Essex	40	TQ6986
Drybeck Cumb	94	NY6615
Drybridge Moray	142	NJ4362
Drybridge N Ayrs	106	NS3536
Drybrook Gloucs	35	SO6417
Dryburgh Border	110	NT5932
Dryhope Border	109	NT2624
Drym Cnwll	2	SW6133
Drymen Stirlg	115	NS4788
Drymuir Abers	143	NJ9046
Drynoch Highld	136	NG4031
Dryslwyn Carmth	32	SN5520
Dryton Shrops	59	SJ5905
Dubford Abers	143	NJ7963
Dublin Suffk	54	TM1669
Duchally Highld	145	NC3817
Duck End Beds	38	TL0544
Duck End Cambs	52	TL2464
Duck End Essex	40	TL6526
Duck's Cross Beds	52	TL1156
Duckend Green Essex	40	TL7223
Duckington Ches	71	SJ4851
Ducklington Oxon	36	SP3507
Duddingston C Edin	117	NT2872
Duddington Nhants	51	SK9800
Duddlestone Somset	20	ST2321
Duddleswell E Susx	16	TQ4628
Duddlewick Shrops	59	SO6583
Duddo Nthumb	110	NT9342
Duddon Ches	71	SJ5164
Duddon Bridge Cumb	86	SD1988
Dudleston Shrops	71	SJ3438
Dudleston Heath Shrops	59	SJ3736
Dudley T & W	103	NZ2573
Dudley W Mids	60	SO9490
Dudley Hill W York	82	SE1830
Dudley Port W Mids	60	SO9691
Dudnill Shrops	47	SO6474
Dudsbury Dorset	12	SZ0798
Dudswell Herts	38	SP9609
Duffield Derbys	62	SK3443
Duffryn Neath	33	SS8495
Dufftown Moray	141	NJ3240
Duffus Moray	141	NJ1668
Dufton Cumb	94	NY6825
Duggleby N York	90	SE8767
Duirinish Highld	137	NG7831
Duisdalemore Highld	129	NG7013
Duisky Highld	130	NN0076
Duke Street Suffk	54	TM0742
Dukestown Blae G	33	SO1410
Dukinfield Gt Man	79	SJ9397
Dulas Angles	68	SH4789
Dulcote Somset	21	ST5644
Dulford Devon	9	ST0706
Dull P & K	125	NN8049
Dullatur N Lans	116	NS7476
Dullingham Cambs	53	TL6357
Dullingham Ley Cambs	53	TL6456
Dulnain Bridge Highld	141	NH9925
Duloe Beds	52	TL1560
Duloe Cnwll	5	SX2358
Dulverton Somset	20	SS9127
Dulwich Gt Lon	27	TQ3373
Dumbarton D & Cb	115	NS3975
Dumbleton Gloucs	47	SP0135
Dumfries D & G	100	NX9776
Dumgoyne Stirlg	115	NS5283
Dummer Hants	24	SU5846
Dumpton Kent	29	TR3966
Dun Angus	135	NO6659
Dunalastair P & K	132	NN7158
Dunan Ag & B	114	NS1571
Dunan Highld	137	NG5828
Dunan P & K	124	NN4757
Dunaverty Ag & B	105	NR6807
Dunball Somset	21	ST3141
Dunbar E Loth	118	NT6778
Dunbeath Highld	151	ND1629
Dunbeg Ag & B	122	NM8833
Dunblane Stirlg	116	NN7801
Dunbog Fife	126	NO2817
Dunbridge Hants	23	SU3226
Duncanston Highld	139	NH5856
Duncanstone Abers	142	NJ5726
Dunchideock Devon	9	SX8787
Dunchurch Warwks	50	SP4871
Duncote Nhants	49	SP6750
Duncow D & G	100	NX9683
Duncrievie P & K	126	NO1309
Duncton W Susx	14	SU9617
Dundee Dund C	126	NO4030
Dundon Somset	21	ST4832
Dundonald S Ayrs	106	NS3634
Dundonnell Highld	145	NH0987
Dundraw Cumb	93	NY2149
Dundreggan Highld	131	NH3214
Dundrennan D & G	99	NX7447
Dundry Somset	21	ST5666
Dunecht Abers	135	NJ7509
Dunfermline Fife	117	NT0987
Dunfield Gloucs	36	SU1497
Dunford Bridge S York	82	SE1502
Dungate Kent	28	TQ9159
Dungavel S Lans	107	NS6537
Dunge Wilts	22	ST8954
Dunglass E Loth	119	NT7671
Dungworth S York	74	SK2789
Dunham Notts	75	SK8074
Dunham Town Gt Man	79	SJ7387
Dunham Woodhouses Gt Man	79	SJ7287
Dunham-on-the-Hill Ches	71	SJ4772
Dunhampstead H & W	47	SO9160
Dunhampton H & W	47	SO8466
Dunholme Lincs	76	TF0279
Dunino Fife	127	NO5311
Dunipace Falk	116	NS8083
Dunk's Green Kent	27	TQ6152
Dunkeld P & K	125	NO0242
Dunkerton Somset	22	ST7159
Dunkeswell Devon	9	ST1407
Dunkeswick W York	82	SE3047
Dunkirk Ches	71	SJ3872
Dunkirk Gloucs	35	ST7885
Dunkirk Kent	29	TR0759
Dunkirk Staffs	72	SJ8152
Dunkirk Wilts	22	ST9962
Dunlappie Angus	134	NO5867
Dunley H & W	47	SO7869
Dunley Hants	24	SU4553
Dunlop E Ayrs	115	NS4049
Dunmaglass Highld	140	NH5922
Dunmere Cnwll	4	SX0467
Dunmore Ag & B	113	NR7961
Dunmore Falk	116	NS8989
Dunn Street Kent	28	TQ7961
Dunnet Highld	151	ND2171
Dunnichen Angus	127	NO5048
Dunning P & K	125	NO0114
Dunnington E R Yk	85	TA1551
Dunnington N York	83	SE6652
Dunnington Warwks	48	SP0654
Dunnockshaw Lancs	81	SD8127
Dunoon Ag & B	114	NS1776
Dunphail Moray	141	NJ0048
Dunragit D & G	98	NX1557
Duns Border	119	NT7853
Duns Tew Oxon	49	SP4528
Dunsa Derbys	74	SK2470
Dunsby Lincs	64	TF1026
Dunscar Gt Man	81	SD7113
Dunscore D & G	100	NX8684
Dunscroft S York	83	SE6409
Dunsdale N York	97	NZ6019
Dunsden Green Oxon	37	SU7377
Dunsdon Devon	18	SS3008
Dunsfold Surrey	14	TQ0035
Dunsford Devon	8	SX8189
Dunshelt Fife	126	NO2410
Dunshillock Abers	143	NJ9848
Dunsill Notts	75	SK4661
Dunsley N York	90	NZ8511
Dunsley Staffs	60	SO8583
Dunsmore Bucks	38	SP8605
Dunsop Bridge Lancs	81	SD6649
Dunstable Beds	38	TL0122
Dunstall Staffs	73	SK1820
Dunstall Common H & W	47	SO8843
Dunstall Green Suffk	53	TL7460
Dunstan Nthumb	111	NU2419
Dunstan Steads Nthumb	111	NU2422
Dunster Somset	20	SS9943
Dunston Lincs	76	TF0662
Dunston Norfk	67	TG2202
Dunston Staffs	72	SJ9217
Dunston T & W	96	NZ2362
Dunston Heath Staffs	72	SJ9017
Dunstone Devon	6	SX5951
Dunstone Devon	7	SX7175
Dunsville S York	83	SE6407
Dunswell E R Yk	85	TA0735
Dunsyre S Lans	117	NT0748
Dunterton Devon	5	SX3779
Dunthrop Oxon	48	SP3528
Duntisbourne Abbots Gloucs	35	SO9607
Duntisbourne Rouse Gloucs	35	SO9805
Duntish Dorset	11	ST6906
Duntocher D & Cb	115	NS4872
Dunton Beds	39	TL2344
Dunton Bucks	38	SP8224
Dunton Norfk	66	TF8830
Dunton Bassett Leics	50	SP5490
Dunton Green Kent	27	TQ5157
Dunton Wayletts Essex	40	TQ6590
Duntulm Highld	136	NG4174
Dunure S Ayrs	106	NS2515
Dunvant Swans	32	SS5993
Dunvegan Highld	136	NG2547
Dunwich Suffk	55	TM4770
Dunwood Staffs	72	SJ9455
Durdar Cumb	93	NY4051
Durgan Cnwll	3	SW7727
Durham Dur	96	NZ2742
Durisdeer D & G	108	NS8903
Durisdeermill D & G	108	NS8804
Durkar W York	82	SE3116
Durleigh Somset	20	ST2736
Durley Hants	13	SU5116
Durley Wilts	23	SU2364
Durley Street Hants	13	SU5217
Durlock Kent	29	TR2757
Durlock Kent	29	TR3164
Durlow Common Gloucs	47	SO6339
Durmgley Angus	127	NO4250
Durn Gt Man	82	SD9416
Durness Highld	149	NC4068
Duror Highld	122	NM9955
Durran Ag & B	122	NM9607
Durrington W Susx	14	TQ1105
Durrington Wilts	23	SU1544
Durris Abers	135	NO7796
Dursley Gloucs	35	ST7598
Dursley Cross Gloucs	35	SO6920
Durston Somset	20	ST2928
Durweston Dorset	11	ST8508
Duston Nhants	49	SP7261
Duthil Highld	140	NH9324
Dutlas Powys	45	SO2177
Dutson Cnwll	5	SX3485
Dutton Ches	71	SJ5779
Duxford Cambs	53	TL4846
Duxford Oxon	36	SP3600
Dwygyfylchi A & C	69	SH7376
Dwyran Angles	68	SH4465
Dyce Aber C	135	NJ8812
Dye House Nthumb	95	NY9358
Dyer's End Essex	53	TL7238
Dyfatty Carmth	32	SN4401
Dyffryn Brdgnd	33	SS8593
Dyffryn Myr Td	33	SO0603
Dyffryn V Glam	33	ST0971
Dyffryn Ardudwy Gwynd	57	SH5823
Dyffryn Castell Cardgn	43	SN7782
Dyffryn Cellwen Neath	33	SN8510
Dyke Devon	18	SS3123
Dyke Lincs	64	TF1022
Dyke Moray	140	NH9858
Dykehead Angus	126	NO2453
Dykehead Angus	134	NO3859
Dykehead N Lans	116	NS8759
Dykehead Stirlg	115	NS5997
Dykelands Abers	135	NO7068
Dykends Angus	133	NO2557
Dykeside Abers	142	NJ7243
Dylife Powys	43	SN8694
Dymchurch Kent	17	TR1029
Dymock Gloucs	47	SO7031
Dyrham Gloucs	35	ST7475
Dysart Fife	117	NT3093
Dyserth Denbgs	70	SJ0578

E

Eachway H & W	60	SO9876
Eachwick Nthumb	103	NZ1171
Eagland Hill Lancs	80	SD4345
Eagle Lincs	76	SK8766
Eagle Barnsdale Lincs	76	SK8865
Eagle Manor Lincs	76	SK8868
Eaglescliffe Dur	96	NZ4215
Eaglesfield Cumb	92	NY0928
Eaglesfield D & G	101	NY2374
Eaglesham E Rens	115	NS5751
Eagley Gt Man	81	SD7112
Eairy IOM	153	SC2977
Eakring Notts	75	SK6762
Ealand Lincs	84	SE7811
Ealing Gt Lon	26	TQ1780
Eals Nthumb	94	NY6756
Eamont Bridge Cumb	94	NY5228
Earby Lancs	81	SD9046
Earcroft Lancs	81	SD6823
Eardington Shrops	60	SO7290
Eardisland H & W	46	SO4158
Eardisley H & W	46	SO3149
Eardiston H & W	47	SO6968
Eardiston Shrops	59	SJ3725
Earith Cambs	52	TL3875
Earl Shilton Leics	50	SP4697
Earl Soham Suffk	55	TM2363
Earl Sterndale Derbys	74	SK0966
Earl Stonham Suffk	54	TM1059
Earl's Croome H & W	47	SO8642
Earl's Down E Susx	16	TQ6419
Earl's Green Suffk	54	TM0366
Earle Nthumb	111	NT9826
Earlestown Mersyd	78	SJ5795
Earley Berks	24	SU7472
Earlham Norfk	67	TG1908
Earlish Highld	136	NG3861
Earls Barton Nhants	51	SP8563
Earls Colne Essex	40	TL8528
Earls Common H & W	47	SO9559
Earlsditton Shrops	47	SO6275
Earlsdon W Mids	61	SP3278
Earlsferry Fife	118	NO4800
Earlsfield Gt Lon	27	TQ2573
Earlsford Abers	143	NJ8334
Earlsheaton W York	82	SE2621
Earlston Border	110	NT5738
Earlston E Ayrs	106	NS4035
Earlswood Surrey	15	TQ2749
Earlswood Warwks	61	SP1174
Earlswood Common Mons	34	ST4594
Earnley W Susx	14	SZ8196
Earnshaw Bridge Lancs	80	SD5222
Earsdon Nthumb	103	NZ1993
Earsdon T & W	103	NZ3272
Earsham Norfk	55	TM3288
Earswick N York	90	SE6157
Eartham W Susx	14	SU9309
Earthcott Gloucs	35	ST6585
Easby N York	90	NZ5708
Easdale Ag & B	122	NM7417
Easebourne W Susx	14	SU9023
Easenhall Warwks	50	SP4679
Eashing Surrey	25	SU9443
Easington Bucks	37	SP6810
Easington Dur	96	NZ4143
Easington E R Yk	85	TA3919
Easington N York	97	NZ7417
Easington Nthumb	111	NU1234
Easington Oxon	37	SU6697
Easington Colliery Dur	96	NZ4344
Easington Lane T & W	96	NZ3646
Easingwold N York	90	SE5269
Easole Street Kent	29	TR2652
Eassie and Nevay Angus	126	NO3344
East Aberthaw V Glam	20	ST0366
East Allington Devon	7	SX7748
East Anstey Devon	19	SS8626
East Anton Hants	23	SU3747
East Appleton N York	89	SE2395
East Ashey IOW	13	SZ5888
East Ashling W Susx	14	SU8107
East Aston Hants	24	SU4445
East Ayton N York	91	SE9985
East Balsdon Cnwll	5	SX2898
East Bank Blae G	33	SO2105
East Barkwith Lincs	76	TF1681
East Barming Kent	28	TQ7254
East Barnby N York	90	NZ8212
East Barnet Gt Lon	27	TQ2795
East Barns E Loth	119	NT7176
East Barsham Norfk	66	TF9133
East Beckham Norfk	66	TG1639
East Bedfont Gt Lon	26	TQ0873
East Bergholt Suffk	54	TM0734
East Bierley W York	82	SE1929
East Bilney Norfk	66	TF9519
East Blatchington E Susx	16	TQ4800
East Bloxworth Dorset	11	SY8894
East Boldon T & W	96	NZ3661
East Boldre Hants	12	SU3700
East Bolton Nthumb	111	NU1216
East Bower Somset	21	ST3237
East Bradenham Norfk	66	TF9308
East Brent Somset	21	ST3451
East Bridgford Notts	63	SK6943
East Briscoe Dur	95	NY9719
East Buckland Devon	19	SS6831
East Budleigh Devon	9	SY0684
East Burnham Bucks	26	SU9584
East Burton Dorset	11	SY8287
East Butsfield Dur	95	NZ1145
East Butterwick Lincs	84	SE8306
East Calder W Loth	117	NT0867
East Carleton Norfk	66	TG1701
East Carlton Nhants	51	SP8389
East Carlton W York	82	SE2143
East Challow Oxon	36	SU3888
East Charleton Devon	7	SX7642
East Chelborough Dorset	10	ST5505
East Chevington Nthumb	103	NZ2699
East Chiltington E Susx	15	TQ3715
East Chinnock Somset	10	ST4913
East Chisenbury Wilts	23	SU1452
East Cholderton Hants	23	SU2945
East Clandon Surrey	26	TQ0651
East Claydon Bucks	49	SP7325
East Clevedon Somset	34	ST4171
East Coker Somset	10	ST5412
East Combe Somset	20	ST1631
East Compton Somset	21	ST6141
East Cornworthy Devon	7	SX8455
East Cote Cumb	92	NY1255
East Cottingwith E R Yk	84	SE7042
East Cowes IOW	13	SZ5095
East Cowick E R Yk	83	SE6620
East Cowton N York	89	NZ3003
East Cramlington Nthumb	103	NZ2776
East Cranmore Somset	22	ST6743
East Creech Dorset	11	SY9382
East Curthwaite Cumb	93	NY3348
East Dean E Susx	16	TV5598
East Dean Gloucs	35	SO6520
East Dean Hants	23	SU2726
East Dean W Susx	14	SU9012
East Dereham Norfk	66	TF9913
East Down Devon	19	SS6041
East Drayton Notts	75	SK7775
East Dulwich Gt Lon	27	TQ3375
East Dundry Somset	21	ST5766
East Ella E R Yk	84	TA0529
East End Beds	38	SP9642
East End Beds	51	TL1055
East End Bucks	38	SP9344
East End E R Yk	85	TA1931
East End E R Yk	85	TA2927
East End Essex	39	TL4210
East End Hants	24	SU4161
East End Hants	12	SZ3696
East End Herts	39	TL4527
East End Kent	17	TQ8335
East End Kent	28	TQ9673
East End Oxon	36	SP3915
East End Somset	34	ST4770
East End Somset	22	ST6746
East Everleigh Wilts	23	SU2053
East Farleigh Kent	28	TQ7353
East Farndon Nhants	50	SP7184
East Ferry Lincs	75	SK8199
East Firsby Lincs	76	TF0085
East Fortune E Loth	118	NT5479
East Garforth W York	83	SE4133
East Garston Berks	36	SU3576
East Ginge Oxon	37	SU4486
East Goscote Leics	63	SK6413
East Grafton Wilts	23	SU2560
East Grange Moray	141	NJ0961
East Green Suffk	55	TM4065
East Grimstead Wilts	23	SU2227
East Grinstead W Susx	15	TQ3938
East Guldeford E Susx	17	TQ9321
East Haddon Nhants	50	SP6668
East Hagbourne Oxon	37	SU5288
East Halton Lincs	85	TA1319
East Ham Gt Lon	27	TQ4283
East Hanney Oxon	36	SU4193
East Hanningfield Essex	40	TL7701
East Hardwick W York	83	SE4618
East Harling Norfk	54	TL9986
East Harlsey N York	89	SE4299
East Harnham Wilts	23	SU1428
East Harptree Somset	21	ST5655
East Hartburn Dur	96	NZ4217
East Hartford Nthumb	103	NZ2679
East Harting W Susx	14	SU7919
East Hatch Wilts	22	ST9228
East Hatley Cambs	52	TL2850
East Hauxwell N York	89	SE1693
East Haven Angus	127	NO5836
East Heath Berks	25	SU7967
East Heckington Lincs	64	TF1944
East Hedleyhope Dur	96	NZ1540
East Helmsdale Highld	147	ND0315
East Hendred Oxon	37	SU4588
East Heslerton N York	91	SE9276
East Hewish Somset	21	ST4064
East Hoathly E Susx	16	TQ5216
East Holme Dorset	11	SY8986
East Holywell T & W	103	NZ3073
East Horndon Essex	40	TQ6389
East Horrington Somset	21	ST5846
East Horsley Surrey	26	TQ0952
East Horton Nthumb	111	NU0330
East Howe Dorset	12	SZ0795
East Huntington N York	83	SE6155
East Huntspill Somset	21	ST3445
East Hyde Beds	38	TL1217
East Ilkerton Devon	19	SS7147
East Ilsley Berks	37	SU4980
East Keal Lincs	77	TF3863
East Kennett Wilts	23	SU1167
East Keswick W York	83	SE3644
East Kilbride S Lans	116	NS6354
East Kimber Devon	5	SX4998
East Kirkby Lincs	77	TF3362
East Knighton Dorset	11	SY8185
East Knowstone Devon	19	SS8423
East Knoyle Wilts	22	ST8830
East Kyloe Nthumb	111	NU0639
East Lambrook Somset	10	ST4318
East Langdon Kent	29	TR3346
East Langton Leics	50	SP7292
East Laroch Highld	130	NN0858
East Lavant W Susx	14	SU8608
East Lavington W Susx	14	SU9416
East Layton N York	89	NZ1609
East Leake Notts	62	SK5526
East Learmouth Nthumb	110	NT8637
East Leigh Devon	8	SS6905
East Leigh Devon	7	SX6852
East Leigh Devon	7	SX7657
East Lexham Norfk	66	TF8517
East Linton E Loth	118	NT5977
East Liss Hants	14	SU7827
East Lockinge Oxon	36	SU4287
East Lound Lincs	75	SK7899
East Lulworth Dorset	11	SY8682
East Lutton N York	91	SE9469
East Lydeard Somset	20	ST1829
East Lydford Somset	21	ST5731
East Malling Kent	28	TQ7056
East Malling Heath Kent	28	TQ6955
East Marden W Susx	14	SU8014
East Markham Notts	75	SK7373
East Martin Hants	12	SU0719
East Marton N York	81	SD9050
East Meon Hants	13	SU6822
East Mere Devon	9	SS9916
East Mersea Essex	41	TM0414
East Molesey Surrey	26	TQ1467
East Morden Dorset	11	SY9194
East Morton D & G	108	NS8800
East Morton W York	82	SE0942
East Ness N York	90	SE6978
East Newton E R Yk	85	TA2638
East Norton Leics	50	SK7800
East Oakley Hants	24	SU5749
East Ogwell Devon	7	SX8370
East Orchard Dorset	11	ST8317
East Ord Nthumb	119	NT9751
East Panson Devon	5	SX3692
East Parley Dorset	12	SZ1097
East Peckham Kent	28	TQ6648
East Pennar Pembs	30	SM9602

East Pennard
Erskine

East Pennard *Somset* 21 ST5937
East Perry *Cambs* 52 TL1566
East Portlemouth *Devon* 7 SX7538
East Prawle *Devon* 7 SX7836
East Preston *W Susx* 14 TQ0602
East Pulham *Dorset* 11 ST7209
East Putford *Devon* 18 SS3616
East Quantoxhead *Somset* 20 ST1343
East Rainham *Kent* 28 TQ8267
East Rainton *T & W* 96 NZ3347
East Ravendale *Lincs* 76 TF2399
East Raynham *Norfk* 66 TF8825
East Rigton *W York* 83 SE3743
East Rolstone *Somset* 21 ST3962
East Rounton *N York* 89 NZ4203
East Rudham *Norfk* 66 TF8228
East Runton *Norfk* 67 TG1942
East Ruston *Norfk* 67 TG3427
East Saltoun *E Loth* 118 NT4767
East Scrafton *N York* 89 SE0884
East Sheen *Gt Lon* 26 TQ2075
East Shefford *Berks* 36 SU3874
East Sleekburn *Nthumb* 103 NZ2883
East Somerton *Norfk* 67 TG4719
East Stockwith *Lincs* 75 SK7894
East Stoke *Dorset* 11 SY8686
East Stoke *Notts* 75 SK7549
East Stour *Dorset* 22 ST8022
East Stourmouth *Kent* 29 TR2662
East Stowford *Devon* 19 SS6326
East Stratton *Hants* 24 SU5440
East Studdal *Kent* 29 TR3149
East Sutton *Kent* 28 TQ8349
East Taphouse *Cnwll* 4 SX1863
East Thirston *Nthumb* 89 NZ1900
East Tilbury *Essex* 28 TQ6877
East Tisted *Hants* 24 SU7032
East Torrington *Lincs* 76 TF1483
East Tuddenham *Norfk* 66 TG0711
East Tytherley *Hants* 23 SU2929
East Tytherton *Wilts* 35 ST9674
East Village *Devon* 8 SS8405
East Wall *Shrops* 59 SO5293
East Walton *Norfk* 65 TF7416
East Water *Somset* 21 ST5350
East Week *Devon* 8 SX6692
East Wellow *Hants* 12 SU3020
East Wemyss *Fife* 118 NT3497
East Whitburn *W Loth* 117 NS9665
East Wickham *Gt Lon* 27 TQ4677
East Williamston *Pembks* 31 SN0904
East Winch *Norfk* 65 TF6916
East Winterslow *Wilts* 23 SU2434
East Wittering *W Susx* 14 SZ7997
East Witton *N York* 89 SE1486
East Woodburn *Nthumb* 102 NY9086
East Woodhay *Hants* 24 SU4061
East Woodlands *Somset* 22 ST7944
East Worldham *Hants* 24 SU7538
East Wretham *Norfk* 54 TL9190
East Youlstone *Devon* 18 SS2715
East-the-Water *Devon* 18 SS4526
Eastbourne *Dur* 89 NZ3013
Eastbourne *E Susx* 16 TV6199
Eastbridge *Suffk* 55 TM4566
Eastbrook *V Glam* 33 ST1671
Eastburn *W York* 82 SE0144
Eastbury *Berks* 36 SU3477
Eastbury *Herts* 26 TQ1092
Eastby *N York* 82 SE0154
Eastchurch *Kent* 28 TQ9871
Eastcombe *Gloucs* 35 SO8904
Eastcote *Gt Lon* 26 TQ1088
Eastcote *Nhants* 49 SP6853
Eastcote *W Mids* 61 SP1979
Eastcott *Cnwll* 18 SS2515
Eastcott *Wilts* 23 SU0255
Eastcourt *Wilts* 35 ST9792
Eastcourt *Wilts* 23 SU2361
Eastdown *Devon* 7 SX8249
Eastend *Essex* 40 TQ9492
Eastend *S Lans* 108 NS9537
Easter Balmoral *Abers* 133 NO2694
Easter Compton *Gloucs* 34 ST5782
Easter Dalziel *Highld* 140 NH7550
Easter Howgate *Mdloth* 117 NT2463
Easter Kinkell *Highld* 139 NH5755
Easter Moniack *Highld* 139 NH5543
Easter Ord *Abers* 135 NJ8304
Easter Pitkierie *Fife* 127 NO5606
Easter Skeld *Shet* 155 HU3144
Easter Softlaw *Border* 110 NT7532
Eastergate *W Susx* 14 SU9405
Easterhouse *C Glas* 116 NS6865
Eastern Green *W Mids* 61 SP2879
Easterton *Wilts* 23 SU0254
Eastertown *Somset* 21 ST3454
Eastfield *N Lans* 116 NS8964
Eastfield *N York* 91 TA0484
Eastgate *Dur* 95 NY9538
Eastgate *Lincs* 64 TF1019
Eastgate *Norfk* 66 TG1423
Eastham *Mersyd* 78 SJ3680
Eastham Ferry *Mersyd* 78 SJ3681
Easthampstead *Berks* 25 SU8667
Easthampton *H & W* 46 SO4063
Easthope *Shrops* 59 SO5695
Easthorpe *Essex* 40 TL9121
Easthorpe *Notts* 75 SK7053
Eastington *Devon* 19 SS7408
Eastington *Gloucs* 36 SP1213
Eastington *Gloucs* 35 SO7705
Eastlands *D & G* 100 NX8172
Eastleach Martin *Gloucs* 36 SP2004
Eastleach Turville *Gloucs* 36 SP1905
Eastleigh *Devon* 18 SS4827
Eastleigh *Hants* 13 SU4519
Eastling *Kent* 28 TQ9656
Eastly End *Surrey* 26 TQ0368
Eastmoor *Norfk* 65 TF7303
Eastney *Hants* 13 SZ6698
Eastnor *H & W* 47 SO7237
Eastoft *Lincs* 84 SE8016
Easton *Berks* 24 SU4172
Easton *Cambs* 52 TL1371
Easton *Cumb* 93 NY2759
Easton *Devon* 8 SX7289
Easton *Dorset* 11 SY6971
Easton *Hants* 24 SU5132
Easton *IOW* 12 SZ3486
Easton *Lincs* 63 SK9326
Easton *Norfk* 66 TG1310
Easton *Somset* 21 ST5147
Easton *Suffk* 55 TM2858
Easton *Wilts* 35 ST8970
Easton Grey *Wilts* 35 ST8887
Easton Maudit *Nhants* 51 SP8858
Easton on the Hill *Nhants* 64 TF0104
Easton Royal *Wilts* 23 SU2060
Easton-in-Gordano *Somset* 34 ST5175
Eastpeek *Devon* 5 SX3494
Eastrea *Cambs* 64 TL2997
Eastriggs *D & G* 101 NY2466
Eastrington *E R Yk* 84 SE7929
Eastrop *Wilts* 36 SU2092
Eastry *Kent* 29 TR3054
Eastshaw *W Susx* 14 SU8724
Eastville *Lincs* 77 TF4056
Eastwell *Leics* 63 SK7728
Eastwick *Herts* 39 TL4311
Eastwood *Essex* 40 TQ8688
Eastwood *Notts* 62 SK4646
Eastwood *W York* 82 SD9726
Eastwood End *Cambs* 65 TL4292
Eathorpe *Warwks* 48 SP3969
Eaton *Ches* 71 SJ5763
Eaton *Ches* 72 SJ8765
Eaton *Leics* 63 SK7928
Eaton *Norfk* 67 TG2006
Eaton *Notts* 75 SK7077
Eaton *Oxon* 37 SP4403
Eaton *Shrops* 59 SO3789
Eaton *Shrops* 59 SO5089
Eaton Bishop *H & W* 46 SO4439
Eaton Bray *Beds* 38 SP9720
Eaton Constantine *Shrops* 59 SJ5906
Eaton Ford *Beds* 52 TL1759
Eaton Green *Beds* 38 SP9621
Eaton Hastings *Oxon* 36 SU2598
Eaton Mascott *Shrops* 59 SJ5305
Eaton Socon *Cambs* 52 TL1759
Eaton upon Tern *Shrops* 72 SJ6523
Eaves Brow *Ches* 79 SJ6393
Eaves Green *W Mids* 61 SP2682
Ebberston *N York* 91 SE8982
Ebbesborne Wake *Wilts* 22 ST9924
Ebbw Vale *Blae G* 33 SO1609
Ebchester *Dur* 95 NZ1055
Ebdon *Somset* 21 ST3664
Ebford *Devon* 9 SX9887
Ebley *Gloucs* 35 SO8205
Ebnal *Ches* 71 SJ4948
Ebnall *H & W* 46 SO4758
Ebrington *Gloucs* 48 SP1840
Ebsworthy Town *Devon* 5 SX5090
Ecchinswell *Hants* 24 SU4959
Ecclaw *Border* 119 NT7568
Ecclefechan *D & G* 101 NY1974
Eccles *Border* 110 NT7641
Eccles *Gt Man* 79 SJ7798
Eccles *Kent* 28 TQ7360
Eccles Green *H & W* 46 SO3748
Eccles on Sea *Norfk* 67 TG4128
Eccles Road *Norfk* 54 TM0189
Ecclesall *S York* 74 SK3284
Ecclesfield *S York* 74 SK3593
Eccleshall *Staffs* 72 SJ8329
Eccleshill *W York* 82 SE1736
Ecclesmachan *W Loth* 117 NT0573
Eccleston *Ches* 71 SJ4162
Eccleston *Lancs* 80 SD5217
Eccleston *Mersyd* 78 SJ4895
Eccleston Green *Lancs* 80 SD5216
Echt *Abers* 135 NJ7405
Eckford *Border* 110 NT7026
Eckington *Derbys* 75 SK4379
Eckington *H & W* 47 SO9241
Ecton *Nhants* 51 SP8263
Ecton *Staffs* 74 SK0958
Edale *Derbys* 74 SK1285
Edburton *W Susx* 15 TQ2311
Edderside *Cumb* 92 NY1045
Edderton *Highld* 146 NH7084
Eddington *Kent* 29 TR1867
Eddleston *Border* 117 NT2447
Eddlewood *S Lans* 116 NS7153
Eden Mount *Cumb* 87 SD4077
Eden Park *Gt Lon* 27 TQ3667
Edenbridge *Kent* 16 TQ4446
Edenfield *Lancs* 81 SD8019
Edenhall *Cumb* 94 NY5632
Edenham *Lincs* 64 TF0621
Edensor *Derbys* 74 SK2469
Edentaggart *Ag & B* 115 NS3293
Edenthorpe *S York* 83 SE6206
Edern *Gwynd* 56 SH2739
Edgarley *Somset* 21 ST5238
Edgbaston *W Mids* 61 SP0684
Edgcombe *Cnwll* 2 SW7133
Edgcott *Bucks* 37 SP6722
Edgcott *Somset* 19 SS8438
Edge *Gloucs* 35 SO8409
Edge *Shrops* 59 SJ3908
Edge End *Gloucs* 34 SO5913
Edge Green *Ches* 71 SJ4851
Edgebolton *Shrops* 59 SJ5721
Edgefield *Norfk* 66 TG0934
Edgefield Green *Norfk* 66 TG0934
Edgefold *Gt Man* 79 SD7005
Edgehill *Warwks* 48 SP3747
Edgerley *Shrops* 59 SJ3518
Edgerton *W York* 82 SE1317
Edgeside *Lancs* 81 SD8322
Edgeworth *Gloucs* 35 SO9406
Edgeworthy *Devon* 19 SS8413
Edgiock *H & W* 48 SP0461
Edgmond *Shrops* 72 SJ7119
Edgmond Marsh *Shrops* 72 SJ7120
Edgton *Shrops* 59 SO3885
Edgware *Gt Lon* 26 TQ1991
Edgworth *Lancs* 81 SD7416
Edial *Staffs* 61 SK0808
Edinample *Stirlg* 124 NN6022
Edinbane *Highld* 136 NG3451
Edinburgh *C Edin* 117 NT2573
Edingale *Staffs* 61 SK2111
Edingham *D & G* 100 NX8363
Edingley *Notts* 75 SK6655
Edingthorpe *Norfk* 67 TG3132
Edingthorpe Green *Norfk* 67 TG3031
Edington *Border* 119 NT8955
Edington *Nthumb* 103 NZ1582
Edington *Somset* 21 ST3839
Edington *Wilts* 22 ST9253
Edington Burtle *Somset* 21 ST3943
Edingworth *Somset* 21 ST3653
Edith Weston *Rutlnd* 63 SK9205
Edithmead *Somset* 21 ST3249
Edlesborough *Bucks* 38 SP9719
Edlingham *Nthumb* 111 NU1109
Edlington *Lincs* 76 TF2371
Edmond Castle *Cumb* 94 NY4958
Edmondsham *Dorset* 12 SU0611
Edmondsley *Dur* 96 NZ2349
Edmondthorpe *Leics* 63 SK8517
Edmonton *Cnwll* 4 SW9672
Edmonton *Gt Lon* 27 TQ3492
Edmundbyers *Dur* 95 NZ0150
Ednam *Border* 110 NT7337
Ednaston *Derbys* 73 SK2341
Edradynate *P & K* 125 NN8751
Edrom *Border* 119 NT8255
Edstaston *Shrops* 59 SJ5132
Edstone *Warwks* 48 SP1861
Edvin Loach *H & W* 47 SO6658
Edwalton *Notts* 62 SK5935
Edwardstone *Suffk* 54 TL9442
Edwardsville *Myr Td* 33 ST0896
Edwinsford *Carmth* 44 SN6334
Edwinstowe *Notts* 75 SK6266
Edworth *Beds* 39 TL2241
Edwyn Ralph *H & W* 47 SO6457
Edzell *Angus* 134 NO6068
Efail Isaf *Rhondd* 33 ST0884
Efail-fach *Neath* 32 SS7895
Efail-rhyd *Powys* 58 SJ1626
Efailnewydd *Gwynd* 56 SH3535
Efailwen *Carmth* 31 SN1325
Efenechtyd *Denbgs* 70 SJ1155
Effgill *D & G* 101 NY3092
Effingham *Surrey* 26 TQ1153
Efflinch *Staffs* 73 SK1816
Efford *Devon* 9 SS8901
Egbury *Hants* 24 SU4352
Egdean *W Susx* 14 SU9920
Egerton *Gt Man* 81 SD7014
Egerton *Kent* 28 TQ9147
Egg Buckland *Devon* 6 SX5057
Eggesford *Devon* 19 SS6811
Eggington *Beds* 38 SP9525
Egginton *Derbys* 73 SK2628
Egglescliffe *Dur* 89 NZ4113
Eggleston *Dur* 95 NY9923
Egham *Surrey* 25 TQ0071
Egham Wick *Surrey* 25 SU9870
Eginswell *Devon* 7 SX8866
Egleton *Rutlnd* 63 SK8707
Eglingham *Nthumb* 111 NU1019
Egloshayle *Cnwll* 4 SX0072
Egloskerry *Cnwll* 5 SX2786
Eglwys Cross *Wrexhm* 71 SJ4740
Eglwys-Brewis *V Glam* 20 ST0068
Eglwysbach *A & C* 69 SH8070
Eglwysfach *Cardgn* 43 SN6996
Eglwyswrw *Pembks* 31 SN1438
Egmanton *Notts* 75 SK7368
Egremont *Cumb* 86 NY0110
Egremont *Mersyd* 78 SJ3192
Egton *N York* 90 NZ8006
Egton Bridge *N York* 90 NZ8004
Eight and Forty *E R Yk* 84 SE8529
Eight Ash Green *Essex* 40 TL9425
Eilanreach *Highld* 129 NG8018
Elan Village *Powys* 45 SN9364
Elberton *Gloucs* 34 ST6088
Elbridge *W Susx* 14 SU9101
Elburton *Devon* 6 SX5353
Elcombe *Wilts* 36 SU1280
Elcot *Berks* 36 SU3969
Elder Street *Essex* 53 TL5734
Eldernell *Cambs* 64 TL3298
Eldersfield *H & W* 47 SO7931
Elderslie *Rens* 115 NS4463
Eldmire *N York* 89 SE4274
Eldon *Dur* 96 NZ2328
Eldwick *W York* 82 SE1240
Elfhill *Abers* 135 NO8085
Elford *Nthumb* 111 NU1831
Elford *Staffs* 61 SK1810
Elgin *Moray* 141 NJ2162
Elgol *Highld* 128 NG5213
Elham *Kent* 29 TR1744
Elie *Fife* 118 NO4900
Elilaw *Nthumb* 111 NT9708
Elim *Angles* 68 SH3584
Eling *Hants* 12 SU3612
Elishaw *Nthumb* 102 NY8595
Elkesley *Notts* 75 SK6975
Elkstone *Gloucs* 35 SO9612
Ella *Abers* 142 NJ6459
Ellanbeich *Ag & B* 122 NM7417
Elland *W York* 82 SE1120
Elland Lower Edge *W York* 82 SE1221
Ellary *Ag & B* 113 NR7376
Ellastone *Staffs* 73 SK1143
Ellel *Lancs* 80 SD4856
Ellemford *Border* 119 NT7260
Ellen's Green *Surrey* 14 TQ0935
Ellenborough *Cumb* 92 NY0435
Ellenbrook *Gt Man* 79 SD7201
Ellenhall *Staffs* 72 SJ8426
Ellerbeck *N York* 89 SE4396
Ellerby *N York* 90 NZ7914
Ellerdine Heath *Shrops* 59 SJ6122
Ellerhayes *Devon* 9 SS9702
Elleric *Ag & B* 123 NN0448
Ellerker *E R Yk* 84 SE9229
Ellers *N York* 82 SE0043
Ellerton *N York* 89 SE2598
Ellerton *E R Yk* 84 SE7039
Ellerton *Shrops* 72 SJ7125
Ellesborough *Bucks* 38 SP8306
Ellesmere *Shrops* 59 SJ3934
Ellesmere Port *Ches* 71 SJ4076
Ellicombe *Somset* 20 SS9844
Ellingham *Hants* 12 SU1408
Ellingham *Norfk* 67 TM3592
Ellingham *Nthumb* 111 NU1725
Ellingstring *N York* 89 SE1783
Ellington *Cambs* 52 TL1671
Ellington *Nthumb* 103 NZ2791
Ellington Thorpe *Cambs* 52 TL1670
Elliots Green *Somset* 22 ST7945
Ellisfield *Hants* 24 SU6446
Ellishader *Highld* 137 NG5065
Ellistown *Leics* 62 SK4310
Ellon *Abers* 143 NJ9530
Ellonby *Cumb* 93 NY4235
Ellough *Suffk* 55 TM4486
Elloughton *E R Yk* 84 SE9428
Ellwood *Gloucs* 34 SO5908
Elm *Cambs* 65 TF4707
Elm Green *Essex* 40 TL7705
Elm Grove *Norfk* 67 TG4803
Elm Park *Gt Lon* 27 TQ5385
Elmbridge *H & W* 47 SO9068
Elmdon *Essex* 39 TL4639
Elmdon *W Mids* 61 SP1783
Elmdon Heath *W Mids* 61 SP1680
Elmer *W Susx* 14 SU9800
Elmer's Green *Lancs* 78 SD5006
Elmers End *Gt Lon* 27 TQ3668
Elmesthorpe *Leics* 50 SP4696
Elmhurst *Staffs* 61 SK1112
Elmley Castle *H & W* 47 SO9841
Elmley Lovett *H & W* 47 SO8769
Elmore *Gloucs* 35 SO7815
Elmore Back *Gloucs* 35 SO7616
Elms Green *H & W* 47 SO7266
Elmscott *Devon* 18 SS2321
Elmsett *Suffk* 54 TM0546
Elmstead Heath *Essex* 41 TM0622
Elmstead Market *Essex* 41 TM0624
Elmstead Row *Essex* 41 TM0621
Elmsted Court *Kent* 29 TR1144
Elmstone *Kent* 29 TR2660
Elmstone Hardwicke *Gloucs* 47 SO9125
Elmswell *E R Yk* 91 SE9958
Elmswell *Suffk* 54 TL9964
Elmton *Derbys* 75 SK5073
Elphin *Highld* 145 NC2111
Elphinstone *E Loth* 118 NT3970
Elrick *Abers* 135 NJ8106
Elrig *D & G* 98 NX3248
Elrington *Nthumb* 102 NY8563
Elsdon *Nthumb* 102 NY9393
Elsecar *S York* 74 SK3899
Elsenham *Essex* 39 TL5326
Elsfield *Oxon* 37 SP5410
Elsham *Lincs* 84 TA0312
Elsick House *Abers* 135 NO8894
Elsing *Norfk* 66 TG0516
Elslack *N York* 81 SD9349
Elson *Hants* 13 SU6002
Elson *Shrops* 59 SJ3735
Elsrickle *S Lans* 108 NT0643
Elstead *Surrey* 25 SU9043
Elsted *W Susx* 14 SU8119
Elsthorpe *Lincs* 64 TF0623
Elstob *Dur* 96 NZ3323
Elston *Lancs* 81 SD5932
Elston *Notts* 63 SK7647
Elston *Wilts* 23 SU0644
Elstone *Devon* 19 SS6716
Elstow *Beds* 38 TL0546
Elstree *Herts* 26 TQ1795
Elstronwick *E R Yk* 85 TA2232
Elswick *Lancs* 80 SD4238
Elswick *T & W* 103 NZ2263
Elsworth *Cambs* 52 TL3163
Elterwater *Cumb* 86 NY3204
Eltham *Gt Lon* 27 TQ4274
Eltisley *Cambs* 52 TL2759
Elton *Cambs* 51 TL0893
Elton *Ches* 71 SJ4575
Elton *Derbys* 74 SK2260
Elton *Dur* 96 NZ4017
Elton *Gloucs* 35 SO7014
Elton *Gt Man* 81 SD7911
Elton *H & W* 46 SO4570
Elton *Notts* 63 SK7638
Elton Green *Ches* 71 SJ4574
Eltringham *Nthumb* 103 NZ0762
Elvanfoot *S Lans* 108 NS9517
Elvaston *Derbys* 62 SK4032
Elveden *Suffk* 54 TL8280
Elvetham Hall *Hants* 25 SU7856
Elvingston *E Loth* 118 NT4674
Elvington *Kent* 29 TR2750
Elvington *N York* 84 SE7047
Elwell *Devon* 19 SS6631
Elwick *Dur* 97 NZ4532
Elwick *Nthumb* 111 NU1136
Elworth *Ches* 72 SJ7361
Elworthy *Somset* 20 ST0834
Ely *Cambs* 53 TL5480
Ely *Cardif* 33 ST1476
Emberton *Bucks* 38 SP8849
Embleton *Cumb* 92 NY1629
Embleton *Dur* 96 NZ4129
Embleton *Nthumb* 111 NU2322
Embo *Highld* 147 NH8192
Embo Street *Highld* 147 NH8091
Emborough *Somset* 21 ST6151
Embsay *N York* 82 SE0053
Emery Down *Hants* 12 SU2808
Emley *W York* 82 SE2413
Emley Moor *W York* 82 SE2313
Emmbrook *Berks* 25 SU8069
Emmer Green *Berks* 37 SU7276
Emmett Carr *Derbys* 75 SK4577
Emmington *Oxon* 37 SP7402
Emneth *Cambs* 65 TF4807
Emneth Hungate *Norfk* 65 TF5107
Empingham *Rutlnd* 63 SK9408
Empshott *Hants* 24 SU7531
Empshott Green *Hants* 24 SU7431
Emsworth *Hants* 13 SU7406
Enborne *Berks* 24 SU4365
Enborne Row *Hants* 24 SU4463
Enchmarsh *Shrops* 59 SO5096
Enderby *Leics* 50 SP5399
Endmoor *Cumb* 87 SD5384
Endon *Staffs* 72 SJ9253
Endon Bank *Staffs* 72 SJ9253
Enfield *Gt Lon* 27 TQ3597
Enfield Lock *Gt Lon* 27 TQ3698
Enfield Wash *Gt Lon* 27 TQ3598
Enford *Wilts* 23 SU1351
Engine Common *Gloucs* 35 ST6984
England's Gate *H & W* 46 SO5451
Englefield *Berks* 24 SU6272
Englefield Green *Surrey* 25 SU9971
Englesea-brook *Ches* 72 SJ7551
English Bicknor *Gloucs* 34 SO5815
English Frankton *Shrops* 59 SJ4529
Englishcombe *Somset* 22 ST7162
Engollan *Cnwll* 4 SW8670
Enham-Alamein *Hants* 23 SU3649
Enmore *Somset* 20 ST2435
Enmore Green *Dorset* 22 ST8523
Ennerdale Bridge *Cumb* 92 NY0615
Enniscaven *Cnwll* 4 SW9659
Enochdhu *P & K* 133 NO0662
Ensay *Ag & B* 121 NM3648
Ensbury *Dorset* 12 SZ0896
Ensdon *Shrops* 59 SJ4017
Ensis *Devon* 19 SS5626
Enson *Staffs* 72 SJ9328
Enstone *Oxon* 48 SP3724
Enterkinfoot *D & G* 108 NS8504
Enterpen *N York* 89 NZ4605
Enville *Staffs* 60 SO8286
Enys *Cnwll* 3 SW7836
Epney *Gloucs* 35 SO7611
Epperstone *Notts* 75 SK6548
Epping *Essex* 27 TL4502
Epping Green *Essex* 39 TL4305
Epping Green *Herts* 39 TL2906
Epping Upland *Essex* 39 TL4404
Eppleby *N York* 89 NZ1713
Eppleworth *E R Yk* 84 TA0131
Epsom *Surrey* 26 TQ2160
Epwell *Oxon* 48 SP3540
Epworth *Lincs* 84 SE7803
Epworth Turbary *Lincs* 84 SE7603
Erbistock *Wrexhm* 71 SJ3541
Erdington *W Mids* 61 SP1191
Eridge Green *E Susx* 16 TQ5535
Eridge Station *E Susx* 16 TQ5434
Erines *Ag & B* 113 NR8575
Erisey *Cnwll* 2 SW7117
Eriska *Ag & B* 122 NM9043
Eriswell *Suffk* 53 TL7278
Erith *Gt Lon* 27 TQ5177
Erlestoke *Wilts* 22 ST9653
Ermington *Devon* 6 SX6353
Erpingham *Norfk* 67 TG1931
Erriottwood *Kent* 28 TQ9459
Errogie *Highld* 139 NH5622
Errol *P & K* 126 NO2422
Erskine *Rens* 115 NS4770

F

Firsdown
Fyning

Firsdown *Dorset*	23	SU2133
Fishbourne *IOW*	13	SZ5592
Fishbourne *W Susx*	14	SU8304
Fishburn *Dur*	96	NZ3632
Fishcross *Clacks*	116	NS8995
Fisher *W Susx*	14	SU8700
Fisher's Pond *Hants*	13	SU4820
Fisher's Row *Lancs*	80	SD4148
Fisherford *Abers*	142	NJ6735
Fisherrow *E Loth*	118	NT3472
Fisherstreet *W Susx*	14	SU9431
Fisherton *Highld*	140	NH7451
Fisherton *S Ayrs*	106	NS2717
Fisherton de la Mere *Wilts*	22	SU0038
Fisherwick *Staffs*	61	SK1708
Fishery Estate *Berks*	26	SU8980
Fishguard *Pembks*	30	SM9537
Fishinghurst *Kent*	28	TQ7537
Fishlake *S York*	83	SE6513
Fishleigh *Devon*	8	SS5405
Fishmere End *Lincs*	64	TF2837
Fishnish Pier *Ag & B*	121	NM6542
Fishpond Bottom *Dorset*	10	SY3698
Fishponds *Bristl*	35	ST6375
Fishpool *Gt Man*	79	SD8009
Fishtoft *Lincs*	64	TF3642
Fishtoft Drove *Lincs*	77	TF3148
Fishwick *Border*	119	NT9151
Fishwick *Lancs*	81	SD5629
Fiskavaig *Highld*	136	NG3334
Fiskerton *Lincs*	76	TF0471
Fiskerton *Notts*	75	SK7351
Fitling *E R Yk*	85	TA2534
Fittleton *Wilts*	23	SU1449
Fittleworth *W Susx*	14	TQ0019
Fitton End *Cambs*	65	TF4313
Fitz *Shrops*	59	SJ4417
Fitzhead *Somset*	20	ST1228
Fitzroy *Somset*	20	ST1927
Fitzwilliam *W York*	83	SE4115
Fiunary *Highld*	121	NM6246
Five Ash Down *E Susx*	16	TQ4723
Five Ashes *E Susx*	16	TQ5525
Five Bells *Somset*	20	ST0642
Five Bridges *H & W*	47	SO6446
Five Lanes *Mons*	34	ST4490
Five Oak Green *Kent*	16	TQ6445
Five Oaks *Jersey*	152	JS0000
Five Oaks *W Susx*	14	TQ0928
Five Roads *Carmth*	32	SN4805
Five Wents *Kent*	28	TQ8050
Fivecrosses *Ches*	71	SJ5276
Fivehead *Somset*	21	ST3522
Fivelanes *Cnwll*	5	SX2280
Flack's Green *Essex*	40	TL7614
Flackwell Heath *Bucks*	26	SU8989
Fladbury *H & W*	47	SO9946
Fladdabister *Shet*	155	HU4332
Flagg *Derbys*	74	SK1368
Flamborough *E R Yk*	91	TA2270
Flamstead *Herts*	38	TL0714
Flansham *W Susx*	14	SU9601
Flanshaw *W York*	82	SE3020
Flappit Spring *W York*	82	SE0536
Flasby *N York*	82	SD9456
Flash *Staffs*	74	SK0266
Flashader *Highld*	136	NG3453
Flaunden *Herts*	26	TL0100
Flawborough *Notts*	63	SK7842
Flawith *N York*	90	SE4865
Flax Bourton *Somset*	21	ST5069
Flaxby *N York*	89	SE3957
Flaxley *Gloucs*	35	SO6815
Flaxmere *Ches*	71	SJ5572
Flaxpool *Somset*	20	ST1435
Flaxton *N York*	90	SE6762
Fleckney *Leics*	50	SP6493
Flecknoe *Warwks*	49	SP5163
Fledborough *Notts*	75	SK8072
Fleet *Dorset*	10	SY6380
Fleet *Hants*	13	SU7201
Fleet *Hants*	25	SU8053
Fleet *Lincs*	64	TF3823
Fleet Hargate *Lincs*	65	TF3925
Fleetend *Hants*	13	SU5006
Fleetwood *Lancs*	80	SD3348
Flemingston *V Glam*	20	ST0169
Flemington *S Lans*	116	NS6559
Flempton *Suffk*	54	TL8169
Fletcher Green *Kent*	16	TQ5349
Fletchersbridge *Cnwll*	4	SX1065
Fletchertown *Cumb*	93	NY2042
Fletching *E Susx*	16	TQ4223
Flexbury *Cnwll*	18	SS2107
Flexford *Surrey*	25	SU9350
Flimby *Cumb*	92	NY0233
Flimwell *E Susx*	17	TQ7131
Flint *Flints*	70	SJ2472
Flint Mountain *Flints*	70	SJ2470
Flint's Green *W Mids*	61	SP2680
Flintham *Notts*	63	SK7445
Flinton *E R Yk*	85	TA2136
Flitcham *Norfk*	65	TF7326
Flitton *Beds*	38	TL0535
Flitwick *Beds*	38	TL0334
Flixborough *Lincs*	84	SE8714
Flixborough Stather *Lincs*	84	SE8614
Flixton *Gt Man*	79	SJ7494
Flixton *N York*	91	TA0479
Flixton *Suffk*	55	TM3186
Flockton *W York*	82	SE2314
Flockton Green *W York*	82	SE2515
Flodden *Nthumb*	110	NT9235
Flodigarry *Highld*	136	NG4671
Flookburgh *Cumb*	87	SD3675
Flordon *Norfk*	66	TM1897
Flore *Nhants*	49	SP6460
Flotterton *Nthumb*	103	NT9902
Flowers Green *E Susx*	16	TQ6311
Flowton *Suffk*	54	TM0846
Flushdyke *W York*	82	SE2820
Flushing *Cnwll*	3	SW8034
Fluxton *Devon*	9	SY0893
Flyford Flavell *H & W*	47	SO9755
Fobbing *Essex*	40	TQ7183
Fochabers *Moray*	141	NJ3458
Fochriw *Caerph*	33	SO1005
Fockerby *Lincs*	84	SE8519
Foddington *Somset*	21	ST5729
Foel *Powys*	58	SH9911
Foel y Dyffryn *Brdgnd*	33	SS8594
Foelgastell *Carmth*	32	SN5414
Foggathorpe *E R Yk*	84	SE7537
Fogo *Border*	110	NT7649
Fogwatt *Moray*	141	NJ2356
Foindle *Highld*	148	NC1948
Folda *Angus*	133	NO1963
Fole *Staffs*	73	SK0437
Foleshill *W Mids*	61	SP3582
Foliejon Park *Berks*	25	SU8974
Folke *Dorset*	11	ST6613
Folkestone *Kent*	29	TR2336
Folkingham *Lincs*	64	TF0733
Folkington *E Susx*	16	TQ5603
Folksworth *Cambs*	52	TL1489
Folkton *N York*	91	TA0579
Folla Rule *Abers*	142	NJ7332
Follifoot *N York*	83	SE3452
Folly Gate *Devon*	8	SX5798
Folly Hill *Surrey*	25	SU8348
Fonmon *V Glam*	20	ST0467
Font-y-gary *V Glam*	20	ST0566
Fonthill Bishop *Wilts*	22	ST9333
Fonthill Gifford *Wilts*	22	ST9231
Fontmell Magna *Dorset*	11	ST8616
Fontmell Parva *Dorset*	11	ST8214
Fontwell *W Susx*	14	SU9407
Foolow *Derbys*	74	SK1976
Foots Cray *Gt Lon*	27	TQ4770
Forbestown *Abers*	134	NJ3513
Forcett *N York*	89	NZ1712
Ford *Ag & B*	122	NM8603
Ford *Bucks*	37	SP7709
Ford *Derbys*	74	SK4080
Ford *Devon*	18	SS4124
Ford *Devon*	6	SX6150
Ford *Devon*	7	SX7940
Ford *Gloucs*	48	SP0829
Ford *Nthumb*	110	NT9437
Ford *Shrops*	59	SJ4113
Ford *Somset*	20	ST0928
Ford *Somset*	21	ST5953
Ford *Staffs*	73	SK0653
Ford *W Susx*	14	SU9903
Ford *Wilts*	35	ST8475
Ford End *Essex*	40	TL6716
Ford Green *Lancs*	80	SD4746
Ford Heath *Shrops*	59	SJ4011
Ford Street *Somset*	20	ST1518
Ford's Green *Suffk*	54	TM0666
Forda *Devon*	8	SX5390
Fordcombe *Kent*	16	TQ5240
Fordell *Fife*	117	NT1588
Forden *Powys*	58	SJ2201
Forder *Devon*	8	SX6789
Forder Green *Devon*	7	SX7967
Fordham *Cambs*	53	TL6370
Fordham *Essex*	40	TL9228
Fordham *Norfk*	65	TL6199
Fordham Heath *Essex*	40	TL9426
Fordingbridge *Hants*	12	SU1414
Fordon *E R Yk*	91	TA0475
Fordoun *Abers*	135	NO7475
Fordstreet *Essex*	40	TL9226
Fordton *Devon*	8	SX8399
Fordwells *Oxon*	36	SP3013
Fordwich *Kent*	29	TR1859
Fordyce *Abers*	142	NJ5563
Forebridge *Staffs*	72	SJ9322
Foremark *Derbys*	62	SK3326
Forest *Guern*	152	GN0000
Forest *N York*	89	NZ2700
Forest Becks *Lancs*	81	SD7851
Forest Gate *Gt Lon*	27	TQ4085
Forest Green *Surrey*	14	TQ1241
Forest Hall *Cumb*	87	NY5401
Forest Hall *T & W*	103	NZ2769
Forest Head *Cumb*	94	NY5857
Forest Hill *Gt Lon*	27	TQ3672
Forest Hill *Oxon*	37	SP5807
Forest Lane Head *N York*	83	SE3356
Forest Lodge *Ag & B*	123	NN2742
Forest Mill *Clacks*	117	NS9694
Forest Row *E Susx*	16	TQ4234
Forest Side *IOW*	13	SZ4889
Forest Town *Notts*	75	SK5662
Forest-in-Teesdale *Dur*	95	NY8630
Forestburn Gate *Nthumb*	103	NZ0696
Forestside *W Susx*	14	SU7612
Forfar *Angus*	127	NO4550
Forgandenny *P & K*	125	NO0818
Forge *Powys*	57	SN7699
Forge Hammer *Torfn*	34	ST2895
Forge Side *Torfn*	34	SO2408
Forgie *Moray*	141	NJ3854
Forgieside *Moray*	142	NJ4053
Forgorig *Border*	110	NT7748
Forgue *Abers*	142	NJ6145
Forhill *H & W*	61	SP0575
Formby *Mersyd*	78	SD3006
Forncett End *Norfk*	66	TM1493
Forncett St Mary *Norfk*	66	TM1694
Forncett St Peter *Norfk*	66	TM1693
Fornham All Saints *Suffk*	54	TL8367
Fornham St Martin *Suffk*	54	TL8567
Fornside *Cumb*	93	NY3220
Forres *Moray*	141	NJ0358
Forsbrook *Staffs*	72	SJ9641
Forse *Highld*	151	ND2234
Forse House *Highld*	151	ND2135
Forshaw Heath *Warwks*	61	SP0873
Forsinain *Highld*	150	NC9148
Forsinard *Highld*	150	NC8942
Forston *Dorset*	11	SY6695
Fort Augustus *Highld*	131	NH3709
Fort George *Highld*	140	NH7656
Fort Hommet *Guern*	152	GN0000
Fort le Marchant *Guern*	152	GN0000
Fort William *Highld*	130	NN1074
Forteviot *P & K*	125	NO0517
Forth *S Lans*	116	NS9453
Forthampton *Gloucs*	47	SO8532
Fortingall *P & K*	124	NN7347
Fortnighty *Highld*	140	NH9350
Forton *Hants*	24	SU4143
Forton *Lancs*	80	SD4851
Forton *Shrops*	59	SJ4316
Forton *Somset*	10	ST3307
Forton *Staffs*	72	SJ7521
Fortrie *Abers*	142	NJ6645
Fortrose *Highld*	140	NH7256
Fortuneswell *Dorset*	11	SY6873
Forty Green *Bucks*	26	SU9291
Forty Hill *Gt Lon*	27	TQ3398
Forward Green *Suffk*	54	TM1059
Fosbury *Wilts*	23	SU3157
Foscot *Oxon*	36	SP2421
Foscote *Nhants*	49	SP6546
Fosdyke *Lincs*	64	TF3133
Fosdyke Bridge *Lincs*	64	TF3232
Foss *P & K*	132	NN7858
Foss-y-ffin *Cardgn*	42	SN4460
Fossebridge *Gloucs*	36	SP0711
Foster Street *Essex*	39	TL4809
Fosterhouses *S York*	83	SE6514
Foston *Derbys*	73	SK1931
Foston *Leics*	50	SP6094
Foston *Lincs*	63	SK8542
Foston *N York*	90	SE6965
Foston on the Wolds *E R Yk*	85	TA1055
Fotherby *Lincs*	77	TF3191
Fothergill *Cumb*	92	NY0234
Fotheringhay *Nhants*	51	TL0593
Foul End *Warwks*	61	SP2494
Foul Mile *E Susx*	16	TQ6215
Foulbridge *Cumb*	93	NY4248
Foulby *W York*	83	SE3917
Foulden *Border*	119	NT9355
Foulden *Norfk*	65	TL7699
Foulridge *Lancs*	81	SD8942
Foulsham *Norfk*	66	TG0324
Fountainhall *Border*	118	NT4249
Four Ashes *Staffs*	60	SJ9108
Four Ashes *Staffs*	60	SO8087
Four Ashes *Suffk*	54	TM0070
Four Ashes *W Mids*	61	SP1575
Four Cabots *Guern*	152	GN0000
Four Crosses *Powys*	58	SJ2618
Four Crosses *Staffs*	60	SJ9509
Four Elms *Kent*	16	TQ4648
Four Foot *Somset*	21	ST5833
Four Forks *Somset*	20	ST2336
Four Gates *Gt Man*	79	SD6407
Four Gotes *Cambs*	65	TF4516
Four Lane End *S York*	82	SE2702
Four Lane Ends *Ches*	71	SJ5561
Four Lanes *Cnwll*	2	SW6838
Four Marks *Hants*	24	SU6735
Four Mile Bridge *Angles*	68	SH2778
Four Oaks *E Susx*	17	TQ8524
Four Oaks *Gloucs*	47	SO6928
Four Oaks *W Mids*	61	SP1098
Four Oaks *W Mids*	61	SP2480
Four Points *Berks*	37	SU5579
Four Roads *Carmth*	32	SN4409
Four Shire Stone *Warwks*	48	SP2232
Four Throws *Kent*	17	TQ7729
Four Wents *Kent*	27	TQ6251
Fourlanes End *Ches*	72	SJ8059
Fourpenny *Highld*	147	NH8094
Fourstones *Nthumb*	102	NY8867
Fovant *Wilts*	22	SU0028
Foveran *Abers*	143	NJ9723
Fowey *Cnwll*	3	SX1251
Fowley Common *Ches*	79	SJ6795
Fowlhall *Kent*	28	TQ6946
Fowlis *Angus*	126	NO3233
Fowlis Wester *P & K*	125	NN9224
Fowlmere *Cambs*	53	TL4245
Fownhope *H & W*	46	SO5834
Fox Corner *Surrey*	25	SU9654
Fox Hatch *Essex*	27	TQ5798
Fox Street *Essex*	41	TM0227
Foxbar *Rens*	115	NS4561
Foxcombe *Devon*	5	SX4887
Foxcote *Gloucs*	35	SP0118
Foxcote *Somset*	22	ST7155
Foxdale *IOM*	153	SC2778
Foxearth *Essex*	54	TL8344
Foxendown *Kent*	27	TQ6466
Foxfield *Cumb*	86	SD2185
Foxham *Wilts*	35	ST9777
Foxhills *Hants*	12	SU3411
Foxhole *Cnwll*	3	SW9654
Foxhole *Swans*	32	SS6694
Foxholes *N York*	91	TA0173
Foxhunt Green *E Susx*	16	TQ5417
Foxley *Nhants*	49	SP6451
Foxley *Norfk*	66	TG0422
Foxley *Wilts*	35	ST8986
Foxley Green *Wilts*	35	ST8985
Foxlydiate *H & W*	47	SP0167
Foxt *Staffs*	73	SK0348
Foxton *Cambs*	52	TL4148
Foxton *Dur*	96	NZ3624
Foxton *Leics*	50	SP7089
Foxton *N York*	89	SE4296
Foxup *N York*	88	SD8676
Foxwist Green *Ches*	71	SJ6268
Foxwood *Shrops*	47	SO6276
Foy *H & W*	46	SO5928
Foyers *Highld*	139	NH4921
Foynesfield *Highld*	140	NH8953
Fraddam *Cnwll*	2	SW5834
Fraddon *Cnwll*	4	SW9158
Fradley *Staffs*	61	SK1513
Fradswell *Staffs*	73	SJ9931
Fraisthorpe *E R Yk*	91	TA1561
Framfield *E Susx*	16	TQ4920
Framingham Earl *Norfk*	67	TG2702
Framingham Pigot *Norfk*	67	TG2703
Framlingham *Suffk*	55	TM2863
Frampton *Dorset*	10	SY6295
Frampton *Lincs*	64	TF3239
Frampton Cotterell *Gloucs*	35	ST6682
Frampton Mansell *Gloucs*	35	SO9202
Frampton on Severn *Gloucs*	35	SO7407
Frampton West End *Lincs*	64	TF3041
Framsden *Suffk*	55	TM1959
Framwellgate Moor *Dur*	96	NZ2644
Frances Green *Lancs*	81	SD6236
Franche *H & W*	60	SO8278
Frandley *Ches*	71	SJ6379
Frank's Bridge *Powys*	45	SO1156
Frankaborough *Devon*	5	SX3991
Frankby *Mersyd*	78	SJ2486
Frankfort *Norfk*	67	TG3024
Franklands Gate *H & W*	46	SO5346
Frankley *H & W*	60	SO9980
Frankton *Warwks*	50	SP4270
Frant *E Susx*	16	TQ5835
Fraserburgh *Abers*	143	NJ9966
Frating *Essex*	41	TM0722
Frating Green *Essex*	41	TM0823
Fratton *Hants*	13	SU6500
Freathy *Cnwll*	5	SX3952
Freckenham *Suffk*	53	TL6672
Freckleton *Lancs*	80	SD4329
Freebirch *Derbys*	74	SK3072
Freeby *Leics*	63	SK8020
Freefolk *Hants*	24	SU4848
Freehay *Staffs*	73	SK0241
Freeland *Oxon*	36	SP4112
Freethorpe *Norfk*	67	TG4005
Freethorpe Common *Norfk*	67	TG4004
Freiston *Lincs*	64	TF3743
Fremington *Devon*	19	SS5132
Fremington *N York*	88	SE0499
French Street *Kent*	27	TQ4552
Frenchay *Gloucs*	35	ST6377
Frenchbeer *Devon*	8	SX6785
Frenich *P & K*	132	NN8258
Frensham *Surrey*	25	SU8441
Freshfield *Mersyd*	78	SD2907
Freshford *Somset*	22	ST7860
Freshwater *IOW*	12	SZ3487
Freshwater Bay *IOW*	12	SZ3485
Freshwater East *Pembks*	30	SS0198
Fressingfield *Suffk*	55	TM2677
Freston *Suffk*	54	TM1638
Freswick *Highld*	151	ND3667
Fretherne *Gloucs*	35	SO7210
Frettenham *Norfk*	67	TG2417
Freuchie *Fife*	126	NO2806
Freystrop *Pembks*	30	SM9511
Friar Waddon *Dorset*	11	SY6486
Friar's Gate *E Susx*	16	TQ4933
Friars' Hill *N York*	90	SE7485
Friday Bridge *Cambs*	65	TF4604
Friday Street *E Susx*	16	TQ6203
Friday Street *Suffk*	55	TM2459
Friday Street *Suffk*	55	TM3351
Friday Street *Suffk*	55	TM3760
Friday Street *Surrey*	14	TQ1245
Fridaythorpe *E R Yk*	90	SE8759
Friden *Derbys*	74	SK1660
Friendly *W York*	82	SE0524
Friern Barnet *Gt Lon*	27	TQ2892
Friesland Bay *Ag & B*	120	NM1954
Friesthorpe *Lincs*	76	TF0683
Frieston *Lincs*	63	SK9347
Frieth *Bucks*	37	SU7990
Friezeland *Notts*	75	SK4750
Frilford *Oxon*	37	SU4497
Frilsham *Berks*	24	SU5473
Frimley *Surrey*	25	SU8757
Frimley Green *Surrey*	25	SU8856
Frindsbury *Kent*	28	TQ7469
Fring *Norfk*	65	TF7334
Fringford *Oxon*	49	SP6029
Frinsted *Kent*	28	TQ8957
Frinton-on-Sea *Essex*	41	TM2320
Friockheim *Angus*	127	NO5949
Friog *Gwynd*	57	SH6112
Frisby on the Wreake *Leics*	63	SK6917
Friskney *Lincs*	77	TF4655
Friskney Eaudike *Lincs*	77	TF4755
Friston *E Susx*	16	TV5598
Friston *Suffk*	55	TM4160
Fritchley *Derbys*	74	SK3552
Frith Bank *Lincs*	77	TF3147
Frith Common *H & W*	47	SO6969
Fritham *Hants*	12	SU2314
Frithelstock *Devon*	18	SS4619
Frithelstock Stone *Devon*	18	SS4518
Frithend *Hants*	25	SU8039
Frithsden *Herts*	38	TL0009
Frithville *Lincs*	77	TF3150
Frittenden *Kent*	28	TQ8140
Frittiscombe *Devon*	7	SX8043
Fritton *Norfk*	67	TG4600
Fritton *Norfk*	67	TM2293
Fritwell *Oxon*	49	SP5229
Frizinghall *W York*	82	SE1435
Frizington *Cumb*	92	NY0316
Frocester *Gloucs*	35	SO7803
Frodesley *Shrops*	59	SJ5101
Frodsham *Ches*	71	SJ5177
Frog End *Cambs*	52	TL3946
Frog End *Cambs*	53	TL5358
Frog Pool *H & W*	47	SO8065
Frogden *Border*	110	NT7628
Froggatt *Derbys*	74	SK2476
Froghall *Staffs*	73	SK0247
Frogham *Hants*	12	SU1612
Frogham *Kent*	29	TR2550
Frogmore *Devon*	7	SX7742
Frognall *Lincs*	64	TF1610
Frogwell *Cnwll*	5	SX3468
Frolesworth *Leics*	50	SP5090
Frome *Somset*	22	ST7747
Frome St Quintin *Dorset*	10	ST5902
Frome Whitfield *Dorset*	11	SY6991
Fromes Hill *H & W*	47	SO6846
Fron *Denbgs*	70	SJ0666
Fron *Gwynd*	56	SH3539
Fron *Gwynd*	68	SH5054
Fron *Powys*	58	SJ2203
Fron *Powys*	58	SO1797
Fron Isaf *Wrexhm*	70	SJ2740
Fron-goch *Gwynd*	70	SH9039
Froncysyllte *Denbgs*	70	SJ2640
Frostenden *Suffk*	55	TM4781
Frosterley *Dur*	95	NZ0237
Froxfield *Beds*	38	SP9733
Froxfield *Wilts*	23	SU2968
Froxfield Green *Hants*	13	SU7025
Fryern Hill *Hants*	13	SU4320
Fryerning *Essex*	40	TL6300
Fryton *N York*	90	SE6874
Fulbeck *Lincs*	76	SK9450
Fulbourn *Cambs*	53	TL5256
Fulbrook *Oxon*	36	SP2513
Fulflood *Hants*	24	SU4730
Fulford *N York*	83	SE6149
Fulford *Somset*	20	ST2029
Fulford *Staffs*	72	SJ9537
Fulham *Gt Lon*	27	TQ2576
Fulking *W Susx*	15	TQ2411
Full Sutton *E R Yk*	84	SE7455
Fullaford *Devon*	19	SS6838
Fullarton *N Ayrs*	106	NS3238
Fuller Street *Essex*	40	TL7416
Fuller Street *Kent*	27	TQ5656
Fuller's End *Essex*	39	TL5325
Fuller's Moor *Ches*	71	SJ4954
Fullerton *Hants*	23	SU3739
Fulletby *Lincs*	77	TF2973
Fullready *Warwks*	48	SP2846
Fullwood *E Ayrs*	115	NS4450
Fulmer *Bucks*	26	SU9985
Fulmodeston *Norfk*	66	TF9930
Fulneck *W York*	82	SE2232
Fulnetby *Lincs*	76	TF0979
Fulney *Lincs*	64	TF2623
Fulstone *W York*	82	SE1709
Fulstow *Lincs*	77	TF3297
Fulwell *Oxon*	36	SP3722
Fulwood *Lancs*	80	SD5431
Fulwood *Notts*	75	SK4757
Fulwood *S York*	74	SK3085
Fulwood *Somset*	20	ST2120
Fundenhall *Norfk*	66	TM1596
Funtington *W Susx*	14	SU8008
Funtley *Hants*	13	SU5608
Funtullich *P & K*	124	NN7526
Furley *Devon*	10	ST2604
Furnace *Ag & B*	114	NN0200
Furnace *Cardgn*	43	SN6895
Furnace *Carmth*	32	SN5001
Furnace End *Warwks*	61	SP2491
Furner's Green *E Susx*	15	TQ4126
Furness Vale *Derbys*	79	SK0083
Furneux Pelham *Herts*	39	TL4327
Further Quarter *Kent*	28	TQ8939
Furtho *Nhants*	49	SP7743
Furze Platt *Berks*	26	SU8782
Furzehill *Devon*	19	SS7245
Furzehill *Dorset*	11	SU0101
Furzehills *Lincs*	77	TF2572
Furzeley Corner *Hants*	13	SU6510
Furzley *Hants*	12	SU2816
Fyfett *Somset*	9	ST2314
Fyfield *Essex*	40	TL5707
Fyfield *Hants*	23	SU2946
Fyfield *Oxon*	36	SU4298
Fyfield *Wilts*	23	SU1468
Fyfield *Wilts*	23	SU1760
Fyfield Bavant *Wilts*	22	SU0125
Fyfield Wick *Oxon*	36	SU4197
Fylingthorpe *N York*	91	NZ9404
Fyning *W Susx*	14	SU8123

G

Goldsworth

Grey Green

Goldsworth *Surrey*	25	SU9958
Goldthorpe *S York*	83	SE4604
Goldworthy *Devon*	18	SS3922
Golford *Kent*	28	TQ7936
Golford Green *Kent*	28	TQ7936
Gollanfield *Highld*	140	NH8053
Gollinglith Foot *N York*	89	SE1481
Golly *Wrexhm*	71	SJ3358
Golsoncott *Somset*	20	ST0239
Golspie *Highld*	147	NC8300
Gomeldon *Wilts*	23	SU1835
Gomersal *W York*	82	SE2026
Gomshall *Surrey*	14	TQ0847
Gonalston *Notts*	63	SK6747
Gonerby Hill Foot *Lincs*	63	SK9037
Gonfirth *Shet*	155	HU3661
Good Easter *Essex*	40	TL6212
Gooderstone *Norfk*	65	TF7602
Goodleigh *Devon*	19	SS6034
Goodmanham *E R Yk*	84	SE8843
Goodnestone *Kent*	28	TR0461
Goodnestone *Kent*	29	TR2554
Goodrich *H & W*	34	SO5719
Goodrington *Devon*	7	SX8958
Goodshaw *Lancs*	81	SD8125
Goodshaw Fold *Lancs*	81	SD8026
Goodstone *Devon*	7	SX7872
Goodwick *Pembks*	30	SM9438
Goodworth Clatford *Hants*	23	SU3642
Goodyers End *Warwks*	61	SP3385
Goole *E R Yk*	84	SE7423
Goole Fields *E R Yk*	84	SE7520
Goom's Hill *H & W*	47	SP0154
Goonbell *Cnwll*	3	SW7249
Goonhavern *Cnwll*	3	SW7853
Goonvrea *Cnwll*	2	SW7149
Goose Green *Essex*	41	TM1327
Goose Green *Essex*	41	TM1325
Goose Green *Gloucs*	35	ST6774
Goose Green *Gt Man*	78	SD5603
Goose Green *Kent*	27	TQ6451
Goose Green *Kent*	28	TQ8437
Goose Green *W Susx*	14	TQ1118
Goose Pool *H & W*	46	SO4636
Goosecruives *Abers*	135	NO7583
Gooseford *Devon*	8	SX6792
Gooseham *Cnwll*	18	SS2316
Goosehill Green *H & W*	47	SO9361
Goosemoor *Somset*	20	SS9635
Goosey *Oxon*	36	SU3591
Goosnargh *Lancs*	81	SD5536
Goostrey *Ches*	79	SJ7770
Gorddinog *A & C*	69	SH6773
Gordon *Border*	110	NT6443
Gordon Arms Hotel *Border*	109	NT3025
Gordonstown *Abers*	142	NJ5656
Gordonstown *Abers*	142	NJ7138
Gore *Powys*	46	SO2558
Gore Pit *Essex*	40	TL8719
Gore Street *Kent*	29	TR2765
Gorebridge *Mdloth*	118	NT3461
Gorefield *Cambs*	65	TF4112
Gores *Wilts*	23	SU1158
Gorey *Jersey*	152	JS0000
Goring *Oxon*	37	SU6080
Goring Heath *Oxon*	37	SU6579
Goring-by-Sea *W Susx*	14	TQ1102
Gorleston on Sea *Norfk*	67	TG5204
Gorrachie *Abers*	142	NJ7358
Gorran *Cnwll*	3	SW9942
Gorran Haven *Cnwll*	3	SX0141
Gorran High Lanes *Cnwll*	3	SW9843
Gorrig *Cardgn*	31	SN4142
Gors *Cardgn*	43	SN6277
Gorse Hill *Wilts*	36	SU1586
Gorsedd *Flints*	70	SJ1576
Gorseinon *Swans*	32	SS5998
Gorseybank *Derbys*	73	SK2953
Gorsgoch *Cardgn*	44	SN4850
Gorslas *Carmth*	32	SN5713
Gorsley *Gloucs*	47	SO6925
Gorsley Common *Gloucs*	47	SO6825
Gorst Hill *H & W*	60	SO7373
Gorstage *Ches*	71	SJ6172
Gorstan *Highld*	139	NH3862
Gorstello *Ches*	71	SJ3562
Gorsty Hill *Staffs*	73	SK1028
Gorten *Ag & B*	122	NM7432
Gorthleck *Highld*	139	NH5420
Gorton *Gt Man*	79	SJ8896
Gosbeck *Suffk*	54	TM1555
Gosberton *Lincs*	64	TF2331
Gosberton Clough *Lincs*	64	TF1929
Gosfield *Essex*	40	TL7829
Gosford *Devon*	9	SY1097
Gosforth *Cumb*	86	NY0603
Gosforth *T & W*	103	NZ2368
Gosland Green *Ches*	71	SJ5758
Gosling Street *Somset*	21	ST5433
Gosmore *Herts*	39	TL1827
Gospel End *Staffs*	60	SO8993
Gospel Green *W Susx*	14	SU9431
Gosport *Hants*	13	SZ6099
Gossard Green *Beds*	38	SP9643
Gossington *Gloucs*	35	SO7302
Goswick *Nthumb*	111	NU0644
Gotham *Notts*	62	SK5330
Gotherington *Gloucs*	47	SO9529
Gotton *Somset*	20	ST2428
Goudhurst *Kent*	28	TQ7237
Goulceby *Lincs*	77	TF2579
Gourdas *Abers*	142	NJ7741
Gourdie *Angus*	126	NO3532
Gourdon *Abers*	135	NO8270
Gourock *Inver*	114	NS2477
Govan *C Glas*	115	NS5465
Goveton *Devon*	7	SX7546
Gowdall *E R Yk*	83	SE6222
Gower *Highld*	139	NH5058
Gowerton *Swans*	32	SS5896
Gowkhall *Fife*	117	NT0589
Gowthorpe *E R Yk*	84	SE7654
Goxhill *E R Yk*	85	TA1844
Goxhill *Lincs*	85	TA1021
Grabhair *W Isls*	154	NB3915
Graby *Lincs*	64	TF0929
Grade *Cnwll*	2	SW7114
Gradeley Green *Ches*	71	SJ5851
Graffham *W Susx*	14	SU9217
Grafham *Cambs*	52	TL1669
Grafham *Surrey*	14	TQ0241
Grafton *H & W*	46	SO4936
Grafton *H & W*	46	SO5761
Grafton *H & W*	47	SO9837
Grafton *N York*	89	SE4163
Grafton *Oxon*	36	SP2600
Grafton *Shrops*	59	SJ4319
Grafton Flyford *H & W*	47	SO9655
Grafton Regis *Nhants*	49	SP7546
Grafton Underwood *Nhants*	51	SP9280
Grafty Green *Kent*	28	TQ8748
Graianrhyd *Denbgs*	70	SJ2156
Graig *A & C*	69	SH8071
Graig *Denbgs*	70	SJ0872
Graig-fechan *Denbgs*	70	SJ1454
Grain *Kent*	28	TQ8876
Grains Bar *Gt Man*	79	SD9608
Grainsby *Lincs*	77	TF2799
Grainthorpe *Lincs*	77	TF3896
Graiselound *Lincs*	75	SK7698
Grampound *Cnwll*	3	SW9348
Grampound Road *Cnwll*	3	SW9150
Gramsdal *W Isls*	154	NF8155
Gramsdale *W Isls*	154	NF8155
Granborough *Bucks*	49	SP7625
Granby *Notts*	63	SK7536
Grand Chemins *Jersey*	152	JS0000
Grandborough *Warwks*	50	SP4966
Grandes Rocques *Guern*	152	GN0000
Grandtully *P & K*	125	NN9153
Grange *Cumb*	93	NY2517
Grange *Kent*	28	TQ7968
Grange *Mersyd*	78	SJ2286
Grange *P & K*	126	NO2625
Grange Crossroads *Moray*	142	NJ4754
Grange Gate *Dorset*	11	SY9182
Grange Hall *Moray*	141	NJ0660
Grange Hill *Gt Lon*	27	TQ4492
Grange Lindores *Fife*	126	NO2516
Grange Moor *W York*	82	SE2215
Grange Villa *Dur*	96	NZ2352
Grange-over-Sands *Cumb*	87	SD4077
Grangehall *S Lans*	108	NS9642
Grangemill *Derbys*	74	SK2457
Grangemouth *Falk*	116	NS9281
Grangepans *Falk*	117	NT0181
Grangetown *N York*	97	NZ5420
Gransmoor *E R Yk*	91	TA1259
Gransmore Green *Essex*	40	TL6922
Granston *Pembks*	30	SM8934
Grantchester *Cambs*	53	TL4355
Grantham *Lincs*	63	SK9135
Granton *C Edin*	117	NT2376
Grantown-on-Spey *Highld*	141	NJ0328
Grantsfield *H & W*	46	SO5260
Grantshouse *Border*	119	NT8065
Grappenhall *Ches*	79	SJ6486
Grasby *Lincs*	85	TA0804
Grasmere *Cumb*	86	NY3307
Grass Green *Essex*	53	TL7338
Grasscroft *Gt Man*	82	SD9704
Grassendale *Mersyd*	78	SJ3985
Grassgarth *Cumb*	93	NY3444
Grassington *N York*	88	SE0063
Grassmoor *Derbys*	74	SK4067
Grassthorpe *Notts*	75	SK7967
Grateley *Hants*	23	SU2741
Gratwich *Staffs*	73	SK0231
Graveley *Cambs*	52	TL2563
Graveley *Herts*	39	TL2327
Gravelly Hill *W Mids*	61	SP1090
Gravelsbank *Shrops*	59	SJ3300
Graveney *Kent*	28	TR0562
Gravesend *Kent*	28	TQ6574
Gravir *W Isls*	154	NB3915
Grayingham *Lincs*	76	SK9396
Grayrigg *Cumb*	87	SD5796
Grays *Essex*	27	TQ6177
Grayshott *Hants*	14	SU8735
Grayson Green *Cumb*	92	NX9925
Grayswood *Surrey*	14	SU9134
Graythorpe *Dur*	97	NZ5227
Grazeley *Berks*	24	SU6966
Greasbrough *S York*	74	SK4195
Greasby *Mersyd*	78	SJ2587
Greasley *Notts*	62	SK4846
Great Abington *Cambs*	53	TL5348
Great Addington *Nhants*	51	SP9675
Great Alne *Warwks*	48	SP1259
Great Altcar *Lancs*	78	SD3305
Great Amwell *Herts*	39	TL3712
Great Asby *Cumb*	94	NY6713
Great Ashfield *Suffk*	54	TL9967
Great Ayton *N York*	90	NZ5610
Great Baddow *Essex*	40	TL7304
Great Badminton *Gloucs*	35	ST8082
Great Bardfield *Essex*	40	TL6730
Great Barford *Beds*	52	TL1351
Great Barr *W Mids*	61	SP0495
Great Barrington *Gloucs*	36	SP2113
Great Barrow *Ches*	71	SJ4768
Great Barton *Suffk*	54	TL8967
Great Barugh *N York*	90	SE7479
Great Bavington *Nthumb*	102	NY9880
Great Bealings *Suffk*	55	TM2348
Great Bedwyn *Wilts*	23	SU2764
Great Bentley *Essex*	41	TM1021
Great Billing *Nhants*	51	SP8162
Great Bircham *Norfk*	65	TF7732
Great Blakenham *Suffk*	54	TM1150
Great Blencow *Cumb*	93	NY4532
Great Bolas *Shrops*	72	SJ6421
Great Bookham *Surrey*	26	TQ1354
Great Bosullow *Cnwll*	2	SW4133
Great Bourton *Oxon*	49	SP4545
Great Bowden *Leics*	50	SP7488
Great Bradley *Suffk*	53	TL6753
Great Braxted *Essex*	40	TL8614
Great Bricett *Suffk*	54	TM0350
Great Brickhill *Bucks*	38	SP9030
Great Bridge *W Mids*	60	SO9892
Great Bridgeford *Staffs*	72	SJ8827
Great Brington *Nhants*	50	SP6665
Great Bromley *Essex*	41	TM0826
Great Broughton *Cumb*	92	NY0731
Great Broughton *N York*	90	NZ5405
Great Budworth *Ches*	79	SJ6677
Great Burdon *Dur*	96	NZ3116
Great Burstead *Essex*	40	TQ6892
Great Busby *N York*	90	NZ5205
Great Canfield *Essex*	40	TL5918
Great Carlton *Lincs*	77	TF4085
Great Casterton *Rutlnd*	63	TF0008
Great Chart *Kent*	28	TQ9841
Great Chatfield *Wilts*	22	ST8563
Great Chatwell *Staffs*	60	SJ7914
Great Chell *Staffs*	72	SJ8652
Great Chesterford *Essex*	39	TL5042
Great Cheverell *Wilts*	22	ST9854
Great Chishill *Cambs*	39	TL4238
Great Clacton *Essex*	41	TM1716
Great Cliffe *W York*	82	SE3015
Great Clifton *Cumb*	92	NY0429
Great Coates *Lincs*	85	TA2309
Great Comberton *H & W*	47	SO9542
Great Comp *Kent*	27	TQ6356
Great Corby *Cumb*	93	NY4754
Great Cornard *Suffk*	54	TL8840
Great Cowden *E R Yk*	85	TA2342
Great Coxwell *Oxon*	36	SU2693
Great Cransley *Nhants*	51	SP8376
Great Cressingham *Norfk*	66	TF8501
Great Crosthwaite *Cumb*	93	NY2524
Great Cubley *Derbys*	73	SK1638
Great Dalby *Leics*	63	SK7414
Great Doddington *Nhants*	51	SP8864
Great Doward *H & W*	34	SO5416
Great Dunham *Norfk*	66	TF8714
Great Dunmow *Essex*	40	TL6222
Great Durnford *Wilts*	23	SU1338
Great Easton *Essex*	40	TL6025
Great Easton *Leics*	51	SP8492
Great Eccleston *Lancs*	80	SD4240
Great Edstone *N York*	90	SE7083
Great Ellingham *Norfk*	66	TM0196
Great Elm *Somset*	22	ST7449
Great Englebourne *Devon*	7	SX7756
Great Everdon *Nhants*	49	SP5957
Great Eversden *Cambs*	52	TL3653
Great Finborough *Suffk*	54	TM0158
Great Fransham *Norfk*	66	TF8913
Great Gaddesden *Herts*	38	TL0211
Great Gidding *Cambs*	52	TL1183
Great Givendale *E R Yk*	84	SE8153
Great Glemham *Suffk*	55	TM3361
Great Glen *Leics*	50	SP6597
Great Gonerby *Lincs*	63	SK8938
Great Gransden *Cambs*	52	TL2655
Great Green *Cambs*	39	TL2844
Great Green *Norfk*	55	TM2889
Great Green *Suffk*	54	TL9155
Great Green *Suffk*	54	TL9365
Great Habton *N York*	90	SE7576
Great Hale *Lincs*	64	TF1442
Great Hallingbury *Essex*	39	TL5119
Great Hanwood *Shrops*	59	SJ4409
Great Harrowden *Nhants*	51	SP8770
Great Harwood *Lancs*	81	SD7332
Great Haseley *Oxon*	37	SP6401
Great Hatfield *E R Yk*	85	TA1842
Great Haywood *Staffs*	73	SJ9922
Great Heck *N York*	83	SE5920
Great Henny *Essex*	54	TL8637
Great Hinton *Wilts*	22	ST9059
Great Hockham *Norfk*	66	TL9592
Great Holland *Essex*	41	TM2019
Great Horkesley *Essex*	41	TL9731
Great Hormead *Herts*	39	TL4029
Great Horton *W York*	82	SE1431
Great Horwood *Bucks*	49	SP7731
Great Houghton *Nhants*	50	SP7958
Great Houghton *S York*	83	SE4206
Great Hucklow *Derbys*	74	SK1777
Great Kelk *E R Yk*	91	TA1058
Great Kimble *Bucks*	38	SP8205
Great Kingshill *Bucks*	26	SU8797
Great Langdale *Cumb*	86	NY2906
Great Langton *N York*	89	SE2996
Great Leighs *Essex*	40	TL7217
Great Limber *Lincs*	85	TA1308
Great Linford *Bucks*	38	SP8542
Great Livermere *Suffk*	54	TL8871
Great Longstone *Derbys*	74	SK2071
Great Lumley *Dur*	96	NZ2949
Great Lyth *Shrops*	59	SJ4507
Great Malvern *H & W*	47	SO7746
Great Maplestead *Essex*	54	TL8034
Great Marton *Lancs*	80	SD3235
Great Massingham *Norfk*	66	TF7922
Great Melton *Norfk*	66	TG1206
Great Meols *Mersyd*	78	SJ2390
Great Milton *Oxon*	37	SP6202
Great Missenden *Bucks*	26	SP8901
Great Mitton *Lancs*	81	SD7138
Great Mongeham *Kent*	29	TR3551
Great Moulton *Norfk*	54	TM1690
Great Munden *Herts*	39	TL3524
Great Musgrave *Cumb*	94	NY7613
Great Ness *Shrops*	59	SJ3919
Great Notley *Essex*	40	TL7421
Great Nurcott *Somset*	20	SS9036
Great Oak *Mons*	34	SO3810
Great Oakley *Essex*	41	TM1927
Great Oakley *Nhants*	51	SP8785
Great Offley *Herts*	38	TL1427
Great Ormside *Cumb*	94	NY7017
Great Orton *Cumb*	93	NY3254
Great Ouseburn *N York*	89	SE4461
Great Oxendon *Nhants*	50	SP7383
Great Oxney Green *Essex*	40	TL6606
Great Pattenden *Kent*	28	TQ7344
Great Paxton *Cambs*	52	TL2063
Great Plumpton *Lancs*	80	SD3833
Great Plumstead *Norfk*	67	TG3010
Great Ponton *Lincs*	63	SK9230
Great Potheridge *Devon*	19	SS5114
Great Preston *W York*	83	SE4029
Great Purston *Nhants*	49	SP5139
Great Raveley *Cambs*	52	TL2581
Great Rissington *Gloucs*	36	SP1917
Great Rollright *Oxon*	48	SP3231
Great Rudbaxton *Pembks*	30	SM9620
Great Ryburgh *Norfk*	66	TF9527
Great Ryle *Nthumb*	111	NU0212
Great Ryton *Shrops*	59	SJ4803
Great Saling *Essex*	40	TL6925
Great Salkeld *Cumb*	94	NY5536
Great Sampford *Essex*	53	TL6435
Great Sankey *Ches*	78	SJ5688
Great Saredon *Staffs*	60	SJ9508
Great Saughall *Ches*	71	SJ3669
Great Saxham *Suffk*	53	TL7862
Great Shefford *Berks*	36	SU3875
Great Shelford *Cambs*	53	TL4651
Great Smeaton *N York*	89	NZ3404
Great Snoring *Norfk*	66	TF9434
Great Somerford *Wilts*	35	ST9682
Great Soudley *Shrops*	72	SJ7229
Great Stainton *Dur*	96	NZ3322
Great Stambridge *Essex*	40	TQ8991
Great Staughton *Cambs*	52	TL1264
Great Steeping *Lincs*	77	TF4364
Great Stonar *Kent*	29	TR3359
Great Strickland *Cumb*	94	NY5522
Great Stukeley *Cambs*	52	TL2274
Great Sturton *Lincs*	76	TF2176
Great Sutton *Ches*	71	SJ3775
Great Sutton *Shrops*	59	SO5183
Great Swinburne *Nthumb*	102	NY9375
Great Tew *Oxon*	48	SP4028
Great Tey *Essex*	40	TL8925
Great Torrington *Devon*	18	SS4919
Great Tosson *Nthumb*	103	NU0200
Great Totham *Essex*	40	TL8611
Great Totham *Essex*	40	TL8713
Great Tows *Lincs*	76	TF2290
Great Urswick *Cumb*	86	SD2674
Great Wakering *Essex*	40	TQ9487
Great Waldingfield *Suffk*	54	TL9144
Great Walsingham *Norfk*	66	TF9437
Great Waltham *Essex*	40	TL6913
Great Warley *Essex*	27	TQ5890
Great Washbourne *Gloucs*	47	SO9834
Great Weeke *Devon*	8	SX7187
Great Weldon *Nhants*	51	SP9289
Great Welnetham *Suffk*	54	TL8759
Great Wenham *Suffk*	54	TM0738
Great Whittington *Nthumb*	103	NZ0070
Great Wigborough *Essex*	41	TL9615
Great Wilbraham *Cambs*	53	TL5557
Great Wishford *Wilts*	23	SU0735
Great Witchingham *Norfk*	66	TG1020
Great Witcombe *Gloucs*	35	SO9114
Great Witley *H & W*	47	SO7566
Great Wolford *Warwks*	48	SP2534
Great Wratting *Essex*	53	TL6848
Great Wymondley *Herts*	39	TL2128
Great Wyrley *Staffs*	60	SJ9907
Great Wytheford *Shrops*	59	SJ5719
Great Yarmouth *Norfk*	67	TG5207
Great Yeldham *Essex*	53	TL7638
Greatfield *Wilts*	36	SU0785
Greatford *Lincs*	64	TF0811
Greatgate *Staffs*	73	SK0539
Greatham *Dur*	97	NZ4927
Greatham *Hants*	14	SU7730
Greatham *W Susx*	14	TQ0415
Greatstone-on-Sea *Kent*	17	TR0822
Greatworth *Nhants*	49	SP5542
Grebby *Lincs*	77	TF4368
Greeba *IOM*	153	SC3081
Green *Denbgs*	70	SJ0668
Green Bank *Cumb*	87	SD3780
Green Cross *Surrey*	14	SU8637
Green Down *Somset*	21	ST5753
Green End *Beds*	38	TL0147
Green End *Beds*	51	TL0864
Green End *Beds*	51	TL1063
Green End *Beds*	52	TL1252
Green End *Cambs*	52	TL2274
Green End *Cambs*	52	TL3856
Green End *Cambs*	53	TL4668
Green End *Cambs*	53	TL4861
Green End *Cambs*	52	TL1683
Green End *Herts*	39	TL2630
Green End *Herts*	39	TL3222
Green End *Herts*	39	TL3333
Green End *Warwks*	61	SP2686
Green Hammerton *N York*	83	SE4556
Green Head *Cumb*	93	NY3649
Green Heath *Staffs*	60	SJ9913
Green Hill *Wilts*	36	SU0686
Green Hills *Cambs*	53	TL6072
Green Lane *Devon*	8	SX7877
Green Lane *H & W*	48	SP0664
Green Moor *S York*	74	SK2899
Green Oak *N York*	84	SE8127
Green Ore *Somset*	21	ST5750
Green Quarter *Cumb*	87	NY4603
Green Street *E Susx*	17	TQ7611
Green Street *Gloucs*	35	SO8915
Green Street *H & W*	47	SO8749
Green Street *Herts*	39	TL4521
Green Street *Herts*	26	TQ1998
Green Street Green *Gt Lon*	27	TQ4563
Green Street Green *Kent*	27	TQ5870
Green Tye *Herts*	39	TL4418
Greenburn *W Loth*	116	NS9360
Greencroft Hall *Dur*	96	NZ1549
Greenend *Oxon*	36	SP3221
Greenfield *Ag & B*	114	NS2490
Greenfield *Beds*	38	TL0534
Greenfield *Flints*	70	SJ1977
Greenfield *Gt Man*	82	SD9904
Greenfield *Highld*	131	NH2000
Greenfield *Oxon*	37	SU7191
Greenford *Gt Lon*	26	TQ1482
Greengairs *N Lans*	116	NS7870
Greengates *W York*	82	SE1937
Greengill *Cumb*	92	NY1037
Greenhalgh *Lancs*	80	SD4035
Greenham *Berks*	24	SU4865
Greenham *Somset*	20	ST0820
Greenhaugh *Nthumb*	102	NY7987
Greenhead *Nthumb*	102	NY6565
Greenheys *Gt Man*	79	SD7104
Greenhill *D & G*	100	NY1079
Greenhill *Falk*	116	NS8279
Greenhill *H & W*	47	SO7248
Greenhill *Kent*	29	TR1666
Greenhill *S Lans*	108	NS9332
Greenhillocks *Derbys*	74	SK4049
Greenhithe *Kent*	27	TQ5875
Greenholm *E Ayrs*	107	NS5437
Greenholme *Cumb*	87	NY5905
Greenhouse *Border*	109	NT5523
Greenhow Hill *N York*	89	SE1164
Greenland *Highld*	151	ND2367
Greenland *S York*	74	SK3988
Greenlands *Bucks*	37	SU7785
Greenlaw *Border*	110	NT7146
Greenlea *D & G*	100	NY0375
Greenloaning *P & K*	125	NN8307
Greenmoor Hill *Oxon*	37	SU6481
Greenmount *Gt Man*	81	SD7714
Greenock *Inver*	115	NS2876
Greenodd *Cumb*	86	SD3182
Greens Norton *Nhants*	49	SP6649
Greensgate *Norfk*	66	TG1015
Greenshields *S Lans*	108	NT0243
Greenside *T & W*	96	NZ1362
Greenside *W York*	82	SE1716
Greenstead *Essex*	41	TM0125
Greenstead Green *Essex*	40	TL8227
Greensted *Essex*	39	TL5403
Greenstreet Green *Suffk*	54	TM0349
Greenway *Gloucs*	47	SO7033
Greenway *H & W*	60	SO7470
Greenway *Somset*	21	ST3124
Greenway *V Glam*	33	ST0573
Greenwich *Gt Lon*	27	TQ3877
Greet *Gloucs*	48	SP0230
Greete *Shrops*	46	SO5770
Greetham *Lincs*	77	TF3070
Greetham *Rutlnd*	63	SK9214
Greetland *W York*	82	SE0821
Gregson Lane *Lancs*	81	SD5926
Greinton *Somset*	21	ST4136
Grenaby *IOM*	153	SC2672
Grendon *Nhants*	51	SP8760
Grendon *Warwks*	61	SP2799
Grendon Green *H & W*	46	SO5957
Grendon Underwood *Bucks*	37	SP6820
Grenofen *Devon*	6	SX4971
Grenoside *S York*	74	SK3393
Greosabhagh *W Isls*	154	NG1593
Gresford *Wrexhm*	71	SJ3454
Gresham *Norfk*	66	TG1638
Greshornish House Hotel *Highld*	136	NG3454
Gressenhall *Norfk*	66	TF9615
Gressenhall Green *Norfk*	66	TF9616
Gressingham *Lancs*	87	SD5769
Gresty Green *Ches*	72	SJ7053
Greta Bridge *Dur*	95	NZ0813
Gretna *D & G*	101	NY3167
Gretna Green *D & G*	101	NY3168
Gretton *Gloucs*	47	SP0030
Gretton *Nhants*	51	SP8994
Gretton *Shrops*	59	SO5195
Grewelthorpe *N York*	89	SE2376
Grey Friars *Suffk*	55	TM4770
Grey Green *Lincs*	84	SE7807

Greygarth

Hardsough

Greygarth *N York*	89	SE1872
Greylake *Somset*	21	ST3833
Greyrigg *D & G*	100	NY0888
Greys Green *Oxon*	37	SU7182
Greysouthen *Cumb*	92	NY0729
Greystoke *Cumb*	93	NY4430
Greystone *Angus*	127	NO5343
Greywell *Hants*	24	SU7151
Gribb *Dorset*	10	ST3703
Gribthorpe *E R Yk*	84	SE7635
Griff *Warwks*	61	SP3689
Griffithstown *Torfn*	34	ST2998
Griffydam *Leics*	62	SK4118
Griggs Green *Hants*	14	SU8231
Grimeford Village *Lancs*	81	SD6112
Grimesthorpe *S York*	74	SK3689
Grimethorpe *S York*	83	SE4109
Grimley *H & W*	47	SO8360
Grimmet *S Ayrs*	106	NS3210
Grimoldby *Lincs*	77	TF3988
Grimpo *Shrops*	59	SJ3526
Grimsargh *Lancs*	81	SD5834
Grimsby *Lincs*	85	TA2710
Grimscote *Nhants*	49	SP6553
Grimscott *Cnwll*	18	SS2606
Grimshader *W Isls*	154	NB4025
Grimshaw *Lancs*	81	SD7024
Grimshaw Green *Lancs*	80	SD4912
Grimsthorpe *Lincs*	64	TF0422
Grimston *E R Yk*	85	TA2735
Grimston *Leics*	63	SK6821
Grimston *Norfk*	65	TF7222
Grimston Hill *Notts*	75	SK6865
Grimstone *Dorset*	10	SY6394
Grimstone End *Suffk*	54	TL9368
Grinacombe Moor *Devon*	5	SX4191
Grindale *E R Yk*	91	TA1271
Grindle *Shrops*	60	SJ7503
Grindleford *Derbys*	74	SK2477
Grindleton *Lancs*	81	SD7545
Grindley Brook *Shrops*	71	SJ5242
Grindlow *Derbys*	74	SK1877
Grindon *Dur*	96	NZ3925
Grindon *Nthumb*	110	NT9144
Grindon *Staffs*	73	SK0854
Grindon Hill *Nthumb*	102	NY8268
Grindonrigg *Nthumb*	110	NT9243
Gringley on the Hill *Notts*	75	SK7390
Grinsdale *Cumb*	93	NY3758
Grinshill *Shrops*	59	SJ5223
Grinton *N York*	88	SE0498
Griomaisiader *W Isls*	154	NB4025
Grishipoll *Ag & B*	120	NM1859
Grisling Common *E Susx*	16	TQ4322
Gristhorpe *N York*	91	TA0981
Griston *Norfk*	66	TL9499
Gritley *Ork*	155	HY5504
Grittenham *Wilts*	36	SU0382
Grittleton *Wilts*	35	ST8580
Grizebeck *Cumb*	86	SD2384
Grizedale *Cumb*	86	SD3394
Groby *Leics*	62	SK5207
Groes *A & C*	70	SJ0064
Groes-faen *Rhondd*	33	ST0680
Groes-Wen *Caerph*	33	ST1286
Groesffordd *Gwynd*	56	SH2739
Groesffordd Marli *Denbgs*	70	SJ0073
Groesllwyd *Powys*	58	SJ2111
Groeslon *Gwynd*	68	SH4755
Groeslon *Gwynd*	68	SH5260
Grogarry *W Isls*	154	NF7739
Grogport *Ag & B*	105	NR8144
Groigearraidh *W Isls*	154	NF7739
Gromford *Suffk*	55	TM3858
Gronant *Flints*	70	SJ0983
Groombridge *E Susx*	16	TQ5337
Grosebay *W Isls*	154	NG1593
Grosmont *Mons*	46	SO4024
Grosmont *N York*	90	NZ8305
Groton *Suffk*	54	TL9641
Grotton *Gt Man*	79	SD9604
Grouville *Jersey*	152	JS0000
Grove *Bucks*	38	SP9122
Grove *Dorset*	11	SY6972
Grove *Kent*	29	TR2362
Grove *Notts*	75	SK7479
Grove *Oxon*	36	SU4090
Grove *Pembks*	30	SM9900
Grove Green *Kent*	28	TQ7856
Grove Park *Gt Lon*	27	TQ4072
Grove Vale *W Mids*	61	SP0394
Grovenhurst *Kent*	28	TQ7140
Grovesend *Gloucs*	35	ST6589
Grovesend *Swans*	32	SN5900
Grubb Street *Kent*	27	TQ5869
Gruinard *Highld*	144	NG9489
Gruinart *Ag & B*	112	NR2966
Grula *Highld*	136	NG3826
Gruline *Ag & B*	121	NM5440
Grumbla *Cnwll*	2	SW4029
Grundisburgh *Suffk*	55	TM2251
Gruting *Shet*	155	HU2749
Gualachulain *Highld*	123	NN1145
Guanockgate *Lincs*	64	TF3710
Guardbridge *Fife*	127	NO4518
Guarlford *H & W*	47	SO8145
Guay *P & K*	125	NN9948
Guestling Green *E Susx*	17	TQ8513
Guestling Thorn *E Susx*	17	TQ8516
Guestwick *Norfk*	66	TG0626
Guide *Lancs*	81	SD7025
Guide Bridge *Gt Man*	79	SJ9297
Guide Post *Nthumb*	103	NZ2585
Guilden Down *Shrops*	59	SO3082
Guilden Morden *Cambs*	39	TL2744
Guilden Sutton *Ches*	71	SJ4468
Guildford *Surrey*	25	SU9949
Guildstead *Kent*	28	TQ8262
Guildtown *P & K*	126	NO1331
Guilsborough *Nhants*	50	SP6772
Guilsfield *Powys*	58	SJ2211
Guilton *Kent*	29	TR2858
Guiltreehill *S Ayrs*	106	NS3610
Guineaford *Devon*	19	SS5537
Guisborough *N York*	97	NZ6015
Guiseley *W York*	82	SE1942
Guist *Norfk*	66	TG0025
Guiting Power *Gloucs*	48	SP0924
Gullane *E Loth*	118	NT4882
Gulling Green *Suffk*	54	TL8256
Gulval *Cnwll*	2	SW4831
Gulworthy *Devon*	6	SX4572
Gumfreston *Pembks*	31	SN1001
Gumley *Leics*	50	SP6889
Gummow's Shop *Cnwll*	4	SW8657
Gun Green *Kent*	17	TQ7731
Gun Hill *E Susx*	16	TQ5614
Gun Hill *Warwks*	61	SP2889
Gunby *Lincs*	63	SK9121
Gunby *Lincs*	77	TF4666
Gunby *E R Yk*	84	SE7035
Gundleton *Hants*	24	SU6133
Gunn *Devon*	19	SS6333
Gunnerside *N York*	88	SD9598
Gunnerton *Nthumb*	102	NY9074
Gunness *Lincs*	84	SE8411
Gunnislake *Cnwll*	6	SX4371
Gunnista *Shet*	155	HU5043
Gunthorpe *Cambs*	64	TF1802
Gunthorpe *Norfk*	66	TG0134
Gunthorpe *Notts*	63	SK6844
Gunton *Suffk*	67	TM5395
Gunville *IOW*	13	SZ4788
Gunwalloe *Cnwll*	2	SW6522
Gupworthy *Somset*	20	SS9734
Gurnard *IOW*	13	SZ4795
Gurnett *Ches*	79	SJ9271
Gurney Slade *Somset*	21	ST6249
Gurnos *Powys*	32	SN7709
Gushmere *Kent*	28	TR0457
Gussage All Saints *Dorset*	11	SU0010
Gussage St Andrew *Dorset*	11	ST9714
Gussage St Michael *Dorset*	11	ST9811
Guston *Kent*	29	TR3244
Gutcher *Shet*	155	HU5499
Guthrie *Angus*	127	NO5650
Guy's Marsh *Dorset*	22	ST8420
Guyhirn *Cambs*	65	TF4003
Guyhirn Gull *Cambs*	65	TF3904
Guyzance *Nthumb*	103	NU2103
Gwaenysgor *Flints*	70	SJ0781
Gwalchmai *Angles*	68	SH3876
Gwastadnant *Gwynd*	69	SH6157
Gwaun-Cae-Gurwen *Carmth*	32	SN6911
Gwbert on Sea *Cardgn*	42	SN1650
Gwealavellan *Cnwll*	2	SW6041
Gwealeath *Cnwll*	2	SW6922
Gweek *Cnwll*	2	SW7026
Gwehelog *Mons*	34	SO3804
Gwenddwr *Powys*	45	SO0643
Gwendreath *Cnwll*	3	SW7217
Gwennap *Cnwll*	3	SW7340
Gwenter *Cnwll*	3	SW7417
Gwernaffield *Flints*	70	SJ2065
Gwernesney *Mons*	34	SO4101
Gwernogle *Carmth*	44	SN5333
Gwernymynydd *Flints*	70	SJ2162
Gwersyllt *Wrexhm*	71	SJ3153
Gwespyr *Flints*	70	SJ1183
Gwindra *Cnwll*	3	SW9552
Gwinear *Cnwll*	2	SW5937
Gwithian *Cnwll*	2	SW5841
Gwredog *Angles*	68	SH4085
Gwrhay *Caerph*	33	ST1899
Gwyddelwern *Denbgs*	70	SJ0746
Gwyddgrug *Carmth*	44	SN4635
Gwynfryn *Wrexhm*	70	SJ2552
Gwystre *Powys*	45	SO0665
Gwytherin *A & C*	69	SH8761
Gyfelia *Wrexhm*	71	SJ3245
Gyrn-goch *Gwynd*	68	SH4048

H

Habberley *H & W*	60	SO8177
Habberley *Shrops*	59	SJ3903
Habergham *Lancs*	81	SD8033
Habertoft *Lincs*	77	TF5069
Habin *W Susx*	14	SU8022
Habrough *Lincs*	85	TA1413
Hacconby *Lincs*	64	TF1025
Haceby *Lincs*	64	TF0236
Hacheston *Suffk*	55	TM3059
Hack Green *Ches*	72	SJ6448
Hackbridge *Gt Lon*	27	TQ2865
Hackenthorpe *S York*	74	SK4183
Hackford *Norfk*	66	TG0502
Hackforth *N York*	89	SE2492
Hackland *Ork*	155	HY3920
Hackleton *Nhants*	51	SP8055
Hacklinge *Kent*	29	TR3454
Hackman's Gate *H & W*	60	SO8978
Hackness *N York*	91	SE9790
Hackness *Somset*	21	ST3345
Hackney *Gt Lon*	27	TQ3484
Hackthorn *Lincs*	76	SK9982
Hackthorpe *Cumb*	94	NY5423
Hacton *Gt Lon*	27	TQ5585
Hadden *Border*	110	NT7836
Haddenham *Bucks*	37	SP7308
Haddenham *Cambs*	53	TL4675
Haddington *E Loth*	118	NT5173
Haddington *Lincs*	76	SK9162
Haddiscoe *Norfk*	67	TM4497
Haddo *Abers*	143	NJ8337
Haddon *Cambs*	64	TL1392
Hade Edge *W York*	82	SE1404
Hadfield *Derbys*	74	SK0296
Hadham Cross *Herts*	39	TL4218
Hadham Ford *Herts*	39	TL4321
Hadleigh *Essex*	40	TQ8187
Hadleigh *Suffk*	54	TM0242
Hadleigh Heath *Suffk*	54	TL9941
Hadley *H & W*	47	SO8564
Hadley *Shrops*	60	SJ6711
Hadley End *Staffs*	73	SK1320
Hadley Wood *Gt Lon*	27	TQ2698
Hadlow *Kent*	27	TQ6350
Hadlow Down *E Susx*	16	TQ5324
Hadnall *Shrops*	59	SJ5220
Hadstock *Essex*	53	TL5644
Hadzor *H & W*	47	SO9162
Haffenden Quarter *Kent*	28	TQ8840
Hafod-y-bwch *Wrexhm*	71	SJ3147
Hafod-y-coed *Blae G*	34	SO2200
Hafodunos *A & C*	69	SH8666
Hafodyrynys *Caerph*	34	ST2298
Haggate *Lancs*	81	SD8735
Haggbeck *Cumb*	101	NY4773
Haggerston *Nthumb*	111	NU0443
Haggington Hill *Devon*	19	SS5547
Haggs *Falk*	116	NS7879
Hagley *H & W*	46	SO5641
Hagley *W Mids*	60	SO9180
Hagmore Green *Suffk*	54	TL9539
Hagnaby *Lincs*	77	TF3462
Hagnaby *Lincs*	77	TF4879
Hagworthingham *Lincs*	77	TF3469
Haigh *Gt Man*	78	SD6009
Haighton Green *Lancs*	81	SD5634
Hail Weston *Cambs*	52	TL1662
Haile *Cumb*	86	NY0308
Hailes *Gloucs*	48	SP0430
Hailey *Herts*	39	TL3710
Hailey *Oxon*	37	SU6485
Hailey *Oxon*	36	SP3512
Hailsham *E Susx*	16	TQ5909
Hainault *Gt Lon*	27	TQ4591
Haine *Kent*	29	TR3566
Hainford *Norfk*	67	TG2218
Hainton *Lincs*	76	TF1884
Hainworth *W York*	82	SE0638
Haisthorpe *E R Yk*	91	TA1264
Hakin *Pembks*	30	SM8905
Halam *Notts*	75	SK6754
Halbeath *Fife*	117	NT1288
Halberton *Devon*	9	ST0112
Halcro *Highld*	151	ND2360
Hale *Ches*	78	SJ4782
Hale *Cumb*	87	SD5078
Hale *Gt Man*	79	SJ7786
Hale *Hants*	12	SU1818
Hale *Somset*	22	ST7427
Hale *Surrey*	25	SU8448
Hale Bank *Ches*	78	SJ4784
Hale Green *E Susx*	16	TQ5514
Hale Nook *Lancs*	80	SD3944
Hale Street *Kent*	28	TQ6749
Halebarns *Gt Man*	79	SJ7985
Hales *Norfk*	67	TM3797
Hales *Staffs*	72	SJ7134
Hales Green *Derbys*	73	SK1841
Hales Place *Kent*	29	TR1459
Halesgate *Lincs*	64	TF3226
Halesowen *W Mids*	60	SO9683
Halesworth *Suffk*	55	TM3877
Halewood *Mersyd*	78	SJ4585
Halford *Devon*	7	SX8174
Halford *Shrops*	59	SO4383
Halford *Warwks*	48	SP2645
Halfpenny *Cumb*	87	SD5387
Halfpenny Green *Staffs*	60	SO8291
Halfpenny Houses *N York*	89	SE2284
Halfway *Berks*	24	SU4068
Halfway *Carmth*	44	SN6430
Halfway *Carmth*	44	SN8232
Halfway *S York*	75	SK4381
Halfway Bridge *W Susx*	14	SU9321
Halfway House *Shrops*	59	SJ3411
Halfway Houses *Kent*	28	TQ9372
Halifax *W York*	82	SE0925
Halistra *Highld*	136	NG2459
Halkirk *Highld*	151	ND1359
Halkyn *Flints*	70	SJ2171
Hall *E Rens*	115	NS4154
Hall Cliffe *W York*	82	SE2918
Hall Cross *Lancs*	80	SD4230
Hall Dunnerdale *Cumb*	86	SD2195
Hall End *Beds*	38	TL0045
Hall End *Beds*	38	TL0737
Hall End *W Mids*	60	SP0092
Hall Glen *Falk*	116	NS8978
Hall Green *W Mids*	61	SP1181
Hall's Green *Essex*	39	TL4108
Hall's Green *Herts*	39	TL2728
Hallam Fields *Derbys*	62	SK4739
Halland *E Susx*	16	TQ4916
Hallaton *Leics*	50	SP7896
Hallatrow *Somset*	21	ST6357
Hallbankgate *Cumb*	94	NY5859
Hallbeck *Cumb*	87	SD6288
Hallen *Gloucs*	34	ST5580
Hallfield Gate *Derbys*	74	SK3958
Hallgarth *Dur*	96	NZ3243
Hallin *Highld*	136	NG2558
Halling *Kent*	28	TQ7063
Hallington *Lincs*	77	TF3085
Hallington *Nthumb*	102	NY9875
Halliwell *Gt Man*	79	SD6910
Halloughton *Notts*	75	SK6951
Hallow *H & W*	47	SO8258
Hallow Heath *H & W*	47	SO8259
Hallrule *Border*	110	NT5914
Hallsands *Devon*	7	SX8138
Hallthwaites *Cumb*	86	SD1885
Halltoft End *Lincs*	64	TF3645
Hallworthy *Cnwll*	4	SX1787
Hallyne *Border*	109	NT1940
Halmer End *Staffs*	72	SJ7948
Halmond's Frome *H & W*	47	SO6747
Halnaker *W Susx*	14	SU9007
Halsall *Lancs*	78	SD3710
Halse *Nhants*	49	SP5640
Halse *Somset*	20	ST1428
Halsetown *Cnwll*	2	SW5038
Halsham *E R Yk*	85	TA2727
Halsinger *Devon*	19	SS5138
Halstead *Essex*	40	TL8130
Halstead *Kent*	27	TQ4861
Halstead *Leics*	63	SK7505
Halstock *Dorset*	10	ST5308
Halsway *Somset*	20	ST1337
Haltcliff Bridge *Cumb*	93	NY3636
Haltham *Lincs*	77	TF2463
Halton *Bucks*	38	SP8710
Halton *Ches*	78	SJ5481
Halton *Lancs*	87	SD5064
Halton *Nthumb*	103	NY9967
Halton *W York*	83	SE3533
Halton *Wrexhm*	71	SJ3039
Halton East *N York*	82	SE0454
Halton Fenside *Lincs*	77	TF4263
Halton Gill *N York*	88	SD8776
Halton Green *Lancs*	87	SD5165
Halton Holegate *Lincs*	77	TF4165
Halton Lea Gate *Nthumb*	94	NY6458
Halton Quay *Cnwll*	5	SX4165
Halton Shields *Nthumb*	103	NZ0168
Halton West *N York*	81	SD8454
Haltwhistle *Nthumb*	102	NY7064
Halvergate *Norfk*	67	TG4106
Halwell *Devon*	7	SX7753
Halwill *Devon*	18	SX4299
Halwill Junction *Devon*	18	SS4400
Ham *Devon*	9	ST2301
Ham *Gloucs*	35	SO9721
Ham *Gloucs*	35	ST6898
Ham *Gt Lon*	26	TQ1772
Ham *Kent*	29	TR3254
Ham *Somset*	20	ST2825
Ham *Somset*	22	ST6748
Ham *Wilts*	23	SU3262
Ham Common *Dorset*	22	ST8125
Ham Green *H & W*	47	SO7544
Ham Green *H & W*	47	SP0163
Ham Green *Kent*	28	TQ8468
Ham Green *Kent*	17	TQ8926
Ham Green *Somset*	34	ST5375
Ham Hill *Kent*	28	TQ6960
Ham Street *Somset*	21	ST5534
Hamble-le-Rice *Hants*	13	SU4806
Hambleden *Bucks*	37	SU7886
Hambledon *Hants*	13	SU6414
Hambledon *Surrey*	25	SU9638
Hambleton *Lancs*	80	SD3742
Hambleton *N York*	83	SE5530
Hambleton Moss Side *Lancs*	80	SD3842
Hambridge *Somset*	21	ST3921
Hambridge *Somset*	21	ST5936
Hambrook *Gloucs*	35	ST6478
Hambrook *W Susx*	14	SU7806
Hamels *Herts*	39	TL3724
Hameringham *Lincs*	77	TF3167
Hamerton *Cambs*	52	TL1379
Hamilton *S Lans*	116	NS7255
Hamlet *Dorset*	10	ST5908
Hamlins *E Susx*	16	TQ5908
Hammerpot *W Susx*	14	TQ0605
Hammersmith *Gt Lon*	26	TQ2378
Hammerwich *Staffs*	61	SK0707
Hammerwood *E Susx*	16	TQ4339
Hammond Street *Herts*	39	TL3304
Hammoon *Dorset*	11	ST8114
Hamnavoe *Shet*	155	HU3735
Hamnavoe *Shet*	155	HU4971
Hampden Park *E Susx*	16	TQ6002
Hampden Row *Bucks*	26	SP8501
Hamperden End *Essex*	40	TL5730
Hampnett *Gloucs*	36	SP0915
Hampole *S York*	83	SE5010
Hampreston *Dorset*	12	SZ0598
Hampsfield *Cumb*	87	SD4080
Hampson Green *Lancs*	80	SD4954
Hampstead *Gt Lon*	27	TQ2685
Hampstead Norrey's *Berks*	37	SU5276
Hampsthwaite *N York*	89	SE2559
Hampt *Cnwll*	5	SX3874
Hampton *Devon*	10	SY2696
Hampton *Gt Lon*	26	TQ1369
Hampton *H & W*	48	SP0243
Hampton *Kent*	29	TR1568
Hampton *Shrops*	60	SO7486
Hampton *Wilts*	36	SU1892
Hampton Bishop *H & W*	46	SO5637
Hampton Green *Ches*	71	SJ5149
Hampton Heath *Ches*	71	SJ5049
Hampton in Arden *W Mids*	61	SP2080
Hampton Loade *Shrops*	60	SO7486
Hampton Lovett *H & W*	47	SO8865
Hampton Lucy *Warwks*	48	SP2557
Hampton on the Hill *Warwks*	48	SP2564
Hampton Poyle *Oxon*	37	SP5015
Hampton Wick *Gt Lon*	26	TQ1769
Hamptworth *Wilts*	12	SU2419
Hamrow *Norfk*	66	TF9124
Hamsey *E Susx*	15	TQ4012
Hamsey Green *Gt Lon*	27	TQ3559
Hamstall Ridware *Staffs*	73	SK1019
Hamstead *IOW*	13	SZ4091
Hamstead *W Mids*	61	SP0592
Hamstead Marshall *Berks*	24	SU4165
Hamsterley *Dur*	95	NZ1156
Hamsterley *Dur*	96	NZ1231
Hamstreet *Kent*	17	TR0033
Hamwood *Somset*	21	ST3756
Hamworthy *Dorset*	11	SY9991
Hanbury *H & W*	47	SO9664
Hanbury *Staffs*	73	SK1727
Hanby *Lincs*	64	TF0231
Hanchet End *Suffk*	53	TL6446
Hanchurch *Staffs*	72	SJ8441
Hand and Pen *Devon*	9	SY0495
Hand Green *Ches*	71	SJ5460
Handale *N York*	97	NZ7215
Handbridge *Ches*	71	SJ4065
Handcross *W Susx*	15	TQ2629
Handforth *Ches*	79	SJ8583
Handley *Ches*	71	SJ4657
Handley *Derbys*	74	SK3761
Handley Green *Essex*	40	TL6501
Handsacre *Staffs*	73	SK0915
Handsworth *S York*	74	SK4186
Handsworth *W Mids*	61	SP0489
Handy Cross *Bucks*	26	SU8590
Hanford *Dorset*	11	ST8411
Hanford *Staffs*	72	SJ8741
Hanging Langford *Wilts*	23	SU0337
Hangleton *E Susx*	15	TQ2607
Hangleton *W Susx*	14	TQ0803
Hanham *Gloucs*	35	ST6472
Hankelow *Ches*	72	SJ6645
Hankerton *Wilts*	35	ST9790
Hankham *E Susx*	16	TQ6105
Hanley *Staffs*	72	SJ8847
Hanley Castle *H & W*	47	SO8442
Hanley Child *H & W*	47	SO6565
Hanley Swan *H & W*	47	SO8142
Hanley William *H & W*	47	SO6766
Hanlith *N York*	88	SD8961
Hanmer *Wrexhm*	71	SJ4539
Hannaford *Devon*	19	SS6029
Hannah *Lincs*	77	TF4979
Hannington *Hants*	24	SU5355
Hannington *Nhants*	51	SP8170
Hannington *Wilts*	36	SU1793
Hannington Wick *Wilts*	36	SU1795
Hanscombe End *Beds*	38	TL1133
Hanslope *Bucks*	38	SP8046
Hanthorpe *Lincs*	64	TF0823
Hanwell *Gt Lon*	26	TQ1579
Hanwell *Oxon*	49	SP4343
Hanworth *Gt Lon*	26	TQ1271
Hanworth *Norfk*	67	TG1935
Happendon *S Lans*	108	NS8533
Happisburgh *Norfk*	67	TG3831
Happisburgh Common *Norfk*	67	TG3728
Hapsford *Ches*	71	SJ4774
Hapton *Lancs*	81	SD7931
Hapton *Norfk*	66	TM1796
Harberton *Devon*	7	SX7758
Harbertonford *Devon*	7	SX7856
Harbledown *Kent*	29	TR1357
Harborne *W Mids*	60	SP0284
Harborough Magna *Warwks*	50	SP4879
Harbottle *Nthumb*	102	NT9304
Harbourneford *Devon*	7	SX7162
Harbours Hill *H & W*	47	SO9565
Harbridge *Hants*	12	SU1410
Harbridge Green *Hants*	12	SU1410
Harbury *Warwks*	48	SP3759
Harby *Leics*	63	SK7431
Harby *Notts*	76	SK8770
Harcombe *Devon*	9	SX8881
Harcombe *Devon*	9	SY1590
Harcombe Bottom *Devon*	10	SY3395
Harden *W Mids*	60	SK0100
Harden *W York*	82	SE0838
Hardenhuish *Wilts*	35	ST9174
Hardgate *Abers*	135	NJ7901
Hardgate *D & Cb*	115	NS5072
Hardgate *D & G*	100	NX8167
Hardgate *N York*	89	SE2662
Hardham *W Susx*	14	TQ0317
Hardhorn *Lancs*	80	SD3537
Hardingham *Norfk*	66	TG0403
Hardingstone *Nhants*	49	SP7657
Hardington *Somset*	22	ST7452
Hardington Mandeville *Somset*	10	ST5111
Hardington Marsh *Somset*	10	ST5009
Hardington Moor *Somset*	10	ST5112
Hardisworthy *Devon*	18	SS2320
Hardley *Hants*	13	SU4205
Hardley Street *Norfk*	67	TG3701
Hardmead *Bucks*	38	SP9347
Hardraw *N York*	88	SD8691
Hardsough *Lancs*	81	SD7920

Hardstoft

Hemley

Hardstoft *Derbys*	**75**	SK4363
Hardway *Hants*	**13**	SU6001
Hardway *Somset*	**22**	ST7234
Hardwick *Bucks*	**38**	SP8019
Hardwick *Cambs*	**52**	TL3758
Hardwick *Lincs*	**76**	SK8675
Hardwick *Nhants*	**51**	SP8469
Hardwick *Norfk*	**55**	TM2289
Hardwick *Oxon*	**36**	SP3806
Hardwick *Oxon*	**49**	SP5729
Hardwick *S York*	**75**	SK4885
Hardwick *W Mids*	**61**	SP0798
Hardwick Green *H & W*	**47**	SO8133
Hardwicke *Gloucs*	**35**	SO7912
Hardwicke *Gloucs*	**47**	SO9027
Hardy's Green *Essex*	**40**	TL9320
Hare Croft *W York*	**82**	SE0835
Hare Green *Essex*	**41**	TM1025
Hare Hatch *Berks*	**37**	SU8077
Hare Street *Essex*	**39**	TL4209
Hare Street *Essex*	**27**	TL5300
Hare Street *Herts*	**39**	TL3929
Harebeating *E Susx*	**16**	TQ5910
Hareby *Lincs*	**77**	TF3365
Harefield *Gt Lon*	**26**	TQ0590
Harehill *Derbys*	**73**	SK1735
Harehills *W York*	**82**	SE3135
Harehope *Nthumb*	**111**	NU0920
Harelaw *Border*	**109**	NT5323
Harelaw *D & G*	**101**	NY4378
Harelaw *Dur*	**96**	NZ1652
Hareplain *Kent*	**28**	TQ8339
Haresceugh *Cumb*	**94**	NY6042
Harescombe *Gloucs*	**35**	SO8310
Haresfield *Gloucs*	**35**	SO8010
Harestock *Hants*	**24**	SU4631
Harewood *W York*	**83**	SE3245
Harewood End *H & W*	**46**	SO5227
Harford *Devon*	**6**	SX6359
Hargate *Norfk*	**66**	TM1191
Hargatewall *Derbys*	**74**	SK1175
Hargrave *Ches*	**71**	SJ4862
Hargrave *Nhants*	**51**	TL0370
Hargrave *Suffk*	**53**	TL7760
Hargrave Green *Suffk*	**53**	TL7759
Harker *Cumb*	**101**	NY3960
Harkstead *Suffk*	**54**	TM1834
Harlaston *Staffs*	**61**	SK2110
Harlaxton *Lincs*	**63**	SK8832
Harle Syke *Lancs*	**81**	SD8635
Harlech *Gwynd*	**57**	SH5831
Harlescott *Shrops*	**59**	SJ4916
Harlesden *Gt Lon*	**26**	TQ2183
Harlesthorpe *Derbys*	**75**	SK4976
Harleston *Devon*	**7**	SX7945
Harleston *Norfk*	**55**	TM2483
Harleston *Suffk*	**54**	TM0160
Harlestone *Nhants*	**49**	SP7064
Harley *S York*	**74**	SK3698
Harley *Shrops*	**59**	SJ5901
Harlington *Beds*	**38**	TL0330
Harlington *Gt Lon*	**26**	TQ0877
Harlington *S York*	**83**	SE4802
Harlosh *Highld*	**136**	NG2841
Harlow *Essex*	**39**	TL4410
Harlow Hill *Nthumb*	**103**	NZ0768
Harlthorpe *E R Yk*	**84**	SE7337
Harlton *Cambs*	**52**	TL3852
Harlyn Bay *Cnwll*	**4**	SW8775
Harman's Cross *Dorset*	**11**	SY9880
Harmby *N York*	**89**	SE1289
Harmer Green *Herts*	**39**	TL2515
Harmer Hill *Shrops*	**59**	SJ4822
Harmondsworth *Gt Lon*	**26**	TQ0577
Harmston *Lincs*	**76**	SK9662
Harnage *Shrops*	**59**	SJ5604
Harnham *Nthumb*	**103**	NZ0781
Harnhill *Gloucs*	**36**	SP0600
Harold Hill *Gt Lon*	**27**	TQ5392
Harold Wood *Gt Lon*	**27**	TQ5590
Haroldston West *Pembks*	**30**	SM8615
Haroldswick *Shet*	**155**	HP6312
Harome *N York*	**90**	SE6481
Harpenden *Herts*	**38**	TL1314
Harpford *Devon*	**9**	SY0990
Harpham *E R Yk*	**91**	TA0861
Harpley *H & W*	**47**	SO6861
Harpley *Norfk*	**65**	TF7825
Harpole *Nhants*	**49**	SP6961
Harpsdale *Highld*	**151**	ND1355
Harpsden *Oxon*	**37**	SU7680
Harpswell *Lincs*	**76**	SK9389
Harpur Hill *Derbys*	**74**	SK0671
Harpurhey *Gt Man*	**79**	SD8501
Harraby *Cumb*	**93**	NY4154
Harracott *Devon*	**19**	SS5527
Harrapool *Highld*	**129**	NG6523
Harrietfield *P & K*	**125**	NN9829
Harrietsham *Kent*	**28**	TQ8652
Harringay *Gt Lon*	**27**	TQ3188
Harrington *Cumb*	**92**	NX9825
Harrington *Lincs*	**77**	TF3671
Harrington *Nhants*	**50**	SP7780
Harringworth *Nhants*	**51**	SP9197
Harriseahead *Staffs*	**72**	SJ8655
Harriston *Cumb*	**92**	NY1541
Harrogate *N York*	**82**	SE3054
Harrold *Beds*	**51**	SP9457
Harrop Dale *Gt Man*	**82**	SE0008
Harrow *Gt Lon*	**26**	TQ1588
Harrow Green *Suffk*	**54**	TL8654
Harrow on the Hill *Gt Lon*	**26**	TQ1587
Harrow Weald *Gt Lon*	**26**	TQ1591
Harrowbarrow *Cnwll*	**5**	SX4070
Harrowden *Beds*	**38**	TL0647
Harrowgate Village *Dur*	**96**	NZ2917
Harston *Cambs*	**53**	TL4250
Harston *Leics*	**63**	SK8331
Harswell *E R Yk*	**84**	SE8240
Hart *Dur*	**97**	NZ4734
Hart Station *Dur*	**97**	NZ4836
Hartburn *Nthumb*	**103**	NZ0885
Hartest *Suffk*	**54**	TL8352
Hartfield *E Susx*	**16**	TQ4735
Hartford *Cambs*	**52**	TL2572
Hartford *Ches*	**71**	SJ6372
Hartford *Somset*	**20**	SS9529
Hartford End *Essex*	**40**	TL6817
Hartfordbridge *Hants*	**25**	SU7757
Hartforth *N York*	**89**	NZ1606
Harthill *Ches*	**71**	SJ4955
Harthill *N Lans*	**116**	NS9064
Harthill *S York*	**75**	SK4980
Hartington *Derbys*	**74**	SK1260
Hartington *Nthumb*	**103**	NZ0288
Hartland *Devon*	**18**	SS2524
Hartland Quay *Devon*	**18**	SS2224
Hartlebury *H & W*	**60**	SO8471
Hartlepool *Dur*	**97**	NZ5032
Hartley *Cumb*	**88**	NY7808
Hartley *Kent*	**27**	TQ6066
Hartley *Kent*	**17**	TQ7634
Hartley *Nthumb*	**103**	NZ3475
Hartley Green *Kent*	**27**	TQ6067
Hartley Green *Staffs*	**72**	SJ9829
Hartley Wespall *Hants*	**24**	SU6958
Hartley Wintney *Hants*	**24**	SU7656
Hartlip *Kent*	**28**	TQ8464
Hartoft End *N York*	**90**	SE7493
Harton *N York*	**90**	SE7061
Harton *Shrops*	**59**	SO4888
Harton *T & W*	**103**	NZ3765
Hartpury *Gloucs*	**47**	SO7924
Hartshead *W York*	**82**	SE1822
Hartshead Moor Side *W York*	**82**	SE1625
Hartshill *Staffs*	**72**	SJ8546
Hartshill *Warwks*	**61**	SP3194
Hartshorne *Derbys*	**62**	SK3221
Hartside *Nthumb*	**111**	NT9716
Hartsop *Cumb*	**93**	NY4013
Hartswell *Somset*	**20**	ST0827
Hartwell *Nhants*	**38**	SP7850
Hartwith *N York*	**89**	SE2161
Hartwood *N Lans*	**116**	NS8459
Hartwoodmyres *Border*	**109**	NT4324
Harvel *Kent*	**28**	TQ6563
Harvington *H & W*	**60**	SO8775
Harvington *H & W*	**48**	SP0549
Harwell *Notts*	**75**	SK6891
Harwell *Oxon*	**37**	SU4989
Harwich *Essex*	**41**	TM2531
Harwood *Dur*	**95**	NY8233
Harwood *Gt Man*	**79**	SD7410
Harwood *Nthumb*	**103**	NZ0189
Harwood Dale *N York*	**91**	SE9695
Harwood Lee *Gt Man*	**81**	SD7411
Harworth *Notts*	**75**	SK6191
Hasbury *W Mids*	**60**	SO9582
Hascombe *Surrey*	**25**	TQ0039
Haselbeach *Nhants*	**50**	SP7177
Haselbury Plucknett *Somset*	**10**	ST4710
Haseley *Warwks*	**48**	SP2367
Haseley Green *Warwks*	**48**	SP2369
Haseley Knob *Warwks*	**61**	SP2371
Haselor *Warwks*	**48**	SP1257
Hasfield *Gloucs*	**47**	SO8227
Hasguard *Pembks*	**30**	SM8509
Haskayne *Lancs*	**78**	SD3508
Hasketon *Suffk*	**55**	TM2450
Hasland *Derbys*	**74**	SK3969
Hasland Green *Derbys*	**74**	SK3968
Haslemere *Surrey*	**14**	SU9032
Haslingden *Lancs*	**81**	SD7823
Haslingden Grane *Lancs*	**81**	SD7522
Haslingfield *Cambs*	**52**	TL4052
Haslington *Ches*	**72**	SJ7355
Hassall *Ches*	**72**	SJ7657
Hassall Green *Ches*	**72**	SJ7858
Hassell Street *Kent*	**29**	TR0946
Hassingham *Norfk*	**67**	TG3605
Hassness *Cumb*	**93**	NY1816
Hassocks *W Susx*	**15**	TQ3015
Hassop *Derbys*	**74**	SK2272
Haste Hill *Surrey*	**14**	SU9032
Haster *Highld*	**151**	ND3251
Hasthorpe *Lincs*	**77**	TF4869
Hastingleigh *Kent*	**29**	TR0945
Hastings *E Susx*	**17**	TQ8209
Hastings *Somset*	**10**	ST3116
Hastingwood *Essex*	**39**	TL4807
Hastoe *Herts*	**38**	SP9209
Haswell *Dur*	**96**	NZ3743
Haswell Plough *Dur*	**96**	NZ3742
Hatch *Beds*	**52**	TL1547
Hatch Beauchamp *Somset*	**20**	ST3020
Hatch End *Beds*	**51**	TL0760
Hatch End *Gt Lon*	**26**	TQ1390
Hatchet Gate *Hants*	**12**	SU3701
Hatching Green *Herts*	**38**	TL1312
Hatchmere *Ches*	**71**	SJ5571
Hatcliffe *Lincs*	**76**	TA2100
Hatfield *H & W*	**46**	SO5959
Hatfield *Herts*	**39**	TL2308
Hatfield *S York*	**83**	SE6609
Hatfield Broad Oak *Essex*	**39**	TL5416
Hatfield Heath *Essex*	**39**	TL5215
Hatfield Peverel *Essex*	**40**	TL7911
Hatfield Woodhouse *S York*	**83**	SE6708
Hatford *Oxon*	**36**	SU3395
Hatherden *Hants*	**23**	SU3450
Hatherleigh *Devon*	**8**	SS5404
Hathern *Leics*	**62**	SK5022
Hatherop *Gloucs*	**36**	SP1505
Hathersage *Derbys*	**74**	SK2381
Hathersage Booths *Derbys*	**74**	SK2480
Hatherton *Ches*	**72**	SJ6847
Hatherton *Staffs*	**60**	SJ9510
Hatley St George *Cambs*	**52**	TL2751
Hatt *Cnwll*	**5**	SX4062
Hattersley *Gt Man*	**79**	SJ9894
Hattingley *Hants*	**24**	SU6437
Hatton *Abers*	**143**	NK0537
Hatton *Angus*	**127**	NO4642
Hatton *Ches*	**78**	SJ5982
Hatton *Derbys*	**73**	SK2130
Hatton *Gt Lon*	**26**	TQ0975
Hatton *Lincs*	**76**	TF1776
Hatton *Shrops*	**59**	SO4790
Hatton *Warwks*	**48**	SP2367
Hatton Heath *Ches*	**71**	SJ4561
Hatton of Fintray *Abers*	**143**	NJ8316
Haugh *E Ayrs*	**107**	NS4925
Haugh *Lincs*	**77**	TF4175
Haugh *W York*	**81**	SD9311
Haugh Head *Nthumb*	**111**	NU0026
Haugh of Glass *Moray*	**142**	NJ4238
Haugh of Urr *D & G*	**100**	NX8066
Haugham *Lincs*	**77**	TF3381
Haughhead Inn *E Duns*	**116**	NS6079
Haughley *Suffk*	**54**	TM0262
Haughley Green *Suffk*	**54**	TM0264
Haughton *Notts*	**75**	SK6872
Haughton *Powys*	**59**	SJ3018
Haughton *Shrops*	**59**	SJ3726
Haughton *Shrops*	**59**	SJ5516
Haughton *Shrops*	**60**	SJ7408
Haughton *Shrops*	**60**	SO6896
Haughton *Staffs*	**72**	SJ8620
Haughton Green *Gt Man*	**79**	SJ9393
Haughton le Skerne *Dur*	**96**	NZ3116
Haughton Moss *Ches*	**71**	SJ5756
Haultwick *Herts*	**39**	TL3323
Haunton *Staffs*	**61**	SK2310
Hautes Croix *Jersey*	**152**	JS0000
Hauxley *Nthumb*	**103**	NU2703
Hauxton *Cambs*	**53**	TL4452
Havannah *Ches*	**72**	SJ8664
Havant *Hants*	**13**	SU7106
Haven *H & W*	**46**	SO4054
Haven Bank *Lincs*	**76**	TF2352
Haven Side *E R Yk*	**85**	TA1827
Havenstreet *IOW*	**13**	SZ5690
Havercroft *W York*	**83**	SE3913
Haverfordwest *Pembks*	**30**	SM9515
Haverhill *Suffk*	**53**	TL6745
Haverigg *Cumb*	**86**	SD1578
Havering-atte-Bower *Essex*	**27**	TQ5193
Haversham *Bucks*	**38**	SP8242
Haverthwaite *Cumb*	**87**	SD3483
Haverton Hill *Dur*	**97**	NZ4822
Havyat *Somset*	**21**	ST4761
Havyatt *Somset*	**21**	ST5338
Hawarden *Flints*	**71**	SJ3165
Hawbridge *H & W*	**47**	SO9049
Hawbush Green *Essex*	**40**	TL7820
Hawcoat *Cumb*	**86**	SD2071
Hawe's Green *Norfk*	**67**	TM2399
Hawen *Cardgn*	**42**	SN3446
Hawes *N York*	**88**	SD8789
Hawford *H & W*	**47**	SO8460
Hawick *Border*	**109**	NT5014
Hawk Green *Gt Man*	**79**	SJ9687
Hawkchurch *Devon*	**10**	ST3400
Hawkedon *Suffk*	**53**	TL7953
Hawkenbury *Kent*	**28**	TQ8045
Hawkeridge *Wilts*	**22**	ST8653
Hawkerland *Devon*	**9**	SY0588
Hawkes End *W Mids*	**61**	SP2982
Hawkesbury *Gloucs*	**35**	ST7686
Hawkesbury *Warwks*	**61**	SP3784
Hawkesbury Upton *Gloucs*	**35**	ST7786
Hawkhill *Nthumb*	**111**	NU2212
Hawkhurst *Kent*	**17**	TQ7530
Hawkhurst Common *E Susx*	**16**	TQ5217
Hawkinge *Kent*	**29**	TR2139
Hawkley *Hants*	**24**	SU7429
Hawkridge *Somset*	**19**	SS8630
Hawksdale *Cumb*	**93**	NY3648
Hawkshaw *Gt Man*	**81**	SD7615
Hawkshead *Cumb*	**87**	SD3598
Hawkshead Hill *Cumb*	**86**	SD3398
Hawksland *S Lans*	**108**	NS8439
Hawkspur Green *Essex*	**40**	TL6532
Hawkstone *Shrops*	**59**	SJ5830
Hawkswick *N York*	**88**	SD9570
Hawksworth *Notts*	**63**	SK7543
Hawksworth *W York*	**82**	SE1641
Hawkwell *Essex*	**40**	TQ8591
Hawley *Hants*	**25**	SU8657
Hawley *Kent*	**27**	TQ5471
Hawling *Gloucs*	**36**	SP0622
Hawnby *N York*	**90**	SE5489
Haworth *W York*	**82**	SE0337
Hawstead *Suffk*	**54**	TL8559
Hawstead Green *Suffk*	**54**	TL8658
Hawthorn *Dur*	**96**	NZ4145
Hawthorn *Hants*	**24**	SU6733
Hawthorn *Rhondd*	**33**	ST0987
Hawthorn Hill *Berks*	**25**	SU8773
Hawthorn Hill *Lincs*	**76**	TF2155
Hawthorpe *Lincs*	**64**	TF0427
Hawton *Notts*	**75**	SK7851
Haxby *N York*	**90**	SE6058
Haxby Gates *N York*	**83**	SE6056
Haxey *Lincs*	**75**	SK7799
Haxey Turbary *Lincs*	**84**	SE7501
Haxted *Surrey*	**16**	TQ4245
Haxton *Wilts*	**23**	SU1449
Hay *Cnwll*	**3**	SW8651
Hay *Cnwll*	**3**	SW9243
Hay *Cnwll*	**3**	SW9552
Hay *Cnwll*	**4**	SW9770
Hay Green *Norfk*	**65**	TF5418
Hay Street *Herts*	**39**	TL3926
Hay-on-Wye *Powys*	**45**	SO2342
Haydock *Mersyd*	**78**	SJ5697
Haydon *Dorset*	**11**	ST6715
Haydon *Somset*	**20**	ST2523
Haydon *Somset*	**22**	ST6853
Haydon Bridge *Nthumb*	**102**	NY8464
Haydon Wick *Wilts*	**36**	SU1387
Haye *Cnwll*	**5**	SX3570
Hayes *Gt Lon*	**26**	TQ0980
Hayes *Gt Lon*	**27**	TQ4066
Hayes End *Gt Lon*	**26**	TQ0882
Hayfield *Ag & B*	**123**	NN0723
Hayfield *Derbys*	**74**	SK0386
Haygate *Shrops*	**59**	SJ6410
Hayhillock *Angus*	**127**	NO5242
Hayle *Cnwll*	**2**	SW5537
Hayley Green *W Mids*	**60**	SO9582
Haymoor Green *Ches*	**72**	SJ6850
Hayne *Devon*	**9**	SS9515
Hayne *Devon*	**8**	SX7685
Haynes *Beds*	**38**	TL0740
Haynes West End *Beds*	**38**	TL0640
Hayscastle *Pembks*	**30**	SM8925
Hayscastle Cross *Pembks*	**30**	SM9125
Haysden *Kent*	**16**	TQ5745
Hayton *Cumb*	**92**	NY1041
Hayton *Cumb*	**94**	NY5157
Hayton *E R Yk*	**84**	SE8245
Hayton *Notts*	**75**	SK7284
Hayton's Bent *Shrops*	**59**	SO5280
Haytor Vale *Devon*	**8**	SX7777
Haytown *Devon*	**18**	SS3814
Haywards Heath *W Susx*	**15**	TQ3324
Haywood *H & W*	**46**	SO4834
Haywood *S York*	**83**	SE5812
Haywood Oaks *Notts*	**75**	SK6055
Hazards Green *E Susx*	**16**	TQ6812
Hazel Grove *Gt Man*	**79**	SJ9287
Hazel Street *Kent*	**28**	TQ6939
Hazel Stub *Suffk*	**53**	TL6544
Hazelbank *S Lans*	**116**	NS8345
Hazelbury Bryan *Dorset*	**11**	ST7408
Hazeleigh *Essex*	**40**	TL8203
Hazeley *Hants*	**24**	SU7458
Hazelford *Notts*	**75**	SK7249
Hazelhurst *Gt Man*	**79**	SD9600
Hazelslade *Staffs*	**60**	SK0212
Hazelton Walls *Fife*	**126**	NO3322
Hazelwood *Derbys*	**62**	SK3245
Hazlemere *Bucks*	**26**	SU8895
Hazlerigg *T & W*	**103**	NZ2372
Hazles *Staffs*	**73**	SK0047
Hazleton *Gloucs*	**36**	SP0718
Heacham *Norfk*	**65**	TF6737
Headbourne Worthy *Hants*	**24**	SU4832
Headbrook *H & W*	**46**	SO2854
Headcorn *Kent*	**28**	TQ8344
Headingley *W York*	**82**	SE2836
Headington *Oxon*	**37**	SP5207
Headlam *Dur*	**96**	NZ1818
Headless Cross *H & W*	**48**	SP0365
Headlesscross *N Lans*	**116**	NS9158
Headley *Hants*	**24**	SU5162
Headley *Hants*	**14**	SU8236
Headley *Surrey*	**26**	TQ2054
Headley Down *Hants*	**14**	SU8336
Headley Heath *H & W*	**61**	SP0676
Headon *Notts*	**75**	SK7476
Heads *S Lans*	**116**	NS7247
Heads Nook *Cumb*	**94**	NY5054
Heage *Derbys*	**74**	SK3750
Healaugh *N York*	**88**	SE0199
Healaugh *N York*	**83**	SE5047
Heald Green *Gt Man*	**79**	SJ8485
Heale *Devon*	**19**	SS6446
Heale *Somset*	**20**	ST2420
Heale *Somset*	**21**	ST3825
Healey *Lancs*	**81**	SD8816
Healey *N York*	**89**	SE1780
Healey *Nthumb*	**95**	NZ0158
Healey *W York*	**82**	SE2719
Healeyfield *Dur*	**95**	NZ0648
Healing *Lincs*	**85**	TA2110
Heamoor *Cnwll*	**2**	SW4631
Heanor *Derbys*	**62**	SK4346
Heanton Punchardon *Devon*	**19**	SS5035
Heapey *Lancs*	**81**	SD5920
Heapham *Lincs*	**76**	SK8788
Hearn *Hants*	**14**	SU8337
Hearts Delight *Kent*	**28**	TQ8862
Heasley Mill *Devon*	**19**	SS7332
Heast *Highld*	**129**	NG6417
Heath *Derbys*	**75**	SK4567
Heath *W York*	**83**	SE3520
Heath and Reach *Beds*	**38**	SP9228
Heath Common *W Susx*	**14**	TQ0915
Heath End *Bucks*	**26**	SU8898
Heath End *Hants*	**24**	SU4161
Heath End *Hants*	**24**	SU5862
Heath End *Leics*	**62**	SK3621
Heath End *Surrey*	**25**	SU8549
Heath End *Warwks*	**48**	SP2360
Heath Green *H & W*	**61**	SP0771
Heath Hall *D & G*	**100**	NX9979
Heath Hayes *Staffs*	**60**	SK0110
Heath Hill *Shrops*	**60**	SJ7613
Heath House *Somset*	**21**	ST4146
Heath Town *W Mids*	**60**	SO9399
Heathbrook *Shrops*	**59**	SJ6228
Heathcote *Derbys*	**74**	SK1460
Heathcote *Shrops*	**72**	SJ6528
Heathencote *Nhants*	**49**	SP7147
Heather *Leics*	**62**	SK3910
Heathfield *Devon*	**8**	SX8376
Heathfield *E Susx*	**16**	TQ5821
Heathfield *N York*	**89**	SE1367
Heathfield *Somset*	**20**	ST1626
Heathstock *Devon*	**9**	ST2402
Heathton *Shrops*	**60**	SO8192
Heatley *Gt Man*	**79**	SJ7088
Heatley *Staffs*	**73**	SK0626
Heaton *Gt Man*	**79**	SD6909
Heaton *Lancs*	**87**	SD4460
Heaton *Staffs*	**72**	SJ9562
Heaton *T & W*	**103**	NZ2666
Heaton *W York*	**82**	SE1335
Heaton Chapel *Gt Man*	**79**	SJ8891
Heaton Mersey *Gt Man*	**79**	SJ8690
Heaton Norris *Gt Man*	**79**	SJ8890
Heaton's Bridge *Lancs*	**80**	SD4011
Heaverham *Kent*	**27**	TQ5758
Heaviley *Gt Man*	**79**	SJ9088
Heavitree *Devon*	**9**	SX9492
Hebburn *T & W*	**103**	NZ3164
Hebden *N York*	**88**	SE0263
Hebden Bridge *W York*	**82**	SD9927
Hebden Green *Ches*	**71**	SJ6365
Hebing End *Herts*	**39**	TL3122
Hebron *Angles*	**68**	SH4584
Hebron *Carmth*	**31**	SN1827
Hebron *Nthumb*	**103**	NZ1989
Heckfield *Hants*	**24**	SU7260
Heckfield Green *Suffk*	**54**	TM1875
Heckfordbridge *Essex*	**40**	TL9421
Heckington *Lincs*	**64**	TF1444
Heckmondwike *W York*	**82**	SE1824
Heddington *Wilts*	**22**	ST9966
Heddon-on-the-Wall *Nthumb*	**103**	NZ1366
Hedenham *Norfk*	**67**	TM3193
Hedge End *Hants*	**13**	SU4912
Hedgerley *Bucks*	**26**	SU9687
Hedgerley Green *Bucks*	**26**	SU9787
Hedging *Somset*	**20**	ST3029
Hedley on the Hill *Nthumb*	**95**	NZ0759
Hednesford *Staffs*	**60**	SJ9912
Hedon *E R Yk*	**85**	TA1928
Hedsor *Bucks*	**26**	SU9086
Hegdon Hill *H & W*	**46**	SO5853
Heglibister *Shet*	**155**	HU3851
Heighington *Dur*	**96**	NZ2422
Heighington *Lincs*	**76**	TF0269
Heightington *H & W*	**60**	SO7671
Heiton *Border*	**110**	NT7130
Hele *Cnwll*	**5**	SX2198
Hele *Devon*	**19**	SS5347
Hele *Devon*	**9**	SS9902
Hele *Devon*	**7**	SX7470
Hele *Somset*	**20**	ST1824
Hele Lane *Devon*	**19**	SS7910
Helensburgh *Ag & B*	**115**	NS2982
Helenton *S Ayrs*	**106**	NS3830
Helford *Cnwll*	**3**	SW7526
Helford Passage *Cnwll*	**3**	SW7626
Helhoughton *Norfk*	**66**	TF8626
Helions Bumpstead *Essex*	**53**	TL6541
Hell Corner *Berks*	**23**	SU3864
Hellaby *S York*	**75**	SK5092
Helland *Cnwll*	**4**	SX0771
Hellandbridge *Cnwll*	**4**	SX0671
Hellescott *Cnwll*	**5**	SX2888
Hellesdon *Norfk*	**67**	TG2010
Hellesvear *Cnwll*	**2**	SW5040
Hellidon *Nhants*	**49**	SP5158
Hellifield *N York*	**81**	SD8556
Hellingly *E Susx*	**16**	TQ5812
Hellington *Norfk*	**67**	TG3103
Helm *Nthumb*	**103**	NZ1896
Helmdon *Nhants*	**49**	SP5943
Helme *W York*	**82**	SE0912
Helmingham *Suffk*	**54**	TM1857
Helmington Row *Dur*	**96**	NZ1835
Helmsdale *Highld*	**147**	ND0315
Helmshore *Lancs*	**81**	SD7821
Helmsley *N York*	**90**	SE6183
Helmswell Cliff *Lincs*	**76**	SK9489
Helperby *N York*	**89**	SE4469
Helperthorpe *N York*	**91**	SE9570
Helpringham *Lincs*	**64**	TF1440
Helpston *Cambs*	**64**	TF1205
Helsby *Ches*	**71**	SJ4975
Helsey *Lincs*	**77**	TF5172
Helston *Cnwll*	**2**	SW6527
Helstone *Cnwll*	**4**	SX0881
Helton *Cumb*	**94**	NY5021
Helwith *N York*	**88**	NZ0702
Helwith Bridge *N York*	**88**	SD8069
Hemblington *Norfk*	**67**	TG3411
Hemel Hempstead *Herts*	**38**	TL0507
Hemerdon *Devon*	**6**	SX5657
Hemingbrough *N York*	**83**	SE6730
Hemingby *Lincs*	**76**	TF2374
Hemingfield *S York*	**83**	SE3801
Hemingford Abbots *Cambs*	**52**	TL2871
Hemingford Grey *Cambs*	**52**	TL2970
Hemingstone *Suffk*	**54**	TM1454
Hemington *Nhants*	**51**	TL0985
Hemington *Somset*	**22**	ST7253
Hemley *Suffk*	**55**	TM2842

Hulme

Keeston

Hulme *Staffs* 72 SJ9345
Hulme End *Staffs* 74 SK1059
Hulme Walfield *Ches* 72 SJ8465
Hulse Heath *Ches* 79 SJ7283
Hulton Lane Ends *Gt Man* 79 SD6905
Hulver Street *Norfk* 66 TF9311
Hulver Street *Suffk* 55 TM4686
Hulverstone *IOW* 13 SZ3984
Humber *Devon* 7 SX8975
Humberston *Lincs* 85 TA3105
Humberstone *Leics* 63 SK6305
Humberton *N York* 89 SE4168
Humbie *E Loth* 118 NT4662
Humbleton *E R Yk* 85 TA2234
Humbleton *Nthumb* 111 NT9728
Humby *Lincs* 63 TF0032
Hume *Border* 110 NT7041
Humshaugh *Nthumb* 102 NY9171
Huna *Highld* 151 ND3573
Huncoat *Lancs* 81 SD7730
Huncote *Leics* 50 SP5197
Hundalee *Border* 110 NT6418
Hundall *Derbys* 74 SK3876
Hunderthwaite *Dur* 95 NY9821
Hundle Houses *Lincs* 77 TF2453
Hundleby *Lincs* 77 TF3966
Hundleton *Pembks* 30 SM9600
Hundon *Suffk* 53 TL7348
Hundred Acres *Hants* 13 SU5911
Hundred End *Lancs* 80 SD4122
Hundred House *Powys* 45 SO1154
Hundred The *H & W* 46 SO5264
Hungarton *Leics* 63 SK6907
Hungate End *Bucks* 38 SP7946
Hunger Hill *Lancs* 80 SD5411
Hungerford *Berks* 23 SU3368
Hungerford *Hants* 12 SU1612
Hungerford *Somset* 20 ST0440
Hungerford Newtown *Berks* 36 SU3571
Hungerstone *H & W* 46 SO4435
Hungerton *Lincs* 63 SK8729
Hungryhatton *Shrops* 72 SJ6626
Hunmanby *N York* 91 TA0977
Hunningham *Warwks* 48 SP3767
Hunnington *H & W* 60 SO9681
Hunny Hill *IOW* 13 SZ4990
Hunsdon *Herts* 39 TL4114
Hunsingore *N York* 83 SE4253
Hunslet *W York* 82 SE3130
Hunsonby *Cumb* 94 NY5835
Hunstanton *Norfk* 65 TF6740
Hunstanworth *Dur* 95 NY9448
Hunston *Suffk* 54 TL9768
Hunston *W Susx* 14 SU8601
Hunston Green *Suffk* 54 TL9866
Hunstrete *Somset* 21 ST6462
Hunsworth *W York* 82 SE1827
Hunt End *H & W* 48 SP0364
Hunt's Corner *Norfk* 54 TM0588
Hunt's Cross *Mersyd* 78 SJ4385
Hunter's Inn *Devon* 19 SS6548
Hunters Quay *Ag & B* 114 NS1879
Hunterston *Ches* 72 SJ6946
Huntham *Somset* 21 ST3426
Hunthill Lodge *Angus* 134 NO4771
Huntingdon *Cambs* 52 TL2471
Huntingdon *H & W* 46 SO2553
Huntingfield *Suffk* 55 TM3374
Huntingford *Dorset* 22 ST8030
Huntington *E Loth* 118 NT4874
Huntington *H & W* 46 SO4841
Huntington *N York* 83 SE6156
Huntington *Staffs* 60 SJ9712
Huntley *Gloucs* 35 SO7219
Huntly *Abers* 142 NJ5339
Hunton *Hants* 24 SU4840
Hunton *Kent* 28 TQ7149
Hunton *N York* 89 SE1892
Hunton Bridge *Herts* 26 TL0800
Hunts Green *Bucks* 38 SP8903
Hunts Green *Warwks* 61 SP1897
Huntscott *Somset* 20 SS9144
Huntsham *Devon* 20 ST0020
Huntshaw *Devon* 19 SS5023
Huntshaw Cross *Devon* 19 SS5222
Huntspill *Somset* 21 ST3145
Huntstile *Somset* 20 ST2633
Huntworth *Somset* 21 ST3134
Hunwick *Dur* 96 NZ1832
Hunworth *Norfk* 66 TG0635
Hurcott *Somset* 10 ST3916
Hurdcott *Wilts* 23 SU1733
Hurdsfield *Ches* 79 SJ9274
Hurley *Berks* 37 SU8283
Hurley *Warwks* 61 SP2495
Hurley Bottom *Berks* 37 SU8283
Hurley Common *Warwks* 61 SP2496
Hurlford *E Ayrs* 107 NS4536
Hurlston Green *Lancs* 80 SD3911
Hurn *Dorset* 12 SZ1296
Hurn's End *Lincs* 77 TF4249
Hursley *Hants* 13 SU4225
Hurst *Berks* 25 SU7973
Hurst *Dorset* 11 SY7990
Hurst *N York* 88 NZ0402
Hurst *Somset* 10 ST4518
Hurst Green *E Susx* 17 TQ7327
Hurst Green *Essex* 41 TM0916
Hurst Green *Lancs* 81 SD6838
Hurst Green *Surrey* 27 TQ3951
Hurst Hill *W Mids* 60 SO9393
Hurst Wickham *W Susx* 15 TQ2816
Hurstbourne Priors *Hants* 24 SU4346
Hurstbourne Tarrant *Hants* 23 SU3853
Hurstley *H & W* 46 SO3548
Hurstpierpoint *W Susx* 15 TQ2716
Hurstway Common *H & W* 46 SO2949
Hurstwood *Lancs* 81 SD8831
Hurtiso *Ork* 155 HY5001
Hurtmore *Surrey* 25 SU9445
Hurworth Burn *Dur* 96 NZ4033
Hurworth-on-Tees *Dur* 89 NZ3009
Hury *Dur* 95 NY9519
Husbands Bosworth *Leics* 50 SP6484
Husborne Crawley *Beds* 38 SP9635
Husthwaite *N York* 90 SE5175
Hut Green *N York* 83 SE5623
Hutcherleigh *Devon* 7 SX7850
Huthwaite *N York* 90 NZ4801
Huthwaite *Notts* 75 SK4659
Huttoft *Lincs* 77 TF5176
Hutton *Border* 119 NT9053
Hutton *Cumb* 93 NY4326
Hutton *E R Yk* 84 TA0253
Hutton *Essex* 40 TQ6395
Hutton *Lancs* 80 SD4926
Hutton *Somset* 21 ST3558
Hutton Bonville *N York* 89 NZ3300
Hutton Buscel *N York* 91 SE9784
Hutton Conyers *N York* 89 SE3273
Hutton Cranswick *E R Yk* 84 TA0252
Hutton End *Cumb* 93 NY4538
Hutton Hall *N York* 90 NZ6014
Hutton Hang *N York* 89 SE1788
Hutton Henry *Dur* 96 NZ4236
Hutton Lowcross *N York* 90 NZ5914
Hutton Magna *Dur* 89 NZ1212
Hutton Mulgrave *N York* 90 NZ8309
Hutton Roof *Cumb* 93 NY3734
Hutton Roof *Cumb* 87 SD5677
Hutton Rudby *N York* 89 NZ4606
Hutton Sessay *N York* 89 SE4776
Hutton Wandesley *N York* 83 SE5050
Hutton-le-Hole *N York* 90 SE7090
Huxham *Devon* 9 SX9497
Huxham Green *Somset* 21 ST5936
Huxley *Ches* 71 SJ5061
Huyton *Mersyd* 78 SJ4490
Hycemoor *Cumb* 86 SD0989
Hyde *Gloucs* 35 SO8801
Hyde *Gt Man* 79 SJ9494
Hyde *Hants* 12 SU1612
Hyde End *Berks* 24 SU7266
Hyde Heath *Bucks* 26 SP9300
Hyde Lea *Staffs* 72 SJ9120
Hyde Park Corner *Somset* 20 ST2832
Hydestile *Surrey* 25 SU9640
Hykeham Moor *Lincs* 76 SK9366
Hylands *Essex* 40 TL6704
Hyndford Bridge *S Lans* 108 NS9141
Hynish *Ag & B* 120 NL9839
Hyssington *Powys* 59 SO3194
Hystfield *Gloucs* 35 ST6695
Hythe *Hants* 13 SU4207
Hythe *Kent* 29 TR1634
Hythe *Somset* 21 ST4452
Hythe End *Berks* 26 TQ0172
Hyton *Cumb* 86 SD0987

I

Ibberton *Dorset* 11 ST7807
Ible *Derbys* 74 SK2457
Ibsley *Hants* 12 SU1509
Ibstock *Leics* 62 SK4009
Ibstone *Bucks* 37 SU7593
Ibthorpe *Hants* 23 SU3753
Iburndale *N York* 90 NZ8707
Ibworth *Hants* 24 SU5654
Icelton *Somset* 21 ST3765
Ickburgh *Norfk* 66 TL8195
Ickenham *Gt Lon* 26 TQ0786
Ickford *Bucks* 37 SP6407
Ickham *Kent* 29 TR2258
Ickleford *Herts* 39 TL1831
Icklesham *E Susx* 17 TQ8716
Ickleton *Cambs* 39 TL4943
Icklingham *Suffk* 53 TL7772
Ickornshaw *N York* 82 SD9642
Ickwell Green *Beds* 52 TL1545
Icomb *Gloucs* 36 SP2122
Idbury *Oxon* 36 SP2319
Iddesleigh *Devon* 19 SS5708
Ide *Devon* 9 SX8990
Ide Hill *Kent* 27 TQ4851
Ideford *Devon* 9 SX8977
Iden *E Susx* 17 TQ9123
Iden Green *Kent* 28 TQ7437
Iden Green *Kent* 17 TQ8031
Idle *W York* 82 SE1737
Idless *Cnwll* 3 SW8147
Idlicote *Warwks* 48 SP2844
Idmiston *Wilts* 23 SU1937
Idridgehay *Derbys* 73 SK2849
Idrigill *Highld* 136 NG3863
Idstone *Oxon* 36 SU2584
Iffley *Oxon* 37 SP5203
Ifield *W Susx* 15 TQ2537
Ifold *W Susx* 14 TQ0231
Iford *Dorset* 12 SZ1393
Iford *E Susx* 15 TQ4007
Ifton *Mons* 34 ST4688
Ifton Heath *Shrops* 59 SJ3237
Ightam *Kent* 27 TQ5956
Ightfield *Shrops* 71 SJ5938
Iken *Suffk* 55 TM4155
Ilam *Staffs* 73 SK1350
Ilchester *Somset* 21 ST5222
Ilderton *Nthumb* 111 NU0121
Ilford *Gt Lon* 27 TQ4486
Ilford *Somset* 10 ST3617
Ilfracombe *Devon* 19 SS5247
Ilkeston *Derbys* 62 SK4641
Ilketshall St Andrew *Suffk* 55 TM3887
Ilketshall St Margaret *Suffk* 55 TM3485
Ilkley *W York* 82 SE1147
Illand *Cnwll* 5 SX2878
Illey *W Mids* 60 SO9881
Illidge Green *Ches* 72 SJ7963
Illingworth *W York* 82 SE0728
Illogan *Cnwll* 2 SW6743
Illston on the Hill *Leics* 50 SP7099
Ilmer *Bucks* 37 SP7605
Ilmington *Warwks* 48 SP2143
Ilminster *Somset* 10 ST3614
Ilsington *Dorset* 11 SY7592
Ilsington *Devon* 7 SX7875
Ilston *Swans* 32 SS5590
Ilton *N York* 89 SE1978
Ilton *Somset* 10 ST3517
Imachar *N Ayrs* 105 NR8640
Immingham *Lincs* 85 TA1814
Immingham Dock *Lincs* 85 TA1916
Impington *Cambs* 53 TL4463
Ince *Ches* 71 SJ4576
Ince Blundell *Mersyd* 78 SD3203
Ince-in-Makerfield *Gt Man* 78 SD5904
Inchbae Lodge Hotel *Highld* 146 NH4069
Inchbare *Angus* 134 NO6065
Incherry *Moray* 141 NJ3055
Inchinnan *Rens* 115 NS4769
Inchlaggan *Highld* 131 NH1701
Inchmichael *P & K* 126 NO2425
Inchnacardoch Hotel *Highld* 131 NH3810
Inchnadamph *Highld* 145 NC2521
Inchture *P & K* 126 NO2728
Inchvuilt *Highld* 139 NH2438
Inchyra *P & K* 126 NO1820
Indian Queens *Cnwll* 4 SW9159
Ingate Place *Suffk* 55 TM4288
Ingatestone *Essex* 40 TQ6499
Ingbirchworth *S York* 82 SE2205
Ingerthorpe *N York* 89 SE2866
Ingestre *Staffs* 72 SJ9724
Ingham *Lincs* 76 SK9483
Ingham *Norfk* 67 TG3926
Ingham *Suffk* 54 TL8570
Ingham Corner *Norfk* 67 TG3927
Ingleborough *Norfk* 65 TF4715
Ingleby *Derbys* 62 SK3426
Ingleby Arncliffe *N York* 89 NZ4400
Ingleby Barwick *N York* 89 NZ4414
Ingleby Cross *N York* 89 NZ4500
Ingleby Greenhow *N York* 90 NZ5706
Ingleigh Green *Devon* 8 SS6007
Inglesbatch *Somset* 22 ST7061
Inglesham *Wilts* 36 SU2098
Ingleston *D & G* 99 NX6048
Ingleston *D & G* 100 NX9865
Ingleton *Dur* 96 NZ1720
Ingleton *N York* 87 SD6972
Inglewhite *Lancs* 80 SD5439
Ingmire Hall *Cumb* 87 SD6391
Ingoe *Nthumb* 103 NZ0374
Ingoldisthorpe *Norfk* 65 TF6832
Ingoldmells *Lincs* 77 TF5668
Ingoldsby *Lincs* 64 TF0129
Ingram *Nthumb* 111 NU0115
Ingrave *Essex* 40 TQ6291
Ingrow *W York* 82 SE0539
Ings *Cumb* 87 SD4498
Ingst *Gloucs* 34 ST5887
Ingthorpe *Lincs* 63 SK9908
Ingworth *Norfk* 67 TG1929
Inkberrow *H & W* 47 SP0157
Inkerman *Dur* 95 NZ1139
Inkhorn *Abers* 143 NJ9239
Inkpen *Berks* 23 SU3664
Inkstack *Highld* 151 ND2570
Inmarsh *Wilts* 22 ST9460
Innellan *Ag & B* 114 NS1570
Innerleithen *Border* 109 NT3336
Innerleven *Fife* 118 NO3700
Innermessan *D & G* 98 NX0862
Innerwick *E Loth* 119 NT7273
Innesmill *Moray* 141 NJ2863
Insch *Abers* 142 NJ6228
Insh *Highld* 132 NH8101
Inskip *Lancs* 80 SD4637
Inskip Moss Side *Lancs* 80 SD4539
Instow *Devon* 18 SS4730
Insworke *Cnwll* 6 SX4252
Intake *S York* 74 SK3884
Inver *Abers* 133 NO2293
Inver *Highld* 147 NH8682
Inver *P & K* 125 NO0142
Inver-boyndie *Abers* 142 NJ6664
Inverailort *Highld* 129 NM7681
Inveralligin *Highld* 138 NG8457
Inverallochy *Abers* 143 NK0365
Inveran *Highld* 146 NH5797
Inveraray *Ag & B* 123 NN0908
Inverarish *Highld* 137 NG5535
Inverarity *Angus* 127 NO4544
Inverarnan *Stirlg* 123 NN3118
Inverasdale *Highld* 144 NG8284
Inveravon *Falk* 117 NS9579
Inverawe *Ag & B* 122 NN0231
Inverbeg *Ag & B* 115 NS3497
Inverbervie *Abers* 135 NO8272
Inverbroom *Highld* 145 NH1883
Invercreran House Hotel *Ag & B* 122 NN0146
Inverdruie *Highld* 132 NH8911
Inveresk *E Loth* 118 NT3471
Inveresragan *Ag & B* 122 NM9835
Inverey *Abers* 133 NO0889
Inverfarigaig *Highld* 139 NH5123
Inverfolia *Ag & B* 122 NM9544
Invergarry *Highld* 131 NH3001
Invergeldie *P & K* 124 NN7327
Invergloy *Highld* 131 NN2288
Invergordon *Highld* 140 NH7068
Invergowrie *P & K* 126 NO3430
Inverguseran *Highld* 129 NG7407
Inverhadden *P & K* 124 NN6757
Inverherive Hotel *Stirlg* 123 NN3626
Inverie *Highld* 129 NG7600
Inverinan *Ag & B* 122 NM9917
Inverinate *Highld* 138 NG9221
Inverkeilor *Angus* 127 NO6649
Inverkeithing *Fife* 117 NT1383
Inverkeithny *Abers* 142 NJ6247
Inverkip *Inver* 114 NS2072
Inverkirkaig *Highld* 145 NC0719
Inverlael *Highld* 145 NH1885
Inverlair *Highld* 131 NN3479
Inverliever Lodge *Ag & B* 122 NM8905
Inverlochy *Ag & B* 123 NN1927
Invermarkie *Abers* 142 NJ4239
Invermoriston *Highld* 139 NH4216
Inverness *Highld* 140 NH6645
Invernoaden *Ag & B* 114 NS1297
Inveroran Hotel *Ag & B* 123 NN2741
Inverquharity *Angus* 134 NO4057
Inverquhomery *Abers* 143 NK0146
Inverroy *Highld* 131 NN2581
Inversanda *Highld* 130 NM9459
Invershiel *Highld* 138 NG9319
Invershin *Highld* 146 NH5796
Invershore *Highld* 151 ND2435
Inversnaid Hotel *Stirlg* 123 NN3308
Inverugie *Abers* 143 NK0948
Inveruglas *Ag & B* 123 NN3109
Inveruglass *Highld* 132 NH8000
Inverurie *Abers* 142 NJ7721
Inwardleigh *Devon* 8 SX5699
Inworth *Essex* 40 TL8717
Iping *W Susx* 14 SU8522
Ipplepen *Devon* 7 SX8366
Ipsden *Oxon* 37 SU6285
Ipstones *Staffs* 73 SK0149
Ipswich *Suffk* 54 TM1644
Irby *Mersyd* 78 SJ2584
Irby in the Marsh *Lincs* 77 TF4663
Irby upon Humber *Lincs* 85 TA1904
Irchester *Nhants* 51 SP9265
Ireby *Cumb* 93 NY2338
Ireby *Lancs* 87 SD6575
Ireland *Beds* 38 TL1341
Ireleth *Cumb* 86 SD2277
Ireshopeburn *Dur* 95 NY8638
Ireton Wood *Derbys* 73 SK2847
Irlam *Gt Man* 79 SJ7294
Irnham *Lincs* 64 TF0226
Iron Acton *Gloucs* 35 ST6783
Iron Bridge *Cambs* 65 TL4898
Iron Cross *Warwks* 48 SP0552
Ironbridge *Shrops* 60 SJ6703
Ironmacannie *D & G* 99 NX6675
Irons Bottom *Surrey* 15 TQ2446
Ironville *Derbys* 75 SK4351
Irstead *Norfk* 67 TG3620
Irthington *Cumb* 101 NY4961
Irthlingborough *Nhants* 51 SP9470
Irton *N York* 91 TA0184
Irvine *N Ayrs* 106 NS3238
Isauld *Highld* 150 NC9865
Isbister *Shet* 155 HU3790
Isfield *E Susx* 16 TQ4417
Isham *Nhants* 51 SP8873
Isington *Hants* 25 SU7842
Islandpool *H & W* 60 SO8780
Isle Abbotts *Somset* 21 ST3520
Isle Brewers *Somset* 21 ST3621
Isle of Dogs *Gt Lon* 27 TQ3779
Isle of Whithorn *D & G* 99 NX4736
Isleham *Cambs* 53 TL6474
Isleornsay *Highld* 129 NG7012
Islesteps *D & G* 100 NX9672
Islet Village *Guern* 152 GN0000
Isley Walton *Leics* 62 SK4224
Islibhig *W Isls* 154 NB0029
Islington *Gt Lon* 27 TQ3184
Islip *Nhants* 51 SP9879
Islip *Oxon* 37 SP5214
Islivig *W Isls* 154 NB0029
Isombridge *Shrops* 59 SJ6113
Istead Rise *Kent* 27 TQ6370
Itchen Abbas *Hants* 24 SU5333
Itchen Stoke *Hants* 24 SU5532
Itchingfield *W Susx* 15 TQ1328
Itchington *Gloucs* 35 ST6587
Itteringham *Norfk* 66 TG1430
Itton *Devon* 8 SX6899
Itton *Mons* 34 ST4995
Ivegill *Cumb* 93 NY4143
Ivelet *N York* 88 SD9398
Iver *Bucks* 26 TQ0381
Iver Heath *Bucks* 26 TQ0283
Iveston *Dur* 96 NZ1350
Ivinghoe *Bucks* 38 SP9416
Ivinghoe Aston *Bucks* 38 SP9517
Ivington *H & W* 46 SO4756
Ivington Green *H & W* 46 SO4656
Ivy Cross *Dorset* 22 ST8623
Ivy Hatch *Kent* 27 TQ5854
Ivy Todd *Norfk* 66 TF8909
Ivybridge *Devon* 6 SX6356
Ivychurch *Kent* 17 TR0327
Iwade *Kent* 28 TQ9067
Iwerne Courtney or
Shroton *Dorset* 11 ST8512
Iwerne Minster *Dorset* 11 ST8614
Ixworth *Suffk* 54 TL9370
Ixworth Thorpe *Suffk* 54 TL9173

J

Jack Green *Lancs* 81 SD5925
Jack Hill *N York* 82 SE1951
Jack's Bush *Hants* 23 SU2636
Jack-in-the-Green *Devon* 9 SY0195
Jacksdale *Notts* 75 SK4451
Jackson Bridge *W York* 82 SE1607
Jackton *S Lans* 115 NS5952
Jacobs Well *Surrey* 25 TQ0053
Jacobstow *Cnwll* 5 SX1995
Jacobstowe *Devon* 8 SS5801
Jameston *Pembks* 30 SS0598
Jamestown *D & Cb* 115 NS3981
Jamestown *Highld* 139 NH4756
Janets-town *Highld* 151 ND3551
Janetstown *Highld* 151 ND1932
Jardine Hall *D & G* 100 NY1088
Jarrow *T & W* 103 NZ3364
Jarvis Brook *E Susx* 16 TQ5329
Jasper's Green *Essex* 40 TL7226
Jawcraig *Falk* 116 NS8475
Jaywick *Essex* 41 TM1413
Jealott's Hill *Berks* 25 SU8673
Jeator Houses *N York* 89 SE4394
Jedburgh *Border* 110 NT6420
Jeffreston *Pembks* 31 SN0906
Jemimaville *Highld* 140 NH7165
Jerbourg *Guern* 152 GN0000
Jerusalem *Lincs* 76 SK9170
Jesmond *T & W* 103 NZ2566
Jevington *E Susx* 16 TQ5601
Jingle Street *Mons* 34 SO4710
Jockey End *Herts* 38 TL0413
Jodrell Bank *Ches* 79 SJ7970
John O'Groats *Highld* 151 ND3872
John's Cross *E Susx* 17 TQ7421
Johnby *Cumb* 93 NY4332
Johnshaven *Abers* 135 NO7967
Johnson's Street *Norfk* 67 TG3717
Johnston *Carmth* 31 SN3919
Johnston *Pembks* 30 SM9310
Johnstone *D & G* 109 NT2400
Johnstone *Rens* 115 NS4263
Johnstonebridge *D & G* 100 NY1092
Johnstown *Wrexhm* 71 SJ3046
Joppa *C Edin* 118 NT3173
Joppa *Cardgn* 43 SN5666
Joppa *S Ayrs* 106 NS4119
Jordans *Bucks* 26 SU9791
Jordanston *Pembks* 30 SM9132
Jordanthorpe *S York* 74 SK3580
Joyden's Wood *Kent* 27 TQ5072
Jubilee Corner *Kent* 28 TQ8447
Jump *S York* 83 SE3801
Jumper's Town *E Susx* 16 TQ4632
Juniper Green *C Edin* 117 NT1968
Jurby *IOM* 153 SC3598
Jurston *Devon* 8 SX6984

K

Kaber *Cumb* 88 NY7911
Kames *Ag & B* 114 NR9771
Kames *E Ayrs* 107 NS6926
Kea *Cnwll* 3 SW8142
Keadby *Lincs* 84 SE8311
Keal Cotes *Lincs* 77 TF3660
Kearby Town End *N York* 83 SE3447
Kearsley *Gt Man* 79 SD7504
Kearsley *Nthumb* 103 NZ0275
Kearsney *Kent* 29 TR2844
Kearstwick *Cumb* 87 SD6079
Kearton *N York* 88 SD9998
Keasden *N York* 88 SD7266
Keason *Cnwll* 5 SX3168
Keaton *Devon* 7 SX6454
Keckwick *Ches* 78 SJ5783
Keddington *Lincs* 77 TF3488
Keddington Corner *Lincs* 77 TF3589
Kedington *Suffk* 53 TL7046
Kedleston *Derbys* 73 SK3040
Keelby *Lincs* 85 TA1610
Keele *Staffs* 72 SJ8045
Keele University *Staffs* 72 SJ8144
Keeley Green *Beds* 38 TL0046
Keelham *W York* 82 SE0732
Keeston *Pembks* 30 SM9019

L

Langrish
Little Airies

Langrish *Hants*	13	SU7023
Langsett *S York*	74	SE2100
Langshaw *Border*	109	NT5139
Langside *P & K*	125	NN7913
Langstone *Hants*	13	SU7204
Langstone *Newpt*	34	ST3789
Langthorne *N York*	89	SE2491
Langthorpe *N York*	89	SE3867
Langthwaite *N York*	88	NZ0001
Langtoft *E R Yk*	91	TA0066
Langtoft *Lincs*	64	TF1212
Langton *Dur*	96	NZ1619
Langton *Lincs*	76	TF2368
Langton *Lincs*	77	TF3970
Langton *N York*	90	SE7966
Langton by Wragby *Lincs*	76	TF1476
Langton Green *Kent*	16	TQ5439
Langton Green *Suffk*	54	TM1474
Langton Herring *Dorset*	10	SY6182
Langton Matravers *Dorset*	11	SZ0078
Langtree *Devon*	18	SS4515
Langtree Week *Devon*	18	SS4715
Langwathby *Cumb*	94	NY5733
Langwell House *Highld*	147	ND1122
Langworth *Lincs*	76	TF0676
Langworthy *Devon*	5	SX4894
Lanieth *Cnwll*	3	SW9752
Lanivet *Cnwll*	4	SX0464
Lank *Cnwll*	4	SX0875
Lanlivery *Cnwll*	4	SX0759
Lanner *Cnwll*	2	SW7139
Lanoy *Cnwll*	5	SX2977
Lanreath *Cnwll*	4	SX1857
Lansallos *Cnwll*	4	SX1751
Lanteglos *Cnwll*	4	SX0882
Lanteglos Highway *Cnwll*	3	SX1453
Lanton *Border*	110	NT6221
Lanton *Nthumb*	110	NT9231
Lapford *Somset*	19	SS7308
Laphroaig *Ag & B*	104	NR3845
Lapley *Staffs*	60	SJ8712
Lapworth *Warwks*	61	SP1671
Larachbeg *Highld*	122	NM6948
Larbert *Falk*	116	NS8582
Larbreck *Lancs*	80	SD4040
Largie *Abers*	142	NJ6131
Largiemore *Ag & B*	114	NR9486
Largoward *Fife*	127	NO4607
Largs *N Ayrs*	114	NS2059
Largybeg *N Ayrs*	105	NS0423
Largymore *N Ayrs*	105	NS0424
Larkbeare *Devon*	9	SY0797
Larkfield *Inver*	114	NS2475
Larkfield *Kent*	28	TQ7058
Larkhall *S Lans*	116	NS7651
Larkhill *Wilts*	23	SU1244
Larling *Norfk*	54	TL9889
Lartington *Dur*	95	NZ0117
Lasborough *Gloucs*	35	ST8294
Lasham *Hants*	24	SU6742
Lashbrook *Devon*	18	SS4305
Lashenden *Kent*	28	TQ8440
Lask Edge *Staffs*	72	SJ9156
Lassodie *Fife*	117	NT1292
Lasswade *Mdloth*	117	NT3065
Lastingham *N York*	90	SE7290
Latcham *Somset*	21	ST4447
Latchford *Herts*	39	TL3920
Latchford *Oxon*	37	SP6501
Latchingdon *Essex*	40	TL8800
Latchley *Cnwll*	5	SX4173
Latebrook *Staffs*	72	SJ8453
Lately Common *Gt Man*	79	SJ6797
Lathbury *Bucks*	38	SP8744
Latheron *Highld*	151	ND2033
Latheronwheel *Highld*	151	ND1832
Lathones *Fife*	127	NO4708
Latimer *Bucks*	26	TQ0099
Latteridge *Gloucs*	35	ST6684
Lattiford *Somset*	22	ST6926
Latton *Wilts*	36	SU0995
Lauder *Border*	118	NT5347
Laugharne *Carmth*	31	SN3010
Laughterton *Lincs*	76	SK8375
Laughton *E Susx*	16	TQ4913
Laughton *Leics*	50	SP6688
Laughton *Lincs*	76	SK8497
Laughton *Lincs*	64	TF0731
Laughton-en-le-Morthen *S York*	75	SK5187
Launcells *Cnwll*	18	SS2405
Launcells Cross *Cnwll*	18	SS2605
Launceston *Cnwll*	5	SX3384
Launton *Oxon*	37	SP6022
Laurencekirk *Abers*	135	NO7171
Laurieston *D & G*	99	NX6864
Laurieston *Falk*	116	NS9179
Lavendon *Bucks*	51	SP9153
Lavenham *Suffk*	54	TL9149
Lavernock *V Glam*	20	ST1868
Laversdale *Cumb*	101	NY4762
Laverstock *Wilts*	23	SU1630
Laverstoke *Hants*	24	SU4948
Laverton *Gloucs*	48	SP0735
Laverton *N York*	89	SE2273
Laverton *Somset*	22	ST7753
Lavister *Wrexhm*	71	SJ3758
Law *S Lans*	116	NS8252
Law Hill *S Lans*	116	NS8251
Lawers *P & K*	124	NN6739
Lawford *Essex*	41	TM0831
Lawford *Somset*	20	ST1336
Lawgrove *P & K*	125	NO0926
Lawhitton *Cnwll*	5	SX3582
Lawkland *N York*	88	SD7766
Lawkland Green *N York*	88	SD7765
Lawley *Shrops*	60	SJ6608
Lawnhead *Staffs*	72	SJ8325
Lawrence End *Herts*	38	TL1419
Lawrenny *Pembks*	30	SN0106
Lawshall *Suffk*	54	TL8654
Lawshall Green *Suffk*	54	TL8853
Lawton *H & W*	46	SO4459
Laxay *W Isls*	154	NB3321
Laxdale *W Isls*	154	NB4234
Laxey *IOM*	153	SC4384
Laxfield *Suffk*	55	TM2972
Laxford Bridge *Highld*	148	NC2346
Laxo *Shet*	155	HU4463
Laxton *E R Yk*	84	SE7925
Laxton *Nhants*	51	SP9596
Laxton *Notts*	75	SK7267
Laycock *W York*	82	SE0341
Layer Breton *Essex*	40	TL9417
Layer Marney *Essex*	40	TL9217
Layer-de-la-Haye *Essex*	41	TL9620
Layham *Suffk*	54	TM0240
Layland's Green *Berks*	23	SU3866
Laymore *Dorset*	10	ST3804
Layter's Green *Bucks*	26	SU9890
Laytham *E R Yk*	84	SE7439
Laythes *Cumb*	93	NY2455
Lazenby *N York*	97	NZ5719
Lazonby *Cumb*	94	NY5439
Le Bigard *Guern*	152	GN0000
Le Bourg *Guern*	152	GN0000
Le Bourg *Jersey*	152	JS0000
Le Gron *Guern*	152	GN0000
Le Haquais *Jersey*	152	JS0000
Le Hocq *Jersey*	152	JS0000
Le Villocq *Guern*	152	GN0000
Lea *Derbys*	74	SK3257
Lea *H & W*	35	SO6521
Lea *Lincs*	75	SK8286
Lea *Shrops*	59	SJ4108
Lea *Shrops*	59	SO3589
Lea *Wilts*	35	ST9586
Lea Bridge *Derbys*	74	SK3156
Lea Heath *Staffs*	73	SK0225
Lea Marston *Warwks*	61	SP2093
Lea Town *Lancs*	80	SD4730
Lea Yeat *Cumb*	88	SD7686
Leachkin *Highld*	140	NH6344
Leadburn *Mdloth*	117	NT2355
Leaden Roding *Essex*	40	TL5913
Leadenham *Lincs*	76	SK9452
Leadgate *Dur*	96	NZ1251
Leadgate *Nthumb*	95	NZ1159
Leadhills *S Lans*	108	NS8815
Leadingcross Green *Kent*	28	TQ8951
Leadmill *Derbys*	74	SK2380
Leafield *Oxon*	36	SP3115
Leagrave *Beds*	38	TL0523
Leahead *Ches*	72	SJ6864
Lealholm Side *N York*	90	NZ7607
Leake *N York*	89	SE4390
Leake Common Side *Lincs*	77	TF3952
Lealholm *N York*	90	NZ7607
Lealt *Highld*	137	NG5060
Leam *Derbys*	74	SK2379
Leamington Hastings *Warwks*	50	SP4467
Leamington Spa *Warwks*	48	SP3265
Leamonsley *Staffs*	61	SK1009
Leamside *Dur*	96	NZ3146
Leap Cross *E Susx*	16	TQ5810
Leasgill *Cumb*	87	SD4983
Leasingham *Lincs*	76	TF0548
Leasingthorne *Dur*	96	NZ2530
Leatherhead *Surrey*	26	TQ1656
Leathley *N York*	82	SE2347
Leaton *Shrops*	59	SJ4618
Leaton *Shrops*	59	SJ6111
Leaveland *Kent*	28	TR0053
Leavenheath *Suffk*	54	TL9537
Leavening *N York*	90	SE7863
Leaves Green *Gt Lon*	27	TQ4161
Lebberston *N York*	91	TA0782
Lechlade *Gloucs*	36	SU2199
Leck *Lancs*	87	SD6476
Leck Gruinart *Ag & B*	112	NR2768
Leckbuie *P & K*	124	NN7040
Leckford *Hants*	23	SU3737
Leckhampstead *Berks*	36	SU4375
Leckhampstead *Bucks*	49	SP7237
Leckhampstead Thicket *Berks*	36	SU4276
Leckhampton *Gloucs*	35	SO9419
Leckmelm *Highld*	145	NH1689
Leckwith *V Glam*	33	ST1574
Leconfield *E R Yk*	84	TA0143
Ledaig *Ag & B*	122	NM9037
Ledburn *Bucks*	38	SP9021
Ledbury *H & W*	47	SO7137
Leddington *Gloucs*	47	SO6834
Ledgemoor *H & W*	46	SO4150
Ledicot *H & W*	46	SO4162
Ledmore Junction *Highld*	145	NC2412
Ledsham *Ches*	71	SJ3574
Ledsham *W York*	83	SE4529
Ledston *W York*	83	SE4328
Ledston Luck *W York*	83	SE4330
Ledstone *Devon*	7	SX7446
Ledwell *Oxon*	49	SP4128
Lee *Devon*	18	SS4846
Lee *Gt Lon*	27	TQ3875
Lee *Hants*	12	SU3617
Lee *Shrops*	59	SJ4032
Lee Brockhurst *Shrops*	59	SJ5427
Lee Chapel *Essex*	40	TQ6987
Lee Clump *Bucks*	38	SP9004
Lee Common *Bucks*	38	SP9103
Lee Green *Ches*	72	SJ6661
Lee Mill *Devon*	6	SX5955
Lee Moor *Devon*	6	SX5762
Lee Street *Surrey*	15	TQ2743
Lee-on-the-Solent *Hants*	13	SU5600
Leebotwood *Shrops*	59	SO4798
Leece *Cumb*	86	SD2469
Leedon *Beds*	38	SP9325
Leeds *Kent*	28	TQ8253
Leeds *W York*	82	SE2932
Leeds Beck *Lincs*	76	TF2065
Leedstown *Cnwll*	2	SW6034
Leek *Staffs*	72	SJ9856
Leek Wootton *Warwks*	48	SP2868
Leeming *N York*	89	SE2989
Leeming *W York*	82	SE0434
Leeming Bar *N York*	89	SE2889
Lees *Derbys*	73	SK2637
Lees *Gt Man*	79	SD9504
Lees *W York*	82	SE0437
Lees Green *Derbys*	73	SK2637
Lees Hill *Cumb*	101	NY5568
Leesthorpe *Leics*	63	SK7813
Leeswood *Flints*	70	SJ2660
Leetown *P & K*	126	NO2121
Leftwich *Ches*	79	SJ6672
Legbourne *Lincs*	77	TF3784
Legburthwaite *Cumb*	93	NY3219
Legerwood *Border*	110	NT5843
Legsby *Lincs*	76	TF1385
Leicester *Leics*	62	SK5804
Leicester Forest East *Leics*	62	SK5202
Leigh *Devon*	19	SS7212
Leigh *Dorset*	10	ST6108
Leigh *Gloucs*	47	SO8626
Leigh *Gt Man*	79	SJ6599
Leigh *H & W*	47	SO7853
Leigh *Kent*	16	TQ5446
Leigh *Shrops*	59	SJ3303
Leigh *Surrey*	15	TQ2246
Leigh *Wilts*	36	SU0692
Leigh Beck *Essex*	40	TQ8183
Leigh Delamere *Wilts*	35	ST8879
Leigh Green *Kent*	17	TQ9033
Leigh Knoweglass *S Lans*	116	NS6350
Leigh Park *Dorset*	12	SZ0299
Leigh Sinton *H & W*	47	SO7750
Leigh upon Mendip *Somset*	22	ST6947
Leigh Woods *Somset*	34	ST5672
Leigh-on-Sea *Essex*	40	TQ8286
Leighland Chapel *Somset*	20	ST0336
Leighterton *Gloucs*	35	ST8290
Leighton *N York*	89	SE1679
Leighton *Powys*	58	SJ2306
Leighton *Shrops*	59	SJ6105
Leighton *Somset*	22	ST7043
Leighton Bromswold *Cambs*	52	TL1175
Leighton Buzzard *Beds*	38	SP9225
Leinthall Earls *H & W*	46	SO4467
Leinthall Starkes *H & W*	46	SO4369
Leintwardine *H & W*	46	SO4074
Leire *Leics*	50	SP5290
Leiston *Suffk*	55	TM4462
Leitfie *P & K*	126	NO2545
Leith *C Edin*	117	NT2776
Leitholm *Border*	110	NT7944
Lelant *Cnwll*	2	SW5437
Lelley *E R Yk*	85	TA2032
Lem Hill *H & W*	60	SO7275
Lemmington Hall *Nthumb*	111	NU1211
Lempitlaw *Border*	110	NT7832
Lemreway *W Isls*	154	NB3711
Lemsford *Herts*	39	TL2212
Lenchwick *H & W*	48	SP0347
Lendalfoot *S Ayrs*	106	NX1390
Lendrick *Stirlg*	124	NN5506
Lendrum Terrace *Abers*	143	NK1141
Lenham *Kent*	28	TQ8952
Lenham Heath *Kent*	28	TQ9149
Lenie *Highld*	139	NH5126
Lennel *Border*	110	NT8540
Lennox Plunton *D & G*	99	NX6051
Lennoxtown *E Duns*	116	NS6277
Lent *Bucks*	26	SU9381
Lenton *Lincs*	64	TF0230
Lenton *Notts*	62	SK5539
Lenwade *Norfk*	66	TG0918
Lenzie *E Duns*	116	NS6572
Leochel-Cushnie *Abers*	134	NJ5210
Leominster *H & W*	46	SO4959
Leonard Stanley *Gloucs*	35	SO8003
Leoville *Jersey*	152	JS0000
Lepe *Hants*	13	SZ4498
Lephin *Highld*	136	NG1749
Leppington *N York*	90	SE7661
Lepton *W York*	82	SE2015
Lerryn *Cnwll*	4	SX1457
Lerwick *Shet*	155	HU4741
Les Arquets *Guern*	152	GN0000
Les Hubits *Guern*	152	GN0000
Les Lohiers *Guern*	152	GN0000
Les Murchez *Guern*	152	GN0000
Les Nicolles *Guern*	152	GN0000
Les Quartiers *Guern*	152	GN0000
Les Quennevais *Jersey*	152	JS0000
Les Sages *Guern*	152	GN0000
Les Villets *Guern*	152	GN0000
Lesbury *Nthumb*	111	NU2311
Leslie *Abers*	142	NJ5924
Leslie *Fife*	126	NO2501
Lesmahagow *S Lans*	108	NS8139
Lesnewth *Cnwll*	4	SX1390
Lessingham *Norfk*	67	TG3928
Lessonhall *Cumb*	93	NY2250
Lestowder *Cnwll*	3	SW7924
Leswalt *D & G*	98	NX0163
Letchmore Heath *Herts*	26	TQ1597
Letchworth *Herts*	39	TL2232
Letcombe Bassett *Oxon*	36	SU3784
Letcombe Regis *Oxon*	36	SU3886
Letham *Angus*	127	NO5348
Letham *Border*	110	NT6709
Letham *Fife*	126	NO3014
Letham Grange *Angus*	127	NO6345
Lethendy *P & K*	126	NO1341
Lethenty *Abers*	142	NJ5820
Lethenty *Abers*	143	NJ8140
Letheringham *Suffk*	55	TM2757
Letheringsett *Norfk*	66	TG0638
Lett's Green *Kent*	27	TQ4559
Lettaford *Devon*	8	SX7084
Letterewe *Highld*	144	NG9571
Letterfearn *Highld*	138	NG8823
Letterfinlay Lodge Hotel *Highld*	131	NN2491
Lettermorar *Highld*	129	NM7389
Letters *Highld*	145	NH1687
Lettershaw *S Lans*	108	NS8920
Letterston *Pembks*	30	SM9429
Lettoch *Highld*	141	NJ0219
Lettoch *Highld*	141	NJ1032
Letton *H & W*	46	SO3346
Letton *H & W*	46	SO3770
Letty Green *Herts*	39	TL2810
Letwell *S York*	75	SK5686
Leuchars *Fife*	127	NO4521
Leumrabhagh *W Isls*	154	NB3711
Leurbost *W Isls*	154	NB3725
Levalsa Moor *Cnwll*	3	SX0049
Levedale *Staffs*	72	SJ8916
Level's Green *Essex*	39	TL4724
Leven *E R Yk*	85	TA1045
Leven *Fife*	118	NO3800
Levencorroch *N Ayrs*	105	NS0021
Levens *Cumb*	87	SD4886
Levens Green *Herts*	39	TL3522
Levenshulme *Gt Man*	79	SJ8794
Levenwick *Shet*	155	HU4021
Leverburgh *W Isls*	154	NG0286
Leverington *Cambs*	65	TF4411
Leverstock Green *Herts*	38	TL0806
Leverton *Lincs*	77	TF4047
Levington *Suffk*	55	TM2339
Levisham *N York*	90	SE8390
Lew *Oxon*	36	SP3206
Lewannick *Cnwll*	5	SX2780
Lewdown *Devon*	5	SX4586
Lewes *E Susx*	15	TQ4110
Leweston *Dorset*	10	ST6312
Leweston *Pembks*	30	SM9322
Lewis Wych *H & W*	46	SO3357
Lewisham *Gt Lon*	27	TQ3774
Lewiston *Highld*	139	NH5129
Lewknor *Oxon*	37	SU7197
Leworthy *Devon*	18	SS3201
Leworthy *Devon*	19	SS6738
Lewson Street *Kent*	28	TQ9661
Lewth *Lancs*	80	SD4836
Lewtrenchard *Devon*	5	SX4586
Lexden *Essex*	41	TL9625
Lexworthy *Somset*	20	ST2535
Ley *Cnwll*	4	SX1766
Ley Hill *Bucks*	26	SP9902
Leybourne *Kent*	28	TQ6858
Leyburn *N York*	89	SE1190
Leycett *Staffs*	72	SJ7946
Leygreen *Herts*	39	TL1624
Leyland *Lancs*	80	SD5422
Leyland Green *Mersyd*	78	SD5500
Leylodge *Abers*	135	NJ7613
Leys *Abers*	143	NK0052
Leys *Angus*	126	NO2537
Leys of Cossans *Angus*	126	NO3849
Leysdown-on-Sea *Kent*	28	TR0370
Leysmill *Angus*	127	NO6047
Leysters *H & W*	46	SO5664
Leyton *Gt Lon*	27	TQ3786
Leytonstone *Gt Lon*	27	TQ3987
Lezant *Cnwll*	5	SX3479
Lezayre *IOM*	153	SC4294
Lezerea *Cnwll*	2	SW6833
Lhanbryde *Moray*	141	NJ2761
Libanus *Powys*	45	SN9925
Libberton *S Lans*	108	NS9943
Liberton *C Edin*	117	NT2769
Lichfield *Staffs*	61	SK1109
Lickey *H & W*	60	SO9975
Lickey End *H & W*	60	SO9772
Lickey Rock *H & W*	60	SO9774
Lickfold *W Susx*	14	SU9226
Liddaton Green *Devon*	5	SX4582
Liddesdale *Highld*	130	NM7759
Liddington *Wilts*	36	SU2081
Lidgate *Derbys*	74	SK3077
Lidgate *Suffk*	53	TL7258
Lidget *S York*	75	SE6500
Lidgett *Notts*	75	SK6365
Lidham Hill *E Susx*	17	TQ8316
Lidlington *Beds*	38	SP9939
Lidsing *Kent*	28	TQ7862
Liff *Angus*	126	NO3332
Lifford *W Mids*	61	SP0580
Lifton *Devon*	5	SX3885
Liftondown *Devon*	5	SX3685
Lighthazles *W York*	82	SE0220
Lighthorne *Warwks*	48	SP3355
Lighthorne Heath *Warwks*	48	SP3555
Lightwater *Surrey*	25	SU9362
Lightwood *Staffs*	72	SJ9241
Lightwood Green *Ches*	71	SJ6342
Lightwood Green *Wrexhm*	71	SJ3840
Lilbourne *Nhants*	50	SP5676
Lilburn Tower *Nthumb*	111	NU0224
Lilleshall *Shrops*	72	SJ7315
Lilley *Berks*	37	SU4479
Lilley *Herts*	38	TL1126
Lilliesleaf *Border*	109	NT5325
Lillingstone Dayrell *Bucks*	49	SP7039
Lillingstone Lovell *Bucks*	49	SP7140
Lillington *Dorset*	10	ST6212
Lilliput *Dorset*	12	SZ0489
Lilstock *Somset*	20	ST1645
Lilyhurst *Shrops*	60	SJ7413
Limbrick *Lancs*	81	SD6016
Limbury *Beds*	38	TL0724
Lime Street *H & W*	47	SO8130
Limebrook *H & W*	46	SO3766
Limefield *Gt Man*	81	SD8012
Limekilnburn *S Lans*	116	NS7050
Limekilns *Fife*	117	NT0883
Limerigg *Falk*	116	NS8571
Limerstone *IOW*	13	SZ4482
Limestone Brae *Nthumb*	95	NY7949
Limington *Somset*	21	ST5422
Limmerhaugh *E Ayrs*	107	NS6127
Limpenhoe *Norfk*	67	TG3903
Limpley Stoke *Wilts*	22	ST7860
Limpsfield *Surrey*	27	TQ4053
Limpsfield Chart *Surrey*	27	TQ4251
Linby *Notts*	75	SK5351
Linchmere *W Susx*	14	SU8630
Lincluden *D & G*	100	NX9677
Lincoln *Lincs*	76	SK9771
Lincomb *H & W*	47	SO8268
Lincombe *Devon*	7	SX7440
Lindal in Furness *Cumb*	86	SD2475
Lindale *Cumb*	87	SD4180
Lindfield *W Susx*	15	TQ3425
Lindford *Hants*	14	SU8036
Lindley *W York*	82	SE1217
Lindley Green *N York*	82	SE2248
Lindores *Fife*	126	NO2616
Lindow End *Ches*	79	SJ8178
Lindridge *H & W*	47	SO6769
Lindsell *Essex*	40	TL6427
Lindsey *Suffk*	54	TL9745
Lindsey Tye *Suffk*	54	TL9845
Liney *Somset*	21	ST3535
Linford *Essex*	40	TQ6779
Linford *Hants*	12	SU1806
Lingbob *W York*	82	SE0935
Lingdale *N York*	97	NZ6716
Lingen *H & W*	46	SO3667
Lingfield *Surrey*	15	TQ3843
Lingley Green *Ches*	78	SJ5588
Lingwood *Norfk*	67	TG3508
Linicro *Highld*	136	NG3966
Linkend *H & W*	47	SO8231
Linkenholt *Hants*	23	SU3657
Linkhill *Kent*	17	TQ8127
Linkinhorne *Cnwll*	5	SX3173
Linktown *Fife*	117	NT2790
Linkwood *Moray*	141	NJ2361
Linley *Shrops*	59	SO3592
Linley Green *H & W*	47	SO6953
Linleygreen *Shrops*	60	SO6898
Linlithgow *W Loth*	117	NS9977
Linshiels *Nthumb*	110	NT8906
Linsidemore *Highld*	146	NH5499
Linslade *Beds*	38	SP9125
Linstead Parva *Suffk*	55	TM3377
Linstock *Cumb*	93	NY4258
Linthurst *H & W*	60	SO9972
Linthwaite *W York*	82	SE1014
Lintlaw *Border*	119	NT8258
Lintmill *Moray*	142	NJ5165
Linton *Border*	110	NT7726
Linton *Cambs*	53	TL5646
Linton *Derbys*	73	SK2716
Linton *H & W*	47	SO6625
Linton *Kent*	28	TQ7550
Linton *N York*	88	SD9962
Linton *Nthumb*	103	NZ2691
Linton *W York*	83	SE3946
Linton Heath *Derbys*	73	SK2816
Linton Hill *Gloucs*	47	SO6624
Linton-on-Ouse *N York*	90	SE4860
Linwood *Hants*	12	SU1809
Linwood *Lincs*	76	TF1186
Linwood *Rens*	115	NS4464
Lional *W Isls*	154	NB5263
Lions Green *E Susx*	16	TQ5518
Liphook *Hants*	14	SU8431
Lipley *Shrops*	72	SJ7330
Liscard *Mersyd*	78	SJ2991
Liscombe *Somset*	19	SS8732
Liskeard *Cnwll*	5	SX2564
Liss *Hants*	14	SU7727
Liss Forest *Hants*	14	SU7828
Lissett *E R Yk*	91	TA1458
Lissington *Lincs*	76	TF1083
Liston *Essex*	54	TL8544
Lisvane *Cardif*	33	ST1883
Liswerry *Newpt*	34	ST3487
Litcham *Norfk*	66	TF8817
Litchard *Brdgnd*	33	SS9081
Litchborough *Nhants*	49	SP6354
Litchfield *Hants*	24	SU4653
Litherland *Mersyd*	78	SJ3397
Litlington *Cambs*	39	TL3142
Litlington *E Susx*	16	TQ5201
Little Abington *Cambs*	53	TL5349
Little Addington *Nhants*	51	SP9673
Little Airies *D & G*	99	NX4248

293

M

Mansfield

Middle Rocombe

Mansfield *E Ayrs* 107 NS6214
Mansfield *Notts* 75 SK5361
Mansfield Woodhouse *Notts* 75 SK5363
Mansriggs *Cumb* 86 SD2980
Manston *Dorset* 11 ST8115
Manston *Kent* 29 TR3466
Manston *W York* 83 SE3634
Manswood *Dorset* 11 ST9708
Manthorpe *Lincs* 63 SK9137
Manthorpe *Lincs* 64 TF0715
Manton *Lincs* 84 SE9302
Manton *Notts* 75 SK6078
Manton *Rutlnd* 63 SK8704
Manton *Wilts* 23 SU1768
Manuden *Essex* 39 TL4926
Manwood Green *Essex* 39 TL5412
Maperton *Somset* 22 ST6726
Maple Cross *Herts* 26 TQ0393
Maplebeck *Notts* 75 SK7060
Mapledurham *Oxon* 37 SU6776
Mapledurwell *Hants* 24 SU6851
Maplehurst *W Susx* 15 TQ1824
Maplescombe *Kent* 27 TQ5664
Mapleton *Derbys* 73 SK1647
Mapleton *Kent* 16 TQ4649
Mapperley *Derbys* 62 SK4342
Mapperley Park *Notts* 62 SK5842
Mapperton *Dorset* 10 SY5099
Mappleborough Green *Warwks* 48 SP0866
Mappleton *E R Yk* 85 TA2243
Mapplewell *S York* 83 SE3210
Mappowder *Dorset* 11 ST7306
Marazanvose *Cnwll* 3 SW7950
Marazion *Cnwll* 2 SW5130
Marbury *Ches* 71 SJ5645
March *Cambs* 65 TL4196
March *S Lans* 108 NS9914
Marcham *Oxon* 37 SU4596
Marchamley *Shrops* 59 SJ5929
Marchamley Wood *Shrops* 59 SJ5831
Marchington *Staffs* 73 SK1330
Marchington Woodlands *Staffs* 73 SK1128
Marchros *Gwynd* 56 SH3125
Marchwiel *Wrexhm* 71 SJ3547
Marchwood *Hants* 12 SU3810
Marcross *V Glam* 20 SS9269
Marden *H & W* 46 SO5146
Marden *Kent* 28 TQ7444
Marden *Wilts* 23 SU0857
Marden Ash *Essex* 27 TL5502
Marden Beech *Kent* 28 TQ7442
Marden Thorn *Kent* 28 TQ7642
Mardens Hill *E Susx* 16 TQ5032
Mardlebury *Herts* 39 TL2618
Mardy *Mons* 34 SO3015
Marefield *Leics* 63 SK7407
Mareham le Fen *Lincs* 77 TF2761
Mareham on the Hill *Lincs* 77 TF2867
Marehay *Derbys* 62 SK3947
Marehill *W Susx* 14 TQ0618
Maresfield *E Susx* 16 TQ4624
Marfleet *E R Yk* 85 TA1429
Marford *Wrexhm* 71 SJ3556
Margam *Neath* 32 SS7887
Margaret Marsh *Dorset* 22 ST8218
Margaretting *Essex* 40 TL6701
Margaretting Tye *Essex* 40 TL6800
Margate *Kent* 29 TR3571
Margnaheglish *N Ayrs* 105 NS0332
Margrie *D & G* 99 NX5950
Margrove Park *N York* 97 NZ6515
Marham *Norfk* 65 TF7009
Marhamchurch *Cnwll* 18 SS2203
Marholm *Cambs* 64 TF1401
Marian-glas *Angles* 68 SH5084
Mariansleigh *Devon* 19 SS7422
Marine Town *Kent* 28 TQ9274
Marionburgh *Abers* 135 NJ7006
Marishader *Highld* 136 NG4963
Maristow *Devon* 6 SX4764
Marjoriebanks *D & G* 100 NY0883
Mark *D & G* 98 NX1157
Mark *Somset* 21 ST3847
Mark Causeway *Somset* 21 ST3547
Mark Cross *E Susx* 16 TQ5010
Mark Cross *E Susx* 16 TQ5831
Mark's Corner *IOW* 13 SZ4692
Markbeech *Kent* 16 TQ4742
Markby *Lincs* 77 TF4878
Markeaton *Derbys* 62 SK3237
Market Bosworth *Leics* 62 SK4002
Market Deeping *Lincs* 64 TF1310
Market Drayton *Shrops* 72 SJ6734
Market Harborough *Leics* 50 SP7387
Market Lavington *Wilts* 22 SU0154
Market Overton *Rutlnd* 63 SK8816
Market Rasen *Lincs* 76 TF1089
Market Stainton *Lincs* 76 TF2279
Market Street *Norfk* 67 TG2921
Market Weighton *E R Yk* 84 SE8741
Market Weston *Suffk* 54 TL9877
Markfield *Leics* 62 SK4809
Markham *Caerph* 33 SO1601
Markham Moor *Notts* 75 SK7173
Markinch *Fife* 126 NO2901
Markington *N York* 89 SE2865
Marks Tey *Essex* 40 TL9023
Marksbury *Somset* 22 ST6662
Markshall *Essex* 40 TL8425
Markwell *Cnwll* 5 SX3758
Markyate *Herts* 38 TL0616
Marl Bank *H & W* 47 SO7840
Marlborough *Wilts* 23 SU1868
Marlbrook *H & W* 46 SO5154
Marlbrook *H & W* 60 SO9774
Marlcliff *Warwks* 48 SP0950
Marldon *Devon* 7 SX8663
Marle Green *E Susx* 16 TQ5816
Marlesford *Suffk* 55 TM3258
Marley *Kent* 29 TR1850
Marley *Kent* 29 TR3353
Marley Green *Ches* 71 SJ5845
Marley Hill *T & W* 96 NZ2058
Marlingford *Norfk* 66 TG1309
Marloes *Pembks* 30 SM7908
Marlow *Bucks* 26 SU8486
Marlow *H & W* 46 SO4076
Marlpit Hill *Kent* 16 TQ4347
Marlpits *E Susx* 16 TQ4528
Marlpits *E Susx* 16 TQ7013
Marlpool *Derbys* 62 SK4345
Marnhull *Dorset* 22 ST7818
Marple *Gt Man* 79 SJ9588
Marple Bridge *Gt Man* 79 SJ9688
Marr *S York* 83 SE5105
Marrick *N York* 88 SE0798
Marros *Carmth* 31 SN2008
Marsden *T & W* 103 NZ3964
Marsden *W York* 82 SE0411
Marsden Height *Lancs* 81 SD8636
Marsett *N York* 88 SD9085
Marsh *Bucks* 38 SP8109
Marsh *Devon* 10 ST2510
Marsh *W York* 82 SE0235
Marsh Baldon *Oxon* 37 SU5699
Marsh Chapel *Lincs* 77 TF3599
Marsh Gibbon *Bucks* 37 SP6422
Marsh Green *Devon* 9 SY0493
Marsh Green *Kent* 16 TQ4344
Marsh Green *Shrops* 59 SJ6014
Marsh Green *Staffs* 72 SJ8858
Marsh Lane *Derbys* 74 SK4079
Marsh Lane *Gloucs* 34 SO5807
Marsh Street *Somset* 20 SS9944
Marsh The *Powys* 59 SO3197
Marshall's Heath *Herts* 39 TL1614
Marshalswick *Herts* 39 TL1608
Marsham *Norfk* 67 TG1923
Marshborough *Kent* 29 TR3057
Marshbrook *Shrops* 59 SO4489
Marshfield *Gloucs* 35 ST7873
Marshfield *Newpt* 34 ST2582
Marshgate *Cnwll* 4 SX1592
Marshland Green *Gt Man* 79 SJ6899
Marshland St James *Norfk* 65 TF5209
Marshside *Mersyd* 80 SD3619
Marshwood *Dorset* 10 SY3899
Marske *N York* 89 NZ1000
Marske-by-the-Sea *N York* 97 NZ6322
Marston *Ches* 79 SJ6775
Marston *H & W* 46 SO3557
Marston *Lincs* 63 SK8943
Marston *Oxon* 37 SP5208
Marston *Staffs* 60 SJ8313
Marston *Staffs* 72 SJ9227
Marston *Warwks* 61 SP2094
Marston *Wilts* 22 ST9656
Marston Green *W Mids* 61 SP1785
Marston Jabbet *Warwks* 61 SP3788
Marston Magna *Somset* 21 ST5922
Marston Meysey *Wilts* 36 SU1297
Marston Montgomery *Derbys* 73 SK1337
Marston Moretaine *Beds* 38 SP9941
Marston on Dove *Derbys* 73 SK2329
Marston St Lawrence *Nhants* 49 SP5341
Marston Stannet *H & W* 46 SO5655
Marston Trussell *Nhants* 50 SP6985
Marstow *H & W* 34 SO5518
Marsworth *Bucks* 38 SP9114
Marten *Wilts* 23 SU2860
Marthall *Ches* 79 SJ7975
Martham *Norfk* 67 TG4518
Martin *Hants* 12 SU0619
Martin *Kent* 29 TR3447
Martin *Lincs* 76 TF1259
Martin *Lincs* 77 TF2466
Martin Dales *Lincs* 76 TF1762
Martin Drove End *Hants* 12 SU0520
Martin Hussingtree *H & W* 47 SO8860
Martindale *Cumb* 93 NY4319
Martinhoe *Devon* 19 SS6648
Martinscroft *Ches* 79 SJ6589
Martinstown *Dorset* 11 SY6489
Martlesham *Suffk* 55 TM2547
Martletwy *Pembks* 30 SN0310
Martley *H & W* 47 SO7560
Martock *Somset* 21 ST4619
Marton *Ches* 71 SJ6267
Marton *Ches* 79 SJ8568
Marton *E R Yk* 85 TA1739
Marton *E R Yk* 91 TA2069
Marton *Lincs* 76 SK8381
Marton *N York* 97 NZ5115
Marton *N York* 89 SE4162
Marton *N York* 90 SE7383
Marton *Shrops* 58 SJ2802
Marton *Warwks* 48 SP4068
Marton-le-Moor *N York* 89 SE3770
Martyr Worthy *Hants* 24 SU5132
Martyr's Green *Surrey* 26 TQ0857
Marwick *Ork* 155 HY2324
Marwood *Devon* 19 SS5437
Mary Tavy *Devon* 5 SX5079
Marybank *Highld* 139 NH4853
Maryburgh *Highld* 139 NH5456
Maryculter *Abers* 135 NO8599
Marygold *Border* 119 NT8159
Maryhill *Abers* 143 NJ8245
Maryhill *C Glas* 115 NS5669
Marykirk *Abers* 135 NO6865
Maryland *Mons* 34 SO5105
Marylebone *Gt Lon* 27 TQ2782
Marylebone *Gt Man* 78 SD5807
Marypark *Moray* 141 NJ1938
Maryport *Cumb* 92 NY0336
Maryport *D & G* 98 NX1434
Marystow *Devon* 5 SX4382
Maryton *Angus* 127 NO6856
Marywell *Abers* 134 NO5895
Marywell *Abers* 135 NO9399
Marywell *Angus* 127 NO6544
Masham *N York* 89 SE2280
Mashbury *Essex* 40 TL6511
Mason *T & W* 103 NZ2073
Masongill *N York* 87 SD6675
Mastin Moor *Derbys* 75 SK4575
Matching *Essex* 39 TL5212
Matching Green *Essex* 39 TL5311
Matching Tye *Essex* 39 TL5111
Matfen *Nthumb* 103 NZ0371
Matfield *Kent* 28 TQ6541
Mathern *Mons* 34 ST5290
Mathon *H & W* 47 SO7346
Mathry *Pembks* 30 SM8832
Matlask *Norfk* 66 TG1534
Matlock *Derbys* 74 SK3059
Matlock Bank *Derbys* 74 SK3060
Matlock Bath *Derbys* 74 SK2958
Matlock Dale *Derbys* 74 SK2959
Matson *Gloucs* 35 SO8515
Matterdale End *Cumb* 93 NY3923
Mattersey *Notts* 75 SK6889
Mattersey Thorpe *Notts* 75 SK6889
Mattingley *Hants* 24 SU7357
Mattishall *Norfk* 66 TG0511
Mattishall Burgh *Norfk* 66 TG0512
Mauchline *E Ayrs* 107 NS4927
Maud *Abers* 143 NJ9148
Maufant *Jersey* 152 JS0000
Maugersbury *Gloucs* 48 SP2025
Maughold *IOM* 153 SC4991
Mauld *Highld* 139 NH4038
Maulden *Beds* 38 TL0538
Maulds Meaburn *Cumb* 94 NY6216
Maunby *N York* 89 SE3586
Maund Bryan *H & W* 46 SO5650
Maundown *Somset* 20 ST0628
Mautby *Norfk* 67 TG4812
Mavesyn Ridware *Staffs* 73 SK0816
Mavis Enderby *Lincs* 77 TF3666
Maw Green *Ches* 72 SJ7057
Maw Green *W Mids* 60 SP0196
Mawbray *Cumb* 92 NY0846
Mawdesley *Lancs* 80 SD4914
Mawdlam *Brdgnd* 32 SS8081
Mawgan *Cnwll* 2 SW7025
Mawgan Cross *Cnwll* 2 SW7024
Mawgan Porth *Cnwll* 4 SW8567
Mawla *Cnwll* 2 SW7045
Mawnan *Cnwll* 3 SW7827
Mawnan Smith *Cnwll* 3 SW7728
Mawthorpe *Lincs* 77 TF4672
Maxey *Cambs* 64 TF1208
Maxstoke *Warwks* 61 SP2386
Maxted Street *Kent* 29 TR1244
Maxton *Border* 110 NT6130
Maxton *Kent* 29 TR3041
Maxwell Town *D & G* 100 NX9676
Maxworthy *Cnwll* 5 SX2593
May Bank *Staffs* 72 SJ8547
May's Green *Oxon* 37 SU7480
May's Green *Surrey* 26 TQ0957
Mayals *Swans* 32 SS6089
Maybole *S Ayrs* 106 NS2909
Maybury *Surrey* 26 TQ0159
Mayes Green *Surrey* 14 TQ1239
Mayfield *E Susx* 16 TQ5826
Mayfield *Mdloth* 118 NT3565
Mayfield *Staffs* 73 SK1545
Mayford *Surrey* 25 SU9956
Mayland *Essex* 40 TL9201
Maynard's Green *E Susx* 16 TQ5818
Maypole *Kent* 29 TR2064
Maypole *Mons* 34 SO4716
Maypole *W Mids* 61 SP0778
Maypole Green *Norfk* 67 TM4195
Maypole Green *Suffk* 54 TL9159
Maypole Green *Suffk* 55 TM2767
Mead *Devon* 18 SS2217
Meadgate *Somset* 22 ST6758
Meadle *Bucks* 38 SP8005
Meadowfield *Dur* 96 NZ2439
Meadowhall *S York* 74 SK3991
Meadowtown *Shrops* 59 SJ3001
Meadwell *Devon* 5 SX4081
Meal Bank *Cumb* 87 SD5495
Mealrigg *Cumb* 92 NY1345
Mealsgate *Cumb* 93 NY2042
Meamskirk *E Rens* 115 NS5455
Meanwood *W York* 82 SE2837
Mearbeck *N York* 88 SD8160
Meare *Somset* 21 ST4541
Meare Green *Somset* 21 ST3326
Meare Green *Somset* 20 ST2922
Mears Ashby *Nhants* 51 SP8366
Measham *Leics* 62 SK3311
Meathop *Cumb* 87 SD4380
Meaux *E R Yk* 85 TA0839
Meavy *Devon* 6 SX5467
Medbourne *Leics* 51 SP8093
Meddon *Devon* 18 SS2717
Meden Vale *Notts* 75 SK5870
Medlam *Lincs* 77 TF3156
Medlar *Lancs* 80 SD4135
Medmenham *Berks* 37 SU8084
Medomsley *Dur* 95 NZ1154
Medstead *Hants* 24 SU6537
Meer Common *H & W* 46 SO3652
Meerbrook *Staffs* 72 SJ9860
Meesden *Herts* 39 TL4332
Meeson *Shrops* 72 SJ6421
Meeth *Devon* 19 SS5408
Meeting Green *Suffk* 53 TL7455
Meeting House Hill *Norfk* 67 TG3028
Meidrim *Carmth* 31 SN2920
Meifod *Powys* 58 SJ1513
Meigle *P & K* 126 NO2844
Meikle Carco *D & G* 107 NS7813
Meikle Earnock *S Lans* 116 NS7053
Meikle Kilmory *Ag & B* 114 NS0560
Meikle Obney *P & K* 125 NO0337
Meikle Wartle *Abers* 142 NJ7230
Meikleour *P & K* 126 NO1539
Meinciau *Carmth* 32 SN4610
Meir *Staffs* 72 SJ9342
Meir Heath *Staffs* 72 SJ9240
Melbourn *Cambs* 39 TL3844
Melbourne *Derbys* 62 SK3825
Melbourne *E R Yk* 84 SE7543
Melbury *Devon* 18 SS3719
Melbury Abbas *Dorset* 22 ST8820
Melbury Bubb *Dorset* 10 ST5906
Melbury Osmond *Dorset* 10 ST5707
Melbury Sampford *Dorset* 10 ST5705
Melchbourne *Beds* 51 TL0265
Melcombe Bingham *Dorset* 11 ST7602
Meldon *Devon* 8 SX5692
Meldon *Nthumb* 103 NZ1183
Meldon Park *Nthumb* 103 NZ1085
Meldreth *Cambs* 52 TL3746
Meldrum *Stirlg* 116 NS7299
Meledor *Cnwll* 3 SW9254
Melfort *Ag & B* 122 NM8313
Melgund Castle *Angus* 127 NO5455
Meliden *Denbgs* 70 SJ0680
Melin Court *Neath* 33 SN8201
Melin-byrhedyn *Powys* 57 SN8198
Melin-y-coed *A & C* 69 SH8160
Melin-y-ddol *Powys* 58 SJ0807
Melin-y-wig *Denbgs* 70 SJ0448
Melinau *Pembks* 31 SN1613
Melkinthorpe *Cumb* 94 NY5525
Melkridge *Nthumb* 102 NY7364
Melksham *Wilts* 22 ST9063
Mell Green *Berks* 37 SU4577
Mellangoose *Cnwll* 2 SW6826
Mellguards *Cumb* 93 NY4445
Melling *Lancs* 87 SD5970
Melling *Mersyd* 78 SD3800
Melling Mount *Mersyd* 78 SD4001
Mellis *Suffk* 54 TM0974
Mellon Charles *Highld* 144 NG8491
Mellon Udrigle *Highld* 144 NG8996
Mellor *Gt Man* 79 SJ9888
Mellor *Lancs* 81 SD6530
Mellor Brook *Lancs* 81 SD6431
Mells *Somset* 22 ST7248
Mells *Suffk* 55 TM4076
Melmerby *Cumb* 94 NY6137
Melmerby *N York* 88 SE0785
Melmerby *N York* 89 SE3376
Melness *Highld* 149 NC5861
Melon Green *Suffk* 54 TL8456
Melplash *Dorset* 10 SY4898
Melrose *Border* 109 NT5434
Melsetter *Ork* 155 ND2689
Melsonby *N York* 89 NZ1908
Meltham *W York* 82 SE1010
Meltham Mills *W York* 82 SE1110
Melton *E R Yk* 84 SE9726
Melton *Suffk* 55 TM2850
Melton Constable *Norfk* 66 TG0432
Melton Mowbray *Leics* 63 SK7518
Melton Ross *Lincs* 84 TA0610
Meltonby *E R Yk* 84 SE7952
Melvaig *Highld* 144 NG7486
Melverley *Shrops* 59 SJ3316
Melverley Green *Shrops* 59 SJ3317
Melvich *Highld* 150 NC8764
Membury *Devon* 10 ST2803
Memsie *Abers* 143 NJ9762
Memus *Angus* 134 NO4259
Menabilly *Cnwll* 3 SX0951
Menagissey *Cnwll* 2 SW7146
Menai Bridge *Angles* 69 SH5571
Mendham *Suffk* 55 TM2782
Mendlesham *Suffk* 54 TM1065
Mendlesham Green *Suffk* 54 TM0963
Menheniot *Cnwll* 5 SX2863
Menithwood *H & W* 47 SO7069
Mennock *D & G* 108 NS8107
Menston *W York* 82 SE1643
Menstrie *Clacks* 116 NS8597
Menthorpe *N York* 84 SE7034
Mentmore *Bucks* 38 SP9019
Meoble *Highld* 129 NM7987
Meole Brace *Shrops* 59 SJ4810
Meonstoke *Hants* 13 SU6119
Meopham *Kent* 27 TQ6466
Meopham Green *Kent* 27 TQ6465
Meopham Station *Kent* 27 TQ6467
Mepal *Cambs* 53 TL4481
Meppershall *Beds* 38 TL1336
Mere *Ches* 79 SJ7281
Mere *Wilts* 22 ST8132
Mere Brow *Lancs* 80 SD4218
Mere Green *H & W* 47 SO9562
Mere Green *W Mids* 61 SP1198
Mere Heath *Ches* 79 SJ6670
Mereclough *Lancs* 81 SD8730
Meresborough *Kent* 28 TQ8264
Mereworth *Kent* 28 TQ6553
Meriden *W Mids* 61 SP2482
Merkadale *Highld* 136 NG3931
Merley *Dorset* 12 SZ0297
Merlin's Bridge *Pembks* 30 SM9414
Merrifield *Devon* 7 SX8147
Merrington *Shrops* 59 SJ4720
Merrion *Pembks* 30 SR9397
Merriott *Somset* 10 ST4412
Merrivale *Devon* 6 SX5475
Merrow *Surrey* 26 TQ0250
Merry Field Hill *Dorset* 12 SU0201
Merry Hill *Herts* 26 TQ1394
Merry Hill *W Mids* 60 SO9286
Merry Lees *Leics* 62 SK4705
Merryhill *W Mids* 60 SO8897
Merrymeet *Cnwll* 5 SX2766
Mersham *Kent* 28 TR0540
Merstham *Surrey* 27 TQ2853
Merston *W Susx* 14 SU8902
Merstone *IOW* 13 SZ5285
Merther *Cnwll* 3 SW8644
Merthyr *Carmth* 31 SN3520
Merthyr Cynog *Powys* 45 SN9837
Merthyr Dyfan *V Glam* 20 ST1168
Merthyr Mawr *Brdgnd* 33 SS8877
Merthyr Tydfil *Myr Td* 33 SO0406
Merthyr Vale *Myr Td* 33 ST0799
Merton *Devon* 19 SS5212
Merton *Gt Lon* 27 TQ2570
Merton *Norfk* 66 TL9098
Merton *Oxon* 37 SP5717
Meshaw *Devon* 19 SS7619
Messing *Essex* 40 TL8918
Messingham *Lincs* 84 SE8904
Metfield *Suffk* 55 TM2980
Metherell *Cnwll* 5 SX4069
Metherin *Cnwll* 4 SX1174
Metheringham *Lincs* 76 TF0661
Methil *Fife* 118 NT3799
Methilhill *Fife* 126 NO3500
Methleigh *Cnwll* 2 SW6226
Methley *W York* 83 SE3926
Methley Junction *W York* 83 SE3925
Methlick *Abers* 143 NJ8537
Methven *P & K* 125 NO0225
Methwold *Norfk* 65 TL7394
Methwold Hythe *Norfk* 65 TL7194
Mettingham *Suffk* 55 TM3689
Metton *Norfk* 67 TG2037
Mevagissey *Cnwll* 3 SX0144
Mexborough *S York* 75 SE4700
Mey *Highld* 151 ND2872
Meyllteyrn *Gwynd* 56 SH2332
Meysey Hampton *Gloucs* 36 SP1100
Miabhig *W Isls* 154 NB0834
Miavaig *W Isls* 154 NB0834
Michaelchurch *H & W* 46 SO5225
Michaelchurch Escley *H & W* 46 SO3134
Michaelchurch-on-Arrow *Powys* 46 SO2450
Michaelston-le-Pit *V Glam* 33 ST1572
Michaelstone-y-Fedw *Newpt* 34 ST2484
Michaelstow *Cnwll* 4 SX0778
Michelcombe *Devon* 7 SX6969
Micheldever *Hants* 24 SU5139
Micheldever Station *Hants* 24 SU5143
Michelmersh *Hants* 23 SU3426
Mickfield *Suffk* 54 TM1361
Mickle Trafford *Ches* 71 SJ4469
Micklebring *S York* 75 SK5194
Mickleby *N York* 90 NZ8012
Micklefield *W York* 83 SE4432
Micklefield Green *Herts* 26 TQ0498
Mickleham *Surrey* 26 TQ1653
Mickleover *Derbys* 73 SK3033
Micklethwaite *Cumb* 93 NY2850
Micklethwaite *W York* 82 SE1041
Mickleton *Dur* 95 NY9623
Mickleton *Gloucs* 48 SP1643
Mickletown *W York* 83 SE4027
Mickley *Derbys* 74 SK3279
Mickley *N York* 89 SE2576
Mickley Green *Suffk* 54 TL8457
Mickley Square *Nthumb* 103 NZ0762
Mid Ardlaw *Abers* 143 NJ9463
Mid Beltie *Abers* 134 NJ6200
Mid Bockhampton *Hants* 12 SZ1796
Mid Calder *W Loth* 117 NT0767
Mid Clyth *Highld* 151 ND2937
Mid Lavant *W Susx* 14 SU8508
Mid Mains *Highld* 139 NH4239
Mid Thorpe *Lincs* 77 TF2672
Mid Yell *Shet* 155 HU5190
Midbea *Ork* 155 HY4444
Middle Assendon *Oxon* 37 SU7385
Middle Aston *Oxon* 49 SP4726
Middle Barton *Oxon* 49 SP4325
Middle Chinnock *Somset* 10 ST4713
Middle Claydon *Bucks* 49 SP7225
Middle Duntisbourne *Gloucs* 35 SO9806
Middle Handley *Derbys* 74 SK4077
Middle Harling *Norfk* 54 TL9885
Middle Kames *Ag & B* 114 NR9189
Middle Littleton *H & W* 48 SP0847
Middle Madeley *Staffs* 72 SJ7745
Middle Maes-coed *H & W* 46 SO3333
Middle Mayfield *Staffs* 73 SK1444
Middle Mill *Pembks* 30 SM8026
Middle Quarter *Kent* 28 TQ8938
Middle Rasen *Lincs* 76 TF0889
Middle Rocombe *Devon* 7 SX9069

Morton

New Leeds

Morton *IOW*	13	SZ6085
Morton *Lincs*	75	SK8091
Morton *Lincs*	64	TF0923
Morton *Norfk*	66	TG1216
Morton *Notts*	75	SK7251
Morton *Shrops*	59	SJ2924
Morton Hall *Lincs*	76	SK8863
Morton Tinmouth *Dur*	96	NZ1821
Morton-on-Swale *N York*	89	SE3291
Morvah *Cnwll*	2	SW4035
Morval *Cnwll*	5	SX2556
Morvich *Highld*	138	NG9621
Morville *Shrops*	60	SO6794
Morville Heath *Shrops*	60	SO6893
Morwenstow *Cnwll*	18	SS2015
Mosborough *S York*	74	SK4281
Moscow *E Ayrs*	107	NS4840
Mose *Shrops*	60	SO7590
Mosedale *Cumb*	93	NY3532
Moseley *H & W*	47	SO8159
Moseley *W Mids*	60	SO9498
Moseley *W Mids*	61	SP0783
Moses Gate *Gt Man*	79	SD7306
Moss *Ag & B*	120	NL9544
Moss *S York*	83	SE5914
Moss *Wrexhm*	71	SJ3053
Moss Bank *Mersyd*	78	SJ5197
Moss Edge *Lancs*	80	SD4243
Moss End *Ches*	79	SJ6778
Moss Side *Cumb*	93	NY1952
Moss Side *Lancs*	80	SD3730
Moss Side *Mersyd*	78	SD3802
Moss-side *Highld*	140	NH8555
Mossat *Abers*	142	NJ4719
Mossbank *Shet*	155	HU4575
Mossbay *Cumb*	92	NX9927
Mossblown *S Ayrs*	106	NS4024
Mossbrow *Gt Man*	79	SJ7089
Mossburnford *Border*	110	NT6616
Mossdale *D & G*	99	NX6670
Mossdale *E Ayrs*	107	NS4904
Mossend *N Lans*	116	NS7460
Mosser Mains *Cumb*	92	NY1125
Mossgiel *E Ayrs*	107	NS4828
Mossknowe *D & G*	101	NY2769
Mossley *Ches*	72	SJ8861
Mossley *Gt Man*	82	SD9701
Mosspaul Hotel *Border*	109	NY3999
Mosstodloch *Moray*	141	NJ3259
Mossy Lea *Lancs*	80	SD5312
Mossyard *D & G*	99	NX5451
Mosterton *Dorset*	10	ST4505
Moston *Gt Man*	79	SD8701
Moston *Shrops*	59	SJ5626
Moston Green *Ches*	72	SJ7261
Mostyn *Flints*	70	SJ1580
Motcombe *Dorset*	22	ST8525
Mothecombe *Devon*	6	SX6047
Motherby *Cumb*	93	NY4228
Motherwell *N Lans*	116	NS7457
Motspur Park *Gt Lon*	26	TQ2267
Mottingham *Gt Lon*	27	TQ4272
Mottisfont *Hants*	23	SU3226
Mottistone *IOW*	13	SZ4083
Mottram in Longdendale *Gt Man*	79	SJ9995
Mottram St Andrew *Ches*	79	SJ8778
Mouilpied *Guern*	152	GN0000
Mouldsworth *Ches*	71	SJ5071
Moulin *P & K*	132	NN9459
Moulsecoomb *E Susx*	15	TQ3307
Moulsford *Oxon*	37	SU5883
Moulsoe *Bucks*	38	SP9141
Moultavie *Highld*	146	NH6371
Moulton *Ches*	79	SJ6569
Moulton *Lincs*	64	TF3023
Moulton *N York*	89	NZ2303
Moulton *Nhants*	50	SP7866
Moulton *Suffk*	53	TL6964
Moulton *V Glam*	33	ST0770
Moulton Chapel *Lincs*	64	TF2918
Moulton Seas End *Lincs*	64	TF3227
Moulton St Mary *Norfk*	67	TG3907
Mount *Cnwll*	3	SW7856
Mount *Cnwll*	4	SX1468
Mount *W York*	82	SE0917
Mount Ambrose *Cnwll*	2	SW7043
Mount Bures *Essex*	40	TL9032
Mount Hawke *Cnwll*	2	SW7147
Mount Hermon *Cnwll*	2	SW6915
Mount Lothian *Mdloth*	117	NT2757
Mount Pleasant *Ches*	72	SJ8456
Mount Pleasant *Derbys*	74	SK3448
Mount Pleasant *Dur*	96	NZ2634
Mount Pleasant *E Susx*	16	TQ4216
Mount Pleasant *H & W*	47	SP0064
Mount Pleasant *Norfk*	66	TL9994
Mount Pleasant *Suffk*	53	TL7347
Mount Sorrel *Wilts*	23	SU0324
Mount Tabor *W York*	82	SE0527
Mountain *W York*	82	SE0930
Mountain Ash *Rhondd*	33	ST0499
Mountain Cross *Border*	117	NT1547
Mountain Street *Kent*	29	TR0652
Mountfield *E Susx*	17	TQ7320
Mountgerald House *Highld*	139	NH5661
Mountjoy *Cnwll*	4	SW8760
Mountnessing *Essex*	40	TQ6297
Mounton *Mons*	34	ST5193
Mountsorrel *Leics*	62	SK5814
Mountstuart *Ag & B*	114	NS1159
Mousehill *Surrey*	25	SU9441
Mousehole *Cnwll*	2	SW4626
Mouswald *D & G*	100	NY0672
Mow Cop *Ches*	72	SJ8557
Mowhaugh *Border*	110	NT8120
Mowmacre Hill *Leics*	62	SK5807
Mowsley *Leics*	50	SP6489
Mowtie *Abers*	135	NO8388
Moy *Highld*	140	NH7634
Moy *Highld*	131	NN4282
Moye *Highld*	138	NG8818
Moyles Court *Hants*	12	SU1608
Moylgrove *Pembks*	42	SN1144
Muasdale *Ag & B*	105	NR6840
Much Birch *H & W*	46	SO5030
Much Cowarne *H & W*	46	SO6147
Much Dewchurch *H & W*	46	SO4831
Much Hadham *Herts*	39	TL4219
Much Hoole *Lancs*	80	SD4723
Much Hoole Town *Lancs*	80	SD4722
Much Marcle *H & W*	47	SO6532
Much Wenlock *Shrops*	59	SO6299
Muchalls *Abers*	135	NO9092
Muchelney *Somset*	21	ST4224
Muchelney Ham *Somset*	21	ST4423
Muchlarnick *Cnwll*	5	SX2156
Mucking *Essex*	40	TQ6881
Muckingford *Essex*	40	TQ6779
Muckleford *Dorset*	10	SY6393
Mucklestone *Staffs*	72	SJ7237
Muckley *Shrops*	59	SO6495
Muckton *Lincs*	77	TF3781
Mucomir *Highld*	131	NN1884
Mud Row *Kent*	28	TR0072
Muddiford *Devon*	19	SS5638
Muddles Green *E Susx*	16	TQ5413
Mudeford *Dorset*	12	SZ1892
Mudford *Somset*	21	ST5719
Mudford Sock *Somset*	21	ST5519
Mudgley *Somset*	21	ST4545
Mugdock *Stirlg*	115	NS5577
Mugeary *Highld*	136	NG4439
Mugginton *Derbys*	73	SK2842
Muggintonlane End *Derbys*	73	SK2844
Muggleswick *Dur*	95	NZ0449
Muir of Fowlis *Abers*	134	NJ5612
Muir of Miltonduff *Moray*	141	NJ1859
Muir of Ord *Highld*	139	NH5250
Muir of Thorn *P & K*	125	NO0637
Muirden *Abers*	142	NJ7054
Muirdrum *Angus*	127	NO5637
Muiresk *Abers*	142	NJ6948
Muirhead *Angus*	126	NO3434
Muirhead *Fife*	126	NO2805
Muirhead *N Lans*	116	NS6869
Muirhouses *Falk*	117	NT0180
Muirkirk *E Ayrs*	107	NS6927
Muirmill *Stirlg*	116	NS7283
Muirshearlich *Highld*	131	NN1380
Muirtack *Abers*	143	NJ9937
Muirton *P & K*	125	NN9211
Muirton Mains *Highld*	139	NH4553
Muirton of Ardblair *P & K*	126	NO1643
Muker *N York*	88	SD9097
Mulbarton *Norfk*	67	TG1901
Mulben *Moray*	141	NJ3550
Mulfra *Cnwll*	2	SW4534
Mulindry *Ag & B*	112	NR3659
Mullacott Cross *Devon*	19	SS5144
Mullion *Cnwll*	2	SW6719
Mullion Cove *Cnwll*	2	SW6617
Mumby *Lincs*	77	TF5174
Muncher's Green *Herts*	39	TL3126
Munderfield Row *H & W*	47	SO6451
Munderfield Stocks *H & W*	47	SO6550
Mundesley *Norfk*	67	TG3136
Mundford *Norfk*	66	TL8093
Mundham *Norfk*	67	TM3397
Mundon Hill *Essex*	40	TL8602
Mungrisdale *Cumb*	93	NY3630
Munlochy *Highld*	140	NH6453
Munnoch *N Ayrs*	114	NS2548
Munsley *H & W*	47	SO6640
Munslow *Shrops*	59	SO5287
Murchington *Devon*	8	SX6888
Murcot *H & W*	48	SP0640
Murcott *Oxon*	37	SP5815
Murcott *Wilts*	35	ST9591
Murkle *Highld*	151	ND1668
Murlaggan *Highld*	130	NN0192
Murrell Green *Hants*	24	SU7455
Murroes *Angus*	127	NO4635
Murrow *Cambs*	64	TF3707
Mursley *Bucks*	38	SP8128
Murston *Kent*	28	TQ9264
Murthill *Angus*	134	NO4657
Murthly *P & K*	126	NO1038
Murton *Cumb*	94	NY7221
Murton *Dur*	96	NZ3847
Murton *N York*	83	SE6452
Murton *Nthumb*	111	NT9748
Murton *T & W*	103	NZ3270
Musbury *Devon*	10	SY2794
Muscoates *N York*	90	SE6879
Musselburgh *E Loth*	118	NT3472
Muston *Leics*	63	SK8237
Muston *N York*	91	TA0979
Mustow Green *H & W*	60	SO8774
Muswell Hill *Gt Lon*	27	TQ2889
Mutehill *D & G*	99	NX6848
Mutford *Suffk*	55	TM4888
Muthill *P & K*	125	NN8717
Mutterton *Devon*	9	ST0205
Muxton *Shrops*	60	SJ7114
Mybster *Highld*	151	ND1652
Myddfai *Carmth*	44	SN7730
Myddle *Shrops*	59	SJ4623
Mydroilyn *Cardgn*	42	SN4555
Mylor *Cnwll*	3	SW8135
Mylor Bridge *Cnwll*	3	SW8036
Mynachlog ddu *Pembks*	31	SN1430
Myndd-llan *Flints*	70	SJ1572
Myndtown *Shrops*	59	SO3989
Mynydd Buch *Cardgn*	43	SN7276
Mynydd Isa *Flints*	70	SJ2563
Mynydd Llandygai *Gwynd*	69	SH6065
Mynydd-bach *Mons*	34	ST4894
Mynydd-bach *Swans*	32	SS6597
Mynyddgarreg *Carmth*	31	SN4208
Mynytho *Gwynd*	56	SH3031
Myrebird *Abers*	135	NO7398
Myredykes *Border*	102	NY5998
Mytchett *Surrey*	25	SU8855
Mytholm *W York*	82	SD9827
Mytholmroyd *W York*	82	SE0126
Mythop *Lancs*	80	SD3634
Myton-on-Swale *N York*	89	SE4366

N

Na Buirgh *W Isls*	154	NG0394
Naast *Highld*	144	NG8283
Nab's Head *Lancs*	81	SD6229
Naburn *N York*	83	SE5945
Naccolt *Kent*	28	TR0544
Nackington *Kent*	29	TR1554
Nacton *Suffk*	55	TM2240
Nafferton *E R Yk*	91	TA0559
Nag's Head *Gloucs*	35	ST8898
Nailbridge *Gloucs*	35	SO6415
Nailsbourne *Somset*	20	ST2128
Nailsea *Somset*	34	ST4770
Nailstone *Leics*	62	SK4106
Nailsworth *Gloucs*	35	ST8499
Nairn *Highld*	140	NH8856
Nalderswood *Surrey*	15	TQ2445
Nancegollan *Cnwll*	2	SW6332
Nancledra *Cnwll*	2	SW4936
Nanhoron *Gwynd*	56	SH2731
Nannerch *Flints*	70	SJ1669
Nanpantan *Leics*	62	SK5017
Nanpean *Cnwll*	3	SW9556
Nanquidno *Cnwll*	2	SW3629
Nanstallon *Cnwll*	4	SX0367
Nant Gwynant *Gwynd*	69	SH6350
Nant Peris *Gwynd*	69	SH6058
Nant-ddu *Powys*	33	SO0014
Nant-glas *Powys*	45	SN9965
Nant-y-Bwch *Blae G*	33	SO1210
Nant-y-caws *Carmth*	32	SN4518
Nant-y-derry *Mons*	34	SO3306
Nant-y-gollen *Shrops*	58	SJ2428
Nant-y-moel *Brdgnd*	33	SS9392
Nant-y-pandy *A & C*	69	SH6973
Nanternis *Cardgn*	42	SN3756
Nantgaredig *Carmth*	32	SN4921
Nantgarw *Rhondd*	33	ST1285
Nantglyn *Denbgs*	70	SJ0061
Nantgwyn *Powys*	45	SN9776
Nantlle *Gwynd*	68	SH5153
Nantmawr *Shrops*	58	SJ2524
Nantmel *Powys*	45	SO0366
Nantmor *Gwynd*	57	SH6046
Nantwich *Ches*	72	SJ6552
Nantyffyllon *Brdgnd*	33	SS8492
Naphill *Bucks*	26	SU8496
Napleton *H & W*	47	SO8648
Nappa *N York*	81	SD8553
Napton on the Hill *Warwks*	49	SP4661
Narberth *Pembks*	31	SN1015
Narborough *Leics*	50	SP5497
Narborough *Norfk*	65	TF7412
Narkurs *Cnwll*	5	SX3255
Nasareth *Gwynd*	68	SH4749
Naseby *Nhants*	50	SP6978
Nash *Bucks*	38	SP7833
Nash *Gt Lon*	27	TQ4063
Nash *H & W*	46	SO3062
Nash *Newpt*	34	ST3483
Nash *Shrops*	46	SO6071
Nash End *H & W*	60	SO7781
Nash Lee *Bucks*	38	SP8408
Nash Street *Kent*	27	TQ6469
Nash's Green *Hants*	24	SU6745
Nassington *Nhants*	51	TL0696
Nastend *Gloucs*	35	SO7906
Nasty *Herts*	39	TL3524
Nateby *Cumb*	88	NY7706
Nateby *Lancs*	80	SD4644
Natland *Cumb*	87	SD5289
Naughton *Suffk*	54	TM0249
Naunton *Gloucs*	48	SP1123
Naunton *H & W*	47	SO8739
Naunton Beauchamp *H & W*	47	SO9652
Navenby *Lincs*	76	SK9858
Navestock *Essex*	27	TQ5397
Navestock Side *Essex*	27	TQ5697
Navidale House Hotel *Highld*	147	ND0316
Navity *Highld*	140	NH7864
Nawton *N York*	90	SE6584
Nayland *Suffk*	54	TL9734
Nazeing *Essex*	39	TL4106
Nazeing Gate *Essex*	39	TL4105
Neacroft *Hants*	12	SZ1896
Neal's Green *Warwks*	61	SP3384
Neap *Shet*	155	HU5058
Near Cotton *Staffs*	73	SK0646
Near Sawry *Cumb*	87	SD3795
Neasden *Gt Lon*	26	TQ2185
Neasham *Dur*	89	NZ3210
Neath *Neath*	32	SS7597
Neatham *Hants*	24	SU7440
Neatishead *Norfk*	67	TG3420
Nebo *A & C*	69	SH8355
Nebo *Angles*	68	SH4690
Nebo *Cardgn*	43	SN5465
Nebo *Gwynd*	68	SH4850
Necton *Norfk*	66	TF8709
Nedd *Highld*	148	NC1331
Nedderton *Nthumb*	103	NZ2382
Nedging *Suffk*	54	TL9948
Nedging Tye *Suffk*	54	TM0149
Needham *Norfk*	55	TM2281
Needham Market *Suffk*	54	TM0855
Needham Street *Suffk*	53	TL7265
Needingworth *Cambs*	52	TL3472
Neen Savage *Shrops*	60	SO6777
Neen Sollars *Shrops*	60	SO6672
Neenton *Shrops*	59	SO6387
Nefyn *Gwynd*	56	SH3040
Neilston *E Rens*	115	NS4857
Nelson *Caerph*	33	ST1195
Nelson *Lancs*	81	SD8638
Nemphlar *S Lans*	116	NS8544
Nempnett Thrubwell *Somset*	21	ST5260
Nenthall *Cumb*	94	NY7545
Nenthead *Cumb*	94	NY7743
Nenthorn *Border*	110	NT6837
Neopardy *Devon*	8	SX7999
Nep Town *W Susx*	15	TQ2115
Nercwys *Flints*	70	SJ2360
Nereabolls *Ag & B*	112	NR2255
Nerston *S Lans*	116	NS6456
Nesbit *Nthumb*	111	NT9833
Nesfield *N York*	82	SE0949
Ness *Ches*	71	SJ3076
Nesscliffe *Shrops*	59	SJ3819
Neston *Ches*	71	SJ2977
Neston *Wilts*	22	ST8668
Netchwood *Shrops*	59	SO6291
Nether Alderley *Ches*	79	SJ8476
Nether Blainslie *Border*	109	NT5443
Nether Broughton *Notts*	63	SK6925
Nether Cerne *Dorset*	11	SY6798
Nether Compton *Dorset*	10	ST5917
Nether Crimond *Abers*	143	NJ8222
Nether Dallachy *Moray*	141	NJ3563
Nether Exe *Devon*	9	SS9300
Nether Fingland *S Lans*	108	NS9310
Nether Handley *Derbys*	74	SK4176
Nether Handwick *Angus*	126	NO3641
Nether Haugh *S York*	74	SK4196
Nether Headon *Notts*	75	SK7477
Nether Heage *Derbys*	74	SK3650
Nether Heyford *Nhants*	49	SP6658
Nether Howcleugh *S Lans*	108	NT0212
Nether Kellet *Lancs*	87	SD5068
Nether Kinmundy *Abers*	143	NK0543
Nether Langwith *Notts*	75	SK5370
Nether Moor *Derbys*	74	SK3866
Nether Padley *Derbys*	74	SK2478
Nether Poppleton *N York*	83	SE5654
Nether Row *Cumb*	93	NY3237
Nether Silton *N York*	89	SE4592
Nether Skyborry *Shrops*	46	SO2873
Nether Stowey *Somset*	20	ST1939
Nether Street *Essex*	40	TL5812
Nether Wallop *Hants*	23	SU3036
Nether Wasdale *Cumb*	86	NY1204
Nether Wellwood *E Ayrs*	107	NS6526
Nether Welton *Cumb*	93	NY3545
Nether Westcote *Gloucs*	36	SP2220
Nether Whitacre *Warwks*	61	SP2392
Nether Whitecleuch *S Lans*	108	NS8319
Netheravon *Wilts*	23	SU1448
Netherbrae *Abers*	143	NJ7959
Netherburn *S Lans*	116	NS7947
Netherbury *Dorset*	10	SY4799
Netherby *Cumb*	101	NY3971
Netherby *N York*	83	SE3346
Nethercleuch *D & G*	100	NY1186
Nethercote *Warwks*	49	SP5164
Nethercott *Devon*	18	SS4839
Nethercott *Devon*	5	SX3596
Netherend *Gloucs*	34	SO5900
Netherfield *E Susx*	16	TQ7019
Netherfield *Leics*	62	SK5816
Netherfield *Notts*	62	SK6140
Netherfield Road *E Susx*	17	TQ7417
Nethergate *Lincs*	75	SK7599
Nethergate *Norfk*	66	TG0529
Netherhampton *Wilts*	23	SU1029
Netherhay *Dorset*	10	ST4105
Netherland Green *Staffs*	73	SK1030
Netherlaw *D & G*	99	NX7444
Netherley *Abers*	135	NO8593
Nethermill *D & G*	100	NY0487
Nethermuir *Abers*	143	NJ9044
Netheroyd Hill *W York*	82	SE1419
Netherplace *E Rens*	115	NS5255
Netherseal *Derbys*	61	SK2812
Netherstreet *Wilts*	22	ST9864
Netherthong *W York*	82	SE1309
Netherthorpe *Derbys*	75	SK4474
Netherton *Angus*	134	NO5457
Netherton *Devon*	7	SX8971
Netherton *H & W*	46	SO5226
Netherton *H & W*	47	SO9941
Netherton *Hants*	23	SU3757
Netherton *N Lans*	116	NS7854
Netherton *Nthumb*	111	NT9807
Netherton *Oxon*	36	SU4199
Netherton *P & K*	126	NO1452
Netherton *Shrops*	60	SO7382
Netherton *Stirlg*	115	NS5579
Netherton *W Mids*	60	SO9488
Netherton *W York*	82	SE1213
Netherton *W York*	82	SE2816
Nethertown *Cumb*	86	NX9907
Nethertown *Highld*	151	ND3578
Nethertown *Lancs*	81	SD7236
Nethertown *Staffs*	73	SK1017
Netherwitton *Nthumb*	103	NZ0990
Nethy Bridge *Highld*	141	NJ0020
Netley *Hants*	13	SU4508
Netley Marsh *Hants*	12	SU3313
Nettacott *Devon*	9	SX8999
Nettlebed *Oxon*	37	SU6986
Nettlebridge *Somset*	21	ST6448
Nettlecombe *Dorset*	10	SY5195
Nettlecombe *IOW*	13	SZ5278
Nettleden *Herts*	38	TL0110
Nettleham *Lincs*	76	TF0075
Nettlestead *Kent*	28	TQ6852
Nettlestead Green *Kent*	28	TQ6850
Nettlestone *IOW*	13	SZ6290
Nettlesworth *Dur*	96	NZ2547
Nettleton *Lincs*	76	TA1100
Nettleton *Wilts*	35	ST8278
Nettleton Shrub *Wilts*	35	ST8277
Netton *Devon*	6	SX5546
Netton *Wilts*	23	SU1336
Neuadd *Carmth*	32	SN7021
Neuadd Fawr *Carmth*	44	SN7441
Neuadd-ddu *Powys*	45	SN9175
Nevendon *Essex*	40	TQ7591
Nevern *Pembks*	31	SN0840
Nevill Holt *Leics*	51	SP8193
New Abbey *D & G*	100	NX9666
New Aberdour *Abers*	143	NJ8863
New Addington *Gt Lon*	27	TQ3763
New Alresford *Hants*	24	SU5832
New Alyth *P & K*	126	NO2447
New Arram *E R Yk*	84	TA0344
New Ash Green *Kent*	27	TQ6065
New Balderton *Notts*	75	SK8152
New Barn *Kent*	27	TQ6169
New Barnet *Gt Lon*	27	TQ2695
New Barton *Nhants*	51	SP8564
New Bewick *Nthumb*	111	NU0620
New Bilton *Warwks*	50	SP4875
New Bolingbroke *Lincs*	77	TF3057
New Boultham *Lincs*	76	SK9670
New Bradwell *Bucks*	38	SP8341
New Brampton *Derbys*	74	SK3771
New Brancepeth *Dur*	96	NZ2241
New Bridge *N York*	90	SE8085
New Brighton *Flints*	70	SJ2565
New Brighton *Mersyd*	78	SJ3093
New Brinsley *Notts*	75	SK4550
New Brotton *N York*	97	NZ6920
New Broughton *Wrexhm*	71	SJ3151
New Buckenham *Norfk*	54	TM0890
New Bury *Gt Man*	79	SD7304
New Byth *Abers*	143	NJ8254
New Costessey *Norfk*	66	TG1810
New Cowper *Cumb*	92	NY1245
New Crofton *W York*	83	SE3817
New Cross *Cardgn*	43	SN6376
New Cross *Gt Lon*	27	TQ3676
New Cross *Somset*	21	ST4119
New Cumnock *E Ayrs*	107	NS6213
New Cut *E Susx*	17	TQ8115
New Deer *Abers*	143	NJ8847
New Delaval *Nthumb*	103	NZ2979
New Delph *Gt Man*	82	SD9907
New Denham *Bucks*	26	TQ0484
New Duston *Nhants*	49	SP7162
New Earswick *N York*	83	SE6155
New Eastwood *Notts*	62	SK4646
New Edlington *S York*	75	SK5398
New Elgin *Moray*	141	NJ2261
New Ellerby *E R Yk*	85	TA1639
New Eltham *Gt Lon*	27	TQ4472
New End *H & W*	48	SP0560
New England *Cambs*	64	TF1801
New Farnley *W York*	82	SE2531
New Ferry *Mersyd*	78	SJ3385
New Fletton *Cambs*	64	TL1997
New Fryston *W York*	83	SE4526
New Galloway *D & G*	99	NX6377
New Gilston *Fife*	127	NO4208
New Grimsby *IOS*	2	SV8815
New Hartley *Nthumb*	103	NZ3076
New Haw *Surrey*	26	TQ0563
New Hedges *Pembks*	31	SN1202
New Herrington *T & W*	96	NZ3352
New Holkham *Norfk*	66	TF8839
New Holland *Lincs*	85	TA0823
New Houghton *Derbys*	75	SK4965
New Houghton *Norfk*	66	TF7927
New Houses *Gt Man*	78	SD5502
New Houses *N York*	88	SD8073
New Hutton *Cumb*	87	SD5691
New Hythe *Kent*	28	TQ7159
New Inn *Carmth*	44	SN4736
New Inn *Torfn*	34	ST3099
New Invention *Shrops*	46	SO2976
New Kelso *Highld*	138	NG9442
New Lakenham *Norfk*	67	TG2307
New Lanark *S Lans*	108	NS8842
New Lane *Lancs*	80	SD4212
New Lane End *Ches*	79	SJ6394
New Langholm *D & G*	101	NY3684
New Leake *Lincs*	77	TF4057
New Leeds *Abers*	143	NJ9954

New Longton
North Fambridge

New Longton *Lancs* 80 SD5025
New Luce *D & G* 98 NX1764
New Malden *Gt Lon* 26 TQ2168
New Marske *N York* 97 NZ6121
New Marston *Oxon* 37 SP5407
New Marton *Shrops* 59 SJ3334
New Mill *Abers* 135 NO7883
New Mill *Cnwll* 2 SW4534
New Mill *Herts* 38 SP9212
New Mill *W York* 82 SE1609
New Mills *Cnwll* 3 SW8952
New Mills *Derbys* 79 SK0085
New Mills *Powys* 58 SJ0901
New Milton *Hants* 12 SZ2495
New Mistley *Essex* 41 TM1131
New Moat *Pembks* 30 SN0625
New Ollerton *Notts* 75 SK6667
New Oscott *W Mids* 61 SP0994
New Oxted *Surrey* 27 TQ3952
New Pitsligo *Abers* 143 NJ8855
New Polzeath *Cnwll* 4 SW9379
New Prestwick *S Ayrs* 106 NS3424
New Quay *Cardgn* 42 SN3959
New Quay *Essex* 41 TM0223
New Rackheath *Norfk* 67 TG2812
New Radnor *Powys* 45 SO2161
New Rent *Cumb* 93 NY4536
New Ridley *Nthumb* 95 NZ0559
New Road Side *N York* 82 SD9743
New Romney *Kent* 17 TR0624
New Rossington *S York* 75 SK6198
New Row *Cardgn* 43 SN7273
New Row *Lancs* 81 SD6438
New Scone *P & K* 126 NO1326
New Sharlston *W York* 83 SE3819
New Shoreston *Nthumb* 111 NU1932
New Silksworth *T & W* 96 NZ3853
New Skelton *N York* 97 NZ6618
New Somerby *Lincs* 63 SK9235
New Spilsby *Lincs* 77 TF4165
New Springs *Gt Man* 78 SD5906
New Stevenston *N Lans* 116 NS7659
New Street *H & W* 46 SO3356
New Swannington *Leics* 62 SK4215
New Thundersley *Essex* 40 TQ7789
New Town *Beds* 52 TL1945
New Town *Dorset* 22 ST8318
New Town *Dorset* 11 ST9515
New Town *Dorset* 11 ST9907
New Town *Dorset* 22 ST9918
New Town *E Loth* 118 NT4470
New Town *E Susx* 16 TQ4720
New Town *Nhants* 51 SP9677
New Town *Somset* 10 ST2712
New Town *Wilts* 36 SU2871
New Tredegar *Caerph* 33 SO1403
New Trows *S Lans* 108 NS8038
New Tupton *Derbys* 74 SK3966
New Village *E R Yk* 84 SE8530
New Walsoken *Cambs* 65 TF4609
New Waltham *Lincs* 85 TA2804
New Whittington *Derbys* 74 SK3975
New Wimpole *Cambs* 52 TL3549
New Winton *E Loth* 118 NT4271
New Yatt *Oxon* 36 SP3713
New York *Lincs* 77 TF2455
New York *N York* 89 SE1963
New York *T & W* 103 NZ3270
New Zealand *Derbys* 62 SK3336
Newall *W York* 82 SE1946
Newark *Cambs* 64 TF2100
Newark *D & G* 107 NS7808
Newark *Ork* 155 HY7142
Newark-on-Trent *Notts* 75 SK7953
Newarthill *N Lans* 116 NS7859
Newbarn *Kent* 29 TR1540
Newbattle *Mdloth* 118 NT3365
Newbie *D & G* 101 NY1764
Newbiggin *Cumb* 93 NY4729
Newbiggin *Cumb* 94 NY5549
Newbiggin *Cumb* 94 NY6228
Newbiggin *Cumb* 86 SD0994
Newbiggin *Cumb* 86 SD2669
Newbiggin *Dur* 95 NY9127
Newbiggin *Dur* 96 NZ1447
Newbiggin *N York* 88 SD9591
Newbiggin *N York* 88 SE0086
Newbiggin-by-the-Sea *Nthumb* 103 NZ3087
Newbiggin-on-Lune *Cumb* 87 NY7005
Newbigging *Angus* 126 NO2841
Newbigging *Angus* 127 NO4237
Newbigging *S Lans* 117 NT0145
Newbold *Derbys* 74 SK3672
Newbold *Leics* 62 SK4019
Newbold on Avon *Warwks* 50 SP4877
Newbold on Stour *Warwks* 48 SP2446
Newbold Pacey *Warwks* 48 SP2957
Newbold Revel *Warwks* 50 SP4580
Newbold Verdon *Leics* 62 SK4403
Newborough *Angles* 68 SH4265
Newborough *Cambs* 64 TF2005
Newborough *Staffs* 73 SK1325
Newbottle *Nhants* 49 SP5236
Newbottle *T & W* 96 NZ3351
Newbourne *Suffk* 55 TM2743
Newbridge *C Edin* 117 NT1272
Newbridge *Caerph* 33 ST2097
Newbridge *Cardgn* 44 SN5059
Newbridge *Cnwll* 2 SW4231
Newbridge *Cnwll* 3 SW7944
Newbridge *D & G* 100 NX9479
Newbridge *Hants* 12 SU2915
Newbridge *IOW* 13 SZ4187
Newbridge *Oxon* 36 SP4001
Newbridge *Pembks* 30 SM9431
Newbridge *Wrexhm* 70 SJ2841
Newbridge Green *H & W* 47 SO8439
Newbridge on Wye *Powys* 45 SO0158
Newbridge-on-Usk *Mons* 34 ST3894
Newbrough *Nthumb* 102 NY8767
Newbuildings *Devon* 8 SS7903
Newburgh *Abers* 143 NJ9659
Newburgh *Abers* 143 NJ9925
Newburgh *Fife* 126 NO2318
Newburgh *Lancs* 78 SD4810
Newburgh Priory *N York* 90 SE5476
Newburn *T & W* 103 NZ1665
Newbury *Berks* 24 SU4766
Newbury *Somset* 22 ST6949
Newbury *Wilts* 22 ST8241
Newby *Cumb* 94 NY5921
Newby *Lancs* 81 SD8146
Newby *N York* 90 NZ5012
Newby *N York* 88 SD7269
Newby *N York* 91 TA0190
Newby Bridge *Cumb* 87 SD3686
Newby Cross *Cumb* 93 NY3653
Newby East *Cumb* 93 NY4758
Newby Head *Cumb* 94 NY5821
Newby West *Cumb* 93 NY3753
Newby Wiske *N York* 89 SE3687
Newcastle *Mons* 34 SO4417
Newcastle *Shrops* 58 SO2582
Newcastle Emlyn *Carmth* 31 SN3040
Newcastle upon Tyne *T & W* 103 NZ2464
Newcastle-under-Lyme *Staffs* 72 SJ8445
Newcastleton *Border* 101 NY4887
Newchapel *Pembks* 31 SN2239
Newchapel *Staffs* 72 SJ8654
Newchapel *Surrey* 15 TQ3641
Newchurch *Blae G* 33 SO1710
Newchurch *H & W* 46 SO3550
Newchurch *IOW* 13 SZ5685
Newchurch *Kent* 17 TR0531
Newchurch *Mons* 34 ST4597
Newchurch *Powys* 45 SO2150
Newchurch *Staffs* 73 SK1423
Newchurch in Pendle *Lancs* 81 SD8239
Newcraighall *C Edin* 118 NT3272
Newdigate *Surrey* 15 TQ1942
Newell Green *Berks* 25 SU8770
Newenden *Kent* 17 TQ8327
Newent *Gloucs* 47 SO7225
Newfield *Dur* 96 NZ2033
Newfield *Dur* 96 NZ2452
Newfield *Highld* 147 NH7877
Newfound *Hants* 24 SU5851
Newgale *Pembks* 30 SM8522
Newgate *Norfk* 66 TG0443
Newgate Street *Herts* 39 TL3005
Newhall *Ches* 71 SJ6145
Newhall *Derbys* 73 SK2820
Newham *Nthumb* 111 NU1728
Newhaven *Derbys* 74 SK1660
Newhaven *E Susx* 16 TQ4401
Newhey *Gt Man* 82 SD9411
Newholm *N York* 90 NZ8610
Newhouse *N Lans* 116 NS7961
Newick *E Susx* 15 TQ4121
Newingreen *Kent* 29 TR1236
Newington *Kent* 28 TQ8564
Newington *Kent* 29 TR1837
Newington *Oxon* 37 SU6096
Newington *Shrops* 59 SO4283
Newington Bagpath *Gloucs* 35 ST8194
Newland *Cumb* 86 SD3079
Newland *E R Yk* 84 TA0631
Newland *Gloucs* 34 SO5509
Newland *H & W* 47 SO7948
Newland *N York* 83 SE6824
Newland *E R Yk* 84 SE8029
Newland *Oxon* 36 SP3609
Newland *Somset* 19 SS8238
Newlandrig *Mdloth* 118 NT3762
Newlands *Border* 101 NY5094
Newlands *Cumb* 93 NY3439
Newlands *Nthumb* 95 NZ0855
Newlands of Dundurcas *Moray* 141 NJ2951
Newlyn *Cnwll* 2 SW4628
Newmachar *Abers* 143 NJ8919
Newmains *N Lans* 116 NS8256
Newman's End *Essex* 39 TL5112
Newman's Green *Suffk* 54 TL8843
Newmarket *Cumb* 93 NY3438
Newmarket *Suffk* 53 TL6463
Newmarket *W Isls* 154 NB4235
Newmill *Border* 109 NT4510
Newmill *Moray* 142 NJ4352
Newmill of Inshewan *Angus* 134 NO4260
Newmillerdam *W York* 83 SE3215
Newmills *C Edin* 117 NT1667
Newmills *Fife* 117 NT0186
Newmills *Mons* 34 SO5107
Newmiln *P & K* 126 NO1230
Newmilns *E Ayrs* 107 NS5337
Newnes *Shrops* 59 SJ3834
Newney Green *Essex* 40 TL6507
Newnham *Gloucs* 35 SO6911
Newnham *H & W* 47 SO6469
Newnham *Hants* 24 SU7053
Newnham *Herts* 39 TL2437
Newnham *Kent* 28 TQ9557
Newnham *Nhants* 49 SP5859
Newnham Paddox *Warwks* 50 SP4983
Newport *Cnwll* 5 SX3285
Newport *Devon* 19 SS5632
Newport *Dorset* 11 SY8895
Newport *Essex* 39 TL5234
Newport *Gloucs* 35 ST7097
Newport *Highld* 151 ND1324
Newport *IOW* 13 SZ5089
Newport *E R Yk* 84 SE8530
Newport *Newpt* 34 ST3188
Newport *Norfk* 67 TG5017
Newport *Pembks* 30 SN0539
Newport *Shrops* 72 SJ7419
Newport Pagnell *Bucks* 38 SP8743
Newport-on-Tay *Fife* 127 NO4228
Newpound Common *W Susx* 14 TQ0627
Newquay *Cnwll* 4 SW8161
Newsam Green *W York* 83 SE3630
Newsbank *Ches* 72 SJ8366
Newseat *Abers* 142 NJ7032
Newsham *Lancs* 80 SD5136
Newsham *N York* 89 NZ1010
Newsham *N York* 89 SE3784
Newsham *Nthumb* 103 NZ3080
Newsholme *Lancs* 81 SD8451
Newsholme *E R Yk* 84 SE7129
Newstead *Border* 109 NT5634
Newstead *Notts* 75 SK5152
Newstead *Nthumb* 111 NU1527
Newtack *Moray* 142 NJ4446
Newthorpe *N York* 83 SE4632
Newtimber *W Susx* 15 TQ2613
Newton *Ag & B* 114 NS0498
Newton *Beds* 39 TL2344
Newton *Border* 110 NT6020
Newton *Brdgnd* 33 SS8377
Newton *Cambs* 65 TF4314
Newton *Cambs* 53 TL4349
Newton *Cardif* 34 ST2378
Newton *Ches* 71 SJ4167
Newton *Ches* 71 SJ5059
Newton *Ches* 71 SJ5375
Newton *Ches* 71 SJ5278
Newton *Cumb* 86 SD2271
Newton *Derbys* 75 SK4459
Newton *H & W* 46 SO3432
Newton *H & W* 46 SO3769
Newton *H & W* 46 SO5153
Newton *Highld* 139 NH5850
Newton *Highld* 140 NH7448
Newton *Highld* 140 NH7866
Newton *Lancs* 80 SD3436
Newton *Lancs* 80 SD4430
Newton *Lancs* 87 SD5974
Newton *Lancs* 81 SD6950
Newton *Lincs* 64 TF0436
Newton *Moray* 141 NJ1663
Newton *Moray* 141 NJ3362
Newton *N York* 90 SE8872
Newton *Nhants* 51 SP8883
Newton *Norfk* 66 TF8315
Newton *Notts* 63 SK6841
Newton *Nthumb* 110 NT9406
Newton *Nthumb* 103 NZ0364
Newton *S Lans* 116 NS6760
Newton *S Lans* 108 NS9331
Newton *Shrops* 59 SJ4234
Newton *Somset* 20 ST1038
Newton *Staffs* 73 SK0325
Newton *Suffk* 54 TL9240
Newton *W Loth* 117 NT0977
Newton *W Mids* 61 SP0393
Newton *W York* 83 SE4527
Newton *Warwks* 50 SP5378
Newton *Wilts* 23 SU2322
Newton Abbot *Devon* 7 SX8571
Newton Arlosh *Cumb* 93 NY2055
Newton Aycliffe *Dur* 96 NZ2724
Newton Bewley *Dur* 97 NZ4626
Newton Blossomville *Bucks* 38 SP9251
Newton Bromswold *Beds* 51 SP9966
Newton Burgoland *Leics* 62 SK3708
Newton by Toft *Lincs* 76 TF0487
Newton Ferrers *Cnwll* 5 SX3466
Newton Ferrers *Devon* 6 SX5548
Newton Ferry *W Isls* 154 NF8978
Newton Flotman *Norfk* 67 TM2198
Newton Green *Mons* 34 ST5191
Newton Harcourt *Leics* 50 SP6497
Newton Heath *Gt Man* 79 SD8700
Newton Hill *W York* 83 SE3222
Newton Kyme *N York* 83 SE4644
Newton Longville *Bucks* 38 SP8431
Newton Mearns *E Rens* 115 NS5355
Newton Morrell *N York* 89 NZ2309
Newton Mountain *Pembks* 30 SM9808
Newton Mulgrave *N York* 97 NZ7815
Newton of Balcanquhal *P & K* 126 NO1610
Newton on Ouse *N York* 90 SE5159
Newton on the Hill *Shrops* 59 SJ4823
Newton on Trent *Lincs* 76 SK8373
Newton Poppleford *Devon* 9 SY0889
Newton Purcell *Oxon* 49 SP6230
Newton Regis *Warwks* 61 SK2707
Newton Reigny *Cumb* 93 NY4731
Newton Row *Highld* 151 ND3449
Newton Solney *Derbys* 73 SK2825
Newton St Cyres *Devon* 9 SX8898
Newton St Faith *Norfk* 67 TG2217
Newton St Loe *Somset* 22 ST7064
Newton St Petrock *Devon* 18 SS4112
Newton Stacey *Hants* 24 SU4140
Newton Stewart *D & G* 99 NX4065
Newton Toney *Wilts* 23 SU2140
Newton Tracey *Devon* 19 SS5226
Newton under Roseberry *N York* 90 NZ5713
Newton Underwood *Nthumb* 103 NZ1486
Newton upon Derwent *E R Yk* 84 SE7149
Newton Valence *Hants* 24 SU7232
Newton Wamphray *D & G* 100 NY1195
Newton-by-the-Sea *Nthumb* 111 NU2325
Newton-le-Willows *Mersyd* 78 SJ5995
Newton-le-Willows *N York* 89 SE2189
Newton-on-the-Moor *Nthumb* 111 NU1705
Newtongarry Croft *Abers* 142 NJ5735
Newtongrange *Mdloth* 118 NT3364
Newtonhill *Abers* 135 NO9193
Newtonloan *Mdloth* 118 NT3362
Newtonmill *Angus* 134 NO6064
Newtonmore *Highld* 132 NN7098
Newtown *Blae G* 33 SO1709
Newtown *Ches* 71 SJ6247
Newtown *Ches* 72 SJ9060
Newtown *Cnwll* 2 SW5729
Newtown *Cnwll* 3 SW7423
Newtown *Cnwll* 3 SX1052
Newtown *Cnwll* 5 SX2978
Newtown *Cumb* 92 NY1048
Newtown *Cumb* 101 NY5062
Newtown *Cumb* 94 NY5224
Newtown *D & G* 107 NS7710
Newtown *Derbys* 79 SJ9984
Newtown *Devon* 9 SY0699
Newtown *Devon* 19 SS7625
Newtown *Dorset* 10 ST4802
Newtown *Dorset* 12 SZ0393
Newtown *Gloucs* 35 SO6702
Newtown *Gt Man* 78 SD5604
Newtown *H & W* 46 SO4757
Newtown *H & W* 46 SO5333
Newtown *H & W* 46 SO6145
Newtown *H & W* 47 SO7037
Newtown *H & W* 47 SO8755
Newtown *H & W* 60 SO9478
Newtown *Hants* 12 SU2710
Newtown *Hants* 24 SU4763
Newtown *Hants* 13 SU6013
Newtown *Highld* 131 NH3504
Newtown *IOW* 13 SZ4290
Newtown *Lancs* 80 SD5118
Newtown *Nthumb* 111 NT9631
Newtown *Nthumb* 103 NU0300
Newtown *Nthumb* 103 NU0425
Newtown *Powys* 58 SO1091
Newtown *Rhondd* 33 ST0598
Newtown *Shrops* 59 SJ4222
Newtown *Shrops* 59 SJ4731
Newtown *Staffs* 60 SJ9904
Newtown *Wilts* 22 ST9129
Newtown *Wilts* 23 SU2963
Newtown Linford *Leics* 62 SK5209
Newtown of Beltrees *Rens* 115 NS3758
Newtown St Boswells *Border* 110 NT5732
Newtown Unthank *Leics* 62 SK4904
Newtyle *Angus* 126 NO2941
Newyears Green *Gt Lon* 26 TQ0788
Newyork *Ag & B* 122 NM9611
Nextend *H & W* 46 SO3357
Neyland *Pembks* 30 SM9605
Niarbyl *IOM* 153 SC2177
Nibley *Gloucs* 35 SO6606
Nibley *Gloucs* 35 ST6982
Nibley Green *Gloucs* 35 ST7396
Nicholashayne *Devon* 9 ST1016
Nicholaston *Swans* 32 SS5288
Nickies Hill *Cumb* 101 NY5367
Nidd *N York* 89 SE3060
Nigg *Aber C* 135 NJ9402
Nigg *Highld* 147 NH8071
Nightcott *Somset* 19 SS8925
Nimlet *Somset* 35 ST7470
Nine Elms *Wilts* 36 SU1085
Nine Wells *Pembks* 30 SM7924
Ninebanks *Nthumb* 94 NY7853
Nineveh *H & W* 47 SO6265
Ninfield *E Susx* 16 TQ7012
Ningwood *IOW* 13 SZ3989
Nisbet *Border* 110 NT6725
Nisbet Hill *Border* 119 NT7950
Niton *IOW* 13 SZ5076
Nitshill *C Glas* 115 NS5260
No Man's Heath *Ches* 71 SJ5148
No Man's Heath *Warwks* 61 SK2808
No Man's Land *Cnwll* 4 SW9470
No Man's Land *Cnwll* 5 SX2756
Noah's Ark *Kent* 27 TQ5557
Noak Bridge *Essex* 40 TQ6990
Noak Hill *Essex* 27 TQ5494
Noblethorpe *W York* 82 SE2805
Nobold *Shrops* 59 SJ4710
Nobottle *Nhants* 49 SP6763
Nocton *Lincs* 76 TF0564
Nogdam End *Norfk* 67 TG3900
Noke *Oxon* 37 SP5413
Nolton *Pembks* 30 SM8618
Nolton Haven *Pembks* 30 SM8618
Nomansland *Devon* 19 SS8313
Nomansland *Wilts* 12 SU2517
Noneley *Shrops* 59 SJ4828
Nonington *Kent* 29 TR2552
Nook *Cumb* 101 NY4679
Nook *Cumb* 87 SD5481
Norbiton *Gt Lon* 26 TQ1969
Norbreck *Lancs* 80 SD3140
Norbridge *H & W* 47 SO7144
Norbury *Ches* 71 SJ5547
Norbury *Derbys* 73 SK1241
Norbury *Gt Lon* 27 TQ3069
Norbury *Shrops* 59 SO3692
Norbury *Staffs* 72 SJ7823
Norbury Common *Ches* 71 SJ5548
Norbury Junction *Staffs* 72 SJ7923
Norchard *H & W* 47 SO8568
Norcott Brook *Ches* 78 SJ6080
Norcross *Lancs* 80 SD3341
Nordelph *Norfk* 65 TF5501
Norden *Gt Man* 81 SD8614
Nordley *Shrops* 60 SO6996
Norham *Nthumb* 110 NT9047
Norland Town *W York* 82 SE0622
Norley *Ches* 71 SJ5772
Norleywood *Hants* 12 SZ3597
Norlington *E Susx* 16 TQ4413
Norman Cross *Cambs* 52 TL1690
Norman's Bay *E Susx* 16 TQ6805
Norman's Green *Devon* 9 ST0503
Normanby *Lincs* 84 SE8816
Normanby *Lincs* 76 SK9988
Normanby *N York* 97 NZ5418
Normanby *N York* 90 SE7381
Normanby le Wold *Lincs* 76 TF1295
Normandy *Surrey* 25 SU9351
Normanton *Derbys* 62 SK3433
Normanton *Leics* 63 SK8140
Normanton *Lincs* 63 SK9446
Normanton *Notts* 75 SK7054
Normanton *Rutlnd* 63 SK9305
Normanton *W York* 83 SE3822
Normanton *Wilts* 23 SU1340
Normanton le Heath *Leics* 62 SK3712
Normanton on Soar *Notts* 62 SK5122
Normanton on the Wolds *Notts* 62 SK6232
Normanton on Trent *Notts* 75 SK7868
Normoss *Lancs* 80 SD3437
Norney *Surrey* 25 SU9444
Norrington Common *Wilts* 22 ST8864
Norris Green *Cnwll* 5 SX4169
Norristhorpe *W York* 82 SE2123
North Anston *S York* 75 SK5184
North Aston *Oxon* 49 SP4828
North Baddesley *Hants* 13 SU3920
North Ballachulish *Highld* 130 NN0560
North Barrow *Somset* 21 ST6129
North Barsham *Norfk* 66 TF9135
North Benfleet *Essex* 40 TQ7588
North Bersted *W Susx* 14 SU9201
North Berwick *E Loth* 118 NT5485
North Bitchburn *Dur* 96 NZ1732
North Blyth *Nthumb* 103 NZ3082
North Boarhunt *Hants* 13 SU6010
North Bockhampton *Hants* 12 SZ1797
North Bovey *Devon* 8 SX7484
North Bradley *Wilts* 22 ST8555
North Brentor *Devon* 5 SX4881
North Brewham *Somset* 22 ST7236
North Bridge *Surrey* 14 SU9636
North Brook End *Cambs* 39 TL2944
North Buckland *Devon* 18 SS4840
North Burlingham *Norfk* 67 TG3609
North Cadbury *Somset* 21 ST6327
North Carlton *Lincs* 76 SK9477
North Carlton *Notts* 75 SK5984
North Cave *E R Yk* 84 SE8932
North Cerney *Gloucs* 35 SP0107
North Charford *Hants* 12 SU1919
North Charlton *Nthumb* 111 NU1622
North Cheam *Gt Lon* 26 TQ2365
North Cheriton *Somset* 22 ST6925
North Chideock *Dorset* 10 SY4294
North Cliffe *E R Yk* 84 SE8736
North Clifton *Notts* 75 SK8272
North Close *Dur* 96 NZ2532
North Cockerington *Lincs* 77 TF3790
North Collingham *Notts* 76 SK8362
North Common *E Susx* 15 TQ3921
North Connel *Ag & B* 122 NM9034
North Cornelly *Brdgnd* 33 SS8181
North Corner *Cnwll* 3 SW7818
North Corry *Highld* 122 NM8353
North Cotes *Lincs* 77 TA3400
North Country *Cnwll* 2 SW6943
North Cove *Suffk* 55 TM4689
North Cowton *N York* 89 NZ2803
North Crawley *Bucks* 38 SP9244
North Cray *Gt Lon* 27 TQ4872
North Creake *Norfk* 66 TF8538
North Curry *Somset* 21 ST3125
North Dalton *E R Yk* 84 SE9351
North Deighton *N York* 83 SE3951
North Duffield *N York* 83 SE6837
North Duntulm *Highld* 136 NG4274
North Elham *Kent* 29 TR1844
North Elkington *Lincs* 77 TF2890
North Elmham *Norfk* 66 TF9820
North Elmsall *W York* 83 SE4712
North End *Cumb* 93 NY3259
North End *Dorset* 22 ST8427
North End *E R Yk* 85 TA1941
North End *E R Yk* 85 TA2831
North End *Essex* 40 TL6618
North End *Hants* 12 SU1016
North End *Hants* 24 SU5828
North End *Hants* 13 SU6502
North End *Leics* 62 SK5715
North End *Lincs* 85 TA1022
North End *Lincs* 85 TA3101
North End *Lincs* 76 TF0499
North End *Lincs* 64 TF2341
North End *Lincs* 77 TF4289
North End *Mersyd* 78 SD3004
North End *Nhants* 51 SP9668
North End *Norfk* 66 TL9992
North End *Nthumb* 103 NU1301
North End *Somset* 21 ST4266
North End *W Susx* 14 SU9703
North End *W Susx* 14 TQ1109
North Erradale *Highld* 144 NG7480
North Evington *Leics* 62 SK6204
North Fambridge *Essex* 40 TQ8597

Plumley

Pyle

Plumley *Ches* 79 SJ7274
Plumpton *Cumb* 94 NY4937
Plumpton *E Susx* 15 TQ3613
Plumpton *Nhants* 49 SP5948
Plumpton End *Nhants* 49 SP7245
Plumpton Green *E Susx* 15 TQ3616
Plumpton Head *Cumb* 94 NY5035
Plumstead *Gt Lon* 27 TQ4478
Plumstead *Norfk* 66 TG1334
Plumstead Green *Norfk* 66 TG1235
Plumtree *Notts* 62 SK6132
Plumtree Green *Kent* 28 TQ8245
Plungar *Leics* 63 SK7634
Plurenden *Kent* 28 TQ9337
Plush *Dorset* 11 ST7102
Plusha *Cnwll* 5 SX2580
Plushabridge *Cnwll* 5 SX3072
Plwmp *Cardgn* 42 SN3652
Plymouth *Devon* 6 SX4754
Plympton *Devon* 6 SX5456
Plymstock *Devon* 6 SX5152
Plymtree *Devon* 9 ST0502
Pockley *N York* 90 SE6385
Pocklington *E R Yk* 84 SE8048
Pode Hole *Lincs* 64 TF2121
Podimore *Somset* 21 ST5424
Podington *Beds* 51 SP9462
Podmore *Staffs* 72 SJ7835
Point Clear *Essex* 41 TM1015
Pointon *Lincs* 64 TF1131
Pokesdown *Dorset* 12 SZ1292
Polapit Tamar *Cnwll* 5 SX3389
Polbain *Highld* 144 NB9910
Polbathic *Cnwll* 5 SX3456
Polbeth *W Loth* 117 NT0264
Polbrock *Cnwll* 4 SX0169
Pole Elm *H & W* 47 SO8450
Pole Moor *W York* 82 SE0615
Polebrook *Nhants* 51 TL0686
Polegate *E Susx* 16 TQ5804
Polelane Ends *Ches* 79 SJ6479
Polesworth *Warwks* 61 SK2602
Polgigga *Cnwll* 2 SW3723
Polglass *Highld* 144 NC0307
Polgooth *Cnwll* 3 SW9950
Polgown *D & G* 107 NS7103
Poling *W Susx* 14 TQ0404
Poling Corner *W Susx* 14 TQ0405
Polkerris *Cnwll* 3 SX0952
Pollard Street *Norfk* 67 TG3332
Pollington *E R Yk* 83 SE6119
Polloch *Highld* 129 NM7668
Pollokshaws *C Glas* 115 NS5661
Pollokshields *C Glas* 115 NS5763
Polmassick *Cnwll* 3 SW9745
Polmear *Cnwll* 3 SX0853
Polmont *Falk* 116 NS9378
Polnish *Highld* 129 NM7582
Polperro *Cnwll* 5 SX2051
Polruan *Cnwll* 3 SX1250
Polsham *Somset* 21 ST5142
Polstead *Suffk* 54 TL9938
Polstead Heath *Suffk* 54 TL9940
Poltalloch *Ag & B* 113 NR8196
Poltescoe *Cnwll* 3 SW7215
Poltimore *Devon* 9 SX9696
Polton *Mdloth* 117 NT2864
Polwarth *Border* 119 NT7450
Polyphant *Cnwll* 5 SX2682
Polzeath *Cnwll* 4 SW9378
Pomathorn *Mdloth* 117 NT2459
Ponde *Powys* 45 SO1037
Ponders End *Gt Lon* 27 TQ3596
Pondersbridge *Cambs* 64 TL2692
Ponsanooth *Cnwll* 3 SW7537
Ponsonby *Cumb* 86 NY0505
Ponsongath *Cnwll* 3 SW7518
Ponsworthy *Devon* 7 SX7073
Pont Cyfyng *A & C* 69 SH7357
Pont Morlais *Carmth* 32 SN5307
Pont Pen-y-benglog *Gwynd* 69 SH6560
Pont Rhyd-sarn *Gwynd* 57 SH8528
Pont Rhyd-y-cyff *Brdgnd* 33 SS8788
Pont Robert *Powys* 58 SJ1012
Pont Walby *Neath* 33 SN8906
Pont-ar-gothi *Carmth* 32 SN5021
Pont-ar-Hydfer *Powys* 45 SN8627
Pont-ar-llechau *Carmth* 44 SN7224
Pont-Ebbw *Newpt* 34 ST2985
Pont-faen *Powys* 45 SN9934
Pont-gareg *Pembks* 31 SN1441
Pont-Nedd-Fechan *Neath* 33 SN9007
Pont-rhyd-y-fen *Neath* 32 SS7994
Pont-rug *Gwynd* 68 SH5162
Pont-y-blew *Wrexhm* 71 SJ3138
Pont-y-pant *A & C* 69 SH7554
Pont-yr-hafod *Pembks* 30 SM9026
Pont-yr-Rhyl *Brdgnd* 33 SS9089
Pontac *Jersey* 152 JS0000
Pontamman *Carmth* 32 SN6312
Pontantwn *Carmth* 32 SN4412
Pontardawe *Neath* 32 SN7204
Pontardulais *Swans* 32 SN5903
Pontarsais *Carmth* 31 SN4428
Pontblyddyn *Flints* 70 SJ2760
Pontdolgoch *Powys* 58 SO0193
Pontefract *W York* 83 SE4521
Ponteland *Nthumb* 103 NZ1672
Ponterwyd *Cardgn* 43 SN7481
Pontesbury *Shrops* 59 SJ3906
Pontesbury Hill *Shrops* 59 SJ3905
Pontesford *Shrops* 59 SJ4106
Pontfadog *Wrexhm* 70 SJ2338
Pontfaen *Pembks* 30 SN0234
Pontgarreg *Cardgn* 42 SN3353
Ponthenry *Carmth* 32 SN4709
Ponthir *Torfn* 34 ST3292
Ponthirwaun *Cardgn* 42 SN2645
Pontllanfraith *Caerph* 33 ST1895
Pontlliw *Swans* 32 SS6199
Pontlottyn *Caerph* 33 SO1106
Pontlyfni *Gwynd* 68 SH4352
Pontnewydd *Torfn* 34 ST2896
Pontnewynydd *Torfn* 34 SO2701
Pontop *Dur* 96 NZ1453
Pontrhydfendigaid *Cardgn* 43 SN7366
Pontrhydygroes *Cardgn* 43 SN7472
Pontrhydyrun *Torfn* 34 ST2997
Pontrilas *H & W* 46 SO3927
Ponts Green *E Susx* 16 TQ6715
Pontshaen *Cardgn* 42 SN4446
Pontshill *H & W* 35 SO6421
Pontsticill *Powys* 33 SO0511
Pontwelly *Carmth* 31 SN4140
Pontyates *Carmth* 32 SN4708
Pontyberem *Carmth* 32 SN5010
Pontybodkin *Flints* 70 SJ2759
Pontyclun *Rhondd* 33 ST0381
Pontycymer *Brdgnd* 33 SS9091
Pontyglasier *Pembks* 31 SN1436
Pontygwaith *Rhondd* 33 ST0094
Pontygynon *Pembks* 31 SN1237
Pontymoel *Torfn* 34 SO2900
Pontypool *Torfn* 34 SO2800
Pontypool Road *Torfn* 34 ST3099
Pontypridd *Rhondd* 33 ST0789
Pontywaun *Caerph* 34 ST2292
Pooksgreen *Hants* 12 SU3710
Pool *Cnwll* 2 SW6641
Pool *IOS* 2 SV8714
Pool *W York* 82 SE2445
Pool Head *H & W* 46 SO5550
Pool of Muckhart *Clacks* 117 NO0000
Pool Quay *Powys* 58 SJ2511
Pool Street *Essex* 53 TL7636
Poole *Dorset* 11 SZ0090
Poole Keynes *Gloucs* 35 ST9995
Poolewe *Highld* 144 NG8580
Pooley Bridge *Cumb* 93 NY4724
Pooley Street *Norfk* 54 TM0581
Poolfold *Staffs* 72 SJ8959
Poolhill *Gloucs* 47 SO7229
Pooting's *Kent* 16 TQ4549
Popham *Hants* 24 SU5543
Poplar *Gt Lon* 27 TQ3780
Poplar Street *Suffk* 55 TM4465
Porchbrook *H & W* 60 SO7270
Porchfield *IOW* 13 SZ4491
Poringland *Norfk* 67 TG2701
Porkellis *Cnwll* 2 SW6933
Porlock *Somset* 19 SS8846
Porlock Weir *Somset* 19 SS8647
Port Appin *Ag & B* 122 NM9045
Port Askaig *Ag & B* 112 NR4369
Port Bannatyne *Ag & B* 114 NS0767
Port Carlisle *Cumb* 101 NY2461
Port Charlotte *Ag & B* 112 NR2558
Port Clarence *Dur* 97 NZ4921
Port Dolgarrog *A & C* 69 SH7766
Port Driseach *Ag & B* 114 NR9973
Port Einon *Swans* 32 SS4685
Port Ellen *Ag & B* 104 NR3645
Port Elphinstone *Abers* 142 NJ7720
Port Erin *IOM* 153 SC1969
Port Gaverne *Cnwll* 4 SX0080
Port Glasgow *Inver* 115 NS3274
Port Henderson *Highld* 137 NG7573
Port Isaac *Cnwll* 4 SW9980
Port Logan *D & G* 98 NX0940
Port Mor *Highld* 128 NM4279
Port Mulgrave *N York* 97 NZ7917
Port Na Craig *P & K* 125 NN9357
Port nan Giuran *W Isls* 154 NB5537
Port nan Long *W Isls* 154 NF8978
Port Nis *W Isls* 154 NB5363
Port of Menteith *Stirlg* 115 NN5801
Port of Ness *W Isls* 154 NB5363
Port Quin *Cnwll* 4 SW9780
Port Ramsay *Ag & B* 122 NM8845
Port Soderick *IOM* 153 SC3472
Port St Mary *IOM* 153 SC2067
Port Sunlight *Mersyd* 78 SJ3384
Port Talbot *Neath* 32 SS7689
Port Tennant *Swans* 32 SS6893
Port Wemyss *Ag & B* 112 NR1651
Port William *D & G* 98 NX3343
Port-an-Eorna *Highld* 137 NG7732
Portachoillan *Ag & B* 113 NR7557
Portavadie *Ag & B* 114 NR9369
Portbury *Somset* 34 ST5075
Portchester *Hants* 13 SU6105
Porteath *Cnwll* 4 SW9679
Portencalzie *D & G* 98 NX0171
Portencross *N Ayrs* 114 NS1748
Portesham *Dorset* 10 SY6085
Portessie *Moray* 142 NJ4366
Portfield Gate *Pembks* 30 SM9215
Portgate *Devon* 5 SX4285
Portgordon *Moray* 142 NJ3964
Portgower *Highld* 147 ND0013
Porth *Cnwll* 4 SW8362
Porth *Rhondd* 33 ST0291
Porth Dinllaen *Gwynd* 56 SH2740
Porth Navas *Cnwll* 3 SW7527
Porth-y-Waen *Shrops* 58 SJ2623
Porthallow *Cnwll* 3 SW7923
Porthallow *Cnwll* 5 SX2251
Porthcawl *Brdgnd* 33 SS8177
Porthcothan *Cnwll* 4 SW8672
Porthcurno *Cnwll* 2 SW3822
Porthgain *Pembks* 30 SM8132
Porthgwarra *Cnwll* 2 SW3721
Porthill *Staffs* 72 SJ8448
Porthkea *Cnwll* 3 SW8242
Porthkerry *V Glam* 20 ST0866
Porthleven *Cnwll* 2 SW6225
Porthmadog *Gwynd* 57 SH5638
Porthmeor *Cnwll* 2 SW4337
Portholland *Cnwll* 3 SW9541
Porthoustock *Cnwll* 3 SW8021
Porthpean *Cnwll* 3 SX0250
Porthtowan *Cnwll* 2 SW6947
Porthwgan *Wrexhm* 71 SJ3846
Porthyrhyd *Carmth* 32 SN5215
Portincaple *Ag & B* 114 NS2393
Portinfer *Jersey* 152 JS0000
Portington *E R Yk* 84 SE7831
Portinnisherrich *Ag & B* 122 NM9711
Portinscale *Cumb* 93 NY2523
Portishead *Somset* 34 ST4675
Portknockie *Moray* 142 NJ4868
Portlethen *Abers* 135 NO9196
Portling *D & G* 92 NX8753
Portloe *Cnwll* 3 SW9339
Portlooe *Cnwll* 5 SX2452
Portmahomack *Highld* 147 NH9184
Portmellon *Cnwll* 3 SX0144
Portmore *Hants* 12 SZ3397
Portnacroish *Ag & B* 122 NM9247
Portnaguran *W Isls* 154 NB5537
Portnahaven *Ag & B* 112 NR1652
Portnalong *Highld* 136 NG3434
Portobello *C Edin* 117 NT3073
Portobello *T & W* 96 NZ2856
Portobello *W Mids* 60 SO9598
Porton *Wilts* 23 SU1836
Portontown *Devon* 5 SX4176
Portpatrick *D & G* 98 NW9954
Portreath *Cnwll* 2 SW6545
Portree *Highld* 136 NG4843
Portscatho *Cnwll* 3 SW8735
Portsea *Hants* 13 SU6300
Portskerra *Highld* 150 NC8765
Portskewett *Mons* 34 ST4988
Portslade *E Susx* 15 TQ2506
Portslade-by-Sea *E Susx* 15 TQ2605
Portslogan *D & G* 98 NW9858
Portsmouth *Hants* 13 SU6400
Portsmouth *W York* 81 SD9026
Portsonachan Hotel *Ag & B* 123 NN0420
Portsoy *Abers* 142 NJ5866
Portswood *Hants* 13 SU4214
Portuairk *Highld* 128 NM4368
Portway *H & W* 46 SO4844
Portway *H & W* 46 SO4935
Portway *H & W* 61 SP0872
Portway *W Mids* 60 SO9787
Portwrinkle *Cnwll* 5 SX3553
Portyerrock *D & G* 99 NX4738
Posbury *Devon* 8 SX8197
Posenhall *Shrops* 59 SJ6501
Poslingford *Suffk* 53 TL7648
Posso *Border* 109 NT2033
Post Green *Dorset* 11 SY9593
Postbridge *Devon* 8 SX6579
Postcombe *Oxon* 37 SP7000
Postling *Kent* 29 TR1439
Postwick *Norfk* 67 TG2907
Potarch *Abers* 134 NO6097
Pothole *Cnwll* 3 SW9750
Potsgrove *Beds* 38 SP9530
Pott Row *Norfk* 65 TF7022
Pott Shrigley *Ches* 79 SJ9479
Pott's Green *Essex* 40 TL9122
Potten End *Herts* 38 TL0109
Potten Street *Kent* 29 TR2567
Potter Brompton *N York* 91 SE9777
Potter Heigham *Norfk* 67 TG4119
Potter Row *Bucks* 26 SP9002
Potter Somersal *Derbys* 73 SK1335
Potter's Cross *Staffs* 60 SO8484
Potter's Forstal *Kent* 28 TQ8946
Potter's Green *E Susx* 16 TQ5023
Potter's Green *Herts* 39 TL3520
Pottergate Street *Norfk* 66 TM1591
Potterhanworth *Lincs* 76 TF0566
Potterhanworth Booths *Lincs* 76 TF0767
Potterne *Wilts* 22 ST9958
Potterne Wick *Wilts* 22 ST9957
Potters Bar *Herts* 26 TL2401
Potters Brook *Lancs* 80 SD4852
Potters Crouch *Herts* 38 TL1105
Potters Green *W Mids* 61 SP3782
Potters Marston *Leics* 50 SP4996
Pottersheath *Herts* 39 TL2318
Potterspury *Nhants* 49 SP7543
Potterton *Abers* 143 NJ9415
Potterton *W York* 83 SE4038
Potthorpe *Norfk* 66 TF9422
Pottle Street *Wilts* 22 ST8140
Potto *N York* 89 NZ4703
Potton *Beds* 52 TL2249
Poughill *Cnwll* 18 SS2207
Poughill *Devon* 19 SS8508
Poulner *Hants* 12 SU1606
Poulshot *Wilts* 22 ST9659
Poulston *Devon* 7 SX7754
Poulton *Gloucs* 36 SP0901
Poulton *Mersyd* 78 SJ3091
Poulton Priory *Gloucs* 36 SP0900
Poulton-le-Fylde *Lancs* 80 SD3439
Pound Bank *H & W* 60 SO7374
Pound Green *E Susx* 16 TQ5123
Pound Green *H & W* 60 SO7578
Pound Green *Suffk* 53 TL7153
Pound Hill *W Susx* 15 TQ2937
Pound Street *Hants* 24 SU4561
Poundffald *Swans* 32 SS5694
Poundgates *E Susx* 16 TQ4928
Poundon *Bucks* 49 SP6425
Poundsbridge *Kent* 16 TQ5341
Poundsgate *Devon* 7 SX7072
Poundstock *Cnwll* 18 SX2099
Pounsley *E Susx* 16 TQ5221
Pouton *D & G* 99 NX4645
Povey Cross *Surrey* 15 TQ2642
Pow Green *H & W* 47 SO7144
Powburn *Nthumb* 111 NU0616
Powderham *Devon* 9 SX9684
Powerstock *Dorset* 10 SY5196
Powfoot *D & G* 100 NY1465
Powhill *Cumb* 93 NY2355
Powick *H & W* 47 SO8351
Powmill *P & K* 117 NT0297
Poxwell *Dorset* 11 SY7384
Poyle *Surrey* 26 TQ0376
Poynings *W Susx* 15 TQ2611
Poynter's Lane End *Cnwll* 2 SW6743
Poyntington *Dorset* 21 ST6520
Poynton *Ches* 79 SJ9283
Poynton *Shrops* 59 SJ5617
Poynton Green *Shrops* 59 SJ5618
Poys Street *Suffk* 55 TM3570
Poyston Cross *Pembks* 30 SM9819
Poystreet Green *Suffk* 54 TL9758
Praa Sands *Cnwll* 2 SW5828
Pratt's Bottom *Gt Lon* 27 TQ4762
Praze-an-Beeble *Cnwll* 2 SW6335
Predannack Wollas *Cnwll* 2 SW6616
Prees *Shrops* 59 SJ5533
Prees Green *Shrops* 59 SJ5531
Prees Heath *Shrops* 71 SJ5538
Prees Higher Heath *Shrops* 59 SJ5635
Prees Lower Heath *Shrops* 59 SJ5732
Preesall *Lancs* 80 SD3647
Preesgweene *Shrops* 59 SJ2936
Pren-gwyn *Cardgn* 42 SN4244
Prendwick *Nthumb* 111 NU0012
Prenteg *Gwynd* 57 SH5841
Prenton *Mersyd* 78 SJ3086
Prescot *Mersyd* 78 SJ4692
Prescott *Devon* 9 ST0814
Prescott *Shrops* 59 SJ4220
Prescott *Shrops* 60 SO6681
Presnerb *Angus* 133 NO1866
Pressen *Nthumb* 110 NT8335
Prestatyn *Denbgs* 70 SJ0682
Prestbury *Ches* 79 SJ8976
Prestbury *Gloucs* 47 SO9723
Presteigne *Powys* 46 SO3164
Prestleigh *Somset* 21 ST6340
Prestolee *Gt Man* 79 SD7505
Preston *Border* 119 NT7957
Preston *Devon* 7 SX7451
Preston *Devon* 7 SX8574
Preston *Devon* 7 SX8962
Preston *Dorset* 11 SY7083
Preston *E Loth* 118 NT5977
Preston *E R Yk* 85 TA1830
Preston *E Susx* 15 TQ3106
Preston *Gloucs* 47 SO6834
Preston *Gloucs* 36 SP0400
Preston *Herts* 39 TL1824
Preston *Kent* 28 TR0260
Preston *Kent* 29 TR2460
Preston *Lancs* 80 SD5329
Preston *Nthumb* 111 NU1825
Preston *Rutlnd* 63 SK8602
Preston *Shrops* 59 SJ5211
Preston *Somset* 20 ST0935
Preston *Suffk* 54 TL9450
Preston *Wilts* 36 SU2774
Preston Bagot *Warwks* 48 SP1765
Preston Bissett *Bucks* 49 SP6529
Preston Bowyer *Somset* 20 ST1326
Preston Brockhurst *Shrops* 59 SJ5324
Preston Brook *Ches* 78 SJ5680
Preston Candover *Hants* 24 SU6041
Preston Capes *Nhants* 49 SP5754
Preston Crowmarsh *Oxon* 37 SU6190
Preston Deanery *Nhants* 50 SP7855
Preston Green *Warwks* 48 SP1665
Preston Gubbals *Shrops* 59 SJ4919
Preston Montford *Shrops* 59 SJ4314
Preston on Stour *Warwks* 48 SP2049
Preston on Tees *Dur* 96 NZ4315
Preston on the Hill *Ches* 78 SJ5780
Preston on Wye *H & W* 46 SO3842
Preston Patrick *Cumb* 87 SD5483
Preston Plucknett *Somset* 10 ST5316
Preston Street *Kent* 29 TR2561
Preston upon the Weald Moors *Shrops* 72 SJ6815
Preston Wynne *H & W* 46 SO5546
Preston-under-Scar *N York* 88 SE0691
Prestonpans *E Loth* 118 NT3874
Prestwich *Gt Man* 79 SD8104
Prestwick *Nthumb* 103 NZ1872
Prestwick *S Ayrs* 106 NS3525
Prestwood *Bucks* 26 SP8700
Prestwood *Staffs* 60 SO8786
Price Town *Brdgnd* 33 SS9391
Prickwillow *Cambs* 53 TL5982
Priddy *Somset* 21 ST5250
Priest Hutton *Lancs* 87 SD5273
Priestacott *Devon* 18 SS4206
Priestcliffe *Derbys* 74 SK1471
Priestcliffe Ditch *Derbys* 74 SK1371
Priestend *Bucks* 37 SP6905
Priestland *E Ayrs* 107 NS5737
Priestley Green *W York* 82 SE1326
Priestweston *Shrops* 59 SO2997
Priestwood Green *Kent* 28 TQ6564
Primethorpe *Leics* 50 SP5293
Primrose Green *Norfk* 66 TG0716
Primrose Hill *Cambs* 52 TL3889
Primrose Hill *Derbys* 75 SK4358
Primrose Hill *Lancs* 78 SD3809
Primrose Hill *W Mids* 60 SO9487
Primrosehill *Border* 119 NT7857
Primsidemill *Border* 110 NT8126
Princes Gate *Pembks* 31 SN1312
Princes Risborough *Bucks* 38 SP8003
Princethorpe *Warwks* 61 SP4070
Princetown *Devon* 6 SX5873
Prinsted *W Susx* 14 SU7605
Prion *Denbgs* 70 SJ0562
Prior Rigg *Cumb* 101 NY4568
Priors Halton *Shrops* 46 SO4975
Priors Hardwick *Warwks* 49 SP4756
Priors Marston *Warwks* 49 SP4957
Priors Norton *Gloucs* 47 SO8624
Priory Wood *H & W* 46 SO2645
Prisk *V Glam* 33 ST0176
Priston *Somset* 22 ST6960
Pristow Green *Norfk* 54 TM1388
Prittlewell *Essex* 40 TQ8687
Privett *Hants* 13 SU6727
Prixford *Devon* 19 SS5536
Probus *Cnwll* 3 SW8947
Prospect *Cumb* 92 NY1140
Prospidnick *Cnwll* 2 SW6431
Protstonhill *Abers* 143 NJ8163
Providence *Somset* 34 ST5370
Prudhoe *Nthumb* 103 NZ0962
Prussia Cove *Cnwll* 2 SW5528
Publow *Somset* 21 ST6264
Puckeridge *Herts* 39 TL3823
Puckington *Somset* 10 ST3718
Pucklechurch *Gloucs* 35 ST6976
Puckrup *Gloucs* 47 SO8836
Puddinglake *Ches* 79 SJ7269
Puddington *Ches* 71 SJ3273
Puddington *Devon* 19 SS8310
Puddledock *Norfk* 66 TM0592
Puddlehill *Herts* 38 TL0023
Puddletown *Dorset* 11 SY7594
Pudsey *W York* 82 SE2232
Pulborough *W Susx* 14 TQ0418
Puleston *Shrops* 72 SJ7322
Pulford *Ches* 71 SJ3758
Pulham *Dorset* 11 ST7008
Pulham Market *Norfk* 55 TM1986
Pulham St Mary *Norfk* 55 TM2085
Pullens Green *Gloucs* 34 ST6192
Pulley *Shrops* 59 SJ4709
Pulloxhill *Beds* 38 TL0634
Pumpherston *W Loth* 117 NT0669
Pumsaint *Carmth* 44 SN6540
Puncheston *Pembks* 30 SN0129
Puncknowle *Dorset* 10 SY5388
Punnett's Town *E Susx* 16 TQ6220
Purbrook *Hants* 13 SU6707
Purbrook Park *Hants* 13 SU6707
Purfleet *Essex* 27 TQ5578
Puriton *Somset* 21 ST3241
Purleigh *Essex* 40 TL8402
Purley *Berks* 37 SU6675
Purley *Gt Lon* 27 TQ3161
Purlogue *Shrops* 46 SO2877
Purlpit *Wilts* 22 ST8766
Purls Bridge *Cambs* 53 TL4786
Purse Caundle *Dorset* 11 ST6917
Purshall Green *H & W* 60 SO8971
Purslow *Shrops* 59 SO3680
Purston Jaglin *W York* 83 SE4319
Purtington *Somset* 10 ST3908
Purton *Gloucs* 35 SO6904
Purton *Gloucs* 35 SO6705
Purton *Wilts* 36 SU0987
Purton Stoke *Wilts* 36 SU0990
Pury End *Nhants* 49 SP7145
Pusey *Oxon* 36 SU3596
Putley *H & W* 47 SO6337
Putley Green *H & W* 47 SO6437
Putloe *Gloucs* 35 SO7709
Putney *Gt Lon* 26 TQ2374
Putron Village *Guern* 152 GN0000
Putsborough *Devon* 18 SS4440
Puttenham *Herts* 38 SP8814
Puttenham *Surrey* 25 SU9247
Puttock End *Essex* 54 TL8040
Puttock's End *Essex* 40 TL5719
Putton *Dorset* 11 SY6480
Puxley *Nhants* 49 SP7542
Puxton *Somset* 21 ST4063
Pwll *Carmth* 32 SN4801
Pwll Trap *Carmth* 31 SN2616
Pwll-du *Mons* 34 SO2411
Pwll-glas *Denbgs* 70 SJ1154
Pwll-y-glaw *Neath* 32 SS7993
Pwllcrochan *Pembks* 30 SM9202
Pwllgloyw *Powys* 45 SO0333
Pwllheli *Gwynd* 56 SH3735
Pwllmeyric *Mons* 34 ST5292
Pydew *A & C* 69 SH8079
Pye Bridge *Derbys* 75 SK4452
Pye Corner *Herts* 39 TL4412
Pye Corner *Newpt* 34 ST3485
Pye Green *Staffs* 60 SJ9813
Pyecombe *W Susx* 15 TQ2813
Pyle *Brdgnd* 33 SS8282

Ridgewood Ryton

Ridgewood *E Susx* 16 TQ4719
Ridgmont *Beds* 38 SP9736
Riding Mill *Nthumb* 103 NZ0161
Ridley *Kent* 27 TQ6164
Ridley *Nthumb* 102 NY7963
Ridley Green *Ches* 71 SJ5554
Ridlington *Norfk* 67 TG3430
Ridlington *Rutlnd* 63 SK8402
Ridlington Street *Norfk* 67 TG3430
Ridsdale *Nthumb* 102 NY9084
Rievaulx *N York* 90 SE5785
Rigg *D & G* 101 NY2966
Riggend *N Lans* 116 NS7670
Righoul *Highld* 140 NH8851
Rigmadon Park *Cumb* 87 SD6184
Rigsby *Lincs* 77 TF4375
Rigside *S Lans* 108 NS8735
Riley Green *Lancs* 81 SD6225
Rileyhill *Staffs* 61 SK1114
Rilla Mill *Cnwll* 5 SX2973
Rillaton *Cnwll* 5 SX2973
Rillington *N York* 90 SE8574
Rimington *Lancs* 81 SD8045
Rimpton *Somset* 21 ST6121
Rimswell *E R Yk* 85 TA3128
Rinaston *Pembks* 30 SM9825
Rindleford *Shrops* 60 SO7395
Ring o'Bells *Lancs* 78 SD4510
Ring's End *Cambs* 65 TF3902
Ringford *D & G* 99 NX6957
Ringinglow *Derbys* 74 SK2883
Ringland *Norfk* 66 TG1313
Ringles Cross *E Susx* 16 TQ4722
Ringlestone *Kent* 28 TQ8755
Ringley *Gt Man* 79 SD7605
Ringmer *E Susx* 16 TQ4412
Ringmore *Devon* 7 SX6546
Ringmore *Devon* 7 SX9272
Ringorm *Moray* 141 NJ2644
Ringsfield *Suffk* 55 TM4088
Ringsfield Corner *Suffk* 55 TM4087
Ringshall *Bucks* 38 SP9814
Ringshall *Suffk* 54 TM0452
Ringshall Stocks *Suffk* 54 TM0551
Ringstead *Nhants* 51 SP9875
Ringstead *Norfk* 65 TF7040
Ringwood *Hants* 12 SU1505
Ringwould *Kent* 29 TR3548
Rinsey *Cnwll* 2 SW5927
Rinsey Croft *Cnwll* 2 SW6028
Ripe *E Susx* 16 TQ5110
Ripley *Derbys* 74 SK3950
Ripley *Hants* 12 SZ1698
Ripley *N York* 89 SE2860
Ripley *Surrey* 26 TQ0556
Riplingham *E R Yk* 84 SE9631
Riplington *Hants* 13 SU6623
Ripon *N York* 89 SE3171
Rippingale *Lincs* 64 TF0927
Ripple *H & W* 47 SO8737
Ripple *Kent* 29 TR3550
Ripponden *W York* 82 SE0319
Risabus *Ag & B* 104 NR3143
Risbury *H & W* 46 SO5455
Risby *Lincs* 84 SE9114
Risby *Suffk* 54 TL8066
Risca *Caerph* 34 ST2391
Rise *E R Yk* 85 TA1542
Riseden *E Susx* 16 TQ6130
Riseden *Kent* 28 TQ7036
Risegate *Lincs* 64 TF2129
Riseholme *Lincs* 76 SK9775
Risehow *Cumb* 92 NY0234
Riseley *Beds* 51 TL0462
Riseley *Berks* 24 SU7263
Rishangles *Suffk* 54 TM1668
Rishton *Lancs* 81 SD7230
Rishworth *W York* 82 SE0318
Rising Bridge *Lancs* 81 SD7825
Risley *Ches* 79 SJ6592
Risley *Derbys* 62 SK4535
Risplith *N York* 89 SE2468
Rivar *Wilts* 23 SU3161
Rivenhall End *Essex* 40 TL8316
River *Kent* 29 TR2943
River *W Susx* 14 SU9323
River Bank *Cambs* 53 TL5368
Riverford *Highld* 139 NH5454
Riverhead *Kent* 27 TQ5156
Rivers Corner *Dorset* 11 ST7712
Rivington *Lancs* 81 SD6214
Roachill *Devon* 19 SS8522
Road Ashton *Wilts* 22 ST8856
Road Green *Norfk* 67 TM2693
Road Weedon *Nhants* 49 SP6359
Roade *Nhants* 49 SP7651
Roadhead *Cumb* 101 NY5174
Roadmeetings *S Lans* 116 NS8649
Roadside *E Ayrs* 107 NS5717
Roadside *Highld* 151 ND1560
Roadwater *Somset* 20 ST0338
Roag *Highld* 136 NG2644
Roan of Craigoch *S Ayrs* 106 NS2904
Roast Green *Essex* 39 TL4632
Roath *Cardif* 33 ST1977
Roberton *Border* 109 NT4214
Roberton *S Lans* 108 NS9428
Robertsbridge *E Susx* 17 TQ7423
Roberttown *W York* 82 SE1922
Robeston Wathen *Pembks* 31 SN0815
Robgill Tower *D & G* 101 NY2471
Robin Hill *Staffs* 72 SJ9057
Robin Hood *Lancs* 80 SD5211
Robin Hood *W York* 83 SE3227
Robin Hood's Bay *N York* 91 NZ9505
Robinhood End *Essex* 53 TL7036
Roborough *Devon* 19 SS5717
Roborough *Devon* 6 SX5062
Roby *Mersyd* 78 SJ4390
Roby Mill *Lancs* 78 SD5107
Rocester *Staffs* 73 SK1039
Roch *Pembks* 30 SM8821
Roch Gate *Pembks* 30 SM8720
Rochdale *Gt Man* 81 SD8913
Roche *Cnwll* 4 SW9860
Rochester *Kent* 28 TQ7468
Rochester *Nthumb* 102 NY8298
Rochford *Essex* 40 TQ8790
Rochford *H & W* 47 SO6268
Rochville *Ag & B* 114 NS2390
Rock *Cnwll* 4 SW9375
Rock *H & W* 60 SO7371
Rock *Neath* 32 SS7893
Rock *Nthumb* 111 NU2020
Rock *W Susx* 14 TQ1213
Rock Ferry *Mersyd* 78 SJ3386
Rock Hill *H & W* 47 SO9569
Rockbeare *Devon* 9 SY0194
Rockbourne *Hants* 12 SU1118
Rockcliffe *Cumb* 101 NY3561
Rockcliffe *D & G* 92 NX8454
Rockcliffe Cross *Cumb* 101 NY3463
Rockesta *Cnwll* 2 SW3722
Rockfield *Highld* 147 NH9282
Rockfield *Mons* 34 SO4814
Rockford *Devon* 19 SS7547
Rockford *Hants* 12 SU1607
Rockgreen *Shrops* 46 SO5275
Rockhampton *Gloucs* 35 ST6593
Rockhead *Cnwll* 4 SX0784
Rockhill *Shrops* 46 SO2978
Rockingham *Nhants* 51 SP8691
Rockland All Saints *Norfk* 66 TL9996
Rockland St Mary *Norfk* 67 TG3104
Rockland St Peter *Norfk* 66 TL9897
Rockley *Notts* 75 SK7174
Rockley *Wilts* 36 SU1571
Rockliffe *Lancs* 81 SD8722
Rockwell End *Bucks* 37 SU7988
Rockwell Green *Somset* 20 ST1220
Rodborough *Gloucs* 35 SO8404
Rodbourne *Wilts* 36 SU1485
Rodbourne *Wilts* 35 ST9383
Rodd *H & W* 46 SO3262
Roddam *Nthumb* 111 NU0220
Rodden *Dorset* 10 SY6184
Roddymoor *Dur* 96 NZ1536
Rode *Somset* 22 ST8053
Rode Heath *Ches* 72 SJ8056
Rode Heath *Ches* 72 SJ8767
Rodel *W Isls* 154 NG0483
Roden *Shrops* 59 SJ5716
Rodhuish *Somset* 20 ST0139
Rodington *Shrops* 59 SJ5814
Rodington Heath *Shrops* 59 SJ5814
Rodley *Gloucs* 35 SO7411
Rodley *W York* 82 SE2236
Rodmarton *Gloucs* 35 ST9498
Rodmell *E Susx* 15 TQ4106
Rodmersham *Kent* 28 TQ9261
Rodmersham Green *Kent* 28 TQ9161
Rodney Stoke *Somset* 21 ST4849
Rodsley *Derbys* 73 SK2040
Rodway *Somset* 20 ST2540
Roe Cross *Gt Man* 79 SJ9896
Roe Green *Gt Man* 79 SD7501
Roe Green *Herts* 39 TL2107
Roe Green *Herts* 39 TL3133
Roecliffe *N York* 89 SE3765
Roehampton *Gt Lon* 26 TQ2273
Roffey *W Susx* 15 TQ1932
Rogart *Highld* 146 NC7202
Rogate *W Susx* 14 SU8023
Roger Ground *Cumb* 87 SD3597
Rogerstone *Newpt* 34 ST2787
Roghadal *W Isls* 154 NG0483
Rogiet *Mons* 34 ST4587
Roke *Oxon* 37 SU6293
Roker *T & W* 96 NZ4058
Rollesby *Norfk* 67 TG4416
Rolleston *Leics* 50 SK7300
Rolleston *Notts* 75 SK7452
Rolleston *Staffs* 73 SK2327
Rolston *E R Yk* 85 TA2144
Rolstone *Somset* 21 ST3962
Rolvenden *Kent* 17 TQ8431
Rolvenden Layne *Kent* 17 TQ8530
Romaldkirk *Dur* 95 NY9922
Romanby *N York* 89 SE3693
Romanno Bridge *Border* 117 NT1647
Romansleigh *Devon* 19 SS7220
Romden Castle *Kent* 28 TQ8941
Romesdal *Highld* 136 NG4053
Romford *Dorset* 12 SU0709
Romford *Gt Lon* 27 TQ5188
Romiley *Gt Man* 79 SJ9490
Romney Street *Kent* 27 TQ5561
Romsey *Hants* 12 SU3521
Romsley *H & W* 60 SO9680
Romsley *Shrops* 60 SO7883
Ronachan *Ag & B* 113 NR7454
Rookhope *Dur* 95 NY9342
Rookley *IOW* 13 SZ5084
Rookley Green *IOW* 13 SZ5083
Rooks Bridge *Somset* 21 ST3652
Rooks Nest *Somset* 20 ST0933
Rookwith *N York* 89 SE2086
Roos *E R Yk* 85 TA2830
Roose *Cumb* 86 SD2269
Roosebeck *Cumb* 86 SD2567
Roothams Green *Beds* 51 TL0957
Ropley *Hants* 24 SU6431
Ropley Dean *Hants* 24 SU6232
Ropley Soke *Hants* 24 SU6533
Ropsley *Lincs* 63 SK9933
Rora *Abers* 143 NK0650
Rorrington *Shrops* 59 SJ3000
Rosarie *Moray* 141 NJ3850
Roscroggan *Cnwll* 2 SW6542
Rose *Cnwll* 3 SW7754
Rose Ash *Devon* 19 SS7921
Rose Green *Essex* 40 TL9028
Rose Green *Suffk* 54 TL9337
Rose Green *Suffk* 54 TL9744
Rose Green *W Susx* 14 SZ9099
Rose Hill *E Susx* 16 TQ4516
Rose Hill *Lancs* 81 SD8231
Roseacre *Lancs* 80 SD4336
Rosebank *S Lans* 116 NS8049
Rosebush *Pembks* 31 SN0729
Rosecare *Cnwll* 4 SX1695
Rosecliston *Cnwll* 4 SW8159
Rosedale Abbey *N York* 90 SE7296
Roseden *Nthumb* 111 NU0321
Rosehall *Highld* 146 NC4702
Rosehearty *Abers* 143 NJ9267
Rosehill *Shrops* 59 SJ4715
Roseisle *Moray* 141 NJ1466
Roselands *E Susx* 16 TQ6200
Rosemarket *Pembks* 30 SM9508
Rosemarkie *Highld* 140 NH7357
Rosemary Lane *Devon* 9 ST1514
Rosemount *P & K* 126 NO1843
Rosenannon *Cnwll* 4 SW9566
Rosenithon *Cnwll* 3 SW8021
Roser's Cross *E Susx* 16 TQ5420
Rosevean *Cnwll* 4 SX0258
Rosevine *Cnwll* 3 SW8736
Rosewarne *Cnwll* 2 SW6036
Rosewell *Mdloth* 117 NT2862
Roseworth *Dur* 96 NZ4221
Roseworthy *Cnwll* 2 SW6139
Rosgill *Cumb* 94 NY5316
Roshven *Highld* 129 NM7078
Roskhill *Highld* 136 NG2744
Roskorwell *Cnwll* 3 SW7923
Roskrow *Cnwll* 3 SW7635
Rosley *Cumb* 93 NY3245
Roslin *Mdloth* 117 NT2763
Rosliston *Derbys* 73 SK2416
Rosneath *Ag & B* 114 NS2583
Ross *D & G* 99 NX6444
Ross *Nthumb* 111 NU1337
Ross-on-Wye *H & W* 46 SO5923
Rossett *Wrexhm* 71 SJ3657
Rossett Green *N York* 82 SE2952
Rossington *S York* 75 SK6298
Rosskeen *Highld* 146 NH6869
Rossland *Rens* 115 NS4370
Roster *Highld* 151 ND2639
Rostherne *Ches* 79 SJ7483
Rosthwaite *Cumb* 93 NY2514
Roston *Derbys* 73 SK1340
Rosudgeon *Cnwll* 2 SW5529
Rosyth *Fife* 117 NT1082
Rothbury *Nthumb* 103 NU0501
Rotherby *Leics* 63 SK6716
Rotherfield *E Susx* 16 TQ5529
Rotherfield Greys *Oxon* 37 SU7282
Rotherfield Peppard *Oxon* 37 SU7182
Rotherham *S York* 75 SK4392
Rothersthorpe *Nhants* 49 SP7156
Rotherwick *Hants* 24 SU7156
Rothes *Moray* 141 NJ2749
Rothesay *Ag & B* 114 NS0864
Rothiebrisbane *Abers* 142 NJ7437
Rothiemay *Moray* 142 NJ5548
Rothiemurchus Lodge *Highld* 133 NH9407
Rothienorman *Abers* 142 NJ7235
Rothley *Leics* 62 SK5812
Rothley *Nthumb* 103 NZ0488
Rothmaise *Abers* 142 NJ6832
Rothwell *Lincs* 76 TF1499
Rothwell *Nhants* 51 SP8181
Rothwell *W York* 83 SE3428
Rothwell Haigh *W York* 83 SE3328
Rotsea *E R Yk* 84 TA0651
Rottal Lodge *Angus* 134 NO3769
Rottingdean *E Susx* 15 TQ3602
Rottington *Cumb* 92 NX9613
Roucan *D & G* 100 NY0277
Roud *IOW* 13 SZ5180
Rough Close *Staffs* 72 SJ9239
Rough Common *Kent* 29 TR1259
Rougham *Norfk* 66 TF8320
Rougham Green *Suffk* 54 TL9061
Roughlee *Lancs* 81 SD8440
Roughley *W Mids* 61 SP1399
Roughpark *Abers* 134 NJ3412
Roughton *Lincs* 77 TF2464
Roughton *Norfk* 67 TG2136
Roughton *Shrops* 60 SO7594
Roughway *Kent* 27 TQ6153
Round Bush *Herts* 26 TQ1498
Round Green *Beds* 38 TL1022
Round Street *Kent* 28 TQ6568
Roundbush *Essex* 40 TL8501
Roundbush Green *Essex* 40 TL5814
Roundham *Somset* 10 ST4209
Roundhay *W York* 83 SE3337
Rounds Green *W Mids* 60 SO9889
Roundstreet Common *W Susx* 14 TQ0528
Roundway *Wilts* 22 SU0163
Roundyhill *Angus* 126 NO3750
Rous Lench *H & W* 47 SP0153
Rousdon *Devon* 10 SY2991
Rousham *Oxon* 49 SP4724
Rout's Green *Bucks* 37 SU7898
Routenbeck *Cumb* 93 NY1930
Routenburn *N Ayrs* 114 NS1961
Routh *E R Yk* 85 TA0942
Row *Cnwll* 4 SX0976
Row *Cumb* 94 NY6234
Row *Cumb* 87 SD4589
Row Ash *Hants* 13 SU5413
Row Green *Essex* 40 TL7420
Rowanburn *D & G* 101 NY4177
Rowardennan Hotel *Stirlg* 115 NS3698
Rowardennan Lodge *Stirlg* 115 NS3598
Rowarth *Derbys* 79 SK0189
Rowberrow *Somset* 21 ST4558
Rowborough *IOW* 13 SZ4684
Rowde *Wilts* 22 ST9762
Rowden *Devon* 8 SX6499
Rowen *A & C* 69 SH7671
Rowfield *Derbys* 73 SK1948
Rowfoot *Nthumb* 102 NY6860
Rowford *Somset* 20 ST2327
Rowhedge *Essex* 41 TM0221
Rowhook *W Susx* 14 TQ1234
Rowington *Warwks* 48 SP2069
Rowland *Derbys* 74 SK2172
Rowland's Castle *Hants* 13 SU7310
Rowland's Gill *T & W* 96 NZ1658
Rowledge *Surrey* 25 SU8243
Rowley *Dur* 95 NZ0848
Rowley *E R Yk* 84 SE9732
Rowley *Shrops* 59 SJ3006
Rowley Green *W Mids* 61 SP3483
Rowley Hill *W York* 82 SE1914
Rowley Regis *W Mids* 60 SO9787
Rowlstone *H & W* 46 SO3727
Rowly *Surrey* 14 TQ0440
Rowner *Hants* 13 SU5801
Rowney Green *H & W* 61 SP0471
Rownhams *Hants* 12 SU3817
Rowrah *Cumb* 92 NY0518
Rows of Trees *Ches* 79 SJ8379
Rowsham *Bucks* 38 SP8417
Rowsley *Derbys* 74 SK2565
Rowstock *Oxon* 37 SU4789
Rowston *Lincs* 76 TF0856
Rowthorne *Derbys* 75 SK4764
Rowton *Ches* 71 SJ4464
Rowton *Shrops* 59 SJ3612
Rowton *Shrops* 59 SJ6119
Rowton *Shrops* 59 SO4180
Rowtown *Surrey* 26 TQ0363
Roxburgh *Border* 110 NT6930
Roxby *Lincs* 84 SE9116
Roxby *N York* 97 NZ7616
Roxton *Beds* 52 TL1554
Roxwell *Essex* 40 TL6408
Roy Bridge *Highld* 131 NN2681
Royal Oak *Dur* 96 NZ2023
Royal Oak *Lancs* 78 SD4103
Royal's Green *Ches* 71 SJ6242
Roydhouse *W York* 82 SE2112
Roydon *Essex* 39 TL4010
Roydon *Norfk* 65 TF7023
Roydon *Norfk* 54 TM1080
Roydon Hamlet *Essex* 39 TL4107
Royston *Herts* 39 TL3540
Royston *S York* 83 SE3611
Royton *Gt Man* 79 SD9107
Rozel *Jersey* 152 JS0000
Ruabon *Wrexhm* 71 SJ3043
Ruaig *Ag & B* 120 NM0747
Ruan High Lanes *Cnwll* 3 SW9039
Ruan Lanihorne *Cnwll* 3 SW8942
Ruan Major *Cnwll* 2 SW7016
Ruan Minor *Cnwll* 2 SW7115
Ruardean *Gloucs* 35 SO6217
Ruardean Hill *Gloucs* 35 SO6317
Ruardean Woodside *Gloucs* 35 SO6216
Rubery *H & W* 60 SO9977
Ruckcroft *Cumb* 94 NY5344
Ruckhall *H & W* 46 SO4637
Ruckhall Common *H & W* 46 SO4539
Ruckinge *Kent* 17 TR0233
Ruckland *Lincs* 77 TF3378
Ruckley *Shrops* 59 SJ5300
Rudby *N York* 89 NZ4706
Rudchester *Nthumb* 103 NZ1167
Ruddington *Notts* 62 SK5732
Ruddle *Gloucs* 35 SO6811
Ruddlemoor *Cnwll* 3 SX0054
Rudford *Gloucs* 35 SO7721
Rudge *Somset* 22 ST8251
Rudgeway *Gloucs* 35 ST6386
Rudgwick *W Susx* 14 TQ0834
Rudhall *H & W* 47 SO6225
Rudheath *Ches* 79 SJ6772
Rudley Green *Essex* 40 TL8303
Rudloe *Wilts* 35 ST8470
Rudry *Caerph* 33 ST2086
Rudston *E R Yk* 91 TA0967
Rudyard *Staffs* 72 SJ9557
Ruecastle *Border* 110 NT6120
Rufford *Lancs* 80 SD4615
Rufforth *N York* 83 SE5251
Rug *Denbgs* 70 SJ0543
Rugby *Warwks* 50 SP5075
Rugeley *Staffs* 73 SK0418
Ruggaton *Devon* 19 SS5545
Ruishton *Somset* 20 ST2625
Ruislip *Gt Lon* 26 TQ0987
Ruletown Head *Border* 110 NT6113
Rumbach *Moray* 141 NJ3852
Rumbling Bridge *P & K* 117 NT0199
Rumburgh *Suffk* 55 TM3481
Rumby Hill *Dur* 96 NZ1634
Rumford *Cnwll* 4 SW8970
Rumford *Falk* 116 NS9377
Rumney *Cardif* 33 ST2178
Rumwell *Somset* 20 ST1923
Runcorn *Ches* 78 SJ5182
Runcton *W Susx* 14 SU8802
Runcton Holme *Norfk* 65 TF6109
Runfold *Surrey* 25 SU8647
Runhall *Norfk* 66 TG0507
Runham *Norfk* 67 TG4610
Runham *Norfk* 67 TG5108
Runnington *Somset* 20 ST1221
Runsell Green *Essex* 40 TL7905
Runshaw Moor *Lancs* 80 SD5319
Runswick *N York* 97 NZ8016
Runtaleave *Angus* 133 NO2867
Runwell *Essex* 40 TQ7594
Ruscombe *Berks* 37 SU7976
Rush Green *Ches* 79 SJ6987
Rush Green *Essex* 41 TM1515
Rush Green *Gt Lon* 27 TQ5187
Rush Green *Herts* 39 TL2123
Rush Green *Herts* 39 TL3325
Rushall *H & W* 47 SO6435
Rushall *Norfk* 55 TM1982
Rushall *W Mids* 60 SK0200
Rushall *Wilts* 23 SU1255
Rushbrooke *Suffk* 54 TL8961
Rushbury *Shrops* 59 SO5191
Rushden *Herts* 39 TL3031
Rushden *Nhants* 51 SP9566
Rushenden *Kent* 28 TQ9071
Rusher's Cross *E Susx* 16 TQ6028
Rushett Common *Surrey* 14 TQ0242
Rushford *Devon* 5 SX4576
Rushford *Norfk* 54 TL9281
Rushlake Green *E Susx* 16 TQ6218
Rushmere *Suffk* 55 TM4986
Rushmere St Andrew *Suffk* 55 TM1946
Rushmoor *Surrey* 25 SU8740
Rushock *H & W* 46 SO3058
Rushock *H & W* 60 SO8871
Rusholme *Gt Man* 79 SJ8594
Rushton *Ches* 71 SJ5863
Rushton *Nhants* 51 SP8482
Rushton *Shrops* 59 SJ6008
Rushton Spencer *Staffs* 72 SJ9362
Rushwick *H & W* 47 SO8254
Rushyford *Dur* 96 NZ2728
Ruskie *Stirlg* 116 NN6200
Ruskington *Lincs* 76 TF0851
Rusland *Cumb* 87 SD3488
Rusper *W Susx* 15 TQ2037
Ruspidge *Gloucs* 35 SO6611
Russ Hill *Surrey* 15 TQ2240
Russel's Green *Suffk* 55 TM2572
Russell Green *Essex* 40 TL7413
Russell's Green *E Susx* 16 TQ7011
Russell's Water *Oxon* 37 SU7089
Rusthall *Kent* 16 TQ5639
Rustington *W Susx* 14 TQ0402
Ruston *N York* 91 SE9583
Ruston Parva *E R Yk* 91 TA0661
Ruswarp *N York* 90 NZ8809
Ruthall *Shrops* 59 SO5990
Rutherford *Border* 110 NT6430
Rutherglen *S Lans* 116 NS6161
Ruthernbridge *Cnwll* 4 SX0166
Ruthin *Denbgs* 70 SJ1258
Ruthrieston *Aber C* 135 NJ9204
Ruthven *Abers* 142 NJ5046
Ruthven *Angus* 126 NO2848
Ruthven *Highld* 140 NH8132
Ruthven *Highld* 132 NN7699
Ruthven House *Angus* 126 NO3047
Ruthvoes *Cnwll* 4 SW9260
Ruthwaite *Cumb* 93 NY2336
Ruthwell *D & G* 100 NY0967
Ruxley Corner *Gt Lon* 27 TQ4770
Ruxton Green *H & W* 34 SO5419
Ruyton-XI-Towns *Shrops* 59 SJ3922
Ryal *Nthumb* 103 NZ0174
Ryall *Dorset* 10 SY4095
Ryall *H & W* 47 SO8640
Ryarsh *Kent* 28 TQ6660
Rycote *Oxon* 37 SP6705
Rydal *Cumb* 87 NY3606
Ryde *IOW* 13 SZ5992
Rye *E Susx* 17 TQ9220
Rye Cross *H & W* 47 SO7735
Rye Foreign *E Susx* 17 TQ8922
Rye Harbour *E Susx* 17 TQ9319
Rye Street *H & W* 47 SO7835
Ryebank *Shrops* 59 SJ5131
Ryeford *H & W* 35 SO6322
Ryehill *E R Yk* 85 TA2225
Ryeish Green *Nhants* 24 SU7267
Ryhall *Rutlnd* 64 TF0310
Ryhill *W York* 83 SE3814
Ryhope *T & W* 96 NZ4152
Rylah *Derbys* 75 SK4667
Ryland *Lincs* 76 TF0179
Rylands *Notts* 62 SK5335
Rylstone *N York* 88 SD9658
Ryme Intrinseca *Dorset* 10 ST5810
Ryther *N York* 83 SE5539
Ryton *N York* 90 SE7975
Ryton *Shrops* 60 SJ7602
Ryton *T & W* 103 NZ1564
Ryton *Warwks* 61 SP4086

Ryton Woodside
Scorborough

Ryton Woodside *T & W* 96 NZ1462
Ryton-on-Dunsmore *Warwks* 61 SP3874

S

Sabden *Lancs* 81 SD7837
Sabine's Green *Essex* 27 TQ5496
Sacombe *Herts* 39 TL3319
Sacombe Green *Herts* 39 TL3419
Sacriston *Dur* 96 NZ2447
Sadberge *Dur* 96 NZ3416
Saddell *Ag & B* 105 NR7832
Saddington *Leics* 50 SP6691
Saddle Bow *Norfk* 65 TF6015
Saddlescombe *W Susx* 15 TQ2711
Sadgill *Cumb* 87 NY4805
Saffron Walden *Essex* 39 TL5438
Sageston *Pembks* 30 SN0503
Saham Hills *Norfk* 66 TF9003
Saham Toney *Norfk* 66 TF8901
Saighton *Ches* 71 SJ4462
St Abbs *Border* 119 NT9167
St Agnes *Border* 118 NT6763
St Agnes *Cnwll* 2 SW7150
St Albans *Herts* 38 TL1407
St Allen *Cnwll* 3 SW8250
St Andrew *Guern* 152 GN0000
St Andrew's Major *V Glam* 33 ST1371
St Andrews *Fife* 127 NO5116
St Andrews Well *Dorset* 10 SY4793
St Ann's *D & G* 100 NY0793
St Ann's Chapel *Cnwll* 5 SX4170
St Ann's Chapel *Devon* 7 SX6647
St Anne's *Lancs* 80 SD3228
St Anthony *Cnwll* 3 SW7825
St Anthony's Hill *E Susx* 16 TQ6201
St Arvans *Mons* 34 ST5296
St Asaph *Denbgs* 70 SJ0374
St Athan *V Glam* 20 ST0167
St Aubin *Jersey* 152 JS0000
St Austell *Cnwll* 3 SX0152
St Bees *Cumb* 86 NX9711
St Blazey *Cnwll* 3 SX0654
St Blazey Gate *Cnwll* 3 SX0653
St Boswells *Border* 110 NT5930
St Brelade *Jersey* 152 JS0000
St Brelades Bay *Jersey* 152 JS0000
St Breock *Cnwll* 4 SW9771
St Breward *Cnwll* 4 SX0977
St Briavels *Gloucs* 34 SO5604
St Bride's Major *V Glam* 33 SS8974
St Brides *Pembks* 30 SM8010
St Brides Netherwent *Mons* 34 ST4289
St Brides super-Ely *Cardif* 33 ST0977
St Brides Wentlooge *Newpt* 34 ST2982
St Budeaux *Devon* 6 SX4558
St Buryan *Cnwll* 2 SW4025
St Catherine *Somset* 35 ST7769
St Catherines *Ag & B* 123 NN1207
St Chloe *Gloucs* 35 SO8401
St Clears *Carmth* 31 SN2816
St Cleer *Cnwll* 5 SX2468
St Clement *Cnwll* 3 SW8543
St Clement *Jersey* 152 JS0000
St Clether *Cnwll* 5 SX2084
St Colmac *Ag & B* 114 NS0467
St Columb Major *Cnwll* 4 SW9163
St Columb Minor *Cnwll* 4 SW8362
St Columb Road *Cnwll* 4 SW9159
St Combs *Abers* 143 NK0563
St Cross South Elmham *Suffk* 55 TM2984
St Cyrus *Abers* 135 NO7464
St David's *P & K* 125 NN9420
St Davids *Pembks* 30 SM7525
St Day *Cnwll* 3 SW7242
St Decumans *Somset* 20 ST0642
St Dennis *Cnwll* 4 SW9557
St Devereux *H & W* 46 SO4431
St Dogmaels *Cardgn* 42 SN1645
St Dogwells *Pembks* 30 SM9727
St Dominick *Cnwll* 5 SX4067
St Donats *V Glam* 20 SS9368
St Edith's Marsh *Wilts* 22 ST9764
St Endellion *Cnwll* 4 SW9978
St Enoder *Cnwll* 3 SW8956
St Erme *Cnwll* 3 SW8449
St Erney *Cnwll* 5 SX3759
St Erth *Cnwll* 2 SW5535
St Erth Praze *Cnwll* 2 SW5735
St Ervan *Cnwll* 4 SW8970
St Ewe *Cnwll* 3 SW9746
St Fagans *Cardif* 33 ST1277
St Fergus *Abers* 143 NK0952
St Fillans *P & K* 124 NN6924
St Florence *Pembks* 31 SN0801
St Gennys *Cnwll* 4 SX1497
St George *A & C* 70 SH9775
St George's *V Glam* 33 ST1076
St George's Hill *Surrey* 26 TQ0862
St Georges *Somset* 21 ST3762
St Germans *Cnwll* 5 SX3657
St Giles in the Wood *Devon* 19 SS5319
St Giles-on-the-Heath *Cnwll* 5 SX3690
St Harmon *Powys* 45 SN9872
St Helen Auckland *Dur* 96 NZ1826
St Helena *Norfk* 66 TG1816
St Helens *Cumb* 92 NY0232
St Helens *E Susx* 17 TQ8212
St Helens *IOW* 13 SZ6289
St Helens *Mersyd* 78 SJ5195
St Helier *Gt Lon* 27 TQ2567
St Helier *Jersey* 152 JS0000
St Hilary *Cnwll* 2 SW5431
St Hilary *V Glam* 33 ST0173
St Hill *Devon* 9 ST0908
St Hill *W Susx* 15 TQ3835
St Illtyd *Blae G* 34 SO2202
St Ippollitts *Herts* 39 TL1927
St Ishmaels *Pembks* 30 SM8307
St Issey *Cnwll* 4 SW9271
St Ive *Cnwll* 5 SX3167
St Ives *Cambs* 52 TL3171
St Ives *Cnwll* 2 SW5140
St Ives *Dorset* 12 SU1204
St James's End *Nhants* 49 SP7460
St James *Norfk* 67 TG2720
St James South Elmham *Suffk* 55 TM3281
St John *Cnwll* 5 SX4053
St John *Jersey* 152 JS0000
St John's *IOM* 153 SC2781
St John's Chapel *Devon* 19 SS5329
St John's Chapel *Dur* 95 NY8837
St John's Fen End *Norfk* 65 TF5312
St John's Highway *Norfk* 65 TF5214
St John's Kirk *S Lans* 108 NS9836
St John's Town of Dalry *D & G* 99 NX6281
St John's Wood *Gt Lon* 27 TQ2683
St Johns *Dur* 95 NZ0633
St Johns *H & W* 47 SO8454
St Johns *Kent* 27 TQ5356
St Johns *Surrey* 25 SU9857
St Jude's *IOM* 153 SC3996
St Just *Cnwll* 2 SW3731
St Just Lane *Cnwll* 3 SW8535
St Just-in-Roseland *Cnwll* 3 SW8435
St Katherines *Abers* 142 NJ7834
St Keverne *Cnwll* 3 SW7921
St Kew *Cnwll* 4 SX0276
St Kew Highway *Cnwll* 4 SX0375
St Keyne *Cnwll* 5 SX2461
St Laurence *Kent* 29 TR3665
St Lawrence *Cnwll* 4 SX0466
St Lawrence *Essex* 41 TL9604
St Lawrence *IOW* 13 SZ5376
St Lawrence *Jersey* 152 JS0000
St Leonard's Street *Kent* 28 TQ6756
St Leonards *Bucks* 38 SP9007
St Leonards *Dorset* 12 SU1103
St Leonards *E Susx* 17 TQ8009
St Levan *Cnwll* 2 SW3822
St Lythans *V Glam* 33 ST1072
St Mabyn *Cnwll* 4 SX0473
St Madoes *P & K* 126 NO1921
St Margaret South Elmham *Suffk* 55 TM3183
St Margaret's at Cliffe *Kent* 29 TR3544
St Margarets *H & W* 46 SO3533
St Margarets *Herts* 39 TL3811
St Margarets Hope *Ork* 155 ND4493
St Marks *IOM* 153 SC2974
St Martin *Cnwll* 5 SX2555
St Martin *Guern* 152 GN0000
St Martin *Jersey* 152 JS0000
St Martin's *P & K* 126 NO1530
St Martin's Green *Cnwll* 3 SW7323
St Martin's Moor *Shrops* 59 SJ3135
St Martins *Shrops* 59 SJ3236
St Mary *Jersey* 152 JS0000
St Mary Bourne *Hants* 24 SU4250
St Mary Church *V Glam* 33 ST0071
St Mary Cray *Gt Lon* 27 TQ4768
St Mary Hill *V Glam* 33 SS9678
St Mary in the Marsh *Kent* 17 TR0627
St Mary's *Ork* 155 HY4701
St Mary's Bay *Kent* 17 TR0827
St Mary's Grove *Somset* 21 ST4669
St Mary's Hoo *Kent* 28 TQ8076
St Marychurch *Devon* 7 SX9166
St Maughans *Mons* 34 SO4617
St Maughans Green *Mons* 34 SO4717
St Mawes *Cnwll* 3 SW8433
St Mawgan *Cnwll* 4 SW8765
St Mellion *Cnwll* 5 SX3965
St Mellons *Cardif* 34 ST2281
St Merryn *Cnwll* 4 SW8874
St Mewan *Cnwll* 3 SW9951
St Michael Caerhays *Cnwll* 3 SW9642
St Michael Church *Somset* 20 ST3030
St Michael Penkevil *Cnwll* 3 SW8541
St Michael South Elmham *Suffk* 55 TM3483
St Michael's on Wyre *Lancs* 80 SD4641
St Michaels *H & W* 46 SO5865
St Michaels *Kent* 17 TQ8835
St Minver *Cnwll* 4 SW9677
St Monans *Fife* 127 NO5201
St Neot *Cnwll* 4 SX1868
St Neots *Cambs* 52 TL1860
St Newlyn East *Cnwll* 3 SW8256
St Nicholas *Pembks* 30 SM9035
St Nicholas *V Glam* 33 ST0974
St Nicholas at Wade *Kent* 29 TR2666
St Ninians *Stirlg* 116 NS7991
St Olaves *Norfk* 67 TM4599
St Osyth *Essex* 41 TM1215
St Ouen *Jersey* 152 JS0000
St Owens Cross *H & W* 46 SO5324
St Paul's Walden *Herts* 39 TL1922
St Pauls Cray *Gt Lon* 27 TQ4768
St Peter *Jersey* 152 JS0000
St Peter Port *Guern* 152 GN0000
St Peter's *Guern* 152 GN0000
St Peter's *Kent* 29 TR3868
St Peter's Hill *Cambs* 52 TL2372
St Petrox *Pembks* 30 SR9797
St Pinnock *Cnwll* 5 SX2063
St Quivox *S Ayrs* 106 NS3723
St Ruan *Cnwll* 2 SW7115
St Sampson *Guern* 152 GN0000
St Saviour *Guern* 152 GN0000
St Saviour *Jersey* 152 JS0000
St Stephen *Cnwll* 3 SW9453
St Stephen's Coombe *Cnwll* 3 SW9451
St Stephens *Cnwll* 5 SX3285
St Stephens *Cnwll* 5 SX4158
St Teath *Cnwll* 4 SX0680
St Tudy *Cnwll* 4 SX0676
St Twynnells *Pembks* 30 SR9597
St Veep *Cnwll* 3 SX1455
St Vigeans *Angus* 127 NO6443
St Wenn *Cnwll* 4 SW9664
St Weonards *H & W* 46 SO4924
Saintbury *Gloucs* 48 SP1139
Salachail *Ag & B* 123 NN0551
Salcombe *Devon* 7 SX7439
Salcombe Regis *Devon* 9 SY1588
Salcott *Essex* 40 TL9413
Sale *Gt Man* 79 SJ7991
Sale Green *H & W* 47 SO9358
Saleby *Lincs* 77 TF4578
Salehurst *E Susx* 17 TQ7524
Salem *Cardgn* 43 SN6684
Salem *Carmth* 44 SN6226
Salem *Gwynd* 69 SH5456
Salen *Ag & B* 121 NM5743
Salen *Highld* 121 NM6864
Salesbury *Lancs* 81 SD6832
Salford *Beds* 38 SP9339
Salford *Gt Man* 79 SJ8197
Salford *Oxon* 48 SP2828
Salford Priors *Warwks* 48 SP0751
Salfords *Surrey* 15 TQ2846
Salhouse *Norfk* 67 TG3114
Saline *Fife* 117 NT0292
Salisbury *Wilts* 23 SU1429
Salkeld Dykes *Cumb* 94 NY5437
Salle *Norfk* 66 TG1024
Salmonby *Lincs* 77 TF3273
Salperton *Gloucs* 36 SP0720
Salph End *Beds* 38 TL0852
Salsburgh *N Lans* 116 NS8262
Salt *Staffs* 72 SJ9527
Salt Cotes *Cumb* 93 NY1853
Salta *Cumb* 92 NY0845
Saltaire *W York* 82 SE1438
Saltash *Cnwll* 6 SX4258
Saltburn *Highld* 146 NH7270
Saltburn-by-the-Sea *N York* 97 NZ6621
Saltby *Leics* 63 SK8526
Saltcoats *Cumb* 86 SD0797
Saltcoats *N Ayrs* 106 NS2441
Saltcotes *Lancs* 80 SD3728
Saltdean *E Susx* 15 TQ3802
Salterbeck *Cumb* 92 NX9926
Salterforth *Lancs* 81 SD8845
Salterswall *Ches* 71 SJ6266
Salterton *Wilts* 23 SU1236
Saltfleet *Lincs* 77 TF4593
Saltfleetby All Saints *Lincs* 77 TF4590
Saltfleetby St Clements *Lincs* 77 TF4691
Saltfleetby St Peter *Lincs* 77 TF4489
Saltford *Somset* 22 ST6867
Salthouse *Norfk* 66 TG0743
Saltley *W Mids* 61 SP1088
Saltmarsh *Newpt* 34 ST3482
Saltmarshe *E R Yk* 84 SE7824
Saltney *Flints* 71 SJ3865
Salton *N York* 90 SE7179
Saltrens *Devon* 18 SS4522
Saltwick *Nthumb* 103 NZ1780
Saltwood *Kent* 29 TR1535
Salvington *W Susx* 14 TQ1205
Salwarpe *H & W* 47 SO8762
Salwayash *Dorset* 10 SY4596
Sambourne *Warwks* 48 SP0662
Sambrook *Shrops* 72 SJ7124
Samlesbury *Lancs* 81 SD5930
Samlesbury Bottoms *Lancs* 81 SD6228
Sampford Arundel *Somset* 20 ST1118
Sampford Brett *Somset* 20 ST0741
Sampford Courtenay *Devon* 8 SS6301
Sampford Moor *Somset* 20 ST1118
Sampford Peverell *Devon* 9 ST0314
Sampford Spiney *Devon* 6 SX5372
Samson's Corner *Essex* 41 TM0818
Samsonlane *Ork* 155 HY6526
Samuelston *E Loth* 118 NT4870
Sanaigmore *Ag & B* 112 NR2370
Sancreed *Cnwll* 2 SW4129
Sancton *E R Yk* 84 SE8939
Sand *Somset* 21 ST4346
Sand Cross *E Susx* 16 TQ5820
Sand Hills *W York* 83 SE3739
Sand Hole *E R Yk* 84 SE8137
Sand Hutton *N York* 90 SE6958
Sand Side *Cumb* 86 SD2282
Sandaig *Highld* 129 NG7102
Sandal Magna *W York* 83 SE3417
Sandale *Cumb* 93 NY2440
Sandavore *Highld* 128 NM4785
Sandbach *Ches* 72 SJ7560
Sandbank *Ag & B* 114 NS1680
Sandbanks *Dorset* 12 SZ0487
Sandend *Abers* 142 NJ5566
Sanderstead *Gt Lon* 27 TQ3461
Sandford *Cumb* 94 NY7316
Sandford *Devon* 8 SS8202
Sandford *Dorset* 11 SY9289
Sandford *Hants* 12 SU1601
Sandford *IOW* 13 SZ5381
Sandford *S Lans* 107 NS7143
Sandford *Shrops* 59 SJ3423
Sandford *Shrops* 59 SJ5833
Sandford *Somset* 21 ST4259
Sandford Orcas *Dorset* 21 ST6220
Sandford St Martin *Oxon* 49 SP4226
Sandford-on-Thames *Oxon* 37 SP5301
Sandgate *Kent* 29 TR2035
Sandhaven *Abers* 143 NJ9667
Sandhead *D & G* 98 NX0949
Sandhill *S York* 75 SK4496
Sandhills *Dorset* 10 ST5800
Sandhills *Dorset* 11 ST6810
Sandhills *Oxon* 37 SP5507
Sandhills *Surrey* 14 SU9337
Sandhills *W Mids* 61 SK0604
Sandhoe *Nthumb* 102 NY9666
Sandhole *Ag & B* 114 NS0098
Sandholme *Lincs* 64 TF3337
Sandholme *E R Yk* 84 SE8230
Sandhurst *Berks* 25 SU8361
Sandhurst *Gloucs* 47 SO8223
Sandhurst *Kent* 17 TQ8028
Sandhurst Cross *Kent* 17 TQ7827
Sandhutton *N York* 89 SE3881
Sandiacre *Derbys* 62 SK4736
Sandilands *Lincs* 77 TF5280
Sandiway *Ches* 71 SJ6070
Sandleheath *Hants* 12 SU1215
Sandleigh *Oxon* 37 SP4701
Sandley *Dorset* 22 ST7724
Sandling *Kent* 28 TQ7557
Sandlow Green *Ches* 72 SJ7865
Sandness *Shet* 155 HU1957
Sandon *Essex* 40 TL7404
Sandon *Herts* 39 TL3234
Sandon *Staffs* 72 SJ9429
Sandon Bank *Staffs* 72 SJ9428
Sandown *IOW* 13 SZ5984
Sandplace *Cnwll* 5 SX2557
Sandridge *Herts* 39 TL1710
Sandridge *Wilts* 22 ST9465
Sandringham *Norfk* 65 TF6928
Sands *Bucks* 26 SU8493
Sandsend *N York* 90 NZ8612
Sandside *Cumb* 87 SD4780
Sandtoft *Lincs* 84 SE7408
Sandway *Kent* 28 TQ8950
Sandwich *Kent* 29 TR3358
Sandwick *Cumb* 93 NY4219
Sandwick *Shet* 155 HU4323
Sandwick *W Isls* 154 NB4432
Sandwith *Cumb* 92 NX9614
Sandwith Newtown *Cumb* 92 NX9614
Sandy *Beds* 52 TL1649
Sandy Bank *Lincs* 77 TF2655
Sandy Cross *H & W* 47 SO6757
Sandy Haven *Pembks* 30 SM8507
Sandy Lane *W York* 82 SE1135
Sandy Lane *Wilts* 22 ST9668
Sandy Lane *Wrexhm* 71 SJ4040
Sandy Park *Devon* 8 SX7189
Sandycroft *Flints* 71 SJ3366
Sandyford *D & G* 101 NY2093
Sandygate *Devon* 7 SX8674
Sandygate *IOM* 153 SC3797
Sandyhills *D & G* 92 NX8855
Sandylands *Lancs* 87 SD4263
Sandylane *Staffs* 72 SJ7035
Sandylane *Swans* 32 SS5589
Sandyway *H & W* 46 SO4925
Sangobeg *Highld* 149 NC4266
Sangomore *Highld* 149 NC4067
Sankey Bridges *Ches* 78 SJ5887
Sankyn's Green *H & W* 47 SO7965
Sanna Bay *Highld* 128 NM4469
Sanndabhaig *W Isls* 154 NB4432
Sannox *N Ayrs* 105 NS0145
Sanquhar *D & G* 107 NS7809
Santon *Cumb* 86 NY1001
Santon *IOM* 153 SC3273
Santon Bridge *Cumb* 86 NY1101
Santon Downham *Suffk* 54 TL8187
Sapcote *Leics* 50 SP4893
Sapey Common *H & W* 47 SO7064
Sapiston *Suffk* 54 TL9175
Sapley *Cambs* 52 TL2474
Sapperton *Derbys* 73 SK1834
Sapperton *Gloucs* 35 SO9403
Sapperton *Lincs* 64 TF0133
Saracen's Head *Lincs* 64 TF3427
Sarclet *Highld* 151 ND3443
Sarisbury *Hants* 13 SU5008
Sarn *Brdgnd* 33 SS9083
Sarn *Gwynd* 56 SH2432
Sarn *Powys* 58 SN9597
Sarn *Powys* 58 SO2090
Sarn-bach *Gwynd* 56 SH3026
Sarn-wen *Powys* 58 SJ2718
Sarnau *Cardgn* 42 SN3150
Sarnau *Carmth* 31 SN3318
Sarnau *Gwynd* 70 SH9639
Sarnau *Powys* 58 SJ2315
Sarnau *Powys* 45 SO0232
Sarnesfield *H & W* 46 SO3750
Saron *Carmth* 31 SN3737
Saron *Carmth* 32 SN6012
Saron *Gwynd* 69 SH5365
Saron *Gwynd* 68 SH4658
Sarratt *Herts* 26 TQ0499
Sarre *Kent* 29 TR2565
Sarsden *Oxon* 36 SP2822
Sarson *Hants* 23 SU3044
Satley *Dur* 95 NZ1143
Satmar *Kent* 29 TR2539
Satron *N York* 88 SD9397
Satterleigh *Devon* 19 SS6622
Satterthwaite *Cumb* 86 SD3392
Satwell *Oxon* 37 SU7083
Sauchen *Abers* 135 NJ7011
Saucher *P & K* 126 NO1933
Sauchieburn *Abers* 135 NO6669
Saul *Gloucs* 35 SO7409
Saundby *Notts* 75 SK7888
Saundersfoot *Pembks* 31 SN1304
Saunderton *Bucks* 37 SP7901
Saunton *Devon* 18 SS4637
Sausthorpe *Lincs* 77 TF3868
Saveock Water *Cnwll* 3 SW7645
Saverley Green *Staffs* 72 SJ9638
Savile Town *W York* 82 SE2420
Sawbridge *Warwks* 50 SP5065
Sawbridgeworth *Herts* 39 TL4814
Sawdon *N York* 91 SE9485
Sawley *Derbys* 62 SK4631
Sawley *Lancs* 81 SD7746
Sawley *N York* 89 SE2467
Sawston *Cambs* 53 TL4849
Sawtry *Cambs* 52 TL1683
Saxby *Leics* 63 SK8219
Saxby *Lincs* 76 TF0086
Saxby All Saints *Lincs* 84 SE9816
Saxelbye *Leics* 63 SK6921
Saxham Street *Suffk* 54 TM0861
Saxilby *Lincs* 76 SK8975
Saxlingham *Norfk* 66 TG0239
Saxlingham Green *Norfk* 67 TM2396
Saxlingham Nethergate *Norfk* 67 TM2297
Saxlingham Thorpe *Norfk* 67 TM2197
Saxmundham *Suffk* 55 TM3863
Saxon Street *Cambs* 53 TL6759
Saxondale *Notts* 63 SK6839
Saxtead *Suffk* 55 TM2665
Saxtead Green *Suffk* 55 TM2564
Saxtead Little Green *Suffk* 55 TM2466
Saxthorpe *Norfk* 66 TG1130
Saxton *N York* 83 SE4736
Sayers Common *W Susx* 15 TQ2618
Scackleton *N York* 90 SE6472
Scaftworth *Notts* 75 SK6691
Scagglethorpe *N York* 90 SE8372
Scalasaig *Ag & B* 112 NR3993
Scalby *E R Yk* 84 SE8429
Scalby *N York* 91 TA0090
Scald End *Beds* 51 TL0457
Scaldwell *Nhants* 50 SP7672
Scale Houses *Cumb* 94 NY5845
Scaleby *Cumb* 101 NY4463
Scalebyhill *Cumb* 101 NY4463
Scales *Cumb* 93 NY3426
Scales *Cumb* 86 SD2772
Scales *Lancs* 80 SD4531
Scalesceugh *Cumb* 93 NY4449
Scalford *Leics* 63 SK7624
Scaling *N York* 90 NZ7413
Scaling Dam *N York* 90 NZ7412
Scalloway *Shet* 155 HU4039
Scamblesby *Lincs* 77 TF2778
Scammonden *W York* 82 SE0515
Scamodale *Highld* 129 NM8373
Scampston *N York* 90 SE8575
Scampton *Lincs* 76 SK9579
Scaniport *Highld* 140 NH6239
Scapegoat Hill *W York* 82 SE0916
Scarborough *N York* 91 TA0488
Scarcewater *Cnwll* 3 SW9154
Scarcliffe *Derbys* 75 SK4968
Scarcroft *W York* 83 SE3541
Scarcroft Hill *W York* 83 SE3741
Scarfskerry *Highld* 151 ND2674
Scargill *Dur* 88 NZ0510
Scarinish *Ag & B* 120 NM0444
Scarisbrick *Lancs* 80 SD3713
Scarness *Cumb* 93 NY2230
Scarning *Norfk* 66 TF9512
Scarrington *Notts* 63 SK7341
Scarth Hill *Lancs* 78 SD4206
Scarthingwell *N York* 83 SE4937
Scartho *Lincs* 85 TA2606
Scawby *Lincs* 84 SE9605
Scawsby *S York* 83 SE5404
Scawthorpe *S York* 83 SE5506
Scawton *N York* 90 SE5483
Scayne's Hill *W Susx* 15 TQ3623
Scethrog *Powys* 45 SO1025
Scholar Green *Staffs* 56 SJ8356
Scholar Green *Staffs* 72 SJ8357
Scholes *Gt Man* 78 SD5905
Scholes *S York* 74 SK3895
Scholes *W York* 82 SE1507
Scholes *W York* 82 SE1625
Scholes *W York* 83 SE3736
Scholey Hill *W York* 83 SE3825
School Aycliffe *Dur* 96 NZ2523
School Green *Ches* 72 SJ6464
School Green *W York* 82 SE1132
School House *Dorset* 10 ST3602
Schoolgreen *Berks* 24 SU7367
Scissett *W York* 82 SE2410
Scleddau *Pembks* 30 SM9434
Sco Ruston *Norfk* 67 TG2821
Scofton *Notts* 75 SK6280
Scole *Norfk* 54 TM1579
Sconser *Highld* 137 NG5132
Scoonie *Fife* 126 NO3801
Scopwick *Lincs* 76 TF0757
Scoraig *Highld* 144 NH0096
Scorborough *E R Yk* 84 TA0145

Scorrier
Shudy Camps

Scorrier Cnwll 3 SW7244
Scorriton Devon 7 SX7068
Scorton Lancs 80 SD5048
Scorton N York 89 NZ2500
Scot Hay Staffs 72 SJ7947
Scot Lane End Gt Man 79 SD6209
Scot's Gap Nthumb 103 NZ0386
Scotby Cumb 93 NY4455
Scotch Corner N York 89 NZ2105
Scotforth Lancs 87 SD4859
Scothern Lincs 76 TF0377
Scotland Lincs 63 TF0030
Scotland W York 82 SE2340
Scotland Gate T & W 103 NZ2584
Scotlandwell P & K 126 NO1801
Scotscalder Station Highld 151 ND0956
Scotsdike Cumb 101 NY3872
Scotsmill Abers 142 NJ5618
Scotstoun C Glas 115 NS5267
Scotswood T & W 103 NZ2063
Scotter Lincs 76 SE8800
Scotterthorpe Lincs 84 SE8701
Scottlethorpe Lincs 64 TF0520
Scotton Lincs 76 SK8899
Scotton N York 89 SE1895
Scotton N York 89 SE3259
Scottow Norfk 67 TG2823
Scoulton Norfk 66 TF9800
Scounslow Green Staffs 73 SK0929
Scourie Highld 148 NC1544
Scouriemore Highld 148 NC1443
Scousburgh Shet 155 HU3717
Scouthead Gt Man 79 SD9605
Scrabster Highld 151 ND1070
Scraesburgh Border 110 NT6718
Scrafield Lincs 77 TF3068
Scrainwood Nthumb 111 NT9808
Scrane End Lincs 64 TF3841
Scraptoft Leics 63 SK6405
Scratby Norfk 67 TG5015
Scrayingham N York 90 SE7359
Scrays E Susx 17 TQ7619
Scredington Lincs 64 TF0940
Screel D & G 92 NX8053
Scremby Lincs 77 TF4467
Scremerston Nthumb 111 NU0049
Screveton Notts 63 SK7343
Scrivelsby Lincs 77 TF2766
Scriven N York 89 SE3458
Scrooby Notts 75 SK6590
Scropton Derbys 73 SK1930
Scrub Hill Lincs 76 TF2355
Scruschloch Angus 133 NO2357
Scruton N York 89 SE2992
Scuggate Cumb 101 NY4474
Sculthorpe Norfk 66 TF8930
Scunthorpe Lincs 84 SE8910
Scurlage Swans 32 SS4687
Sea Somset 10 ST3412
Sea Palling Norfk 67 TG4226
Seaborough Dorset 10 ST4206
Seabridge Staffs 72 SJ8343
Seabrook Kent 29 TR1835
Seaburn T & W 96 NZ4059
Seacombe Mersyd 78 SJ3290
Seacroft Lincs 77 TF5661
Seacroft W York 83 SE3635
Seadyke Lincs 64 TF3236
Seafield Highld 136 NG4743
Seafield W Loth 117 NT0066
Seaford E Susx 16 TV4899
Seaforth Mersyd 78 SJ3297
Seagrave Leics 62 SK6117
Seagry Heath Wilts 35 ST9581
Seaham Dur 96 NZ4149
Seahouses Nthumb 111 NU2231
Seal Kent 27 TQ5556
Seal Sands Dur 97 NZ5324
Seale Surrey 25 SU8947
Seamer N York 90 NZ4910
Seamer N York 91 TA0183
Seamill N Ayrs 114 NS2047
Searby Lincs 85 TA0705
Seasalter Kent 29 TR0864
Seascale Cumb 86 NY0301
Seathwaite Cumb 93 NY2312
Seathwaite Cumb 86 SD2295
Seatle Cumb 87 SD3783
Seatoller Cumb 93 NY2413
Seaton Cnwll 5 SX3054
Seaton Cumb 92 NY0130
Seaton Devon 9 SY2490
Seaton Dur 96 NZ3949
Seaton E R Yk 85 TA1646
Seaton Kent 29 TR2258
Seaton Nthumb 103 NZ3276
Seaton Rutlnd 51 SP9098
Seaton Burn T & W 103 NZ2373
Seaton Carew Dur 97 NZ5229
Seaton Delaval Nthumb 103 NZ3075
Seaton Ross E R Yk 84 SE7840
Seaton Sluice Nthumb 103 NZ3376
Seatown Dorset 10 SY4291
Seave Green N York 90 NZ5500
Seaview IOW 13 SZ6291
Seaville Cumb 92 NY1553
Seavington St Mary Somset 10 ST4014
Seavington St Michael Somset 10 ST4015
Sebastopol Torfn 34 ST2998
Sebergham Cumb 93 NY3641
Seckington Warwks 61 SK2507
Sedbergh Cumb 87 SD6591
Sedbury Gloucs 34 ST5493
Sedbusk N York 88 SD8891
Sedge Fen Suffk 53 TL6684
Sedgeberrow H & W 48 SP0238
Sedgebrook Lincs 63 SK8537
Sedgefield Dur 96 NZ3528
Sedgeford Norfk 65 TF7036
Sedgehill Wilts 22 ST8627
Sedgley W Mids 60 SO9193
Sedgley Park Gt Man 79 SD8202
Sedgwick Cumb 87 SD5186
Sedlescombe E Susx 17 TQ7818
Sedrup Bucks 38 SP8011
Seed Kent 28 TQ9456
Seend Wilts 22 ST9460
Seend Cleeve Wilts 22 ST9360
Seer Green Bucks 26 SU9692
Seething Norfk 67 TM3197
Sefton Mersyd 78 SD3501
Sefton Town Mersyd 78 SD3400
Seghill Nthumb 103 NZ2874
Seighford Staffs 72 SJ8825
Seion Gwynd 69 SH5466
Seisdon Staffs 60 SO8495
Selattyn Shrops 58 SJ2633
Selborne Hants 24 SU7433
Selby N York 83 SE6132
Selham W Susx 14 SU9320
Selhurst Gt Lon 27 TQ3267
Selkirk Border 109 NT4728
Sellack H & W 46 SO5627
Sellafirth Shet 155 HU5198
Sellan Cnwll 2 SW4230
Sellick's Green Somset 20 ST2119
Sellindge Kent 29 TR0938
Selling Kent 28 TR0456
Sells Green Wilts 22 ST9462
Selly Oak W Mids 61 SP0482
Selmeston E Susx 16 TQ5007
Selsdon Gt Lon 27 TQ3562
Selsey W Susx 14 SZ8593
Selsfield Common W Susx 15 TQ3434
Selside Cumb 87 SD5399
Selside N York 88 SD7875
Selsted Kent 29 TR2144
Selston Notts 75 SK4553
Selworthy Somset 20 SS9246
Semer Suffk 54 TL9946
Semington Wilts 22 ST8960
Semley Wilts 22 ST8926
Send Surrey 26 TQ0155
Send Marsh Surrey 26 TQ0355
Senghenydd Caerph 33 ST1190
Sennen Cnwll 2 SW3525
Sennen Cove Cnwll 2 SW3526
Sennybridge Powys 45 SN9228
Serlby Notts 75 SK6389
Sessay N York 89 SE4575
Setchey Norfk 65 TF6313
Setley Hants 12 SU3000
Seton Mains E Loth 118 NT4275
Settle N York 88 SD8163
Settlingstones Nthumb 102 NY8468
Settrington N York 90 SE8370
Seven Ash Somset 20 ST1533
Seven Kings Gt Lon 27 TQ4587
Seven Sisters Neath 33 SN8208
Seven Springs Gloucs 35 SO9617
Seven Star Green Essex 40 TL9325
Seven Wells Gloucs 48 SP1134
Sevenhampton Gloucs 36 SP0321
Sevenhampton Wilts 36 SU2090
Sevenoaks Kent 27 TQ5255
Sevenoaks Weald Kent 27 TQ5250
Severn Beach Gloucs 34 ST5484
Severn Stoke H & W 47 SO8644
Sevick End Beds 51 TL0954
Sevington Kent 28 TR0340
Sewards End Essex 53 TL5738
Sewardstonebury Gt Lon 27 TQ3995
Sewell Beds 38 SP9922
Sewerby E R Yk 91 TA1968
Seworgan Cnwll 2 SW7030
Sewstern Leics 63 SK8821
Sexhow N York 89 NZ4706
Sezincote Gloucs 48 SP1731
Sgiogarstaigh W Isls 154 NB5461
Shabbington Bucks 37 SP6606
Shackerstone Leics 62 SK3706
Shacklecross Derbys 62 SK4234
Shackleford Surrey 25 SU9345
Shade W York 81 SD9323
Shader W Isls 154 NB3854
Shadforth Dur 96 NZ3440
Shadingfield Suffk 55 TM4384
Shadoxhurst Kent 28 TQ9737
Shadwell Norfk 54 TL9383
Shadwell W York 83 SE3439
Shaftenhoe End Herts 39 TL4037
Shaftesbury Dorset 22 ST8623
Shaftholme S York 83 SE5708
Shafton S York 83 SE3911
Shafton Two Gates S York 83 SE3910
Shalbourne Wilts 23 SU3163
Shalcombe IOW 13 SZ3985
Shalden Hants 24 SU6941
Shalden Green Hants 24 SU7043
Shaldon Devon 7 SX9372
Shalfleet IOW 13 SZ4189
Shalford Essex 40 TL7229
Shalford Surrey 25 TQ0047
Shalford Green Essex 40 TL7127
Shallowford Staffs 72 SJ8729
Shalmsford Street Kent 29 TR0954
Shalstone Bucks 49 SP6436
Shamley Green Surrey 14 TQ0343
Shandford Angus 134 NO4962
Shandon Ag & B 114 NS2586
Shandwick Highld 147 NH8575
Shangton Leics 50 SP7196
Shankhouse Nthumb 103 NZ2778
Shanklin IOW 13 SZ5881
Shap Cumb 94 NY5615
Shapwick Dorset 11 ST9301
Shapwick Somset 21 ST4138
Shard End W Mids 61 SP1588
Shardlow Derbys 62 SK4330
Shareshill Staffs 60 SJ9406
Sharlston W York 83 SE3918
Sharlston Common W York 83 SE3919
Sharman's Cross W Mids 61 SP1279
Sharnal Street Kent 28 TQ7974
Sharnbrook Beds 51 SP9959
Sharneyford Lancs 81 SD8824
Sharnford Leics 50 SP4891
Sharnhill Green Dorset 11 ST7105
Sharoe Green Lancs 80 SD5333
Sharow N York 89 SE3371
Sharp Green Norfk 67 TG3820
Sharpenhoe Beds 38 TL0630
Sharperton Nthumb 102 NT9503
Sharpness Gloucs 35 SO6702
Sharpthorne W Susx 15 TQ3732
Sharptor Cnwll 5 SX2573
Sharpway Gate H & W 47 SO9565
Sharrington Norfk 66 TG0337
Shatterford H & W 60 SO7981
Shatterling Kent 29 TR2658
Shaugh Prior Devon 6 SX5463
Shave Cross Dorset 10 SY4198
Shavington Ches 72 SJ6951
Shaw Berks 24 SU4768
Shaw Gt Man 79 SD9308
Shaw W York 82 SE0235
Shaw Wilts 22 ST8965
Shaw Wilts 36 SU1185
Shaw Common Gloucs 47 SO6826
Shaw Green Herts 39 TL3032
Shaw Green Lancs 80 SD5218
Shaw Green N York 82 SE2652
Shaw Hill Lancs 81 SD5720
Shaw Mills N York 89 SE2562
Shawbost W Isls 154 NB2646
Shawbury Shrops 59 SJ5521
Shawclough Gt Man 81 SD8914
Shawdon Hill Nthumb 111 NU0813
Shawell Leics 50 SP5480
Shawford Hants 13 SU4625
Shawforth Lancs 81 SD8920
Shawhead D & G 100 NX8675
Shawsburn S Lans 116 NS7750
Shear Cross Wilts 22 ST8642
Shearington D & G 100 NY0266
Shearsby Leics 50 SP6290
Shearston Somset 20 ST2830
Shebbear Devon 18 SS4409
Shebdon Staffs 72 SJ7625
Shebster Highld 150 ND0164
Sheddens E Rens 115 NS5757
Shedfield Hants 13 SU5613
Sheen Derbys 74 SK1161
Sheep Hill Dur 96 NZ1757
Sheep-ridge W York 82 SE1519
Sheepbridge Derbys 74 SK3674
Sheepscar W York 82 SE3134
Sheepscombe Gloucs 35 SO8910
Sheepstor Devon 6 SX5667
Sheepwash Devon 18 SS4806
Sheepwash Nthumb 103 NZ2585
Sheepway Somset 34 ST4976
Sheepy Magna Leics 61 SK3201
Sheepy Parva Leics 62 SK3301
Sheering Essex 39 TL5014
Sheerness Kent 28 TQ9174
Sheerwater Surrey 26 TQ0461
Sheet Hants 13 SU7524
Sheffield Cnwll 2 SW4526
Sheffield S York 74 SK3587
Sheffield Bottom Berks 24 SU6469
Sheffield Green E Susx 15 TQ4125
Shefford Beds 38 TL1439
Shegra Highld 148 NC1860
Sheinton Shrops 59 SJ6003
Shelderton Shrops 46 SO4077
Sheldon Derbys 74 SK1768
Sheldon Devon 9 ST1208
Sheldon W Mids 61 SP1584
Sheldwich Kent 28 TR0156
Sheldwich Lees Kent 28 TR0156
Shelf W York 82 SE1228
Shelfanger Norfk 54 TM1083
Shelfield W Mids 61 SK0302
Shelfield Warwks 48 SP1263
Shelfield Green Warwks 48 SP1261
Shelford Notts 63 SK6642
Shelford Warwks 50 SP4288
Shellacres Border 110 NT8943
Shelley Essex 39 TL5505
Shelley Suffk 54 TM0238
Shelley W York 82 SE2011
Shelley Far Bank W York 82 SE2010
Shellingford Oxon 36 SU3193
Shellow Bowells Essex 40 TL6007
Shelsley Beauchamp H & W 47 SO7363
Shelsley Walsh H & W 47 SO7263
Shelton Beds 51 TL0368
Shelton Norfk 67 TM2291
Shelton Notts 63 SK7844
Shelton Shrops 59 SJ4613
Shelton Green Norfk 55 TM2390
Shelton Lock Derbys 62 SK3730
Shelton Under Harley Staffs 72 SJ8139
Shelve Shrops 59 SO3399
Shelwick H & W 46 SO5242
Shenfield Essex 40 TQ6095
Shenington Oxon 48 SP3742
Shenley Herts 26 TL1800
Shenley Brook End Bucks 38 SP8335
Shenley Church End Bucks 38 SP8336
Shenleybury Herts 26 TL1801
Shenmore H & W 46 SO3937
Shennanton D & G 98 NX3363
Shenstone H & W 60 SO8673
Shenstone Staffs 61 SK1004
Shenstone Woodend Staffs 61 SK1101
Shenton Leics 61 SK3800
Shepeau Stow Lincs 64 TF3012
Shephall Herts 39 TL2623
Shepherd's Bush Gt Lon 26 TQ2380
Shepherd's Green Oxon 37 SU7183
Shepherds Cnwll 3 SW8154
Shepherds Patch Gloucs 35 SO7304
Shepherdswell Kent 29 TR2647
Shepley W York 82 SE1909
Shepperdine Gloucs 35 ST6295
Shepperton Surrey 26 TQ0766
Shepperton Green Surrey 26 TQ0767
Shepreth Cambs 52 TL3947
Shepshed Leics 62 SK4819
Shepton Beauchamp Somset 10 ST4017
Shepton Mallet Somset 21 ST6143
Shepton Montague Somset 22 ST6831
Shepway Kent 28 TQ7753
Sheraton Dur 96 NZ4435
Sherborne Dorset 10 ST6316
Sherborne Gloucs 36 SP1614
Sherborne Somset 21 ST5855
Sherborne Causeway Dorset 22 ST8323
Sherborne St John Hants 24 SU6255
Sherbourne Warwks 48 SP2661
Sherburn Dur 96 NZ3142
Sherburn N York 91 SE9576
Sherburn Hill Dur 96 NZ3342
Sherburn in Elmet N York 83 SE4933
Shere Surrey 14 TQ0747
Shereford Norfk 66 TF8829
Sherfield English Hants 23 SU2922
Sherfield on Loddon Hants 24 SU6858
Sherfin Lancs 81 SD7925
Sherford Devon 7 SX7844
Sherford Dorset 11 SY9193
Sheriff Hutton N York 90 SE6566
Sheriffhales Shrops 60 SJ7512
Sheringham Norfk 66 TG1543
Sherington Bucks 38 SP8846
Shermanbury W Susx 15 TQ2019
Shernborne Norfk 65 TF7132
Sherril Devon 7 SX6874
Sherrington Wilts 22 ST9639
Sherston Wilts 35 ST8586
Sherwood Notts 62 SK5643
Shettleston C Glas 116 NS6464
Shevington Gt Man 78 SD5408
Shevington Moor Gt Man 78 SD5410
Shevington Vale Gt Man 78 SD5309
Sheviock Cnwll 5 SX3755
Shibden Head W York 82 SE0928
Shide IOW 13 SZ5088
Shidlaw Nthumb 110 NT8037
Shiel Bridge Highld 138 NG9318
Shieldaig Highld 137 NG8154
Shieldhill D & G 100 NY0385
Shieldhill Falk 116 NS8976
Shieldhill House Hotel S Lans 108 NT0040
Shields N Lans 116 NS7755
Shielfoot Highld 129 NM6670
Shielhill Angus 134 NO4257
Shielhill Inver 114 NS2472
Shifford Oxon 36 SP3701
Shifnal Shrops 60 SJ7407
Shilbottle Nthumb 111 NU1908
Shildon Dur 96 NZ2226
Shillford E Rens 115 NS4556
Shillingford Devon 20 SS9824
Shillingford Oxon 37 SU5992
Shillingford Abbot Devon 9 SX9088
Shillingford St George Devon 9 SX9087
Shillingstone Dorset 11 ST8211
Shillington Beds 38 TL1234
Shillmoor Nthumb 110 NT8807
Shilton Oxon 36 SP2608
Shilton Warwks 61 SP4084
Shilvinghampton Dorset 10 SY6284
Shimpling Norfk 54 TM1583
Shimpling Suffk 54 TL8651
Shimpling Street Suffk 54 TL8753
Shincliffe Dur 96 NZ2940
Shiney Row T & W 96 NZ3252
Shinfield Berks 24 SU7368
Shingay Cambs 52 TL3046
Shingle Street Suffk 55 TM3642
Shinnersbridge Devon 7 SX7862
Shinness Highld 146 NC5215
Shipbourne Kent 27 TQ5952
Shipbrookhill Ches 79 SJ6771
Shipdham Norfk 66 TF9507
Shipham Somset 21 ST4457
Shiphay Devon 7 SX8965
Shiplake Oxon 37 SU7678
Shiplake Row Oxon 37 SU7478
Shiplate Somset 21 ST3556
Shipley Derbys 62 SK4444
Shipley Shrops 60 SO8095
Shipley W Susx 15 TQ1421
Shipley W York 82 SE1537
Shipley Bridge Surrey 15 TQ3040
Shipley Hatch Kent 28 TR0038
Shipmeadow Suffk 55 TM3790
Shippea Hill Station Cambs 53 TL6484
Shippon Oxon 37 SU4898
Shipston on Stour Warwks 48 SP2540
Shipton Bucks 49 SP7727
Shipton Gloucs 36 SP0318
Shipton N York 90 SE5558
Shipton Shrops 59 SO5692
Shipton Bellinger Hants 23 SU2345
Shipton Gorge Dorset 10 SY4991
Shipton Green W Susx 14 SZ8099
Shipton Moyne Gloucs 35 ST8989
Shipton-on-Cherwell Oxon 37 SP4716
Shipton-under-Wychwood Oxon 36 SP2817
Shiptonthorpe E R Yk 84 SE8543
Shirburn Oxon 37 SU6995
Shirdley Hill Lancs 80 SD3612
Shire Cumb 94 NY6135
Shire Oak W Mids 61 SK0504
Shirebrook Derbys 75 SK5267
Shiregreen S York 74 SK3691
Shirehampton Bristl 34 ST5376
Shiremoor T & W 103 NZ3171
Shirenewton Mons 34 ST4793
Shireoaks Notts 75 SK5580
Shirkoak Kent 17 TQ9435
Shirl Heath H & W 46 SO4359
Shirland Derbys 74 SK4058
Shirlett Shrops 59 SO6497
Shirley Derbys 73 SK2141
Shirley Gt Lon 27 TQ3565
Shirley Hants 13 SU4014
Shirley W Mids 61 SP1278
Shirrell Heath Hants 13 SU5714
Shirven Ag & B 113 NR8784
Shirwell Devon 19 SS6037
Shirwell Cross Devon 19 SS5936
Shiskine N Ayrs 105 NR9129
Shittlehope Dur 95 NZ0039
Shobdon H & W 46 SO4062
Shobley Hants 12 SU1806
Shobrooke Devon 9 SS8601
Shoby Leics 63 SK6820
Shocklach Ches 71 SJ4349
Shocklach Green Ches 71 SJ4349
Shoeburyness Essex 40 TQ9385
Sholden Kent 29 TR3552
Sholing Hants 13 SU4511
Shoose Cumb 92 NY0127
Shoot Hill Shrops 59 SJ4112
Shop Cnwll 18 SS2214
Shop Cnwll 4 SW8773
Shop Street Suffk 55 TM2268
Shopwyke W Susx 14 SU8805
Shore Gt Man 81 SD9216
Shoreditch Gt Lon 27 TQ3382
Shoreditch Somset 20 ST2422
Shoreham Kent 27 TQ5161
Shoreham-by-Sea W Susx 15 TQ2105
Shoreswood Nthumb 110 NT9446
Shorley Hants 13 SU5726
Shorncote Gloucs 35 SU0296
Shorne Kent 28 TQ6971
Shorne Ridgeway Kent 28 TQ6970
Short Heath W Mids 60 SJ9700
Short Heath W Mids 61 SP0992
Shorta Cross Cnwll 5 SX2857
Shortbridge E Susx 16 TQ4521
Shortfield Common Surrey 25 SU8442
Shortgate E Susx 16 TQ4915
Shortlanesend Cnwll 3 SW8047
Shorwell IOW 13 SZ4583
Shoscombe Somset 22 ST7156
Shotesham Norfk 67 TM2499
Shotgate Essex 40 TQ7592
Shotley Suffk 55 TM2335
Shotley Bridge Dur 95 NZ0953
Shotley Gate Suffk 41 TM2433
Shotley Street Suffk 55 TM2335
Shotleyfield Nthumb 95 NZ0553
Shottenden Kent 28 TR0454
Shottermill Surrey 14 SU8832
Shottery Warwks 48 SP1854
Shotteswell Warwks 49 SP4245
Shottisham Suffk 55 TM3244
Shottle Derbys 74 SK3149
Shottlegate Derbys 62 SK3147
Shotton Dur 96 NZ3625
Shotton Dur 96 NZ4139
Shotton Flints 71 SJ3168
Shotton Nthumb 110 NT8430
Shotton Nthumb 103 NZ2277
Shotton Colliery Dur 96 NZ3941
Shotts N Lans 116 NS8759
Shotwick Ches 71 SJ3371
Shougle Moray 141 NJ2155
Shouldham Norfk 65 TF6709
Shouldham Thorpe Norfk 65 TF6607
Shoulton H & W 47 SO8159
Shover's Green E Susx 16 TQ6530
Shraleybrook Staffs 72 SJ7849
Shrawardine Shrops 59 SJ3915
Shrawley H & W 47 SO8065
Shreding Green Bucks 26 TQ0280
Shrewley Warwks 48 SP2167
Shrewsbury Shrops 59 SJ4912
Shrewton Wilts 23 SU0743
Shripney W Susx 14 SU9302
Shrivenham Oxon 36 SU2389
Shropham Norfk 66 TL9893
Shrub End Essex 41 TL9723
Shucknall H & W 46 SO5842
Shudy Camps Cambs 53 TL6244

Shurdington

South Radworthy

Shurdington *Gloucs* 35 SO9218
Shurlock Row *Berks* 25 SU8374
Shurnock *H & W* 48 SP0360
Shurrery *Highld* 150 ND0458
Shurrery Lodge *Highld* 150 ND0456
Shurton *Somset* 20 ST2044
Shustoke *Warwks* 61 SP2290
Shut End *W Mids* 60 SO9089
Shut Heath *Staffs* 72 SJ8621
Shute *Devon* 9 SS8900
Shute *Devon* 10 SY2597
Shutford *Oxon* 48 SP3840
Shuthonger *Gloucs* 47 SO8935
Shutlanger *Nhants* 49 SP7249
Shutt Green *Staffs* 60 SJ8709
Shutterton *Devon* 9 SX9679
Shuttington *Warwks* 61 SK2505
Shuttlewood *Derbys* 75 SK4673
Shuttlewood Common *Derbys* 75 SK4773
Shuttleworth *Lancs* 81 SD8017
Siabost *W Isls* 154 NB2646
Siadar *W Isls* 154 NB3854
Sibbertoft *Nhants* 50 SP6882
Sibdon Carwood *Shrops* 59 SO4183
Sibford Ferris *Oxon* 48 SP3537
Sibford Gower *Oxon* 48 SP3537
Sible Hedingham *Essex* 53 TL7734
Sibley's Green *Essex* 40 TL6128
Siblyback *Cnwll* 5 SX2372
Sibsey *Lincs* 77 TF3550
Sibsey Fenside *Lincs* 77 TF3452
Sibson *Cambs* 51 TL0997
Sibson *Leics* 61 SK3500
Sibster *Highld* 151 ND3253
Sibthorpe *Notts* 75 SK7273
Sibthorpe *Notts* 63 SK7645
Sibton *Suffk* 55 TM3669
Sicklesmere *Suffk* 54 TL8760
Sicklinghall *N York* 83 SE3648
Sid Cop *S York* 83 SE3809
Sidbrook *Somset* 20 ST2527
Sidbury *Devon* 9 SY1391
Sidbury *Shrops* 60 SO6885
Sidcot *Somset* 21 ST4257
Sidcup *Gt Lon* 27 TQ4672
Siddick *Cumb* 92 NY0031
Siddington *Ches* 79 SJ8470
Siddington *Gloucs* 36 SU0399
Sidemoor *H & W* 60 SO9571
Sidestrand *Norfk* 67 TG2539
Sidford *Devon* 9 SY1390
Sidlesham *W Susx* 14 SZ8599
Sidlesham Common *W Susx* 14 SZ8599
Sidley *E Susx* 17 TQ7408
Sidmouth *Devon* 9 SY1287
Siefton *Shrops* 59 SO4883
Sigford *Devon* 7 SX7773
Sigglesthorne *E R Yk* 85 TA1545
Sigingstone *V Glam* 33 SS9771
Signet *Oxon* 36 SP2410
Silchester *Hants* 24 SU6261
Sileby *Leics* 62 SK6015
Silecroft *Cumb* 86 SD1381
Silfield *Norfk* 66 TM1299
Silian *Cardgn* 44 SN5751
Silk Willoughby *Lincs* 64 TF0542
Silkstead *Hants* 13 SU4424
Silkstone *S York* 82 SE2805
Silkstone Common *S York* 82 SE2904
Silksworth *T & W* 96 NZ3752
Silloth *Cumb* 92 NY1153
Silpho *N York* 91 SE9692
Silsden *W York* 82 SE0446
Silsoe *Beds* 38 TL0835
Silton *Dorset* 22 ST7829
Silver End *Beds* 38 TL1042
Silver End *Essex* 40 TL8119
Silver Street *H & W* 61 SP0776
Silver Street *Kent* 28 TQ8760
Silver Street *Somset* 21 ST5432
Silverburn *Mdloth* 117 NT2060
Silverdale *Lancs* 87 SD4674
Silverdale *Staffs* 72 SJ8146
Silverdale Green *Lancs* 87 SD4674
Silverford *Abers* 142 NJ7763
Silvergate *Norfk* 66 TG1727
Silverlace Green *Suffk* 55 TM3160
Silverley's Green *Suffk* 55 TM2976
Silverstone *Nhants* 49 SP6743
Silverton *Devon* 9 SS9502
Silverwell *Cnwll* 3 SW7448
Silvington *Shrops* 47 SO6279
Simmondley *Derbys* 74 SK0293
Simonburn *Nthumb* 102 NY8773
Simons Burrow *Devon* 9 ST1416
Simonsbath *Somset* 19 SS7739
Simonstone *Lancs* 81 SD7734
Simonstone *N York* 88 SD8791
Simprim *Border* 110 NT8445
Simpson *Bucks* 38 SP8836
Simpson Cross *Pembks* 30 SM8919
Sinclair's Hill *Border* 119 NT8150
Sinclairston *E Ayrs* 107 NS4716
Sinderby *N York* 89 SE3482
Sinderhope *Nthumb* 95 NY8451
Sinderland Green *Gt Man* 79 SJ7389
Sindlesham *Berks* 25 SU7769
Single Street *Gt Lon* 27 TQ4359
Singleborough *Bucks* 49 SP7631
Singleton *Lancs* 80 SD3838
Singleton *W Susx* 14 SU8713
Singlewell *Kent* 28 TQ6570
Sinkhurst Green *Kent* 28 TQ8142
Sinnarhard *Abers* 134 NJ4713
Sinnington *N York* 90 SE7485
Sinton *H & W* 47 SO8160
Sinton Green *H & W* 47 SO8160
Sipson *Gt Lon* 26 TQ0777
Sirhowy *Blae G* 33 SO1410
Sissinghurst *Kent* 28 TQ7937
Siston *Gloucs* 35 ST6875
Sitcott *Devon* 5 SX3691
Sithney *Cnwll* 2 SW6328
Sithney Common *Cnwll* 2 SW6428
Sithney Green *Cnwll* 2 SW6429
Sittingbourne *Kent* 28 TQ9063
Six Ashes *Staffs* 60 SO7988
Six Bells *Blae G* 34 SO2202
Six Mile Bottom *Cambs* 53 TL5756
Six Mile Cottages *Kent* 29 TR1344
Six Rues *Jersey* 152 JS0000
Sixhills *Lincs* 76 TF1787
Sixpenny Handley *Dorset* 11 ST9917
Sizewell *Suffk* 55 TM4762
Skaill *Ork* 155 HY5806
Skares *E Ayrs* 107 NS5317
Skateraw *E Loth* 119 NT7375
Skeabost *Highld* 136 NG4148
Skeeby *N York* 89 NZ1902
Skeffington *Leics* 63 SK7402
Skeffling *E R Yk* 85 TA3719
Skegby *Notts* 75 SK4961
Skegby *Notts* 75 SK7869
Skegness *Lincs* 77 TF5663
Skelbo *Highld* 147 NH7895
Skelbo Street *Highld* 147 NH7994
Skelbrooke *S York* 83 SE5012
Skeldyke *Lincs* 64 TF3337
Skellingthorpe *Lincs* 76 SK9272
Skellorm Green *Ches* 79 SJ9281
Skellow *S York* 83 SE5310
Skelmanthorpe *W York* 82 SE2310
Skelmersdale *Lancs* 78 SD4606
Skelmorlie *N Ayrs* 114 NS1967
Skelpick *Highld* 150 NC7256
Skelston *D & G* 100 NX8285
Skelton *Cumb* 93 NY4335
Skelton *N York* 89 NZ0900
Skelton *N York* 97 NZ6618
Skelton *N York* 89 SE3668
Skelton *N York* 83 SE5756
Skelton *E R Yk* 84 SE7625
Skelwith Bridge *Cumb* 87 NY3403
Skendleby *Lincs* 77 TF4369
Skene House *Abers* 135 NJ7610
Skenfrith *Mons* 34 SO4520
Skerne *E R Yk* 84 TA0455
Skerray *Highld* 149 NC6563
Skerricha *Highld* 148 NC2350
Skerton *Lancs* 87 SD4763
Sketchley *Leics* 50 SP4292
Sketty *Swans* 32 SS6292
Skewen *Neath* 32 SS7296
Skewsby *N York* 90 SE6270
Skeyton *Norfk* 67 TG2425
Skeyton Corner *Norfk* 67 TG2527
Skiall *Highld* 150 ND0267
Skidbrooke *Lincs* 77 TF4393
Skidbrooke North End *Lincs* 77 TF4395
Skidby *E R Yk* 84 TA0133
Skigersta *W Isls* 154 NB5461
Skilgate *Somset* 20 SS9827
Skillington *Lincs* 63 SK8925
Skinburness *Cumb* 92 NY1256
Skinflats *Falk* 116 NS9082
Skinidin *Highld* 136 NG2247
Skinners Green *Berks* 24 SU4465
Skinningrove *N York* 97 NZ7119
Skipness *Ag & B* 114 NR9057
Skipper's Bridge *Cumb* 101 NY3783
Skiprigg *Cumb* 93 NY3945
Skipsea *E R Yk* 85 TA1654
Skipsea Brough *E R Yk* 85 TA1454
Skipton *N York* 82 SD9851
Skipton-on-Swale *N York* 89 SE3679
Skipwith *N York* 83 SE6638
Skirlaugh *E R Yk* 85 TA1439
Skirling *Border* 108 NT0739
Skirmett *Bucks* 37 SU7790
Skirpenbeck *E R Yk* 84 SE7456
Skirwith *Cumb* 94 NY6132
Skirwith *N York* 87 SD7073
Skirza *Highld* 151 ND3868
Skitby *Cumb* 101 NY4465
Skittle Green *Bucks* 37 SP7703
Skulamus *Highld* 129 NG6622
Skullomie *Highld* 149 NC6161
Skyborry Green *Shrops* 46 SO2674
Skye Green *Essex* 40 TL8722
Skye of Curr *Highld* 141 NH9924
Skyreholme *N York* 88 SE0660
Slack *Derbys* 74 SK3362
Slack *W York* 82 SD9728
Slack Head *Cumb* 87 SD4978
Slack Side *W York* 82 SE1430
Slackcote *Gt Man* 82 SD9709
Slackholme End *Lincs* 77 TF5370
Slacks of Cairnbanno *Abers* 143 NJ8445
Slad *Gloucs* 35 SO8707
Slade *Devon* 19 SS5046
Slade *Devon* 9 ST1108
Slade *Somset* 19 SS8327
Slade End *Oxon* 37 SU5990
Slade Green *Kent* 27 TQ5276
Slade Heath *Staffs* 60 SJ9106
Slade Hooton *S York* 75 SK5288
Sladen *Derbys* 74 SK0771
Slades Green *H & W* 47 SO8134
Sladesbridge *Cnwll* 4 SX0171
Slaggyford *Nthumb* 94 NY6752
Slaid Hill *W York* 83 SE3240
Slaidburn *Lancs* 81 SD7152
Slaithwaite *W York* 82 SE0813
Slaley *Derbys* 74 SK2757
Slaley *Nthumb* 95 NY9657
Slamannan *Falk* 116 NS8572
Slapton *Bucks* 38 SP9320
Slapton *Devon* 7 SX8245
Slapton *Nhants* 49 SP6446
Slattocks *Gt Man* 79 SD8808
Slaugham *W Susx* 15 TQ2528
Slaughterford *Wilts* 35 ST8473
Slawston *Leics* 50 SP7894
Sleaford *Hants* 25 SU8038
Sleaford *Lincs* 64 TF0645
Sleagill *Cumb* 94 NY5919
Sleap *Shrops* 59 SJ4826
Sleapford *Shrops* 59 SJ6315
Sleasdairidh *Highld* 146 NH6496
Sledge Green *H & W* 47 SO8134
Sledmere *E R Yk* 91 SE9364
Sleight *Dorset* 11 SY9898
Sleightholme *Dur* 88 NY9510
Sleights *N York* 90 NZ8607
Slepe *Dorset* 11 SY9293
Slerra *Devon* 18 SS3124
Slickly *Highld* 151 ND2966
Sliddery *N Ayrs* 105 NR9323
Sligachan *Highld* 136 NG4829
Sligrachan *Ag & B* 114 NS1791
Slimbridge *Gloucs* 35 SO7303
Slindon *Staffs* 72 SJ8232
Slindon *W Susx* 14 SU9608
Slinfold *W Susx* 14 TQ1131
Sling *Gwynd* 69 SH6066
Slingsby *N York* 90 SE6974
Slip End *Beds* 38 TL0718
Slip End *Herts* 39 TL2837
Slipton *Nhants* 51 SP9579
Slitting Mill *Staffs* 73 SK0217
Slockavullin *Ag & B* 113 NR8297
Slogarie *D & G* 99 NX6568
Sloley *Norfk* 67 TG2923
Sloncombe *Devon* 8 SX7386
Sloothby *Lincs* 77 TF4970
Slough *Berks* 26 SU9879
Slough Green *Somset* 20 ST2719
Slough Green *W Susx* 15 TQ2826
Slumbay *Highld* 138 NG8938
Slyfield Green *Surrey* 25 SU9952
Slyne *Lancs* 87 SD4765
Smailholm *Border* 110 NT6436
Small Dole *W Susx* 15 TQ2112
Small Heath *W Mids* 61 SP1085
Small Hythe *Kent* 17 TQ8930
Small Wood Hey *Lancs* 80 SD3948
Smallbridge *Gt Man* 81 SD9115
Smallbrook *Devon* 9 SX8698
Smallbrook *Gloucs* 34 SO5900
Smallburgh *Norfk* 67 TG3324
Smalldale *Derbys* 74 SK0977
Smalldale *Derbys* 74 SK1781
Smalley *Derbys* 62 SK4044
Smalley Common *Derbys* 62 SK4042
Smalley Green *Derbys* 62 SK4043
Smallfield *Surrey* 15 TQ3143
Smallridge *Devon* 10 ST3001
Smallthorne *Staffs* 72 SJ8850
Smallways *N York* 89 NZ1111
Smallwood *Ches* 72 SJ8060
Smallworth *Norfk* 54 TM0080
Smannell *Hants* 23 SU3749
Smardale *Cumb* 88 NY7308
Smarden *Kent* 28 TQ8742
Smarden Bell *Kent* 28 TQ8742
Smart's Hill *Kent* 16 TQ5242
Smeafield *Nthumb* 111 NU0937
Smearisary *Highld* 129 NM6476
Smeatharpe *Devon* 9 ST1910
Smeeth *Kent* 29 TR0739
Smeeton Westerby *Leics* 50 SP6892
Smelthouses *N York* 89 SE1964
Smerral *Highld* 151 ND1733
Smestow *Staffs* 60 SO8591
Smethwick *W Mids* 60 SP0287
Smethwick Green *Ches* 72 SJ8063
Smisby *Derbys* 62 SK3418
Smith End Green *H & W* 47 SO7752
Smith Green *Lancs* 80 SD4955
Smith's End *Herts* 39 TL4037
Smith's Green *Essex* 40 TL5721
Smith's Green *Essex* 53 TL6640
Smitheclose *IOW* 13 SZ5391
Smithfield *Cumb* 101 NY4465
Smithies *S York* 83 SE3508
Smithincott *Devon* 9 ST0611
Smithstown *Highld* 144 NG7977
Smithton *Highld* 140 NH7145
Smithy Bridge *Gt Man* 81 SD9215
Smithy Green *Ches* 79 SJ7474
Smithy Green *Gt Man* 79 SJ8785
Smithy Houses *Derbys* 62 SK3846
Smockington *Leics* 50 SP4589
Smoo *Highld* 149 NC4167
Smythe's Green *Essex* 40 TL9218
Snade *D & G* 100 NX8485
Snailbeach *Shrops* 59 SJ3702
Snailwell *Cambs* 53 TL6467
Snainton *N York* 91 SE9282
Snaith *E R Yk* 83 SE6422
Snake Pass Inn *Derbys* 74 SK1190
Snape *N York* 89 SE2684
Snape *Suffk* 55 TM3959
Snape Green *Mersyd* 80 SD3813
Snape Street *Suffk* 55 TM3958
Snaresbrook *Gt Lon* 27 TQ4089
Snarestone *Leics* 62 SK3409
Snarford *Lincs* 76 TF0482
Snargate *Kent* 17 TQ9928
Snave *Kent* 17 TR0129
Sneachill *H & W* 47 SO9053
Snead *Powys* 59 SO3192
Sneath Common *Norfk* 54 TM1689
Sneaton *N York* 91 NZ8907
Sneatonthorpe *N York* 91 NZ9006
Snelland *Lincs* 76 TF0780
Snelston *Derbys* 73 SK1543
Snetterton *Norfk* 66 TL9991
Snettisham *Norfk* 65 TF6834
Snibston *Leics* 62 SK4114
Snig's End *Gloucs* 47 SO7828
Snitter *Nthumb* 103 NU0203
Snitterby *Lincs* 76 SK9894
Snitterfield *Warwks* 48 SP2159
Snitterton *Derbys* 74 SK2760
Snittlegarth *Cumb* 93 NY2138
Snitton *Shrops* 46 SO5575
Snoadhill *Kent* 28 TQ9442
Snodhill *H & W* 46 SO3240
Snodland *Kent* 28 TQ7061
Snoll Hatch *Kent* 28 TQ6648
Snow End *Herts* 39 TL4032
Snow Street *Norfk* 54 TM0981
Snowden Hill *S York* 74 SE2600
Snowshill *Gloucs* 48 SP0933
Soake *Hants* 13 SU6611
Soar *Cardif* 33 ST0983
Soar *Powys* 45 SN9731
Soberton *Hants* 13 SU6116
Soberton Heath *Hants* 13 SU6014
Sockbridge *Cumb* 94 NY4926
Sockburn *Dur* 89 NZ3406
Sodom *Denbgs* 70 SJ0971
Sodylt Bank *Shrops* 71 SJ3439
Soham *Cambs* 53 TL5973
Soham Cotes *Cambs* 53 TL5775
Solas *W Isls* 154 NF8074
Solbury *Pembks* 30 SM8912
Soldon *Devon* 18 SS3210
Soldon Cross *Devon* 18 SS3210
Soldridge *Hants* 24 SU6535
Sole Street *Kent* 28 TQ6567
Sole Street *Kent* 29 TR0949
Solihull *W Mids* 61 SP1679
Sollers Dilwyn *H & W* 46 SO4255
Sollers Hope *H & W* 46 SO6132
Sollom *Lancs* 80 SD4518
Solva *Pembks* 30 SM8024
Solwaybank *D & G* 101 NY3077
Somerby *Leics* 63 SK7710
Somerby *Lincs* 84 TA0606
Somercotes *Derbys* 74 SK4253
Somerford *Dorset* 12 SZ1793
Somerford Keynes *Gloucs* 35 SU0195
Somerley *W Susx* 14 SZ8198
Somerleyton *Suffk* 67 TM4897
Somersal Herbert *Derbys* 73 SK1335
Somersby *Lincs* 77 TF3472
Somersham *Cambs* 52 TL3678
Somersham *Suffk* 54 TM0848
Somerton *Oxon* 49 SP4928
Somerton *Somset* 21 ST4928
Somerton *Suffk* 54 TL8153
Somerwood *Shrops* 59 SJ5614
Sompting *W Susx* 15 TQ1505
Sonning *Berks* 37 SU7575
Sonning Common *Oxon* 37 SU7180
Sonning Eye *Oxon* 37 SU7476
Sontley *Wrexhm* 71 SJ3347
Sopley *Hants* 12 SZ1596
Sopworth *Wilts* 35 ST8286
Sorbie *D & G* 99 NX4346
Sordale *Highld* 151 ND1462
Sorisdale *Ag & B* 120 NM2763
Sorn *E Ayrs* 107 NS5526
Sortat *Highld* 151 ND2863
Sosgill *Cumb* 92 NY1024
Sotby *Lincs* 76 TF2078
Sots Hole *Lincs* 76 TF1264
Sotterly *Suffk* 55 TM4484
Sotwell *Oxon* 37 SU5890
Soughton *Flints* 70 SJ2466
Soulbury *Bucks* 38 SP8826
Soulby *Cumb* 93 NY4625
Soulby *Cumb* 88 NY7411
Souldern *Oxon* 49 SP5231
Souldrop *Beds* 51 SP9861
Sound Muir *Moray* 141 NJ3652
Soundwell *Gloucs* 35 ST6575
Sourton *Devon* 8 SX5390
Soutergate *Cumb* 86 SD2281
South Acre *Norfk* 66 TF8114
South Alkham *Kent* 29 TR2441
South Allington *Devon* 7 SX7938
South Alloa *Falk* 116 NS8791
South Ambersham *W Susx* 14 SU9120
South Anston *S York* 75 SK5183
South Ascot *Berks* 25 SU9268
South Ashford *Kent* 28 TR0041
South Baddesley *Hants* 12 SZ3596
South Bank *N York* 97 NZ5320
South Bank *N York* 83 SE5950
South Barrow *Somset* 21 ST6028
South Beddington *Gt Lon* 27 TQ2863
South Beer *Cnwll* 5 SX3091
South Benfleet *Essex* 40 TQ7787
South Bersted *W Susx* 14 SU9300
South Bockhampton *Dorset* 12 SZ1795
South Bowood *Dorset* 10 SY4498
South Bramwith *S York* 83 SE6211
South Brent *Devon* 7 SX6960
South Brewham *Somset* 22 ST7236
South Broomhill *Nthumb* 103 NZ2499
South Burlingham *Norfk* 67 TG3807
South Cadbury *Somset* 21 ST6325
South Carlton *Lincs* 76 SK9476
South Carlton *Notts* 75 SK5883
South Cave *E R Yk* 84 SE9230
South Cerney *Gloucs* 36 SU0497
South Chard *Somset* 10 ST3205
South Charlton *Nthumb* 111 NU1620
South Cheriton *Somset* 22 ST6924
South Church *Dur* 96 NZ2128
South Cleatlam *Dur* 96 NZ1218
South Cliffe *E R Yk* 84 SE8735
South Clifton *Notts* 75 SK8270
South Cockerington *Lincs* 77 TF3888
South Collingham *Notts* 75 SK8261
South Cornelly *Brdgnd* 33 SS8280
South Cove *Suffk* 55 TM4981
South Creake *Norfk* 66 TF8536
South Crosland *W York* 82 SE1112
South Croxton *Leics* 63 SK6810
South Dalton *E R Yk* 84 SE9645
South Darenth *Kent* 27 TQ5669
South Duffield *N York* 83 SE6833
South Elkington *Lincs* 77 TF2988
South Elmsall *W York* 83 SE4711
South End *E R Yk* 85 TA3918
South End *H & W* 47 SO7444
South End *Hants* 12 SU1015
South End *Lincs* 85 TA1120
South End *Norfk* 54 TL9990
South Erradale *Highld* 137 NG7471
South Fambridge *Essex* 40 TQ8694
South Fawley *Berks* 36 SU3880
South Ferriby *Lincs* 84 SE9820
South Field *E R Yk* 84 TA0225
South Godstone *Surrey* 15 TQ3648
South Gorley *Hants* 12 SU1610
South Gosforth *T & W* 103 NZ2467
South Green *Essex* 41 TM0319
South Green *Essex* 40 TQ6893
South Green *Kent* 28 TQ8560
South Green *Norfk* 66 TG0510
South Green *Suffk* 54 TM1775
South Gyle *C Edin* 117 NT1871
South Hanningfield *Essex* 40 TQ7497
South Harting *W Susx* 14 SU7819
South Hayling *Hants* 13 SZ7299
South Hazelrigg *Nthumb* 111 NU0532
South Heath *Bucks* 26 SP9101
South Heighton *E Susx* 16 TQ4402
South Hetton *Dur* 96 NZ3845
South Hiendley *W York* 83 SE3912
South Hill *Cnwll* 5 SX3272
South Hill *Somset* 21 ST4726
South Hinksey *Oxon* 37 SP5104
South Hole *Devon* 18 SS2220
South Holmwood *Surrey* 15 TQ1744
South Hornchurch *Gt Lon* 27 TQ5183
South Huish *Devon* 7 SX6941
South Hykeham *Lincs* 76 SK9364
South Hylton *T & W* 96 NZ3556
South Kelsey *Lincs* 76 TF0498
South Kessock *Highld* 140 NH6547
South Killingholme *Lincs* 85 TA1416
South Kilvington *N York* 89 SE4284
South Kilworth *Nhants* 50 SP6081
South Kirkby *W York* 83 SE4410
South Knighton *Devon* 7 SX8172
South Kyme *Lincs* 76 TF1749
South Lawn *Oxon* 36 SP2814
South Leigh *Oxon* 36 SP3909
South Leverton *Notts* 75 SK7881
South Littleton *H & W* 48 SP0746
South Lopham *Norfk* 54 TM0481
South Luffenham *Rutlnd* 63 SK9301
South Malling *E Susx* 16 TQ4210
South Marston *Wilts* 36 SU1987
South Merstham *Surrey* 27 TQ2952
South Middleton *Nthumb* 111 NT9923
South Milford *N York* 83 SE4931
South Milton *Devon* 7 SX7042
South Mimms *Herts* 26 TL2201
South Molton *Devon* 19 SS7125
South Moor *Dur* 96 NZ1951
South Moreton *Oxon* 37 SU5688
South Mundham *W Susx* 14 SU8700
South Muskham *Notts* 75 SK7957
South Newbald *E R Yk* 84 SE9035
South Newington *Oxon* 48 SP4033
South Newton *Wilts* 23 SU0834
South Normanton *Derbys* 75 SK4456
South Norwood *Gt Lon* 27 TQ3368
South Nutfield *Surrey* 15 TQ3049
South Ockendon *Essex* 27 TQ5983
South Ormsby *Lincs* 77 TF3675
South Ossett *W York* 82 SE2819
South Otterington *N York* 89 SE3787
South Owersby *Lincs* 76 TF0693
South Park *Surrey* 15 TQ2448
South Perrott *Dorset* 10 ST4706
South Petherton *Somset* 10 ST4316
South Petherwin *Cnwll* 5 SX3181
South Pickenham *Norfk* 66 TF8504
South Pill *Cnwll* 6 SX4259
South Pool *Devon* 7 SX7740
South Poorton *Dorset* 10 SY5297
South Quarme *Somset* 20 SS9236
South Queensferry *C Edin* 117 NT1378
South Radworthy *Devon* 19 SS7432

Sutcombemill

Thearne

Sutcombemill Devon 18 SS3411
Suton Norfk 66 TM0999
Sutterby Lincs 77 TF3872
Sutterton Lincs 64 TF2835
Sutton Beds 52 TL2247
Sutton Cambs 51 TL0998
Sutton Cambs 53 TL4479
Sutton Devon 8 SS7202
Sutton Devon 7 SX7042
Sutton E Susx 16 TV4999
Sutton Gt Lon 27 TQ2564
Sutton Kent 29 TR3349
Sutton Mersyd 78 SJ5393
Sutton N York 83 SE4925
Sutton Norfk 67 TG3823
Sutton Notts 75 SK6784
Sutton Notts 63 SK7637
Sutton Oxon 36 SP4106
Sutton Pembks 30 SM9115
Sutton S York 83 SE5512
Sutton Shrops 59 SJ3527
Sutton Shrops 59 SJ5010
Sutton Shrops 72 SJ6631
Sutton Shrops 60 SO7386
Sutton Staffs 72 SJ7622
Sutton Suffk 55 TM3046
Sutton W Susx 14 SU9715
Sutton at Hone Kent 27 TQ5569
Sutton Bassett Nhants 50 SP7790
Sutton Benger Wilts 35 ST9478
Sutton Bingham Somset 10 ST5410
Sutton Bonington Notts 62 SK5024
Sutton Bridge Lincs 65 TF4721
Sutton Cheney Leics 50 SK4100
Sutton Coldfield W Mids 61 SP1295
Sutton Courtenay Oxon 37 SU5094
Sutton Crosses Lincs 65 TF4321
Sutton Fields Notts 62 SK4926
Sutton Grange N York 89 SE2873
Sutton Green Oxon 36 SP4107
Sutton Green Surrey 25 TQ0054
Sutton Green Wrexhm 71 SJ4048
Sutton Howgrave N York 89 SE3179
Sutton in Ashfield Notts 75 SK4958
Sutton in the Elms Leics 50 SP5193
Sutton Lane Ends Ches 79 SJ9270
Sutton Maddock Shrops 60 SJ7201
Sutton Mallet Somset 21 ST3736
Sutton Mandeville Wilts 22 ST9828
Sutton Manor Mersyd 78 SJ5190
Sutton Marsh H & W 46 SO5544
Sutton Montis Somset 21 ST6224
Sutton on Sea Lincs 77 TF5281
Sutton on the Hill Derbys 73 SK2333
Sutton on Trent Notts 75 SK7965
Sutton Poyntz Dorset 11 SY7083
Sutton Scansdale Derbys 75 SK4468
Sutton Scotney Hants 24 SU4639
Sutton St Edmund Lincs 64 TF3613
Sutton St James Lincs 65 TF3918
Sutton St Nicholas H & W 46 SO5245
Sutton Street Kent 28 TQ8055
Sutton upon Derwent E R Yk 84 SE7047
Sutton Valence Kent 28 TQ8149
Sutton Veny Wilts 22 ST9041
Sutton Waldron Dorset 11 ST8615
Sutton Weaver Ches 71 SJ5479
Sutton Wick Oxon 37 SU4894
Sutton Wick Somset 21 ST5759
Sutton-in-Craven N York 82 SE0043
Sutton-on-Hull E R Yk 85 TA1232
Sutton-on-the-Forest N York 90 SE5864
Sutton-under-Brailes Warwks 48 SP3037
Sutton-under-Whitestonecliffe N York 90 SE4882
Swaby Lincs 77 TF3877
Swadlincote Derbys 73 SK2919
Swaffham Norfk 66 TF8108
Swaffham Bulbeck Cambs 53 TL5562
Swaffham Prior Cambs 53 TL5764
Swafield Norfk 67 TG2832
Swainby N York 89 NZ4701
Swainshill H & W 46 SO4641
Swainsthorpe Norfk 67 TG2101
Swainswick Somset 22 ST7668
Swalcliffe Oxon 48 SP3737
Swalecliffe Kent 29 TR1367
Swallow Lincs 85 TA1703
Swallow Beck Lincs 76 SK9467
Swallow Nest S York 75 SK4585
Swallowcliffe Wilts 22 ST9627
Swallowfield Berks 24 SU7264
Swallows Cross Essex 40 TQ6198
Swampton Hants 24 SU4150
Swan Green Ches 79 SJ7373
Swan Street Essex 40 TL8927
Swan Village W Mids 60 SO9892
Swanage Dorset 12 SZ0378
Swanbourne Bucks 38 SP8026
Swanbridge V Glam 20 ST1667
Swancote Shrops 60 SO7494
Swanland E R Yk 84 SE9928
Swanley Kent 27 TQ5168
Swanley Village Kent 27 TQ5369
Swanmore Hants 13 SU5716
Swannington Leics 62 SK4116
Swannington Norfk 66 TG1319
Swanpool Garden Suberb Lincs 76 SK9569
Swanscombe Kent 27 TQ6074
Swansea Swans 32 SS6592
Swanton Abbot Norfk 67 TG2625
Swanton Morley Norfk 66 TG0117
Swanton Novers Norfk 66 TG0231
Swanton Street Kent 28 TQ8759
Swanwick Derbys 74 SK4053
Swanwick Hants 13 SU5109
Swarby Lincs 64 TF0440
Swardeston Norfk 67 TG2002
Swarkestone Derbys 62 SK3728
Swarland Nthumb 103 NU1602
Swarland Estate Nthumb 103 NU1603
Swarraton Hants 24 SU5636
Swartha W York 82 SE0546
Swarthmoor Cumb 86 SD2777
Swaton Lincs 64 TF1337
Swavesey Cambs 52 TL3668
Sway Hants 12 SZ2798
Swayfield Lincs 63 SK9922
Swaythling Hants 13 SU4416
Sweet Green H & W 47 SO6462
Sweetham Devon 9 SX8899
Sweethaws E Susx 16 TQ5028
Sweetlands Corner Kent 28 TQ7845
Sweets Cnwll 4 SX1595
Sweetshouse Cnwll 4 SX0861
Swefling Suffk 55 TM3463
Swepstone Leics 62 SK3610
Swerford Oxon 48 SP3731
Swettenham Ches 72 SJ8067
Swffryd Blae G 33 ST2198
Swift's Green Kent 28 TQ8744
Swiftsden E Susx 17 TQ7328
Swilland Suffk 54 TM1852
Swillbrook Lancs 80 SD4834
Swillington W York 83 SE3830
Swimbridge Devon 19 SS6230
Swimbridge Newland Devon 19 SS6030
Swinbrook Oxon 36 SP2812
Swincliffe N York 89 SE2458
Swincliffe W York 82 SE2027
Swincombe Devon 19 SS6941
Swinden N York 81 SD8554
Swinderby Lincs 76 SK8663
Swindon Gloucs 47 SO9325
Swindon Nthumb 102 NY9799
Swindon Staffs 60 SO8690
Swindon Wilts 36 SU1484
Swine E R Yk 85 TA1335
Swinefleet E R Yk 84 SE7621
Swineford Gloucs 35 ST6969
Swineshead Beds 51 TL0565
Swineshead Lincs 64 TF2340
Swineshead Bridge Lincs 64 TF2242
Swiney Highld 151 ND2335
Swinford Leics 50 SP5679
Swinford Oxon 37 SP4408
Swingfield Minnis Kent 29 TR2142
Swingfield Street Kent 29 TR2343
Swingleton Green Suffk 54 TL9647
Swinhill S Lans 116 NS7748
Swinhoe Nthumb 111 NU2128
Swinhope Lincs 76 TF2196
Swinithwaite N York 88 SE0489
Swinmore Common H & W 47 SO6741
Swinscoe Staffs 73 SK1247
Swinside Cumb 93 NY2421
Swinstead Lincs 64 TF0122
Swinthorpe Lincs 76 TF0680
Swinton Border 110 NT8347
Swinton Gt Man 79 SD7701
Swinton N York 89 SE2179
Swinton N York 90 SE7573
Swinton S York 75 SK4599
Swithland Leics 62 SK5512
Swordale Highld 139 NH5765
Swordland Highld 129 NM7891
Swordly Highld 150 NC7463
Sworton Heath Ches 79 SJ6884
Swyddffynnon Cardgn 43 SN6966
Swynnerton Staffs 72 SJ8535
Swyre Dorset 10 SY5288
Sycharth Powys 58 SJ2025
Sychnant Powys 45 SN9777
Sychtyn Powys 58 SH9907
Sydallt Flints 71 SJ3055
Syde Gloucs 35 SO9511
Sydenham Gt Lon 27 TQ3671
Sydenham Oxon 37 SP7301
Sydenham Damerel Devon 5 SX4176
Sydenhurst Surrey 14 SU9534
Syderstone Norfk 66 TF8332
Sydling St Nicholas Dorset 10 SY6399
Sydmonton Hants 24 SU4857
Sydnal Lane Shrops 60 SJ8005
Syerston Notts 63 SK7447
Syke Gt Man 81 SD8915
Sykehouse S York 83 SE6316
Syleham Suffk 55 TM2078
Sylen Carmth 32 SN5106
Symbister Shet 155 HU5462
Symington S Ayrs 106 NS3831
Symington S Lans 108 NS9935
Symonds Yat H & W 34 SO5515
Symondsbury Dorset 10 SY4493
Sympson Green W York 82 SE1838
Synderford Dorset 10 ST3803
Synod Inn Cardgn 42 SN4054
Syre Highld 149 NC6943
Syreford Gloucs 35 SP0220
Syresham Nhants 49 SP6241
Syston Leics 62 SK6211
Syston Lincs 63 SK9240
Sytchampton H & W 47 SO8466
Sywell Nhants 51 SP8267

T

Tabley Hill Ches 79 SJ7379
Tackley Oxon 37 SP4719
Tacolneston Norfk 66 TM1495
Tadcaster N York 83 SE4843
Taddington Derbys 74 SK1471
Taddington Gloucs 48 SP0831
Taddiport Devon 18 SS4818
Tadley Hants 24 SU6061
Tadlow Cambs 52 TL2847
Tadmarton Oxon 48 SP3937
Tadwick Somset 35 ST7470
Tadworth Surrey 26 TQ2257
Tafarn-y-bwlch Pembks 31 SN0834
Tafarn-y-Gelyn Denbgs 70 SJ1961
Tafarnaubach Blae G 33 SO1210
Taff's Well Cardif 33 ST1283
Tafolwern Powys 57 SH8902
Tai'r Bull Powys 45 SN9925
Taibach Neath 32 SS7788
Tain Highld 151 ND2266
Tain Highld 147 NH7781
Tairbeart W Isls 154 NB1500
Takeley Essex 40 TL5621
Takeley Street Essex 39 TL5421
Tal-y-Bont A & C 69 SH7668
Tal-y-bont Gwynd 57 SH5921
Tal-y-bont Gwynd 69 SH6070
Tal-y-cafn A & C 69 SH7871
Tal-y-coed Mons 34 SO4115
Tal-y-garn Rhondd 33 ST0379
Tal-y-llyn Gwynd 57 SH7109
Tal-y-Waun Torfn 34 SO2604
Talachddu Powys 45 SO0833
Talacre Flints 70 SJ1183
Talaton Devon 9 SY0699
Talbenny Pembks 30 SM8411
Talbot Green Rhondd 33 ST0382
Talbot Village Dorset 12 SZ0793
Taleford Devon 9 SY0997
Talerddig Powys 58 SH9300
Talgarreg Cardgn 42 SN4251
Talgarth Powys 45 SO1533
Taliesin Cardgn 43 SN6591
Talisker Highld 136 NG3230
Talke Staffs 72 SJ8253
Talke Pits Staffs 72 SJ8353
Talkin Cumb 94 NY5557
Talla Linnfoots Border 108 NT1320
Talladale Highld 144 NG9170
Tallaminnock S Ayrs 106 NX4098
Tallarn Green Wrexhm 71 SJ4444
Tallentire Cumb 92 NY1035
Talley Carmth 44 SN6332
Tallington Lincs 64 TF0908
Tallwrn Wrexhm 71 SJ2947
Talmine Highld 149 NC5863
Talog Carmth 31 SN3325
Talsarn Cardgn 44 SN5456
Talsarnau Gwynd 57 SH6135
Talskiddy Cnwll 4 SW9165
Talwrn Angles 68 SH4877
Talwrn Wrexhm 71 SJ3847
Talybont Cardgn 43 SN6589
Talybont-on-Usk Powys 33 SO1122
Talysarn Gwynd 68 SH4952
Talywern Powys 57 SH8200
Tamer Lane End Gt Man 79 SD6401
Tamerton Foliot Devon 6 SX4761
Tamworth Staffs 61 SK2003
Tamworth Green Lincs 64 TF3842
Tan Hill N York 88 NY8906
Tan Office Green Suffk 53 TL7858
Tan-y-Bwlch Gwynd 57 SH6540
Tan-y-fron A & C 70 SH9564
Tan-y-fron Wrexhm 71 SJ2952
Tan-y-groes Cardgn 42 SN2849
Tancred N York 89 SE4558
Tancredston Pembks 30 SM8826
Tandlemuir Rens 115 NS3361
Tandridge Surrey 27 TQ3750
Tanfield Dur 96 NZ1855
Tanfield Lea Dur 96 NZ1854
Tangiers Pembks 30 SM9518
Tangley Hants 23 SU3252
Tangmere W Susx 14 SU9006
Tankerness Ork 155 HY5109
Tankersley S York 74 SK3499
Tankerton Kent 29 TR1166
Tannach Highld 151 ND3247
Tannachie Abers 135 NO7884
Tannadice Angus 134 NO4758
Tanner Green H & W 61 SP0874
Tannington Suffk 55 TM2467
Tannochside N Lans 116 NS7061
Tansley Derbys 74 SK3259
Tansor Nhants 51 TL0590
Tantobie Dur 96 NZ1754
Tanton N York 90 NZ5210
Tanwood H & W 60 SO9074
Tanworth in Arden Warwks 61 SP1170
Tanygrisiau Gwynd 57 SH6945
Taobh Tuath W Isls 154 NF9989
Taplow Bucks 26 SU9182
Tarbert Ag & B 113 NR6551
Tarbert Ag & B 113 NR8668
Tarbert W Isls 154 NB1500
Tarbet Ag & B 123 NN3104
Tarbet Highld 148 NC1649
Tarbet Highld 129 NM7992
Tarbock Green Mersyd 78 SJ4687
Tarbolton S Ayrs 107 NS4327
Tarbrax S Lans 117 NT0255
Tardebigge H & W 47 SO9969
Tardy Gate Lancs 80 SD5425
Tarfside Angus 134 NO4879
Tarland Abers 134 NJ4804
Tarleton Lancs 80 SD4520
Tarlscough Lancs 80 SD4314
Tarlton Gloucs 35 ST9599
Tarnock Somset 21 ST3752
Tarns Cumb 92 NY1248
Tarnside Cumb 87 SD4390
Tarporley Ches 71 SJ5562
Tarr Somset 19 SS8632
Tarr Somset 20 ST1030
Tarrant Crawford Dorset 11 ST9203
Tarrant Gunville Dorset 11 ST9213
Tarrant Hinton Dorset 11 ST9311
Tarrant Keynston Dorset 11 ST9204
Tarrant Launceston Dorset 11 ST9409
Tarrant Monkton Dorset 11 ST9408
Tarrant Rawston Dorset 11 ST9306
Tarrant Rushton Dorset 11 ST9305
Tarring Neville E Susx 16 TQ4403
Tarrington H & W 46 SO6140
Tarskavaig Highld 129 NG5810
Tarves Abers 143 NJ8631
Tarvie P & K 133 NO0164
Tarvin Ches 71 SJ4966
Tarvin Sands Ches 71 SJ4967
Tasburgh Norfk 67 TM1996
Tasley Shrops 60 SO6894
Taston Oxon 36 SP3521
Tatenhill Staffs 73 SK2021
Tathall End Bucks 38 SP8246
Tatham Lancs 87 SD6069
Tathwell Lincs 77 TF3182
Tatsfield Surrey 27 TQ4156
Tattenhall Ches 71 SJ4858
Tatterford Norfk 66 TF8628
Tattersett Norfk 66 TF8429
Tattershall Lincs 76 TF2157
Tattershall Bridge Lincs 76 TF1956
Tattershall Thorpe Lincs 76 TF2159
Tattingstone Suffk 54 TM1337
Tattingstone White Horse Suffk 54 TM1338
Tatworth Somset 10 ST3205
Tauchers Moray 141 NJ3749
Taunton Somset 20 ST2224
Taverham Norfk 66 TG1613
Taverners Green Essex 40 TL5618
Tavernspite Pembks 31 SN1812
Tavistock Devon 6 SX4874
Taw green Devon 8 SX6597
Tawstock Devon 19 SS5529
Taxal Derbys 79 SK0079
Taychreggan Hotel Ag & B 123 NN0421
Tayinloan Ag & B 105 NR6946
Taynton Gloucs 35 SO7222
Taynton Oxon 36 SP2313
Taynuilt Ag & B 122 NN0031
Tayport Fife 127 NO4628
Tayvallich Ag & B 113 NR7487
Tealby Lincs 76 TF1590
Team Valley T & W 103 NZ2459
Teangue Highld 129 NG6609
Teanord Highld 140 NH5964
Tebay Cumb 87 NY6104
Tebworth Beds 38 SP9926
Tedburn St Mary Devon 8 SX8194
Teddington Gloucs 47 SO9633
Teddington Gt Lon 26 TQ1670
Tedstone Delamere H & W 47 SO6958
Tedstone Wafer H & W 47 SO6759
Teesport N York 97 NZ5423
Teesside Park N York 97 NZ4618
Teeton Nhants 50 SP6970
Teffont Evias Wilts 22 ST9931
Teffont Magna Wilts 22 ST9932
Tegryn Pembks 31 SN2233
Teigh Rutlnd 63 SK8615
Teigncombe Devon 8 SX6787
Teigngrace Devon 7 SX8574
Teignmouth Devon 7 SX9473
Teindside Border 109 NT4408
Telford Shrops 60 SJ6908
Tellisford Somset 22 ST8055
Telscombe E Susx 15 TQ4003
Telscombe Cliffs E Susx 15 TQ4001
Tempar P & K 124 NN6857
Templand D & G 100 NY0886
Temple C Glas 115 NS5469
Temple Cnwll 4 SX1473
Temple Mdloth 117 NT3158
Temple Balsall W Mids 61 SP2076
Temple Bar Cardgn 44 SN5354
Temple Cloud Somset 21 ST6257
Temple End Suffk 53 TL6650
Temple Ewell Kent 29 TR2844
Temple Grafton Warwks 48 SP1255
Temple Guiting Gloucs 48 SP0928
Temple Hirst N York 83 SE6024
Temple Normanton Derbys 74 SK4167
Temple Pier Highld 139 NH5330
Temple Sowerby Cumb 94 NY6127
Templecombe Somset 22 ST7022
Templeton Devon 19 SS8813
Templeton Pembks 31 SN1111
Templetown Dur 95 NZ1050
Tempsford Beds 52 TL1653
Ten Mile Bank Norfk 65 TL5996
Tenbury Wells H & W 46 SO5968
Tenby Pembks 31 SN1300
Tendring Essex 41 TM1424
Tendring Green Essex 41 TM1325
Tendring Heath Essex 41 TM1326
Tenpenny Heath Essex 41 TM0820
Tenterden Kent 17 TQ8833
Terling Essex 40 TL7715
Tern Shrops 59 SJ6216
Ternhill Shrops 59 SJ6332
Terregles D & G 100 NX9377
Terrington N York 90 SE6770
Terrington St Clement Norfk 65 TF5520
Terrington St John Norfk 65 TF5314
Terry's Green Warwks 61 SP1073
Teston Kent 28 TQ7053
Testwood Hants 12 SU3514
Tetbury Gloucs 35 ST8993
Tetbury Upton Gloucs 35 ST8895
Tetchill Shrops 59 SJ3932
Tetcott Devon 5 SX3396
Tetford Lincs 77 TF3374
Tetney Lincs 77 TA3100
Tetney Lock Lincs 85 TA3402
Tetsworth Oxon 37 SP6801
Tettenhall W Mids 60 SJ8800
Tettenhall Wood W Mids 60 SO8899
Tetworth Cambs 52 TL2253
Teversal Notts 75 SK4861
Teversham Cambs 53 TL4958
Teviothead Border 109 NT4005
Tewel Abers 135 NO8085
Tewin Herts 39 TL2714
Tewkesbury Gloucs 47 SO8932
Teynham Kent 28 TQ9662
Thackley W York 82 SE1738
Thackthwaite Cumb 92 NY1423
Thackthwaite Cumb 93 NY4225
Thakeham W Susx 14 TQ1017
Thame Oxon 37 SP7005
Thames Ditton Surrey 26 TQ1567
Thamesmead Gt Lon 27 TQ4780
Thanington Kent 29 TR1356
Thankerton S Lans 108 NS9738
Tharston Norfk 66 TM1894
Thatcham Berks 24 SU5167
Thatto Heath Mersyd 78 SJ5093
Thaxted Essex 40 TL6131
The Bank Ches 72 SJ8457
The Bank Shrops 59 SO6199
The Beeches Gloucs 36 SP0302
The Biggins Cambs 53 TL4788
The Blythe Staffs 73 SK0428
The Bourne H & W 47 SO9856
The Braes Highld 137 NG5234
The Bratch Staffs 60 SO8693
The Broad H & W 46 SO4961
The Brunt E Loth 118 NT6873
The Bungalow IOM 153 SC3986
The Bush Kent 28 TQ6649
The Butts Gloucs 35 SO8916
The Chequer Wrexhm 71 SJ4840
The City Beds 52 TL1159
The City Bucks 37 SU7896
The Common Oxon 48 SP2927
The Common Wilts 35 SU0285
The Corner Kent 28 TQ7041
The Corner Shrops 59 SO4387
The Cronk IOM 153 SC3395
The Den N Ayrs 115 NS3251
The Flatt Cumb 101 NY5678
The Forge H & W 46 SO3459
The Forstal E Susx 16 TQ5435
The Forstal Kent 28 TQ8946
The Forstal Kent 28 TR0438
The Fouralls Shrops 72 SJ6831
The Green Cumb 86 SD1884
The Green Essex 40 TL7719
The Grove H & W 47 SO8741
The Haven W Susx 14 TQ0830
The Haw Gloucs 47 SO8427
The Hill Cumb 86 SD1783
The Hirsel Border 110 NT8240
The Holt Berks 37 SU8078
The Leacon Kent 17 TQ9833
The Lee Bucks 38 SP9004
The Lhen IOM 153 NX3801
The Lochs Moray 141 NJ3062
The Middles Dur 96 NZ2051
The Moor Kent 17 TQ7529
The Mumbles Swans 32 SS6187
The Mythe Gloucs 47 SO8934
The North Mons 34 SO5206
The Neuk Abers 135 NO7397
The Quarry Gloucs 35 ST7499
The Quarter Kent 28 TQ8844
The Reddings Gloucs 35 SO9121
The Rookery Staffs 72 SJ8555
The Ross P & K 124 NN7621
The Sands Surrey 25 SU8846
The Shoe Wilts 35 ST8074
The Smithies Shrops 60 SO6897
The Spike Cambs 53 TL4848
The Spring Warwks 61 SP2873
The Square Torfn 34 ST2796
The Stair Kent 16 TQ6047
The Stocks Kent 17 TQ9127
The Straits Hants 25 SU7839
The Strand Wilts 22 ST9259
The Thrift Herts 39 TL3139
The Towans Cnwll 2 SW5538
The Vauld H & W 46 SO5349
The Wyke Shrops 60 SJ7206
Theakston N York 89 SE3085
Thealby Lincs 84 SE8917
Theale Berks 24 SU6471
Theale Somset 21 ST4646
Thearne E R Yk 85 TA0736

Theberton Torbreck

Theberton *Suffk* 55 TM4365
Thedden Grange *Hants* 24 SU6839
Theddingworth *Leics* 50 SP6685
Theddlethorpe All Saints *Lincs* 77 TF4688
Theddlethorpe St Helen *Lincs* 77 TF4788
Thelbridge Cross *Devon* 19 SS7911
Thelnetham *Suffk* 54 TM0178
Thelveton *Norfk* 54 TM1681
Thelwall *Ches* 79 SJ6587
Themelthorpe *Norfk* 66 TG0524
Thenford *Nhants* 49 SP5241
Theobald's Green *Wilts* 23 SU0268
Therfield *Herts* 39 TL3337
Thetford *Norfk* 54 TL8783
Thethwaite *Cumb* 93 NY3744
Theydon Bois *Essex* 27 TQ4499
Thicket Prior *E R Yk* 83 SE6943
Thickwood *Wilts* 35 ST8272
Thimbleby *Lincs* 77 TF2470
Thimbleby *N York* 89 SE4495
Thingwall *Mersyd* 78 SJ2784
Thirkleby *N York* 89 SE4778
Thirlby *N York* 90 SE4883
Thirlestane *Border* 118 NT5647
Thirlspot *Cumb* 93 NY3118
Thirn *N York* 89 SE2185
Thirsk *N York* 89 SE4281
Thirtleby *E R Yk* 85 TA1634
Thistleton *Lancs* 80 SD4037
Thistleton *Rutlnd* 63 SK9118
Thistley Green *Suffk* 53 TL6676
Thixendale *N York* 90 SE8460
Thockrington *Nthumb* 102 NY9578
Tholomas Drove *Cambs* 65 TF4006
Tholthorpe *N York* 89 SE4766
Thomas Chapel *Pembks* 31 SN1008
Thomas Close *Cumb* 93 NY4340
Thomas Town *Warwks* 48 SP0763
Thomastown *Abers* 142 NJ5736
Thompson *Norfk* 66 TL9296
Thong *Kent* 28 TQ6770
Thoralby *N York* 88 SE0086
Thoresby *Notts* 75 SK6371
Thoresthorpe *Lincs* 77 TF4577
Thoresway *Lincs* 76 TF1696
Thorganby *Lincs* 76 TF2097
Thorganby *N York* 83 SE6841
Thorgill *N York* 90 SE7096
Thorington *Suffk* 55 TM4174
Thorington Street *Suffk* 54 TM0035
Thorlby *N York* 82 SD9653
Thorley *Herts* 39 TL4718
Thorley *IOW* 12 SZ3689
Thorley Houses *Herts* 39 TL4620
Thorley Street *IOW* 12 SZ3788
Thormanby *N York* 90 SE4974
Thorn's Flush *Surrey* 14 TQ0440
Thornaby-on-Tees *N York* 97 NZ4518
Thornage *Norfk* 66 TG0536
Thornborough *Bucks* 49 SP7433
Thornborough *N York* 89 SE2979
Thornbury *Devon* 18 SS4008
Thornbury *Gloucs* 35 ST6390
Thornbury *H & W* 47 SO6259
Thornbury *W York* 82 SE1933
Thornby *Cumb* 93 NY2851
Thornby *Nhants* 50 SP6775
Thorncliff *Staffs* 73 SK0158
Thorncombe *Dorset* 10 ST3703
Thorncombe Street *Surrey* 25 SU9941
Thorncott Green *Beds* 52 TL1547
Thorncross *IOW* 13 SZ4381
Thorndon *Suffk* 54 TM1469
Thorndon Cross *Devon* 8 SX5394
Thorne *S York* 83 SE6812
Thorne *Somset* 10 ST5217
Thorne St Margaret *Somset* 20 ST1020
Thornecroft *Devon* 7 SX7767
Thornehillhead *Devon* 18 SS4116
Thorner *W York* 83 SE3740
Thornes *Staffs* 61 SK0703
Thornes *W York* 83 SE3219
Thorney *Bucks* 26 TQ0379
Thorney *Cambs* 64 TF2804
Thorney *Notts* 76 SK8572
Thorney *Somset* 21 ST4223
Thorney Hill *Hants* 12 SZ2099
Thorney Toll *Cambs* 64 TF3404
Thornfalcon *Somset* 20 ST2823
Thornford *Dorset* 10 ST6012
Thorngrafton *Nthumb* 102 NY7865
Thorngrove *Somset* 21 ST3632
Thorngumbald *E R Yk* 85 TA2026
Thornham *Norfk* 65 TF7343
Thornham Magna *Suffk* 54 TM1070
Thornham Parva *Suffk* 54 TM1072
Thornhaugh *Cambs* 64 TF0600
Thornhill *Caerph* 33 ST1584
Thornhill *D & G* 100 NX8795
Thornhill *Derbys* 74 SK1983
Thornhill *Hants* 13 SU4612
Thornhill *Stirlg* 116 NN6600
Thornhill *W York* 82 SE2518
Thornhill Lees *W York* 82 SE2419
Thornhills *W York* 82 SE1523
Thornholme *E R Yk* 91 TA1164
Thornicombe *Dorset* 11 ST8703
Thornington *Nthumb* 110 NT8833
Thornley *Dur* 95 NZ1137
Thornley *Dur* 96 NZ3639
Thornley Gate *Cumb* 95 NY8356
Thornliebank *E Rens* 115 NS5559
Thorns *Suffk* 53 TL7455
Thorns Green *Gt Man* 79 SJ7884
Thornsett *Derbys* 79 SK0086
Thornthwaite *Cumb* 93 NY2225
Thornthwaite *N York* 89 SE1758
Thornton *Angus* 126 NO3946
Thornton *Bucks* 49 SP7435
Thornton *E R Yk* 84 SE7645
Thornton *Fife* 117 NT2897
Thornton *Lancs* 80 SD3342
Thornton *Leics* 62 SK4607
Thornton *Lincs* 77 TF2467
Thornton *Mersyd* 78 SD3301
Thornton *N York* 89 NZ4713
Thornton *Nthumb* 111 NT9547
Thornton *Pembks* 30 SM9007
Thornton *W York* 82 SE0932
Thornton Curtis *Lincs* 85 TA0817
Thornton Dale *N York* 90 SE8383
Thornton Green *Ches* 71 SJ4473
Thornton Heath *Gt Lon* 27 TQ3168
Thornton Hough *Mersyd* 78 SJ3080
Thornton in Lonsdale *N York* 87 SD6873
Thornton le Moor *Lincs* 76 TF0496
Thornton Rust *N York* 88 SD9689
Thornton Steward *N York* 89 SE1787
Thornton Watlass *N York* 89 SE2385
Thornton-in-Craven *N York* 81 SD9048
Thornton-le-Beans *N York* 89 SE3990
Thornton-le-Clay *N York* 90 SE6865
Thornton-le-Moor *N York* 89 SE3988
Thornton-le-Moors *Ches* 71 SJ4474
Thornton-le-Street *N York* 89 SE4186
Thorntonhall *S Lans* 115 NS5955
Thorntonloch *E Loth* 119 NT7574
Thornwood Common *Essex* 39 TL4604
Thornydykes *Border* 110 NT6148
Thornythwaite *Cumb* 93 NY3922
Thoroton *Notts* 63 SK7642
Thorp Arch *W York* 83 SE4345
Thorpe *Derbys* 73 SK1550
Thorpe *E R Yk* 84 SE9946
Thorpe *Lincs* 77 TF4981
Thorpe *N York* 88 SE0161
Thorpe *Norfk* 67 TM4398
Thorpe *Notts* 75 SK7649
Thorpe *Surrey* 26 TQ0168
Thorpe Abbotts *Norfk* 55 TM1979
Thorpe Acre *Leics* 62 SK5119
Thorpe Arnold *Leics* 63 SK7720
Thorpe Audlin *W York* 83 SE4715
Thorpe Bassett *N York* 90 SE8673
Thorpe Bay *Essex* 40 TQ9185
Thorpe by Water *Rutlnd* 51 SP8996
Thorpe Common *S York* 74 SK3895
Thorpe Constantine *Staffs* 61 SK2508
Thorpe End *Norfk* 67 TG2810
Thorpe Green *Essex* 41 TM1623
Thorpe Green *Lancs* 81 SD5923
Thorpe Green *Suffk* 54 TL9354
Thorpe Hesley *S York* 74 SK3796
Thorpe in Balne *S York* 83 SE5910
Thorpe in the Fallows *Lincs* 76 SK9180
Thorpe Langton *Leics* 50 SP7492
Thorpe Larches *Dur* 96 NZ3826
Thorpe le Street *E R Yk* 84 SE8343
Thorpe Lea *Surrey* 26 TQ0170
Thorpe Malsor *Nhants* 51 SP8378
Thorpe Mandeville *Nhants* 49 SP5244
Thorpe Market *Norfk* 67 TG2436
Thorpe Morieux *Suffk* 54 TL9453
Thorpe on the Hill *Lincs* 76 SK9065
Thorpe on the Hill *W York* 82 SE3126
Thorpe Salvin *S York* 75 SK5281
Thorpe Satchville *Leics* 63 SK7311
Thorpe St Andrew *Norfk* 67 TG2508
Thorpe St Peter *Lincs* 77 TF4860
Thorpe Thewles *Dur* 96 NZ3923
Thorpe Tilney *Lincs* 76 TF1257
Thorpe Underwood *N York* 89 SE4659
Thorpe Underwood *Nhants* 50 SP7981
Thorpe Waterville *Nhants* 51 TL0281
Thorpe Willoughby *N York* 83 SE5731
Thorpe-le-Soken *Essex* 41 TM1722
Thorpeness *Suffk* 55 TM4759
Thorpland *Norfk* 65 TF6108
Thorrington *Essex* 41 TM0919
Thorverton *Devon* 9 SS9202
Thrales End *Beds* 38 TL1116
Thrandeston *Suffk* 54 TM1176
Thrapston *Nhants* 51 SP9978
Threapland *Cumb* 92 NY1539
Threapland *N York* 88 SD9860
Threapwood *Ches* 71 SJ4344
Threapwood *Staffs* 73 SK0342
Threapwood Head *Staffs* 73 SK0342
Threave *S Ayrs* 106 NS3306
Three Ashes *H & W* 34 SO5122
Three Bridges *W Susx* 15 TQ2837
Three Burrows *Cnwll* 3 SW7446
Three Chimneys *Kent* 28 TQ8238
Three Cocks *Powys* 45 SO1737
Three Crosses *Swans* 32 SS5794
Three Cups Corner *E Susx* 16 TQ6320
Three Gates *H & W* 47 SO6862
Three Hammers *Cnwll* 5 SX2287
Three Holes *Norfk* 65 TF5000
Three Lane Ends *Gt Man* 79 SD8309
Three Leg Cross *E Susx* 16 TQ6831
Three Legged Cross *Dorset* 12 SU0805
Three Mile Cross *Berks* 24 SU7167
Three Mile Stone *Cnwll* 3 SW7745
Three Miletown *W Loth* 117 NT0675
Three Oaks *E Susx* 17 TQ8314
Threehammer Common *Norfk* 67 TG3419
Threekingham *Lincs* 64 TF0836
Threepwood *Border* 109 NT5143
Threlkeld *Cumb* 93 NY3125
Threshfield *N York* 88 SD9863
Thrigby *Norfk* 67 TG4612
Thringarth *Dur* 95 NY9322
Thringstone *Leics* 62 SK4217
Thrintoft *N York* 89 SE3192
Thriplow *Cambs* 53 TL4346
Throapham *S York* 75 SK5387
Throckenhalt *Lincs* 64 TF3509
Throcking *Herts* 39 TL3330
Throckley *T & W* 103 NZ1566
Throckmorton *H & W* 47 SO9850
Throop *Dorset* 11 SY8292
Throop *Dorset* 12 SZ1195
Throphill *Nthumb* 103 NZ1285
Thropton *Nthumb* 103 NU0202
Throsk *Stirlg* 116 NS8591
Througham *Gloucs* 35 SO9108
Throughgate *D & G* 100 NX8784
Throwleigh *Devon* 8 SX6690
Throwley *Kent* 28 TQ9955
Throwley Forstal *Kent* 28 TQ9854
Thrumpton *Notts* 62 SK5031
Thrumpton *Notts* 75 SK7080
Thrumster *Highld* 151 ND3345
Thrunscoe *Lincs* 85 TA3107
Thrunton *Nthumb* 111 NU0810
Thrup *Oxon* 36 SU2999
Thrupp *Gloucs* 35 SO8603
Thrupp *Oxon* 37 SP4716
Thrushelton *Devon* 5 SX4487
Thrushesbush *Essex* 39 TL4909
Thrussington *Leics* 63 SK6515
Thruxton *H & W* 46 SO4334
Thruxton *Hants* 23 SU2945
Thrybergh *S York* 75 SK4695
Thulston *Derbys* 62 SK4031
Thundersley *Essex* 40 TQ7988
Thurcaston *Leics* 62 SK5610
Thurcroft *S York* 75 SK4988
Thurdon *Cnwll* 18 SS2810
Thurgarton *Norfk* 66 TG1834
Thurgarton *Notts* 75 SK6949
Thurgoland *S York* 82 SE2901
Thurlaston *Leics* 50 SP5099
Thurlaston *Warwks* 50 SP4670
Thurlbear *Somset* 20 ST2621
Thurlby *Lincs* 76 SK9061
Thurlby *Lincs* 64 TF0916
Thurlby *Lincs* 77 TF4776
Thurleigh *Beds* 51 TL0558
Thurlestone *Devon* 7 SX6742
Thurlow *Suffk* 53 TL6750
Thurloxton *Somset* 20 ST2730
Thurlstone *S York* 82 SE2303
Thurlton *Norfk* 67 TM4198
Thurlwood *Ches* 72 SJ8057
Thurmaston *Leics* 62 SK6109
Thurnby *Leics* 63 SK6403
Thurne *Norfk* 67 TG4015
Thurnham *Kent* 28 TQ8057
Thurning *Nhants* 51 TL0882
Thurning *Norfk* 66 TG0729
Thurnscoe *S York* 83 SE4505
Thursby *Cumb* 93 NY3250
Thursden *Lancs* 81 SD9034
Thursford *Norfk* 66 TF9833
Thursley *Surrey* 25 SU9039
Thurso *Highld* 151 ND1168
Thurstaston *Mersyd* 78 SJ2484
Thurston *Suffk* 54 TL9265
Thurston Clough *Gt Man* 82 SD9707
Thurston Planch *Suffk* 54 TL9364
Thurstonfield *Cumb* 93 NY3156
Thurstonland *W York* 82 SE1610
Thurton *Norfk* 67 TG3200
Thurvaston *Derbys* 73 SK2437
Thuxton *Norfk* 66 TG0307
Thwaite *N York* 88 SD8998
Thwaite *Suffk* 54 TM1168
Thwaite Head *Cumb* 87 SD3490
Thwaite St Mary *Norfk* 67 TM3395
Thwaites *W York* 82 SE0741
Thwaites Brow *W York* 82 SE0740
Thwing *E R Yk* 91 TA0470
Tibbermore *P & K* 125 NO0423
Tibbers *D & G* 100 NX8696
Tibberton *Gloucs* 35 SO7521
Tibberton *H & W* 47 SO9057
Tibberton *Shrops* 72 SJ6820
Tibbie Shiels Inn *Border* 109 NT2420
Tibenham *Norfk* 54 TM1389
Tibshelf *Derbys* 75 SK4461
Tibthorpe *E R Yk* 84 SE9555
Ticehurst *E Susx* 16 TQ6830
Tichborne *Hants* 24 SU5730
Tickencote *Rutlnd* 63 SK9809
Tickenham *Somset* 34 ST4571
Tickford End *Bucks* 38 SP8843
Tickhill *S York* 75 SK5993
Ticklerton *Shrops* 59 SO4890
Ticknall *Derbys* 62 SK3523
Tickton *E R Yk* 84 TA0541
Tidbury Green *W Mids* 61 SP1075
Tidcombe *Wilts* 23 SU2858
Tiddington *Oxon* 37 SP6404
Tiddington *Warwks* 48 SP2255
Tidebrook *E Susx* 16 TQ6130
Tideford *Cnwll* 5 SX3559
Tideford Cross *Cnwll* 5 SX3461
Tidenham *Gloucs* 34 ST5595
Tideswell *Derbys* 74 SK1575
Tidmarsh *Berks* 24 SU6374
Tidmington *Warwks* 48 SP2538
Tidpit *Hants* 12 SU0718
Tiers Cross *Pembks* 30 SM9010
Tiffield *Nhants* 49 SP7051
Tigerton *Angus* 134 NO5364
Tigh a Ghearraidh *W Isls* 154 NF7172
Tigharry *W Isls* 154 NF7172
Tighnabruaich *Ag & B* 114 NR9873
Tigley *Devon* 7 SX7660
Tilbrook *Cambs* 51 TL0869
Tilbury *Essex* 27 TQ6476
Tilbury Green *Essex* 53 TL7441
Tile Cross *W Mids* 61 SP1687
Tile Hill *W Mids* 61 SP2777
Tilehouse Green *W Mids* 61 SP1776
Tilehurst *Berks* 24 SU6673
Tilford *Surrey* 25 SU8743
Tilgate *W Susx* 15 TQ2734
Tilgate Forest Row *W Susx* 15 TQ2632
Tilham Street *Somset* 21 ST5535
Tillers Green *Gloucs* 47 SO6932
Tillicoultry *Clacks* 116 NS9197
Tillietudlem *S Lans* 116 NS8045
Tillingham *Essex* 41 TL9904
Tillington *H & W* 46 SO4644
Tillington *W Susx* 14 SU9621
Tillington Common *H & W* 46 SO4545
Tilly *Essex* 40 TL5926
Tillybirloch *Abers* 135 NJ6807
Tillycairn *Abers* 134 NO4697
Tillyfourie *Abers* 135 NJ6412
Tillygreig *Abers* 143 NJ8822
Tillyrie *P & K* 126 NO1006
Tilmanstone *Kent* 29 TR3051
Tiln *Notts* 75 SK7084
Tilney All Saints *Norfk* 65 TF5618
Tilney High End *Norfk* 65 TF5617
Tilney St Lawrence *Norfk* 65 TF5414
Tilshead *Wilts* 23 SU0347
Tilstock *Shrops* 59 SJ5437
Tilston *Ches* 71 SJ4650
Tilstone Bank *Ches* 71 SJ5659
Tilstone Fearnall *Ches* 71 SJ5660
Tilsworth *Beds* 38 SP9824
Tilton on the Hill *Leics* 63 SK7405
Tiltups End *Gloucs* 35 ST8497
Timberland *Lincs* 76 TF1258
Timbersbrook *Ches* 72 SJ8962
Timberscombe *Somset* 20 SS9542
Timble *N York* 82 SE1853
Timewell *Devon* 20 SS9625
Timpanheck *D & G* 101 NY3274
Timperley *Gt Man* 79 SJ7888
Timsbury *Hants* 23 SU3424
Timsbury *Somset* 22 ST6758
Timsgarry *W Isls* 154 NB0534
Timsgearraidh *W Isls* 154 NB0534
Timworth *Suffk* 54 TL8669
Timworth Green *Suffk* 54 TL8669
Tincleton *Dorset* 11 SY7692
Tindale *Cumb* 94 NY6159
Tindale Crescent *Dur* 96 NZ1927
Tingewick *Bucks* 49 SP6532
Tingley *W York* 82 SE2826
Tingrith *Beds* 38 TL0032
Tinhay *Devon* 5 SX3985
Tinker's Hill *Hants* 24 SU4047
Tinkersley *Derbys* 74 SK2664
Tinsley *S York* 74 SK4090
Tinsley Green *W Susx* 15 TQ2839
Tintagel *Cnwll* 4 SX0588
Tintern Parva *Mons* 34 SO5200
Tintinhull *Somset* 21 ST4919
Tintwistle *Derbys* 79 SK0197
Tinwald *D & G* 100 NY0081
Tinwell *Rutlnd* 63 TF0006
Tipp's End *Norfk* 65 TL5095
Tippacott *Devon* 19 SS7647
Tiptoe *Hants* 12 SZ2597
Tipton *W Mids* 60 SO9492
Tipton Green *W Mids* 60 SO9592
Tipton St John *Devon* 9 SY0991
Tiptree *Essex* 40 TL8916
Tiptree Heath *Essex* 40 TL8815
Tir-y-fron *Flints* 70 SJ2859
Tirabad *Powys* 45 SN8741
Tiretigan *Ag & B* 113 NR7162
Tirley *Gloucs* 47 SO8328
Tirphil *Caerph* 33 SO1303
Tirril *Cumb* 94 NY5026
Tisbury *Wilts* 22 ST9429
Tisman's Common *W Susx* 14 TQ0632
Tissington *Derbys* 73 SK1752
Titchberry *Devon* 18 SS2427
Titchfield *Hants* 13 SU5405
Titchfield Common *Hants* 13 SU5206
Titchmarsh *Nhants* 51 TL0279
Titchwell *Norfk* 65 TF7643
Tithby *Notts* 63 SK6937
Titley *H & W* 46 SO3360
Titmore Green *Herts* 39 TL2126
Titsey *Surrey* 27 TQ4054
Tittensor *Staffs* 72 SJ8738
Tittleshall *Norfk* 66 TF8921
Titton *H & W* 60 SO8370
Tiverton *Ches* 71 SJ5560
Tiverton *Devon* 9 SS9512
Tivetshall St Margaret *Norfk* 54 TM1787
Tivetshall St Mary *Norfk* 54 TM1686
Tivington *Somset* 20 SS9345
Tivy Dale *S York* 82 SE2707
Tixall *Staffs* 72 SJ9722
Tixover *Rutlnd* 51 SK9700
Toab *Shet* 155 HU3811
Toadhole *Derbys* 74 SK3856
Toadmoor *Derbys* 74 SK3451
Tobermory *Ag & B* 121 NM5055
Toberonochy *Ag & B* 122 NM7408
Tobha Mor *W Isls* 154 NF7536
Tocher *Abers* 142 NJ6932
Tochieneal *Moray* 142 NJ5165
Tockenham *Wilts* 36 SU0379
Tockenham Wick *Wilts* 36 SU0381
Tocketts *N York* 97 NZ6217
Tockholes *Lancs* 81 SD6623
Tockington *Gloucs* 34 ST6086
Tockwith *N York* 83 SE4652
Todber *Dorset* 22 ST7919
Todburn *Nthumb* 103 NZ1295
Toddington *Beds* 38 TL0128
Toddington *Gloucs* 48 SP0333
Todds Green *Herts* 39 TL2226
Todenham *Gloucs* 48 SP2335
Todhills *Angus* 127 NO4239
Todhills *Cumb* 101 NY3762
Todhills *Dur* 96 NZ2133
Todmorden *W York* 81 SD9324
Todwick *S York* 75 SK4984
Toft *Cambs* 52 TL3656
Toft *Ches* 79 SJ7576
Toft *Lincs* 64 TF0717
Toft *Shet* 155 HU4376
Toft *Warwks* 50 SP4770
Toft Hill *Dur* 96 NZ1528
Toft Hill *Lincs* 77 TF2462
Toft Monks *Norfk* 67 TM4294
Toft next Newton *Lincs* 76 TF0388
Toftrees *Norfk* 66 TF8927
Tofts *Highld* 151 ND3668
Toftwood *Norfk* 66 TF9811
Togston *Nthumb* 103 NU2402
Tokavaig *Highld* 129 NG6011
Tokers Green *Oxon* 37 SU7077
Tolastadh *W Isls* 154 NB5347
Toldavas *Cnwll* 2 SW4226
Toldish *Cnwll* 4 SW9259
Toll Bar *S York* 83 SE5507
Tolland *Somset* 20 ST1032
Tollard Farnham *Dorset* 11 ST9515
Tollard Royal *Wilts* 11 ST9417
Tollbar End *W Mids* 61 SP3675
Toller Fratrum *Dorset* 10 SY5797
Toller Porcorum *Dorset* 10 SY5698
Toller Whelme *Dorset* 10 ST5101
Tollerton *N York* 90 SE5164
Tollerton *Notts* 62 SK6134
Tollesbury *Essex* 40 TL9510
Tolleshunt D'Arcy *Essex* 40 TL9211
Tolleshunt Knights *Essex* 40 TL9114
Tolleshunt Major *Essex* 40 TL9011
Tolpuddle *Dorset* 11 SY7994
Tolsta *W Isls* 154 NB5347
Tolvan *Cnwll* 2 SW7028
Tolver *Cnwll* 2 SW4832
Tolworth *Gt Lon* 26 TQ1966
Tomaknock *P & K* 125 NN8721
Tomatin *Highld* 140 NH8028
Tomchrasky *Highld* 131 NH2512
Tomdoun *Highld* 131 NH1500
Tomich *Highld* 146 NC6005
Tomich *Highld* 139 NH3027
Tomich *Highld* 139 NH5348
Tomich *Highld* 146 NH6971
Tomintoul *Moray* 141 NJ1619
Tomlow *Warwks* 49 SP4563
Tomnacross *Highld* 139 NH5141
Tomnavoulin *Moray* 141 NJ2126
Tompkin *Staffs* 72 SJ9451
Ton *Mons* 34 SO3301
Ton *Mons* 34 ST3695
Ton-teg *Rhondd* 33 ST0986
Tonbridge *Kent* 16 TQ5846
Tondu *Brdgnd* 33 SS8984
Tonedale *Somset* 20 ST1321
Tong *Kent* 28 TQ9556
Tong *Shrops* 60 SJ7907
Tong *W York* 82 SE2230
Tong Green *Kent* 28 TQ9853
Tong Norton *Shrops* 60 SJ7908
Tong Street *W York* 82 SE1930
Tonge *Leics* 62 SK4223
Tongham *Surrey* 25 SU8848
Tongland *D & G* 99 NX6954
Tongue *Highld* 149 NC5956
Tongue End *Lincs* 64 TF1518
Tongwynlais *Cardif* 33 ST1382
Tonna *Neath* 32 SS7798
Tonwell *Herts* 39 TL3316
Tonypandy *Rhondd* 33 SS9991
Tonyrefail *Rhondd* 33 ST0188
Toot Baldon *Oxon* 37 SP5600
Toot Hill *Essex* 27 TL5102
Toot Hill *Hants* 12 SU3818
Toothill *Wilts* 36 SU1183
Tooting *Gt Lon* 27 TQ2771
Tooting Bec *Gt Lon* 27 TQ2872
Top End *Beds* 51 TL0362
Top of Hebers *Gt Man* 79 SD8607
Top-y-rhos *Flints* 70 SJ2558
Topcliffe *N York* 89 SE3976
Topcroft *Norfk* 67 TM2693
Topcroft Street *Norfk* 67 TM2691
Topham *S York* 83 SE6217
Toppesfield *Essex* 53 TL7437
Toppings *Gt Man* 81 SD7213
Toprow *Norfk* 66 TM1698
Topsham *Devon* 9 SX9688
Torbeg *N Ayrs* 105 NR8929
Torboll *Highld* 147 NH7599
Torbreck *Highld* 140 NH6441

313

Vennington
Wellesbourne Mountford

Vennington *Shrops*	59	SJ3309
Venny Tedburn *Devon*	8	SX8297
Venterdon *Cnwll*	5	SX3675
Ventnor *IOW*	13	SZ5677
Venton *Devon*	6	SX5956
Vernham Dean *Hants*	23	SU3356
Vernham Street *Hants*	23	SU3457
Vernolds Common *Shrops*	59	SO4780
Verwood *Dorset*	12	SU0809
Veryan *Cnwll*	3	SW9139
Veryan Green *Cnwll*	3	SW9140
Vickerstown *Cumb*	86	SD1868
Victoria *Blae G*	33	SO1707
Victoria *Cnwll*	4	SW9861
Victoria *S York*	82	SE1705
Vidlin *Shet*	155	HU4765
Viewfield *Moray*	141	NJ2864
Viewpark *N Lans*	116	NS7061
Vigo *Kent*	27	TQ6361
Ville la Bas *Jersey*	152	JS0000
Villiaze *Guern*	152	GN0000
Vinehall Street *E Susx*	17	TQ7520
Vines Cross *E Susx*	16	TQ5917
Virginia Water *Surrey*	25	TQ0067
Virginstow *Devon*	5	SX3792
Virley *Essex*	40	TL9414
Vobster *Somset*	22	ST7048
Voe *Shet*	155	HU4062
Vowchurch *H & W*	46	SO3636
Vulcan Village *Ches*	78	SJ5894

W

Wackerfield *Dur*	96	NZ1522
Wacton *Norfk*	66	TM1791
Wadborough *H & W*	47	SO9047
Waddesdon *Bucks*	37	SP7416
Waddeton *Devon*	7	SX8756
Waddicar *Mersyd*	78	SJ3999
Waddingham *Lincs*	76	SK9896
Waddington *Lancs*	81	SD7343
Waddington *Lincs*	76	SK9764
Waddon *Devon*	9	SX8879
Waddon *Dorset*	10	SY6285
Wadebridge *Cnwll*	4	SW9972
Wadeford *Somset*	10	ST3110
Wadenhoe *Nhants*	51	TL0183
Wadesmill *Herts*	39	TL3617
Wadhurst *E Susx*	16	TQ6431
Wadshelf *Derbys*	74	SK3170
Wadswick *Wilts*	22	ST8467
Wadworth *S York*	75	SK5696
Waen *Denbgs*	70	SH9962
Waen *Denbgs*	70	SJ1065
Waen *Powys*	58	SJ2319
Waen Fach *Powys*	58	SJ2017
Waen-pentir *Gwynd*	69	SH5766
Waen-wen *Gwynd*	69	SH5768
Wagbeach *Shrops*	59	SJ3602
Wainfelin *Torfn*	34	SO2701
Wainfleet All Saints *Lincs*	77	TF4959
Wainfleet Bank *Lincs*	77	TF4759
Wainford *Norfk*	55	TM3490
Wainhouse Corner *Cnwll*	4	SX1895
Wains Hill *Somset*	34	ST3970
Wainscott *Kent*	28	TQ7470
Wainstalls *W York*	82	SE0428
Waitby *Cumb*	88	NY7508
Waithe *Lincs*	77	TA2800
Wake Green *W Mids*	61	SP0982
Wakefield *W York*	83	SE3320
Wakerley *Nhants*	51	SP9599
Wakes Colne *Essex*	40	TL8928
Wal-wen *Flints*	70	SJ2076
Walberswick *Suffk*	55	TM4974
Walberton *W Susx*	14	SU9705
Walbottle *T & W*	103	NZ1666
Walbutt *D & G*	99	NX7468
Walby *Cumb*	101	NY4460
Walcombe *Somset*	21	ST5546
Walcot *Lincs*	84	SE8720
Walcot *Lincs*	64	TF0635
Walcot *Lincs*	76	TF1356
Walcot *Shrops*	59	SJ5912
Walcot *Shrops*	59	SO3485
Walcot *Warwks*	48	SP1358
Walcot *Wilts*	36	SU1684
Walcot Green *Norfk*	54	TM1280
Walcote *Leics*	50	SP5683
Walcott *Norfk*	67	TG3532
Walden *N York*	88	SE0082
Walden Head *N York*	88	SD9880
Walden Stubbs *N York*	83	SE5516
Walderslade *Kent*	28	TQ7663
Walderton *W Susx*	14	SU7910
Walditch *Dorset*	10	SY4892
Waldley *Derbys*	73	SK1236
Waldridge *Dur*	96	NZ2549
Waldringfield *Suffk*	55	TM2845
Waldron *E Susx*	16	TQ5419
Wales *S York*	75	SK4882
Wales *Somset*	21	ST5824
Walesby *Lincs*	76	TF1392
Walesby *Notts*	75	SK6870
Walford *H & W*	46	SO3872
Walford *H & W*	34	SO5820
Walford *Shrops*	59	SJ4320
Walford *Staffs*	72	SJ8133
Walford Heath *Shrops*	59	SJ4419
Walgherton *Ches*	72	SJ6948
Walgrave *Nhants*	51	SP8071
Walhampton *Hants*	12	SZ3396
Walk Mill *Lancs*	81	SD8729
Walkden *Gt Man*	79	SD7302
Walker *T & W*	103	NZ2864
Walker Fold *Lancs*	81	SD6741
Walker's Green *H & W*	46	SO5247
Walker's Heath *W Mids*	61	SP0578
Walkerburn *Border*	109	NT3637
Walkeringham *Notts*	75	SK7792
Walkerith *Lincs*	75	SK7892
Walkern *Herts*	39	TL2826
Walkerton *Fife*	126	NO2301
Walkhampton *Devon*	6	SX5369
Walkington *E R Yk*	84	SE9936
Walkley *S York*	74	SK3388
Walkwood *H & W*	48	SP0364
Wall *Cnwll*	2	SW6036
Wall *Nthumb*	102	NY9168
Wall *Staffs*	61	SK1006
Wall End *Cumb*	86	SD2383
Wall End *H & W*	46	SO4457
Wall Heath *W Mids*	60	SO8889
Wall Houses *Nthumb*	103	NZ0368
Wall under Haywood *Shrops*	59	SO5092
Wallacetown *S Ayrs*	106	NS2703
Wallacetown *S Ayrs*	106	NS3422
Wallands Park *E Susx*	15	TQ4010
Wallasey *Mersyd*	78	SJ2992
Wallend *Kent*	28	TQ8775
Waller's Green *H & W*	47	SO6739
Wallhead *Cumb*	101	NY4660
Wallingford *Oxon*	37	SU6089
Wallington *Gt Lon*	27	TQ2864
Wallington *Hants*	13	SU5806
Wallington *Herts*	39	TL2933
Wallington Heath *W Mids*	60	SJ9903
Wallis *Pembks*	30	SN0125
Wallisdown *Dorset*	12	SZ0694
Walliswood *W Susx*	14	TQ1138
Walls *Shet*	155	HU2449
Wallsend *T & W*	103	NZ2966
Wallthwaite *Cumb*	93	NY3526
Wallyford *E Loth*	118	NT3671
Walmer *Kent*	29	TR3750
Walmer Bridge *Lancs*	80	SD4724
Walmersley *Gt Man*	81	SD8013
Walmestone *Kent*	29	TR2559
Walmley *W Mids*	61	SP1393
Walmley Ash *W Mids*	61	SP1492
Walmsgate *Lincs*	77	TF3677
Walpole *Somset*	20	ST3042
Walpole *Suffk*	55	TM3674
Walpole Cross Keys *Norfk*	65	TF5119
Walpole Highway *Norfk*	65	TF5114
Walpole St Andrew *Norfk*	65	TF5017
Walpole St Peter *Norfk*	65	TF5016
Walrow *Somset*	21	ST3447
Walsall *W Mids*	60	SP0198
Walsall Wood *W Mids*	61	SK0403
Walsden *W York*	81	SD9321
Walsgrave on Sowe *W Mids*	61	SP3881
Walshall Green *Herts*	39	TL4430
Walsham le Willows *Suffk*	54	TM0071
Walshaw *Gt Man*	81	SD7711
Walshaw *W York*	82	SD9731
Walshford *N York*	83	SE4153
Walsoken *Norfk*	65	TF4710
Walston *S Lans*	117	NT0545
Walsworth *Herts*	39	TL1930
Walter Ash *Bucks*	37	SU8398
Walters Green *Kent*	16	TQ5140
Walterston *V Glam*	33	ST0671
Walterstone *H & W*	46	SO3425
Waltham *Kent*	29	TR1048
Waltham *Lincs*	85	TA2603
Waltham Abbey *Essex*	27	TL3800
Waltham Chase *Hants*	13	SU5614
Waltham Cross *Herts*	27	TL3600
Waltham on the Wolds *Leics*	63	SK8024
Waltham St Lawrence *Berks*	37	SU8276
Waltham's Cross *Essex*	40	TL6930
Walthamstow *Gt Lon*	27	TQ3689
Walton *Bucks*	38	SP8936
Walton *Cambs*	64	TF1702
Walton *Cumb*	101	NY5264
Walton *Derbys*	74	SK3568
Walton *Leics*	50	SP5987
Walton *Powys*	46	SO2559
Walton *Shrops*	59	SJ5818
Walton *Shrops*	46	SO4679
Walton *Somset*	21	ST4636
Walton *Staffs*	72	SJ8528
Walton *Staffs*	72	SJ8932
Walton *Suffk*	55	TM2935
Walton *W Susx*	14	SU8104
Walton *W York*	83	SE3516
Walton *W York*	83	SE4447
Walton *Warwks*	48	SP2853
Walton Cardiff *Gloucs*	47	SO9032
Walton East *Pembks*	30	SN0223
Walton Elm *Dorset*	11	ST7717
Walton Grounds *Nhants*	49	SP5135
Walton Lower Street *Suffk*	55	TM2834
Walton on the Hill *Surrey*	26	TQ2255
Walton on the Naze *Essex*	41	TM2522
Walton on the Wolds *Leics*	62	SK5919
Walton Park *Somset*	34	ST4172
Walton West *Pembks*	30	SM8612
Walton-in-Gordano *Somset*	34	ST4273
Walton-le-Dale *Lancs*	81	SD5628
Walton-on-Thames *Surrey*	26	TQ1066
Walton-on-the-Hill *Staffs*	72	SJ9520
Walton-on-Trent *Derbys*	73	SK2118
Walwen *Flints*	70	SJ1179
Walwen *Flints*	70	SJ1771
Walwick *Nthumb*	102	NY9070
Walworth *Dur*	96	NZ2318
Walworth *Gt Lon*	27	TQ3277
Walworth Gate *Dur*	96	NZ2320
Walwyn's Castle *Pembks*	30	SM8711
Wambrook *Somset*	10	ST2907
Wampool *Cumb*	93	NY2454
Wanborough *Surrey*	25	SU9348
Wanborough *Wilts*	36	SU2082
Wandel *S Lans*	108	NS9427
Wandon End *Herts*	38	TL1322
Wandsworth *Gt Lon*	27	TQ2574
Wangford *Suffk*	55	TM4679
Wanlip *Leics*	62	SK5910
Wanlockhead *D & G*	108	NS8712
Wannock *E Susx*	16	TQ5703
Wansford *Cambs*	64	TL0799
Wansford *E R Yk*	84	TA0656
Wanshurst Green *Kent*	28	TQ7645
Wanstead *Gt Lon*	27	TQ4088
Wanstrow *Somset*	22	ST7141
Wanswell *Gloucs*	35	SO6801
Wantage *Oxon*	36	SU3988
Wants Green *H & W*	47	SO7557
Wapley *Gloucs*	35	ST7179
Wappenbury *Warwks*	48	SP3769
Wappenham *Nhants*	49	SP6245
Warbleton *E Susx*	16	TQ6018
Warborough *Oxon*	37	SU5993
Warboys *Cambs*	52	TL3080
Warbreck *Lancs*	80	SD3238
Warbstow *Cnwll*	5	SX2090
Warburton *Gt Man*	79	SJ7089
Warcop *Cumb*	94	NY7415
Ward End *W Mids*	61	SP1188
Ward Green *Suffk*	54	TM0464
Warden *Kent*	28	TR0271
Warden *Nthumb*	102	NY9166
Warden Law *T & W*	96	NZ3649
Warden Street *Beds*	38	TL1244
Wardhedges *Beds*	38	TL0635
Wardington *Oxon*	49	SP4846
Wardle *Ches*	71	SJ6156
Wardle *Gt Man*	81	SD9116
Wardley *Gt Man*	79	SD7602
Wardley *Rutlnd*	51	SK8300
Wardley *T & W*	96	NZ3061
Wardlow *Derbys*	74	SK1874
Wardsend *Ches*	79	SJ9382
Wardy Hill *Cambs*	53	TL4782
Ware *Herts*	39	TL3514
Ware Street *Kent*	28	TQ7956
Wareham *Dorset*	11	SY9287
Warehorne *Kent*	17	TQ9832
Waren Mill *Nthumb*	111	NU1434
Warenford *Nthumb*	111	NU1328
Warenton *Nthumb*	111	NU1030
Wareside *Herts*	39	TL3915
Waresley *Cambs*	52	TL2554
Waresley *H & W*	60	SO8470
Warfield *Berks*	25	SU8872
Warfleet *Devon*	7	SX8750
Wargate *Lincs*	64	TF2330
Wargrave *Berks*	37	SU7978
Warham *H & W*	46	SO4838
Warham All Saints *Norfk*	66	TF9541
Warham St Mary *Norfk*	66	TF9441
Wark *Nthumb*	110	NT8238
Wark *Nthumb*	102	NY8577
Warkleigh *Devon*	19	SS6422
Warkton *Nhants*	51	SP8979
Warkworth *Nhants*	49	SP4840
Warkworth *Nthumb*	111	NU2406
Warlaby *N York*	89	SE3491
Warland *W York*	82	SD9420
Warleggan *Cnwll*	4	SX1569
Warleigh *Somset*	22	ST7964
Warley Town *W York*	82	SE0524
Warlingham *Surrey*	27	TQ3658
Warmanbie *D & G*	101	NY1969
Warmbrook *Derbys*	73	SK2853
Warmfield *W York*	83	SE3720
Warmingham *Ches*	72	SJ7061
Warmington *Nhants*	51	TL0790
Warmington *Warwks*	49	SP4147
Warminster *Wilts*	22	ST8745
Warmley *Gloucs*	35	ST6673
Warmsworth *S York*	75	SE5400
Warmwell *Dorset*	11	SY7585
Warndon *H & W*	47	SO8856
Warnford *Hants*	13	SU6223
Warnham *W Susx*	15	TQ1533
Warnham Court *W Susx*	15	TQ1533
Warningcamp *W Susx*	14	TQ0307
Warninglid *W Susx*	15	TQ2426
Warren *Ches*	79	SJ8870
Warren *Pembks*	30	SR9397
Warren Row *Berks*	37	SU8180
Warren Street *Kent*	28	TQ9252
Warren's Green *Herts*	39	TL2628
Warrenby *N York*	97	NZ5825
Warrenhill *S Lans*	108	NS9438
Warrington *Bucks*	51	SP8953
Warrington *Ches*	78	SJ6088
Warriston *C Edin*	117	NT2575
Warsash *Hants*	13	SU4906
Warslow *Staffs*	74	SK0858
Warsop *Notts*	75	SK5667
Warsop Vale *Notts*	75	SK5467
Warter *E R Yk*	84	SE8750
Warter Priory *E R Yk*	84	SE8449
Warthermaske *N York*	89	SE2078
Warthill *N York*	83	SE6755
Wartling *E Susx*	16	TQ6509
Wartnaby *Leics*	63	SK7123
Warton *Lancs*	80	SD4128
Warton *Lancs*	87	SD4972
Warton *Nthumb*	103	NU0002
Warton *Warwks*	61	SK2803
Warwick *Cumb*	93	NY4656
Warwick *Warwks*	48	SP2865
Warwick Bridge *Cumb*	93	NY4756
Warwicksland *Cumb*	101	NY4577
Wasbister *Ork*	155	HY3932
Wasdale Head *Cumb*	86	NY1808
Wash *Derbys*	74	SK0682
Wash *Devon*	7	SX7665
Washaway *Cnwll*	4	SX0369
Washbourne *Devon*	7	SX7954
Washbrook *Somset*	21	ST4250
Washbrook *Suffk*	54	TM1142
Washfield *Devon*	9	SS9315
Washfold *N York*	88	NZ0502
Washford *Somset*	20	ST0541
Washford Pyne *Devon*	19	SS8111
Washingborough *Lincs*	76	TF0170
Washington *T & W*	96	NZ3155
Washington *W Susx*	14	TQ1112
Washwood Heath *W Mids*	61	SP1088
Wasing *Berks*	24	SU5764
Waskerley *Dur*	95	NZ0445
Wasperton *Warwks*	48	SP2658
Wasps Nest *Lincs*	76	TF0764
Wass *N York*	90	SE5579
Watchet *Somset*	20	ST0743
Watchfield *Oxon*	36	SU2490
Watchfield *Somset*	21	ST3446
Watchgate *Cumb*	87	SD5398
Watchill *Cumb*	93	NY1842
Watcombe *Devon*	7	SX9267
Watendlath *Cumb*	93	NY2716
Water *Devon*	8	SX7580
Water *Lancs*	81	SD8425
Water Eaton *Oxon*	37	SP5112
Water Eaton *Staffs*	60	SJ9011
Water End *Beds*	38	TL0637
Water End *Beds*	38	TL1047
Water End *Beds*	38	TL1051
Water End *Essex*	53	TL5840
Water End *Herts*	38	TL0310
Water End *Herts*	39	TL2304
Water End *E R Yk*	84	SE7938
Water Fryston *W York*	83	SE4726
Water Newton *Cambs*	51	TL1097
Water Orton *Warwks*	61	SP1790
Water Stratford *Bucks*	49	SP6534
Water Street *Neath*	32	SS8083
Water Yeat *Cumb*	86	SD2889
Water's Nook *Gt Man*	79	SD6605
Waterbeach *Cambs*	53	TL4965
Waterbeach *W Susx*	14	SU8908
Waterbeck *D & G*	101	NY2477
Watercombe *Dorset*	11	SY7585
Waterden *Norfk*	66	TF8836
Waterend *Cumb*	92	NY1122
Waterfall *Staffs*	73	SK0851
Waterfoot *Lancs*	81	SD8321
Waterfoot *S Lans*	115	NS5655
Waterford *Herts*	39	TL3114
Watergate *Cnwll*	4	SX1181
Waterhead *Cumb*	87	NY3703
Waterhead *E Ayrs*	107	NS5411
Waterheads *Border*	117	NT2451
Waterhouses *Dur*	96	NZ1841
Waterhouses *Staffs*	73	SK0850
Wateringbury *Kent*	28	TQ6853
Waterlane *Gloucs*	35	SO9204
Waterloo *Cnwll*	4	SX1072
Waterloo *Derbys*	74	SK4163
Waterloo *Dorset*	11	SZ0193
Waterloo *H & W*	46	SO3447
Waterloo *Highld*	129	NG6623
Waterloo *Mersyd*	78	SJ3298
Waterloo *N Lans*	116	NS8154
Waterloo *Norfk*	67	TG2219
Waterloo *P & K*	125	NO0537
Waterloo *Pembks*	30	SM9803
Waterloo Cross *Devon*	9	ST0514
Waterloo Port *Gwynd*	68	SH4964
Waterlooville *Hants*	13	SU6809
Watermillock *Cumb*	93	NY4422
Waterperry *Oxon*	37	SP6206
Waterrow *Somset*	20	ST0525
Waters Upton *Shrops*	59	SJ6319
Watersfield *W Susx*	14	TQ0115
Waterside *Bucks*	26	SP9600
Waterside *Cumb*	93	NY2245
Waterside *E Ayrs*	107	NS4308
Waterside *E Ayrs*	107	NS4843
Waterside *E Duns*	116	NS6773
Waterside *Lancs*	81	SD7123
Waterside *S York*	83	SE6714
Waterstock *Oxon*	37	SP6305
Waterston *Pembks*	30	SM9305
Watford *Herts*	26	TQ1196
Watford *Nhants*	50	SP6069
Wath *N York*	89	SE1467
Wath *N York*	89	SE3277
Wath upon Dearne *S York*	75	SE4300
Watlington *Norfk*	65	TF6111
Watlington *Oxon*	37	SU6894
Watnall *Notts*	62	SK5046
Watten *Highld*	151	ND2454
Wattisfield *Suffk*	54	TM0074
Wattisham *Suffk*	54	TM0151
Watton *Dorset*	10	SY4591
Watton *E R Yk*	84	TA0150
Watton *Norfk*	66	TF9100
Watton Green *Norfk*	66	TF9201
Watton-at-Stone *Herts*	39	TL3019
Wattons Green *Essex*	27	TQ5295
Wattston *N Lans*	116	NS7770
Wattstown *Rhondd*	33	ST0193
Wattsville *Caerph*	33	ST2091
Wauldby *E R Yk*	84	SE9629
Waulkmill *Abers*	135	NO6492
Waunarlwydd *Swans*	32	SS6095
Waunfawr *Cardgn*	43	SN6081
Waunfawr *Gwynd*	68	SH5259
Waungron *Swans*	32	SN5901
Waunlwyd *Blae G*	33	SO1806
Wavendon *Bucks*	38	SP9137
Waverbridge *Cumb*	93	NY2249
Waverton *Ches*	71	SJ4663
Waverton *Cumb*	93	NY2247
Wawne *E R Yk*	85	TA0936
Waxham *Norfk*	67	TG4426
Waxholme *E R Yk*	85	TA3229
Way *Kent*	29	TR3265
Way Village *Devon*	19	SS8810
Way Wick *Somset*	21	ST3862
Waye *Devon*	7	SX7771
Wayford *Somset*	10	ST4006
Waytown *Dorset*	10	SY4797
Weacombe *Somset*	20	ST1140
Weald *Cambs*	52	TL2259
Weald *Oxon*	36	SP3002
Wealdstone *Gt Lon*	26	TQ1589
Wear Head *Dur*	95	NY8539
Weardley *W York*	82	SE2944
Weare *Somset*	21	ST4152
Weare Giffard *Devon*	18	SS4721
Wearne *Somset*	21	ST4228
Weasdale *Cumb*	87	NY6903
Weasenham All Saints *Norfk*	66	TF8421
Weasenham St Peter *Norfk*	66	TF8522
Weaste *Gt Man*	79	SJ8098
Weatheroak Hill *H & W*	61	SP0674
Weaverham *Ches*	71	SJ6174
Weaverslake *Staffs*	73	SK1319
Weaverthorpe *N York*	91	SE9670
Webb's Heath *Gloucs*	35	ST6873
Webbington *Somset*	21	ST3855
Webheath *H & W*	48	SP0266
Webton *H & W*	46	SO4136
Wedderlairs *Abers*	143	NJ8532
Wedding Hall Fold *N York*	82	SD9445
Weddington *Kent*	29	TR2959
Weddington *Warwks*	61	SP3693
Wedhampton *Wilts*	23	SU0557
Wedmore *Somset*	21	ST4347
Wednesbury *W Mids*	60	SO9895
Wednesfield *W Mids*	60	SJ9400
Weecar *Notts*	75	SK8266
Weedon *Bucks*	38	SP8118
Weedon Lois *Nhants*	49	SP6046
Weeford *Staffs*	61	SK1403
Week *Devon*	19	SS5727
Week *Devon*	19	SS7316
Week *Devon*	7	SX7862
Week *Somset*	20	SS9133
Week St Mary *Cnwll*	5	SX2397
Weeke *Devon*	8	SS7606
Weeke *Hants*	24	SU4630
Weekley *Nhants*	51	SP8881
Weel *E R Yk*	84	TA0639
Weeley *Essex*	41	TM1422
Weeley Heath *Essex*	41	TM1520
Weem *P & K*	125	NN8449
Weeping Cross *Staffs*	72	SJ9421
Weethley *Warwks*	48	SP0555
Weeting *Norfk*	53	TL7788
Weeton *E R Yk*	85	TA3520
Weeton *Lancs*	80	SD3834
Weeton *N York*	82	SE2847
Weetwood *W York*	82	SE2737
Weir *Lancs*	81	SD8625
Weir Quay *Devon*	6	SX4365
Weirbrook *Shrops*	59	SJ3424
Welbeck Abbey *Notts*	75	SK5574
Welborne *Norfk*	66	TG0610
Welbourn *Lincs*	76	SK9654
Welburn *N York*	90	SE7267
Welbury *N York*	89	NZ3902
Welby *Lincs*	63	SK9738
Welches Dam *Cambs*	53	TL4686
Welcombe *Devon*	18	SS2318
Weldon Bridge *Nthumb*	103	NZ1398
Welford *Berks*	24	SU4073
Welford *Nhants*	50	SP6480
Welford-on-Avon *Warwks*	48	SP1452
Welham *Leics*	50	SP7692
Welham *Notts*	75	SK7281
Welham Green *Herts*	39	TL2305
Well *Hants*	24	SU7646
Well *Lincs*	77	TF4473
Well *N York*	89	SE2681
Well End *Bucks*	26	SU8888
Well End *Herts*	26	TQ2098
Well Fold *W York*	82	SE2024
Well Head *Herts*	39	TL1727
Well Hill *Kent*	27	TQ4963
Well Town *Devon*	9	SS9009
Welland *H & W*	47	SO7940
Welland Stone *H & W*	47	SO8138
Wellbank *Angus*	127	NO4737
Wellbury *Herts*	38	TL1329
Wellesbourne *Warwks*	48	SP2855
Wellesbourne Mountford *Warwks*	48	SP2755